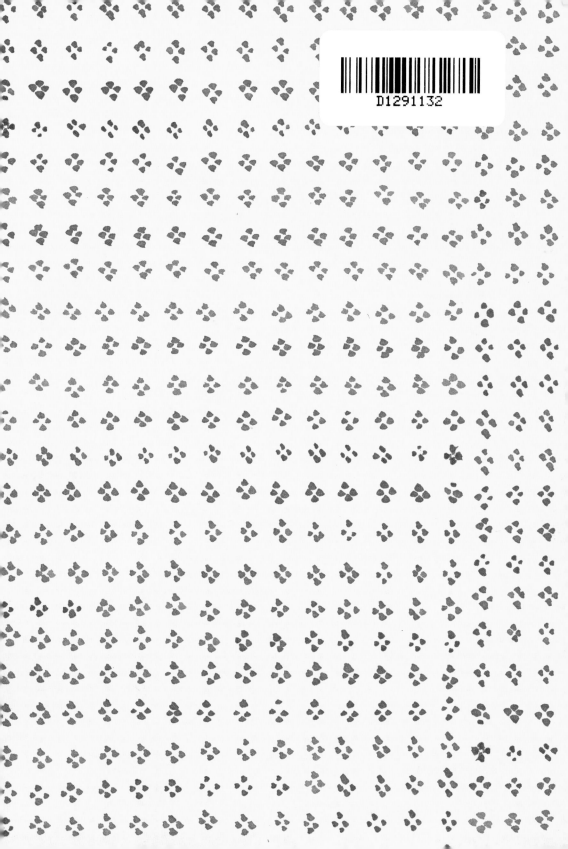
D1291132

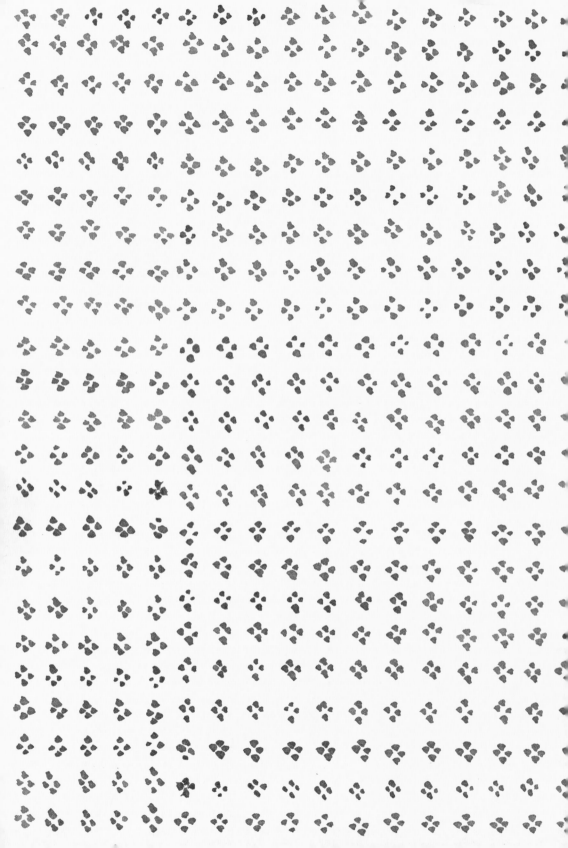

DEC 0 3 2014

blue
rider
press

The Blue Mountains Public Libra
L.E. Shore Memorial Library
Thornbury, Ontario N0H 2P0

Women in Clothes

# Women in Clothes

+

SHEILA HETI, HEIDI JULAVITS,
LEANNE SHAPTON & 639 OTHERS

ASSOCIATE EDITOR: MARY MANN

BLUE RIDER PRESS

A MEMBER OF PENGUIN GROUP (USA)

NEW YORK

blue
rider
press

Published by the Penguin Group
Penguin Group (USA) LLC
375 Hudson Street
New York, New York 10014

USA · Canada · UK · Ireland · Australia
New Zealand · India · South Africa · China

penguin.com
A Penguin Random House Company

Copyright © 2014 by Sheila Heti, Heidi Julavits, Leanne Shapton

Penguin supports copyright. Copyright fuels creativity, encourages diverse voices,
promotes free speech, and creates a vibrant culture. Thank you for buying an authorized
edition of this book and for complying with copyright laws by not reproducing, scanning,
or distributing any part of it in any form without permission. You are supporting writers
and allowing Penguin to continue to publish books for every reader.

Blue Rider Press is a registered trademark and its colophon is a trademark
of Penguin Group (USA) LLC

ISBN 978-0-399-16656-3

Printed in the United States of America
1  3  5  7  9  10  8  6  4  2

BOOK DESIGN BY LEANNE SHAPTON, KATE RYAN,
AND CLAIRE NAYLON VACCARO

Some names of individuals have been changed.

—

# CONTENTS

## SURVEYS

## COLLECTIONS

## WEAR AREAS

## COMPLIMENTS

Clothing pattern paintings – *Emily Hass*

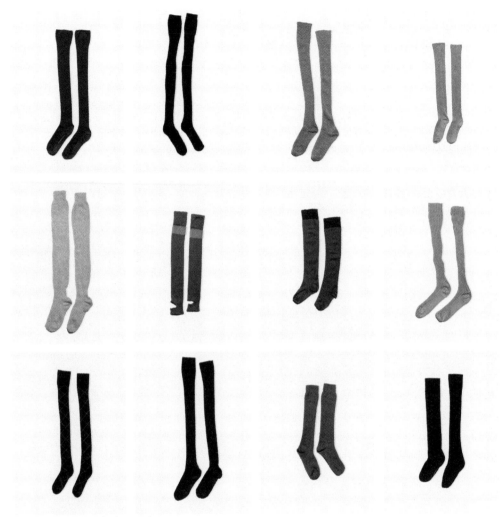

*LUISE STAUSS*'s over-the-knee socks

# CLOTHING GARDEN

*Skype meeting. Leanne and Heidi are in Leanne's studio in New York. Sheila is in her apartment in Toronto. Leanne has recently cut her hair.*

**SHEILA:** Oh my god, look at your hair!

**LEANNE:** I know. *(laughs)*

**SHEILA:** I love it, I love it! It's so good.

**LEANNE:** Are you wearing fur?

**SHEILA:** No, I'm wearing a throw.

**HEIDI:** I have no new hair to share, no new hair. Sheila, are you growing your bangs out?

**SHEILA:** Not intentionally.

**LEANNE:** This is how our book should start: Hi, are you growing your bangs out? What are you wearing, are you wearing fur? We're like a bunch of chickens squawking at each other!

**SHEILA:** You look like Peter Pan.

**HEIDI:** Have you ever had short hair like this before?

**LEANNE:** Not this short. Well, when I was ten.

**HEIDI:** Yeah, that's the last time I had short hair, too. Sheila, have you ever had short-short, pixie-short, boy-short, hair?

**SHEILA:** Yeah, in high school I had like concentration-camp short. That's what my mother called it.

**HEIDI:** Oh my god.

**LEANNE:** So wait, in terms of how we want to write the introduction, I like the essays we wrote a year ago when we first started thinking about the book. I think we should

just rewrite those to some degree. And I also like your idea, Sheila, of talking about what's happened to us since we began the project.

**HEIDI:** So why don't we, right now, ask each other questions that we can use as connective tissue in the intro? So I might say, Sheila, how did you get dressed this morning, what did you think about that's different from what you might have thought about eight months ago?

**SHEILA:** Well, I didn't really get dressed.

**SHEILA** *Until this year, I never put much thought into clothes. I bought my silk 1930s ivory-colored wedding dress in about half an hour, made impatient by the task. I wore black shoes that hardly matched, but which were in my closet already.*

*What changed to make me more interested in dressing? I suppose it was that (a few years after my divorce) I began living with a man who cares a lot about dressing and clothes. I had never, up close, seen what that looks like. I'd always assumed the well-dressed just happened to be that way—not that it was an area of life that people excelled in because they applied thought, attention, and care to it. Living with my boyfriend, I began to see that dressing was like everything else: those who dress well do so because they spend some time thinking about it.*

*Clothes and style became more interesting to me. For someone who is fascinated by how people relate to one another, it's hard to overlook personal style as a way we speak to the world. One day I just decided, Today is the day I'm going to figure out how to dress. I biked to a bookstore—one of those very big bookstores—*

3

*and went to the section where there were fashion and style books, looking for one that would tell me what women thought about as they shopped and dressed. But there was nothing like that. There were books about Audrey Hepburn and books filled with pictures from* Vogue, *but nothing that felt useful to me at all. I thought, I'll have to make this a project. I decided to begin by asking some of the women I knew the very questions I'd hoped to find answered in a book.*

+

FROM: Sheila Heti
DATE: Sun, Apr 8, 2012, at 1:00PM
SUBJECT: fashion survey
TO: Heidi Julavits
Hey Heidi, I might write a little piece about women's fashion and I was wondering if I could bug you (as a fashionable lady!) to fill out my survey. Please answer as many times and in as much detail as possible to each question listed (if you're interested!). xo Sheila
ps: I was partly inspired to think about dressing after reading your latest novel. Also, I'm not sure if the q's are exactly right.

QUESTION 1 What are some dressing rules that you have for yourself, that you wouldn't recommend to other people necessarily, but which you follow?

QUESTION 2 What are some dressing or clothing rules that you think every woman should follow?

QUESTION 3 What are the shopping habits you follow? Ex: are you always looking? do you only look for particular items when you need them? do you shop online? do you save up for great pieces?

QUESTION 4 Which people from culture, past and present, do you admire or have you admired, fashion-wise? Are there any people you took as models who you tried to emulate, even if only in details, not the whole?

QUESTION 5 Are you a fan of certain brands and labels, and if so, what are they?

QUESTION 6 What is dressing about, for you? What are you trying to do or achieve when you dress up?

FROM: Heidi Julavits
DATE: Sun, Apr 8, 2012, at 7:45PM
SUBJECT: Re: fashion survey
TO: Sheila Heti
hey sheila! sorry i've been on west coast and not online—but i LOVE these questions!!!! maybe you and i should write a women's fashion book that isn't stupid like all women's fashion books. i was just reading in three cities and believe me, i gave questions like this way too much thought—actually packed a whole suitcase and wore the same outfit for two days, and on the third i wore a dress i bought in seattle, which was white and see-through (muslin, basically), and i hadn't brought any white underthings, just black, and the store woman suggested that i "own it," so i did, and wore the dress with very visible black underwear to a reading and i kind of liked that the people in the audience might think that they knew something about me that i didn't know about myself.

On Fri, Apr 20, 2012, at 7:38PM, Sheila Heti wrote:
I think this could be a great book collaboration! I was trying to find a smart women's fashion philosophy (philosophy of style) book this weekend, and not one! I love your black-underwear story. I've added some more questions. Are we missing anything? Do you think any should be cut?

QUESTION 7 How does makeup fit into all this for you?

QUESTION 8 What's the situation with your hair?

QUESTION 9 Describe what you're wearing on your body and face, and how your hair is done, right this moment.

FROM: Heidi Julavits
DATE: Sat, Apr 21, 2012, at 9:25AM
SUBJECT: Re: fashion survey
TO: Sheila Heti

i think these are all great! i'm just going to throw some other questions out there that may cant this in an "identity" direction:

QUESTION 10 Do you ever find yourself channeling an old outfit of your mother's (i.e., from your childhood), and is this a good or bad thing? (but maybe we don't want to drag mothers into this.)

Also, the idea of sharing clothes—I had a roommate once in my twenties and our closets became essentially conjoined—and even though I was the greater benefitee of this arrangement, the whole idea made me sort of uncomfortable, and I found it to be a boundary I didn't like negotiating. Thus,

QUESTION 11 Do you share clothes with friends or roommates?

and QUESTION 12 What are the rules about "copying" an obviously original look? Say if your friend wears a down vest over a bikini top . . . Can you copy it? Or is it only ok to copy from strangers? xx

FROM: Sheila Heti
DATE: Sat, Apr 21, 2012, at 10:19AM
SUBJECT: others
TO: Heidi Julavits

Heidi, I think we should ask Leanne Shapton if she wants to be in on this project. Leanne would be wonderful to get to pass the survey around, as she knows many people in lots of different countries, and many artists, too. Perhaps she could also provide illustrations, if we wanted them, and do the cover and lettering inside.

Already Leanne has added some good ideas (I sent her a survey, too). She thought there shouldn't be photographs of the women we're profiling. That made me start thinking about the book differently.

I think the one thing we want to steer away from is pronouncements on fashion from people like Coco Chanel or Diane von Furstenberg ("A woman's style is in direct proportion to her misery" or whatever, i just made that up). I think we'll want regular women, not only the most fashionable. People who aren't that fashionable may be quite smart, nevertheless, about what they have on. We should send surveys to whoever we're curious about and inspired to learn about and hear from. xo S

On Sun, Apr 22, 2012, at 11:03PM, Heidi Julavits wrote:
i so admire leanne and would kill to work with her.

LEANNE *First I took cues on how to dress from my brother and drawings from children's books. Then, as a teenager, from movies. I knew other girls knew more than me. I had subscriptions to* Seventeen *and* Sassy *and loved looking at and reading them, but could not relate.*

*Then at twenty-eight I bought a bikini with another tomboyish friend. A magazine could never have convinced me to buy a bikini, but the afternoon I shared with this friend did.*

*When I started dating my future husband, he was the editorial director of an international stable of magazines. Many of the women he had dated were fashion editors, models, or socialites, women who knew how to put themselves together and wore and could afford beautiful clothes. Women who were photographed. During our first years together he bought me designer clothes, which I wore uneasily.*

*I dove into fashion magazines and read them regularly for the next seven years, absorbing the language of promotion and hype and enthusiasm. I met designers and muses and terrifically photogenic people and went to fashion parties and the Met Ball and the Oscars and places where what women wear is noticed and noted. There was constant gushing about clothes* and style, and beauty and power. But to me, only a handful of people looked truly great.

✛

**SHEILA** *A problem I've always had with fashion magazines is that women are encouraged to copy other women. While I suspect that many men enjoy copying other men (consider the idea of the alpha male and beta males), and while part of what makes a man "superior" is how close he can get to "embodying manliness" (in clothing terms: the suit), I feel it's the opposite for a woman. The most compelling women are the ones who are distinctive, who are most like themselves and least like other women. There is no other Marilyn Monroe. There is no other Anaïs Nin. And being as iconic and inimitable as they were would be better than being like either one of them. It's almost as if fashion magazines don't understand what a woman wants. I think she wants to be unique among women, a creature unlike any other.*

✛

**HEIDI** *I don't check out men on the street. I check out women. I am always checking out women because I love stories, and women in clothes tell stories. For years I watched other women to learn how I might someday be a woman with a story.*

*Even when I was very young, I knew I wanted to be a writer, and I wanted to be stylish, because to be stylish was to be poised on the precipice between reality and fiction. I grew up in a house that bordered a private school I didn't attend. These girls, and the clothing they wore, told stories about places to which I otherwise had no access. To understand their style was to be a tourist in the habits and traditions of a strange world. To watch them was not terribly different from reading a book. I learned that style isn't what you wear, it's how you wear it. I learned from one girl that I should wear my big wool sweaters inside out so that the threads*

and seams were revealed. I learned from another girl that instead of tying my anorak arms around my waist when I wasn't wearing it, I could tie them with one arm over one shoulder and one arm under the other, so that the sleeves crossed my chest diagonally.

*But style, I also learned, is not about strictly copying others, because style is not transferable. There are too many variables. I once followed a woman down the street in New York. She wore white clogs and a flowered headscarf and a long skirt. She had high cheekbones and a long neck; she looked like an early-twentieth-century immigrant from Eastern Europe who'd just arrived at Ellis Island, though of course she was probably an artist who lived in Brooklyn. I loved her style but knew that I couldn't pull off a headscarf. My cheekbones aren't high enough. My neck is too short. But the white clogs, those could contribute a small and beneficial mutation to my existing wardrobe. I bought a pair. Twelve years later, I wear them still.*

✛

**JANUARY 8, 2014**
*Skype meeting.*

**SHEILA:** So right now I'm wearing this, like, black silk slip that I wore to bed last night, and then because it's sort of cold here I put on these black tights, without feet, and then this scarf. Because I was only going to be seeing you guys over Skype, I didn't feel the need to get dressed today. But I think it looks better than . . . like probably, a year ago, I would have been in a sweatshirt. I don't know. I basically feel like if you guys came into the house now, I wouldn't be embarrassed.

**HEIDI:** Wait, you *would* or you *would not* be embarrassed if we came into your house?

**SHEILA:** Wouldn't. Even though it's basically pajamas, it's still an outfit.

**HEIDI & LEANNE:** *(laugh)*

SHEILA: I have a little more appreciation for the aesthetics of an outfit, and take more pleasure in it. I guess a year ago I thought there would be some big change in me once the book was done, but it's more like a slight shift in the way I see things. I now feel like—my choices are my choices and that's good and that's enough. I realized there was nothing so terribly wrong with me. Whereas a year ago I felt like there was something terribly wrong with the way I approached clothes.

LEANNE: Right.

SHEILA: I think other women have that same feeling, too. Yet reading all the surveys makes me see that none of us are doing anything terribly wrong, and that realization gives you the confidence to make deliberate choices.

LEANNE: I don't care in the same way about dressing anymore, and that's interesting to me, and it's probably got to do with childbirth and having your body torn apart, but I agree with what you're saying—you just have that thing on and you're not going to be embarrassed.

HEIDI: For me what's changed is, well, I always thought that aspiring to have the right clothes and style meant trying to look like somebody else. But now my aspiration is to look like some former version of myself in a specific time or place. Not like "I wish I was fourteen again, so I'm gonna wear hot pants"—not that I ever wore hot pants when I was fourteen—but it's more about trying to have some sort of emotional connection to a part of myself that I feel I could lose touch with if I don't re-inhabit it every once in a while.

LEANNE: I love the idea of a version of yourself.

HEIDI: It's not just an age thing, it's also a place thing. This has been coming up a lot in the last few weeks because we lived in Berlin this fall, and I really don't like being home. For four months I had worn only what I brought in this one suitcase, and while I never thought, "Ugh, I'm bored, I wish I had my other clothes," I did have these moments of missing certain items, and occasionally I'd think, "I'm so excited to get home and put them on." But instead I've come home and I just keep living out of my suitcase, which three weeks later I still haven't unpacked. And those things I thought I missed so much, I haven't even pulled them out of my closet.

SHEILA: Why?

HEIDI: The only analogy is like, when you haven't seen your boyfriend or your husband or your partner in a month or more and then you see them and you have to have sex with them again. You want to have sex again! But the first time can actually be sort of awkward, and you put it off a bit sometimes, and then you're like "Fuck it, we just have to have sex now, get this over with." I'm sort of having that with the shirts in my closet.

SHEILA & LEANNE: *(laugh)*

HEIDI: I open the closet and I'm like, "Oh, I know we know each other really well, but I'm just not ready to have sex with you yet."

LEANNE: Have sex with your clothes already!

✛

LEANNE *After those seven years immersed in women's fashion magazines, I still dress as I always have—in used men's clothes and lots of vintage—but I can afford better vintage, and can appreciate great design after paying attention to it. I still buy fashion magazines. I cut them up, responding to what I'm drawn to, and paste these clippings into scrapbooks. In this way, I've tailored my formerly uneasy relationship to the fashion world.*

*Skype meeting.*

**LEANNE:** Have I told you about my stoner/gay theory? Like, everything successful has to have some aspect of stoner and some aspect of gay.

**HEIDI:** Male or female?

**LEANNE:** Both.

**SHEILA:** You mean successful in fashion or successful in anything?

**LEANNE:** Anything. Just that, if you look at a painting, a book, a room, a meal . . . things that really appeal to me have a certain laid-back quality and also a certain kind of truth and surrender, and I realize it's because I am not a stoner and I am not gay, yet I probably want to be a bit of both. So now I sort of dress like I want to impart a little bit of stoner into my wardrobe and a little bit of gay. That's where it's left me, because they are versions of myself that I'll probably never be. So rather than how you, Heidi, are going, I want to be a version of me, I'm going, My dream version is just me, but that little bit more stoner, and that little bit more gay. I want to give expression to it in some small way. So like today . . .

**HEIDI:** Yeah, let's talk about the stoner/gay aspects today.

**LEANNE:** Today my stoner aspect is maybe these army pants, and maybe the gay aspect is . . .

**HEIDI:** . . . the dandy boots?

**LEANNE:** I love equestrian wear—there's a sort of S&M aspect to it. And it's all a little bit androgynous.

+

**SHEILA** *My boyfriend talked about his interest in clothes (and my recent interest) as a "hobby" and said that the important thing about a hobby is that it allows you to relate to people you wouldn't normally relate to. It gives you something to say to everyone you share that hobby with, which is important—to have something to say to anyone you might encounter in the world. I had never before thought about an interest in clothes as a "hobby" or that this was one of the important functions of a hobby.*

+

*Skype meeting.*

**HEIDI:** You know, a couple of years ago I decided I was going to be a gardener—I wanted to have a garden in my backyard. And I'm by no means a professional decorator or a stylist or anything, but I have some, possibly incorrect, sense of myself as a person with an aesthetic point of view. I figured, How hard will it be for me to make a garden? I'll just go out and plant one. I gave no thought to making things grow, mind you, which I also could not do. My focus was more about how—inside this little container of land—can you create something visually pleasing. Then I realized I had never in my life, not once, looked at gardens! So I thought: Well, okay, where have I put my visual energies, where have I paid attention? And that's when I realized: I've paid attention to women—at the expense of gardens, I guess. How women dress and present themselves is a subject of study, and for better or worse it's where I've put my energies. That knowledge I'd gained felt really sedimentary, really layered, and it gave me more appreciation for the topic of dressing as something worthy of excavation or exploration. Seeing my thoughts about dressing from that angle—of trying to figure out how to grow a garden—ennobled all that learning in a way I'd never considered before.

LEANNE: Maybe we should call it "Clothing Garden." *(laughs)*

SHEILA: What, the whole book?

LEANNE: Or the intro. Maybe it should be a German word—*Clothinggarten.*

HEIDI: It could be a German compound word!

LEANNE: And actually, when you think about it, a clothes garden, it does make sense. It's seasonal, and you do all these things, and then you prune away and you plant stuff and you nurture stuff . . .

HEIDI: *(laughs)* It's true!

SHEILA: It's interesting that we've all said the same thing of nothing much having changed in the past year. Like, in a nice way, there was no dramatic difference, we just feel a little more confidence and a little more ourselves.

LEANNE: It makes me think—like the way your hairstyle always defaults to whatever hair you have, there's probably a default to how individual women present themselves in dress. No makeover's going to actually work, because you'll just default to who you are, ultimately.

SHEILA: What's been kind of a revelation is seeing that other women think about this stuff not so differently from me, and have some of the same problems, the same anxieties. It makes it a bit more pleasurable knowing that everything you're feeling you share with other women. It makes the act of getting dressed seem more like a communal thing.

LEANNE: So thinking back to when you wanted to go to a store to find the book to tell you how to care about your clothes and be stylish and stuff—if this is that book, then what we're saying is: Don't bother reading this, you're fine?

HEIDI: *(laughs)* Stop reading here! Read no further unless you want to remain exactly who you are.

SHEILA: Well, or even that the cultural difficulty of being a woman is that you feel you have to be a certain kind of woman. I experience the conversations in this book as a liberation from that. To me it's also talking about how it's okay to have your own identity in the face of all this pressure to have some other identity. Working on the book and seeing women on the street, I immediately began to feel I loved them more because I could see inside them in a new way. I had a new way of interpreting their outsides.

HEIDI: What reading the surveys made me want are beliefs. Not rules or guidelines or tips, but beliefs. I was struck by how many people had idiosyncratic and highly personalized beliefs about clothing and its role in their lives. To me, that felt so . . . I don't want to say spiritual, but it felt like people's habits of mind were on display.

LEANNE: I think what these conversations do is eliminate a certain amount of nervousness and shame around dressing. We're surrounded by tons of imagery on a daily basis that says: Here are all these things you should admire, and things you can do to mask your insecurities and body, and you should not admit to feeling weird about this stuff. And this book is one huge admission. People might get some relief with it.

SHEILA: What kind of relief?

LEANNE: Just the relief of saying, "Yeah, I'm anxious about this, too." Or, "Look! Now I don't have to be anxious about this anymore!" Everyone is capable of feeling intimidated or scared or nervous about what they're wearing, and feeling judged by or judgmental of others, and admitting to that gives such relief. You can laugh about it. ✕

9

*TANIA VAN SPYK*'s dress sets part I

# QUESTIONS

*The book is based on a survey we invited women worldwide to complete.*
*The survey consisted of an ever-evolving list of questions.*

What is the most transformative conversation you have ever had with someone on the subject of fashion or style? • With whom do you talk about clothes? • Do you think you have taste or style? Which one is more important? What do these words mean to you? • Do you have style in any areas of your life aside from fashion? • Do you have a unified way of approaching your life, work, relationships, finances, chores, etc.? Please explain. • Would you say you "know what you like" in the area of fashion and clothing? If so, do you also know what you like in other areas of life, that is, are you generally good at discernment? If you're not so sure about your clothing choices, would you say you're better in other areas, or the same? Can you say where your discernment comes from, if you have it (or where the lack comes from, if you don't have it), and why? • Can you say a bit about how your mother's body and style have been passed down to you or not? • What is your cultural background, and how has that influenced how you dress? • Did your parents teach you things about clothing, care for your clothing, dressing, or style? What lessons do you remember? Did they tell you things directly, or did you just pick things up? • What sorts of things do you do, clothing- or makeup- or hair-wise, to feel sexy or alluring? • What are some things you admire about how other women present themselves? • Many people say they want to feel "comfortable," or that they admire people who seem "confident." What do these words really mean to you? • Do you care about lingerie? • Do you notice women on the street? If so, what sort of women do you tend to notice? What sort do you tend to admire? If not admiration, what is the feeling that a compelling woman on the street gives you? • If dressing were the only thing you did, and you were considered an expert and asked to explain your style philosophy, what would you say? • What is really beautiful, for you, in general? • What do you consider very ugly? • Are you generally a good judge of whether what you buy will end up being worn? Have you figured out how to know in advance? • When you look at yourself before going out, and you are trying to see yourself from the outside, what is this "other person" like? What does she like, dislike, what sorts of judgments does she have? Is this "outer eye" based on someone you know or knew once? • What's your process getting dressed in the morning? What are you considering? • What are you trying to achieve when you dress? • What, for you, is the difference between dressing and dressing up? • If you had to wear a "uniform," what would it look like? • What would you say is "you," and what would you say is "not you"? • Do you remember a time in your life when you dressed quite differently from how you do now? Can you describe it and what it was all about for you? • What sorts of things do you do, clothing-, makeup-, or hair-wise, to feel professional? • How do you conform to or rebel against the dress expectations at your workplace? • How do institutions affect the way you dress? • Do you have a dress code, a school uniform, or a uniform that you wear for an extracurricular activity? • Are there ways in which you conform to or rebel against these uniforms? • Is it comforting or constraining to have a uniform? • Was there a moment in your life when something "clicked" for you about fashion or dressing or makeup or hair? What was it? Why did it happen then, do you think? • Are there any dressing tricks you've invented or learned that make you feel like you're getting away with something? • What are some dressing rules that you wouldn't necessarily recommend to others but that you follow? • Are there any dressing rules you'd want to convey to other women? • What is an archetypal outfit for you, one that you could have happily worn at any point in your life? What do you like about it? • Do you ever wish you were a man or could dress like a man or had a man's body? Was there ever a time in the past? • If there was one country or culture or era that you had to live in, fashion-wise, what would it be? • Do you consider yourself photogenic? • When you see yourself in photographs, what do you think? • Send a photograph of your mother from the time before she had children, and tell us what you see. • Are there any figures from culture, past or present, whose style you admire or have drawn from? • Have you ever had a dream that involved clothes? • What would be a difficult or uncomfortable look for you to try to achieve? • Have you stolen, borrowed, or adapted any dressing ideas or actual items from friends or family? • Have you ever successfully given someone a present of jewelry or clothing that you continue to feel good about? • Were you ever given a present of clothing or jewelry that especially touched you? • If you were totally comfortable with your body, or your body was a bit closer to what you wish it was like, what would you wear? • When do you feel at your most attractive? • Is there anyone you are trying to attract or repel when you dress? • Do you like to smell a certain way? • What do you think of perfume? Do you wear it? • What's the situation with your hair? • Please describe your body. • Please describe your mind. • Please describe your emotions. • What are some things you need to do to your body or clothes in order to feel presentable? • How does makeup fit into all this for you? • What are you wearing on your body and face, and how is your hair done, right at this moment? • Is there a certain look you feel you're expected to like that you have absolutely no interest in? What is it? Why aren't you interested? • What are your closet and drawers like? Do you keep things neat, etc.? • Can you describe in a basic way what you own, clothing- and jewelry-wise? • What is your favorite piece of clothing or jewelry that you own? • Tell us about something in your closet that you keep but never wear. What is it, why don't you wear it, and why do you keep it? • Is there any fashion trend you've refused to participate in, and if so, why? • Looking back at your purchases over the past five to fifteen years, can you generalize about what sorts of things were the most valuable to buy? • Is there an item of clothing that you once owned but no longer own and still think about or wish you had? What was it and what happened to it and why do you want it back? • If you had to throw out all your clothes but keep one thing, what would you keep? • If you were building up your wardrobe from nothing, what would you do differently this time? • What's the first "investment" item you bought? Do you still own or wear it? • Was there ever an important or paradigm-shifting purchase in your life? • What item of clothing are you still (or have you forever been) on the hunt for? • Do you remember the biggest waste of money you ever made on an item of clothing? • Was there a point in your life when your style changed dramatically? What happened? • Do you address anything political in the way you dress? • Did you ever buy an article of clothing without giving it much thought, only to have it prove much more valuable as time went on? What was the item, and what happened? • Did you ever buy an item of clothing or jewelry certain that it would be meaningful to you, but it wasn't at all? What was it, and what happened? • How and when do you shop for clothes? • Do you have any shopping rules you follow? • How does how you dress play into your ambitions for yourself? • How does money fit into all this? • Are there any clothing (or related) items that you have in multiple? Why do you think you keep buying this thing? • Is there an article of clothing, some makeup, or an accessory that you carry with you or wear every day? • Can you recall some times when you have dressed a particular way to calm yourself or gain a sense of control over a situation that scared you? • Do you remember the first time you were conscious of what you were wearing? Can you describe this moment and what it was about? • Did anyone ever say anything to you that made you see yourself differently, on a physical and especially sartorial level? • In what way is this stuff important, if at all? ✕

*CLAUDIA DEY*'s fedoras

# GOOD MORNING

ELIF BATUMAN

Last summer, when I was living in Istanbul, Sheila Heti asked me to compliment a series of women on their clothes and record our subsequent conversations. The women were supposed to be strangers, and I was supposed to meet them in elevators. There were many, many reasons why I never did end up asking strange women about their clothes in elevators in Istanbul. The only place where I used the elevator was at the gym. I felt like the women at my gym already weren't that crazy about me, and to be honest, their clothes were nothing special. I did once compliment the Pilates instructor, a former ballerina, whose insistence on relaxing and natural breathing seemed somehow fraught with anxiety, on her amazing earrings: one of the tiny silver studs was connected, by a long, fine chain, to an equally fine necklace. I didn't have a tape recorder, but luckily she just smiled politely. She was folding "resistance bands."

Later that week, I had lunch with the writer Elif Şafak. We had first met some months earlier, when she accidentally walked into me at a huge dinner in London. She had been walking backward, for some reason. This was our second meeting. She was wearing marvelous clothes, about which I remember only that each article had a different texture, everything looked expensive, and all of it was black, though it was July. When I told her how wonderful she looked, she gave me a look full of compassion and, reaching across the table, wordlessly squeezed my hands.

All summer, antigovernment protests raged in Istanbul, and in cities all over the country. My apartment was often full of tear gas, and also full of journalists and protesters and, on one occasion, a protester's small, demanding dog. One journalist had come from Bulgaria; most mornings starting at seven, he was reporting to Bulgarian national radio, speaking very loudly, since it wasn't a good line. Every day, one or the other of my parents called, urging me to come home to the U.S. early. Nobody was sleeping, or getting any work done. Feeling overwhelmed, I packed a bag and took a commuter ferry to Heybeliada, an island in the Sea of Marmara. Though Heybeliada is in the Istanbul municipality, stepping off the boat was like landing on a different planet. There were no police vehicles, no police, no protesters, no gas masks, no gas, no graffiti. It was as if the past weeks had never happened.

"Where are all the police?" I asked when I reached the pension where I had booked a room.

"We have four police on the island," the owner replied. "They mostly concern themselves with picnickers."

When I stepped outside the next morning, a beautiful orange cat rubbed up against my leg. The sun seemed to pour over your whole body in a way that was full of love. Walking downhill toward the sea, past the ruined white Ottoman houses that resembled, with their gingerbread trim, heaps of old lace, I came upon a woman sitting on the curb. In her forties, deeply tanned, she wore a headscarf, and a severe expression. As I approached, I felt that she was actually glowering at me.

"Good morning," I said cheerfully, hoping to defuse the atmosphere, even as I wondered whether the woman was religious, and how the people who lived here felt about women traveling alone.

The woman's face was suddenly, utterly transformed, by what I realized was a smile. "Good morning," she said, beaming. "I was just admiring your skirt. That's why I was looking at you like that." ✕

# WOMEN LOOKING AT WOMEN

*"Sometimes I'll see a woman dressed in a way that makes me think we must be similar, like in another world we'd be friends."* —SASHA ARCHIBALD

**ANN IRELAND** Often, I'll spot a woman crossing the road who is wearing just the narrow gray-black pants I want. Or sneakers that are just one color with no ugly stripes. Maybe I could get away with that Indian dress! Those Jesus sandals are just the ticket—I bet they're comfortable, too. Then I crave it, a sort of low-level fever that won't lift until I've located the desired item and seen whether it works for me, too.

**VANESSA BERRY** A woman selling vegetables at a market stall once complimented me on my wool shirt. Every time I looked back she was looking at me. I took it as a good sign that I should wear this shirt when I want to impress someone.

**ALESIA PULLINS** I like complimenting other black women—women of color in general—because I feel like a lot of times the only people giving us compliments are other women of color. It's not a conscious thing where I'm like, "I'm going to go in here and find the two black girls and load them down with compliments." It's just something I tend to do because I realize, "Look, I see what you're doing over there, I see what you're working with, and I like it."

**ANA KINSELLA** When I was about nineteen, my friend and I were sitting outside the lecture theatre, smoking cigarettes and commenting on every girl who walked by and what she was wearing. We thought we were very

cool and trendy and edgy. In retrospect we were idiots and I in particular looked like a fashion-crazed fool. But after an hour or so we figured out that the girls we considered the best-dressed were not the girls who wore the clothes we may have coveted most, but the ones who had a consistent style, a steady palette, and knew the silhouettes that worked best for them. I realized then that style is about knowing what you like and why you like it, more than anything else.

**GRACE DENTON** In university, there was a girl who lived on my floor. She once came to my room and asked if her outfit looked okay. In the natural way young girls have with people they don't really know yet, I said, "Yeah, you look great!" She was probably wearing something middle-of-the-road and vaguely hippy. Then I asked, "How about me?" as a kind of social exchange. She said, "Hmmm, yeah, I don't know. You kind of look like you're trying to look wacky." This was a horrific revelation. Who the fuck . . . ! Why did she . . . ! I was wearing a polka-dot spaghetti-strap dress I loved, with a T-shirt underneath. It later became apparent that she had multiple social strangenesses, but the comment stuck. I still occasionally look at myself with her eyes and think, "Okay, trying too hard, take it back a step." This makes me sad.

**JILL MARGO** In my early twenties, there were a bunch of girls who swapped clothes or, rather, borrowed clothes from our most alpha female, who was very communally minded. They were considered lucky clothes—the ones that got us laid. Recently, I saw a photo from back then of my friend in one of the outfits. There is no way those things looked as good on any of us as they looked on her. What were we thinking?

OLLA NAJAH AL-SHALCHI In high school, I started wearing a hijab, and was still trying to find a way of dressing like my peers, while also respecting my religion. So I would wear black pants, a beige shirt, a vest that was black and beige, and a beige hijab. But I love color, and this outfit was boring and lacked color. However, one day my friends told me that my outfit looked "sophisticated." This got me thinking about how I didn't really need to care about dressing like my peers. Dressing "sophisticated" made me feel better about the clothes I was wearing.

KELLEY HOFFMAN It's not just my clothing that changed my first year working at *Vogue*. I also picked up cues on how to speak and act. Whenever my editor would ask me to do something, I'd say casually, "No problem!" But when I heard another intern, who was much more sophisticated than I was, say, "Of course," to this same editor, I thought it sounded much more refined, so I started saying "Of course," too.

JOSS LAKE My ex-girlfriend said, "You don't have style, you have styles." I'd always felt like I was failing to construct a coherent style—so it became a sort of Whitmanian mantra, not only for fashion, but for my personhood: "I contain multitudes. I contain multitudes."

STELLA BUGBEE Sometimes when I see a woman with particular charm or confidence or just interesting personal habits, I actually want to be her. And it's not one kind of

woman. Wildly different people inspire that kind of interest and awe. I never think that way about men, though.

AREV DINKJIAN For the past few summers, I worked at an Armenian Youth Federation camp. My outfits consisted of gym shorts, a dirty T-shirt, old tennis shoes, a messy bun, and a face with no makeup. It's less than glamorous, yet I leave each year with more confidence than ever. I'm surrounded by girls who look up to me, who mimic my every move, who want to look and be just like me. They tell me every day that I'm beautiful and ask me to do their hair and pick out their dresses for the dances. I feel at my best because they look up to me in my most natural state. And I find them just as beautiful.

LILI OWEN ROWLANDS I live with four girls and our wardrobes are an extension of each other. However, I find there's a competitiveness in it. I love to borrow but hate to lend. Sometimes I make up excuses about wanting to wear items of my own wardrobe so others can't wear them. I never understand where this sheer meanness comes from, but it happens and I hate it. I fear our slow homogenization. I've started wearing lots of yellow because I have told myself it suits only my colouring. I like to make a point of this sporadically at dinner: "Yellow only really works with a dark fringe."

KRISTI GOLDADE Last August, I was at an art fair and there was this Russian woman. She looked so pretty and dainty, her hair was cut in this shiny black bob, and she had a scarf around her neck. She was with her husband and kid. More than her look, I wanted her essence—it was so artistic and effortless. So in November, I cut my hair into a bob and now I try to do the seamless, sophisticated thing. I'm into it as a form.

**UMM ADAM** When I was thirteen, I dressed like all my friends in a simple shalwar kameez with a dupatta around my neck. There were a few girls in my school who wore the hijab, but I thought that was a little too extreme. I did not look down on them or think they were old-fashioned. I respected their style, but felt that style was not for me. One day, my mom was showing me pictures from her trip to the U.S. and I was a little surprised to see that there were Muslim girls there who wore hijab. My mom said, "I wish you could cover like them." That's when I put my dupatta on my head and decided to wear hijab.

**SZILVIA MOLNAR** I love noticing women who have a panoramic view of their environment when they're walking down the street. Women who are engaged in the moment and are interested in looking at who or what is around them.

**HEATHER MALLICK** When I was a child, we were on the subway in Montreal and I saw a beautiful black-haired young woman with perfect skin. She was in a red skirt with polka dots and was biting into a pistachio ice cream with her perfect large white teeth. I stared in awe and thought, "One day I will move to the city and live in my own apartment and dress like her." Who was that woman? I think about her often.

**AMANDA M.** At school, a Muslim girl spoke about why she chose the burka. She said, "You American girls have it rough. You constantly have to be thinking about what looks good on you, how to look hot, how to hide flaws. You're slaves to fashion. I'm never self-conscious about how sexy I look." When I see women in full coverings now, I wonder, "Are they freer than I am?"

**HELEN DeWITT** Once in Paris a woman pulled up to the curb in a red Ferrari to exclaim over a pair of black stretch trousers with a white faux-Chinese-character pattern which I had bought for ten quid in the Roman Road.

**DIANA BECKER** I was in line at the Guggenheim with my favorite cousin, who is a stylist. There was a woman in front of us and we couldn't understand her. She had a beautiful sixty-something face but she felt like a girl. Her outfit was perfect, her body svelte, not yoga-tight or anything extreme. We were obsessed with her and labeled her one of the "young-old." We still hunt for them and wonder if weather or cultures inspire more of them. What's their secret? Do they have good taste, or is it their mental state, diet, exercise? And why are they mostly not American? ✕

*LYDIA BURKHALTER*'s gray sweatshirts

# Leopoldine Core

*What do you admire about how other women present themselves?*

I admire well-groomed women whose clothes are clean and fit them perfectly. Conversely, I admire women who rock a more feral look. I can't decide which of these women I'd like to be. Clean or dirty? I pinball between the two.

*When do you feel at your most attractive?*

I feel attractive when I don't have any zits and when I'm having a good hair day. Hair and skin are the top priorities for me. But I feel spectacular when I'm wearing a dress because I like the air on my legs and I can wear my boots with the little heel. If I wear a dress and have exposed legs, I like a big sweater on top, kind of hanging off me, like a Kurt Cobain sweater. I can also feel very attractive in jeans and sneakers and an old stained hoodie with no makeup. That feels very youthful, and I'm turned on by the idea of someone being drawn to the face I actually have, the clothes I actually own. If someone likes me

all raggedy, I feel powerful, like I don't need much, and that's hot. Okay, I'm now realizing when I feel the most attractive. It's when I'm wearing someone else's well-chosen and wonderfully lived-in clothes. Like when I borrow a friend's shirt or pants or shoes. I look in the mirror while wearing these clothes and think, "I would never have known to buy this." And then I walk out into the world wearing whatever it is with a certain feeling—a sexy feeling.

*Are there any clothing (or related) items that you have in multiple?*

What I have a lot of is pajamas. Nightgowns are important to me, too, because I spend more time inside than out. Being in bed feels the most natural to me, I even write in bed. I grew up in a very cluttered apartment; my mother was a hoarder. The only uncluttered place was my bed, so I learned to do everything there. I have many flannel pajama bottoms and many large sleep shirts, which are just oversized T-shirts that are

soft from being washed so many times. I also call these shirts "eating shirts" because it doesn't matter if you spill, they are already so stained. I think I keep collecting these things because I like being naked but not totally naked. I like for there to be a loose wall between me and the world. I can't wear regular clothes while I'm home. It doesn't matter what time it is, when I get home I immediately strip down and put on pajamas or just underwear and a robe. I find regular clothes really restricting. I can't really relax until I'm wearing something loose and crawling into bed.

*How long does it take you to get dressed?*

It actually takes me a very long time to get ready, but I never feel a sense of urgency in the morning. I often leave late and with the sense that I look like shit. A good breakfast is very important to me. Making my egg and toast and tea comes first, then I make my way to my dresser and start rooting around. I think it takes me forty-five minutes including all the distractions along the way.

*What are some dressing rules you wouldn't necessarily recommend to others but you follow?*
I follow my mood and that can get me into trouble. I'll arrive somewhere and suddenly feel like a slob. The thing is that I can't get all tarted up if I feel depressed or lazy or if I'm too immersed in a creative project or a TV show. I wouldn't recommend this personality or soul or whatever it is that chooses my clothes. I'm hopelessly inconsistent and weirdly vain. I'll curl up with myself at home and think, "God, you're gorgeous," then at the party I'll realize it really would have been a good idea to take a shower.

*What are some dressing or shopping rules you think every woman should follow?*
Don't buy anything to prove yourself to a sneering salesperson in a fancy store. In upscale stores I've so often felt judged to the point of purchasing clothes I didn't truly want or need. I did this to prove I wasn't poor or a thief (even though I am poor and used to be a thief). Sometimes that devil head is my own and it's telling me I need a $300 sweater. But I don't. That said, I think it's important to get a few really nice, sometimes pricey items. I have these Swedish clog boots that were sort of expensive but I adore them

and wear them everywhere. I think the biggest mistake you can make is to buy a lot of crap, like thirty things off a sale rack rather than a few beautiful items. I think it's our demented way of getting to feel rich, buying tons of cheap little junky dresses. It feels so much saner to have a lean wardrobe you dig.

*Is there a dressing thing you wish women would stop doing?*
I wish women would stop fetishizing notions of perfection. Look at American *Vogue*—it's so safe. We are ashamed of our excess and that is the saddest thing in the world. It's why women keep getting nose jobs. They take the most beautiful thing about themselves and lop it off so they look like everyone else. In fashion it's the same. Anyone who gets an outfit perfectly right turns me off. Or I don't even notice them. It's "offness" that is key in fashion, I think. On a more specific note, I find the "It Bag" repulsive. Often I'll see one swinging on the arm of a wealthy woman in a tracksuit—it's a charmless staple of female wealth. And think about what a purse really is: an externalized pussy or womb. So to have the "right" one and the most expensive one—that sends a chill up my body. Taste is a wink, not a thud.

*Are there any dressing tricks you've invented or learned that make you feel like you're getting away with something?*
"Skater" dresses are hugely flattering on me. They hug the ribs, with a free-flowing skirt over the lower belly, so I can eat a huge dinner and my bloated stomach will be obscured.

*What is the most transformative conversation you have ever had on the subject of fashion or style?*
I remember talking to my ex-girlfriend about our experience of each other when we first met. I was wearing a striped button-down shirt, jeans, and navy Keds. My hair was tamely side-parted and I had daubed the purplish caves under my eyes with concealer. She said I looked like an intense private-school girl. "So I looked smart?" I asked. "Oh, definitely." I've had so many conversations like that, where someone describes me to me and I think, "How could that be me?" I looked intense to her because I was nervous. Although I am intense, I mean, she was right. Instantly she struck me as a genius because of all the things that she said. It didn't matter that she was wearing a holey old T-shirt, she was an intellectual. She was the intellectual in the old shirt and it made the shirt special. I still remember that shirt.

It was gray and battered and sheer. It's burned in my mind.

*Would you rather be perceived as having great taste or great style?*
When I think of taste, I think of the home. People with great taste have the right furniture, that kind of thing. It seems like a whole religion. "Style" feels looser to me, and sexier. I think of partial strangers saying this: "You have such great style!" It's the thing we say about the traveling circus that is our bodies. I love for people to look at how I move through the world and think, "Wow."

*Do you consider yourself photogenic?*
No. I think I look moon-faced and shadowy in photographs. Ghoulish and sad, like someone who works in a factory. The truth is that I panic when someone whips out a camera. And of course I try to suppress that horrible ringing feeling but I can't. It's the face of fear that represents me in most photographs. I think I'm beautiful in action, so that loss of my animation has always been deeply unflattering.

*What is your favorite piece of clothing or jewelry that you own?*
This might sound absurd, but right now it's my bra. I've had horrible luck with bras but this one fits like a glove. It's a Lithuanian bra

my ex bought for me last year when she was teaching there. I still can't believe she just looked at it and knew. I think it's a teen bra, and it's hideous, purple with yellow, orange, and blue stripes, but it feels perfect.

*What's the first "investment" item you bought?*
A pair of $200 shoes for my high school graduation. They were black with ribbons that tied up my legs, and my toes spilled out the front. They were a mistake, but at the time I was proud of how expensive they were.

*Was there a point when your style changed dramatically?*
When I was fifteen, my mother and I parted ways. Before, I had lived in an apartment in Manhattan with her, where she slowly went crazy. Eventually she was so dysfunctional that she had to move to L.A. and live in her brother's guest room. I moved with a friend of the family upstate to finish high school. I went from going to LaGuardia High, where you could wear a bathing suit without getting in trouble, to a really repressed high school with a dress code and no queers in sight. I went from dressing in an exciting way to dressing in a bland, brand-hungry way. It was sad. Before I moved there, I was making shirts out of stockings. I had oxblood Doc Martens, cool vintage old-lady coats, and weird little

dresses that were my mom's from the '70s. I was awesome. But upstate I became this nobody in, like, Steve Madden platform boots.

*What is the difference between dressing and dressing up?*
Dressing is just finding something comfortable and leaving the house. Dressing up is a more strenuous journey. It means rubbing scented oils into my frizzy hair and putting on some makeup. It means wearing a dress and my little clog boots and some sheer black stockings (Wolford are the best).

*Do you care about lingerie?*
I do, though not in an ambitious way. If someone were to buy lingerie for me I would wear it. But I'm more interested in finding well-fitting underwear and bras. I think cotton underwear can be sexier. Sometimes lingerie feels old-ladyish. I also don't like how certain "sexy" underwear is so tiny. I like more coverage on my ass.

*What are you trying to achieve when you dress for the world?*
Some days I want to be invisible. Other days I want to look interesting and pretty and like an animal. Looking unraveled but not too unraveled feels sexy and smart. It's part of being a writer. I like looking like someone who was probably lying around with her thoughts for a while and

then took a shower and groomed herself a little.

*How has your background influenced how you dress?*
I grew up in the East Village in the '90s. It was a dirty, stylish time. The goal was always to stand out and look different, not to aspire to be one kind of woman. Punk felt right. When I was young and pretty, there was a part of me that wanted to destroy that image. I was realizing that the corridor of women is all YES and I wanted to say NOOO. But I also wanted certain boys to want to fuck me, so it got confusing. I wore a lot of eyeliner and hoped to be ravaged.

*Have you ever dressed a certain way to gain a sense of control?*
When I feel too exposed, I put on a loose button-up sweater and instantly relax. My skin is pinkish, and color floods to the surface if I'm having a feeling. It's like looking right into my thoughts, and that can make me nervous. Frequently at an event I'll cover my naked arms.

*What are you wearing on your body and face, and how is your hair done, right at this moment?*
Shu Uemura oil on my hair and coconut Skin Trip lotion on my body. Then I put aloe gel on my face to calm the pinkness. I'm wearing an illuminating concealer under my eyes, some mascara and blush. I also use a Chanel eyebrow pencil to shape and define. Some days, I won't wear any makeup at all.

*What are some things you do to feel presentable?*
Shaving my armpits is important. It feels so good to get clean and smooth there. I need to wash my face and clean my teeth. I always floss. My shirt should be clean because a dirty shirt is a stinky shirt.

*Is there a part of your body that feels most distinctly you?*
I like my back. It's slender and muscly and pretty. I think it's the most sexual part of me.

*Would you ever do anything like cosmetic surgery?*
No, that scares me too much. Cosmetic surgery is actually really dangerous. You open yourself up to all sorts of infections. And then usually you look crazy.

*How do you care for your body?*
I don't exercise much. I try to eat lots of vegetables and lean meats and I take various green pills. But I have off months of swigging coffee and eating lots of candy. It takes its toll on me when I do that. I try to steer clear of inflammatory foods. Cucumber juice is excellent for my mood and skin.

*Do you have a unified way of approaching your life, work, relationships, finances, and chores?*
I think I'm a bird in a wind tunnel, and I'm working on it. I'm not as organized as I'd like, but my passions are deep and true and they move me to work really hard. I'm an intense little candle. If I love you it's really like a light coming from the bottom of my soul and you have my full attention. Same with a poem or story. Then other parts of my life suffer. I'll forget to pay Con Ed and suddenly it's dark.

*How important is all this?*
I hate when people say they don't care about clothes, because it's a lie. It's like when writers say they don't care about plot. Lie. We are always asking for something when we get dressed. Asking to be loved, to be fucked, to be admired, to be left alone, to make people laugh, to scare people, to look wealthy, to say I'm poor, I love myself. It's the quiet poem in the waiting room, on the subway, in the movie of our lives. It's a big fucking deal.

*Please say anything you like about yourself.*
I'm a feminist. I'm bisexual. And at twenty-eight, I'm more myself than I've ever been. What I mean is that the inside is pouring out more than ever before. Maybe twenty-eight is the magic year. The year of my lion heart. ✕

# YOU DON'T KNOW WHAT I DEAL WITH

## THE WOMEN FROM THE PODCAST BLACK GIRLS TALKING

ALESIA: What are your favorite fabrics?

FATIMA: Leather.

AURELIA: Leather is always great.

ALESIA: Yeah. Leather, chiffon, lace, sequins . . .

AURELIA: Tulle, I love tulle. I have no place in my life for tulle. But I love it.

RAMOU: Oh, I totally want to have a tulle wedding dress. My wedding dress is gonna have to have tulle.

AURELIA: I love the Pinterest boards with girls wearing tulle skirts and jean jackets, but that wouldn't function in my life.

ALESIA: I own a custom-made tutu! It has like three different pinks: hot pink, regular pink, and like a petal pink. And it has a black bow belt. Really, it's awesome. It was my birthday tutu. I think for a while I was going some shit and I just really needed something that made me feel all right, and I was like, "I'll get a tutu!"

RAMOU: Now I wanna wear tulle for my birthday this year!

AURELIA: You should. But I will just say, with the tutu—you can either wear a tiara on your birthday or a tutu. You can't do both.

*(Everyone laughs.)*

FATIMA: Aurelia, how would you describe your personal style?

AURELIA: Oh my god, I don't know. Maybe a post-apocalyptic Audrey Hepburn My Little Pony sort of thing.

FATIMA: That sounds amazing!

AURELIA: Yeah, I kinda landed somewhere between Audrey Hepburn and Stevie Nicks.

ALESIA: I wear dark clothes because I think they look great on me. Also, it's an homage to Janet Jackson. Her *Control* era, the *Rhythm Nation* era . . .

FATIMA: She looked great.

ALESIA: She'd always been the chubby kid with the chubby face, and that's how I've looked most of my life. But she didn't wear baggy stuff, she wasn't trying to hide her body. She embraced her curves, and everything she wore, it looked like it was tailor-made for her. She may have had insecurities, but you couldn't tell it in the way she dressed. I think that's been my style inspiration for who knows how long, with little adjustments here and there.

FATIMA: For me it's sort of a three-pronged thing between nineties Morticia Addams—like in the *Addams Family* movie—and Grace Jones, because I'm very drawn to androgynous kinds of looks, and Diana Ross, because I love that really glam stuff.

ALESIA: I spend a lot of time on my eyelashes, and it's definitely because of Diana.

AURELIA: I love lashes. Solange is a little bit further left-field than I am in my day-to-day life, but I wish I could dress like her on the regular. But my life doesn't really allow for that.

RAMOU: I love Solange, but you're right. I could not wear what she wears every day and make it work for me. I used to be really into accessories, like I would overaccessorize. And since I've cut my hair, I'm pretty much all about my earrings. But when I first cut it, I was very self-conscious about still appearing feminine, so I'd wear these big, very girly earrings. . . .

ALESIA: Me, too. When my hair started transitioning to natural, I wasn't comfortable with not having straight hair anymore, and I would try to girly it up a bit by wearing huge, chunky, feathery, neon, sparkly earrings. Like, "Hey, I'm still a girl!"

RAMOU: I was definitely like that.

AURELIA: I didn't do the big chop. I got a weave, and I had a big curly weave until my hair grew out enough that I wanted to wear it out.

ALESIA: That takes a lot of patience. I was, like, ready to rock my stuff immediately.

AURELIA: I did cut all of my hair off a while after that, but that was a fashion statement for me. I knew what I was going to look like. I think it's because my mother and my aunt had really short hair, like these boy cuts, and I always thought they were so gorgeous, so I was like, "I want to be like my mom and cut all my hair off." But then I grew it all out because I thought my boobs were too big, and it made my head look really small. *(Everyone laughs.)*

ALESIA: I went natural because I thought my head was too big, and wearing my hair straight was making me look odd. Everyone was always, "You have the best hair, it's so thick, you should just wear it." And I was like, "You don't know what you're talking about. You don't know what I deal with." But then I'd notice that when I had a curly weave, I looked really great, like my head looked proportional, so I finally decided to do it. But then I had a little problem where I just didn't feel like I looked . . . presentable.

RAMOU: I think, especially for black girls, it can be very contentious—natural or not natural—and people are very sensitive about their hair. But I'm realizing that before I cut my hair, it was more about my own worries. Like, nobody cared about my hair. And now that I've cut it, I just feel more confident with it, and it feels like more of a style, because I was very self-conscious when it was straight. It was very damaged and I would straighten it all the time and I would always wear it pulled back. So it's a whole different look for me. I do get a lot of compliments on my hair now.

AURELIA: I got more compliments when I cut all my hair off, which was weird. I thought it was gonna be the opposite. When I cut all my hair off, I got a hundred percent more attention from men. But at some point I decided that's not how I want to look anymore, so I grew it out. I constantly have this idea in my head of what I want to look like, and I just go with that.

ALESIA: There's four different types of hair on my head—like, curl patterns. I'd say my hair ranges from 3c to 4c. When I let it do its own thing, no one wants to see that, apparently, because I get no compliments. Other black women are like, "Good for you!" But I know they would never do it. But when I have my hair in twisties or a braid-out, where there's a defined pattern, I get a lot of compliments and I'm just like: "Save it. I know why you're complimenting me!"

FATIMA: My confidence grew when I stopped straightening my hair and started wearing it in its natural state. One, probably just because I was less exhausted from all this damn straightening, you know? *(laughs)* I looked better because I looked fresher— I was getting more sleep! And I wasn't constantly worried in the summer, when it's humid, about my hair going back to its natural curly state, or if it rained—all that stuff you worry about when your hair's straightened. It just went out the window. I've now cut it after about five years of growing it out, and I realized I should have kept it short the entire time, because I once again feel very free. There's this idea about very long, curly hair, and it being ideal, and I think I bought into that, even though it was more work for me, because it didn't really have a shape.

RAMOU: It's funny, we all have these similar hair journeys. I think the problem is . . . I know for me, I didn't grow up with a lot of black girlfriends with natural hair, or black girlfriends period. So part of my struggle with cutting off my hair was I felt, Oh I don't know anybody else who's going through this. But it does seem like this is a very kind of common thing that black girls go through.

ALESIA: What's really sad about that is that, yeah, I didn't have a community of black girls until very late in life. I mean, I'm not sixty, but until recently. Especially when I was transitioning from relaxed hair to natural hair, I was looking for a community to guide me through it, and I was lucky enough that I found someone who gave me this book called *Thank God I'm Natural* that's written by a black woman who has all these natural recipes and she tells you what to do straight up. Because looking at the blogs, they were so vicious, it's a miracle I didn't just say whatever and put my hair in a fake Yaki weave or something.

AURELIA: I went natural because there were enough people out in the world, at the point when I decided to do it, who were natural, so I got to see it more and say, Wait a minute, this is exactly what I'm trying to accomplish getting these relaxers every six weeks and getting straw sets. It looks exactly the same!

ALESIA: That's an advantage of living in an area that's populated by actual black people. *(laughs)* You get to see other black people living relatively normal lives, with bangin' hair. I only found natural communities because I was having scalp issues and I knew it was probably related to getting relaxers, and I was just Googling, and I was like, What else can I do? Then I found natural hair, and I kind of just waded my way through the murk.

ALESIA: I think that's why when I see someone in a really bad . . . sorry to keep talking about bad weaves, but they're ruining our community. *(laughs)* It's a real problem, you guys! When I see people who have terrible weaves, I'm just like, Look, there's a better way. Which probably comes off as weird, but . . .

FATIMA: My hair now looks healthy and it has a style, and it's manageable, and I just feel better. I just feel more like myself.

RAMOU: I think in the last few years I've also figured out what my style is. I sometimes like looking at fashion blogs and seeing trends, and figuring out which trends work for me and which don't. But I'm also somebody that, if I like a trend, I'm not going to stop wearing it next season or whatever, right?

AURELIA: Yeah. When you find something you like, it goes into your personal fashion library.

RAMOU: Like leopard. I'm never going to stop wearing leopard. I'm just always going to wear leopard, I think.

ALESIA: I'm so with you on that.

RAMOU: I'm wearing leopard underwear right now!

ALESIA: Most of my lingerie is leopard. My favorite nightie is this leopard-print Betsey Johnson negligee. It's got hot-pink bows on it, it's so tacky, it's so Peg Bundy, I love it.

AURELIA: That sounds amazing, are you kidding me? ✕

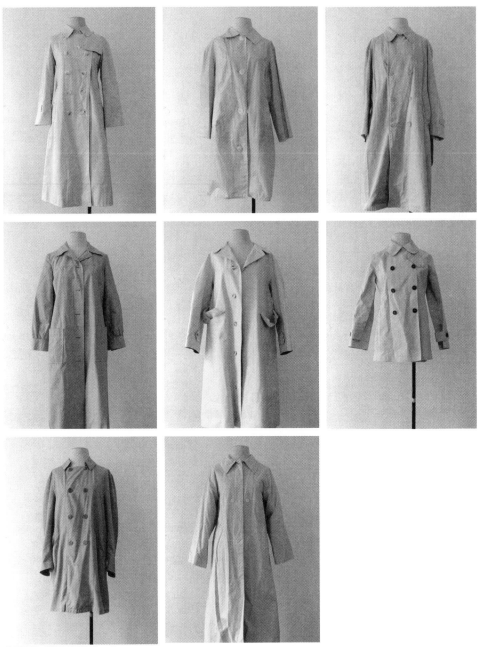

*ODETTE HENDERSON*'s raincoats

# I'M ALWAYS ON THE FLOOR AND WORKING

FASHION DESIGNER **MONA KOWALSKA** OF A DÉTACHER SPEAKS TO
**HEIDI JULAVITS** & WRITER/CHILDBIRTH EDUCATOR **CERIDWEN MORRIS**

**CERIDWEN:** When you think about clothes, do you think more about day-to-day, practical, non-event-focused dressing?

**MONA:** I don't really care so much about looking sexy or smart. People want to feel a certain way. That is almost more important than how things look. So I try everything on, because I want the clothing to feel a specific way. I do all my own pattern-making, I do all my own muslins. I like to feel strong in my clothes.

**CERIDWEN:** I just turned forty-five, and the look that's being pitched to me is about being MILF-y, sexy—but whatever you do, don't look like you're forty-five. Like the idea of being a capital-W Woman is not so great. We should all look twenty-eight.

**MONA:** And the result is these terrible human collages. Sometimes you see someone from the back and they're all worked out and wearing skinny jeans and then they turn around . . .

**HEIDI:** Eep! And they're seventy!

**MONA:** I'd prefer someone dressed in a dowdy way.

**CERIDWEN:** I feel like the stuff you design is younger than anything else out there, in the sense that it's childhood young. I recently tried on your dress with the ruching around the bottom. You said the design was inspired by the act of tucking your dress into your underwear.

**MONA:** My assistant from Australia always tucked her dress into her underwear. I thought, That is so smart, so I did it, too! Now if I'm wearing something fluid in the summer I always tuck it into my underpants, because I'm always on the floor and working.

**CERIDWEN:** There's this youthful aspect to your clothing and at the same time it's very much about being a grown-up woman. Everyone else is seeking to be right in the middle, at twenty-eight. Which, by the way, is a wonderful age.

**HEIDI:** It's not a wonderful age, actually.

**CERIDWEN:** It's a rough age, that's true. Thirty is a bit better.

**HEIDI:** I feel like forty is the best age.

**MONA:** I was at a dinner in France recently. Most of the women at the table were in their late fifties, and at some point somebody said, "What age would you go back to?" And all of them said forty. It was amazing. They could have said anything! They could have made themselves sixteen. Everyone said forty. You're at the top of your game, you're at the top of your career, you're at the top sexually. But here in America we don't have this appreciation. I don't find America particularly youthful, for all the emphasis on youth.

**HEIDI:** You really appreciate the influence of older women.

**MONA:** That ruched-bottom dress came from the "Grandma's House" collection. I feel like one's grandmother is a big clothing influence.

**HEIDI:** More than one's mother?

**MONA:** I think so. A grandmother is your first contact with vintage. Grandmas are pile-ups of the old thing, the acrylic thing, the crazy thing. There's the thrill of sorting through Grandmother's stuff.

HEIDI: What was your grandmother like?

MONA: She was a very elegant woman. One of the things in the collection inspired by her was this big wallet. She used to wear a big wallet between her bosoms. When she needed money, she would, just like a magician with a rabbit, pull this wallet out of the top of her dress.

CERIDWEN: I store lots of things in my bra. I have my phone in there. Credit cards, money, keys. When you don't have pockets, you have to stick it somewhere.

HEIDI: Was your mother an influence?

MONA: My mother was head of an atelier. There were two companies that dressed all of Poland under Communism, and my mother worked for one of them. She had a lot of private clients, so there were always women in and out. You know, wives of party members, who could afford to have clothing made. Our apartment was the size of your pocket, so when someone arrived, that's what was happening that day. I remember her doing wedding dresses. She thought it was a particular kind of gift to make a wedding dress.

CERIDWEN: Have you ever made a wedding dress?

MONA: I made one for one of my oldest customers, a person who supported me when I first opened. But I would never do it again.

HEIDI: You had misgivings about the dress?

MONA: I didn't. I just don't have a lot of connection to the idea of the wedding dress. I planned my wedding in two days. I wore a '40s silver jacket and black pants. So I wasn't connected to the intensity of choosing a wedding dress. You know, when a person is trying on a wedding dress, we say it looks nice, and then we have to start over and say it again. It's this "You look great" loop that goes on for two hours.

CERIDWEN: I have one of your sweaters and it's a little itchy, and there's something about the itchiness that's so intentionally contrary to the Juicy Couture comfy adult sweatpants culture.

MONA: I wear those sweaters on bare skin because I'm such a maniac. I always say, It's nice to feel your clothes. If something's a little tight on your bum, I don't think that that's an issue. You'll walk differently that day. Like a little panty line, and that funny way of walking . . .

HEIDI: I love the panty-line detail. When you moved to Baltimore, was your mother still making your clothing?

MONA: Not so much. We moved in the 1970s, when I was nine.

CERIDWEN: Baltimore has a specific aesthetic—the whole John Waters thing. Was that relevant for you at all? Or '70s American culture in general?

MONA: Just '70s American culture in general. I really have an appreciation for that era. That was when we finally took the remaining stuffing out of the clothes. After the '80s, it's more about bulking up again, but in the '70s we were almost naked. There was this feeling: a little bit naked—powerful and naked. If I think about clothing, the 1970s is one of the decades for which I have a deep appreciation. I think it's the decade that influences me the most. Although it's less about the way the clothing looked. It's more about that feeling of a sense of freedom. No bras, a natural body, you'd always see somebody's nipple. I have a girlfriend, she has a big bosom, and if the dress permits it, she'll go without a bra. I think that looks great.

HEIDI: Do you wear bras ever?

MONA: No. I mean, I'm so tiny!

HEIDI: You work in the back of your store. Do you ever come to the front and give customers advice when they're trying on your clothes?

MONA: Generally I try not to give advice. I don't really want to worm my way into people's lives and closets in that way. If I say something to a customer, it's usually along the lines of "That dress looks really beautiful with your hair color," because I think sometimes people don't see those things. Someone with dark hair will try on a navy dress, and all of a sudden their hair has this blue cast and it looks really beautiful. But rarely do I give advice like "You should wear this with this," because I don't know. I don't know what people should wear. You don't know about people's lives.

**HEIDI:** Do you ever learn things from watching people try on the clothes?

**MONA:** Women love pockets. Sometimes when we do sales, a buyer will try something on and I'll see her do this *(hands-searching-for-pockets gesture)*, and then I will add pockets.

**HEIDI:** Are there other people who've inspired you?

**MONA:** I worked for Sonia Rykiel in Paris, and she was really into the accidental discovery. She was the first person who did the inside-out seams. I think she just put her sweater on inside out one day. As a designer, you pay attention to these accidents.

**CERIDWEN:** What are some of your best accidental discoveries?

**MONA:** One day I walked out of the shop and saw an older woman with her raincoat on. She'd put her dickey on over her raincoat, and I thought, Ah!

**HEIDI:** What's a dickey?

**MONA:** It's just a little partial shirt, it usually has a turtleneck, and you wear it under things. But she wore it over her coat, and I thought, "She couldn't find her scarf and so she just threw that on." She was a little Hispanic old lady, she wasn't doing a "look." I pay attention to older women. I find they just do these things.

**CERIDWEN:** What was the first thing you owned that you were excited about?

**MONA:** I remember some jumpsuits I had when I was in high school. I had one that was made in India.

**CERIDWEN:** Did you listen to the Abba record *Arrival*? The Abba ladies really worked the jumpsuit.

**MONA:** I had immigrant parents, so we had no music at the house. When I said I wanted a backpack, they were like, Oh my god, no, you're going to look like a runaway. So I couldn't carry a backpack or wear jeans.

**HEIDI:** Do you always wear heels?

**MONA:** I prefer heels. Last week I wore Birkenstocks and at the end of the day I just felt so bad about myself. Like, Okay, my feet don't hurt, but my morale is really low. I think I'd rather have feet that hurt a little bit but a higher morale.

**HEIDI:** Do you think about how the body gets canted differently depending on the heel height? That posture becomes part of the whole look.

**MONA:** I have one pair of try-on shoes, they're a pair of old Miu Miu shoes that have a high heel and a very simple banded front. They are in horrible condition, they are so beat, but if I try on a muslin and those shoes are not there, I am almost in tears. I turn over the whole back room, like, "We gotta find the try-on shoes!" There's something about the way these shoes sort out my body—all of a sudden it's the proportion I want to see. It's that extra three inches on the leg. It's not about the shoe so much. It's the proportion that shoe creates.

**CERIDWEN:** Since I've got bigger boobs, I like to wear bigger shoes. Because if I come down to a point, I'm feel like I'm teetering.

**MONA:** If you made your hair big, then it would be nice to teeter.

**HEIDI:** Do you ever make super-delicate shoes?

**MONA:** I prefer a strong, sexy shoe. I like things that aren't just one thing. When you accomplish that in a design, it allows everyone to find themselves in it. I like these dualities. They're open-ended somehow. People will come in and they'll say of a dress, "It reminds me of something my mother used to wear." That sense of finding yourself in something is important. That's where the resonance comes from.

**CERIDWEN:** Sometimes you need fishnets to balance the wool sweater.

**MONA:** I think about the very beautiful woman who dresses down. She could dress up and be a total babe. But people like a more complicated presentation of themselves, I find.

**HEIDI:** How do you balance wanting your aesthetic to be embraced by many women with that proprietary feeling of, "Hey, fuck, that's my look."

**MONA:** I only have one thing about which I feel proprietary. When I wear men's shirts, I turn the collar in. I have a friend who does it and it makes me crazy. It brings out the teenager in me. You know why I resent it so much? Because I share everything. For example, I make a little dish rack for my house, and then I make it for the store because it works so great. I share everything! So that collar thing makes me so crazy. I want to say, "Let me just have this one thing." Oh, it just makes me so cross, you have no idea. ✕

## "WATCH"

*Shibuya, Tokyo. Saturday night in a department store. Two young Japanese saleswomen stand together. One is wearing a black miniskirt, tights, and a loose gray sweater. She is also wearing a watch with a brown leather band and, in its face, golden exposed gears and parts.*

**KATE:** I like your watch!

**WOMAN:** Oh, thank you!

*(The woman and her coworker giggle.)*

**HER COWORKER** *(in Japanese)*: Her watch is handmade.

*(The woman holds it up for the others to see more closely.)*

**WOMAN:** Handmade by an artist in Japan.

**KATE:** It's beautiful.

**WOMAN:** Thank you! ✕

## WEAR AREAS | GINTARE PARULYTE

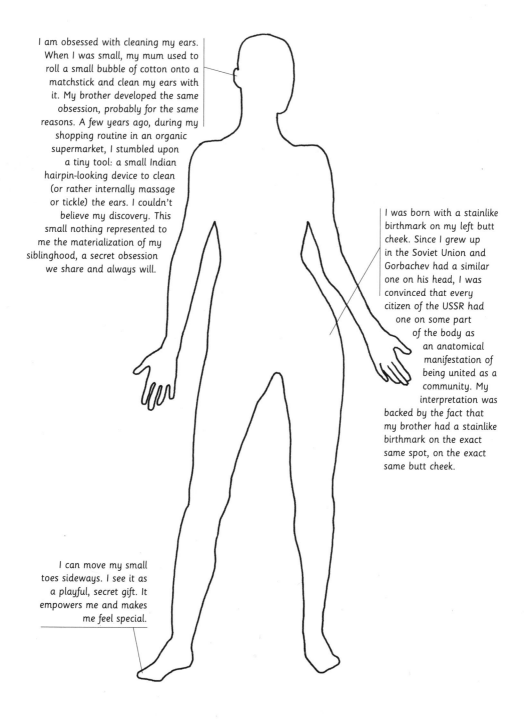

I am obsessed with cleaning my ears. When I was small, my mum used to roll a small bubble of cotton onto a matchstick and clean my ears with it. My brother developed the same obsession, probably for the same reasons. A few years ago, during my shopping routine in an organic supermarket, I stumbled upon a tiny tool: a small Indian hairpin-looking device to clean (or rather internally massage or tickle) the ears. I couldn't believe my discovery. This small nothing represented to me the materialization of my siblinghood, a secret obsession we share and always will.

I was born with a stainlike birthmark on my left butt cheek. Since I grew up in the Soviet Union and Gorbachev had a similar one on his head, I was convinced that every citizen of the USSR had one on some part of the body as an anatomical manifestation of being united as a community. My interpretation was backed by the fact that my brother had a stainlike birthmark on the exact same spot, on the exact same butt cheek.

I can move my small toes sideways. I see it as a playful, secret gift. It empowers me and makes me feel special.

*KATE RYAN*'s tote bags

# BREASTS

*"I rebel against the idea of pleasing men, but I think lingerie is beautiful, especially on women over fifty."* —ELLEN RODGER

**KRISTINA ANNE GYLLING** I'm pretty happy and comfortable with my body. I wish my breasts were bigger so that I could wear dresses that had bust cups or a bustline that accentuates the breasts. When I see women wearing those types of dresses, it embodies a certain part of womanhood that I don't think I'll ever experience. I think I'll feel like I'm trapped in a little girl's body forever.

**MEGHAN BEAN FLAHERTY** I care a great deal about lingerie. Where I fail in clothing, I ace all tests of underlace. I have a pathological desire to match the bra and panties, the silk stockings to the garter belt. Each new piece becomes a character in me—a heroine, an ingenue, a bawd. I keep them in a perfumed box.

**TALITA S.** My mum is sort of anti-bra. She wears Lycra tops and says anything else gives breast cancer. I used to wear Lycra tops when I was younger, but I felt embarrassed about it. My lack of decent bras made me feel like less of a woman. So when I moved to London, the first thing I bought was a bra. I went to the shop that makes bras "by appointment to Her Majesty the Queen" and had a fitting, then spent 180 pounds on a bra at Agent Provocateur. It is still the only piece of actual lingerie I own—that bra and the matching panties—and it always gives me a buzz to wear it. If I have to wear old or dirty underwear, I spend the whole day missing a big chunk of my self-confidence.

**ZARA GARDNER** Lately I'm very interested when women deliberately present themselves as small-chested by wearing an unpadded bra. I see this as an act of liberation, rejecting how men and society might wish them to look. I'm small-breasted myself and gradually moving toward bras that are about support over cleavage. I feel it's a sign of growing confidence and strength somehow.

**TAMARA SCHIFF** I think smaller breasts would be more conducive to the types of tops I like to wear. I wish I could go braless with certain tops without feeling inappropriate. It's not my style to dress in a sexy manner, but sometimes I think my boobs, which honestly aren't even that big, make things a little more va-va-voom than I would like them to be.

**KRISTY HELLER** I travel the country with the Renaissance Festival. My circuit takes me from North Carolina to Arizona to Minnesota to Louisiana, and everywhere in between. Every weekend I dress up in "garb" and everything I put on for the shows accentuates the female form; waists are taken in, hips are lush and womanly, breasts are everywhere. When women put on an outfit like this, they can feel this incredible surge of power.

**JUDE STEWART** Getting a real bra fitting is no joke when you're expecting. Those boobs really do swell on you, for a surprisingly long time, and going braless occasionally becomes a thing of the past. I used to wear a

36B and am now a 36C at least. I hate the smoothly robotic-neutral color of most maternity bras, but it's too much effort to fight that tendency entirely.

**ASHLEY C. FORD** My breasts are always bigger than I think. I look fertile. I'm not.

**SZILVIA MOLNAR** I have an almost bodily memory of a new sweater I got one Christmas. I was fourteen, and my mother had knitted me a cream-colored sweater that came out a lot tighter than planned. I liked it, but it was the first time I let my quite newly budded breasts get so much recognition. I felt they were exposed to the world for the first time, since the sweater held on to them so tightly. I ended up only wearing that sweater at home during the holidays.

**EMILY BROTMAN** In high school, girls with names like Molly and Cate wore sports bras that curved fantastically around their shoulder blades—I could see through their gym shirts when it rained. It made their chests look taut and perky.

**REN JENDER** In a cruisey, sexual way, I like women with generous bodies, perhaps because even at my heaviest I've never had big hips or breasts.

**BETH FOLLETT** If I find a brassiere that suits me, I buy two or three, as it seems almost a Murphy's Law that bras I really like will become obsolete in two years. I am not a standard bra size and I've had trouble finding bras that truly fit. I don't want to wear my breasts like bullets.

**MIMI CABELL** My ex-boyfriend really liked it when I wore a garter belt and stockings, and he would get really turned on, but as he got turned on, I would sort of shrink away into myself. I knew that he was into me in

the lingerie, but it was hard. I guess I feel at odds with the way that sexy is portrayed, because the closer I get to how I think I should be presenting myself, the less like myself I feel. I feel like an alien, or not alive, or nothing at all.

**RACHEL WEEKS** When I worked at this nonprofit to help garment workers, there was a faction of women there who could not believe we were considering partnering with a manufacturer that was making bras for Victoria's Secret. I mean, these women were just *livid*. And I sat there and I thought to myself: Every woman in this room is wearing a bra. And do they have any idea where that bra was made? Like, are all their bras ethically sourced? I doubt it. It's one of the most complicated garments in the world to make—it has over thirty-five components, and it's a very complicated piece of apparel with a global sourcing story.

**CARISSA HALSTON** I have a very small back and a very large front. How I wish I could buy a $10 or $15 bra from H&M. I can't even buy a $40 bra from Lane Bryant. Because I'm a 32F, my back is too small to shop in plus-size stores and my cup size is too large to get a bra anywhere else. And if I wear the wrong-size bra, my posture is awful and my clothes fit me like a tarp.

**MARIE MYUNG-OK LEE** I don't enjoy wearing bras. I also think they are bad for your health, so I keep my eye out for clothes that suit this. I'm Asian, so I have small breasts and can get away with this more than women with larger cargo.

**KATHRYN BOREL** I never let a button-up shirt bulge around my boobs. You know when that little opening is created between two buttons? Fuck that. To myself I will say, "Suck it up, get a larger size."

**ROXANE GAY** I would get a breast reduction and lift. I want the girls to fly high.

**KATE ZAMBRENO** I have a rather large bust but a small frame—the last measurement at a bra fitting was a 32DDD. I have to buy new bras every six months, otherwise I am already on the last hook and everything's stretched. My bras are like military equipment. It's a really costly thing I have to do. I know that when my clothes don't fit then I need to buy new bras.

**JASON BARKER** Trying to pass as male with 38DD breasts was quite a challenge, so I wore a tight elasticated binder to keep my boobs strapped to my chest and then a beige fleece vest on top, like a psychological binder on the outside. There's a photo of me standing outside the pork pie shop in Skipton and the outline of flattened breasts is quite clear, like I'm trying to smuggle two very large pita breads under my clothes. Then, last autumn, I bought myself a padded sleeveless jacket from a shop that sells outdoor gear and I loved the whole shop. The clothes are all presented according to purpose. There are no tricky patterns or designs, nothing to call attention to the wearer in a "Look at me in my new clothes—I think I look great!" sort of way. The huge photos they have of bearded men and laughing women enjoying the outdoors were very appealing—to be free from fashion and free from the pressure to "express myself" through clothing. Truth is, I just want to look like everybody else. ✕

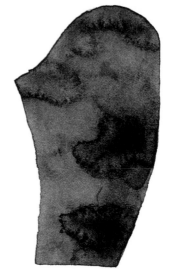

*DOROTHY PLATT*'s wrap skirts

# STAYING HOME

ROSE WALDMAN

From my closet I pull out a straight black skirt, my go-to on most days. I choose a cream-colored T-shirt to go with it, then the lace blouse I always wear over the T-shirt to hide the fatty bulges on my back. A perfectly good outfit—in Williamsburg, among my fellow Hasidim, that is. But for tonight's event, I'm feeling doubtful. The outfit seems too overdone. Too formal. The blouse goes back. So does the shirt.

I try a dark purple T-shirt instead. Now I look somber. Off it goes. I want something summery, light. I'll be conspicuous enough wearing long sleeves in ninety-degree weather among the halter tops I imagine everyone else will be wearing. I try the cropped white shell with the turquoise cotton sweater. I like it. Maybe this will work.

Tonight's event is a reading at a gallery by one of my fiction workshop classmates. When I got the invite, I e-mailed her, *I'll be there. Can't wait!* But in the end, I don't go. All the shilly-shallying over clothes has been for nothing. As usual, at the last minute I chicken out.

Some clarifications before I continue:

When I use the word "T-shirt," I am talking about the "Hasidic T-shirt," which is the same thing as a regular T-shirt but the sleeves are longer.

Cropped shells are also a Hasidic invention. They are long-sleeved T-shirts that end in an elastic below the bust. They're quite brilliant, actually. We can now buy pretty much any sleeveless top, wear it with a cropped shell, and voilà—instant sleeves!

After supper, I lie down on the couch with my sudoku and feel a bit guilty. I should be out there supporting my fellow writers, especially this woman, who is one of the loveliest people I know. Here's how I justify staying home:

I'm generally not a night person. After six p.m., my body and brain stop cooperating with me. So it's not really my fault, but my body's.

I squeeze a lot into my days. I deserve to relax with a book or a crossword puzzle or sudoku in the evenings.

It's really hot and humid out there, and I'm allergic to humidity. It always puts me in a foul mood.

I have so many obligations in my real life—my Hasidic life—weddings, bar mitzvahs, engagement parties, charity events, and so on, that I cannot get out of attending, that it's not my fault if I have no energy for these extracurricular experiences.

These reasons aren't bad. And they're also true. But they're not the real reasons. Or at least, not the only reasons.

The fact is, I'm self-conscious at these events. In my panty hose, long skirt, long-sleeved top, and wig, I feel like "that girl." My rational mind tells me that in New York City, where people dye their hair green and wear knee-high boots in the dead heat of summer, my Hasidic wear barely merits a second glance. But like most people, I operate by emotion, not rationality. And my emotional self feels conspicuous and self-conscious.

These days, when people compete for ever more imaginative ways to make themselves stand out, when all of life is one big exhibition and if it's not on Facebook and Twitter it's like it never happened, I suppose many people would enjoy standing out. But that's because they don't have to stand out. Standing out is their luxury, not their necessity.

It bothers me that I didn't go to the reading. Clothes should not have such power. ✕

*Bird*

*Doris*

*Gossips*

*Rooster*

*Princess*

*Tulip tree*

*Les violons*

*Spring rain*

*Deer season*

*White trellis*

*Field flowers*

*Flower heads*

*Scattered pins*

*Vegetable patch*

*Orange blossom*

*Triangles and lines*

*Pennies from heaven*

# YOUR JEWELRY IS YOUR STOMACH

## NOVELIST KIRAN DESAI SPEAKS TO HEIDI JULAVITS

**HEIDI:** You recently mentioned that you're at a fashion crossroads.

**KIRAN:** Yes, but also a life crossroads. I realized that I've been doing everything wrong. *(laughs)*

**HEIDI:** Let's start with clothes and then we can explore the other aspects of your wrongness.

**KIRAN:** I grew up in India, so you have to learn a whole new way of doing clothes when you move to the West. Fashions don't carry over, so if you fly between places you will inevitably look wrong in the country you're going to. Definitely going to India you look bad if you go in your Western clothes. Everyone comments on how awful you look right away. The sky is different, the street is different, the dust is different—only Indian clothes work.

**HEIDI:** So do you have both of those wardrobes?

**KIRAN:** No, I don't. I always look wrong when I go back to India. But then, I feel extremely unhappy in New York, too.

**HEIDI:** New York is where I've always felt the most wrong. Even when I manage to feel right on occasion, if I see a picture of myself when I felt right, I look horrible to myself.

**KIRAN:** I feel ashamed of myself when I feel right in New York, because there's something wrong with this place. I'm always stunned when I walk into a party

and I find all these women are really wearing little high heels, and girls are dressed in tiny clothes that look really horrible in fact, and they're so miserable in the cold of winter, wearing tiny little high heels in the snow. These women have no pride.

**HEIDI:** Many people see saris as being more uniform, if they don't have an eye for where the differences lie, where personal flair comes in.

**KIRAN:** That's right. It's in the way you tie them. But also, every tiny community and all the weaving families, they have a code of symbols, and the patterns can be handed down six, seven generations. They're so complex. The wedding sari will have its own special symbols—it's this huge code. They're beautiful. The plants and shells and creatures and birds . . . I miss that, because in America, you don't have animals all over your clothes. Well, you do sometimes, but I'm not a fan of leopard print.

**HEIDI:** Just actual leopards.

**KIRAN:** I lament having to give up Indian clothing now that I'm here. It's one of the most fun things about being an Indian woman. But it's really time-consuming. All these people manage to have clothes like that because they have servants. With the saris, you wash these great lengths of fabric, then you hang them on huge lines or down your balcony, then you starch them and then someone stands on one end and you stand on the other end and you pull it to make it tight and starchy, and then it's ironed. So it's a lot of work.

**HEIDI:** I never think of saris as being starched. I think of them as being more flowing.

**KIRAN:** Well, the cotton ones are starched. Traditionally they're dipped in rice water and then starched, so you walk around so stiffly. Then gradually the humidity and sun get to them and they become really crumply.

**HEIDI:** They wilt.

**KIRAN:** Starched clothes also sound so different. I once interviewed weavers in different parts of India, and they were telling me how important the sound of silk is. If two women are going through a door together, and they rub saris, they should make a *kssshh*. They complained that cheap Chinese silks are flooding the market. They don't have the right sound. It should be rustling.

**HEIDI:** Instead of that nylon-y, slick sound. Do you have recollections of learning what to wear once you moved to England, then America?

**KIRAN:** I remember starting to wear the most basic T-shirts and jeans and being unhappy in them. If you haven't grown up wearing a lot of jeans, they're very uncomfortable.

**HEIDI:** They have grommets on them. That dig into your body!

**KIRAN:** Why did they become so popular? Remember after September 11, when everyone was terrified that anyone who looked strange in New York would summarily shoot something? Well, my aunt has only worn saris her whole life, and

her son told her, "You've got to try to wear jeans." So they put her into jeans and she couldn't sit down. *(laughs)* I kept saying, "Sit down," and she'd say, "I can't!" *(laughs)*

**HEIDI:** So what made your misery come to a head?

**KIRAN:** I don't know. It was building and building and I realized I'm not . . . *anything*. I'm not living the life I want. I'm not living according to my ideals of life. I'm just sort of embarrassing myself. One option for me now is to come up with a kind of uniform.

**HEIDI:** And you feel that figuring out a uniform is a starting point?

**KIRAN:** Well, you have to have some sort of self-respect in the end that doesn't alter depending on where you go, which place you travel to. Ideally, the uniform would be something I'm happy in, that's not dull, but also that I could wear all the time.

**HEIDI:** Gustav Klimt used to work in a blue caftan. It was a painter's smock, and it was linen, and almost looked like a monk's robe.

**KIRAN:** With exciting fabric, you could wear that with your long johns in the winter! I feel like when I find the right thing, I'm really going to go for it and stick with it, because it's taken me until age forty-two to be in this miserable place.

**KIRAN:** I'm writing a story right now about these women going to visit the family jewelry in the bank—these precious stones mixed with beads and glass. That was your inheritance, and it mattered a lot, as any Indian woman knows. And the grandmother keeps giving it away to the granddaughters, then reclaiming it because she can't bear to let it go because . . . it's like her stomach is missing. I've seen it so strongly, the jealousy, greed—having to pass on your jewelry, feeling your jewelry is your stomach, in a way. It's that much the center of your life—your saris, your jewels. There are women in my family—their eyes, their entire expression changes as soon as they're in front of a sari or old jewels they've handed down. Something really old comes up. I remember my grandmother had these jewels, and whenever she had to give one away, she felt like an organ was missing.

**HEIDI:** And she had to give it away because . . .

**KIRAN:** Because you inherited it. You have to give it to a daughter when she gets married.

**HEIDI:** So in the story you're writing, they're going to visit the jewelry in the bank?

**KIRAN:** Yes.

**HEIDI:** That's fascinating—the survival worry that, as a woman, you're only worth what you show up with. Like you have this clothing, and this dowry with these linens, and these jewels.

**KIRAN:** Yes. I have some jewelry that was divided among all us grandchildren, and I have my grandmother's nose ring. It's huge—it covers your whole mouth. Why don't I wear that? ╳

# MOTHERS AS OTHERS | PART 1

*Send a photograph of your mother from the time before she had children and tell us what you see.*

*TENKI TENDUFLA*

*DORA VOGEL*

Born in Darjeeling, India, my mother flew across the world to New York at nineteen. It was 1951 and she was the first Tibetan to travel to the U.S. to study medicine. She attended medical school at Columbia University and became a pediatrician and mother of four. I love this photo because it captures my mother's courage and ambition, her intelligence and poise, and her love of glamour and beauty. Looking at her leather gloves, white trench coat, stylish bag, the elegant shoes on display, I can smell her perfume, see her flawless red lipstick and arched brows, hear her delightful—and delighted—laugh. Whether in a Tibetan chuba dress, lab coat, or tailored suit and pearls, my mother was always stunning. When this photo was taken, she might have just finished a week of cramming for finals or come from an all-nighter in the lab. Perhaps she was on her way to meet friends for a showing of *Cry, the Beloved Country* at the Bijou Theatre, or out for sake and sukiyaki at the Miyako Restaurant on 56th Street. **ANN TASHI SLATER**

This is my mother and two of her sisters in their hometown of Regina, Saskatchewan, Canada. It's 1945, three years before she met my dad. Mom is the one in the foreground with the goofy sunglasses and striped shirt. At that point in her life, I think she felt happy. She enjoyed her job as a secretary and was still living at home, with few worries or responsibilities aside from her job. The first time I saw this photograph, the image of my mother jolted me. Never in her life did I witness any inkling of lightheartedness, especially not as we kids were growing up. Seldom do I recall her laughing or smiling. What was missing from her life? How sad that she chose not to confide in us. **BEV SANDELL GREENBERG**

CLAIRE GRIFFIN

BERNADETTE CHEE GEK KHENG

This is a picture of my mother in Palm Beach, Queensland, in 1979. She is the brunette. Her sister, the blonde, would die of cancer at age sixteen soon after this picture was taken. The cancer metastasized from the thin brown right arm in the foreground of this picture. My mother sometimes looks at this picture and tries to find evidence of the cancer inside, but can't. Every summer they would buy matching bikinis and flirt with the surfers together. **MADELEINE STACK**

This photo was taken in the late 1960s, when my mother was about twenty years old. It's a bit scary how much I looked like my mother when I was the same age. When I look at this photo, my mum looks so young and innocent and carefree. This was before she was married, before she had even met my father, before she had children and possibly even before she had started work. In this photo, she had just finished school forever and was on holiday in Kuching, East Malaysia. She looks so happy, and stylish too. Look at her fashionable flared pants matched with the watch and groovy sandals. My mother is great at putting together an outfit. In this photo, I see so much potential and a bright future for my mother. **CHANG SHIH YEN**

DR. AGNES VAGO

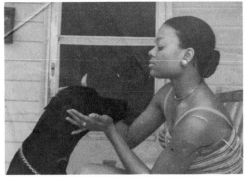

LYNNE HARRIS

I fell in love with my mom in my mid-twenties. I remember going out with her for coffee and kind of staring at her the way I'd stare at a boy I was falling in love with. Before that, our relationship had been a little difficult. I'm pretty sure this is a picture my father took of her when they were newly married. The picture is from a series. It seems like she's possibly thinking about something else as she's dancing for him. Probably work. My mom is one of the hardest-working people I have ever known. She was always in her study, eyes in a microscope. Her face has a serious cast. She's around twenty-four here, having just moved to Toronto from Hungary; she was studying to be a pathologist. That dress is great. I'm always looking for dresses like that. I move like my mother and have her body—especially her feet and hands. It troubled me when I noticed it as a girl, but now it makes me feel warm and closer to her. **SHEILA HETI**

This is a photograph of my mother in the seventies. She wasn't yet a wife or a mother. Here I see a woman who is confident in herself in a way that doesn't require too much adornment or finery. She looks like a woman who is not afraid to take chances, or to fall down and make mistakes, a woman who is confident, self-assured, and vulnerable in a way that's evident in her dress. Her hair is pulled back, her earrings are simple button-style clip-ons. I know it's summer because of her bronzed skin. She's wearing a striped cotton tank top and jeans, and is possibly braless. I think the beauty of this picture of my mother is that she's beautiful without trying to be. You can see it in the smoothness of her skin, the dip of her clavicle, the angles of her jaw. There's a tenderness in the way she's holding the dog's head, a regal bearing in her posture that mirrors the dog's long neck. I imagine her life was just beginning at this point, that she was a young woman ready and willing to face the challenges and opportunities the world had to offer her. **LYDIA JOHNSON**

KATHRYN HUEY

JUDY CAMPE

When I look at this photograph of my mother, I think how pretty she was, and I remember her soft skin and how good she always smelled. I also think how glamorous she looked in her Chicago & Southern stewardess uniform. The reality of the job was less than glamorous, however, with stewardesses crowded together cooking in-flight meals on stoves located behind the cockpit. Many of her stories involved wildly bumpy flights on propeller planes and passengers running out of airsickness bags. And she never failed to add that because of the altitude and the not-so-pressurized cabins, when passengers got sick, everything they brought up was bright chartreuse. In the fifties, chartreuse was a popular color for little girls' dresses, but not for mine. Still, my mother must have felt that being a "career girl," as she called it, was exciting, as she kept that uniform hanging in the back of her closet in four different houses until she died. I still have her enameled stewardess pin, and I wear it on a coat occasionally because I like it. I still have the leather buttons with brass wings, too, just waiting for the right jacket to come along. **KATE McMULLAN**

This is my mom, in her twenties, during her "hippie phase." She died in 1997, so looking at this photo makes me feel a lot of complicated things—wistful, sad, admiring, curious. I mostly take after my dad, and my mom was always this glamorous figure to me growing up. When she was young she sort of resembled Brigitte Bardot; I sort of resemble the cartoon Daria. I'll never manage to re-create her beauty myself, but I do find myself examining her photos for traces of me; maybe something in the eyes, I think. **JENNIFER CROLL**

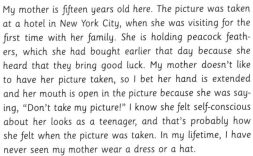

MARCÈLE LAMARCHE

RUTH GAIS

My mother is fifteen years old here. The picture was taken at a hotel in New York City, when she was visiting for the first time with her family. She is holding peacock feathers, which she had bought earlier that day because she heard that they bring good luck. My mother doesn't like to have her picture taken, so I bet her hand is extended and her mouth is open in the picture because she was saying, "Don't take my picture!" I know she felt self-conscious about her looks as a teenager, and that's probably how she felt when the picture was taken. In my lifetime, I have never seen my mother wear a dress or a hat.

**CLAUDIA EVE BEAUCHESNE**

I've always loved this photograph of my mother, which was taken when she was in her early twenties. I recognize her smile, and I recognize my face in hers, though I think she has a more beautiful smile. It flatters me that people look at the photo and think it's me. I like her clothes, which are things I'd wear today. I have a good idea of what her life was like back then, because my mother has told me a lot about her personal life, and I've asked her about it, too. This photograph seems to represent a moment of happiness, separate from the concerns and problems (and joys) that would come in the rest of her life. That must be part of why I like it, because she seems forever in that moment, and I can just reach back and join her there.

**CLARE NEEDHAM**

*CHRISTINE ANDREA CAVIGLIA*

Before she was a mother, before she was a widow, before she remarried, before she had cancer twice, before she lost her own parents. Before, before, before. I love this picture for a number of reasons. For one, my mother isn't wearing pants. Also, she always dyed her hair whatever color she wanted. And even though she's holding a bunch of dead fish, she's got on some rings and a headscarf that matches her bathing suit. This somehow defines my mother—up for anything while wearing a cute outfit. And the fish, the fish! My whole family fishes and hunts, so I don't even know who caught these fish—my Italian grandfather, some cousin, some uncle, maybe even her. I do know, however, that my father didn't catch those fish. My mother didn't know him yet. She was still married to her first husband, and he was still healthy. In this photo, my mamma is a twenty-three-year-old newlywed married to her college sweetheart, Jim Marsh. The following year, 1970, she would get pregnant with my oldest brother. The year after that, she would become pregnant with my other brother, and then about ten years after this photo was taken, Jim would be gone. She was just thirty-four when he died, and had two young boys. There's a lot I don't know about that time in my mother's life—the time she spent getting to know and getting to love and then ultimately having to lose Jim, but when I look at pictures from those early years of their life together, I see how young she was, and I see how much she loved him. And even though I wouldn't be here if that hadn't happened, these photos make me so sad that she had to lose him. Of course, my father lost Jim, too. They were in the Navy together, and that is how my dad would eventually come to meet my mother. So when I see this picture, I see my fun, spunky mother, but I also see a young woman who has no idea what she is about to endure, lose, gain, and bring into the world, and who has no idea that she'll eventually have a daughter who adores her, by a man she has yet to meet. **CAROLANN MADDEN**

DIANE MARKWAT

YUNGWHA KIM

My mom is not a poser. She doesn't wear makeup, she didn't pierce my or my sisters' ears when we were babies, she never got involved with the parking lot moms and their glamour politics. She never has a cheesy smile. I believe this photo depicts her holding a bouquet caught at someone's wedding, and the connotations of catching the bouquet, to me, speaks of the inevitability of her betrothment, but moreover of her motherhood. She's a natural nurse and nurturer. A sense of fun and her individuality weren't separate from her desire to create a family. In photos, she always manages to convey this omniscient sense of knowing. She doesn't draw attention to herself. Her humor speaks for itself. She's fair and unassuming, quick and wicked. She has this incredible ability to let a joke sink in for a few seconds before laughing at it—there's this smirk that creeps onto her poker face, then she gives it away. **JACLYN BRUNEAU**

My mother came to the States at the age of seventeen from war-devastated South Korea immediately following the Korean War. She attended Pine Manor Junior College, then Mount Holyoke. She married my father, who attended Amherst College, six years later. I love this photograph of her because she looks so glamorous and beautiful, but also because she was modeling for some Junior League function, and I think it's kind of amusing and awesome that she should be asked to model for the Junior League so soon after arriving in this country. **KATHERINE MIN**

*JUSTYNA MATUSIAK*

This is my mother, nineteen, on the beach in Rynia, Poland, with her cousin and a boy with a transistor radio. My mom is the one with fake eyelashes and headband, smoking a cigarette, being badass. I'm looking into this strange (and familiar) young woman's life, uninvited, even though later on, she became familiar and mine—became my complicated mom. I love how feisty she is here, and how self-aware and sexual she is. She looks like this in most pictures from that time, and always with those fake lashes on. Brigitte Bardot. Her bikini is like something from *Blow-Up*. I know that she was really popular with boys but that she didn't fall in love easily, so she probably buried a couple of hearts in that pile of sand. The woman next to her, her cousin, was someone she grew up with—they were like sisters—and she died a few years ago from breast cancer. That killed my mom a little, too. Looking at this picture, I think of that and how it's nice to know that they had no idea in 1970. **JOWITA BYDLOWSKA**

LAUREL LEE

This is a picture of my mom, Laurel Lee, on her wedding day. She's in her wedding out-fit—jeans and a checked shirt to match my dad's. Recently, my grandma told me they didn't actually get married by the justice of the peace until later, but this is the day they made roast goat. This is the day everyone came to my grandparents' farm. I see my mom intensely listening. She still looks like that a lot, but here she's looking at my dad like that. They got divorced when I was five. I've never seen her look at him with (what I imagine to be) deep admiration. I bet my mom was happy at this time in her life. She was twenty-two, a star art student marrying a star of their artists' circle. My dad was playing the clarinet then. She was about to start her grown-up life with this beautiful, exciting man. Still, there had to be doubt. My mom is a lesbian. She's been out since the divorce, and now she's finally at home in the San Francisco Bay area. There had to have been some fear, something telling her, even then, "This isn't really it." My mom started out thinking she was going to paint and have babies and be lovers with a man in small-town Wisconsin. Her style in this photo tells that story. She's alternative, yes. What a rebel! How liberating, getting married in jeans! But she's linked to a man. My mom ended up making provocative art on the other side of the country. She wore a strap-on and neon duct-taped flare-legged pants to the San Francisco Dyke March. That style tells a different story, a story that says that sometimes life screeches to a halt on the highway and drives you across a field. **AURORA SHIMSHAK**

GWENN THOMAS

CHO BOK NIM

My mom was a dancer before she became an artist (and an artist before she became a mother). I love looking at this photo. Pure fancy and flight. She is literally flying through the air! In her I see so much joy as she uses her body. It also makes me feel a little jealous. **JOANA AVILLEZ**

I'm not sure how old my mom is here, but I'm guessing around twenty-five. She had me when she was twenty-seven, so this is my mom when she was still living in Korea, but probably right before she moved to New York with my dad, and before she got pregnant with me. This is my favorite picture of her and this is actually kind of the way I dress right now: a mix of tomboy/boyfriend clothes. I love that clunky Walkman she has around her neck. It must have been like three pounds back then. I also love her pose; she is so cool! I think my dad is the one who took this photo of her. **JINNIE LEE**

ELLIE CSEPREGI

HELGA KERN

My mom's past is something I've only begun to scrape. She's gone through a lot, lived in many cities, had many jobs. I don't think she had much stability until she had kids. Her life was oriented around the theater and poetry scenes of whatever city she was living in at the time. This photograph has always been really elusive to me, and I've always been fascinated by it. I think what's most interesting about it is that it's staged. At the same time, it seems like it's a staging of who my mom actually was. It feels like she's performing her own personality, like she put on a leather jacket and lit up a cigarette to become herself. It's so performative and so dramatic. It doesn't take itself seriously, but it also takes itself very seriously. It's hard to read, but that's exactly my mom. **EMILY COYLE**

My mother never talked much about dressing up or going out. That's why I like this picture of her, where you can spot her in party mood. She had an eye for the casual and was always quick in picking the things she liked. A simple shirt, a necklace, a tiny black watch; above all: no fuss. When she married my father in 1980, she drove from Constance to Zurich's Bahnhofstrasse. She found a dark green dress by Christian Dior with a green leather belt. She tried it on, it fit her perfectly, and she bought it right away. It cost 500 Swiss francs, and at the ceremony she wore it with a summer hat. **FRIEDERIKE SCHILBACH**

SUSAN MARVEL

MILDRED WOLSKY STEINBOCK

I love this photo of my mum. She was between eighteen and twenty when it was taken, and when I was growing up, it represented what I wanted to look like, the era I wanted to live in, and the confidence I could potentially have. I love her stripey top. **GRACE DENTON**

I see a beautiful woman who spent her life completely unaware of that fact, who was as uncomfortable with her height as she was with the rest of her body. **JEANIE KIMBER**

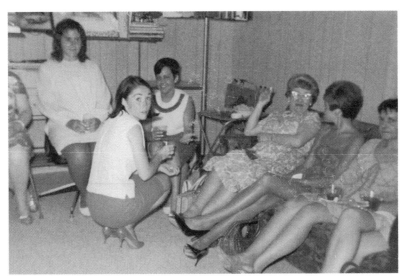

*RITA MARIA RAUCH*

She's 19. She's a virgin. She's getting married. She's working class. She's the eldest of five. She's just bought her first car. A powder blue Mustang with tan interior. It's new. She's paid for it herself. She's a secretary at Hanna-Barbera Studio in Hollywood. That's where she met *him*. A trumpet player on a record date. Age, 37.

She's the good kid. The one that never gets into trouble. Her parents tell him, "she's the pick of the litter." (Did she hear that? Did she cry?) Her parents like to drink and smoke. She never will. She wants to become something different...do things differently. She'll not only breast feed, she'll become a leader in La Leche League. She'll insist on natural childbirth, despite 32 hours labor and a baby that's 3 weeks past-due. No sugar. No junk food. NO soda pop. She's self-conscious, but she feels kind of hot. She's shy. A faint memory of 10th grade acne dusts high set cheekbones. She has a great body. Not an ounce of fat and yet she wears a white panty girdle attached to her stockings. She made that skirt.

At 35, she'll leave him. Her father will tell her he loves her for the very first time. She'll hang up quickly so he won't hear her cry. She will lose her only son at 40—a boy not yet 18. She'll smile through a glassy eye and say she's lucky. She's Rita and she's kind of a phantom... unknown and unknowable...fragile and fierce. Something like love. **LAURA PETERSON** ✕

# MAGICAL

SADIE STEIN

Though I've had a lot of clothes in my life, a few have stood out—not the most beautiful or most flattering, just pieces that, for one reason or another, at a certain moment in my life were invested with special powers—had the capacity to transform me every time I put them on.

The first was from Urban Outfitters. I bought it the August before my freshman year of college. It was a synthetic black party dress with a vaguely '70s cut, sweetheart neck, and Lycra underdress. The moment I put it on, I saw in the mirror the college woman I wanted to be. Not the nerdy, frowsy frump who'd been ignored by a high school crush and who shopped for clothes with her mom at the Salvation Army, but a sophisticated woman of the world with a curvaceous figure. I first wore the dress to an event for incoming students, and as I donned it, I donned my new persona: confident and assured. I wore the dress every chance I got. I wore it to parties and lectures—whenever I needed to feel pretty or adult or confident. I'm convinced it netted me a boyfriend. Being cheap, the dress soon showed the effects of wear, and its sleek lines were marred by the lumpy proof of my inexpert repairs. But its magic, to me, remained undimmed. Then, when I was twenty-one, I lost the dress somewhere in London. I was briefly bereft. But it was meant to be. The dress's work was done. It had disappeared, never to be seen again.

It was three years before I found the dress's heir. Dress 2 was a more sophisticated affair. In fact, it was the most expensive piece of clothing I'd ever owned. It was brown wool, severely tailored, with a tulip skirt that clung, then flared, and a high neckline saved from dowdiness by a keyhole, and a series of gold buttons at the neck and wrist. I coveted Dress 2 for months before saving up enough to buy it on sale. It entered my life around the time I took an office job, and seemed the perfect uniform for an efficient and asexual girl Friday. It became my trademark around the office, and lent itself to the slightly arcane, wisecracking patter I favored at the time. My boyfriend was out of the country that year, and I liked that the dress signaled that I was independent and unavailable. Dress 2, in short, made me feel like a million bucks. Then one day my boss showed up at work and, after casually saying, "I have a new dress," removed her coat to reveal . . . Dress 2. Albeit on a taller and more stunning frame. I was dumbfounded and hurt. I retired Dress 2 and got another job. In due course, the dress also disappeared. In a move perhaps? Who knows. I combed my apartment for weeks hoping it might turn up, but its work, too, was done.

Dress 3 came into my life at a low point. I'd been nursing a badly broken heart, and was scrawny and ill-groomed. For my birthday, the owner of the clothing shop where I worked gave me a dress I had been coveting for months. Broke, I had been unable to do more than gaze at it longingly. When I opened the box and saw Dress 3 staring up at me, tears came to my eyes. It was the beginning of a new era. Dress 3 is the most utilitarian of the three. It's a denim shirtwaist dress with a faint primary-colored check and a sash. It's a sleeper: you don't notice it, just the woman beneath. When I first got it, I wore it everywhere, at least three days a week. And when I finally started dating, I wore it for dates. I was wearing it when I ran into my ex and his new girlfriend. I was wearing it when I had my first kiss with the guy to whom I would later become engaged, and also when I first met his family. It never failed me.

That dress never disappeared. I know exactly where it is in my closet. It has hung there for more than two years, unworn. This past summer, I pulled it out. I was going on a date—the first I'd been on in seven years—and for a moment, I wondered if the ghostly old magic would assuage my nerves. It was slightly worn around the edges, but it still looked okay when I put it on—a flattering, nice dress. For a few moments I considered wearing it, then unbuttoned it and hung it back in the closet. I needed something new. But what? You can't force magic. ✕

# MANDATES OF PLACE

*"I dress to withstand the elements. I dress to be as interesting as the Tate. I dress to insert myself into social strata, to be accepted, to pass."* —CAITLYNN CUMMINGS

**ALEXI CHISLER** I try to limit buying clothes for myself when I'm at home. This is because when I travel, I often feel like I'm a different person, or I'm willing to try out being a new person. So the clothes I buy don't usually suit me for very long after I return.

**DORETTA LAU** My family is Chinese. Once, in Hong Kong, I was wearing a button-down plaid shirt when it was 18°C. Everyone else was wearing woolen turtlenecks and heavy scarves, and a family friend called my mother to tell her I showed up at tea looking like a slut.

**ELIZABETH KAISER** Everywhere I've lived has nudged me into a uniform—clogs look good in Washington but dowdy in New Orleans; fluorescents look amazing in the South but tacky in the Northwest. That's one of the reasons I hate flying. Whatever you're wearing when you get on the plane looks terrible once you've arrived at your destination. Vacation packing is a chore for this reason. I never pack the right outfits.

**MADELEINE STACK** I went to art school and was suddenly surrounded by devastatingly cool people. I had to learn to dress one way for up to forty-eight hours as life became much more spontaneous. I had to be dressed for any eventuality.

**POPPY TOLAND** My friend Emily and I were traveling in southern China. We went to a village, Shidong. The girls showed us these beautiful embroidered belts and waistcoats they'd spent days and days making and were incredibly proud of, and their silver jewelry and headdresses. Before, I'd always thought being overly interested in fashion and spending a lot of time, money, and effort on looking good was frivolous and to be avoided. After that visit, Emily and I decided that dressing up was an essential, human, female behavior and that it turned life into a celebration.

**GISELA WILLIAMS** Berlin winters are indescribably oppressive and endless. From late November to March, the city is a place of pure darkness. One day, on a fall trip to the States, I saw a pair of UGGs covered in bright blue sequins in a shop on Broadway in Manhattan. I have always hated UGGs, I swore I would never buy a pair, but I immediately bought them. No matter how dark it is outside in Berlin, my UGGs sparkle like enormous sapphire disco balls on my feet.

**TASHA COTTER** I once spent a summer in Paris. Slowly little cultural details began to sink in. French women focus on skin care. They present a more natural version of themselves to the world. I adopted these things into my life. It may sound silly, but I even stopped drinking soda. I drank more water. I was hungry for a way to live, and in Paris I had found something like a code to go by.

**ANAHIT ORDYAN** Most Armenian women like to be dressed up. An American once told me her impression was that the women in Armenia are going to a theater performance early in the mornings, not to work.

**LEIGH MCMULLAN ABRAMSON** Until I was fifteen, I did not care about "street clothes" because I only thought about what I looked like in the ballet studio. I did have some amazing leotards back then. We all competitively ordered them from a seamstress in New Jersey. They would have velvet on top around the boobs and cotton on the bottom, or be shiny with keyhole backs. I deeply regret not having saved them, but I threw them all out the day I quit, in a moment of catharsis. Anyway, after I quit and went to high school, I realized that I needed actual clothes. My first day at the new school I wore brown corduroy overalls and Doc Martens because my mother told me it was cool. I had no idea. I got to school and all the girls were in *Clueless* outfits. I was mortified.

**SUSAN SWAN** I think my sense of style took a great leap when I was at McGill University in Montreal. I was in a cosmopolitan city for the first time in my life and far away from my traditional family. I could suddenly be myself, and I loved the feeling of freedom. I was six-two and I had this extremely short boyfriend and he had two extremely tall friends. We used to go everywhere together and people expected me to be with one of the tall men. The four of us would do an umbrella dance at parties. I'd swing around on the arms of the big men (all of us dancing with opened umbrellas) and then would end up kissing the little guy. People were shocked. It was a lot of fun playing with their assumptions. I had been a shy, awkward teenager. After the umbrella dance, I never looked back. A sense of personal style and learning to use my height for theatrical effect came together at that time.

**INGRID SATELMAJER** When I was eight, my family moved from the New York City area to the Finger Lakes region. We left behind shopping malls for cornfields and cow pastures. I showed up at a one-room schoolhouse— a place where the boys would spit onto a wood-burning stove in the winter—wearing a dapper three-piece outfit, tan skirt, tan vest, patterned blouse, *and* a tan beret. I can't remember ever wearing that outfit again. When my best friend from Pearl River showed up to visit the next year, my mom made us matching calico dresses with bonnets. We wore them to church.

**ANA OTTMAN** After my divorce, I moved from stuffy Washington, D.C., to Austin, Texas. I started to experiment with showing more skin and wearing more color. Now when I look at pictures of myself from D.C., I feel like I'm looking at a stranger in these dark, professional clothes.

**JUSTIN VIVIAN BOND** When I moved to San Francisco, in my twenties, I finally let my hair grow and began expressing my gender in a much more honest way. I started wearing skirts and dressing a lot like Elizabeth Montgomery on *Bewitched*. Then I moved to New York and started playing in rock clubs and wearing harder, more rock looks that were appropriate for the clubs and punk bars in the East Village during the '90s. Now I only like to wear clothes that are "aggressively neutral"—serious tailoring but mostly consisting of colors that resonate with sand and the sea.

**SOPHIE ZEITZ** I spent a year in boarding school in Maine. The school was very small and remote, and so different from the public high school in West Germany (backcombed hair! hot-pink lipstick! blue eye shadow!). I did not know anything about the fashion structures and codes in a small American prep school, where the cool people were into the Grateful Dead. When my mother picked me up at the Frankfurt airport a year later, her heart must have sunk. I was wearing tie-dye, baggy clothes, Indian jewelry, and no makeup. She did not comment on my new look, but a couple of weeks later she got me a set of black underwear. To me, this seemed an awkwardly frivolous object. White cotton had been the thing to wear in Maine.

SAADA AHMED The major turning point in my own personal style was when I lived with my college roommate Barbara from Spain. She showed me how just because things look bad on a hanger doesn't mean they will look bad on you. Then I went to Madrid with her for four months, and seeing how people dressed there, and how free they seemed, really made an impression on me.

KRISTI GOLDADE When I was fresh out of undergrad (wearing baggy dresses and combat boots), I went to live and teach in Ukraine. The women there bought a few expensive outfits and took good care of them. You'd wear your nice outfit to work and the minute you got home, you'd hang it up and put on sweatpants. About a month in, the supervising teacher took me aside and asked that I wear more feminine clothes. I was so ashamed that the next weekend, I traveled solo to the capital and bought a new wardrobe: high-heeled boots, shiny black pants, sheer tops. After that, people trusted me more and let me into their homes and got to know me as a person. Some of my fellow Peace Corps volunteers gave me such grief for wearing these clothes and makeup. One girl proposed they nickname me "Rita Hayworth." They continued to wear their Tevas and bulky backpacks and to think they were better, as if their staunch individualism made them more American and therefore better women. ✕

## "DRESS"

*Bookstore, bestseller table. A woman helps her friend choose a gift.*

STARLEE: Your dress is amazing.

FIRST WOMAN: Thank you!

SECOND WOMAN: It's homemade in Slovenia. She's from Slovenia. She has a wonderful friend. She makes all of her dresses. . . .

STARLEE: Looks perfect.

FIRST WOMAN: I'll tell her! She'll be happy.

SECOND WOMAN: It's totally for her body. The way they do it over there, the women have all their clothing made. It's like, this isn't off the rack.

STARLEE: Is that common?

SECOND WOMAN: Yes, it's what the women do.

FIRST WOMAN: It's not so common anymore.

STARLEE: How did you guys meet?

SECOND WOMAN: We met at a course here in New York.

FIRST WOMAN: I work in pharmaceuticals.

SECOND WOMAN: I'm a therapist. Can I give you my card? This is great! Things are supposed to happen, in this moment in time. ✕

*LISA NAFTOLIN*'s swimsuits

# MAYBE A LOT OF PEOPLE DON'T DO THIS

**LY KY TRAN** *as told to Heidi Julavits*

I'm originally from South Vietnam. My father had been a lieutenant, then in 1975 he was captured, when he was eighteen or nineteen. He remained a prisoner of war for ten years. Then he met my mother after he was released, and they had my three older brothers and me. We had the opportunity to come to the United States in 1993 through the Humanitarian Operation program. I was three. Our apartment was on the border of Ridgewood and Bushwick in Brooklyn, and we still have that apartment. When we first got here, nobody knew the language, so it was really tough for us. The way my father referred to objects was by their brand name. He would say, "Oh, look at this Whirlpool that we have," in reference to the refrigerator. Our sewing machine was "the Mitsubishi."

I think it was his way of becoming more Americanized. If he would write letters back home, he'd say, "We just got a Whirlpool." Back home there was definitely no refrigerator. Something about the brand name made it so legitimate: We're in America, we have this brand-name thing. Even though we found it on the street—nobody had to know!

My father, he took night courses to learn how to speak English, and he eventually got a degree in computer literacy. But then he couldn't find a job at all. My mother sold every single bit of jewelry she had, but we were emaciated, we were starving, and there was no Vietnamese community here in New York City. It was very difficult to find a Vietnamese person to speak to. We arrived in the winter and I remember my brother, his fingertips turned blue. There's this disease called Secondary Raynaud's Disease, it's sort of like frostbite, your blood vessels constrict to the point where there's just no blood flowing to the tips of your fingers. We had to go to the hospital. It was really frightening.

We found work about six or seven months after we arrived, and it was through the one Vietnamese friend my father knew. The friend said, "There's this great opportunity, you can make so much money from it." So this person came to our home and spoke to us. He was very clean-shaven, and had on a suit, and he sells us this idea, this American dream: You can become rich doing this! And my father said, "Yes, sign us up! Where do we go, when do we begin?" And he said, "No no no, that's the great perk of this program, you don't actually go anywhere, we bring everything to you." Which, of course, that makes it even better! But it was just to cover up their operation, because the government wouldn't be able to find out a single location where this was taking place.

So the next weekend we get this huge shipment—about six boxes, huge cardboard boxes—and inside were these different types of fabrics. My father called this guy and said, "I don't really know how to do this," and they said, "Right right right, we're going to get you this brand-new Mitsubishi sewing machine, and an iron—we're going to get you all these things." Little did we know that we actually had to pay them back for these things with our first month's work.

So we had to read the instructions, which were in English, on how to make a cummerbund or how to make a tie. My brothers were enrolled in school, so they were starting to learn the language, and my father was very smart. He immediately figured out the quickest way to make these things. You separate the materials, you put all the materials together in the shape of a cummerbund, and I will sew, and you will take these cummerbunds coming down the bottom of the sewing machine and separate them, and cut them up using a blade. We would cycle. When one of us got tired of doing one thing, we'd be like, "Okay, your turn!" I don't remember exactly the figures, but that first night my parents and three brothers and I made about three hundred cummerbunds.

My father called the guy and he's like, "I have such good news for you, in one night we made so much! Can you please tell me how much that would earn us?" And the man says, "Oh yeah, that's amazing! I think you get about . . . twenty dollars." And my father said, "I'm sorry . . . what? Wait, I don't understand." And the man's like, "Yeah, yeah, twenty dollars, it's really good money." So my father, he's completely devastated, he says, "You lied to us, why? This is not a lot of money. My entire family worked. We didn't even sleep!" The guy says, "I'm sorry, welcome to America, this is the way it is." So my parents had no choice. They didn't know how to speak the language. This was their only connection to American society or whatever.

When my brothers and I found out how much money we made through the telephone call, we were like, "Oh my god! How many bags of chips would that get us? Ice cream, we can have ice cream!" We were so excited. But we saw the looks on our parents' faces, and we were like, "Wait . . . you're upset? But we're so happy! What's going on here?"

There were a lot of mishaps initially. My father's finger would get caught in the needle of the sewing machine. And even my mother—she would sew by hand in Vietnam, but this was a huge machine we had no idea how to work. Even just changing the different spools of the thread was really difficult for us. My hair actually got caught in the machine once, at which point my father was just like, "I'm cutting your hair." So my hair . . . I looked like a boy for ten years.

Every weekend or two a guy would come by and pick up everything we had made. I think our first batch that we made, the guy said, "Oh, you know, it's a little crooked here, the tag is in the wrong place." But they didn't say, "We're not paying you for this one because it's crooked." I mean, they were paying us a dollar for every twenty-four cummerbunds we made, so I don't think it was too much of a loss for them if one or two were a little crooked.

In terms of us realizing at some point that it was illegal, I don't think that happened until much later on. When I was old enough to go to school—because I was only three when we started doing this—there would be all these little kids developing calluses on their fingers from writing, and we had all these cuts and bruises on our fingers from doing sweatshop labor. We didn't even know this was something that was outside the norm for everybody. We didn't think it was different. We literally thought all the other kids were doing the same thing. We realized that we were different in the sense that we were emaciated, our hair was falling out, our teeth were black and rotten, so to that extent we were like: Okay, we are different. And obviously we can't speak English very well. But in terms of what went on at home, we didn't even realize. And we were really good students somehow, even though we didn't have a chance to do our homework at home—we always did our homework in school. We didn't realize that other students were doing their homework at home. We thought it was interesting that it was called homework.

So yeah, I think sometime in middle school, in the eighth grade, was the first time I went over to a friend's house. I was never allowed to go to anybody else's house because my parents were just really afraid—the Vietnamese people in New York, when we first landed, they were like, "Don't go anywhere, your daughter will be raped, your son will be kidnapped—never go anywhere if it's dark outside, don't go outside of your home," so we said, "Okay! Oh my goodness, it's a crazy jungle out here."

But I was like, "I just want to see her house for ten minutes. I'm curious." So I walked into her house—this was one of my best friends, Veronica—and I asked her, "Where are all the ties and cummerbunds?" She's like, "What are you talking about?" "You know, the stuff you make." She was like, "What are you talking about? I don't make anything." And that's when I started to realize, Oh, maybe some people don't do this. Then sometime in high school I started to realize, Okay, maybe a lot of people don't do this. *(laughs)*

It wasn't until tenth or eleventh grade that I realized, "Wow, we were exploited." But to us it was almost . . . we weren't angry at this guy. It was just sort of inter-esting, like, Wow, we lived this life that people write about and talk about in his-tory, this whole sweatshop thing.

What's interesting about our expe-rience, and I feel like very few people talk about this, but as children, we never thought our lives sucked. Even when we were starving, it was never like, "Oh my god, we're starving," it was just like, "Oh, there's just some rice, okay." I mean, we were children, and everything was magi-cal. We made games out of everything. Even when it was two a.m. and we were up making these cummerbunds, we might sing songs to each other. Everything was a game to us, so we never thought, "Oh, our lives suck." It was just part of being an American. Like, Wow, we're here together and we're making these cummerbunds? And these fabrics are so colorful. . . . I always felt that there was sort of a win-dow between us—my brothers and I on the outside, looking in at my parents, and being very confused a lot of the time, be-cause we had all this wonder and they seemed really miserable.

But we were all in this situation to-gether. I think we were all victims in a way, even the man in the suit. Because he was just fulfilling the role. I mean, we were upset in that initial moment when we realized, Okay, this is not the amaz-ing life we thought we would live in America. But at the same time we were grateful. This money that we made from the sweatshop labor, even though it didn't buy us a lot of clothes, it did buy us some clothes and food. We weren't starving to death. And we kept a roof over our heads. So ultimately we were very grateful for it. And to this day my parents are still grateful.

I believe I was twelve when the opera-tion terminated.

I wish I could say that I give a lot of thought to where my clothing comes from these days. Sometimes when I see "Made in Vietnam," I'll joke around with my friends, "Oh, my cousins made this." And my friends are like, "Oh my god, how could you say that," and I'm like, "Well, I *can* say that." I probably made a lot of the ties that the men are wearing in the street. ✕

# LET ONE DREAM COME TRUE

KATIE KITAMURA

### MONDAY

**9:26** Kenzo Eye-print silk-crepe shirt, $440 on net-a-porter .com. KENZO's all-seeing eye is a prominent motif for Fall '13. It alludes to the strength of extra vision and also to a spiritual protection from above. **9:28** Carven Bamboo-print crinkled-sateen dress, $650 on net-a-porter.com. Cut from lightweight crinkled-sateen, this piece gently flares from the hips for a flattering lady-like shape. **9:37** Acne Powder convertible down-filled parka, $900 on net-a-porter.com. Acne's water repellent canvas parka offers two styles in one. Give yours a downtown take with heels and leather pants. **12:46** Stella McCartney Aubrey Dress, £870 on stellamccart-ney.com. Double chalk stripe dress in wool stretch featuring a circular front insert adding volume and movement. **12:47** Stella McCartney Pin Stripe Dress, £810 on stellamccartney .com. Luxurious soft wool knit-ted dress in pin stripe with an asymmetric hem, long sleeved and ribbed trims. **16:03** Filson Duffle Bag in Medium, $325.00 on filson.com. Pack for a long weekend in this spacious, inde-structible duffle bag. Features two inside pockets at each end, leather pulls, leather grip with two-snap closure. Made in USA.

**21:05** Stella McCartney Single Breasted Long Wool Coat, Current Bid $446.00 on ebay. com. UTTERLY GORGEOUS, ABSOLUTELY NEARLY NEW condition (it was owned by a MAJOR HOLLYWOOD WIFE/ ACTRESS who obviously BARELY wears her things at all)—ULTRA SCOOOORE!!!!!! **22:18** Acne White Shirt, Current Bid $5.99 on ebay.com. All cotton. I don't like to iron.

### TUESDAY

**9:50** Giambattista Valli Leopard-print stretch-jersey pants, $750 on net-a-porter.com. Parisian girl meets Manhattan boy was the theme of Giambattista Valli's Pre-Fall '13 collection—cue glamor and androgyny in equal measure. **10:50** Marni Cotton Front Pocket Wide Leg Pant, $99 $525 on gilt.com. This item is final sale and non-returnable. **10:51** Marni Cotton High Rise Pant, $99 $560 on gilt.com. This item is final sale and non-returnable. **11:00** Alexander McQueen Bible Book Show embellished leather box clutch, $3975 on net-a-porter.com. The new bag for evening is a divine clutch—the ornate detailing is nothing short of artful. **11:38** Maison Martin Margiela cement-effect coated knee boots, Origi-nal price $1395 NOW $559.95 60% OFF on theoutnet.com.

**13:47** Vionnet Chunky-knit merino wool sweater, $1305 on net-a-porter.com. The striking silhouette wowed us on the runway, so keep it in focus with slimline pants and pin heels. **13:53** Charlotte Olympia Kitty Cat–Embroidered Velvet Flat Slipper, $595 on neimanmarcus. com. The whimsical cat design brings all the eye-catching style of the designer's stunning plat-forms, but with a flat heel. **13:54** Charlotte Olympia Kitty Cat– Embroidered Velvet Flat Slipper, Current Bid $259.65 on ebay. com. Free shipping! Bid now so you can get a deal. **14:41** Acne Black Merino Wool Long Sleeve Chunky Sweater, Current Bid $31.00 on ebay.com. I live in South Florida and I definitely wore this sweater once. Might even have been twice. It's in excellent condition. **21:43** Equip-ment Liliane washed-silk pajama set, $388 on net-a-porter.com. Luxe sleepwear is our ultimate indulgence. Complete with a matching pouch, they're a fabulous treat.

### WEDNESDAY

**10:26** See By Chloé Herringbone wool-blend coat, $1095 on net-a-porter.com. Heritage fabrics are a key style story for fall. This oversized style is crafted with soft touches of alpaca and mohair. **10:28** Chalayan

Wool-blend coat, $1780 on net-a-porter.com. This season, the runways were awash with menswear-inspired coats. The key to nailing this trend is all in the proportions. **10:29** A.P.C. Wool-blend peacoat, $575 on net-a-porter.com. A.P.C. Atelier de Production et de Création is all about cool, classic pieces that you can build your wardrobe with. Warm without being too bulky. **10:31** Kenzo Oversized faux fur coat, $840 on net-a-porter.com. Work two of the season's most important trends—statement-making coats and rich texture—at the same time. The restrained navy hue tempers the playful spirit of this piece. **15:34** Isabel Marant for H&M Coat, £99.99 on vogue.co.uk. Pieces that echo Marant's Parisian bohemian aesthetic perfectly. Start making your wish list now, before the collection lands in stores on November 14. **20:45** Acne Black Merino Wool Long Sleeve Chunky Sweater, Current Bid $86 on ebay.com. Saved to watch list. **20:46** Charlotte Olympia Kitty Cat–Embroidered Velvet Flat Slipper, Current Bid $274.65 on ebay.com. Saved to watch list.

### THURSDAY
**10:45** Acne Black Merino Wool Long Sleeve Chunky Sweater, Current Bid $86 on ebay.com. Saved to watch list. **10:45** Charlotte Olympia Kitty Cat–Embroidered Velvet Flat Slipper, Current Bid $274.65 on ebay.com. Saved to watch list. **11:54** Stella McCartney Cable-knit wool miniskirt, Original Price $785 NOW $250.02 68% OFF on theoutnet.com. **11:56** Peter Pilotto

Eleni printed stretch-crepe pencil skirt, $795 on net-a-porter.com. The clean silhouette emphasizes the design duo's masterful kaleidoscopic print. Make the sea-green pattern pop. **12:00** Jil Sander Leather envelope clutch, $510 on net-a-porter.com. Jil Sander's black leather style is coolly understated—free from any embellishment or branding save a subtly embossed designer stamp. **12:03** Carven Wool Sweater Dress, Original price $900 NOW $270 70% OFF on theoutnet.com. **14:45** Maison Martin Margiela Perforated leather Oxford brogues, $875 on net-a-porter.com. Wear this sleek black leather pair with matching prints. **14:53** Eugenia Kim Sammy hat, $~~220~~ $59 on barneyswarehouse.com. Mohair and wool blend trapper hat with leather ties. **19:22** Acne Black Merino Wool Long Sleeve Chunky Sweater, Current Bid $86 on ebay.com. It is ending soon, so bid now before you miss out! **19:31** Acne Black Merino Wool Long Sleeve Chunky Sweater, Current Bid $91 on ebay.com. You're the highest bidder on the item but you're close to being outbid. **19:35** Acne Black Merino Wool Long Sleeve Chunky Sweater, Winning Bid $97.00 on ebay.com. You didn't win this auction.

### FRIDAY
**10:37** Band of Outsiders Leather-trimmed Atari 2600 printed cotton-voile shirt, $375 on net-a-porter.com. The geometric print is inspired by graphics from video games originally played on the Atari 2600 console system. We recommend wearing this semi-sheer style with a

neutral camisole. **10:53** American Vintage Nine Nile Falls angora-blend sweater, $235 on net-a-porter.com. Knitted from luxuriously soft black angora-blend, American Vintage's midweight sweater has a distinctly fluffy feel. **10:58** Midweight Full Zip Hooded Sweatshirt, $79 on americangiant.com. This will become your go-to hoodie. **21:26** Pablo Bronstein for Opening Ceremony Silk Scarf, $150 on openingceremony.us. This season, British artist Pablo Bronstein has created a not-so-typical silk scarf specially for OC. Represented by Herald St—one of Carol and Humberto's favorite galleries in London—Pablo is known for his fantastical architectural paintings. **21:36** Peter Jensen Mini Spend Sweatshirt, $175 on openingceremony.us. Danish architect Arne Jacobson seems like an unlikely inspiration for Peter Jensen's pre-Fall collection, but his timeless ideas with a modernist twist fit right in with the brand's aesthetic. **21:42** Peter Jensen Nina Crewneck, $235 on openingceremony.us. For fall, Peter Jensen was inspired by notorious British lottery winner Vivian Nicholson and her bittersweet entrance into pop culture. **21:44** Steve J & Yoni P Double Breasted Check Coat, $705 on openingceremony.us. Spike up your Mohawk and pull out your best shoes. For Fall, design duo Steve J & Yoni P put a glam spin on fashion's year of punk. **21:54** Proenza Schouler Small Pony Lunch Bag, $1150 on openingceremony.us. Proenza Schouler's simple Lunch Bag clutch gets a little furry for fall! This basic bag adds just the right amount of texture to any outfit.

**8:42** Sophie Hulme Textured leather and brass box clutch, $430 on net-a-porter.com. Finished with the brand's signature polished brass hardware, this contemporary piece also comes with a playful gold-tone ice cream spoon! **8:44** Kenzo Eye-embellished cotton shirt, $410 on net-a-porter. com. Supersized proportions strike the perfect note this season. Take your cue from the runway and wear it tucked into a skirt. **15:30** 3.1 Phillip Lim Oversized Embroidered Bomber Jacket, $269 $675 on gilt.com. Your waitlisted item is available. Just One. **22:21** A.P.C. Metallic Mini Skirt, $99 $325 on barneyswarehouse. com. Metallic mini skirt in abstract detail with short pleated waistband and hidden back zip. All sales final. **22:22** Maison Martin Margiela Rubber Oxford, $219 $795 on barneyswarehouse.com. Textured rubber six-eye round toe oxford. All sales final. **22:26** Miu Miu Laceless Oxford, $239 $595

on barneyswarehouse.com. Smooth leather round toe laceless oxford with tonal stitching. All sales final. **22:30** Lanvin Stitched Wingtip Oxford, $239 $595 on barneyswarehouse .com. Suede taper toe lace-up oxford with stitched wingtip and cap toe. Tonal laces and grosgrain trim at vamp. All sales final. **22:47** KENZO Cloud Print Vans Slip-Ons, $125 on openingceremony.us. Printed shoe game on point! Carol and Humberto have once more Kenzofied classic Vans styles and we can't get enough.

**SUNDAY**

**17:13** Gudrun & Gudrun 1.176 Sweater traditional blue, $380 on thecools.com. This is one style from our best selling series. So simple and yet so special. The first model in white and brown (100.101) is known in Denmark from the TV series "Forbrydelsen" (the crime) and sold in Japanese specialty stores year after year. **17:14** Gudrun & Gudrun 1.101 Sweater Traditional, $350 on thecools.com. This is our best selling item ever—so simple and yet so special. It

is especially known as Sarah Lund's favorite sweater in the Danish TV series "The Killing" where it was worn by the main character Sarah Lund in both season 1 and 3. The sweater is available in other colors, you just have to write which color you like to purchase in the comment of the order, and we will send it to you. **17:16** Gudrun and Gudrun 1.108 Sweater traditional alpa, $350 on thecools.com. The colour range is different in that way that it is only made by the natural colour of the animals, such as the pattern that is iconic. Currently used by Sarah Linden in the American version of The Killing. **20:27** Gudrun and Gudrun 2.131 Sweater with knots, $360 on thecools. com. Relaxed in a sophisticated and elegant way. The sweater is perfect when you want to be trendy without being too loud. **20:33** Gudrun and Gudrun 1.819 Sweater landscape-rose, $400 on thecools.com. We all dream a lot. Here is something to dream about. The amazing Gudrun & Gudrun multicoloured dream sweater. Let one dream come true. ✕.

---

**SURVEY** *How does makeup fit into all this for you?*

If I know someone well, I don't feel like I have to wear makeup around them. —VANESSA BERRY • When I am bored or nervous, I paint my face like it's a blank page. I switch my nail polish weekly, like starting a new chapter. —MAYA FUHR • I've worn lipstick every day since I was eleven years old. —RACHEL KUSHNER • I started wearing makeup when I was a spokesperson for the pro-choice movement. I realized that I looked washed-out if I appeared on TV without makeup. Later I was a TV host with professional hair and makeup and a wardobe allowance. For eight years, I was a high-maintenance woman. It was fun at first, but then I started to feel the oppression, especially with the makeup. —JUDY REBICK • I impulse-buy makeup that I don't wear often, despite my hatred of useless impulse purchases. —VALERIE STIVERS • A former coworker used to obsess about how creamy the skin on my face is. It made me really uncomfortable. —GINA SHELTON • I have been experimenting with bright, intense lipstick lately. I finally feel adult enough to wear it. —BETH STUART ✕

*AMY ROSE SPIEGEL*'s false eyelashes worn over the course of one week

# ECONOMICS OF STYLE

*"There was one explicit lesson my grandparents taught me,*
*which was to never look like 'the poor soul.'"* —RACHEL TUTERA

**ALLISON D.** Last year, I drew my sister-in-law's name in our annual family Christmas gift draw. She's impossible to buy for because she is rich and has expensive taste, and I am the opposite. I'm not rich and I don't have expensive taste. My style is probably more like a woman's adaptation of a feminine gay man's wardrobe, except maybe not as stylish. I took my sister—who is poor, but has expensive taste—to an antique shop, where she enthusiastically helped me pick out a few pieces of vintage jewelry she thought our sister-in-law would like. Christmas morning, our sister-in-law opened the package, and it was clear she thought it was a totally shitty gift. When I saw the jewelry in her hand, it just looked so different to me—ugly and cheap. It ruined the day for me, honestly.

**DALE MEGAN HEALEY** I paid full price for a pair of clog boots in Williamsburg. I knew exactly how much money was in my bank account and that I was spending about half of it on these shoes. I told the saleswoman that they cost almost half my rent, but they were just so beautiful. "Well, if they're not an impulse buy, you should go for it!" she said. When I finally paid for them I expected someone to congratulate me or hand me a certificate.

**IMAN BIBARS** I often appear in the media, so if I'm attending an important event, I take extra care to coordinate my outfit, my makeup, and my jewelry. I will also have my hair and nails done the day before. I like to look good, even if I'm just going to the office. I'm fortunate that I have a driver and do not have to commute to the office as, living in Egypt, if I had to travel any distance to work without a driver, I would have to consider other factors when dressing, sexual harassment being prominent here.

**ASHLEY C. FORD** My mother had me perpetually covered in tulle for the first two years of my life. When my father went to prison, she refused to adjust the way she dressed me and my brother. As a single mother, she had sacrificed a lot of resources so her children never "looked" poor—even if we were.

**CLAUDIA EVE BEAUCHESNE** It's difficult to express personal style through clothing or the way you decorate a space, when you live out of a suitcase and occupy spaces for short periods of time, spaces that have been decorated by other people. I suppose a personal style can emerge from transience, but my transience hasn't been consistent enough for me to build a style around it. I see expressing personal style in everyday life as a luxury. It implies you occupy a space consistently enough to "make it your own" and have a readily available selection of clothes or objects to choose from and add to and subtract from. It also implies you're willing to spend time thinking about how to express yourself through the selection and arrangement of clothing, furniture, and so on.

**SUSAN GLOUBERMAN** I love that anyone can dress creatively for very little money.

**JENNY TROMSKI** I used to steal a lot of clothing when I was fat. I was convinced I was entitled to the few things that looked good on me.

**MOLLY MURRAY** I grew up in a family without much money; my mother's disdain for vulgar people who shopped at the mall was a reflection of her vestigial hippie principles, but also an attempt to make good taste out of sour grapes, since we couldn't afford to shop in malls.

**MARY PEELEN** I was in my twenties, when, shortly after arriving in Bangkok with a backpack and very little money, I bought a sarong. At first I thought it was just a pretty piece of cloth, but it turned out to be an item I would wear daily for nearly three years, buying a new one when the old one got too many holes. In India it was called a lungi or a dhoti, but it served all the same functions. Depending on how you fold and tie it, it is a long skirt or a miniskirt, a strapless dress (with variations), harem pants, a scarf, a turban, a belt, a shawl, a towel, a sheet, a pillow, a curtain, a tablecloth, a suitcase, or a shelter from the sun when arranged over some sticks on the beach. Kind of a hippie item, to be sure, but by far the most versatile thing I've ever owned.

**AMANDA MILLER** I come from a line of low-maintenance ladies. Solid United Church stock. Short hair, flat shoes, trousers or A-line skirts, minimal makeup, no fragrance. The women in the family still carry the baggage of a community that believed that fancy things were for lazy, spoiled women with the wrong values in their hearts.

**SHEILAH RAY COLEMAN** From a young age, I was aware of the luxuries in other households—girls whose mothers took them shopping for clothes, who vacationed at Disney or in the Bahamas. Our parents viewed these other families' values as moral failings (they were labor activists and professors). On the positive side, our household was incredibly rich with people stopping by all the time—writers, artists, and musicians—and with talk of politics and books and ideas. I remember as a little girl telling my dad I thought a friend's mom was beautiful. I told him how I loved that sometimes she wore an amazing pair of green leather trousers. He rolled his eyes and said green leather pants did not equal beauty; they only made her nouveau riche.

**MALWINA GUDOWSKA** I grew up in a Polish household. As a child, my mother wanted to be a professional launderer. I now work in the UK in the fashion industry, which pays horribly—an irony that is not lost on anyone I work with, since none of us can afford the clothing we write about.

**STEPHANIE P.** I think I'd dress better if I had money. Someone gave my mom a gift certificate to Bloomingdale's for $100, and she gave it to me, and I went to find something. I ended up in the Theory section, and I tried on about six or seven things. They were way out of my price range, but were so well constructed, and fit my body type exactly, and I felt like a new person in them. I felt confident and really excited; I nearly felt like I was under the influence of some kind of drug. I think the price had a lot to do with it—it was like stepping into a different life for a moment, a life where I'd be rich enough to afford these clothes, where I wouldn't lie awake at night worrying about money, where I could choose a job I loved instead of feeling trapped in a job to pay the bills, and where I could focus on my real priorities—spending time with family and friends, creative fulfillment, meaningful, impactful work. I felt so devastated at having to put the clothes back. I did get to buy one item that didn't turn out to be too expensive with the gift certificate and a sale, but it was just like . . . this little fantasy.

**RACHEL KUSHNER** When I was nineteen, my roommate was a wealthy girl from Oak Park, Illinois, and she had this impeccable preppy style and her life seemed to revolve around fine-tuning the style, which was truly "timeless" and not marred by the temptations of trend and fashion. She said her style was nothing compared with that of her mother and grandmother, and that "it takes a lifetime." It does not really take a lifetime, I realized. It takes being born into a family that has a lot of money and a lot of taste. You cannot just go and get that kind of look. It's only available to the right class. And even then . . .

**SOFIA SAMATAR** When I was in high school, my uncle gave me a hundred-dollar bill. I never had much spending money, so I was thrilled. I went to the mall, to all the cheapest stores, and got ten things—skirts, tops, leg warmers, all kinds of stuff! I was so proud of myself for making the most of that money. When I was telling the story in the dorm (I went to a boarding school), another girl said—not in a mean way, just sort of contemplative, "I would have bought one sweater and one bottle of perfume." It blew my mind that you could think of clothes that way—as special, beloved articles, not this mass noun that you had to get as much of as possible.

**BONNIE MORRISON** My dad cared a lot about me being dressed "presentably." This came from growing up black in a working-class family in the '50s. The sentiment was that how you dressed was important to how black people in general were perceived—sort of like a team wearing suits when they travel for away games. It ended up translating to his favoring a preppy look for me when I was growing up. What could be more deracinating than polo shirts and seersucker? ✕

**SURVEY** *I feel most attractive when . . .*

I think there was a study done about how women look different on each day of their menstrual cycle, and I am definitely more beautiful when I am ovulating.—EMMA MADNICK • Straight out of the shower, ovulating, three sips into a dirty dry martini. —LISA GUNNING • I feel my most attractive when I'm not premenstrual, in the spring or summer, in a dress, when I have a fun manicure and some interesting footwear, riding my bike. —ZOE WHITTALL • I feel best about myself during those ten days— two weeks after my period every month. —LEINI IRELAND • Ovulation equals glowy. PMS equals dumpy. I am a creature of biology. —JILL MARGO

Covered in salt, after a day swimming in the ocean. —JOANA AVILLEZ • Summer, summer, summer. When it's humid-hot out, and my hair is curly and I have a tan, and am wearing hardly any makeup or clothes. —THERESA PAGEOT • On holidays to sunny, warm places. —SARAH ILLENBERGER • Always in the summer. In a dress and sandals that are somehow effortless, my hair up in a bun, and only lip gloss. —REBECCA ACKERMANN • At the beginning of summer, when I have just gotten a bit of color on my skin and I can wear dresses and bright lipsticks. —ADINA GOLDMAN • In the summer, when I've been outside all day. —CATHERINE LACEY ✕

*ANNIE McDONALD*'s clogs

# RASPBERRIES, BLUEBERRIES, STRAWBERRIES

ARTIST **MAKIKO YAMAMOTO** SPEAKS TO
FILMMAKER **STEPHANIE COMILANG**

**STEPHANIE:** So you were talking about all the little things that Japanese people like so much.

**MAKIKO:** Yeah, they want to keep them around, and they want to show them off. For example, Japanese people want to name something, to say, "Oh, this is mine."

**STEPHANIE:** They want to personalize their things?

**MAKIKO:** I think so. In Japan there are so many choices, mobile phones or an Xbox, shoes, everything, but still they want to show, "This is mine, not yours."

**STEPHANIE:** To make it their own.

**MAKIKO:** Or because they can't express their feelings with words but they can send some messages.

**STEPHANIE:** When I was living in Tokyo in 2004, the fashion was so incredible. It was wild. Like wow, I couldn't believe it.

**MAKIKO:** Yeah. Crazy.

**STEPHANIE:** People were doing whatever they wanted with fashion. Was it more intense then than it is now?

**MAKIKO:** I don't know. After I entered university, I just wanted to focus on my work, so there was no space to think about fashion. Before that, I was wearing a Lolita fashion.

**STEPHANIE:** Lolita?

**MAKIKO:** Mm-hmm.

**STEPHANIE:** Why?

**MAKIKO:** Because, okay, so it's gonna be a big long story.

**STEPHANIE:** I'm ready.

**MAKIKO:** It's very personal. Okay, so when I was in primary school, I hated everything. I hated people. I wanted to kill everyone. Because I couldn't share anything with my friends, my teachers, no one agreed with me, my opinions.

**STEPHANIE:** No one agreed with you?

**MAKIKO:** No. If I say, "Oh teacher, I don't think so—" No. I was not allowed to say anything personal. Then I asked my friend, "What do you think? Because I don't think he's right, my teacher." My friend says, "Oh, no no—if the teacher says something you have to go for it." So at one point, I decided to do something weird.

**STEPHANIE:** What was the weird thing?

**MAKIKO:** I dig. The graves.

**STEPHANIE:** You were digging graves? You were a grave-digger. *(laughs)* Really?

**MAKIKO:** Of the animals. Or fishes. Like, all the classes had some pets in primary school. Then of course the friends got scared. "What is she doing? I don't know, she must be crazy or something."

**STEPHANIE:** How old were you?

**MAKIKO:** Ten.

**STEPHANIE:** Oh, you were young.

**MAKIKO:** Very young. I really wanted to protect myself from others. "Don't come to my world." So I started wearing Lolita fashion. Because now I'm living on another planet, so you can't speak to me.

STEPHANIE: Ah, you were separating yourself from everyone else. That was your way.

MAKIKO: Yes.

STEPHANIE: So what is Lolita fashion?

MAKIKO: You have to wear so many layers. Oh, it's heavy.

STEPHANIE: But what is Lolita fashion based on?

MAKIKO: I don't know. They are based on raspberries, blueberries, strawberries. Also, very European.

STEPHANIE: Like old European? Victorian?

MAKIKO: Yeah, kind of.

STEPHANIE: So what would you wear?

MAKIKO: Dresses. Hats. Tall hats with ribbon. It's not cute.

STEPHANIE: It's kind of cute, though. *Kawaii*, for me, is equal to what's cool. People in North America, they want to look cool. I think it means the same thing.

MAKIKO: It means: I'm different to the others, or unique, or . . . ?

STEPHANIE: Yeah. In some ways. But cool sort of means, I'm not really trying, I just look like this, it's my style. I'm not trying.

MAKIKO: Oh yeah?

STEPHANIE: I think that's maybe where the origins of cool came from. The idea of cool.

MAKIKO: That's a recent concept, no?

STEPHANIE: I think it came out of the fifties in North America. Like James Dean. I don't know. Where does *kawaii* come from?

MAKIKO: It was the big movement in 2004, that whole *kawaii* culture.

STEPHANIE: Girls in Tokyo always try to be *kawaii*, they always want to be cute. And for me it's like, I don't want to be cute. It's very different.

MAKIKO: Yeah it is different, I'm sure. *Kawaii*, it doesn't mean unique. *Kawaii* means standard.

STEPHANIE: But what makes someone *kawaii*?

MAKIKO: A bit naive, number one. And number two, not too crazy. If you're too crazy, it's not *kawaii*, it's not *kawaii* at all. But number three, if you are a perfect person, it's not *kawaii*.

STEPHANIE: If you're a what?

MAKIKO: A perfect person. Because you demand . . . and men cannot get you, because you are a perfect person.

STEPHANIE: Oh, you sort of need to be helped.

MAKIKO: Yes. That's *kawaii*.

STEPHANIE: Okay, I see. Like, "Oh, I can't open this thing, can you help me, please?"

MAKIKO: Oh yes. That's *kawaii*. Do you think it's cute?

STEPHANIE: Sort of. It's cute in a way that a child is cute.

MAKIKO: *(laughs)* Yeah.

STEPHANIE: What do people think if a girl is sexy? Or what do men think of women who are very independent and strong and who can do things on their own?

MAKIKO: Cool. I think so, yeah.

STEPHANIE: What do women want to be?

MAKIKO: *(sighs)* This century they can choose which life they want to take. If you want to be a cool lady, you can take that way. If you don't have any ideas how to live your life, then you can be *kawaii* person. *(laughs)* No? There are two options.

STEPHANIE: Only two.

MAKIKO: There are some exceptions, I'm sure.

STEPHANIE: So say I'm walking down the street. Are people trying to read what I am?

MAKIKO: Compared to London, I'm sure. I'm a hundred percent sure Japanese people care more than English people, because they're not good at expressing themselves. So they need to read people's clothing to see what they are thinking. I think they are very good at watching people.

STEPHANIE: Right. I definitely get looked at here. I was in a store today, and I just got such looks.

MAKIKO: What kind of store did you go to?

STEPHANIE: It wasn't really my kind of store. I was just looking for black jeans.

MAKIKO: Did you find it?

STEPHANIE: I can't find them.

MAKIKO: Why? I'm sure it's easy to find.

STEPHANIE: It's not. I have no idea why. But I went into this store that was more feminine, and all the girls that were working there were looking me up and down, and I was like, Ugh.

MAKIKO: Really.

STEPHANIE: Because my style is not feminine. It's kind of tomboy in some ways, it's harder. Also, I don't look Japanese.

MAKIKO: You don't like it, no?

STEPHANIE: It's not a problem. I know I look different. Also, we're in Kyoto, which is smaller.

MAKIKO: Black jeans. That's weird. No, I'm sure it's very easy to find here.

STEPHANIE: But Lolita style. Why did you stop?

MAKIKO: Mm, because it's too heavy for me. And it's not easy to move.

STEPHANIE: And how old were you when you started and how old were you when you stopped?

MAKIKO: Thirteen until fifteen. I wanted people to give attention to me, but—as you can imagine—if you are wearing Lolita fashion, everyone pays attention to that person, no? So I said, No, this didn't work.

STEPHANIE: Were there other Lolita people you hung out with?

MAKIKO: One person, yes.

STEPHANIE: Did that connect you in a way?

MAKIKO: I think so, because they are outsiders. So in a way I could share my ideas, yes.

STEPHANIE: That's a normal teenage way of rebelling—to dress different? It's like getting a piercing or dyeing your hair. Then what?

MAKIKO: Then? I was different from the other girls, and somehow they started asking me my advice, like, "Oh, I lost my way," or "I love this guy very much but he doesn't like me, so what can I do," or "I'm in big trouble with my family, what should I do?" I was the person . . .

STEPHANIE: . . . who people would talk to?

MAKIKO: Yeah, because I was different compared to my other classmates. So then, of course, I really wanted to help them, but at the same time I thought, Okay, yeah yeah yeah, I know what you need, but I can't do anything because you need to decide what you want to do for your future. So I listened to their worries, and then I just made charms.

STEPHANIE: What do you mean? What did you make them with?

MAKIKO: I don't remember, but they still have it. Like, something very small. Small. Sometimes drawings, or sometimes objects. And every time I gave a charm to my classmate, they got so happy and one week later they came to me saying, "Oh thank you very much, okay, now I'm okay, thank you so much."

STEPHANIE: Really?

MAKIKO: Mm-hmm. And I thought *(intakes breath)*, Okay, I have something I can do to people. And I realized, Okay, I really, really realized, I want to do something to help people by giving something I can make for them. That's the big start of changing my life. Then I don't need to wear thick layers. Yeah. ✕

*ANDREA WALKER*'s floral-print shirts

# Lena Dunham

*What item of clothing, makeup, or accessory do you carry with you or wear every day?*
I wear my mother's vintage rose-gold Art Deco bow ring and a lot of ChapStick.

*What are some shopping habits or rules that you follow?*
I try to only buy things I really need and can see myself in again and again. Otherwise I will end up with what my dad calls "rainbow chaps and unicorn hats." That rule goes down the toilet when I have an emergency and need tights or underpants, and then anything goes.

*What are you wearing on your body and face, and how is your hair done, right at this moment?*
I am sitting naked on my striped ottoman. Haven't washed my hair in two days. Nails are black and white and chipping mightily.

*How does makeup fit into this?*
Makeup can make me feel polished but it also makes me feel dirty, like when you were little and your parents slathered you in enough sunscreen that it felt like a catsuit. I often want to rush home to scrub my face at the end of the night. But I recognize the difference between me with and me without makeup, even if I resent it.

*What's the situation with your hair?*
I cut it all off a year ago, and it was the best thing I ever did in my life. I have always hated my hair—it's dry and ornery and has no pleasing qualities. But suddenly, short, it has unveiled itself as pretty okay hair!

*Please describe your figure.*
On good days I am sturdy bordering on slim and on less good days I am chubby. On all days I have a high waist, a wide ass and fairly long legs. I feel lucky to have thin wrists and ankles, and less lucky to have three rolls of flesh on my stomach that don't budge even in the face of extreme measures. I show myself naked on television a lot, but then I also had a terrible dream last night that my parents and sister had an intervention on me because my face was getting fat. They said I had gained "five to the face." It's all good.

*When do you feel most attractive?*
I feel most attractive at work, directing a scene that I'm not acting in—headphones on, monitor in front of me, focused on the frame and giving calm orders. I once saw a video of the late director Adrienne Shelly speaking about being a female filmmaker, and she called moving around set "a really sexy feeling." I also love to wear nightclothes—to be just showered (so that I am no longer what my boyfriend calls "a dirtbag") with clean teeth, pretending to read a book until he comes to bed.

*What is an archetypal outfit for you; one you could have happily worn at any time in your life?*
A party dress, velvet or wool, with thick nubby tights and flats. A good hooded coat. It makes me feel like I have put in proper effort but could get down on the floor or go out on a secret mission on a moment's notice.

*Is there any fashion trend you've refused to participate in?*
I just won't go there with a gaucho pant. I like a weird pant just as much as the next girl who grew up near

the Issey Miyake store, but that feels like it's a rejection of everything great about having lady legs.

*Would you rather be perceived as having great taste or great style?*
Great style. Taste, to me, implies you pick out the products that look and smell the best, you give great gifts, you know what's in style, and people believe you when you recommend a store. Style is a feeling that no one else could have put on what you're wearing that day because it sprang forth from your unique neon mind. I don't always have the best taste. My friend Jemima says I'm like a man who has decided to rifle through his wife's closet and cross-dress for the first time, selecting everything pink and shiny. She also says I am good to shop for because anything I'm handed I cry out, "I needed one of these!" But I do try to let people know I am with them, I am really with them, based on what I wear to meet them.

*What is the most transformative conversation you have ever had on the subject of style?*
I think just watching Jemima get dressed in high school, the ease of it, the confidence to make a strange move or perform some strange cultural appropriations or wear her pajamas with a heeled boot, gave me the juice that will drive my style for my whole life. My mother always wants to talk about clothes (she will call me up and say, "What's your thought on oxfords?"), and it makes me insane, even though I love her look (think bejeweled ventriloquist dummy).

*What are some dressing rules you wouldn't necessarily recommend to others but you follow?*
I like to be a character—schoolgirl, new lesbian, lapsed nun, Miami mistress. Not everyone needs that added layer, but it helps me.

*What are you trying to do or achieve when you dress?*
I want to inhabit the part I am playing that day—be it businesswoman, girlfriend with a life of her own, daughter at a holiday party, writer in a coffee shop. It's mortifying but true.

*What are some dressing or clothing rules you think every woman should follow?*
Wear things you feel confident in, that you don't have to tug at. Choose colors that make you happy. Be warm enough (but not too warm). I'd say stay comfortable, but the epic shoes may be worth it.

*What do you admire about how other women present themselves?*
I am easily impressed by women who smell fresh, with clean nail beds and many small minimalist rings. Those effects seem hard for me to achieve.

*Are there any dressing tricks that make you feel like you are getting away with something?*
I worked with one stylist who puts a tight belt *inside* the dress. She says it cinches you for photos and then you can take it off for the party. But it makes me feel like a big dumb liar, honestly, and then I just have to remeet my real waist again at the fucking party.

*What's the first "investment" item you bought, and why?*
I know this! I know this! It was a Marc by Marc Jacobs leopard-print trench coat (circa 2003), and I still cherish it. About twice a year it makes an appearance, and it still gives me the same "I'm here for the cocktail party" feeling it did when I was seventeen.

*What is your favorite piece of clothing or jewelry?*
I have a nightshirt my friend Addie left at my house in kindergarten before she moved to Rome. It used to come down to my ankles and now it comes to approximately just above my ass crack. It's covered in satiny, loving elephants.

*What item of clothing are you still on the hunt for?*
I am always looking for the denim jacket that makes me

feel like someone else's high school crush or role model. I imagine I'd walk a puppy in it, or put it on over my commitment ceremony dress to dance at the party later on.

*How has your background affected how you dress?*
I'm half Russian Jew and half *Mayflower* Wasp and the Wasp half makes me feel qualified to wear a lot of slouchy collared shirts and what my great-aunt Doad calls "dungarees." The Russian Jew half wants Chanel C's on everything, including the pillows.

*Do you look like your mother?*
I don't. We used to have the same teeth—freak-tiny incisors and big buck fronts—but she capped hers. Her hennaed hair is so smooth and always smells like shampoo no matter what. Other people say we have similar faces and stances. Somehow, even though I'm fives inches shorter and weigh ten pounds more, we can wear the same clothes. They just "project" differently, as my father would say. (If it were up to him we'd all dress like boy toddlers.)

*What is the difference between dressing and dressing up?*
It should probably be a greater divide, because I think of dressing up as just dressing with more uncomfortable variables. A great daytime

outfit gives me infinitely more pleasure than a nighttime look—at night it's like "Duh, you look great because you worked on it for hours and are probably wearing an under-dress constructed of Spanx and duct tape."

*What are things you need to do in order to feel presentable?*
A stain makes me want to go home immediately. It just feels like a big fat sign reading YOU GUYS, I'M FALLING APART.

*Do you have style in areas of your life other than fashion?*
Home design is my favorite hobby. I love arranging tchotchkes, sticking the perfect picture above the telephone table (see? I have a telephone table!). My style in that department is orderly mayhem. I hate leaving my home, and I want everyone else to feel the same way. I dream of a real home where each floor is thematically unified and intense. I also want a dirty-sexy toilet at some point.

*What dressing ideas or items have you stolen or borrowed from people you know?*
Jenni Konner runs my TV show with me and she is the most stylish woman I know. Just the way her jeans sit on her hips looks cool to me. I'm embarrassed to say that right after I met her I bought the exact same purse she had, and a bunch

of striped T-shirts because I'd seen a stack in her closet. Somehow all her shoes look like the coolest shoe in a fancy children's store, and I've never been able to mimic it. She's a really good mom, and that's stylish.

*What would you say is "you" and what would you say is "not you"?*
Me: undone hair, cardigans, collars, showing my knees, a clunky flat, a witty print, full-size underwear, a little strip of belly showing "by accident," and a tit falling out of a dress, honestly by accident. Not me (which doesn't mean I don't do it): stick-straight hair, boot-cut pants, turtlenecks, big-lady bags, tube tops, pointy toes, bangles, going to bars.

*How important is all this?*
Really important because no one can see me without seeing me, ya know? I feel I was put on this earth for a number of reasons, one of them being that I got the chance to see Sarah Jessica Parker in *Once Upon a Mattress* on Broadway in 1997. But the biggest reason is to help normalize a certain kind of body (and, therefore, all bodies) and the accompanying concerns. So even when I want to look beautiful, I want to look like myself. Even when I am uncomfortable, I want to look comfortable. ✕

## A MAP OF MY FLOOR | LEANNE SHAPTON

**OCCASION** *Taking part in a panel discussion of* Withnail and I *at the Brooklyn Academy of Music. The bedroom floor displays the following tried and discarded items:*

**1** Vintage tweed jacket, shrunk in washing machine, one arm needs repair, not enough time to mend, too rustic and outdoorsy for the occasion. **2** Red-and-white miniskirt, bought in mall near Olympic Park, London, totally wrong. **3** Vintage purple-and-black woven pumps from Toronto, stand out too much. **4** Vintage red Balmain A-line bouclé dress, fits well over baby bump and flattering but too *Umbrellas of Cherbourg*—too daytime. **5** Vintage Roger Vivier flats, found at an estate sale for $5, love but make legs look stumpy. **6** Margaret Howell lace-ups, immediately too collegiate preppy and remind me of something my friend Trish would wear to work. **7** Annoyed by the soles of my secondhand Louboutins, hate how they announce themselves, must paint soles black. **8** Vintage pink dress, still too large for second trimester, save for later in pregnancy. **9** Beige cardigan, feels suburban and boring. **10** Neon-pink dress, too modern and breezy. **11** Bespoke tweed jacket from Ireland, cheap buttons always disappoint slightly, looks like office wear. **12** Purple vintage sweater, right color, wrong shape. **13** Blue polka-dot knit cardigan, tight in the arms. **14** Vintage green knit cardigan, on theme for film about English countryside, but heavy and tends to itch. **15** White canvas sneakers, too casual and dirty. **16** Chanel flats, daytime. **17** Raincoat, wrong length. **18** Jogging pants, out of the question. **19** Tweed jacket, too much structure and too pale to wear over navy jumpsuit, looks weird over red dress.

**WORN** *Vintage floor-length navy jumpsuit with a beaded waistband. Worn with cowboy-style boots.*

# SURVEY DIARY NO. 1

MARY MANN

*Associate editor Mary Mann read and organized the surveys we received.*
*These are excerpts from the diaries she kept.*

### JUNE 7

Surveys tend to come in waves and each wave tends to have its own trend. Today I read three different surveys that all mentioned the appeal of menswear. After being in those three brains I was hankering to do the same, so I wore my boyfriend's shirt to dinner with friends. I walked to the restaurant, and on the way it started to rain hard. I was wearing waterproof boots, fortunately, but I kept worrying about messing the shirt up. New York is really gross in the rain, and he cares for his clothes more than I care for mine.

### JUNE 8

Reading five to ten surveys each day puts me inside the style brains of five to ten people. The effect is that when I leave the apartment, I'm looking at people and thinking about them more as I walk down the street. Two young women walking side by side have no underwear lines under their summer dresses, and they walk like they know this looks good. I catch myself looking at myself in a shop window. Goddamnit. In one of the surveys, someone wrote that her mom's advice was to look at yourself *before* leaving the house so you don't become "one of those women" who checks herself out in windows. I make a note to buy a full-length mirror.

High heels are the great survey divider. Some women see them as a symbol of patriarchy, hobbling women, making them unable to run. Others see heels—and specifically the ability to walk in heels—as a superpower. So many surveys mention women who walk well in heels as style icons, and those people who do walk well in heels seem to know this in their surveys. The women who write about wearing heels actually come across as extra-confident throughout the survey. What came first, the confidence or the footwear? Does style confidence carry over into other parts of life? How does one learn to walk in heels?

In the East Village tonight I saw a lot of women in heels and some clunked around or swayed, always on the verge of toppling, but one woman walked in them as though she was built to do so. I was drawn to her. She seemed like she would actually be faster than those of us in flats, maybe an effect of the leopardlike slinkiness that a good high-heeled walk bestows.

Older women frequently write that they're unhappy with their aging bodies, and say that they now dress for utility rather than style. Some don't see the point of taking time to dress bodies they're unhappy with, while others actively desire invisibility. Yet young women frequently write that they are inspired by fashionable older women. This disconnect makes me sad. I wish I could give these surveys to some of the older women and show them that dressing with style does not become pointless with age. In fact, it's probably the opposite.

I wonder if this is a new thing, this youthful veneration of stylish older women, and if it will change how young women today think about style and bodies as they age. How great that would be! That's probably part of why it's important for me to think about this stuff now. I'm building a foundation of style.

After all this reading and thinking about the power of high heels, I've decided to teach myself to wear them by getting comfortable in narrow wedges first. I wore them all day today and felt extra-special, like a kid in Sunday clothes. End result: blisters. Even with trains, I did walk at least three miles by the end of the day, and that seems pretty good for the first day of wedges.

Today I called my mom and we talked about style. As a young mom, her style was antistyle. She felt really strongly that she didn't want her daughters to think they had to dress a certain way to be valued, so she wore a lot of T-shirts with environmental messages on them, and encouraged thrift over fashion. She told me that in hospice, where she works, "you notice. sometimes people are happier when they're wearing their favorite thing. Obviously, they can't go anywhere. Nobody is going to see them. But still. It makes a difference."

### JUNE 15

Reading surveys makes me want new clothes. Or new ways to wear my old clothes, which, for me, is better. So yesterday I wore an old blue tube dress as a long skirt, with a black camisole. I think it felt especially good because it was a new silhouette for me. I usually wear knee-length or mid-thigh skirts and loose yoga tops (the kind that could double as maternity tops). It felt so good that I wore the exact same thing today on a trip to the Barnes Collection in Philly with Grace and Rachel. Grace said I looked sassy.

There's so much potential in my closet, but it's hard to use it right. When I figure out one outfit that clicks, I wear it for days in a row because it's so hard to find that perfect combination. It's like being a good curator—like Barnes—getting the combination of everything so right that nobody even questions it; making a hard thing look easy. ✕

**SURVEY** *I feel most attractive when . . .*

When I'm dirty from hard work. No matter how nicely I might dress up for a special occasion, I never feel as attractive as I do when I'm covered with paint or dirt or grease. —STEPHANIE AVERY • When I look most like an architecture student. —LILI OWEN ROWLANDS • I feel most attractive after I've accomplished something. That confident glow that you get from being creative—it's like my eyes grow wider, my skin more luminous, and my heart more open. It doesn't really matter what I'm wearing at those moments. —MAYA FUHR • I feel prettiest when I paint, and am convinced that concentration becomes me. Though no one is ever there to witness it, I feel beautiful when I am rosy, flush, and focused. —AGNES BARLEY

I really like that look of blurred makeup the next morning. —IVY KNIGHT • In the morning. —SARAH WHIDDEN • When I get out of bed in the morning and have on only underpants and a T-shirt and I walk to the bathroom and see my body in the mirror, every single day this same thought pops up: You are skinnier than you think. —PETRA KRUIJT • In the morning, looking in the bathroom mirror, once I am completely ready to leave but have not left yet. —CAROLINE EICK • I feel most attractive the moment right after leaving the house in the morning. —FAITH HARDEN • When I'm just about to leave the house in the morning. —AMÉLIE SNYERS • Looking in the mirror, dressed, about to leave the house. —MADELEINE STACK ✕

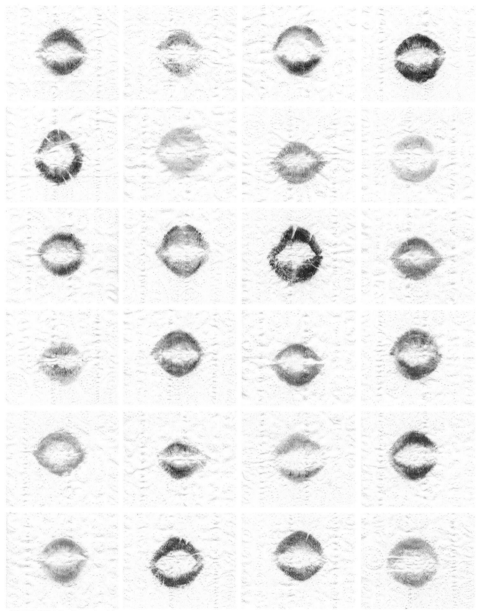

*JOYCE WALL*'s lipsticks blots

# IT'S THIS MYSTERY, ISN'T IT?

### WRITER & JOURNALIST JULIET JACQUES
### SPEAKS TO SHEILA HETI

**SHEILA:** I feel like a name is something that you wear, and I wonder how you chose your name.

**JULIET:** It came to me when I was about ten years old. I'd never liked the name my parents gave me, and I think one reason was because it was a male name that didn't have an obvious female equivalent, and I just had the name Juliet in my head. I think I liked the literary connotations of it, even though I'd never read Shakespeare, so you know, from a very young age I was sort of pretending to be more cultured and intelligent than I was. And I would write—on scraps of paper or whatever—*My name is Juliet*, then cross it out because I wasn't allowed to be called Juliet. Then, in my twenties, I was living in Brighton and had started to come out as transgender but not transsexual yet, and I started gradually going out as a woman more and more. And sometimes my friends would say, "What do you want to be called?" I didn't have that much confidence in this name, so I said, "Well, what do you want to call me?" And that's quite a risky strategy, right? That could have ended friendships. Luckily it never turned out too bad. A friend of mine once called me Mina—I was reading Mina Loy at the time—and I really, really liked that. But when I started transitioning, I had to make a decision and stick with it, so it was Juliet. It instinctively felt as right at twenty-seven as it did when I was ten.

**SHEILA:** And your last name, Jacques, was

that also chosen?

**JULIET:** Well, pronounce it "Jakes," but that's a pen name. I only use it for my writing and my online presence. It's my grandmother's maiden name. Her birth name was Millicent Hilda Jacques. She hated how aristocratic it sounded. So she married my granddad, whose surname was Buckell, and she took the first name Betty.

**SHEILA:** Betty Buckell?

**JULIET:** Yes, she took this very unassuming name. She was from an aristocratic family, and somebody a generation or two above blew all the money through gambling or drink or bad business decisions, I don't know what exactly. So she became this lower-middle-class working woman, and ended up taking this name to match, and two generations later I've taken her original maiden name. *(laughs)* I'm as petit bourgeois as she was, and thanks to her, I've given myself a much more . . .

**SHEILA:** . . . aristocratic?

**JULIET:** Worldly-sounding name.

**SHEILA:** What was the name you were given, if you want to say?

**JULIET:** I'd rather not.

**SHEILA:** Okay. I don't need to know your name, but I'm curious about why you choose not to tell people.

**JULIET:** There's a long history of the media and just people in everyday life having this kind of prurient interest in transgender and transsexual people's old names, which, you know, clearly serves to kind of undermine them. Also, the name carries a lot of very difficult associations for me. I really hate hearing it.

**SHEILA:** Do you think people want to know trans people's old names in order to, like, resurrect that other person or something?

**JULIET:** Yeah. Or because they don't feel your identity is valid. You know, they just won't accept it, and having that old name makes it easier for them to be like, Well, no, you're not Juliet, you're *that* person, which obviously is the opposite of how I feel.

**SHEILA:** Right. Knowing their old name . . . that is actually a lot of power.

**JULIET:** People often ask me which point in the transition felt like the biggest rupture in my life, and they often assume it was the surgery, but no. The sex reassignment surgery was quite near the end of the process. I already felt a lot more female, my mannerisms had changed, the way I dressed had changed, my social role had really changed. The biggest rupture was changing my name.

**SHEILA:** Do you think it's a good thing to do? I mean, obviously in your situation it's a lot more necessary, but for a woman changing her name to a different woman's name . . .

**JULIET:** I don't see why not. But changing your first name is a socially difficult thing to do, and there's this custom of your parents giving you your first name, so to change it feels kind of like a rejection of them. When I wrote to my parents, coming out as transsexual and telling them I was Juliet, I did say, "Look, I'm so sorry to have to do this, but I hope you can understand." And in the end they did, and the first time my parents called me Juliet was a really, really big moment. For a long time they

just called me J, and they hit on Jules after a while and that was okay—I understand why it was so difficult for them. But the first time my dad called me Juliet, after a year or eighteen months, it was a really incredible moment. More than anything, it felt like things were starting to work again between us, after this really, really difficult negotiation of who I was and who they wanted me to be. That was really special, it was really important.

•

**JULIET:** For a long time, I felt sort of caught somewhere between male and female, and to be honest, I still do. So I had these three identities. One of them was the young, sort of teenage male me, all punk bands and football and, you know, stand-up comedy, and I was quite Bolshy and angry—

**SHEILA:** Quite what?

**JULIET:** Bolshy. It's short for Bolshevik, actually. *(laughs)* You know, quite politically motivated with a very strong sense of injustice. Then I had this kind of degendered identity, which was my initials and my surname, and I was writing on literature and film and music and things. That was my transitional identity between the male one and the female one. Then I came up with this name Juliet Jacques, and I had this image of myself as somebody who would write about my gender identity and feminism and sex and sexuality, as well as all the things I'd been interested in before, and in this process of integrating all those sides of my person, the female identity ended up strongest. It took a long time. When I started living as female, I just thought: Can I still go to football matches, can I still dress in a certain way, can I still behave in a certain way, what's socially acceptable for me to talk about, which of these gestures are appropriate or not appropriate? And I'd learned a body language and a way of talking to help me pass as male when I needed to, and then I had to unlearn that. Then convincing somebody that actually I was female was quite difficult.

SHEILA: Right. So, like, hand gestures . . . Would you even say you gesture differently now?

JULIET: I'm not sure. I think I probably do. I had some speech and language therapy, and the premise behind it in Britain is that women are socially policed to behave with a lot more restraint, so we learn different ways of sneezing. And I sneeze now in this way where I try not to sneeze loudly, where when I was living as a male, I didn't do that.

SHEILA: So, as a feminist, why did you choose to be that kind of conventionally socialized woman?

JULIET: Yeah, well, I chose to explore the possibility of being it—then broke back out of it again. A bit like Picasso—everyone always says that he could paint as he did because he'd learned how to paint classically. *(laughs)* I think lots of women are taught those things—either in their schools or in their families or just by people in the street or by aggressive men or whatever. Why shouldn't I know who the entire Norwich City team was from twenty years ago, or talk about things in an authoritative way or sneeze loudly if I need to? But because I'd spent a lot of my mid-twenties reading feminist literature and engaged with those ideas, and then this weird thing of taking on what I was told in this speech and language therapy, or that people on the street would tell me, or that friends would tell me—about how I comported myself—I began not only instinctively thinking, This is bullshit, but also having this quite developed theoretical base for thinking, No, this is bullshit.

SHEILA: Right. It's complicated because if you want to pass, you have to adopt some of those mannerisms.

JULIET: Exactly. And I would get beaten up if I didn't. The first summer that I lived as a woman was 2009—and it was quite a hot summer, and I don't like the summer anyway, I get depressed in hot weather, it really floors me—my body language was quite depressed, and I was nervous and scared all the time, because this was an incredibly vulnerable time: you've just come out, you're worried about your friends and family rejecting you, things being a lot harder at your job, maybe even losing it,

---

CONVERSATION *Four women at a clothing swap.*

**CHRISTINE MUHLKE:** I love this, but I just don't wear it.  **HEIDI JULAVITS:** Let me see. Whoa! It's not you. **LEANNE SHAPTON:** That's a little big on you.  **CHRISTINE:** Big coats are in for fall.  **LEANNE:** These are the things I take out every year and I'm like . . . **HEIDI:** You wonder about them.  **LEANNE:** Who wants a drink and pizza?  **HEIDI:** Here are the things that I really want somebody to want, but don't feel pressure at all.  **CHRISTINE:** Heidi, those boots are wicked! And they're not you?  **HEIDI:** You don't even know—I stalked these things for so fucking long.  **CHRISTINE:** I remember you stalking them.  **HEIDI:** I sent the link to you, I sent the link to everybody. I finally found them, I bought them—they just don't fit me.  **EVERYONE:** Aww.  **HEIDI:** Because of my bunions.  **CHRISTINE:** What is a bunion?  **HEIDI:** It's this. *(shows a bunion)*  **CHRISTINE:** Who has slightly smaller feet?  **LEANNE:** Maybe Gaby?  **CHRISTINE:** Maybe Gaby.  **HEIDI:** It's such a shame.  **KERRY DIAMOND:** I think you should cut the toe open.  **HEIDI:** It's not even the toe! I don't know what it is about these things that

and people beating you up. And a lot of the time I would get the clothing codes wrong. I hadn't started the hormone therapy, so my hair was thinner, and my face was more male and my skin tone was harsher, all these physical signifiers of maleness. But also not feeling comfortable in my own skin or my own clothes. So I'd walk around town wearing quite a lot of makeup and stuff because I'd been told it would help me pass. But then, of course, it would attract a lot of attention. There were a few times when groups of young men would pick up on how I looked, and just humiliate me in the street, yell and laugh and point at me and stuff—throw things every now and again. And I felt completely defenseless, and it made me really angry and really sad, and I didn't have any outlet for it, so I got more depressed and the body language would get more defeated, which just made it worse. I was so glad when the winter came around, because I could just wrap myself in hats, which hid my hairline, and big coats, which made my body shape less obvious, and I never really got hassled in the winter, it was always in the summer. And it was partly because I didn't know how to dress for the summer, and partly because it just makes you more conspicuous.

**SHEILA:** Yeah. Most women probably get hassled more in the summer because of all the flesh.

**JULIET:** Well, exactly, and lots of men see summer as a real treat, because they get to see things they wouldn't normally. With the football fans I used to talk to on the message boards, when I was in my mid-twenties and was living as male, I'd go on about how much I hated the summer, and a lot of the guys I used to talk to would be like, "But women in short skirts!"—or "birds in short skirts" would be the term they used. It was interesting to get this insight into straight sexism, because that was always one of the best things about summer for these guys, "birds in short skirts." The second summer was a bit easier, but not that much easier, but then by the third summer I sort of worked out what would attract scrutiny and what wouldn't, and spent the whole summer wearing cotton trousers that weren't too hot. I realized that if I wasn't showing off my legs, actually people looked at me a lot less.

**SHEILA:** You don't wear much makeup now.

**JULIET:** No, I try not to be over-the-top. For anyone who presents as female in our society, your appearance gets scrutinized at a really unbearable level, and for trans women that's the truth to a huge degree. It's a double bind: you get attacked if you're

---

aren't quite right, but . . . *(Attention shifts.)* **CHRISTINE:** Oo, that's pretty. **HEIDI:** That *is* pretty. **KERRY:** I kind of brought more designer stuff. **LEANNE:** *(Pulling out of her own pile.)* This is what I chose for you, Kerry, and I think you should experiment with it, because I was like, "Who in the group is basically gonna look beautiful in this?" It's trousers and a top. **HEIDI:** It's trousers?! **LEANNE:** Yes, it's a pantsuit. And I just think you'd look great. **KERRY:** I'll take 'em. **LEANNE:** See, the pants, they're not pleated. It's a little bit like Mia in *The Great Gatsby.* **CHRISTINE:** Ooo. *(Pizza break.)* **LEANNE:** You've got some good stuff, Christine, look at how pretty this is! I feel like I've seen you in this. **HEIDI:** That's so you, why are you getting rid of it!? **CHRISTINE:** I just don't wear it anymore. And I have it in brown. *(New item.)* **HEIDI:** Wow. **CHRISTINE:** Heidi, teach in that. **HEIDI:** Oh my god, that is insane. **CHRISTINE:** It's Bob Mackie from the Leona Helmsley auction. Kerry, would you just do me . . . will you try on the Bob Mackie? **KERRY:** I'm highly confident I won't be taking it. **CHRISTINE:** It has covered buttons! **KERRY:** It looks like it would be a little tiny on me, but it's really cute and sexy.

not feminine enough, because you're not trying to pass, or because you're not really committed to this whole thing.

**SHEILA:** Attacked by other trans people?

**JULIET:** Other trans people, men, feminists, other women, whoever. This stuff seems to cut across gender categories. So you get attacked for not being feminine enough—like if I went out with my friends and dressed or acted in a way they thought was too male, they would tell me. But if I was overly feminine, I got attacked for reiterating gender stereotypes and being socially conservative.

**SHEILA:** Do you have the sense, walking through the streets as a woman, versus when you walked through the streets as a man, that it's different?

**JULIET:** Oh god, absolutely. I hardly ever got street harassment as a man. The first year I lived in London, when I moved in with my friend Helen, she was like, "Never walk down this street"—which is a shortcut to our house—"at night." And there's a part of me, the sort of pretransitional part of me, and I guess the feminist part as well, that just said, That's bullshit. Why shouldn't I? Then one night I thought someone was gonna rape me, actually. This guy came on to me, and grabbed me and kissed me, and told me his name. I'd met so many people

in London recently that he was playing on whether or not I'd recognize him. He said, "I'm Gino," and I said, "I don't think I know you." And of course, rather than just walk on, I dithered, and he grabbed me and kissed me and said, "Where are you going?" and I said, "I'm going home." And he heard a male voice and said, "Look, are you a man or a girl?" and I just flicked my hand at him and walked off, and luckily he didn't follow me home, but I was absolutely terrified. This kind of social space opens up where I'm kind of below male or female, and it's absolutely terrifying. If you're being read as a man, and another man is annoyed with you, he's probably gonna fight you. And you can be prepared for that—like my tactic would be to run away. And if you're being treated as a woman, there might be a modicum of respect for you. But if they're treating you as below either of those things, then that's terrifying—all bets are off.

•

**JULIET:** A real challenge for trans women is the social stereotype that we dress like our grandmothers or something, that we dress well behind our times. In the beginning, I was trying not to fall into that, and trying to find a way of dressing as a woman in her

---

**HEIDI:** Oh my god! But you have the stature to pull it off. It's crazy. It's so crazy! **KERRY:** I'm so not taking it. **LEANNE:** Kerry, please? **KERRY:** No. *(New item.)* **HEIDI:** I say too short. **LEANNE:** You do? **HEIDI:** I say too short! *(New item.)* **LEANNE:** I think we should each go through our things and present them. Like, "Here's the thing, here's who I think should have it," you know? I could start with these shoes. **HEIDI:** Okay, present your shoes. **LEANNE:** I traded these with Louisa for some clogs, and I don't, I can't, wear them. **CHRISTINE:** Heidi. Heidi's the clog mistress. **HEIDI:** I'm cloggy. **KERRY:** Those are pretty. **LEANNE:** eBay purchase. **KERRY:** I can't do a wedge. I don't know why. *(Heidi tries on a pair of boots with difficulty.)* **LEANNE:** You could cut the shoe in the front, but not the back, because in back it would . . . don't you think? Or on the side? **HEIDI:** Oh maybe like a zip? Or a magnet? **KERRY:** Or what about a sock? **HEIDI:** A sock. It could slide right on with a sock. **LEANNE:** I think cutting maybe a snip in the front would make it fit. **KERRY:** I would try a sock first, before you do any boot cutting. **HEIDI:** Boot episiotomy! **KERRY:** Someone e-mailed me today and was like,

twenties that felt natural and not contrived, and also individualistic and right for me. It was really difficult, and I made loads of mistakes, obviously.

**SHEILA:** What were some of the mistakes?

**JULIET:** When I was twenty-two, I wore a dress with a floral print to a nightclub, and somebody told me, "You dress like my mum," and I was really upset by that. When I started transitioning, I wore this really, really short dress to work one day, and this woman came up to me and said, "Look, if you were on my team, I'd have sent you home." And I felt awful about that, and it was really early on, and I felt so insecure. I was terrified of getting it wrong. I was always wearing black, things that weren't very colorful or didn't have a lot of personality. But I had a few friends whose style I liked, so I asked them to come shopping with me. I would keep picking things out, and they would say, "No, that's too dowdy," or "It's too young," or "It's too conservative," or "It's over-the-top." It was like dressing by consensus. *(laughs)* My friend Laura, who I used to work with in a jewelry shop—when I told her I was transitioning, she got really excited and she started offering to give me loads of old clothes. When she took me shopping, I turned up in a pair of shoes that were falling to pieces and a horrible bag I'd bought from a charity shop, and she took one look at me and said, "Right, the first thing we're doing is getting rid of the bag and the shoes." Basically she just took ownership of it, it was like a project for her. Which I was quite happy with. She turned clothes shopping from this terrifying ordeal into something life-affirming and fun. We bought a whole new wardrobe, and we symbolically threw away the bag and the shoes at the end. *(laughs)* It just felt amazing.

**SHEILA:** What are some of your favorite pieces that you own?

**JULIET:** I have this great gray dress that I love wearing in winter, it's long-sleeved, V-necked—not a particularly exciting piece of clothing, but something you can have good fun accessorizing. I have no idea where it came from, it just sort of appeared in my wardrobe. I don't know if I took it by mistake from someone that I shouldn't have. There's that and one other piece of clothing that I've got, which is this sort of transparent dress, quite long, and it's got this kind of silver pattern on it, and there's sort of metal attached to the dress. And I don't know where that one came from, either. These are my two favorite items of clothing! That I didn't buy, no one

---

"I'm sorry to bother you, I know you're probably packing," and I was like, Psh, I'll be packing at midnight. **CHRISTINE:** When do you guys go to Berlin? **HEIDI:** Tomorrow. **CHRISTINE:** Oh my gosh. **HEIDI:** I'm so so so tired of packing that I'm just like, You know what? We'll wake up in the morning and something will go in a suitcase and hopefully the children will have pants. *(New item.)* **KERRY:** Those are great. **HEIDI:** I would never wear them. **CHRISTINE:** You need a green trench coat with them. **HEIDI:** I would never wear them. **KERRY:** Why? I'm telling you, they scream Berlin! They're weirdly comfortable. I've worn them since, like, 1999. **HEIDI:** Yeah, it's not— **KERRY:** I'm telling you, you'll get to Berlin and you'll be like, "Damn, I should have brought those boots." **HEIDI:** I don't know. How much do you walk there? **KERRY:** Like in New York. **HEIDI:** All right, I'm gonna keep them on for a while. Ech, I have one bunion rubbing. *(New item.)* **CHRISTINE:** Oo I like it! **HEIDI:** No. The lederhosen and the bunny ears are just too much. *(New item.)* **KERRY:** I also brought these little shoes that are amazing but don't fit me. **HEIDI:** Oh my god. **LEANNE:** Those

gave me, I don't know where they're from!

SHEILA: *(laughs)* The closet genie!

JULIET: Yeah! It's baffling. *(laughs)*

SHEILA: I feel like that about some of my clothes, but I've been acquiring a woman's wardrobe my entire life. Within the past five years, to have two items turn up mysteriously, that's amazing.

JULIET: That never happens to me with men's clothes! Not once. You know, I wouldn't open my chest of drawers and be like, "Oh, I've got a new T-shirt, I wonder where that's from." So yeah, I don't know, it's this mystery, isn't it?

SHEILA: *(laughs)* Yeah. When do you feel most attractive?

JULIET: Oh god, good question. That's been a big problem for me, to be honest. Gender dysphoria and sexual attraction, they're really difficult things to navigate. So when do I feel the most attractive? In the evening, definitely. I prefer there to not be too much light. I feel more attractive in the dark. *(laughs)* Last year this woman I'd only just met took an interest in me really quickly, and she said, "Look, tomorrow, I'd love to give you a makeover and take some photos." She was a singer and an amateur makeup artist, and she took some pictures of me, and they're my favorite pictures of me. It was when I saw the photos, actually, that I probably felt the most attractive. Something else I did quite early on—some female friends of mine invited me to a clothes swap. I said, "Look, I don't really have anything to give away," and they were like, "No, fine, it's cool," so I went and joined in with everyone—dressing up in different things, trying things on, discarding things. Nobody had a problem with me being there at all. I felt totally accepted as one of the women there, and that was one of the earliest moments where I thought, Okay, this is gonna work. This is gonna be all right. ✕

---

are gorgeous. HEIDI: They're beautiful. They're insane. LEANNE: They're incredible. I think they might fit you, Christine. HEIDI: But she's got bunions. I've got bunions, we've all got bunions. *(New item.)* KERRY: Here's some Céline jeans that I wanted so badly and I thought they looked great in the dressing room, but I've just never liked how they looked. LEANNE: I have a pile of weird jeans. KERRY: I think in my head I've always wanted to be that seventies girl with the big jeans, but I just don't have the body shape for them. CHRISTINE: These are like . . . below my crack line! KERRY: I know, they're low-rise. *(New item.)* LEANNE: My boobs just do not, they're not agreeing, you know what I mean? HEIDI: Your boobs are not agreeing with what? LEANNE: With anything. HEIDI: You don't think they're agreeing with that dress? *(Later.)* HEIDI: Anyway, what I learned from looking at these old photographs is that all these things I thought had happened because I had kids had almost always been there. I'm not joking, all this stuff I had blamed on my children, it was like, Oh, I always had that vein. Even when I was twenty. ✕

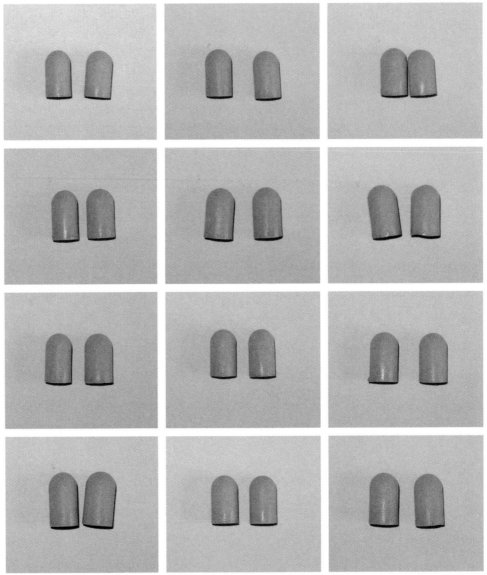

*VERONICA MANCHESTER*'s earplugs used over the course of one week

# ADVICE AND TIPS

*"You'll never look like you've fallen apart completely if you're wearing a good pair of shoes."* —SASHA GORA

**JYTZA GUZMAN** I never try on my clothes beforehand and I know that no one would ever follow that rule because it sounds crazy, but for some reason, I have this sense where I know if something is going to look good on me. I'll put it on the day of the event and everything is perfectly fine.

**JENNIFER ARMBRUST** Clothes that list more than one fiber are undesirable. Too many fiber types seems like a sad statement of late-stage capitalism, like, "We had some surplus angora, nylon, and elastane lying around so we threw in five percent of each with your wool sweater. Hope you like it!"

**MARGAUX WILLIAMSON** Wear whatever makes you less sad and feels right when it's on. Don't wear too many things that serve no function. Wear what you can wear on a bicycle. Wear what you can run in or survive in if necessary. If something feels right, wear it all the time. Don't look too cool. Keep some things in!

**MAYA FUHR** I have never shopped online, and to be honest, I don't understand it. The fun of shopping to me is feeling every piece of fabric, jumping to the colors that intrigue me, trying them on in a relaxed fashion, taking my time to decide if this is a good "investment" and if I could see it hanging on my very own hanger, then walking out with a little bag in my hand. I am obsessed with shopping for secondhand clothing. Nobody else has it, and it has a story that comes with it. Spending money excessively on really expensive pieces sort of ruins shopping for me, because you feel a certain guilt afterward. Some of my favorite pieces were five dollars. No matter what, I think that the wrists should be shown, and the ankles too! Just rolling a big sweater at the cuffs makes the whole look more elegant and feminine. My dad always said, "If the colors go together in a flower, then they work together in an outfit." I agree. Colors that you see in nature, or in a flower garden, give a tremendous spectrum: mustard yellow, browns, beiges, dusty pinks, greens. The bright colors that pop in flowers, like red or yellow, those are usually the colors in my wardrobe that stand out. I like "timeless" pieces, so that each purchase is an investment and adds to the collection that is my wardrobe. If something is in style and obviously will not last, there is no point in buying it.

**PATRICIA MARX** My mother said red and black was for drum majorettes.

**AUDREY GELMAN** When wearing a skirt or slacks, I often tuck my shirt into my underwear. It's a trick my mother taught me to hold shirts into place. After moving in with my boyfriend, he witnessed me pulling up pants with my underwear over my shirt, and asked if I was having a seizure.

**CAILIN HILL** There was a time when I first moved to New York when I blew money on dumb shit like $1,200 heels and $700 coats. I reflect on these occurrences as huge regrets. If you're going to blow a huge chunk of dough on designer goods, make sure it's "timeless," like a black pump. I wore those neon-orange platforms *twice* before I decided I was over them. I always try to look a little too dressed down for events. And if I really need makeup, I just stop by Sephora and use theirs. I don't fuck around with mascara testers, though.

**KARIMA CAMMELL** So many psychological problems fell away when I started tailoring my clothes to my body instead of the other way around.

**SARAH NICOLE PRICKETT** I believe contradictions make you attractive. So if I wear something short, it's not also tight, or if it's both short and tight, I wear it with old boots. If I wear skinny pants, I usually wear big sweaters, and if I have a fancy dress on, I like it when my nails chip. I love a gorgeous necklace with an old gray shirt. Try on many things, and stop saying, "Oh, that's not me," or "I could never." So boring! TRY. It's fun sometimes to have on one thing that feels off or like you borrowed it from someone else. It shows you're not that precious about yourself, and it throws the rest of you, the "real you," into relief.

**ANA ZIR** My mother-in-law once said, "Save all the pictures of yourself you hate. In thirty years you'll think you looked fabulous." She was right.

**LIANE BALABAN** Dressing is about helping yourself do the work you were put on this earth to do. Everyone has their own relationship to beauty, but I would say: Don't be obvious. Try not to buy things that are mass-produced. Flea markets, church bazaars, or local boutiques are good. Curate rather than shop. Your wardrobe should be a collection of beloved pieces you wear for decades. When you witness beauty, it's visceral—there is no second guessing it. Plato says that feeling of absolute knowing can inspire the beholder to quest after a similar revelation in other dis-

ciplines of life—poetry or music or science, for example. The ultimate experience of eros, then, is one that inspires you to live in a questioning, questing way, seeking truth in all areas of life. Ergo, true beauty turns you into a philosopher!

**ERIKA THORMAHLEN** When I was younger, I believed in a reverse psychology of dressing: a night out on the town meant a black wool turtleneck or a skirt worn over pants for maximum coverage. I wore a grey cashmere turtleneck and a white knee-length slip skirt to the Playboy Mansion when I was nineteen. (Though part of me wishes I had worn a baby-doll nightgown in those early, slamming-body days when I shook hands with Hef.)

**HEIDI HOWARD** I feel like the biggest part of style is making do with what you have.

**ANU HENDERSON** I'm with the French, who supposedly believe that less is more when it comes to makeup, and that a healthy complexion shouldn't be covered with foundation. I spend much more on moisturizers and facials than I ever would on makeup. The more I look like a messy, pretty boy, the more attractive I feel. I actually break most rules: loose threads hang from where I sewed buttons; bleach stains on a new tunic, from cleaning floors; torn pockets and holes in the cashmere shirt I refuse to stop wearing. The joke about men wearing their underwear till it's in shreds is true for me and clothes. I suppose in my head I'm imagining I look like a disheveled adult matchstick-seller. This is acceptable so long as the clothes are clean, so say I. It's advisable to strike some balance between being comfortable and captivating. I once met Isabella Rossellini, who was stunning in her usual uniform of an Italian men's suit; however, when she crossed her legs, I saw that she was wearing white tube socks, which I found reassuring. ✕

# ANYONE CAN LOOK COOL

MUSICIAN **KIM GORDON** OF SONIC YOUTH

SPEAKS TO NOVELIST & EDITOR **CHRISTOPHER BOLLEN**

**CHRIS**: I want to talk about when you were starting out as a musician. What were you wearing at the time?

**KIM**: I was just really poor at the time. *(laughs)* My mom grew up during the Depression and she really never bought new clothes. So all my life, I bought clothes from thrift stores, or she made them. I had kind of a mishmash fashion. I was kind of a tomboy because of my older brother. Button-downs and '70s corduroy flares or boot-cuts.

**CHRIS**: I feel like women who have older brothers tend to have a more tomboyish look. Some of the brothers' clothes mix in with theirs.

**KIM**: Yeah, that's possible. But when I started performing, I really got into the idea of playing against type. We were playing this very dissonant music, so I liked the idea of wearing a dress onstage because it didn't really look punk rock or hard rock. It was kind of vulnerable. I think you have to make yourself vulnerable in order to do a good performance.

**CHRIS**: That's interesting, because rock 'n' roll has a history of costumes involving armor or shields or vectors of confusion. But you were trying to go in the opposite direction. You were trying to open up.

**KIM**: I didn't have a persona. I was just being normal. When we went to England, that was really baffling to them. Everyone had personas. That was how they escaped the class system.

**CHRIS**: Were people surprised that you weren't going with the standard punk rock look of ripped leather, safety pins . . .

**KIM**: I guess. Being a woman in music you were meant to present yourself as a freak or something.

**CHRIS**: So you would wear dresses. With what kind of shoes?

**KIM**: Motorcycle boots. I was always influenced by people like Anita Pallenberg or Marianne Faithfull. People like that.

**CHRIS**: Do you still try to find vulnerability with what you wear on stage?

**KIM**: I guess. I don't know. I have this one dress I wore in 1991 when we did the tour that was in the film *1991: The Year Punk Broke*. It was this striped dress that looked very casual and sporty, but it was also really short, and at every show I would sweat and it would shrink and get shorter and shorter.

**CHRIS**: So the dress became a document of your stage performances. Did you notice a big difference when you went from living in Los Angeles to living in New York?

**KIM**: Yeah. In a way it was really hard for me to find my fashion groove in New York. As soon as I moved back East, my hair turned dark and I was wearing glasses all the time. I just felt really nerdy. I didn't know how to dress for the cold.

**CHRIS**: Were there people in New York you knew well, or was it lonely?

**KIM**: I didn't really know that many people. I had just met the artist Dan Graham and he introduced me to other people. And

I had one friend who was the sister of a friend of mine in high school. You know, it was like that.

CHRIS: I wonder about the genesis of the fashion label you started.

KIM: Oh, X-Girl. We knew the X-Large guys through Mike D and the Beastie Boys. I think Daisy [von Furth] was actually working at the X-Large store, and one of the brothers knew that we talked about going to thrift stores together and looking for 517 boot-cut cords and perfect-fitting T-shirts. He asked Daisy if she'd be interested in doing a girls' line, and she asked me if I would do it with her. Daisy was into really preppy stuff, which was part of her teenage world growing up. Mine was more like '60s and '70s stuff. So it was a mix. The other thing I was really into was the look of Godard movies and Anna Karina and that timeless '60s way of dressing.

CHRIS: Was there a specific kind of girl you had in mind as a customer?

KIM: We wanted to make shapes that any size girl would look good in. It was a reaction to all the really baggy streetwear coming out of the boys' skater world. Everything was so big. We wanted to do things like the perfect A-line skirt or an A-line dress. If you're a big girl, it's better to wear something that is more fitted. It was tomboyish and cool, I guess.

Sort of Françoise Hardy–ish.

CHRIS: X-Girl was concurrent with high fashion exploding, as well as the supermodel ideal and extreme beauty. Did it feel like you were presenting the other option?

KIM: X-Girl was more low-key about fashion. But it was totally non-grunge. There were clean and deliberate lines. There were no muddy colors.

CHRIS: You've mentored a lot of women in terms of style and attitude. I know you probably don't want to claim that. (laughs) Has anyone said you've been an influence on them—younger women, or women of any age?

KIM: Um, I've heard that. (laughs)

CHRIS: Does that surprise you?

KIM: Kind of, yeah. But I don't really feel anything from that. I don't like becoming too self-conscious about what I'm doing. And I guess I feel that I'm always still evolving. I don't really know what I am, exactly. In my mind I'm much younger than I am. (laughs) You know, it's great.

CHRIS: Do you think your style had anything to do with the fact that you were playing with men? You probably had more male peers than women peers back then.

KIM: In the beginning, I did wear lots of T-shirts. I remember Mark Arm from

---

SURVEY  *What's the situation with your hair?*

You noticed, eh? My hair is thick—thicker than any hairdresser I've ever been to has seen. So thick it takes about twenty-four hours to dry after I've washed it, and if I used a hair dryer I'd be standing there, pointing it at my head for a few hours. So I don't. I wash it before bed and wake up and it's usually still damp. My hormones fuck it up constantly—dry one day, greasy another day. I tend to avoid the hairdresser like I avoid the dentist. I find it takes so much time. My hair also grows very slowly. It grows out thick instead of long. Sigh. —MICHELLE BERRY • Oh, fucking heck, I hate my hair. —AMANDA MILLER • Used to be bright blue. Now short, I sometimes wear it in four braids. Normally a ponytail. —ADA EZE • It's spaghetti straight. It's great to tie in a knot, but for everything else it is too straight and heavy. I hate blow dryers. I think in an ideal world, where I had a hairstylist every day (and more hours to kill), I could look ravishingly fantastic. But in my life, I just take a rubber band every day and tie my hair in a knot.

Mudhoney saying to me once, "How come you don't wear T-shirts anymore?" I felt like I exhausted that. One gets sick of wearing band shirts. It probably has something to do with not wanting to be too flashy. When I think of style icons or people who were influential, I think more about Chloë [Sevigny]. To me, she was very adventurous and creative.

CHRIS: It's sort of an unfair thing that happens to women more than men, but if you're considered stylish as a woman, there's this expectation that you're always going to show up at a party and be stylish.

KIM: That you're going to what, I'm sorry?

CHRIS: Show up at every event or party and be stylish. There will always be someone who'll want to take your picture.

KIM: Oh yeah, that's a whole other world that I've only dipped my toe into. It's very strange. You can't just go somewhere, you know.

CHRIS: Do you ever feel, "I have to dress up for this thing, I'm going to have to take it to number ten on the register."

KIM: No, though I do feel like I want to look good. It's very hard to just look good. Also, you don't know how your outfit is going to photograph.

CHRIS: I know. Sometimes you match blacks that seem like they're suitable enough, and then someone takes a picture of you and you look at it in the bright light and it's disturbingly different.

KIM: I wore this Rodarte dress that they gave to me to wear to the *Girls* premiere.

CHRIS: Was it something you chose or—I know Kate and Laura Mulleavy at Rodarte admire you, so . . . ?

KIM: They sent it to me, and I was like, "Well, if I don't wear it here, then where am I going to wear it?" You know, aside from my living room. *(laughs)*

CHRIS: Is it strange to have people send you clothes—that whole fame and fashion complex where it's like, "We need you to wear this. . . . Now go out and smile in it"?

KIM: I mean, I know them and they're friends. I really like what they do and I could never afford to buy their stuff. And it's fun to wear their dresses. But they're the only ones. . . . *(laughs)* Nobody sends me things to wear.

CHRIS: You were also in that Yves Saint Laurent ad.

KIM: Oh yeah, that's true.

CHRIS: I hope you got some clothes out of that. Is that something that's strange for you? Doing those campaigns?

KIM: Hedi [Slimane, creative director of Yves Saint Laurent] asked me and my daughter, although they never ran her

---

—SOPHIE ZEITZ • It's frustrating at the moment. I used to have my hair done once a month, but I am not working anymore, so I am not able to do this. Which is horrible! At the moment I have not been to the hairdresser in six months. —ALIYA JACOBS • I'm forty-two and getting gray, so I'm putting a little red in it, which I really like. —JEANA DELROSSO • It's in the awkward place between two lengths. Then there is the onion sprout. —MEGHAN BEAN FLAHERTY • I have an expensive sandy-blond long bob with bangs. My hair changes a lot. (I own a hair salon.) —JOHANNA FATEMAN • My mom used to comb it with a bristle brush and it was a disaster. When I got older and learned that curly hair needs a wide-tooth comb, things got better. My husband loves it very long, so I wore it like that for a few years. He would comb it for me. I once had a boyfriend, though, who said I *had* to have long hair, so I nearly shaved it off. —MELANIE PAGE • My hair is in dreads down below my navel. —RAINBOW MOOON • It's thick, dark, coarse, and wiry, and it grows out from my head in the Asian fashion. I think the only hair that truly works for me is long, witchy hair.

pictures. I was disappointed, because she looked amazing.

CHRIS: Do you see a shift in the way fashion is treated today from when you first started out?

KIM: As a visual artist, I just like to look at clothes. I'm comfortable with being associated with fashion. I'm not a designer. I don't think of myself in that way. But I'm interested in the whole machinery of fashion and how it relates with culture. There was that show at the Met this year . . . *Impressionism, Fashion, and Modernity*. It was one of the best shows I've ever seen. I don't know if you've ever read Émile Zola's book *The Ladies' Paradise*. It describes the beginning of consumerism and the first department store and how the department store is this big machine in the neighborhood and how the owner feels like he has the ladies' pleasure and he's in control of it and whipping it up into a frenzy.

CHRIS: People forget that, especially in the case of Manet and Renoir, those paintings are about fashion. The fashion element has been completely eclipsed in art history, but those artists were basically presenting new ways of dressing and new styles and the culture that was being built around it.

KIM: And showing how those styles allowed women to go out in public. Like the day dress. Showing a woman sitting at a café having a beer by herself, I find all of that really fascinating.

CHRIS: Do you think the machinery is good for women?

KIM: I mean, it just *is*. Now men are pulled in, too. The metro male. It's beginning to be as big of a market for men, and men are now involved in consumerism in that way. It's just part and parcel of the whole consumerist society.

CHRIS: Do you think there's less of an opportunity to revolt now? That there are fewer opportunities for young people to be creative?

KIM: It's become all so democratic. Anyone can look cool. Which is great. But it's harder and harder to find things that are really authentic or to create your own identity. I think it's become about smaller gestures. That's how you make fashion your own. I mean, I look at the way my daughter dresses, and she's kind of minimalist, tomboyish.

CHRIS: She doesn't borrow your clothes?

KIM: Oh, she does. But she always has to make it her own. She isn't an overconsumer. She seems to have much more of a sense of style than I did at that age. I think she probably has a better innate sense of what looks good. She's just a cool girl. ✕

---

—JILLIAN TAMAKI • Absolute war ever since I dyed it green when I was eleven and fucked it up forever. —TALITA S. • The higher the hair, the closer to God! I'm very into volume. —ALICIA BERNLOHR • After years of confusion, I finally understand my hair. It's all thanks to one hairdresser. My hair is wavy, but it was always being cut straight and styled straight. I've used straightener so much of my life that I actually think it started to damage my hairline. But one day I went to this hairdresser who gave me a cute medium-length cut with the intention that the hair would wave or curl in whatever direction. She threw a little curling cream in and told me to twirl it and voilà! I now officially have one of the easiest hair regiments of anyone I know. —JENNIFER CARROLL • It's in an okay state right now. I used to wear it very long and completely flat-ironed (for all of high school). I have curly hair, though, so this took forever. I now wear it short and curly. It's sort of triangle-shaped. I cut my own hair. I like it. —LINDSAY ALLISON RUOFF • I would love to have long hair, but it looks bad on me. My hair is cut in a short bob that I call the "mom cut." —KRISTIN SJAARDA ✕

## WEAR AREAS | RIVKA GALCHEN

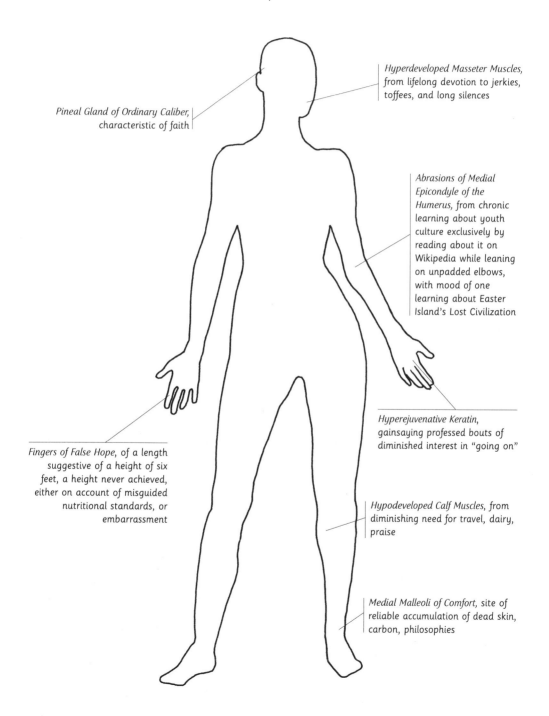

Hyperdeveloped Masseter Muscles, from lifelong devotion to jerkies, toffees, and long silences

Pineal Gland of Ordinary Caliber, characteristic of faith

Abrasions of Medial Epicondyle of the Humerus, from chronic learning about youth culture exclusively by reading about it on Wikipedia while leaning on unpadded elbows, with mood of one learning about Easter Island's Lost Civilization

Hyperejuvenative Keratin, gainsaying professed bouts of diminished interest in "going on"

Fingers of False Hope, of a length suggestive of a height of six feet, a height never achieved, either on account of misguided nutritional standards, or embarrassment

Hypodeveloped Calf Muscles, from diminishing need for travel, dairy, praise

Medial Malleoli of Comfort, site of reliable accumulation of dead skin, carbon, philosophies

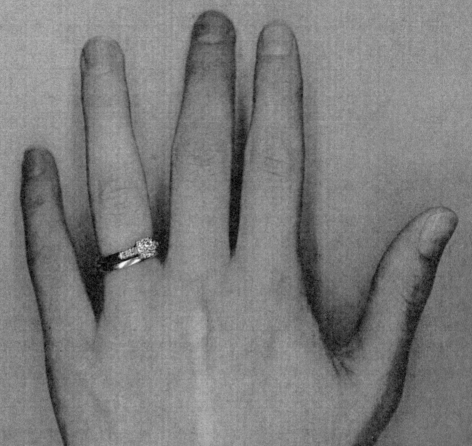

## RING CYCLE | FIFTEEN WOMEN IN A NEWSPAPER OFFICE PHOTOCOPY THEIR HANDS AND TALK ABOUT THEIR RINGS

**HONOR JONES** The engagement ring was my grandmother's, and when she died, my oldest cousin got the ring. This cousin called Daniel and said, "No pressure, but if you're going to propose to Honor, do you want this ring?" One of our friends was going to Cincinnati and so he stopped in Pittsburgh and got the ring and brought it back to New York. I really loved my grandmother, so it is really special to me. It's from the forties. There's one funny story about the ring. Apparently, my grandmother lost it for a while and couldn't find it anywhere. The family was moving to a new city, and their last day in the house, my youngest aunt was hungry, but everything had been packed except for an old box of cereal. When she poured it out, the ring fell out, too! The wedding ring is just a ring that went with it. We got it together, Daniel and I.

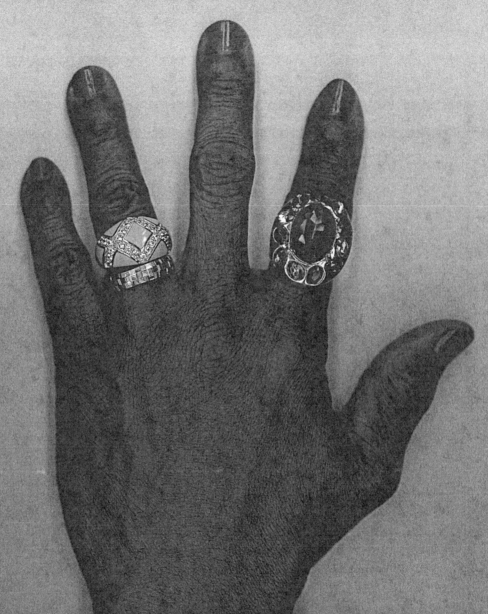

**INELL WILLIS** The gold one is a wedding band. The original wedding band has been lost. I also like to buy ten-dollar, fifteen-dollar rings at flea markets, like this purple one. I like purple, it's a royal color. You always hear Oprah talking about "We're royal women." I don't remember where I got this turquoise one from. It's a dome shape, but it doesn't catch on my gloves. I like the colors. I'm into bright colors. None of these are heirloom. My mother has a ton of rings. You can see the aging process in her hands and fingers, which seem to be shrinking and twisting with arthritis. I look at her hands and think, My hands will look like that someday.

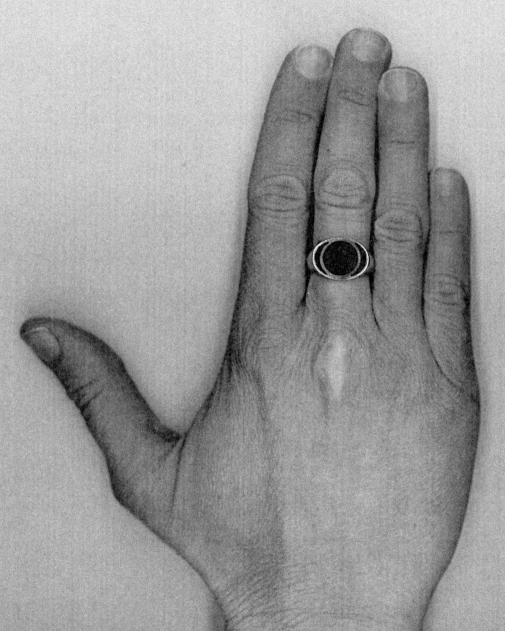

**CAROLINE HIRSCH** It was originally my grandmother's. I did meet her, but she died before I really got to know her. I visited my aunt in Deauville, she came across the ring and said, "You're the one with little hands, maybe this one will fit you." It did, and I've been wearing it ever since. My grandmother was a painter; apparently we had quite a bit in common, and similar taste in rings. I like that it's kind of an eye.

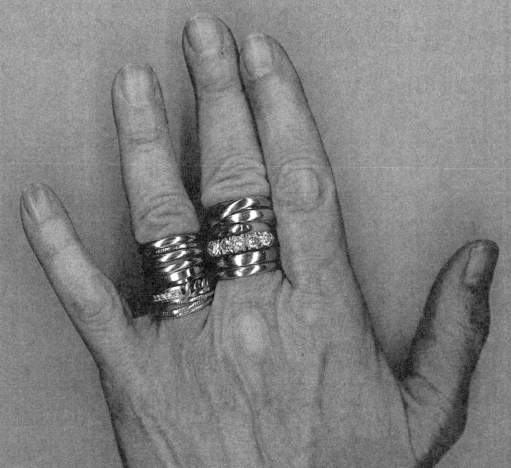

**RUTH LA FERLA** I have three rings from my family here. My mother's wedding ring. My father's wedding ring that she had lying around. Then, years later—because, as with many couples, they couldn't afford diamonds or whatever—he got her this one, so that's also my mother's ring. My mother gave me the two wedding rings, but when she died I got the diamond one. I wear it a lot. Then sandwiched in there is a dolphin I bought last summer in Greece, in Corfu, just because it was like an emblem of Greece, of Corfu. Then—so tight because I've put so many rings on— that's a Cartier triple band I bought as self-indulgence sometime in the seventies. If I bought it now, it would cost a lot more. I do switch them around a lot; I choked my fingers today. These are part of ten, these skinny little things; they look kind of tribal, they are Me&Ro, they're gold. I mix gold and fake and everything. This one with the chain is from a flea market in Chicago. That's just some old ring, but I knew it would look okay stacked; I love stacking them for some reason. People say with Taurus your power is in your throat, so you should wear a big chunky necklace or something, but I feel armed when I wear a lot of rings, and I switch them around.

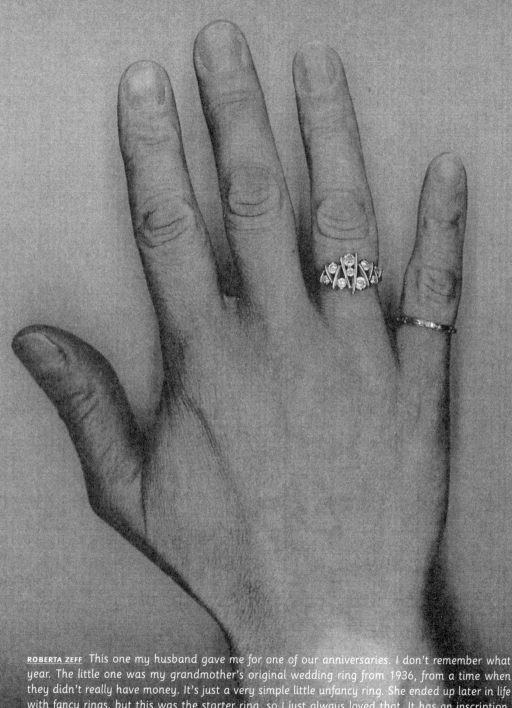

**ROBERTA ZEFF** This one my husband gave me for one of our anniversaries. I don't remember what year. The little one was my grandmother's original wedding ring from 1936, from a time when they didn't really have money. It's just a very simple little unfancy ring. She ended up later in life with fancy rings, but this was the starter ring, so I just always loved that. It has an inscription. It has my grandparents' initials and the date of their wedding: H.P. to C.L., 2-1-36.

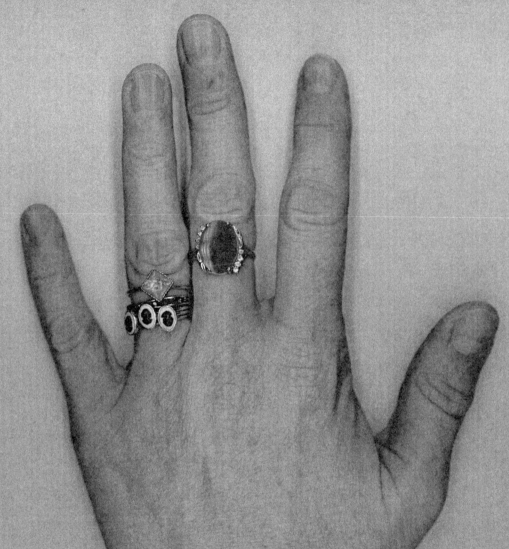

**MAURA EGAN**  So this ring I got in Vietnam five or six years ago, in Saigon. I was by myself, it was my birthday, and I was there for work, it was so hot and very chaotic and I was tired and ready to come home. I was like, I'm just going to go buy myself a birthday present. I bought this in a random store and it wasn't super-expensive. People say, "That's your ring from Vietnam," like it's some fancy, fancy ring, but it's not. These are from an artist who casts the objects you get out of a bubble-gum machine. These were plastic cameos that she set in gold. They're from a store in SoHo called Legacy. I've always gone there, and I've been buying her stuff for years and years. I've never met her. She's a Brooklyn artist. She did all three and they're stackable. Then this—I guess I buy a lot of my own jewelry—I've always liked black diamonds, and I like rose gold, and I bought this two years ago, as a present to myself. All my jewelry is a present to myself. No man's ever bought me jewelry, because you know what? Every time they do I never like it. So I buy my own stuff, which is probably a control issue.

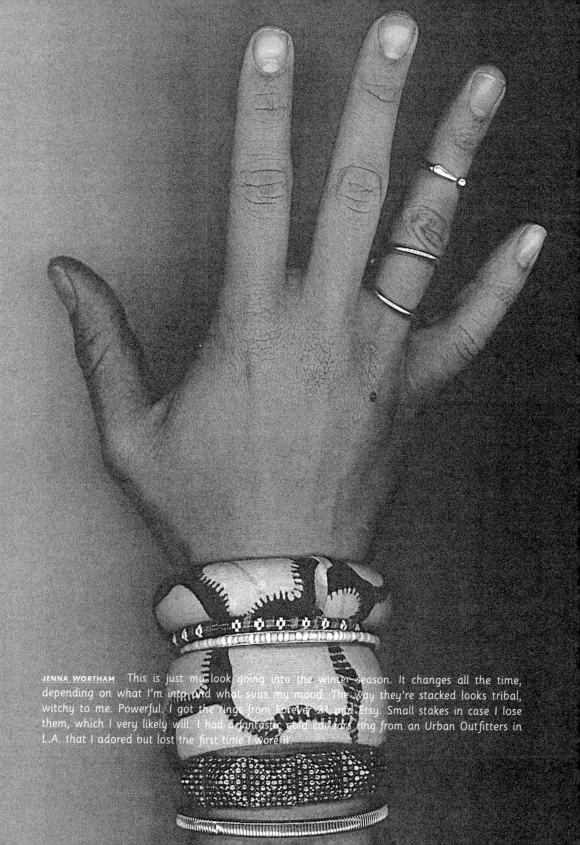

**JENNA WORTHAM** This is just my look going into the winter season. It changes all the time, depending on what I'm into and what suits my mood. The way they're stacked looks tribal, witchy to me. Powerful. I got the rings from Forever 21 and Etsy. Small stakes in case I lose them, which I very likely will. I had a fantastic gold cat-ears ring from an Urban Outfitters in L.A. that I adored but lost the first time I wore it.

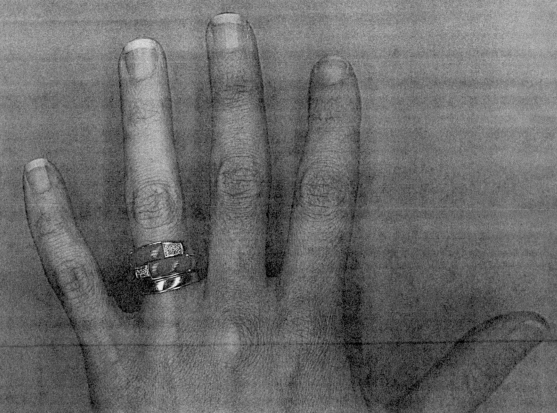

**ALEXANDRA JACOBS**  The one on the bottom is just my wedding ring. We got it at one of those 47th Street places, someplace called, like, A Thousand and One Engagement Rings. The second one, which looks like two but is actually only one, my husband got for me for our tenth anniversary, and it's coral and diamonds. I love it because—he didn't do this intentionally, but maybe subconsciously—to me it suggests us and our two children, who are of course the diamonds. But I love it, I adore it. And coral is not my usual—I usually go with a cool palette—but I love it, I love it. He was choosing between two. I wear a lot of costume jewelry, and the reason he picked coral—believe me, he didn't pluck that out of his head—is that I had this big flamboyant Kenneth Jay Lane ring with lots of little orange faux-coral beads. It's a big honker. He was considering two rings and was like, Oh, she likes coral, and one of them was like the Lane one but real, and the other was this one. And he could not decide, so he consulted with a dear friend of mine and she picked this one. So not only does it represent us and our children, but that a friend was involved in choosing it makes me very happy. The sister I never had. In the winter, when I think more about what I'm wearing, I wear it at least once every two weeks. It's a great ring. It goes with a lot—tweeds—it's amazing what you can make into a neutral when you want to. I wear it less in the summer because I'm scared of losing it. In the summer, I tend to wear more costume jewelry because of pools and the travel. I admire those women of yesteryear who would wear their jewelry all the time, but I'm too scared. I lose stuff all the time and I cannot lose this. It's a little stressful managing it, because if I lost it that would be devastating. My nails look good. I've been taking biotin.

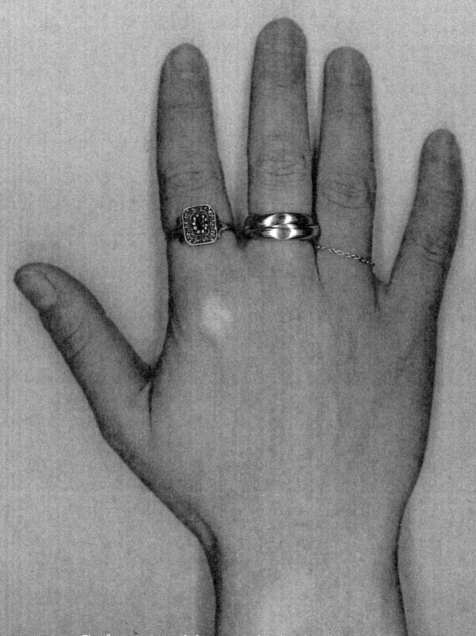

**AURÉLIE PELLISSIER** The first one is a gift from my godmother that she gave me a very long time ago. It was a ring that her husband had given her when they first met. The second ring, my boyfriend gave to me for our tenth anniversary, it's a Trinity ring. The last one is a gift from a friend; it had a little emerald in it but I lost it, so I wear it as a little chain.

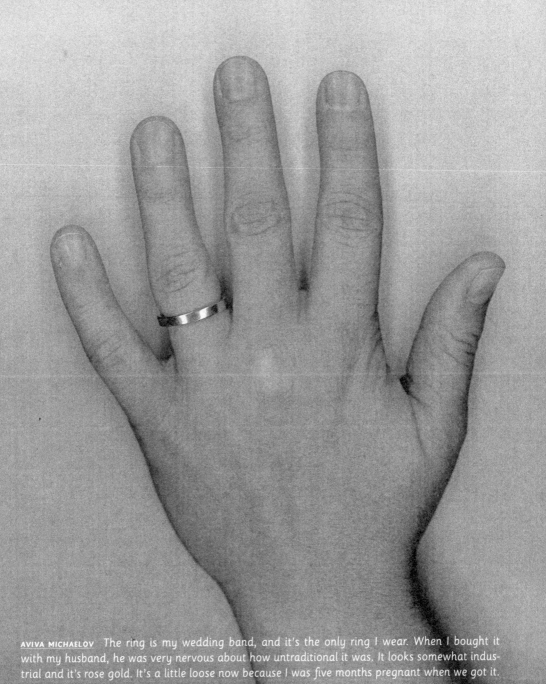

**AVIVA MICHAELOV** The ring is my wedding band, and it's the only ring I wear. When I bought it with my husband, he was very nervous about how untraditional it was. It looks somewhat industrial and it's rose gold. It's a little loose now because I was five months pregnant when we got it.

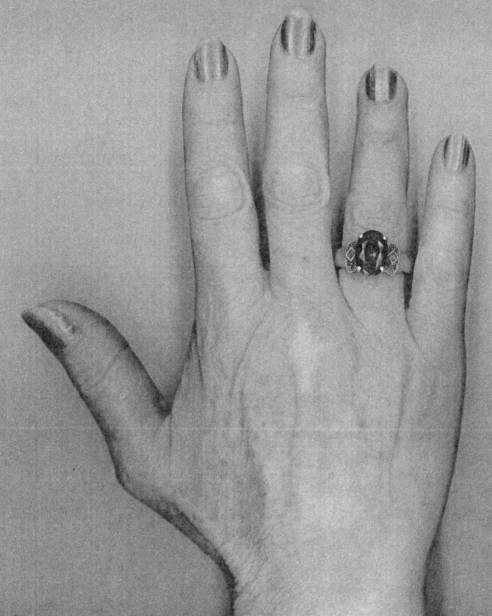

**DEBORAH AUER** I got it on Bleecker Street probably about ten years ago, and the thing is, when I bought it, it was quite garish, and had little black stones in it, which have all fallen out. Nobody talked about it, because it was just "bling," and it's one of those semiprecious green stones. It was really flashy and trashy-looking. As it got dirtier and older, people would go, "Wow, look at that great ring!" My nephew says, "Wow, is that an emerald?" Yeah, if it was an emerald we'd be taking a car service. That's the best thing about it. I always wear rings. I don't feel dressed if I don't have rings on, so even if I'm late for work, I put on a ring.

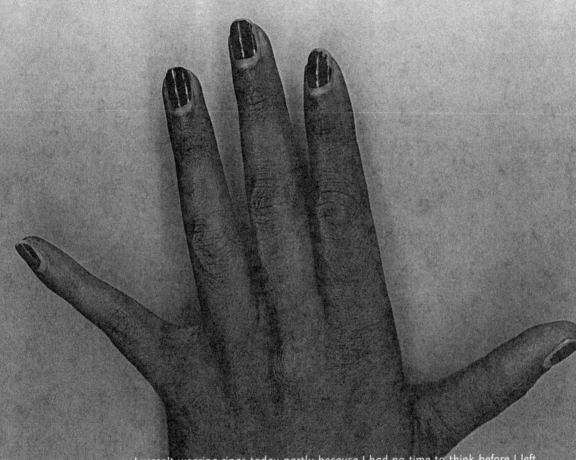

**SNIGDHA KOIRALA**  I wasn't wearing rings today partly because I had no time to think before I left the house, and also because my nails are a mess and I felt like there was too much going on with my nails a mess—wearing the bracelet, not having had time to think about which ring I wanted to wear. So I came to work completely bare. But this is a bracelet that I wear pretty much every day. This is what I'm in love with right now. The bracelet is something that I saw just clicking around online, and it's from this interesting program. I believe Cory Booker, mayor of Newark, is doing this "gun-buyback" program, which encourages people to turn in their guns. Then a company called Jewelry for a Cause takes some of those guns, melts them down, and turns them into beautiful artifacts. They have the gun ID number as well as the city on them. I thought it was cool. I like toe rings. You have to get really comfortable ones, otherwise you get all sorts of things poking into your toe.

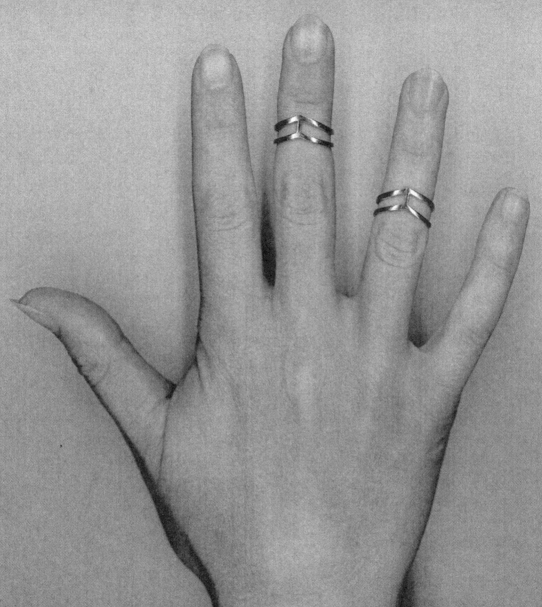

**ALEXANDRA ZSIGMOND** These are a recent acquisition, actually, and I'm interested now in wearing rings high. Low on one hand and high on the other. Just for a contrast. Sometimes I'll wear on the same hand a ring that's lower—I don't have that today—but there's just something very delicate and elegant about wearing rings higher up. I got the idea from a friend of mine who lives in Berlin. She was always wearing rings like this and I thought it was really cool so I adopted it. She was a roommate of mine, she had great style, and we were always getting inspired by each other.

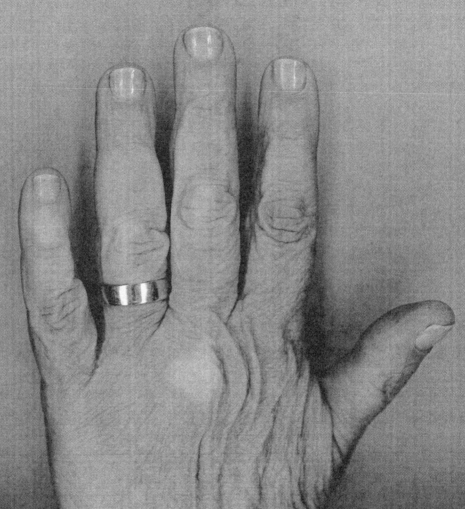

**GAIL COLLINS** We got married in 1970, and of course we didn't have any money or anything, so we went to Caldor's, which I don't think exists anymore, but it was like Kmart, and it was the only big store in Amherst. They had these rings. They were something like forty dollars each. And that's what we bought. Years later—five, ten years ago, for our anniversary—my husband replaced them. So I now have a ring that's much more expensive that looks exactly like the ones we got in Caldor's.

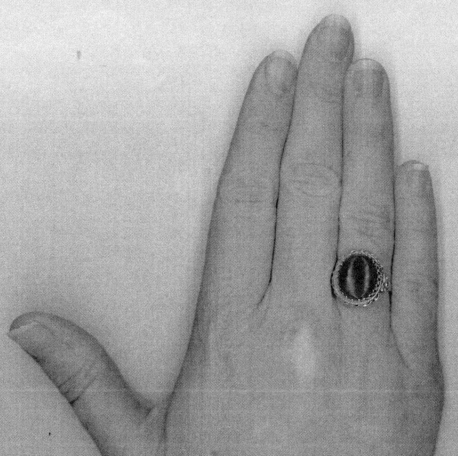

**SARAH WILLIAMSON** I was very, very close to my grandmother, she and my mom raised me, but she was as important as my mom. When she passed away we went to her safety deposit box; she had a lot of jewelry and gold because she and my grandfather were antique dealers. I saw this ring and right away I thought, I have to have this ring. So I took it. I never took it off except during the 2004 Bush election. I went to vote that day and I put it in the zippered pocket of a hoodie sweatshirt. I lost it for two years and was sad for two years. I cried every time I thought about it. And then I was in my closet and saw the hoodie and thought, "I haven't worn that forever," and I opened the pocket and found the ring. Now I never take it off. She had far nicer and probably more valuable things in the deposit box, but it wasn't about that to me. I love the whole design of it and feel like it suits me. It's my grandma to me and it's very special to me. I really got along with my grandma, we did everything together. I'm sad because she never got to see me in my twenties, or even now when I'm in my thirties. She only saw a much younger version of me.

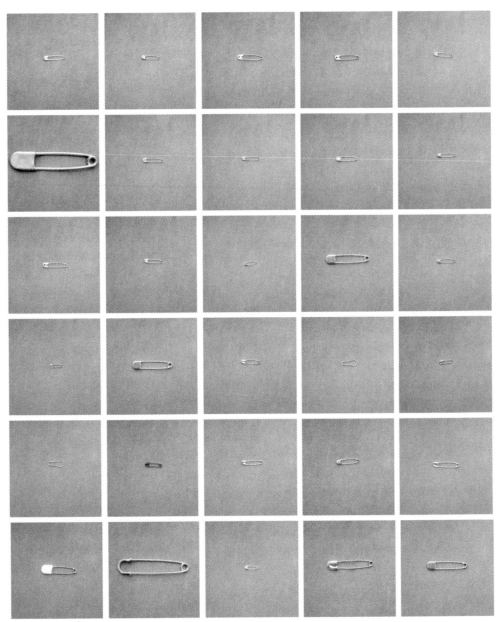

*MAE PANG*'s safety pins

# WHAT I WORE TO FALL IN LOVE

### SARAH NICOLE PRICKETT

**APRIL 5**

My name is on the list: Sarah Nicole plus Alexandra. Everybody calls her Alex, but when I e-mail the party host to ask if my out-of-town friend can come, I say Alexandra to make her sound Russian, taller. He says of course.

The theme of the party is "'80s wedding." I have on a pair of bright silver Doc Martens, twice worn, that I ordered on a three a.m. slowdown from Adderall. I wanted to sleep, so I smoked weed, and when I still wasn't sleepy, I went to Etsy. Now I own the only pair of bright silver Docs I've seen.

I don't go to the party. Alex should be Alex, and I should be Sarah, the girl from Canada who didn't sleep with the life-partnered man.

Instead we drink at Noah's apartment, where I am staying while he's out of town. We smoke indoors. Alex is fading. I'm flickering. I text Dana to ask if she's still at Black Market, and when she says yes, I ask who with. She says Jesse. Is Jesse single, I text. I never ask if anyone's single. I'm in a mild panic because (1) I'm not sleeping; (2) I'm only sleeping with this one guy; (3) I can't only be sleeping with this one guy, who is supposed to be my friend, and who is not even answering my texts. I hate the fit of the jeans I'm wearing: skinny, tight, dark blue, a medium rise. They make me feel like I've recently lost the baby weight. Noah has a navy cashmere sweater, and although I dislike a V-neck I need something soft in the chill. He also has a great varsity jacket from a school he didn't attend. When I put it on, it's like I have an older brother.

When I get to Black Market, Dana is leaving, and Jesse is drunk. Jesse's gorgeous.

I first saw him at the very end of January. I was feeling thinner and bold—I'd started boxing lessons—in a black leather bustier, vintage; a silk-and-wool kilt, both French navy and French; an old blazer. My shoes were these badass buckled things that clomped like hell and made my calves look like I might be a waif. I was dead hot. Jesse did not say hello.

In February, I held an erotic reading at a clothing store on Grand, and wore a dress I'd bought on final sale at $170. Still too much but it's silk, this startling say-yes green, a girl-proud thing, tied at the waist and falling in tiers to my knee. At Dana's invitation, Jesse came not to the reading but afterward to the bar, where he doesn't remember meeting me at all.

The third time I saw him was in March at our friend Dana's birthday, and I wore a long white man's shirt with skinny, soft gray jeans and those silver Docs for the second time. Jesse came for a cigarette with me, but we didn't talk at all. He did not know my name.

But tonight I show up to Black Market in basic-ass jeans and boys' clothes and a lick of feral eyeliner, and Jesse looks at me and thinks I'm so pretty. It's like he never saw me before, and maybe he didn't.

<hr>

### APRIL 25

Two weeks before the book party of a woman we both know, Jesse asked me to be his date. I did not believe in dating but wanted to go. Plus, who was I to say no to something two weeks in advance.

The day of the party, I cry for six or seven hours. My eyes turn to snake bites. We're to meet at a bar before the party. I think, I'll skip it. But just fifty-some minutes after the time I promised to meet him, I turn the corner onto West 13th in: my number-one comfort item, a light gray sweater, stitched like a sweatshirt and bought for $200; the shortest skirt I can find, which is my roommate's and even shorter on me, me being both leggier and hippier than she is; a pair of $30 sunglasses from Prince Street; the badass shoes. To further hide the crying, I've circled my eyes with smudgy, ink-blue eyeliner, like the total on a diner receipt. I lift my chin. But then he's sitting on the steps, smoking and reading, and he looks up at me and he just has this *mouth*. When he asks if I'm all right, he says I don't have to answer or talk

about it, and when I say I'm fine, he smiles and pretends I'm not lying. It is pretty much the best thing he could do.

<hr>

### MAY 3

I miss nine calls from Stephanie. At ten a.m. I'm meant to get in the car and drive with her and her husband and a photographer to her house in the Hamptons. I've never been to the Hamptons. Also, it seems impossible that I would leave Jesse now. I call Stephanie and tell her I'm sorry, but it turns out I'm in love. PRICKETT, she says. Bring him. But seriously, get on the train.

Jesse buys sparkling wine and I buy snacks and we meet in Fort Greene Park after I make us miss the train. We catch the next one. He likes my dress, which I haven't worn since August. It is sky denim with white paisley leaves all over, like polka dots, and a figure skater's shape, and when I twirl, it flies upward, but has just enough weight to stay decent. I like it, too.

<hr>

### MAY 11

This afternoon I stopped to buy jewelry at a twee self-adornment store that isn't really my taste. I bought a vintage costume ring with a tiny baby "sapphire" and two rhinestones. It only fits my ring finger, so that's where I wore it. I stepped outside, the sky broke, and in four blocks I was bone-soaked, laughing. Untouchable. Jesse said he'd meet me at seven.

At six-fifteen, I changed for the party. The dress code was "silver," and although

I own silver Docs and a silver-threaded Anna Sui dress and three shades of silver nail polish, I decided to do things in blue. My nails were Lego blue, the same blue as one block of a color-blocked dress I choose. It's light and sleek; I felt dolphin-ish. Because the dress is long and the slit so high, it's a bit much for daylight with heels. So black sandals, flat. I walk quickly, listening to "Midnight City," and for the very first time I'm not late.

Blue is Jesse's favorite color, and he hasn't read *Bluets*, the Maggie Nelson book, so I bring it to him and he's happy. He's never been so happy. Neither have I. He says he would marry me tomorrow. I say yes. We're smoking outside and then we go back in-side and sit down and I'm explaining to him my tattoos and he says, Will you marry me? I say yes and it's a different answer. It is the one time a word is enough.

I go to a dinner party with all these women, mostly writers, some of whom are the most radical anarcho-femmes I know. I tell them I'm getting married and they all want to see my ring. For a second I have no idea what they're talking about, and then I have to explain that the ring I'm wearing I bought myself, by accident, for six dollars. If Jesse had bought me a diamond ring, brand-new, from a store neither of us had ever been in, I think I would have had to say no.

### MAY 19

Today is Lara and Hugh's wedding. I've only known Lara for three or four years, from Toronto, but still I cannot think of a person I'd be happier to see in a $12,000 dress. I mean that.

The wedding is on the top, skylit floor of the Gramercy Park Hotel. A few days before, I decide—definitely—to wear a stiff, sleeveless crop top in pure white *broderie an-glaise*. I'll wear it with slim black pants and tall black heels and straighten my hair to a high gloss and put on my silver choker, even though it's been missing for months.

The day of the wedding, it rains. The white top seems stupid and overpriced. At home I consider a blood-orange silk Acne dress that falls just so, or would if

SURVEY *Is there an article of clothing, some makeup, or an accessory that you carry or wear every day?* Liquid eyeliner. —BRONWYN CAWKER • Vaseline rose-tinted balm. —BRYENNE KAY • I'm never without my The Row leather backpack. It holds my heels and my model book during the day. I always have a tiny Given-chy mascara on me. The one with three balls. —CAILIN HILL • Bobby pins. I have unruly red curly hair that occasionally requires a bobby pin to keep it under wraps. —ABI SLONE • My brown vinyl computer bag with golden-brown leather straps. —LARA AVERY • My wedding rings. —ADRIENNE BUTIKOFER • I carry a "Rainbow Viewfinder" in my wallet that my dad gave me when I was a kid. It's just a piece of cellophane-ish paper cut in a circle—you look through it and see rainbows playing off light. Its obvious metaphor is what makes it such a good talisman. —JOANA AVILLEZ • I usually have one of my coats in tow, just in case it gets cold, which it's bound to do in San Francisco. —ANISSE GROSS • My glasses. —MEGAN FRANKLYNE • My

it didn't feel so impossible on my hips. I bought it at my very skinniest, four years ago, when I was mostly a style reporter. At some point, my mind became a more pressing concern than my flesh, and now I'm just not sure about the dress. Anyway, it needs to be dry-cleaned. Ditto the jade-and-blue Kenzo skirt I wore on my birthday. Ditto the pinky-pale Jeremy Laing shift dress, edged in black, $400 for the sample. It's an investment piece, I told my ex, Graeme, borrowing from the fashion editor's lexicon when he asked how much I'd paid. How, he wanted to know. Does it turn into four of them?

But inevitably I wear the best top I ever bought (off eBay, actually). It's made of soft, itchy, iron-gray wool, cut on the bias into a long, one-armed swirl. Everywhere it's tight, but not too tight. My tits look great. I wear it with six-inch Aldo heels designed for the brand by Patrik Ervell—they have rubber spike heels, a bulbous platform, and a Mary Jane strap, and they are hideous—and a navy polyes-

ter ball skirt I got for $10 on the Joe Fresh sale rack two years ago.

After the ceremony come speeches, and dinner courses, and cigarettes in the atrium, then somebody orders coke and Jesse comes and I know all the words to all the Beyoncé songs. It's two a.m. The Toronto guests want to keep going, but I live here and I've learned, I think, to leave when you least want to leave.

So we leave. In a tote bag, I've brought the old denim shirt and black jeans and a pair of all-white Converse. We look for cops. I change on the street—this is when I really feel superheroic. We scale the black iron fence into Gramercy Park, which is gated for the exclusive use of the surrounding, superrich residents. It has recently come to my attention that the only hobby I have is trespassing. I dress—black baseball hat, white Converse—with that in mind.

### JUNE 4

It's hot as a fucking jungle. I wear a sliplike light pink top, chiffon, that my roommate bought from Zara, and a black leather skirt

---

glasses! —MEGAN PATTERSON • These days it is a green cashmere toque I bought from Holt Renfrew six years ago. It has a few small holes in it, but it is the warmest article of clothing that I own. Plus, I spent $70 on it, so I can't bring myself to replace it until it is completely in tatters. —ANU HENDERSON • I always have rice paper for a quick dabbing in case my skin gets oily. —AREV DINKJIAN • My heart necklace, which I bought for myself from an artist in Brooklyn. It was a kind of present to help me feel complete on my own, rather than waiting for a man to buy me things. —ALEXI CHISLER • No. —CLEO PERRY • Underwear and my phone. —DANKA HALL • Nothing, really, although I find it very difficult to wear something that has absolutely no pockets. —BETH STUART • Red lipstick. —CAT TYC • Sleep mask would be a funny answer. —EILEEN MYLES • Perfume and my headscarf. —IMOGEN DONATO • I wear a plain silver chain with almost every outfit. —KRISTINA ANNE GYLLING • I wear a red ring that my boyfriend gave me for Christmas a couple years ago every day. If I forget it, I feel nervous that I've lost it. It's this vintage piece that

that was gorgeous and sultry till I cut half of it off with scissors. Now it's slutty. After a meeting I go to a cheap salon and get nails as white as Wite-Out. Durga, my soulmate, does her nails white all the time, and I rarely get a manicure without texting her. This time I also text Jesse. White, I say, 'cause it'll look so good on your dick.

#### JUNE 27

In Chinatown, my lease is up, I'm moving. Jesse comes to help me and I'm wearing a white Hanes T-shirt, a pair of purplish-gray shorts I never run in (while packing I find that I own three pairs of gym shorts, probably because whenever I decide to exercise, I've forgotten the last time I did), and running shoes I ordered custom from Nike. He looks at the running shoes. He says, "Do your . . . running shoes have your initials on them?" I say, "Yes. This is the person you're marrying," and we laugh.

#### JULY 5

I am on Fire Island to work. Jesse says he'll take a photo of me, and though I prefer to take photos of myself almost without exception, if there is an exception, he's it.

I'm wearing a tomato-red bikini, shiny the way all bathing suits are when you get them free from American Apparel. I never understand how bikinis contrive to make you look, with so little material, so much worse than you do naked, but they do. Over it I put on an old striped shirt. I have a hundred striped shirts, or ten, but this one is loose and soft and mannish and also feminine, the way its stripes look painted on. It's ink-blue and a dirty white. A favorite.

Jesse takes the photos. He doesn't say anything about the shirt.

Later, he tells me about the photo he saw when he Googled me. It was taken in the winter of 2010, in Palm Springs. I was blonde. My hair full of salt. I had white sunglasses and a Bloody Mary and fresh red nails and I was wearing the same striped shirt. He told his roommate, Dan, that there was something he knew: that I would be someone for him. ✕

---

I really like. It made me realize he has good taste. —CATHERINE LACEY • My eyebrow kit. I usually use a dark brown, but sometimes I do a faintly bluish black, a very orangey brown, or an extremely electric blue. They frame my face in a way my natural brows never could. —JACLYN BRUNEAU • Céline bag, Clé de Peau concealer. —AUDREY GELMAN • Medical bracelet. —ELIZABETH PERKINS • When I've forgotten to put on earrings, I often feel bereft. —POPPY TOLAND • A gold bracelet, my watch, and groomed eyebrows. —JOSIE HO • I am never without the following: a Moleskine notebook, my phone, a good pen (it must write well), a good bag (it must hold more things than you can tell). —ALY MARGARETS • Pendant with camel. —GINI ALHADEFF • A hair tie. —GLYNDA ALVES • I wear a small strand of pearls my parents gave me when I was seventeen. It's not an expensive example of its kind, and it actually has no "style" as such. But it's like, the more I wear it, the more it becomes an appropriate item. —JESSICA JOHNSON • I always have a scarf. —AMY RUDERSDORF • A smile is the best accessory. —SAGAN MacISAAC ✕

*SHEILA HETI*'s nail polish

# A SCHMATTE LOOKS GOOD

PRESCHOOL TEACHER **DINA GOLDSTEIN** SPEAKS WITH
HER SON, RADIO HOST **JONATHAN GOLDSTEIN**

**JONATHAN:** When do you feel at your most attractive?

**DINA:** I don't know. Some days I look in the mirror and I say, "I'm so pretty." And other times I look in the mirror and I have to look away because I'm so ugly.

**JONATHAN:** Those are extreme poles. What influences that?

**DINA:** I have creases on my face and they're very pronounced, I need a hair dye . . . I don't know. I just feel I'm not pretty that day.

**JONATHAN:** It doesn't have to do with maybe the way Dad's treating you or anything like that?

**DINA:** No.

**JONATHAN:** Okay, are there any items of clothing that you have in multiple, and why do you think you keep buying this thing?

**DINA:** I have a lot of fancy jackets and I go to this place where they're really cheap and they're really pretty. They're so pretty I feel I have to have them.

**JONATHAN:** How many jackets do you have?

**DINA:** Maybe eight to ten. And I love costume jewelry. Especially if it's a bargain, then I really love it! *(laughs)*

**JONATHAN:** What is it that you like about it?

**DINA:** I don't know. It's crazy. I can't even explain it. I take them out every so often and I spread them on the bed and I look at them and it gives me so much pleasure. I get enormous pleasure from just looking at my jewelry. More pleasure from that garbage than from my real jewelry.

**JONATHAN:** Really?

**DINA:** It's a sickness, I know. I hardly even wear them. I just like owning them.

**JONATHAN:** Okay. What are some shopping rules you think every woman should follow?

**DINA:** Buy what looks good on you, not what's in style. Buy things that are not going to go out of style.

**JONATHAN:** What doesn't go out of style?

**DINA:** Black pants never go out of style. Turtlenecks haven't gone out of style.

**JONATHAN:** Are there any dressing tricks you've invented or learned that make you feel like you're getting away with something?

**DINA:** Yes! That's a very good question. When I just wear an ordinary T-shirt that I buy in Walmart for five dollars and I drape a scarf around it, I look dressed up.

**JONATHAN:** Oh, so the trick is the scarf?

**DINA:** That's what I think. It makes me look like I'm dressed up. A schmatte looks good.

**JONATHAN:** Would you rather be perceived as having great taste or great style?

**DINA:** I think I don't have great taste. I'd like to have great style, because people who are stylish always look good no matter what they wear, they just know how to put themselves together. If I had something really important, like if I was visiting the Queen, I would have to take someone with me to help me choose a dress.

JONATHAN: If you were going to be meeting with a queen, what would be your look?

DINA: I don't know. I have no idea.

JONATHAN: Scarf and a T-shirt?

DINA: No! You see, I would have to have somebody tell me.

JONATHAN: Who would you ask?

DINA: Somebody who looks good all the time. I have this girl Louise who works at the day care, she always puts herself together very nicely. I look at the girls at work and I see what they wear. I don't care, I just copycat. Otherwise how the hell do I know what's in style?

JONATHAN: Do you think fashion is a waste of money? Or a waste of time?

DINA: No. It's not a waste of money or time.

JONATHAN: Okay, what do you admire about how other women present themselves?

DINA: They just look well put-together. A lot of people wear their good clothes to work. When I buy something new, I save it. What I'm saving it for, God only knows. I'm afraid I'll get paint on it, so what? It's meant to be worn. Enjoy what you have now! So it gets dirty, so I buy another one. I didn't pay a million dollars for these garbage clothes.

JONATHAN: Are there any figures from culture, past or present, whose style you admire or have drawn from?

DINA: (sighs) I don't remember, Jonathan. I haven't gone to the movies in years.

JONATHAN: What's the first "investment" item that you bought?

DINA: When I was forty my parents bought me a fur coat.

JONATHAN: And do you still wear it?

DINA: No, it's in the garage. I didn't take really good care of it. It smells like the garage.

JONATHAN: How many seasons did you wear it?

DINA: Oh, a long time, I loved it. But fur coats—you have to send them to storage or put them in a cedar closet, which I did not.

JONATHAN: Do you think there's a reason why you lost interest in it?

DINA: I don't know. People were talking about how bad it is to wear fur and that sort of stuff.

JONATHAN: So you lost the taste. Do you remember the biggest waste of money you ever made on a clothing purchase?

DINA: I've wasted a lot of money. I'll buy something, like a long top, because I think, "Oh, I'm going to wear it with tights." And I never wear it, so that's a waste of money.

JONATHAN: How much money was that waste?

DINA: Twenty dollars. I never spend more than twenty dollars on my clothes. (laughs)

JONATHAN: What's the most expensive item you've ever bought?

DINA: Oh, the dress for Margie's wedding. Four, five, six hundred dollars. When you get married, I'll spend the same thing.

JONATHAN: (quietly) Okay, I'll count on it. Was there a point in your life when your style changed dramatically?

DINA: When I got married I stopped dressing to kill. When I was nineteen, I went to Florida and I had an outfit for every day! I loved to look nice. Oh my God, clothes were so important to me. It was everything. When I got married, I had a closet full of clothes with the tags on that I had never even worn because I was buying and buying.

JONATHAN: So what happened to that impulse?

DINA: I don't know. I just suddenly lost interest once I got married. Weird, eh?

JONATHAN: You don't have insight as to why? Was it because you'd gotten married, so you didn't feel like you had to attract somebody?

DINA: I guess. I couldn't stop buying when I was single. I just couldn't stop buying.

JONATHAN: If Dad was more complimentary, would you have felt encouraged to continue?

DINA: No. He thinks that I'm dressed nice and I'm happy.

JONATHAN: Is it nice to be with someone who kind of doesn't care?

DINA: Yes, of course.

JONATHAN: Do you care about lingerie?

DINA: No, not at all.

JONATHAN: Okay. What are you trying to do or achieve when you dress?

DINA: People think more of you if you dress nicely, this is what I've heard. I guess I do dress nicely for other women. I want to look as nice as everyone else.

JONATHAN: When you were younger, you were a bank teller. Did you dress . . . ?

DINA: Oh yes, I used to stand on my high heels all day long, I don't know how I ever did it. That's how everybody dressed. You wore high heels and dresses. That was fifty-two years ago, oh my God.

JONATHAN: Okay, what is your cultural background and how has that influenced how you dress?

DINA: Well, I'm Jewish. How has that influenced me? I guess I dress like other Jewish women. But I don't look like those well-kept women. They all look sort of alike, and they all have makeup. They wear their hair in a ponytail, their clothes are just so, and their shoes are the latest . . . I can't be that type.

JONATHAN: Do you judge those people?

DINA: No, of course not.

JONATHAN: Can you talk about how your mother's way of dressing has influenced you?

DINA: Well, I used to borrow a lot of my mother's clothes when I was in my thirties. I always liked what she wore, and our figures were similar, so if I had somewhere to go—like a wedding or something—I would always borrow her dresses. She would say, "Why don't you buy your own?"

JONATHAN: How would you answer her?

DINA: "I like yours."

JONATHAN: I've seen a few photos of her mother, who seemed like a put-together, fancy lady.

DINA: Yes. She would never go out of the house looking like a mess. She always fixed herself up. My other grandmother didn't fix herself up at all. I think I take after her more.

JONATHAN: Is that something you decided on, or is that just the way you're built?

DINA: That's just the way I'm built. But I wouldn't leave the house without my pancake on my face.

JONATHAN: Oh, so you do put on makeup.

DINA: Not now! Then! Now I don't care.

JONATHAN: What's the situation with your hair?

DINA: Lately I dye it darker. A little bit red.

JONATHAN: Does Dad notice these things?

DINA: Yeah, he does.

JONATHAN: Do you like when he notices? Most people like to be noticed, to get compliments . . .

DINA: No, I don't care. He's good, I don't care.

JONATHAN: Describe your figure.

DINA: I have thin legs and a big belly.

JONATHAN: (laughs) That's not . . . You're very unkind to yourself.

**DINA:** I am, aren't I?

**JONATHAN:** Is there any article of clothing, piece of makeup, or accessory that you wear or carry with you every day?

**DINA:** No.

**JONATHAN:** I guess Purell doesn't count.

**DINA:** I guess not.

**JONATHAN:** Would you ever do anything like cosmetic surgery?

**DINA:** I used to think about it, but now I don't even think about it.

**JONATHAN:** Really? For what?

**DINA:** I would have liked to have my nose fixed. I find it not nice. But I find that people who have their nose fixed are not as pretty as they were before, so now I think God gave you the nose because it fits in your face.

**JONATHAN:** Do you have a unified way of approaching your life?

**DINA:** Appreciate what you have. Some people are smart enough to know what they have and they appreciate it. They don't let it go by. They're lucky and they know it. That's what I'm trying to say. You have to know it.

**JONATHAN:** Can you speak to how all this is important?

**DINA:** It makes life more interesting. It's nice to go somewhere and think, "Oh, I look nice," as opposed to, "Oh, I see a hole in my dress."

**JONATHAN:** Okay, please say anything you'd like about your life that might put this survey into some sort of context.

**DINA:** I don't know. I'm very happy.

**JONATHAN:** It makes me a little bit sad when I hear you be harsh with yourself.

**DINA:** Aw. Actually, sometimes I'm really—I'm in love with myself sometimes. *(laughs)* ✕

---

## "JEANS"

*(Dog barking)*

**STARLEE:** Are your knees cold?

**WOMAN:** No. I know it's weird, but I'm sort of used to it.

**STARLEE:** Did you make the holes yourself?

**WOMAN:** No. I bought them this way. *(laughs)*

**STARLEE:** They look good!

**WOMAN:** Thank you. I know it's ridiculous to buy them, but you couldn't make them yourself. I mean, you could, but not that perfect.

**STARLEE:** Because by the time they ripped naturally, they'd be all stretched out. Did they reinforce them to make them not rip more?

**WOMAN:** No, which is also what I kind of like about them, they just sort of do their thing.

**STARLEE:** Do you think someone would have to be your height for them to hit the knee just right?

**WOMAN:** Yeah, I think because I have long legs they hit in the best place.

**STARLEE:** Do you ever try and find jeans with the holes in a different place?

**WOMAN:** Oh no, that's just too much. *(laughs)* ✕

# CALAMITY

RENEE GLADMAN

I began the day "a woman in clothes" wanting to be a woman in clothes, because Danielle had had a certain body all her life. And I had had a certain body, but where she had regained the body of her life, which she had temporarily lost, such that she carried a memory of the other body but didn't have to see it, I had this body, which had been mine for a long time, but which may not have been my body, in that sense of Danielle's—a body she liked to drape in clothes. My body was wearing the red pajamas and hers the dark green and hers made a shape around her butt with a line bisecting, and the line wrote "ass" all over everything. My line wrote "penis-pocket," because of the slit, the pouch at the front of the red pajamas. And the day was getting on. I was wondering how to be a woman in my red pajamas and thick red wool sweater, my skin-tight pajamas, my striped sweater. I was wondering how, if the bell rang, I would run down the stairs a woman in clothes, as if someone had written a story about our day, where we stayed on this side of the snow that was falling, and the inside was our city. We wanted a city full of living, so we walked quickly back and forth in front of the full-length mirror. She swished past me; I swished past her, with hours passing. We were women in clothes for a time (despite my undershirt being tucked into my skintights), and this made you want to get to know a person. "You are red everything," she said, looking all the way to my socks. But my slit, my pocket, made me shy and I was dizzy from the speed of my walking: I was in my skintight pajamas and carried, in them, a voluptuous body that was probably an impostor. My sweater sat on top of my belly; my socks slid across the floor. I was red-black-red-red-black in that order and something else in reverse. Then several hours passed. "She was now in a white shirt," wrote the story, "a blouse, intersected by blue infinitely. And though the woman was dressed . . ." it carried on. And though Danielle was now in bed—I began writing my own story—she was wearing jeans, and this was her body. To find mine, I had to push my hand through the slit, the pouch of the red pajamas, and show the ring on my middle finger: it was something along the road to getting there; it was a feminine gesture—if you looked only at the grace of the hand—an accessory. ✕

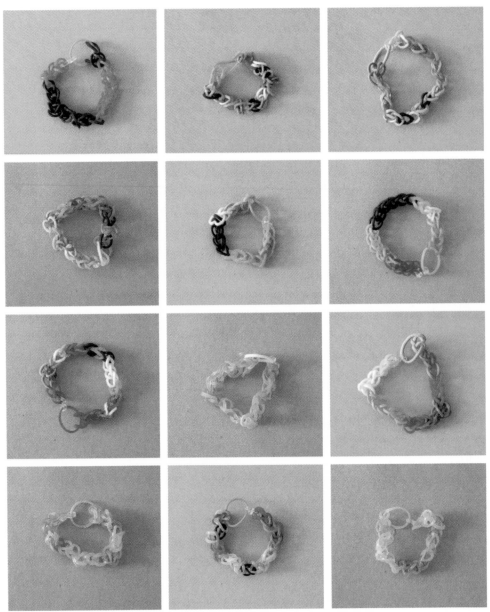

*DELIA MARCUS*'s friendship bracelets

# DRESS FOR SUCCESS

*"I wear bicycle gloves at the computer as if it were professional writing gear."*—ANN BOGLE

**GENEVIEVE FERRIER** I'm a doctor and I read somewhere that patients don't want their doctor to look like a successful business-woman. That liberated me from buying any more "dress for success" suits that women were told to wear in the eighties. But patients also don't want you to look like a clue-less frump. So I have a casual professional look that shows off my own style.

**RONNIE ANGEL POPE** Once, I dressed up in this crazy, kooky, wild outfit with the intention of going into Vivienne Westwood's shop in Cardiff and asking for a job. I went in, looked at the clothes, looked at the people, and after smiling nervously, just walked out. I was so, so, so nervous. Even to this day, it still makes me shake just thinking about it. I haven't been back since.

**JOANNA WALSH** By the time I was six, I'd for-mulated a theory: The good people grow up to be men, and the bad people grow up to be women. Men had so many rewards, I thought, and women so few, that I could intuit no other reasonable explanation. So I bullied my mother into buying me boys' shoes throughout primary school, and in dresses, I felt fundamentally uncomfortable. When I started doing readings in public, I was unable to wear anything but pants or overalls. As I'm not particularly butch, the effect tended toward the cute, but in the overalls I've been erotically as well as profes-sionally successful. When I launched a col-lection of stories recently at a bookshop in Paris, I wore a dress for the first time—one I bought on impulse the day before. It's hardly ultra-feminine, but it's perhaps a sign that I feel more relaxed about marrying the idea of "femininity" with an event at which I'd like to achieve a degree of professional success.

**ALESIA PULLINS** Sometimes I feel like no mat-ter how I present myself, I look threatening. I think it's just because I am a black wom-an. So sometimes I'll want to dress to seem more approachable. Like for job interviews or meetings or something that's more cor-porate, I tend to wear lighter colors, even though I don't really feel it in my soul.

**AMY BONNAFFONS** I had a terrible temp job at a real estate office where I was completely invisible except to the openly sexist boss. I coped by adopting a fake persona. I wore ugly slacks and button-down shirts. I bought dorky non-corrective glasses for five dollars at CVS. I decided that if I looked not like "myself" but like an uninteresting temp, it would be the uninteresting temp-girl charac-ter who did the job, not me. I felt I was put-ting one over on everybody.

**HIMANEE GUPTA-CARLSON** After I finished my first marathon in 2000, I wore the finisher T-shirt as a nightshirt for about a month. I re-discovered the shirt in August as I was train-ing for my tenth marathon, which also was my first one in five years. I wore it to sleep every night for about a month before the marathon, to remember that first one and to inspire and psych up myself.

**MARILYN BOOTH** I remember having to dress very formally for a job interview that was going to last two days. I was freaked out about making sure I felt comfortable, so I bought two suits. Though I got the job, I can't stand to wear them now because they remind me of the stress.

**ZOE WHITTALL** I have never really achieved a polished look no matter what I'm wearing. There is always some cat hair adhered to me, or too many bruises on my legs, I have split ends. I'm five feet tall, and I've never had defined triceps. Clothing can't change those things about me.

**ANA ZIR** My world is hospice patients and their families. First, I want to present professionalism, openness, warmth, and cleanliness, but also a little style that sets me apart from the other nurses on the unit, whether that means matching clogs or the latest scrubs with the latest gizmos and gadgets in my pockets. I hope they remember me not just for what I do, but because I left a positive impression by the way I dressed. People do notice. Even very sick ones.

**REBECCA ACKERMANN** I work in a field, technology, where there are very few women and even fewer in power positions. It's cool for dudes to wear flip-flops and T-shirts, but I've found that it really helps me project authority when I dress up slightly. It's so strange to me that dressing down can signal power for men but never for women.

**JAGODA WARDACH** My first year at university in Poland, it was just after my trip to New York, and I had so many nice things. I was like, Okay, now I'm at the university, I have to reinvent my style—'cause I'm not a high school student anymore. I was nineteen and I felt this responsibility to be a real student. I had so many new things to wear, and then I found myself isolated from the group, because the girls were jealous. I heard them sometimes saying, "Oh, there's our star coming," but I was not—I just wasn't wearing clothes that I would wear to the club.

**ANITA POWELL** When I went to my last job interview (for the job I currently have) I wore a classic, rather boring interview suit. The boss was surprised because I had been working for her as a freelancer for six months and she was used to seeing me in my normal, more elaborate attire. I told her I felt I should show that I appreciated the seriousness of this situation, then showed her how I had paired the suit with my bright red shoes. She said, "Oh good, I wanted to make sure it was actually you so I can offer you this job."

**MELISSA HENDERSON** I grew up around educated black people who ingrained in me that style and dressing well were key factors to success and combating stereotypes. I never go out of the house with my hair not done.

**ALEXA S.** This week I packed only party dresses for what turned out to be a very informal film market. All the men were in jeans. I hope they didn't think I was trying to look sexy because my projects were shit.

**ELISSA SCHAPPELL** We focus so much in politics on what women look like—look at the Hillary Clinton headband debacle, or the focus on Michelle Obama's wearing sleeveless dresses that show off her ripped arms, or Wendy Davis in her white suit and pink sneakers. Does anyone ever say: Given that Mitch McConnell appears to have been separated at birth from one of the Sneetches, he should replace his eyeglasses with a pair that makes him look less goggle-eyed? Or that Justice Roberts would look less dumpy if he ditched the made-in-China blue suit and showed off his toned ass?

**LAURA SNELGROVE** Recently, I've started to consciously dress in a more "professional" manner when I attend prenatal appointments. I noticed that when I was dressed in my usual casual summer style, I was treated like a helpless teen mother. I was talked down to and about as if I wasn't in the room. I had to fight to have my questions answered. I've since made the switch to dressing as though I'm coming from an office, and I find that I'm spoken to more directly and as though I may have done my research. I resent having to do this.

**MOLLY MURRAY** Toward the end of graduate school, I was interviewed for an academic job by a woman who I knew to be sleeping with my then boyfriend. What to wear? I opted for radical neutrality so that I could look with a maximally critical eye at what she was wearing (clearly the intellectual content of the interview was not foremost in my mind). I was bitchily gratified to see that she had on "interesting" shoes, and I left the room feeling smug and triumphant, even though I didn't get the job and she ended up with the boyfriend.

**PAIGE V. LYNN** When I moved from L.A. to D.C., I had to buy clothes that accommodated actual weather. I also started working in politics, and I received a lot of conflicting advice on how a professional female lawyer should dress, including a debate about the necessity of stockings at all times. I heard that ponytails, braids, and hair worn down were "too sexy" for the workplace, and I was told by career counselors that at certain conservative firms, ladies should never wear a pantsuit, lest you remind some elderly hiring partner of Hillary Clinton. I have officially stopped caring, and the only rule I adhere to is closed-toed shoes in court and a blazer at all times in the office.

**ALICIA BERNLOHR** My roommate gave me a black Dolce & Gabbana skirt suit that was a gift from her old boss at Merrill Lynch. Her boss was a really successful but kind of evil female stockbroker. She was brilliant but ruthless! At one point, she gave my roommate a few things she didn't need anymore, including this gorgeous D&G suit. Apparently she said, "I'm giving this to you, but you can't ever sell it. I'll know if you do!" The suit was too big for my roommate and she eventually quit the job. But she was afraid (karmically) of selling the suit, so she gave it to me. It fits me perfectly. When I put it on, a weird sort of heightened ambition comes over me. I've never owned something so expensive and beautifully cut. It makes me feel like I'm channeling this bad bitch from Merrill Lynch. I've worn the suit to two job interviews, and I've gotten job offers each time! So the magic really works. ✕

# YES? | VARIOUS WOMEN

# I DO CARE ABOUT YOUR PARTY

UMM ADAM

What I think of as my style is very different from how many other people view me and my style. If you saw me outside my home, you would see a lady draped in loose clothing of dull colors (I wear mostly a jilbab, or loose pants and a long, very loose shirt with a big hijab covering my head and chest, covering almost to my navel). Some see this style as extremist, some see this as oppression, some see it as out of style, not knowing what style is. They think it's old-fashioned. Some see me as being very pious and religious. But I don't see myself or my style in any of these ways.

I feel life is very precious and there is a lot to be done. I don't have time to spend or waste worrying about how I look and what people think about me based on my clothing. I believe the purpose of clothing, as defined by God in the Quran, is to cover your body and for beautification. As long as my body is covered properly, I am fine. As for beautification, I believe it is very different from the way women understand it today. It does not mean making your body attractive (especially to the other gender). Clothes beautify you by covering your body, giving you human dignity. Animals don't wear clothes. The earliest humans covered themselves with leaves and animal hide. As the human race became more and more civilized, the quantity and quality of clothes increased and improved. It was a sign of civilization and dignity to wear more clothes and cover yourself more. Religion had a role in this, as God ordained humans to live in dignity, and all religions that originated from the revelation from God asked for modest clothing.

All through history, aristocratic women would wear long, loose clothing and even cover their heads with a hat or scarf. Lower-class women—workers, servants, slaves— would wear less clothing. Clothing was seen as a symbol of civilization and dignity, which I believe it is, and is the right of every woman, not just the upper class or more religious ones.

The Industrial Revolution and the feminist movement made women feel that to be equal to men, they had to be like men. One way women found to do this was by shedding their clothes. This coincided with the decline of religion. Men took advantage of this, and to please their own instinctive desires had the women undress more and more in the name of modernization. Yes, I believe men took advantage of women and made them slaves of their desires. This was no freedom—it was slavery. Why is it that when there is a party, a dance, women wear spaghetti-string dresses and try to show more of their body, and make their bodies attractive with make-up and all, while men cover up in a suit and tie, even closing the top button? I call this a loss of feminine dignity and the slavery of women to men's desires, while men get to keep the dignity that civilization gave humankind. It's not fair.

I believe my clothing is meant to cover. When I cover myself, I am passing on a message to others, saying:

I respect myself, my body is precious and beautiful, I know that, but it is none of your business. It is my private business and I respect my privacy and will allow only those whom I please to allow into that private space. I do not think you have any right to get any pleasure off of my body. I am a free woman and refuse to be a slave of your desires. You cannot control what I wear to please your desires. My interaction with you is not physical. I have a brain and a soul and am an intelligent individual, and that's what you need to interact with. I have my personal dignity and space and you need to stay out of it.

Now, I am not the only woman who makes such a statement. Every woman—when she goes for a job interview or business meeting, or when she stands for election in public office, dresses in business attire—wears modest clothing according to cultural standards. She wants to come across as confident and wants people to have confidence in her abilities. Hillary Clinton never went campaigning in a spaghetti-strap dress. I am always on official business, and I want people to judge me by my brains; if I am in the comfort of my home and relaxing with family, or in my bedroom in an intimate situation, I dress accordingly. I believe my body is too precious to be displayed in public. We don't display our precious belongings in public, do we? We keep them protected, in safe conditions. There is a place and time for everything, and the public arena is not the place to display the beautiful body.

I also have the confidence that God has created me—and every woman and man—beautiful. We are all beautiful, internally and externally, in our own special way. We don't need to do anything to our body to make it look beautiful. It already is. As you may have guessed, I do not wear makeup. I have nothing to make up for. You make up for mistakes, for something that is deficient. God made no mistakes when He made me. He made me perfect. Sorry if I sound arrogant or overconfident, but I am confident about my appearance. Why wouldn't I be? I was created by the most perfect—my Lord—in perfection, and I don't need any man, clothing designer, or makeup artist to tell me what is perfect.

I don't fall for the false standards set by society, by cultures that have dominated the world, or by others who are human just like me.

I don't wear foundation to look whiter or heels to look taller or colored contacts, or pluck my eyebrows into some odd shape or color my nails into colors that are not human, or have plastic surgery to look different from how I am. If society thinks white skin, blond hair, blue eyes, tallness, and a skinny waist are beautiful, then that's their problem. They can go ahead and create their Barbie dolls in that image, but I'm not their Barbie doll and they are not going to impose any image on me.

I take care of the body God gave me and respect it by keeping it clean and watching my diet—not to maintain a figure that pleases the eyes of others, but to protect it from disease. I give my body the quantity and quality of food it was created to consume.

So that's my style. I feel bad for women who spend hours dressing every day, and days or months planning what they will wear for a party and how they can look more attractive, then look so uncomfortable in those tight clothes and high heels and can barely walk or bend down to pick up an item. When I see what the women on billboards, commercials, and game shows are wearing, it really aches my heart.

I mean no offense to anyone, but it hurts me to see the bodies of these innocent women being used to sell products. And they are made to believe that this is freedom. This is slavery. I feel a sense of freedom that I do not have that burden on me, of making myself attractive to others all the time. When I go to a party after spending an extra ten minutes planning what to wear, trying to match my hijab to my jilbab and finding a scarf in my closet that is not my regular cotton, and maybe adding an embroidered shawl for color and accent, I feel like I am telling my host, I do care about your party. ✕

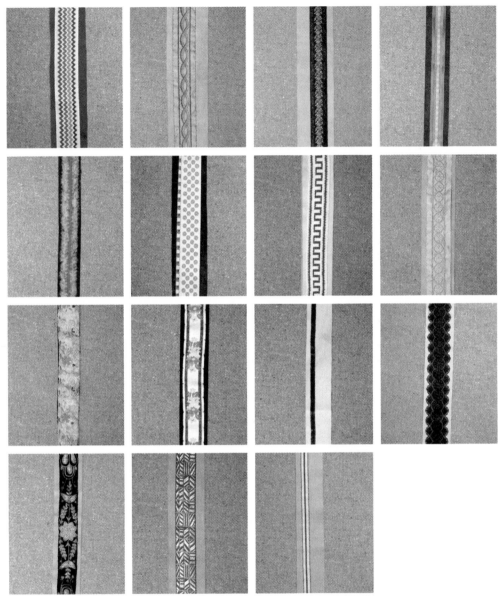

*TIFT MERRITT*'s handmade guitar straps

# COLOR

*"I bought a hot-pink dress a month before I was due. I loved how I felt, like a car won by the top seller at Mary Kay."* —ANN IRELAND

<u>AMY ROSE SPIEGEL</u> I think it's important to have one red detail: a purse, a hair bow, shoes. I think of it like a red door on an otherwise plain house, and how elegant that always seems.

<u>ADRIENNE BUTIKOFER</u> I was scouted to move to Toronto to model after high school. I went to castings but never got a job, and at the same time I was told that my personality was shitty. I went to a rave at one point and did E. It did not turn out well. It was like, "Holy fuck, I *do* suck. I am a huge loser." So I moved to Thunder Bay, where my parents were living in a cabin in the woods, and I cried a lot. But I had a revelation— that people created identities for themselves, and part of my personal pain was that I had never done that. I needed to finally commit to an identity. So I thrifted and re-vamped my wardrobe and wore nothing but brown for two years. Brown seemed like the most uncool choice, the weakest color. I felt weak and helpless at the time. Then I had a therapist in university who spelled it out for me. He said that people normally associate depression with black, but that the truly depressed wear brown. Hearing that made it something to strive against. The transition was pretty slow, but around two or three years later, I had a lighthearted, colorful wardrobe, and I remember feeling awesome about it. I stayed away from all brown for a long time, but then a few years later I started wearing wooden charms on a necklace on a daily basis. Having that bit of brown around my neck made me feel grounded.

<u>GILLIAN KING</u> When I was in art school, and I realized that painting was my medium of choice, I began dressing in a palette similar to my paintings. I was obsessed with dyeing my hair different colors, and for about a year or two my head was the rotating colors of the rainbow.

<u>MEGAN HUSTAD</u> For a brief spell in the eight-ies, my mother took the lessons in Carole Jackson's *Color Me Beautiful* very seriously. The premise is that every person is a Win-ter, Summer, Spring, or Autumn, depending on skin tone, hair color, and eye color, and if one stuck to the approved colors in her sea-sonal palette, she would look prettier. Wear the wrong shade of green—you risked looking sallow, like a wallflower. But the right shade of green brought sparks to your eyes, a blush to your cheeks. A woman armed with this knowl-edge about what she looked best in wouldn't be tempted by trends, and would be less likely to buy something she liked in the store, only to never feel good about wearing it for rea-sons she couldn't quite articulate. I guess the idea was that it would save you money.

<u>MEGAN B.</u> As a child, I was told over and over how beautiful my auburn hair was, so I refused to color or treat it in any way my entire life. Well, until my mid-thirties. Then it started to turn brown. I would say to people,

"Well, as a redhead, I have to be careful in the sun," and they'd tilt their heads in confusion. "Redhead?" My identity as a redhead is actually very important to me, it turns out.

NICOLE LAVELLE One winter my friend Elizabeth said, "I am going to wear only gray this year." She did it, and it worked, and she didn't have to think about clothes. I tried it too, but it made me feel upset.

VICTORIA HAF I have found a lot of great things in Barcelona's streets, but one night I was walking with my husband, talking about how it had been a long time since we had found something good on the street, and he said, "The reason we don't find things anymore is that we've stopped wishing for them." I had this list of things I wanted (a bike, an accordion, a hammock), and I had found all of them on the street, and I thought: "He's right, I wish I could find something today," and on the way home I found a cardboard box full of red things, red toys, a red feather boa—it seemed like props from a play or something, and there was this beautiful red Valentino dress missing a button and with some holes, but it was so easy to fix and it fits me perfectly.

SARA HABEIN I was the one kid with black ballet shoes, and I made my mother look for an all-black backpack and a black toothbrush. It probably all started as a way to be contrary, because I still insist on being contrary about certain things.

LAUREN BRIDE A few years ago, I was having some intense psychological pain. I have always loved clouds as a symbol, and that summer, alone and upset, I began looking often at photos of clouds. Then I moved on to looking at pictures of whipped cream, heaps of feathers, cotton wool, froth on waves, marshmallows . . . I wondered what they shared. I realized they were all fluffed with air, so what I was seeing was a frame for the air. I thought about how this was true for everything, though not with air as a common denominator, but empty space. I believed if I could focus on the parts of myself that were made of empty space, it might cure me of my mental pain. So I saved the images I found online of those fluffy, pale things, and I created zoomed-in shots, and printed them on white long-sleeved cotton shirts. I wore the shirts with white skirts and white shoes all summer. I wanted to be like the white space left after a person is cut out of a photograph. Wearing white all the time and walking into the world in those clothes caused the world to treat me with a bit more gentleness, so that was soothing for me. When I saw people I knew, they would ask me about the shirts and I told them what the pictures were of, and about the idea of empty space, without going into how miserable and wild I was feeling. People were very kind to me, and it generated dreamy, warm conversations that were comforting to have.

SASHA GREY I've often had recurring dreams about rescuing someone or something in the ocean while wearing an all-white tuxedo that gets weighed down by the water, making it nearly impossible for me to save this person or thing.

COLLEEN ASPER For about five years, I have worn only black, white, and gray. This began as an unpremeditated inclination and morphed into a decision when I found myself routinely traveling for work, and realized that it ensured all my clothes matched and I always looked somewhat dressed up. Now I travel less regularly but have come to feel squeamish about wearing color, as it presents all these options that represent potential commitments that I am not ready for.

**KARI LARSEN** I don't like when people comment on my wearing a piece that departs from black. I would rather they not comment at all.

**BRIAN McCLOSKEY** I would obsessively check *The Ricki Lake Show*'s guest request page. When I saw an invitation casting people in "unconventional marriages," I wrote: "I am a transvestite; I got married in a dress." The producers contacted me immediately! For the important day, I chose a red Calvin Klein pleated A-line dress—fun, flattering, and filling me with confidence. On the day of the show, the wardrobe lady burst into the dressing room in a panic and announced, "You can't wear red! Ricki's wearing red today!" I had to change into my backup outfit—a conservative gray Calvin Klein dress. We walked onto the stage, took our places on Ricki's couch, and answered a few questions. Ricki asked if what I was wearing held any special significance. I told her no—I had planned to wear something red but was told to change since someone else on the show was already wearing red. The audience cracked up. Ricki responded with mock horror. Clutching her red blouse, she exclaimed, "I would have taken this off!" Ricki Lake offered to take her top off for me. It was the greatest moment of my life. ✕

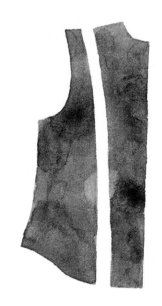

*PAVIA ROSATI*'s cashmere V-neck sweaters and cardigans

# YOU'RE NEVER GOING TO GET THAT MONEY BACK

**JULIET LANDAU-POPE** *as told to Sheila Heti*

I am a declutter coach. When people take me into their bedroom and open up a wardrobe, they often say, "Ah! I would never let my mother see this!" or "My closest friends would never see this!" It's a really big thing to display your most personal belongings to someone.

A lot of women feel very bad about having too many clothes, or not enough clothes, or too many certain kinds of clothes. The most common issues I encounter are around weight and body size. The vast majority of women have clothes that don't fit them, and the majority have a fantasy that at some mythical point they'll go back to being a size they were. So they keep that favorite pairs of jeans, or their pre-maternity clothes, or clothes that have never been worn but that they bought because they wanted to slim down into them. They have a fantasy that they will be a certain size one day. It can be very painful, confronting that reality.

Sometimes people hold on to things because they're very expensive and they feel like, "Well, I've invested a great deal of money in this, therefore I have to hold on to it." In that case, I say, "Whatever you spent on it, you're never going to get that money back. And in fact, what's happening now is it's reminding you of the guilt that you paid so much."

I work very closely with clients to help them find a meaningful way of parting with stuff. If they've lost a relative to cancer, maybe there's a charity that's raising money for medical research. I never talk about throwing anything out.

People find it very difficult to just show me things without telling me stories—every item has a story. If I'm talking to an older woman or a mum, she'll start telling me a story, and I'll say, "I'm sure your daughters would love to hear that, or your sisters. There must be someone in the family who would love to hear that story." By holding on to the thing, they are keeping the story to themselves rather than sharing it, so one of the things I encourage people to do is write the stories down or record them or find some way of documenting them so the story is not lost, while the thing can be given to someone who's actually going to make use of it.

Something I especially encounter with older people is fear of losing the memory. They're afraid if they give away the physical item, they'll lose the memory that's attached to it.

Sometimes people hold on to clothes that have been given to them by people they don't like—ex-husbands! Somebody said to me the other day, "I can't give away that coat. I wore it to my brother's funeral." I said to her, "Do you want to be reminded of your brother's funeral every time you open the door?"

People are often very uneasy if there's space on a shelf or in a wardrobe—they feel they have to fill it up.

I work with people who are Jewish, Muslim, all sorts of religions, and it's interesting to see how cultural identity plays out in their wardrobes. I was with somebody last week—a professional woman in her thirties from a Hindu family—who had two wardrobes in her bedroom. She said to me, "This is my Indian wardrobe, and these are my regular clothes"—that's how she described it. Everything from formal wear to party clothes to underwear—two completely different sets of lingerie!

That was really stark, but we all have different sets of wardrobes, and I think what many women find difficult is to negotiate those different identities. I'm struck over and over again by the number of women who tell me that they don't actually enjoy wearing their clothes. They wear what they need to wear, but they don't particularly like it. I've noticed that when someone culls a wardrobe and reduces it to things that are comfortable and that fit and are flattering, it's a different experience altogether to look in the closet. We lose track of who we are sometimes, and that's reflected in the wardrobe, because we keep clothes for all sorts of reasons, not just because we wear them. ✕

# WORN

*"I am trying to get used to the idea that you wear things and they wear out and you find new things. It's okay."* —MIMI CABELL

CATHERINE MAROTTA My grandmother gave me cashmere sweaters from Costco. In college I would wear them every Friday, when I was most tired, because there were so comfortable, yet they would still make me feel put-together and sophisticated. I met my best friend for coffee every Friday, and we would call them my Friday sweaters. I wore them until they had holes in the sleeves.

NATALIA ELTSOVA In the USSR, you had a thing, you wore it, you spoiled it, you fixed it—until it would be used for mopping floors or something like that. We had a great respect for things, and the opposite side of it was the fear of spoiling things. Once I had a fight with a girl in school and she took my jacket from the hook and threw it on the floor. It was more offensive than if she had tried to beat me up. Another time I had this pair of velvet pants I really liked. And guess what? I sat on a heater in the school corridor and there was gum stuck to it. Because of the material my pants were made of, I never got rid of that damn gum, and that was some stress.

MASHA TUPITSYN I used to paint or clean my apartment in my best dresses. As a result, I ruined a lot of clothes with paint and bleach stains.

DALE MEGAN HEALEY On New Year's Eve, I went to a party in a treehouselike mansion. I got stoned and walked in the mud and ruined my Nina Z clogs. I kept telling myself it was

worth it—I can't stop myself from having experiences for the sake of preserving my clothes. Still, those clogs were sort of a big purchase. Saving up and finally buying those shoes felt like kissing a crush.

ANNEMIEKE BEEMSTER LEVERENZ I try to not dress in something that would be more important to me than having a good time. I wouldn't want to stop doing something for fear that my outfit would get ruined or weird-looking in the act of having fun.

KARI LARSEN I'm wearing a holey T-shirt and my eyeliner is pulled down my cheeks because I rubbed my eyes and forgot I was wearing any.

SARAH MANGUSO A friend gave me a dark blue shirtdress six years ago that I wear all the time. She got it at Walmart. I wear it with good leather boots. I wore it to demonstrate against Bush II in Rome. I wore it to give a reading in Gainesville, and I wore it yesterday. And the day before. A friend's sick dog peed all over it once. It has pockets.

ISHA KAZEMI I remember my mom getting very excited to buy Eid outfits for me when I was very little. She bought a white dress for me when I was around five or six. It was made of satin with thread patterns in the fabric. It was so beautiful and I was so excited to wear it because I was rarely allowed to wear white. I did inevitably stain it, because I was an active child, prone to rolling around in the grass. But I remember feeling very beautiful in that Eid.

**EMILY SPIVACK** At the Chelsea Flea Market about eight years ago, I splurged on an antique black lucite mourning ring with an embedded photograph of a stranger—a woman. I loved that ring. I liked that I could shower with it, which is important as I can't be bothered to take off my jewelry when I shower or sleep. I wore it a bunch, then it broke. I got it fixed and it broke again in a way that was unrepairable. I made a conscious decision that I would no longer care about that ring. I put it in a box and I'm not sure where it is now.

**ALLISON D.** I once had a light blue T-shirt that I got from a street vendor in Edinburgh. It was majorly pitted-out and fraying at the seams, but I loved it. I also had a navy blue zip hoodie that had been my mom's. It had bleach stains. Then there was this peachy sweatshirt I adored for the same reason: it was comfortable and worn. It was a gift from my mom's friend Terry. She was so cool, and that coolness extended to this sweatshirt. I want these worn things back. I miss having clothing that I feel connected to.

**AGNES BARLEY** I wore a pale pink ribbon around my waist under my clothing for many years. It occasionally migrated to the outside to serve as a belt, but I did not take it off. I slept in it. I bathed in it. It was mostly invisible, but I enjoyed the pink line encircling me like a little secret, making me feel pretty. I'm not sure quite how this came about. I may have unconsciously been inspired by an extended family from Bangladesh who lived above me on the Lower East Side in New York. The children would climb down the fire escape and into my apartment and I became good friends with them and one of their aunts. She was a young woman par-

ticularly interested in my clothing because she wore only saris. She wore pages of the Koran in a small pocket on a leather string tied around her waist. I was struck by the idea that one should wear one's beliefs in this way, and I wondered what I would wear in that sense. Years later, the pink ribbon was a sort of abstract prayer and a reminder of myself. Friends were aware of the ribbon as time went by and often tried to give me ribbons as gifts, but I only ever wore my one ribbon. My boyfriend loved it, too. The funniest thing is that my mom liked to wear a red patent-leather belt under her clothes in kindergarten. She apparently refused to take it off and cinched it as tight as she could. So it may be hereditary.

**MADELEINE STACK** White dresses are irresistible to me, clean and minimal, with sneakers or flat sandals. The best thing is floating angelic through a wrecking-ball party in rustling white skirts, sitting in the grass, dancing too hard with muddy barefoot smears, and having red wine thrown all over you. To wake up to a Pollock the morning after.

**SASHA WISEMAN** I had a yellow sundress in my late teens that I wore every warm New England day for probably three years. I remember going on a very long bike ride to a friend's wedding in a park and collapsing on the ground when I finally arrived. I landed under a tree that shed staining berries, and later spent hours sewing heart-shaped patches of silk onto every smudge since I didn't know how to do laundry effectively. I was in a band then, and in every picture I have of our summer tour, I'm wearing that dress.

**MONA KOWALSKA** Sometimes people will buy something pristine and think, It'll be nice as soon as I fuck it up. People say it all the time, because they're uncomfortable with the purity or integrity or whatever it is. I guess

I travel too much and see poor people too much to appreciate that sentiment. In Peru you can see that people have hand-washed their clothes and ironed them and taken care of them and it means something to them. So when I hear people be like, "I just want to fuck this expensive thing up," I'm a bit like, "No!"

**SOFIA SAMATAR** I got a Strawberry Shortcake nightgown when I was maybe ten years old. It was Christmas and we had a fire in the fireplace, and my younger brother and I were hanging out in front of it, and probably messing with it, and a spark leaped out onto my nightgown and burned a hole in it. I just held the fabric stretched out and shrieked: "IT'S BURNING A HOLE IN MY NIGHTIE!" It went through the fabric so fast! My brother and I were dying with laughter. We still think it's a funny story, but what it's about to me now is the sensation of wearing something totally synthetic and surprising. You couldn't guess what it would do.

**EMILY K.** There was this light blue cotton T-shirt I stole from my best friend that had a picture of a sailboat in dark blue and then the phrase: no friggin' in the riggin'. It got armpit stains, then I cut the sleeves off and wore that thing to shreds.

**TISHANI DOSHI** I had a lovely green batik silk dress with puffy sleeves and a black trim that I paid a bit for. I was once at a party where there was a lot of dancing and I was being thrown around the dance floor, and one of the sleeves ripped off. I tried to make it a strapless number by removing both sleeves, but the dress was never quite the same. I still have it in my cupboard. I keep it as a reminder that the dress had a good life, and to buy more clothes like that and less of the kinds that hang like ghosts in the wardrobe. ✕

# THE OUTFIT IN THE PHOTOGRAPH | I

*Nonie, Nene, Inday, and Judy Pacificador, sisters in the Philippines, 1952*

**NONIE (FAR LEFT):** I'm wearing my mother's duster, we called it a duster, a house dress, it's just something that we used for cleaning around. Like an apron dress that you wear. It was green and white. It was very, very comfortable, very loose, like a muumuu, but short.

**NENE:** These were just our regular play clothes, nothing special, and this had a blue top part with a printed white texture on white. It wasn't a hand-me-down, it was probably sewn by my aunt.

**INDAY:** I don't remember this dress, I was about seven. It was white, I don't really recall anything about it.

**JUDY:** I loved this dress because it had big pockets. And we didn't have a lot of toys, so we'd go around in the streets and we'd pick up stuff. We'd pick up seeds or sticks, tamarind seeds, and we'd use that for currency or whatever. So I loved pockets because I could fill them up with as much stuff as I could carry.

**INDAY:** It was so hot we didn't wear shoes. We might have had some flip-flops.

**NONIE:** We had a washerwoman, she came every week.

**INDAY:** She washed at the waterfall and did the ironing. She wrapped it up and tied it and carried it back on her head and dried it under the sun. This lady lived in a house with another lady and there was only one husband. The other lady sold meat. One walked around the town with her meat, and the other one did the washing and ironing. It was so funny, they only had the one husband.

**NENE:** The washerwoman had the kid.

# *I* ALWAYS LIKED THE PEARL SNAP

**NIKKI HAUSLER** *as told to Mary Mann*

I work in the police department as an animal control officer. I wear a uniform that's issued by my employers—tactical pants, tactical boots, and, depending on the season, a short-sleeved or long-sleeved button-up two-pocket shirt. I'm not trying to look like a hottie. I do have my ears double-pierced, so I wear studs from time to time. My wedding ring I don't wear to work. I had that drilled into my head because we had a family friend who wore his wedding ring at a grain elevator where he worked. He had gotten up on a truck, and when he jumped down, his wedding ring got stuck on something and it ripped his finger off.

Tactical pants are what the guys wear when they're going on SWAT team assignments. They've got two big pockets below the regular pockets to carry gear in. I have to carry a notebook in one of those pockets, and in the other I have a hand Taser. I've never had to use it. Knock on wood I never will have to. I've got a Velcro underbelt that holds on to a big leather belt that holds all the other equipment I have for my job. I carry Mace and what animal control officers call bite sticks—things that I can swing out and protect myself with. And a cell phone, key ring . . . there's a lot of equipment. The main thing is it's a huge pain to go to the restroom with it on. *(laughs)*

I've always, always been a tomboy. I grew up on a ranch, and from the time I could start dressing myself, it was always jeans, a button-up shirt, and boots. That's what I'm comfortable in. A while back, my husband was looking in my closet and he was like, "Nikki, you don't even own a dress!" *(laughs)* He made me go buy a dress. I quite frankly hate to shop and I don't like the styles back in the stores, so I just went out and got a little black dress. I figured I was safe with a little black dress.

I have always been terrible about buying clothes. The women in my family, we're not built like most women. I'm not gonna say that word "fat," but we're bigger-boned. I go to the men's department, because the way they make women's clothes, they don't fit right for me. I have huge biceps because of my farming and ranching background, and I can't tell you how frustrated I am with the jeans industry right now, because I cannot go to the women's side and find a pair of jeans that are just a pair of jeans. They're all thin, low-cut, low-rise, and I'm sorry, but there are people in this world who are not into that. I don't need blingetty-bling on my ass. They're trying to make that the focal point of all of the women in the world, and I think that's wrong. I know I have a nice butt, but I don't need to be showing it off. And god forbid I ever find a pair, I have to pay eighty bucks or ninety bucks for 'em. Whereas if I just go over to the men's side, I can find a pair that make me happy for just twenty-five or thirty bucks.

I'm only forty-two, but I started getting gray hair early—I think after my first husband died. I had a lot of stress in my life then. I try to dye it every six months or so. Actually, I have a box sitting on my kitchen table. I was thinking about dyeing it tonight when I get done with chores and stuff. But there's a part of me that's always thinking, "How healthy is it to put those chemicals on my head?"

Anyway, when I was on the ranch it was so easy. We had to wear jeans because we did all of our work on horseback, and you're not going to wear shorts or sweats on a horse. My dad has always been my hero. Even as a little girl, I always wanted to be my dad. That's why it wasn't a problem for me to dress that way, because he was my hero and I wanted to be just like him. My dad's favorite saying is, "In this world there are takers and there are care-takers." He raised me and Travis both to be caretakers.

My dad would have never, ever allowed my brother or me to go outside to work in anything but jeans and a button-up shirt. Obviously boots come in handy during the summer months because of snakes and cactus. Also a button-up shirt with pockets because I like to carry a pen. A lot of times you have to write down a calf number or how many cattle you have in one pen or another. And I'm a smoker, so it's nice to have my cigarettes right there. I always liked the pearl snap button shirts. When you're stretching fence, you don't want a short-sleeved shirt on because you've got barbed wire and god forbid it breaks and comes flinging back at you.

You also want a good pair of leather gloves. Fencing is pretty tough, with the barbs, so we wear leather gloves to protect our hands, and a belt to hang the pliers on.

My dad is probably one of the last remaining true cowboys in the area. He now works part-time for a farmer. I didn't go with the cowboy hat, but I'd always have on a ball cap to protect my face from the sun. The wind is blowing forty miles an hour today, and I'm sure wherever my dad is, he's wearing his cowboy hat. I can never figure out how he keeps it on his head. Mine always blew right off. ✕

## WEAR AREAS | ANA BUNČIĆ

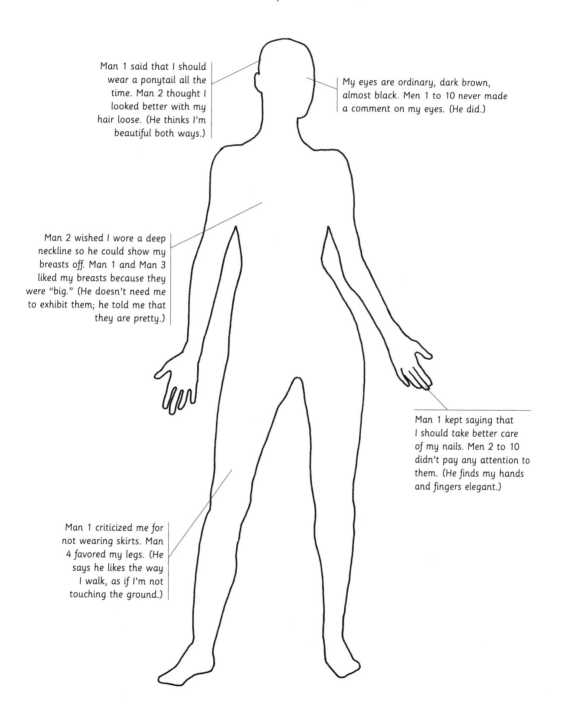

Man 1 said that I should wear a ponytail all the time. Man 2 thought I looked better with my hair loose. (He thinks I'm beautiful both ways.)

My eyes are ordinary, dark brown, almost black. Men 1 to 10 never made a comment on my eyes. (He did.)

Man 2 wished I wore a deep neckline so he could show my breasts off. Man 1 and Man 3 liked my breasts because they were "big." (He doesn't need me to exhibit them; he told me that they are pretty.)

Man 1 kept saying that I should take better care of my nails. Men 2 to 10 didn't pay any attention to them. (He finds my hands and fingers elegant.)

Man 1 criticized me for not wearing skirts. Man 4 favored my legs. (He says he likes the way I walk, as if I'm not touching the ground.)

*SHEILA O'SHEA*'s hand-me-downs from her mother

# Sherwin Tjia

*Please describe your figure.*
Full disclosure: I'm a male cross-dresser. I'm a skinny man who's thickened around the belly because of beer and an inactive lifestyle.

*What's the situation with your hair?*
Right now it's long on the top and buzzed on both sides. There was a moment when I realized that I had Rihanna's haircut and I was delighted to fit in.

*When do you feel at your most attractive?*
I feel I look my best when I'm cross-dressed. I wear this strapless satiny black dress that's ruched around the hips. It's terrifically comfortable. I wish I'd bought a few of them. When I dress as a man, I tend to wear the same outfit. It's almost like a uniform. When I find a shirt I like, I will buy multiples of it. I have twenty-two of one shirt, eleven of another. In terms of dresses, I tend to buy the same kind of dress—a little black dress.

*What are some dressing rules you think all women should follow?*
I am not a big believer in rules, unless they are useful. Fashion is a terrible place that promises you can look like a peacock if you like, but the second you do, people will make fun of you.

*Would you rather be perceived as having great taste or great style?*
I think today, for someone to say that you have good taste means that you're rich enough to adorn yourself with all these brand names. But if you are someone who has style, you are turning yourself into a very particular brand. Your own name is your brand name when you have style.

*Are there dressing tricks that make you feel like you're getting away with something?*
I wear a whole chassis of things underneath a dress. I have fake hips, a fake bum, I corset up my belly, and I have a bra that holds silicone breast forms. These are the only things that give me any curves at all.

*Who are some people from culture whose style you admire?*
I remember when Björk appeared on some awards show to sing a song and she was in this dress that resembled a giant dead swan. Its neck curled up and around her own neck and its head rested on her right boob. I remember being blown away by that dress. It, more than anything, made fashion more artful to me.

*Are there times when you dressed to calm yourself?*
I'm scared a lot, so I more often wear clothes to protect me. I like having a lot of layers between me and the world. I get self-conscious when people look at me. I like attention, but handle it better when it comes obliquely, through admiration of the things I make.

*Is there an item of clothing you no longer own, but which you still think about?*
When I was six or seven I had this Batman outfit and I would wear these black high-heeled boots that my mom didn't wear anymore. I adored them. I was conscious of the fact that boys weren't supposed to wear them, but I enjoyed them immensely. Then one day I couldn't find them and my mom told me that she'd thrown them out, and it broke my heart. Now I have an entire collection of sexy high-heeled black boots. ✕

# THIRTY-SIX WOMEN | MIRANDA JULY

*Six strangers wear one another's favorite outfits.*

*Featuring Ziva Serkis–Naumann, Rosemary Hochschild, Nyjia Jones, Tabatha Rajendra, Molly Ringwald, and Kimber Hall. Photographs by Michael Schmelling*

## A MAP OF MY FLOOR | HEIDI JULAVITS

**OCCASION** *Funeral for a close family friend, rural New Hampshire, February. The bedroom floor displays the following tried and discarded items:*

**1** Liz Claiborne silk jumpsuit. The woman who died was sexy into her seventies. I want to look sexy in her honor, but also because I'll be seeing her favorite nephew at the service. I've had a crush on him since 1983, i.e., since the year this jumpsuit was produced. I believe she would have been happy if I'd married him, so I might dress as though this is still a possibility (even though he and I are happily married to other people). **2** Sixties double-knit wool jersey dress (Karlana) with white leather trim and belt. Last time I wore it was to a wedding and the couple is now divorced. **3** Commes des Garçons black tulle skirt. Too bleak-girl-at-the-prom. Too like I'm trying to perform, before an audience, my sadness. **4** A Détacher kimono-sleeved jacket. I bought this a few years ago at a sample sale thinking, "I'll wear this a lot when I'm older." I guess I am not yet old enough. **5** Vintage B. Altman ankle-length knit wool dress. Also sixties. I wore this with Miu Miu nautical sandals to a literary awards ceremony. I did not win, but Uma Thurman checked me out approvingly and I took that as the greater honor. **6** Sixties French sailor pants. Fear I might look like an extra in Guy Maddin's "Sissy-Boy Slap-Party." Also, the funeral is in the mountains and nowhere near the sea. There will be enough cognitive dissonance with this woman now gone. **7** Another sixties knit wool dress (Cordon of Philadelphia). Black and brown stripes. I feel bouncy like Snoopy whenever I put it on. This is either the best or the worst thing to wear when one plans to cry a lot.

**WORN** *Agnés B. dress, black cardigan, long wool socks, white pleather ankle boots.*

# IF NOTHING ELSE,
# I HAVE AN ETHICAL GARTER

HUMAN RIGHTS JOURNALIST **MAC McCLELLAND** SPEAKS TO **SHEILA HETI**

**MAC:** When I was a teenager, I saw this documentary about abuses at overseas Gap factories, and it simultaneously opened my eyes and ruined my life—being an embarrassingly avid Gap shopper at that time. *(laughs)*

**SHEILA:** Do you remember what you thought about where your clothes came from before seeing that film?

**MAC:** I'd never thought about it. You wear clothes starting when you're a baby, right? Unless you're educated in some way about where clothes come from, there's no reason you'd look at your OshKosh overalls and think, I wonder if a child slave made these.

**SHEILA:** Can you tell me what you mean when you say "child slave"?

**MAC:** Underage workers, not in school, making some obscenely low wage. A million workers squeezed into tiny dorm spaces crammed with beds, not allowed to leave, no windows or heating or air-conditioning, not being able to take breaks, people getting hurt, people working crazy long shifts . . . The thing everyone in a sweatshop has in common is that they are poor, they desperately need a job, and it's the best or the only job they can get.

**SHEILA:** Right.

**MAC:** So I stopped shopping at the Gap—huge sacrifice for a teenager in the nineties *(laughs)*—and I found a way to self-righteously insert the topic into conversations. Then, of course, one day I was soapboxing to this woman who had

worked in Cambodia for years and years—this is a white lady I'm talking about, an aid worker—and she was like, "When people boycott those factories or get them shut down, all those workers lose their jobs." She'd worked with women who'd lost factory jobs and thus had to become prostitutes. She was like, "Buy anything you want from the Gap. Fuck it."

**SHEILA:** Do you have any idea what percentage of the clothes people buy in the West is produced overseas in these kinds of conditions?

**MAC:** Almost nothing is made in the United States. Which is not to say that all overseas factories are hellholes, but there's very little oversight and regulation, so it's impossible to know what kind of conditions your Made in non-USA clothes are produced in. Not to say that if we moved a portion of the textile industry back to the States, the workers wouldn't also be treated like shit here, of course.

**SHEILA:** Right.

**MAC:** We do all sorts of terrible things to our own warehouse and factory workers. Because in general, people want to have jobs, and they'd rather have shitty jobs than no jobs. At one point in college, I was hell-bent on buying overpriced American Apparel clothes because they're made in the States, but where does the fabric come from? Also, it turns out Dov Charney is allegedly a sexual terrorist. What's a girl to do?

SHEILA: So what do you do personally in terms of your own shopping choices?

MAC: Well, I hardly ever shop because I hate having things. *(laughs)* But when I do have to buy clothes—so like, I'm not in a position where I have to go to Old Navy for a five-dollar T-shirt, but even if I'm going to go to Saks . . . Okay, obviously I don't have that much money. But if I was to go to a J.Crew, who says those clothes don't come out of those same factories? They still do. It's not like across the street they have a different row of Saks factories that are really fancy and have air-conditioning and flavored water that the workers can sip all day, and they can take a lot of breaks. The clothes at Saks are probably made with better materials, and that's where your money is going—plus design, branding, things like that. But some of them could be made in the same conditions. So it doesn't necessarily make any difference whether I'm going to buy a five-dollar shirt or a five-hundred-dollar shirt.

SHEILA: What if you buy from a boutique where the owner makes the clothes herself?

MAC: Sure, right. When I lived in San Francisco, there were definitely stores on Valencia that upwardly mobile hipsters would go to, where people designed and made their own stuff, and I actually do own a dress made by this girl in Pittsburgh. I paid a hundred dollars for it and I thought that was great. But that choice is not open to all consumers, not just for price purposes, but because if you don't live in a boutiquey hipster area—

SHEILA: But then there's Etsy—

MAC: Right, I wasn't thinking about that. So for example, my garter—this is really embarrassing, but when I got married, my husband really wanted me to have the garter, and I was like, "Where am I going to get a garter?" 'Cause Victoria's Secret—I mean, they specifically have had very serious child-labor and slave-labor accusations in the past. But maybe I'm just turning all the ex–Victoria's Secret workers into prostitutes because I'm not supporting Victoria's Secret factories! Anyway, I went on Etsy and some gal—I don't know where—made a garter and sent it to my house and I was like, This is great.

SHEILA: Your ethical garter.

MAC: That's right. If nothing else, I have an ethical garter.

SHEILA: Okay, so there's sweatshops, and then there's the distribution of clothing items within America. Tell me a bit about Amazon and how most people get their clothes shipped to them.

MAC: Well, this whole process—there's not a clean step in it, right? Because yes, you *could* buy your clothes online. But then you're probably buying it from some mega-place. Do people buy a lot of clothes on Amazon?

SHEILA: I imagine people must, and even if you don't buy clothes there, you buy cosmetics—

MAC: Accessories, sure. And even if you're not buying it specifically from Amazon, chances are very high that any distributor of clothing will use some sort of mega-warehouse to get those orders fulfilled. And in those giant warehouses, a lot of times the workers are not paid very well, or they're temporary workers, which is this big new trend. Because if you have "temporary workers," even if you keep them for three years, they're basically on contract, which means you don't have to give them vacation or health insurance or raises or other things that people might be interested in having, and they can work under extremely demanding and physically damaging conditions. They could be doing a lot of repetitive actions or things that could cause permanent injuries in some cases. But then if you think about retail, there have been a lot of complaints in recent years against retail companies for worker abuses. They're forcing people not to work full-time hours, so that they don't have to give them benefits, and that makes it not a living wage. So you can't win. How can you win? It's so hard.

SHEILA: You were saying you don't like to have much stuff. Is that related at all to what we're talking about?

MAC: It is a bit related, yes. Also, I used to work for a moving company, so I spent a lot of time in people's houses, packing up their things, and just being overwhelmed by the amount of shit people had that they didn't need. So I think it probably started a little bit there. *(laughs)* Then I have some weird disaster issues, like I lived in New Orleans during Hurricane Katrina. To me, things that you have are just things you will lose or could lose, so don't get attached to them. But yeah, if I'm going to go shopping, I do think about all these things. It's kind of hard to turn your brain off. And if you're keeping these things in mind while you're shopping, is shopping, like, *fun*? Not really. Okay, I just looked up the Abercrombie scandal. They were keeping employees down to one shift per week, and the employees would have to call in every day to see if they were working or not.

SHEILA: So they can't have any other job.

MAC: Right. You're on call for your fifty-five-dollar shift. You couldn't have another job, and you wouldn't be able to plan your finances if you had no idea how many days per week you were going to work.

SHEILA: What's the motivation for having people call in every day to find out their shift?

MAC: I'm not entirely sure about retail, but that's a thing they do in big warehouses. There, people call in because they don't want to pay one cent to a worker they don't absolutely need. There's real-time updating—they have software that tells them: This is how many orders we have. Then they can calculate the exact number of humans they'll need to fill them, and then they will order those people by the day.

SHEILA: When you saw this documentary as a teenager, was that the dawning of your consciousness about global politics and labor unions?

MAC: It had a lot to do with it. Because it was astounding to me that here I am, spending my whole life shopping in the Gap, and my parents are coming with me, and they're shopping at the Gap, and my parents are considered to be intelligent people. And when I'm in the Gap, there's a hundred other people in the Gap. So how are we all just walking around the Gap having no idea? It's such a big deal. You're buying these clothes. You're supporting these companies in this industry.

SHEILA: So when you, in your head, map the world, and you see America and India and China and all these places, in terms of clothing and in terms of these issues, what's the structure you see? What do you visualize?

MAC: I visualize cheap labor—and originally, when people set up these factories in China, they were pulling people out of the fucking hillsides, you know? But now that the game's been going on for a while, the workers in China are getting more organized and they're demanding higher wages and they see the news and they know that they're being underpaid, so their wages are way up. I was talking to an economist and he was telling me that there was this mad rush to get into Vietnam because China was so expensive—though compared with the United States, it's nothing. But for sure, any place that has a desperate and very poor population in the East, there are a lot of factories. I picture older, heavier white men walking around, possibly with hard hats on, you know? Touring factories and setting up connections and hustling. Then all that stuff gets shipped on these huge containers into our ports. Then there's us in the United States, where we care about this stuff, but at the same time our own wages have been stagnant for decades. So you have a huge population of people who, even if they're not so enthusiastic about foreign workers being exploited for their benefit so they can have cheaper clothes, don't have the money to buy anything that's more expensive because their own wages are low and their cost of living is very high. It's just reinforcing demand for cheap, cheap, super-cheap clothes. But even when you're buying more expensive stuff, it doesn't mean it was produced in better conditions. And H&M, oh my god, I can't even be in an H&M. I feel like I'm having a heart attack in there. It smells like . . . do you know what I'm talking about?

SHEILA: It smells like what?

MAC: It smells! To me it smells like diesel or something—gas fumes and textile chemicals. It smells like a terrible factory. The smell, and the amount of clothes, and how cheap they are, and how totally disposable they are—everything sort of comes together for me in there and it makes me feel overwhelmed and sad. Urban Outfitters—I have the same thing. Every time I walk in there I'm just like, oh my god, it smells like plastic and chemicals and bad news and bad politics and I just *(laughs)* I don't want to be there. I sound like a crazy person, by the way. But it's frustrating because there's no good answer, you know?

SHEILA: But it's still better for people to know about these things, right?

MAC: *(long pause)* Sure, yeah. It's the first step. Admitting you have a problem.

SHEILA: Can you see a future when there isn't a place in the world where there's incredibly cheap, exploited labor?

MAC: If you think about how many poor countries there are in the world, and how many poor people there are, that would take a very long time. Of course, once you bring all those factories into countries, it does build up their economies, and the more you do that, the more you have to end up paying people, but then you're like, "Oh no, we ruined this for ourselves! These people have a standard of living now! We have to leave!" Then the companies go somewhere else. And wages are only part of it. There's no oversight, or very little oversight, so people end up dying in factory fires. And trying to figure out what the conditions are that produced, say, your Apple products—there's so much corruption and so many levels of outsourcing that it's almost impossible to nail down what's really happening and fix it. Will we move toward that eventually? I don't know. We haven't yet—and the Industrial Revolution was a really long time ago. *(laughs)*

SHEILA: Okay, let me ask this, because I'm stuck on the idea that you don't like owning much. What do you own? How does your house look different from the houses you packed up?

MAC: Until two years ago, I had in my apartment in San Francisco—I'd lived in it for years and years, and I was a professional adult woman, so I had the means to buy furniture—but I had a mattress that I bought for thirty dollars, 'cause it was junk, and I had a tiny table that someone was throwing out of a garage. I only had garbage furniture in my house, and I only had three pieces.

**SHEILA:** Right.

**MAC:** But then I got married, and my husband is French, and I was like, "I can't have a European with all his aesthetic sensibilities move into my garbage apartment." *(laughs)* I wanted to make it look more like a home. So now I have a few pieces of furniture. But in terms of clothes, I have maybe ten sweaters. The latest I bought in probably 2007. Fuck, which is seven years ago. And the two sweaters I wear most often, they're J.Crew, and I got them for Christmas in 2003. See, I really hate shopping.

**SHEILA:** Do you take very good care of your clothes to make them last?

**MAC:** One of those J.Crew sweaters is in pretty bad shape. It has a very visible mustard stain that it's had for five of the last ten years. And the other one is getting super-threadbare in the elbows.

**SHEILA:** *(laughing)* I keep having this line from a sixties women's magazine in my head, like, "And yet she still managed to find a husband, ladies!"

**MAC:** *(laughing)* Yeah, my husband still married me, even though I never change my clothes. We met when I was reporting in Haiti and I was wearing a five-year-old American Apparel T-shirt, and it definitely had holes in it. But he thought I looked beautiful! ✕

*GWEN SMITH*'s concert T-shirts

# UNINTENTIONAL

*"Mainly, I'm just trying to keep what I'm wearing from being a problem."* —MARY DUENWALD

**EILEEN MYLES** During the Iraq war I had a crew cut and just absently bought a camouflage duffel bag and started getting treated really well and I realized it wasn't that they thought I was a man. It was that I was willing to die for my country.

**LAUREN SPENCER KING** My grandmother was a painter. She always had on so many colors, and the more jewelry the better. She had terrible arthritis and had this theory that wearing these huge intricate rings on every finger would distract people from the way her hands looked, but instead it just made them want to look closer.

**SANAA ANSARI KHAN** When I was about eight years old, we went together as a family to a party at my parents' friend's home. My mom dressed me in a pink frilly dress with bells. They jingled every time I moved. It caught the attention of the other kids at the party, and before I knew it, they were sifting through the layers of my dress to see where the noise was coming from.

**MARION LARSEN** When I took my first job as an addictions counselor, my clients were a group of black homeless women. They spoke very rapidly and used slang I didn't understand. I tried to dress "professionally" to appear as if I understood things much better than I really did. I had to laugh when I heard them say of me, "Well, here comes Mary Poppins with her pearls."

**LYDIA JOHNSON** I bought my sister a slinky red dress to wear on dinner dates with her husband when she was pregnant. She didn't like it at all. I wanted her to feel beautiful and put-together but hadn't considered any issues she might have had with her body or self-image while pregnant. Who wants to wear something tight and uncomfortable when you're growing a tiny human?

**ELIZABETH KAISER** I was living in Florida and bought a dress as a laugh. It was fluorescent and hooker-ish. I told people it was my "Italian prostitute" dress. I wore it to the most fun party, where I ended up befriending a police officer who took me for a moonlit ride on his horse!

**OLIVIA S.** In second grade, my Girl Scout troop decided to complete the fashion badge. The activity was a field trip to a department store where we would pick out clothes, try them on, and hold a little fashion show with the outfits we put together. I picked out a polo shirt and khaki pants because it was what I wore every day and I had never really thought about wearing anything else. I was so embarrassed when all the other girls came out of the dressing rooms in crazy frilly dresses and scarves and hats. I still have a photo of my seven-year-old self walking down the "catwalk" in my plain polo shirt.

**AMY RUDERSDORF** I grew up with artistic aunties. I remember as a kid seeing one auntie's leg hair poking out of her magenta tights. I've never forgotten it. It says a lot about who she is, probably without her even knowing it.

**MICHELLE GARRETT** One time in junior high, I tried wearing a new pair of overalls, which was not something I'd ever worn before. My best friend told me they made me look pregnant.

**MARTHA McCARTY** An 18-carat gold fingernail was a gift from my sister after a low (post-divorce) point in my life. She said I needed to wear something fun and frivolous. I naively paraded around, conspicuously flashing the nail glued to my pinkie finger, until someone told us a gold fingernail is used to scoop cocaine. I wear it still.

**ALICIA BERNLOHR** In American *Vogue*, a young designer said she liked to wrap duct tape around her breasts for a makeshift bandeau bikini top and write "Chanel" on it in Sharpie to wear to the beach. Was this some kind of joke? I have no clue, but Anna Wintour really printed it in her magazine. I decided to use a roll of silver duct tape as a strapless bra under a tube top to visit friends in Toulouse, France. We all went out to a hip bar downtown. I felt really grown-up, drinking cocktails and flirting with French men. Then I realized everyone was looking at me. My tube top had slipped down. The tight loops of duct tape emerged. It didn't even seem like some cool S&M bondage thing. It just looked bizarre.

**SARAH STEINBERG** In my very early twenties I acquired my grandfather's old "Russian hat." It was a dark brown fur, boxy, it covered my ears, and it was tall enough to give me three more inches. I wore it all the time. I wore it to class, to the pub after class. Once I wore it to see a band, and from the audience I fell in love with the drummer, to whom I introduced myself after the show. I wouldn't have had the confidence to do that if it hadn't been for the hat. He walked me home after the show, then told all his friends that we had sex. ✕

# SURVEY ANSWERED WITH PHRASES FROM MY DIARY

SHEILA HETI

*Are there any dressing rules you want to convey to other women?*
Sometimes all a woman needs to look stylish is to be standing in front of some beautiful flowers.

*Are there any dressing tricks that make you feel like you're getting away with something?*
For me, the more I care, the worse I look.

*Do you address anything political in the way that you dress?*
Was it just about keeping warm?

*Do you have style in any areas of your life apart from fashion?*
I always want a relationship that feels like a block of steel—but perhaps consider instead: love that feels like the thinnest man's undershirt, in many places ripping.

*Have you ever stolen or adapted dressing ideas or items from friends or family?*
I'm happy to wear something that Margaux likes, or Leanne likes, or Kathryn likes, because I like them.

*How do you shop?*
It looks good.

*How do institutions affect the way you dress?*
I feel like half the reason I got married was because I wanted to wear a wedding band.

*How does makeup fit into all this for you?*
But I didn't mind being dead, because I had been an artist.

*If you were asked to explain your style philosophy, what would you say?*
There's something to be said for the person who does not discern. Something to be said for the truly democratic heart that can see the good everywhere.

*If you had to throw out all your clothes but keep one thing, what would you keep?*
When I was in Istanbul, Elif and I came up with a game. We would ask each other questions, knowing what the other person's answer revealed. For instance, if I asked her, "What is your favorite movie?" what I was thinking was, "Your answer will tell me what the plot of the next book you write will be." At one point Elif asked me, "What is your favorite article of clothing?" and I said, "A simple dress." She said, "That is your life in Toronto." It made sense to me: I can come to Toronto and slip it on—my friends are here, my family is here, my work is here, my boyfriend is here.

*If you were totally comfortable with your body, what would you wear?*
Whatever is beautiful and falling apart.

*In what way is this stuff important, if at all?*
Kate Moss wrote a poem.

*Please describe your emotions.*
I went out last night in New York to meet all my friends looking like this—tears and bra and all.

*Please describe your mind.*
Part of me was curious to live out this other self, to discover her, but a greater part of me was relieved to think I didn't have to—that no one was creeping up behind me to rip away the life I have—meaning I should get rid of it now so I don't have to suffer when it all inevitably falls apart.

*Was there a moment in your life when something "clicked" for you about fashion or dressing?*
Marilyn Monroe had help.

*What is the most transformative conversation you ever had on the subject of fashion or style?*
Your present is a lovely dress that's all in one piece, Elif wrote, to remind me.

*Was there ever an important or paradigm-shifting purchase in your life?*
It cost $350 in a fancy part of town.

*What are some things you do to feel sexy or alluring?*
This morning, jaywalking, I crossed in front of the truck of an old man.

*What are things you admire about other women?*
I always try to be a "pretty girl," but I admire someone like Margaux, whose image is far more complex.

*What are your drawers and closets like?*
On the plane to Coral Gables, Florida, I made a list of all the clothes I own: two hundred items. My plan is to edit my closet this way—whatever I forgot to write down, I'll give away.

*What do you consider beautiful?*
I could build up my aesthetic from looking at a tree.

*What do you consider ugly?*
No ugliness.

*What do you think of perfume? Do you wear it?*
I asked him the other day if he would mind if I grew out my armpit hair.

*What is an archetypal outfit for you, one you could have happily worn at any point in your life?*
I thought, "I want to go home now," and took the streetcar back to my apartment, back to my neighborhood.

*What is your process for getting dressed in the morning? What are you considering?*
I don't want to look like Audrey Hepburn.

*With whom do you talk about clothes?*
This is something I have never done. ✕

## "GLASSES"

*Mary steps onto the elevator at her university at the same time as a short, brown-haired woman wearing glasses with periwinkle-blue frames. They ride one floor down together.*

**MARY:** I really like your glasses.

**WOMAN:** Thank you!

**MARY:** The colored frames look so cool. I always want to get a pair like that.

**WOMAN:** Yeah, I have a few. I like to match them to my outfit whenever I can.

*Mary notices that the woman is also wearing shoes with periwinkle-blue squares.* ✕

*HEIDI JULAVITS*'s striped shirts

# Milena Rosa

*I did the survey with my daughter. She's always been very deliberate about her clothes. She's five.*
—SASHA ARCHIBALD

*Do you remember the first time you were conscious of what you were wearing?*
I am always conscious of what I am wearing.

*What lessons did your parents teach you about clothing or style?*
Don't pull them or they will sometimes rip. You might have some fancy clothes that you want to wear but you didn't wear it because your mom and dad said no.

*Did you ever buy an article of clothing without giving it much thought, only to find it much more valuable as time went on?*
Yes, this dress. First I didn't really like it because there's too many flowers, but then I said I like flowers and this dress became my favorite. Also, this hat. I didn't like it at first, because I thought my eye color wasn't green, but then I saw my eye color and it was green and it matched the hat, so then I liked it.

*Did you ever buy an item of clothing, certain it would be meaningful to you, but it wasn't?*
First I loved this hat for my doll. It came in a box and I love the doll. Then when I saw that it didn't fit my doll, I didn't really like the hat anymore.

*Looking back at your purchases over the past five years, can you generalize about which were the most valuable things to buy?*
These sparkly sneakers. I like them because they are so sparkly except the holes where the laces go, and the bottom is pink, and there's a white stripe and a pink stripe but the part I like most is the bottom. It's my favorite sneakers and they're sparkly, and sparkly is my favorite. But they don't fit yet 'cause they're too big. Also, my dress-up shoes. I like them 'cause everywhere is sparkly except the bow and it's white sparkly and red sparkly and some more white sparkly and there's also yellow and golden sparkles and they have high heels and they're only for dress-up or I used them

for Halloween. I feel happy and I feel like I look really beautiful.

*Did anyone ever say anything that made you see yourself differently, on a physical or sartorial level?*
One time someone said, "I like your shoes!" and one time someone said, "I like your dress!" and one time someone said, "I like your sparkly pants and your hair" and everything that I am.

*Were you ever given a present of clothing that really touched you?*
Yes, my aunt Jarmila gave me a shirt with little beads and it sparkles in the sun and I like it so much and it's long-sleeved. I want to show you how I wear it. *(She leaves to put it on.)*

*Have you ever successfully given someone a present of jewelry or clothing that you feel good about?*
I made a special thing for my friend Langston and I sent it to him and I felt good about it. It was some jewelry that I didn't really want anymore. I glued it to the paper. I think he liked it.

*What sorts of things do you do to feel sexy or alluring?*
Making braids and doing a four-river or three-river hairstyle. Or a ponytail.

*What sorts of women do you tend to notice in the streets?*
I like the clothes in my family the best. My mommy and daddy is my family. And my friends.

*What is really beautiful for you, in general?*
My fancy dresses, my dress-up dresses, and my rings and everything I have that's really pretty.

*What do you consider very ugly?*
*(She goes to the bathroom and gets the bathroom tub plug.)*
This. This thing is really ugly.

*Would you say you "know what you like" in the area of fashion and clothing?*
Sometimes I know what I like, and sometimes I don't really know, 'cause I forgot right then what I like.

*How does makeup fit into all this?*
I want to wear makeup when I'm like a teenager, or a grown-up. I would like to wear blue makeup and red makeup and green makeup and lipstick. And ChapStick, too.

*What's with your hair?*
It's exactly how I like it.

I like my hair more than anyone else's. My hair is blond and turning brown. The thing that I like is how short it is. It's okay if it changes colors but I want it to be as short as it is forever.

*Please describe your body.*
I don't really know what to say.

*Please describe your mind.*
Sometimes my mind tells me what to do but I don't do it 'cause I can't. Like sometimes I need to go potty and my mind screams, "Go potty! Go potty! Go potty!" but I can't 'cause there's not a bathroom. That's very weird. Sometimes my mind says, "Go potty!" in a baby voice, and it cries, too, when I can't go potty. My mind pretends it's a baby.

*Please describe your emotions.*
Sometimes when I'm happy I actually feel sad but I'm really happy. But then when I'm sad, I change and start to feel like I'm funny.

*What are some things you need to do in order to feel presentable?*
I sometimes want to go to school with fancy clothes but my mom says, No, no no no no. I try to wear them anyway but my mom takes them off. Also, I wear clean underwear every day. I had a playdate yesterday with a boy. It was so fun 'cause he wore my underwear and I

wore his underwear. He was pretending he was a girl and I was pretending I was a girl that didn't have any girl underwear so I had to wear boy underwear. It was so fun.

*What are you wearing on your body and face, and how is your hair done, right at this moment?*
I'm wearing a little-princess costume. It has sparkles, it's yellow, it has short sleeves, and there used to be two little things stuck on it but one broke off. I have Snow White shoes that I wear with it.

*Is there anything that came to mind while filling this out that you wanted to say?*
I want to add another thing to the ugly question. *(She leaves to retrieve a toothbrush.)* This is also very ugly. ✕

## WEAR AREAS | JINNIE LEE

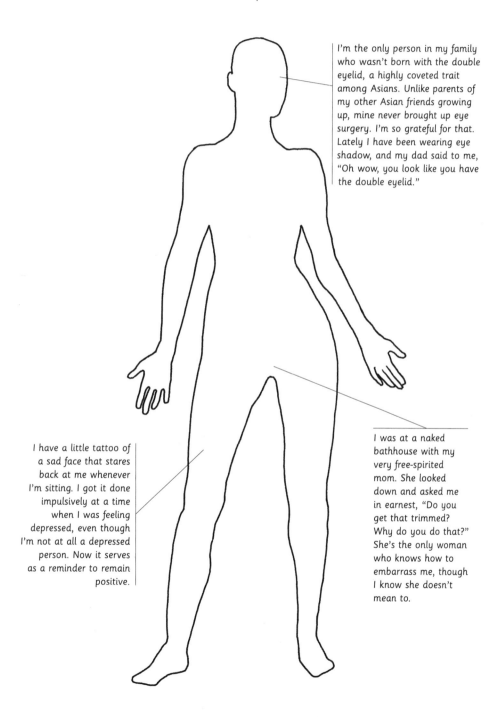

I'm the only person in my family who wasn't born with the double eyelid, a highly coveted trait among Asians. Unlike parents of my other Asian friends growing up, mine never brought up eye surgery. I'm so grateful for that. Lately I have been wearing eye shadow, and my dad said to me, "Oh wow, you look like you have the double eyelid."

I have a little tattoo of a sad face that stares back at me whenever I'm sitting. I got it done impulsively at a time when I was feeling depressed, even though I'm not at all a depressed person. Now it serves as a reminder to remain positive.

I was at a naked bathhouse with my very free-spirited mom. She looked down and asked me in earnest, "Do you get that trimmed? Why do you do that?" She's the only woman who knows how to embarrass me, though I know she doesn't mean to.

*JULIA LEACH*'s jean jackets

# THE SURFER IS NOTHING
# WITHOUT THE WAVE

### ART HISTORIAN **ALEXANDER NAGEL** SPEAKS TO **SHEILA HETI**

SHEILA: Tell me about the relationship between the words "style" and "stylus."

ALEX: "Style" comes from the word "stylus," which refers to a writing or drawing instrument. So I love that "style" immediately has a few meanings. It is the instrument, and by extension the hand that moves it, and also the trace left by the hand and instrument. When we talk about style, we are always talking about those things. When we say, "She has such great style," we mean the clothes, but not just the clothes. We also mean the sensibility that chose the clothes, and the body that found the clothes to suit it and that moves inside the clothes.

SHEILA: If people choose clothes they can't move in, can they have style?

ALEX: Since stylus is also the name of the needle of a record player, it suggests that without ease of movement, registration is unclear. You don't hear the music. Without ease, there is no style. That's not to say that all style is fluid. We've all seen people who manage their awkwardness into a style, and that is hugely charming, but I would say there is an accuracy in the registration even there. They have found a way to turn their awkwardness into a way of navigating the world. Style is all about agency, about marking the world in a certain way. But there is also a receptive moment in style. Style is the way we let the world move through us. Think of a surfer. The surfboard is a stylus, cutting a path through the wave. The surfer finds an individual path—no two

surfers will find the same path through the swell and curl. And the surfer is nothing without the wave. Without that energy, that force, the surfer can't carve her path. The same relation exists in the sphere of clothing. Someone with style is irreducible, yet she is always in a powerful relation to her moment. Even if she adopts styles from other eras, or comes up with a style that has never been seen before, she needs the wave of the surrounding culture to do it. That's why certain periods seem better suited to producing stylish responses than others.

SHEILA: Why?

ALEX: Because certain waves are better than others.

SHEILA: How well suited is our period to producing a stylish response, do you think? Or which periods were well suited?

ALEX: I think the optimal condition for a good style era, like the twenties or sixties, is a combination of lots of sudden change, but also a good deal of incipient codification in the new expressions. That seems to create the right kind of tension.

SHEILA: That sounds like right now.

ALEX: But I don't see a lot of radical new now. Of course, fashion has always been backward-looking—Shakespeare has one of his characters talk about the "young hotbloods" hunting for new looks in old stained-glass windows and tapestries—but these days it seems more backward-looking than normal. There's a lot of recycling from a pretty well-established menu.

**SHEILA:** Yet now is a time of sudden and radical change. There's unprecedented information access, more global communication. You'd think that would change things somehow—be a big, powerful wave.

**ALEX:** Then why haven't we seen anything as radical as flappers or hippies? Lots of waves go unsurfed.

**SHEILA:** What are hipsters?

**ALEX:** Hipsters are part of the retrospective culture I was talking about, archivists of past styles.

**SHEILA:** Do you think style is related more to one's character or to one's body?

**ALEX:** I think style is the state in which one feels the least separation between one's character and one's body. There's no question that style is a kind of armor. We need it to get through the world. But it's a fluid armor.

**SHEILA:** When you think of style, do you think of it in terms of how one conducts conversations, and who one chooses as one's friends, and so on?

**ALEX:** Yes. Since style is the marking instrument in movement, it courses through many things.

**SHEILA:** Can you think of any figures from history who had style in life and dress?

**ALEX:** Jimi Hendrix is a good example. It's surprising to hear him speak in interviews, as he is so sweet and unassuming, but then you realize that is part of the style. The guitar-playing combines flamboyance and discreetness in the same way the person does.

**SHEILA:** Is it possible to have style without thinking about one's culture?

**ALEX:** No, I don't think so. May I quote Gilles Deleuze, pretentiously?

**SHEILA:** Yes!

**ALEX:** *Creuser dans la langue une langue étrangère et porter tout le langage vers une limite musicale—c'est ça avoir un style.* "To carve out within language another foreign language and to take all of language to a musical limit—that is to have style." That pretty well describes Jimi Hendrix playing "The Star-Spangled Banner."

**SHEILA:** Do you think people with style think about it and cultivate it, the way one can alter one's own handwriting?

**ALEX:** As young humans we learn to navigate the world—a very difficult ballet. We get so good that it becomes almost totally automatic. But then we go to a foreign country, or have some of our parameters messed with, and we have to start over, at least partly. I think people with style maintain a sense of that starting over always, a sense of knowing how to do it, but also learning how to do it at all times.

**SHEILA:** I love this idea that people with style are always relearning. It can be depressing to discover oneself wearing, as a grown-up, what one liked back in high school.

**ALEX:** That's what distinguishes the stylists. They change, they're alive. That sense of always relearning means the stylists are not just unconsciously inhabiting whatever their prevailing way is. They are conscious. But they're not self-conscious, overthinking beings. They have *sprezzatura.* They are philosophers in that they are a little outside—but their philosophy is entirely practical.

**SHEILA:** What is philosophy, to you?

**ALEX:** It is reflection. It responds to reality and turns it around a bit. Philosophers think through what is taken for granted by most people. I called the stylists "practical philosophers" because they have that, but their activity is not in their thinking, rather their thinking is in their style, in the way they move, dress, inhabit the world.

**SHEILA:** Has being newly in love changed your style, your way of moving through the world?

**ALEX:** I think so. People have been remarking on how well I look. And I definitely feel a greater suppleness, a sense of being a finer, more receptive instrument.

**SHEILA:** Yes, your body language is so different with her in the room.

**ALEX:** She is so strong and individual, she fills the room.

**SHEILA:** You have to respond to the wave that is her. She is your new wave.

**ALEX:** Yes, we navigate around each other. ✕

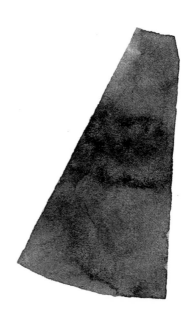

## STYLUS | MICAH LEXIER

I've always been interested in other people's handwriting, and have made a number of artworks, often in steel or acrylic, using handwritten names. In preparation for these artworks I ask a person to write his or her name in black pen on a piece of paper many times so I'll have some options to choose from. Instead of signatures, I like to have them handwrite their name as a way of presenting themselves. These sample sheets are the written equivalent of the changing room or one's bedroom, where one tries on different clothes or looks.

Jean
Jean
Jean
Jean
Jean
Jean
Jean
Jean
Jean

Jean
Jean
Jean
Jean
Jean
~~Jean~~
Jean
Jean
Jean
Jean

Jean
Jean
Jean
Jean
Jean
Jean
Jean
Jean

Andrena Morrish ANDRENA.M.

AMorrish ~~Andrena~~ Andrena Morrish

Andrena Morrish AMorrish Andrena.M.

Andrena Morrish ANDRENA MORRISH

Andrena Morrish Andrena Morrish

Andrena Morrish Andrena Morrish

AM. Andrena.M. Andrena Morrish

ANDRENA MORRISH Andrena Morrish

Andrena Morrish. ANDRENA . MORRISH.

mandy   mandy   mandy   mandy

mandy   mandy   mandy   mandy

mandy   mandy   mandy   mandy

mandy   mandy   mandy   mandy

mandy   mandy   mandy

mandy   mandy   mandy   mandy

mandy   mandy   mandy

mandy   mandy

mandy   mandy

mandy mandy

mandy mandy mandy mandy

mandy mandy mandy mandy

mandy mandy mandy mandy

mandy mandy mandy mandy

mandy mandy mandy mandy

mandy mandy mandy mandy mandy

mandy mandy mandy mandy mandy

mandy mandy mandy mandy mandy

mandy mandy mandy mandy

mandy mandy mandy mandy

mandy

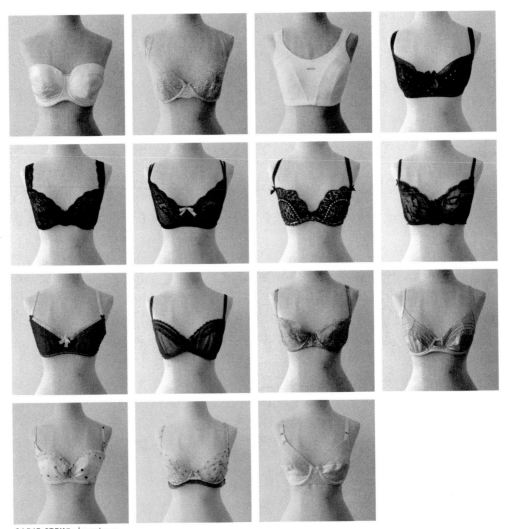

*SADIE STEIN*'s brassieres

# I DIDN'T BUY THE BABY ANY CLOTHING

## MAD MEN WRITER SEMI CHELLAS SPEAKS TO SHEILA HETI

SHEILA: I'm so interested in the idea of a "deep style" and how everyone has one—even if a person is not aware of what it is. I think it cuts across everything you do. Can we figure out yours?

SEMI: I feel like I have no style. I feel like a human collage. I moved to L.A. suddenly. I had a job interview on Friday and I started on Monday. We quickly got a place online, and I put a note on Facebook that said we needed furniture, and so many people offered us furniture. The only thing we ended up buying was a TV. *(A baby cries.)*

SHEILA: Were the baby clothes donated, too?

SEMI: Yeah, I didn't buy the baby any clothing. So now we have this hilarious house, and nothing goes together because it's all from different people. I had this myth in my head that in Toronto my home was stylish and I was put-together, but then I realized that it wasn't true—my furniture has always been donated.

SHEILA: Do you think there's any similarity between that and how you've handled your career?

SEMI: I've always operated on the idea that all I needed was the ability to say no—to make enough money to say no to stuff I didn't want to do—which is slightly different from saying there's stuff you do want to do. I sometimes feel like I should be more self-directed, but when I am, I feel like I'm in a safe zone. When I let myself be open to what other people think I should do, it's more interesting to me.

SHEILA: Does that correspond to how you dress?

SEMI: Yeah. I have one friend here who gives me clothes she doesn't want anymore. They're never clothes I'd buy, but they're much more interesting than the clothes I *would* buy, and I like wearing them. Most of my clothes have been hand-me-downs. People say, "Buy a jacket that will last you forever," and I think of how every time I did that, I abandoned it in some city.

SHEILA: Your romantic relationships—are they like your furniture and your clothes and your career? Have they also been "given" to you?

SEMI: Well, I was never interested in getting married. I never pursued relationships in the abstract, or cared if I ended up in a long-term relationship. I definitely never had a desire to have a wedding. I hate to say this, but with relationships I've often—like with cities—walked away when I felt ready to. Even with intense emotional relationships, I've had a tendency to leave them behind like litter, as I've done with my clothes and places I've lived. But when I found true love with Mike, it wasn't convenient, it was actually a lot of work, and it was one of the few relationships where I worked at it and went back to it and rode out the bad stuff.

SHEILA: Do you understand why you stuck it through with Mike?

SEMI: A big change came over me in the last few years, where I started to take on bigger commitments and be less afraid of them. Until I was thirty-eight, I thought, "I'm never having children!" because I thought I wouldn't be able to make that commitment to caring for them. Then something changed where I suddenly saw that I could. I had my first child at forty and my second at forty-three. I signed a contract with *Mad Men* for three years, and I'd never signed on to do anything for three years in a row, ever. I feel like I used to have this secret list in the back of my mind, of men I would be with, and places I would live, and no commitments I had would ever interfere with the fact of the list. Then Mike and I broke up for a year in the middle of our relationship, and I lost track of where he was in the world. During that time, I had an opportunity to cross something off my list, and I walked away from it. And it was the complete disintegration of the list. 'Cause I was like, "If I'm walking away from *this* . . ." Sea changes come over your personality—they literally do. After that, I reconciled with Mike and had a child and bought a house in Toronto, and it seemed like everything was going to settle down. I had this ratty old couch from my grandma, and I had it reupholstered. It was a huge outlay of money and commitment. Then, six months later, we had to move across the country, and we left the couch and everything behind. It made me realize that having a baby doesn't settle you down or give you a sense of what you're going to look like moving through your life.

SHEILA: So your style is to abandon a cohesive style in order to experience the extremes of life more fully, or to experience surprise more fully?

SEMI: I think so. To always try to keep things, myself, in the unknown. I think that's true.

SHEILA: How do you approach writing a script? Because writing for *Mad Men*—it's like these characters have been handed to you or donated to you like baby clothes.

SEMI: And my feature career has been adaptations of books. It's similar writing for a TV show, where you're working with found material. I can't believe I'm saying all this out loud. I feel so insecure about this— that my own imagination needs so much exterior material. I'm envious of artists who seem to work from a more internal place.

SHEILA: I can think of a number of people who could never live with mismatched furniture or hand-me-down clothes. What's going on at the core of you that links and normalizes and understands all these disparate elements?

SEMI: That's a question I have always wrestled with. I've always been able to put everything I own into a package and move it. Portability is my aesthetic at some level. Do you remember the cartoon that had a portable hole, a black circle you could go through or throw stuff in? I've always been obsessed with that image—this flat, black circle that can contain multitudes. The only thing I think I know about myself is that I can keep moving. I can always land in a city and figure it out. But there's a deep insecurity in me that there is no *there* there.

SHEILA: So the black hole is you?

SEMI: I think it kind of is. But it's actually an illusion. It's a 2-D flat circle that you can put all this stuff into and everything will disappear. Then you can tear the circle off and move it again. I guess it's an image of myself and aesthetic.

SHEILA: How do you work?

SEMI: This is interesting, thinking about this makes me feel like I have more of a pattern. I always try to have a room of my

Bag with toiletries

Computer bag

Set bag

Backpack / baby carrier

Breast pump bag

Diaper bag

at eleven at night I felt: I really have to go home now. I'd been away for twelve hours, backpacking around the city, and I had the newspaper, and a book I'd bought, and the breast milk, and I got home and dumped it all. I need to take everything and go somewhere that's not mine.

**SHEILA:** I'm so different. I need to be alone in my room. I'd hate to work away from my room.

**SEMI:** I've always spent a lot of time alone, being unaccountable. My whole aesthetic of living—a profound solitariness is part of it. For a long time, I had a really crappy apartment in New York, and sometimes if I was in a bad mood in Toronto, I would get on a train to New York without telling anyone. I loved living that way. Now I have kids and I can't go anywhere without five diaper bags and eight changes of clothes, but sometimes when I'm with Mike and the kids, doing something random, I'll have a profound sense of: These are my people, this is my tribe. It's not necessarily what you would think of as love—it's not a mushy, sentimental feeling, but a fierce "We're in this together" feeling. But saying that, I feel all itchy, like I should run and jump on a train.

**SHEILA:** But if it's your tribe, it becomes part of what you take with you. It becomes part of your identity and part of yourself.

**SEMI:** That's right. A tribe is very portable. This is part of what I'm taking with me. ✕

own and a desk and a space, but I always end up writing in the most uncomfortable, shitty cafés, where the coffee is bad and the bagels are worse. I fit everything I need into a backpack, and when I have to write, I grab my backpack and go wherever. Yesterday I set off to meet a friend for work with my backpack and breast pump and maxi pads to stuff my bra, and we went to a café and worked for ninety minutes, then I went to pump my boobs, then I went to another café and worked, then I went somewhere else, and

*MIRANDA PURVES*'s shirts with Peter Pan collars

# Young Kim

*What is the most transformative conversation you have ever had with someone on the subject of fashion or style?*
The bulk of my formative adult years—twelve years from the age of twenty-six—were spent with my boyfriend, Malcolm McLaren, until his death. We were extremely close, and at a certain point in our relationship, I believe we somehow became the same. This is why I think our relationship worked. As an artist—which Malcolm quintessentially was—he was naturally a narcissist. (Perhaps I am one, too.) But as we somehow became one ("We have to be the same," Malcolm would often insist), it enabled our relationship to constantly strengthen. In the last few years of his life, we never disagreed on anything—people, food, fashion, art, design, politics, film, books, ideas . . . We might have different personal preferences (for example, I don't like heavy political war films), but we would agree on our assessments of them. (Liking something is different from recognizing

that it is good.) Ultimately I believe we influenced each other equally. I was influenced by him and he was influenced by me. I can't imagine having more transformative conversations about style or fashion with anyone than I had with Malcolm. We used to talk about clothes all the time. He knew so much about fashion—from the historical to the practical, everything about the great couturiers and the fashion movements in pop culture. But he could get his hands dirty, too. He knew how things should be made—all the different techniques of fabrication, cloth, cut, et cetera. Looking at a pair of trousers flat, he could tell if they would suit you. Once, in Zurich, he took the bottle opener in the hotel and wedged it into a new pair of shoes (mine) to stretch them out. He knew exactly what he was doing. We both loved clothes and were obsessed by them. We loved shopping and looking . . . at everything, not just clothes. I often joked that shopping was our favorite exercise—shopping for cheese, shopping for wine, shopping for

linens, shopping for books, shopping for objects and furniture, shopping for clothes . . . We always went shopping together. The only problem was, I would get bored more easily shopping for men's clothes than he would for women's clothes. Men's clothes are just not as interesting! He would insist always that I come into the dressing room with him while he tried things on, and would reproach me when I started to get bored.

*When do you feel most attractive?*
When my skin is clear, my hair manageable, and I have the right complete outfit for the occasion.

*Are there any clothing items that you have in multiple?*
I don't buy things in multiple, but in the past fifteen years, I have had two special pairs of boots that I have replaced when they became completely worn-out. I am on the second generation of both. (I hope they will continue to be manufactured so I can keep replacing them.) One is a pair of black patent-leather Courrèges

go-go boots, which I wear in the rain. They are not necessarily intended for inclement weather, but they are durable enough for a rainy walk in the city. I love them because, first of all, no one wears them. Furthermore, I think the design is chic and timeless. I like the fact that they are unchanged from the sixties and still beautifully made in France. The spacey style is always cheery on a rainy day, and the surprising lightness allows one to trot around dodging raindrops. The other is a pair of traditional sealskin boots from Norway with soles like tire treads, lined in shearling with bright red laces. They are the best footwear for snow. Malcolm originally bought them for me at the Swedish shop in Paris next to the Brasserie Lipp. (He had worn sealskin boots himself in the seventies.) When I tried to replace them recently, I discovered they were now banned in Europe, so I had to get a Norwegian friend to bring them from Norway for me. I happen to have a Balenciaga white rabbit coat banded in horizontal strips of red felt, which I often wear with the boots. Once I wore this coat during a France–England football game in Paris and realized I looked like an England supporter.

*What's your process getting dressed in the morning?*
I do not get dressed until I am going out. Since I work at home, this can mean the afternoon. I will wear a slip until then. However, when I am getting dressed, because of global warming, the first thing I do is check a weather site that charts the weather hour by hour. If I am going to an important appointment, I will have already thought through what I will wear. In the film *Shame*, a character tells her date that she spent an entire hour deciding what to wear. When I brought up this scene with the director of the film, Steve McQueen, he explained it was to show how much effort she had put into the evening. He looked a bit shocked when I told him that I would never have waited until an hour before dressing for an important date to decide what to wear; I would have started working this out as soon as the date was set—and enjoyed every minute of mulling it over. If I am not going anywhere special, then I probably am in a groove with one set of looks or another. I go in phases.

*What are some dressing rules you follow?*
For me, the most important dressing rule is to think in entire outfits—dress, belt, stockings, shoes, jewelry, coat, scarf, gloves, bag. Once I have the outfit down, I don't have to worry about it. It's a bit of a luxury, but then again, it isn't, because if you don't have the right top for the skirt, you will never wear the skirt. Malcolm taught me to do this. He said he didn't understand why girls never thought in outfits but in separates. However, when I first met him, I was just a student and didn't have the means to buy many pieces at once. I tend to stick to one designer or another. (This is probably also due to Malcolm, who felt that a designer has a vision and you shouldn't tamper with it. The designer, as artist, would have conceived the various elements of the collection to marry together.) At the end of the nineties, until she stopped her brand, I wore Martine Sitbon head to toe. After a few wandering years mixing it up with Margiela, Marni, Lanvin, and Dries, I settled on Nicolas Ghesquière and Balenciaga. There is something about Ghesquière's aesthetic and cut that suits me like no other designer. It can be a crazy rock-'n'-roll showpiece or a severe Edition suit or simply a T-shirt, but for me, it's just magic. Since he's left Balenciaga, everyone has been asking me what I will wear.

*Do you think you have taste or style? What do these words mean to you?*
I think I have good taste and style. Taste can be about a specific thing. Style is about more than one element—it

is more of a painted canvas, an environment, or perhaps simply a feeling. It takes more creativity to have style. I believe there is such a thing as good taste and bad taste, good style and bad style. There are many kinds of good taste and good style, but there is definitely a demarcation on what is good and bad. Then, of course, there is no style and no taste.

*Are you photogenic?*
I am not, and I am relieved when others agree! I think I am terrible at posing, though maybe I am not as bad as I think, because I have posed a number of times for photographers, including a topless picture and a nude series, which have both been published. (But you can't see my face!) I am about to pose for a series of portraits wearing Louis Vuitton S/S 2013 for Alessandro Raho, a British painter. Personally, my favorite pictures of myself tend to be candid shots.

*What are some things you admire about how other women present themselves?*
Poise, carriage, manner of speaking, true style—not one based on status symbols and manners.

*Are there any figures from culture, past or present, whose style you admire or have drawn from?*

Aside from Malcolm, I imagine my list is the same as most people's—Hitchcock movies from the sixties, Audrey Hepburn, Coco Chanel, Faye Dunaway in *The Thomas Crown Affair*. I think the woman with the best style today is Kate Moss. She gets it right every time, and it's not just because she's Kate Moss that she looks great. She really has amazing inherent style.

*How do you shop for clothes?*
There are a few shops I like and I visit them regularly. The best city to shop for fashion is Paris, without a doubt. In Paris, it takes days to cover all the shops— hosiery shops, lingerie shops, glove shops, dress shops, shoe shops, bag shops, jewelry shops, antique shops, many of the original couture houses and flagship stores. In New York or in London, you can cover them all in an afternoon. I don't shop with the mission to find something. I shop to see what's going on. Like everyone, whenever I actually need something urgently, I can never find it, but in terms of fashion, you have a better chance in Paris than anywhere else. Many women complain they can't find anything they want; my problem is, I can always find something I want. I think you have to constantly look to find good things. Different shops stock different things,

and they come out at different times. Unless you're looking, you'll miss the right—or best—things. So maybe I never stop shopping.

*Do you have any shopping rules?*
Try not to make mistakes. Think it over. Better to get a few great pieces of quality you will wear for a long time rather than a lot of random, poorly made ones that you might never wear or that will fall apart.

*What is your favorite piece of clothing or jewelry?*
My most precious piece is probably a tiny antique pearl necklace—most likely a child's—from Hancocks in Burlington Arcade in London. It was a gift from Malcolm, who loved the idea that it was so tiny he felt only I could wear it. Also, because I am from Long Island, Malcolm associated me with Oyster Bay and oysters and hence pearls. In regard to my favorite piece of clothing, it's difficult to say, but perhaps it is my black waxed-cotton trench coat from Lanvin. It is a raincoat that actually is not only pretty but waterproof and light and that breathes, unlike vinyl. The British, in particular, seem to like it, maybe because the mackintosh is such an inherent part of British culture.

*What's the first "investment item" you bought?*
I hate the term "investment item." This is a modern term that strips fashion of its romance and artistry and makes it cold and corporate. Fashion should be bought because one loves it and looks wonderful in it, not because it is an "investment." I have never thought of fashion, or anything else in this way. I find it cynical and depressing.

*Do you care about lingerie?*
Yes, though it is a luxury. It is easier to indulge in it in France, as there is quite pretty and decent-quality lingerie at all price points. I prefer natural fiber to synthetics, and I really care about quality and French manufacturing. Most of my lingerie is silk or cotton from a sweet little boutique in Paris called Fifi Chachnil. Naturally, I wash it by hand. I hate wearing bras, so I don't go as far as the French, who insist on matching bras and panties—though I have a few sets. But then again, the French are known for going braless, too!

*How does how you dress play into your ambitions for yourself?*
Clothes have always been very important to me. Since I was a small child, I was aware of clothes and had very strong feelings about them. My mother and father both have excellent taste and care about clothes, too. Though we didn't indulge in any nonessentials, my parents would buy clothes—especially for us children. People often think fashion is frivolous, but it isn't—at least for some of us. Clothes give you confidence and power to do things you might not be able to do otherwise. It puts you into a role. This even applies to uniforms in war. (Malcolm told me the head of a uniform factory in Poland explained that the Nazis understood fashion and designed great uniforms—which this factory had produced. When the Stalinists took over, they were smart enough to simply change the color. This man said that if Mao had had better uniforms, he would have been more successful.) People perceive you differently and treat you differently. How I dress has literally changed my life. At the same time, I dress for myself, not others.

*What is your cultural background, and how has that influenced how you dress?*
I am what is called a 1.5-generation Korean immigrant. Because of this, I was brought up with a certain formality, which includes emphasis on presentation and the idea that how you look communicates respect (or lack thereof) toward others. It is more close to European culture than American culture, in which, as far as I am concerned, anything goes and comfort is overrated! I was raised to wash things properly (for example, hand-wash, air-dry), and to mend and iron. My roommates were bemused when I arrived at Yale with an iron, an ironing board, a drying rack, a soaking bucket, and a sewing kit.

*Can you say a bit about how your mother's body and style have been passed down to you, or not?*
Why do you think only a mother's style and body can be passed on to a woman? My mother was a great beauty and has good style. She is right in thinking I look better in more formal and structured clothes than casual clothes, though she chose to buy me my first pair of stretch jeans in bubble-gum pink and a graffiti-print shirt when I was thirteen. However, in terms of body, I am exactly like my father. We have the same slight bone structure and we even have the same beauty mark on our lower left eyelid. People always think we are identical, though I don't see it. As in the Korean saying my mother uses, "You can't deceive the seed!" My father also has a great eye and taste.

*Can you recall times when you have dressed a particular way*

*to calm yourself or gain a sense of control over a situation?*
Clothes are my greatest material pleasure. Nothing makes me as happy as a beautiful new dress. When people have suggested I see a therapist for my grief, I have answered (quite truthfully) that I prefer to spend the money on clothes. They give me great pleasure, serve a purpose, and help me with my work. (I often say I have clothes instead of assistants!) Once, when I was in high school, I received an unfair grade on my report card. I went psychosomatically blind. My mother picked me up, calmed me, took me clothes shopping, and I recovered.

*How does makeup fit into this?*
I don't wear much makeup. I'm not very good with it. A bit of eyeliner and mascara. Sometimes lipstick or gloss, sometimes foundation and powder. However, I do love costume parties and enjoy going all the way on such occasions, including the makeup.

*What's with your hair?*
You would think someone who is artistic and good with her hands would be good at dealing with hair. I am terrible at styling hair and I am relieved that I have figured out a simple twisted chignon, which I don't intend to change. Once Malcolm threatened

to cut my hair while I slept. He said he'd done that to Vivienne Westwood and gave her her signature look. I told him I would kill him if he dared do such a thing and I would also shave off one of his eyebrows. That was the end of that idea!

*Please describe your figure.*
I am, as Malcolm called me, "a stick insect." I have relatively long limbs and digits, and a long neck, to which Malcolm attributed my chronic neck and shoulder problems. As for my bow legs, he surmised that my ancestors must have ridden horses through the steppes with Genghis Khan.

*Is there any article of clothing, makeup, or accessory you carry with you every day?*
I always carry a Smythson page-per-day diary in my bag.

*Do you have style in any areas of your life aside from fashion?*
Yes. I have specific ideas about food, design, and behavior, which accorded with Malcolm's and ran into our work. A friend described our life as a *Gesamtkunstwerk*, which is probably accurate. Neither of us was materialistic and we chose things from the heart. Quality of life was important to us, as was integrity. We never amassed much beyond a few clothes and books. We made it a point to acquire things of

good quality, made mainly in Europe, that would last. (I hate disposables.) There was an inherent pragmatism and simplicity but also a certain romantic and whimsical quality to our life together. Our home in Paris, which was originally the studio of my favorite painter, Kees van Dongen, reflected our overall aesthetic philosophy. I had it photographed just after Malcolm died, to have a record.

*What would be a difficult look for you to try to achieve?*
I look terrible in anything hippie-ish or trashy. For instance, caftans or Cavalli.

*How is this stuff important?*
It's not important to everyone, and there is nothing wrong in its not being important to someone. But it is important to some of us.

*Where were you born and where do you live now?*
Seoul, Korea. I live between New York and Paris.

*Are you single, married?*
I am single since Malcolm passed away. He is in fact the only relationship I have ever had. I do not have children. I have never cared about them. Perhaps this is why I could give everything to Malcolm and be his best friend. He called me his "buddy with breasts." ✕

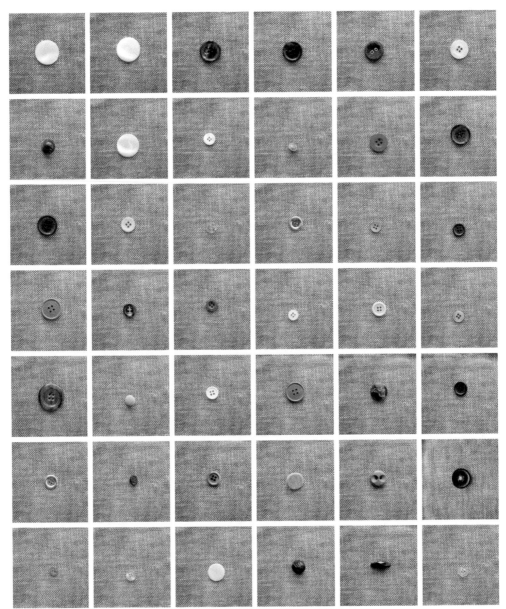

*JEMIMA TRUMAN*'s spare buttons

# MODEST AND NAKED

*"My mother wanted me to know that when she was sixteen, any skirt with a hem that extended past the fingertips was considered too long."*—MEGAN HUSTAD

**AUGUSTA LEE** I dress more conservatively at church than I do during the week. I feel like it's a meat market and a fashion show when I go to church. Girls dress up to try and get married.

**EUFEMIA FANTETTI** I was just leaving my toddler days behind me, and I'd been woken up from an early-afternoon nap. I looked out between the bars of my crib and saw two children staring at me. My mother announced that my cousins from Montreal had come to visit. I was wearing an undershirt and pajama bottoms, and I remember feeling intensely exposed. I turned away from everyone in embarrassment.

**SASHA ARCHIBALD** My parents are ultraconservative Christians and had tons of rules about clothing. I remember I had to change one day because I was wearing leggings with a tight sweater. It was strange because I didn't think the outfit pushed the boundaries of modesty. I needed them to explain why it was immodest. It was always my mom's job to convey what I was allowed to wear or not, but my mom and dad would confer on the decision. When I went to high school dances, all three of us had to go shopping together, and of course nothing cute was modest enough.

**E. M. HECTOR** My evil twin tells me, "Think of those ladies you see with their 'stuff' hanging out. Is that what you want to look like? What would your mother say if she saw you wearing that? Is that what you want everyone to see?"

**ALICIA BERNLOHR** My parents worked for the American government and we lived overseas, and we were supposed to represent the United States wherever we went. This meant I could not dye my hair magenta or have a septum ring. I have never completely recovered from my early style censorship, and my tastes at the office are still fairly modest and unassuming, so as not to draw too much attention to myself. Because of this, my rebellions are small but extremely important. For example, I have white tube socks that say, above the ankle, I DON'T GIVE A FUCK. No one knows this but me. I'm in a good mood whenever I wear them.

**DOROTHY DENISOFF** I don't show bra straps and nipples, and you won't see a G-string when I bend over. I do show cleavage, but no belly shirts that announce my rolls.

**SASHA GREY** When I ended my first long-term relationship, I was nervous about dating. Living in L.A. doesn't help, so I decided to dress in combat boots and leather jackets every time I went out. I like to dress up and be wanted, but at this time I didn't know what I wanted, so I didn't want to project myself in that way. I guess I have disdain for young women who dress half naked but scowl when you glance their way.

**LUCY BIRLEY** At fifty-five it's a bit weird if you show a lot of flesh and wear short skirts and things. I don't think that's a good look, really. I think it's quite sad.

**LAUREN REITER** I remember going up to the door of my friend's house when I was five. I was topless, since it was summertime, and their German nanny or relative opened the door and gave me the most withering look, which even then I understood as a condemnation of my nakedness.

**CLAIRE O.** I remember my mother telling me that clothes are fine, but she has always preferred the way she looks naked. I liked that.

**GINA SHELTON** I am more concerned with modesty than the look of my body. I'm afraid I'll flash people or appear awkward. How do women walk and move so confidently in miniskirts? What will people think of me in a tiny dress?

**CATHY DE LA CRUZ** This past summer, I lived for a month at a retreat center, Esalen, in Big Sur, California. I learned to relax, enjoy myself, and get comfortable with my naked body in public. On Fridays, I would work all day doing something very unglamorous like cleaning cabins, then at four or five p.m., I would go to the heated outdoor swimming pool overlooking the ocean and just strip off my work clothes and jump in completely naked in front of whoever was around. By the end of my time at Esalen, I felt so comfortable in my own skin that when the guy I was dating came to visit me, I had never felt sexier or more attractive. I wasn't one bit self-conscious about my naked body. It made the sex so much better.

**EMILY COYLE** I love seeing bodies and finding out how different and odd and complicated they are. It's always exciting for me, so I imagine it must also be exciting for the person I'm with. I think, "Your body is so you, and mine is so me!" That always makes me feel okay about anything I might otherwise feel less okay about—my tummy, my stupidly long legs.

**REN JENDER** I've always wished that toplessness were legal for women in my state, and didn't draw as much attention as in the states where it is legal, especially during heat waves.

**HILARY PROSSER** I went through a nudist period and for a long time I didn't wear any underwear. I guess it was about feeling unrestrained. I did quite a lot of unintentional nudity as my clothing fixes were always sloppy and there were many times when the safety pin holding my outfit together completely gave way. I must have caused embarrassment to a lot of people, not least my parents, who had to endure my nude-cooked dinners. ✕

## WEAR AREAS | ADITI SADEQA RAO

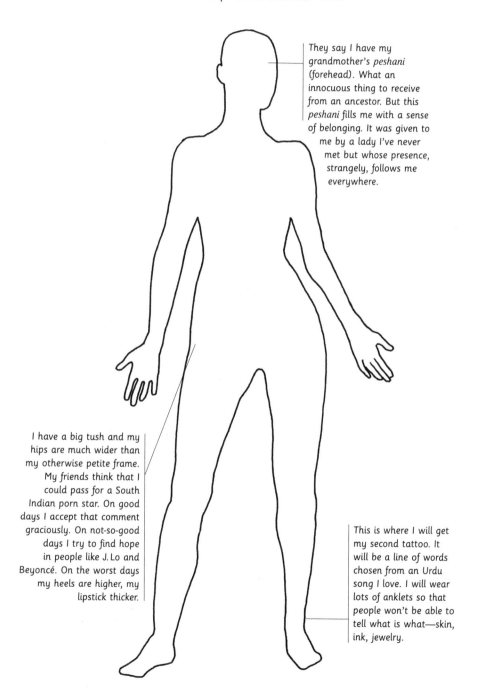

They say I have my grandmother's *peshani* (forehead). What an innocuous thing to receive from an ancestor. But this *peshani* fills me with a sense of belonging. It was given to me by a lady I've never met but whose presence, strangely, follows me everywhere.

I have a big tush and my hips are much wider than my otherwise petite frame. My friends think that I could pass for a South Indian porn star. On good days I accept that comment graciously. On not-so-good days I try to find hope in people like J. Lo and Beyoncé. On the worst days my heels are higher, my lipstick thicker.

This is where I will get my second tattoo. It will be a line of words chosen from an Urdu song I love. I will wear lots of anklets so that people won't be able to tell what is what—skin, ink, jewelry.

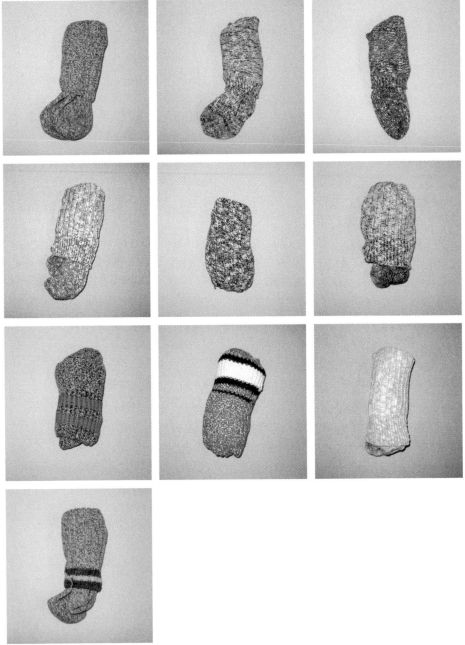

*LISA PRZYSTUP*'s marled socks

# 1989

**CATH LE COUTEUR** *as told to Heidi Julavits*

I started university in '89. This was a time of AIDS, a time of much sadness, a time, too, when queer nightlife in Sydney celebrated sex, style, and play while the media was telling us that being gay meant we were going to die.

It was still pre-treatments. So many guys were dying. Dressing up at night was a way to take action against the AIDS horror and stigma. One shouldn't underestimate the power this kind of style activism had. Sydney became renowned as the activist place where HIV prevention evolved from abstinence to safe sex.

The goal when we dressed up was to be as outrageous and in-your-face as possible. Also more sexual than ever. A really important aspect was to acknowledge sex and desire as still integral to gay identity—humor and fun, too. People would go out in the most brilliant outfits, like all Burberry plaid—face, skin, hair, bag, shoes. My friend Nic tied a clear plastic tube around his waist and filled it with water and live goldfish. Car Crash Victim was a costume I really liked—I'd go out like I had just been hit by a car. Or as Ken from Ken and Barbie. Or I would dress up as a cupid boy angel with glittery wings and smuggle Ecstasy and fags into the hospitals to the gay guys who were seriously ill. These guys had pneumonia and collapsed lungs and they were like, "Keep bringing me fags." My friends and I did that a lot. In our cupid outfits, we were basically saying, "Here we are with our love! Here we are with our Ecstasy for you. We're here to make you happy. You might be dying, but you're gonna go out feeling fucking great." That was part of our duty, really.

Brenton Heath-Kerr, this amazing artist who died in '95, aged thirty-three—he was famous for his gingham-print look. In fact, he was the one who kicked off the all-one-pattern outfits, as in all polka dots or plaids or stripes, hair and skin included. Toward the end he did a show dressed in a full-body skeleton outfit, holding a drip. He'd perform in nightclubs, skinny as fuck. He was in real physical pain by then, but so defiant, so brave. It was dark, we were all on drugs, it was messy and super-sad, but it was also extraordinary.

There was also an explosion of what we used to call sex subculture parties, boys and girls mixed up all the time, so "queer" really took on its identity as a practice and a community and an activist group. Every possible sex practice you can think of was explored at these parties. The idea of multiple representations was very much a part of things. In the lesbian community, girls were reading glamour mags and wearing leather and lots of lipstick and playing around with being femme or butch or combination or trans or whatever. It was all about a fluid identity and politics—not the old-school "You can't shave under your arms and you've got to wear dungarees if you've got any lesbian integrity." It was about the girls' going designer, wanting fast and loose sex, aping the boys in that way.

Then there were these dance productions we'd put on twice a year. Boy George, Kylie Minogue, those kinds of people would headline. Grace Jones. The shows would go all through the night—till seven. We'd spend three months rehearsing for this one night. The tryouts were fierce. In one show I wore the brushes of a red broom as a mohawk, and red leather shorts, and my tits were popping out of this red bra thing. That was not an outfit I'd wear normally— it was too girly for me. I wouldn't go around with my tits out. Lots of girls did on a regular basis. I loved men's suits. I've always loved men's suits.

I was working as a waitress. Daytime was jeans and a T-shirt. But we'd knock off from waitressing or whatever, meet around four, and people would start asking, "What's your outfit?" This was for a normal Tuesday night. Outfits required hours of thought and cheap solutions. We would trip down to the hardware store because there were always amazing things, like chains and ropes and flags, plumber bits and tubes; then we'd go to the cheapest supermarket and get Glad wrap and foil. You were never allowed to borrow people's ideas. Don't *ever* do that. You had to be totally original. You could repeat your own outfits, but you certainly couldn't repeat someone else's. Nic, I remember, had this amazing bathing cap, fuck knows how he found it, it was a *Jaws* bathing cap, the head of the shark with the open mouth bouncing around when he walked. He painted his torso blue and wore a blue tutu and hard-core blue leather boots. And I remember him getting into a fight the following week when someone else wore the same shark cap. He was like, "You fuck," and the other guy said, "Bitch, it looks different," and Nic said, "Take it off right now! It's mine!" It mattered.

Of course, it wasn't always fun and easy to be dressed this way. Along one strip of Oxford Street—our gay mile— and Darlinghurst—our gay ghetto—it was fine, but outside that it was not great. I remember once I was walking toward a group of drunk guys, fifteen, sixteen years old, there were about six or seven of them, and I was in a wetsuit jacket and an Astro Boy tee. I recognized really quickly that this was not a great scenario. I was like, *They're drinking, they're checking me out, and there's a group of them.* I was trying to work out where to cross the street, but if I crossed, it might draw more attention to me. So I was like, *No, I'm on a straight line here. I'm holding the course.* Within ten feet, the first aggressive comment came: "Are you a boy or a girl?" I waited until I got really close, then I said, "Yes," and kept walking. ✕

# IF YOU LIKE IT, I LIKE IT MORE

NEWLYWEDS **TALITA** & **BEN** IN A CAR DURING LONDON RUSH HOUR

**BEN**: If something interesting's going on, it doesn't matter what you're wearing, obviously.

**TALITA**: Interesting? Like what?

**BEN**: Well, if we're having a conversation.

**TALITA**: Then it doesn't matter what I'm wearing?

**BEN**: Yeah, because it's not the thing. But if nothing's going on . . . what it does is it adds something. It adds a certain level of enjoyment to a day if you're wearing something nice. So, you know, there's a hundred thousand times a day I will just glance around and look at you, and if you're wearing something nice, I might think: Oh, that looks nice. I will get enjoyment throughout the day.

**TALITA**: Moment to moment.

**BEN**: Yeah, moment to moment. I'll keep getting a thrill out of looking at you. There's a part of me that likes to think you're not doing it just for me, because then it feels stupid, like I've asked you to do this and you're doing it for me, rather than you like feeling sexy, too. Part of the experience is: If you like it, I like it more. If you don't like it, I don't want you to do it. Though I secretly want you to do it. But I also want you to like it.

**TALITA**: This is all something I wasn't that switched on to until I met you. But it's something that's changed a bit since I met you, my style and the clothes I wear. Like, I'll wear high heels a lot more often, and it's something, before I met you, that I

would wear maybe once a year to some really posh thing.

**BEN**: I don't mind the idea that I've turned you on to a way of enjoying that—

**TALITA**: Yeah. Because I love that interaction with you.

**BEN**: And it's a thing you can play with. It fulfills a bit of a fantasy of mine, and I also feel really grateful because I feel like you're doing it for me. You don't have to, but you are. And you're willing.

**TALITA**: Every time I get dressed I think: Do I look good for you? Which to me is a very welcome thing in my life, something to get dressed for. Like when I was at school, I actually enjoyed having uniforms because I thought: I'm wearing this for a purpose, which is being a student. I enjoyed that because it's better than just waking up every day and opening your wardrobe and having all those questions.

**BEN**: I think mistakes initially were made, in that you thought: I have to do this, otherwise he's not going to love me. And I thought: I really want a guarantee that she's prepared to do that because it's important to me. It got to be too much pressure. But I think without the pressure, it just kind of works out nicely.

**TALITA**: Yeah, we've found enjoyment. Of course, there is an element of neurosis, but I think we've sort of worked it in our favor.

**BEN**: When we first met, I spent a lot of money on nice clothes and boots and everything for you. But that hasn't carried on. It was like: Okay, you have that. It's not like you have to get loads more clothes. It really is like a bit of a uniform, I guess. Without the horrible connotation, which is that you have to do it.

TALITA: To me it is a sort of fantasized neurosis. Like one of those really rich bastards who have a . . . I don't know, a swimming pool in their basement full of gold coins or something. When you have the ability to do that, the means, you can sort of roll in your neurosis.

BEN: For me it's just a sexual-enjoyment thing. I mean, why else would I care what you're wearing?

TALITA: Would you have that with me wearing a really expensive coat and that flannel shirt that you really like, that hangs on my boobs nicely?

BEN: It depends. . . . I guess the sex thing is all about fantasy. The fantasy of like, You're that woman I always wanted and I never thought I could have. Like a woman wearing a really sexy jacket and really nice boots and everything. Where I grew up and among the people I grew up with, nobody was interested in that. So I guess it becomes a fantasy: Wow, I'm actually with somebody like that. It sounds more neurotic than it is.

TALITA: No, I think I understand.

BEN: Once I found it, I was afraid: Oh my god, I'm going to become a horrible person if I indulge in it. It's going to be this insatiable black hole of desire that twists you into something I don't like and you don't like, either. That's the fear: that I would be happy to buy you clothes every day and tweak what you have every morning and spend half an hour saying, Oh no, don't do this, don't do that. But actually it's not like that.

TALITA: Yeah, it's more relaxed once you've had the lack out of the way.

BEN: Once I allowed it. There's this feeling that the reason it's bad is that you're never going to be satisfied. But remember I told you about my watch? I was never happy with the watch I had, and I wanted something that I really liked. It wasn't an obsession, but it was something I thought about. Then I saved up and bought this really nice Cartier watch, which I really liked. And then I thought, Okay, it's going to wear off and I'm going to feel guilty about it, because I'm going to want the next thing. But it didn't happen like that at all. I still get a lot of pleasure every time I look at it, pretty much the same as when I first bought it. It's the same with you.

TALITA: Part of the reason why I do it is to get it out of the way, because I know that if there was any sort of resistance to it, it would become a problem.

BEN: That doesn't sound good.

TALITA: I mean, you do agree with me. It would be a bigger problem if I said, No, fuck that, it's not important for me. It would be a bigger problem than if I just did it.

BEN: Yeah, absolutely.

TALITA: And if I just do it, then there's room for me enjoying it.

BEN: How many times have I mentioned it in the last five months?

TALITA: Not very often, it's true. We've spent days in our pajamas when you didn't say anything, whereas in the past there was all that tension of, you know, Can you do your hair?

BEN: I think clothes are just one of the ways where you can express something different and look different, and it's exciting to look fresh, to look like a new person.

TALITA: That threatens me.

BEN: Does it? But if you wear the same thing every day, it becomes completely irrelevant what you're wearing, it's just you. Because you can change, it makes me look at you afresh. I think also it's worth mentioning that I'm an incredibly aesthetic person. The aesthetics of things are extremely important to me.

TALITA: True.

BEN: When I first met you, your sense of style was really not that switched on, because you thought: Oh, I don't have an attractive body.

TALITA: I wouldn't say that. I just hated spending money on clothes, so I'd get clothes from my mum.

BEN: What I'm saying is that the relationship you had with your body was distorted, as it is for most women: they think they look a particular way and the most important thing is to hide that feature they don't like, so they plan an outfit completely around a feature they don't like, and actually it's totally irrelevant. It creates something way more obvious.

TALITA: What are you trying to say? What's your point? Because—how do I explain this? I think how I felt was: If I can just try to convey this not-readiness in me, this girly thing, I don't really have to think very much about who I want to be or what I want to show. There was all sorts of hiding. But I don't think it was from being ashamed of certain things, it was more from not being particularly proud of anything, and therefore wanting to avoid the whole question of being a woman and owning it. Like when girls started wearing high heels and makeup. They were very ready for it, and I wasn't, I think.

BEN: A few girls I've been with, they've all felt like they can't be that person, or they've missed the chance to do it. In some way they've missed the boat, and it's too embarrassing, or it's too much effort to admit that actually, yeah, I want that. Because they've been left behind in a way. So they turn it into reversal—I don't want it anyway—and actually they secretly do. Like girls I'd help with shopping, they'd be really shocked that they could look like they wanted to.

TALITA: Because of body image?

BEN: No, because of some factor that happened in the teenage years. I don't know what, I've never really discussed it, but maybe everyone else was being really enthusiastic about high heels and makeup, and you don't feel like you can. You think: I'm not that attractive. Or you're not

---

SURVEY *Do you remember the first time you were conscious of what you were wearing?*
When I got my First Communion dress at age seven. —EITHNE BARRON • I remember being four years old and unable to choose between a yellow and a pink pair of underwear. So I wore them both right on top of each other! Now I'm an underwear designer. —DAPHNE JAVITCH • I remember a time when I tied a piece of a T-shirt to my shoe. I thought it was an innovative bit of Pippi Longstocking–influenced shabby-chic. The kids at school made fun of me. They said, "You thought you'd be so cool if you'd tie a rag to your shoe, didn't you?" I was horribly ashamed that they saw right through me. I thought I was smarter than them, but they were smarter than me. —GABRIELLE BELL • I remember going to a Saturday art class with my mom where we painted fish with fabric paint and then pressed them against white T-shirts so that the image of the fish would appear on the shirt. —SIBYL S. • I wore my first training bra at a sleepover party. I didn't need one.

hanging out with the cool kids, so you don't enter that "Hey, I can do this" confidence.

TALITA: I don't think I wore shit clothes.

BEN: Let's say for example, my mum. She was always, I can't wear high heels, they don't fit my feet, they don't look good, I look stupid. She had this whole thing she'd repeated to herself since she was a teenager. Then I bought her a pair of high heels for her birthday, and she was over the moon. She thought she looked really sexy, she felt super-good, it was like: Wow, I get to be a girl who wears heels! Oh my god, I never thought I could! It was all in her head. She just had this whole mental blockage about it.

TALITA: Yeah, like my mental blockage.

BEN: I'm not saying you have a huge mental blockage. But with a lot of women, I've noticed this latent desire to be that person.

TALITA: I don't think I've ever had a latent desire that I didn't think I could fulfill. I think my mental block was more about "I'm superficial if I do this." If I'm wearing something that is sort of blatantly sexy, I think I look dumb. I think I look smarter if I'm wearing something that's kind of shit.

BEN: Maybe it's a fear of being laughed at because you're trying.

TALITA: Or not taken seriously. That is such a key feeling to girls growing up—you're supposed to be really sexy, inhumanely sexy, but if you look like you're trying to be sexy, you can very easily feel ridiculous.

BEN: That's the thing. It takes a leap into "Not only am I sexy, I know I'm sexy, I'm proud of it, and I'm going to own it," which is like a super-confident, powerful position.

TALITA: Yeah, it's very easy to avoid all that if you're a man. You can just not . . .

BEN: Exactly. No one cares. There's no: Hey, I want to show my sexuality. If you go too far, people think you're gay. And that's it.

TALITA: Yeah, there isn't really a way to express your sexuality as a man. I think it's true. I don't know what it means.

BEN: It means I just have to keep buying you clothes because I can't buy myself them.

TALITA: *(laughs)* I'm the loving, accepting wife of a transvestite. ✕

---

When I went to change for bed, all the girls giggled and made fun of me for wearing a bra. They were jealous, I know now, but I immediately threw the bra out. —M. WHITEFORD • In preschool we had a "Backwards Day" where we were told to come to school wearing our clothes backwards. This is the first time I remember having any intentionality behind getting dressed. I was self-conscious about wanting to fit in and be backwards enough—I didn't want to do it wrong. I think it was supposed to be a fun day, but I was so anxious about all the changes it would require and how to navigate them that I nearly vomited. —ALISSA NUTTING • I was about four years old and I was wearing a dress my grandmother had gotten for me. I loved my grandmother but I hated that dress. My mom took us to Anthony's Fish Restaurant for a nice lunch, and I refused to eat. Wearing that dress felt like the end of the world. My mom tells me that was the moment when she realized she would never dress me again. —CLAIRE COTTRELL • Wonder Woman underoos, 1979. I was three years old. I wanted them very badly because I believed if I wore them I would be Wonder Woman. —EMILY RABOTEAU ✕

# BILLIONAIRE CLIENTS

IDA LIU, MANAGING DIRECTOR AND HEAD OF NORTH AMERICA ASIAN
CLIENTS GROUP FOR CITI PRIVATE BANK, SPEAKS TO **HEIDI JULAVITS**

**HEIDI:** What do you wear to work? Is there a dress code at your office?

**IDA:** Formal business attire. I wear suits and dresses to work.

**HEIDI:** Are these guidelines written down anywhere? How do you learn them?

**IDA:** There are no explicit rules to formal business attire, but there are certainly guidelines to help you make the right choices, such as taking cues from colleagues and other industry professionals. I always followed the rule "Dress for the job you want to have."

**HEIDI:** How do you define "power suit"? Do you wear powers suits?

**IDA:** A power suit is a suit that gives you extra confidence and makes you feel great. If you don't feel great, you won't be performing to your max. Tailoring and fit are key! You can't go wrong with a black power suit—it also allows the audience to focus on you and your message.

**HEIDI:** Can you express personal flair when wearing a power suit? Or is the suit flair enough?

**IDA:** For me it's more about an interesting detail on the suit—an asymmetrical cut, appliqués, interesting buttons—and less about loud prints or loud colors. I'm not suggesting that you suppress your personal style. But you don't want your audience to be focused on your outfit rather than what you have to say. First impressions are formed within a few seconds, and nonverbal visual cues are extremely important.

**HEIDI:** Can you think of a time when what a person was wearing diluted the message?

**IDA:** I had a meeting with a woman who was wearing a super-heavy sparkly necklace, and I kept focusing on the necklace and wondering: It must be so heavy, it's such an interesting color, wow, that is so big! And while it was a gorgeous piece and would have been great to wear on the weekends or for a party, it was incredibly distracting to encounter it in the workplace.

**HEIDI:** How many suits do you own?

**IDA:** That's a hard question! I've been an investment banker since I graduated from college. I have a *lot* of suits. I have very specific taste and I am a very quick and decisive shopper.

**HEIDI:** How has the idea of business attire evolved in the past few decades?

**IDA:** Women are dressing more feminine. There's nothing wrong with skirt suits and there's nothing wrong with dresses. We can get away with a bare leg in the summer as long as we're wearing closed-toe shoes. When I worked in Asia, there was such heat and humidity, we wore a lot of short-sleeved dresses and suits.

**HEIDI:** What's an example of something you'd never wear to work?

**IDA:** I'd never wear something loud or outspoken. When you're having important investment discussions with billionaire clients, you don't want them to spend time focused on what you're wearing. You don't want them thinking, *Why is she wearing that loud print?*

# **STAINS** | LEANNE SHAPTON

*Various women's stains*

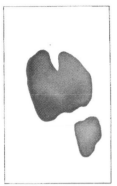

*French toast on coat sleeve.*

*Bicycle grease and hydraulic fluid on sweatshirt cuff.*

*Bleach on corduroy pant leg.*

*Tomato soup on shirt.*

*Ink on back of bra.*

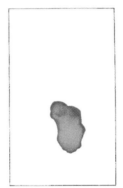

*Oil on kurta.*

*Blood, urine, hydrogen peroxide on back of coat.*

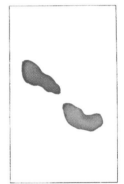

*Ink on jumpsuit.*

*Unknown.*

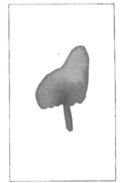

*Housepaint on boot toe.*

*Mascara on pillowcase.*

*Tahini on cable-knit sweater.*

*Ink on elbow of sweatshirt.*

*Armpit sweat on summer blouse.*

*Food spilled on T-shirt while cooking.*

*Bicycle grease on jeans.*

*Olive oil on silk shirt.*

*Yogurt on jeans.*

*Buttered bagel on coat lap.*

*Toothpaste on cardigan.*

*Coffee on jean jacket.*

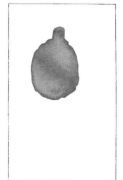

*Unknown stain on purse.*

*Oil paint on coveralls.*

*Blood on underpants.*

*BAY GARNETT*'s leopard-print tops

# PROTECTION

*"I find life rather terrifying, so I tend to dress to feel invisible and, in turn, safe. This makes me sound a little crazy, but I am not."* —ROXANE GAY

**ANNIE REBEKAH GARDNER** I dress protectively. Outside, people have told me I walk like a "dude," and that they daren't approach me because I look like I'm going to kill somebody.

**CLARE NEEDHAM** When I lived on the Mount of Olives in East Jerusalem, I would deliberately plan outfits that made me look as unattractive and asexual as possible. I would wear my boyfriend's shirts, which were baggy and loose. Once I even tried to wear his jeans. It was better to pull my hair back, to keep my nails unpainted, and to try to draw as little attention to myself as possible. None of these disguises really worked—I was still harassed. But choosing to dress myself in a modest way gave me the illusion of control.

**NINA MOOG** I usually wear eye shadow when I'm stressed. When I wrote my master's dissertation, I wore mascara every day. I am unsure what this means, exactly.

**BRYENNE KAY** In grade eight, my mother said I looked like a prostitute. I'd just grown boobs and hadn't realized that men noticed. I was wearing the same clothes I'd always worn, I just looked more womanly. What did she say, exactly? That I was trying to be a predator, when really I was the prey, and that the clothes I wore could affect my safety. Thanks, Mom!

**LORI HANDELMAN** I was severely abused in my childhood and lived on the street for three years in high school to get away from my terrible home. It took me a few decades to learn that I did not have to hide myself, that I could dress in an attractive way and still be safe, even be seen by others, by men, without too much danger. Dressing is really only now becoming fun and a pleasure. I am fifty-four years old.

**CARLA DU PREE** When I'm not quite up to feelin' folks, the big sunglasses come out and stay on, and with a tilt of an upward chin, folks don't say much. I don't allow them in.

**AURELIA BELFIELD** Fashion is a weapon. Fashion is 100 percent a weapon in my life.

**WEDNESDAY LUPYPCIW** When I was in grades eight to ten, I used to make "wearable-art sculptures" out of anything I found lying around, and wear them to school. There was a yellow fringe face-veil mounted onto wire antlers, a molded skirt made out of Sweet Valley High books, and a silk shirt with a rusted-wrench pattern, worn with the actual rusty wrench. Stuff like that. I was really shy. The sculptures were a way to make sure no one talked to me.

**JENNY DAVIDSON** I took up endurance sports in a big way six or seven years ago, and as much as things like bike shorts are unflattering, there is so much clarity about what's the best style and color. I will wear bright colors for safety without a qualm. I wish I could wear a navy blue boiler suit and have a shaved head, but if I did those things, they would attract attention rather than repel it.

**THERESA PAGEOT** I own one really expensive item. It's a really sexy blazer with these huge power-pockets. If I'm going somewhere I'm scared of, or where I feel like I don't really belong, I'll wear that blazer for a hit of courage.

**JOHANNA ADORJÁN** Once I was called by a friend who told me that the man I loved had just walked into a party in the company of another woman. He had minutes ago left my apartment, claiming he was tired and needed to go home to sleep. I immediately got dressed to confront him. I chose my highest-heeled shoes, and it felt a bit like dressing in war gear, like wearing armor. Also, they made me taller, which was exactly how I needed to feel. Unfortunately, when I arrived at the party, he had already left.

**MONIQUE AUBÉ** I wear a necklace every day. It's a volcanic stone from Mount Hekla in Iceland, which was thought to be the very gates of hell during the middle ages.

**JESSICA JOHNSON** Once I worked for a difficult woman who was a TV star. She always had hair and makeup done before going on a plane or doing anything in public. Although the superficiality of our world isn't lost on me, I realized that some security comes from knowing a professional has done your look, which leaves you much more confident in being your true self and getting the job done. So my favorite thing is to get a beautiful blowout, and then go and be a big weirdo.

**KATE SHEPHERD** I distrust anything that looks different from things I already own.

**LAURA SNELGROVE** My favorite dress at age three was a floral dress with tiny puffed sleeves. The smocking on the bodice allowed me to pull the neckline all the way over my head when in a seated tucked position, which felt like a secret hiding spot. It's my first memory of recognizing the potential for protection in clothing.

**ELEANOR JOHNSTON** When I lived in Kitchener, it had the highest rape stats per capita in Canada. I put heel and toe cleats on my ox-blood oxfords thinking I'd sound bigger and more forceful when I was walking home late from the library. Seemed to work.

**SADIE STEIN** There have been moments when I have felt insecure with women—with an ex's new flame, or someone I find intimidating—and I have found myself offering them something in my closet that I suddenly feel they must have. "It's never really been me," I might say, or, "I've been waiting for the right person to give it to." Sometimes these clothes are expensive, even beloved. They are always disarmed, and exclaim at my generosity. Then I feel slightly ashamed, because I am conscious of a rush of euphoria and relief: the balance of power has shifted.

**NATASHA HUNT** If you want to play into the shittiest and most irritating of racial stereotypes, I'm the token black girl. I've usually been one of a few brown kids in whatever circles I run in, so I tend to stand out. I think I wanted some semblance of control over my own feelings of belonging, of being the only one and occasionally gawped at. If you dress yourself as the "misfit," it becomes safer to interact in a world that has arbitrarily placed you as an outsider.

**CLAIRE COTTRELL** I used to be terrified of flying and I'd try to intuitively feel what I should wear. If I wore the right thing, the flight would be okay, and I'd get to wherever I was going. If I didn't, disaster would strike. I don't do that anymore. It's a very dangerous place to be. ✕

# THE PINK PURSE

EMILY GOULD

In the early spring of 2004, I was twenty-two and had just received my first tax refund. I didn't have any money, but I was close to money all the time. At the slick corporate publishing offices on the Upper West Side where I worked, the profit-and-loss statements were for hundreds of thousands of dollars, which it was my job to calculate, and I fetched coffee for established authors and agents—daily interactions that reassured me that my modest circumstances were only temporary. The hazy future would deliver me a big payday, so there was no need to save. I spent every penny I earned, which was easy to do: rent took most of it, food pretty much covered the rest.

When I unexpectedly got a check in the mail from the federal government for $342, I went out to buy a large, rectangular, pale pink Marc by Marc Jacobs handbag.

Why a purse? Why pale pink? Why Marc by Marc Jacobs? In 2004, Marc anything was the ultimate status symbol for a specific kind of New York City woman, the kind I aspired to be: someone with natural charisma, a cool job, effortless and understated sexiness, and plenty of cash. These garments seemed to represent a reaction against the blingy, logo-obsessed late nineties–early aughts. They were a credible imitation of clothes you'd find in a thrift store, but perfected and updated with better quality and cooler details: cashmere instead of polyester, and clever prints that invited a second glance or started a conversation ("Are those foxes?").

By the time I received the check, I had been lusting after those clothes for years. I felt a purse that I would carry every day would cast the glamour of Marc over my entire existence and transform my thrifted clothes into their classier renditions.

So I dressed in what I considered to be a subtle-yet-glamorous outfit, something the kind of person who frequented West Village designer boutiques would wear for a day of casual shopping: slouchy flat black boots, tight black jeans (then fashionably low-waisted), vintage black velvet blazer over a shrunken black perfectly worn-out and semitransparent T-shirt.

No one greeted me when I walked in the door of Marc Jacobs. I tried to make subtle, casual, "I'm not a shoplifter" eye contact with the pretty, dark-haired salesgirl, who was wearing an outfit like mine except with a halo around it, that intangible aura of expensiveness that designer clothes have. She didn't smile back.

"Let me know if I can help you find anything," she said without a question mark.

She closely monitored me as I picked up purses and modeled them one by one in the mirror.

I did my best to ignore her as I faux-casually compared price tags. The larger, heavier bags that I really wanted were $500 or $700, but after only a few minutes in the store that was starting to seem normal. The pink purse had soft leather and pretty clasp details, an inner pocket for my wallet and phone, and two outer pockets that could hold the many lip balm–type products I was equipped with at all times. I chose it quickly. I carried it to the register and paid with cash. I did not at that innocent time possess a credit card.

The purse made its debut at work the next day. As the editor in chief's assistant, I had a cubicle just outside his office. Everyone waiting to see him had to linger in my cube region, chatting with me. The women—all the important editors were women—treated me with a mix of admiration and exasperation. The most glamorous, P, was the first to notice my purse—casually hanging from a handle on the file cabinet behind me.

"Oh my god. Is that Marc by Marc Jacobs?"

"It is. I bought it with my tax refund."

She looked at me with a mixture of condescension and compassion. "Wow. Well, you're lucky. I wish I could go out and buy myself a Marc Jacobs purse."

I felt genuinely confused. "What's stopping you?"

She sighed. "When you're married, when you have a child, you'll understand."

I'm still not married and I do not have children, but I do understand. I had spied on every document that crossed my boss's desk, so I knew her approximate salary—it was a number that seemed enormous to me then, and still seems healthy now, except I know people with that salary who struggle to pay their mortgage in studio apartments in this beautiful, appalling city. Back then I had felt betrayed by P. If she couldn't buy a Marc by Marc Jacobs purse, what was I working toward? She owed it to me, to all us assistants, to give us something to aspire to. She owed it to us to dress for the job and the life we wanted.

Six years later—not half as secure, materially or otherwise, as my twenty-two-year-old self assumed I'd be—I set out a bunch of my belongings on my friend's Fort Greene stoop, including the once pink purse. Despite repeated professional cleanings, the color hadn't held up to the heavy wear I inflict on all my possessions. Also, pale pink is an impractical color for something you're going to set down on the grimy subway floor. The purse had lost its rectangular shape and sat slumped in a leathery pile. I sold it for $10 and, along with some other things, netted $40 that day—cash I needed and felt lucky to have. ✕

# CLOTHES ON THE GROUND

**JULIA WALLACE** *& translator Kuch Naren*

There are more than 400,000 garment workers in Cambodia, concentrated in a vast and growing sweep of factories in the dusty outskirts of Phnom Penh. The majority of these workers are female and rural, having been enticed by the prospect of a regular monthly wage to leave their farming families and move to the big city, or what passes for it. Migrant garment workers usually live in makeshift wooden barracks that spring up like mushrooms in factory districts, each room large enough to admit only a hard raised platform that serves as a bed, and a few personal belongings. Toilets and cooking facilities are usually shared. Factories transport the women to and from work in rickety flatbed trucks, cattle-car style. Dozens of workers are crammed into each truck, standing room only, for miles along the country's pitted and potholed highways. The trucks crash and overturn frequently. The cost of this rudimentary transport is deducted from their monthly salaries.

In Cambodia, below a smattering of brand-name chain stores such as Mango and Giordano, there are malls, which sell nondescript but fashionable clothes in unbranded stalls. Below the malls, there are the local *phsar*, the markets. And below the *phsar*, there is *krom chhat*: literally, under the umbrella. These are either secondhand garments or the cheapest possible factory-made goods, often imported from China. They are the only clothes garment workers can afford—sold out in the street, strewn on tarps spread out beneath umbrellas. The most brightly and gaudily dyed fabrics are the least expensive ones.

As a journalist in Cambodia, I have been interviewing garment workers about their lives for more than three years, but I never thought to interview them about what they wear, although I have often been struck by their de facto uniform: blue jeans, trucker hats, and screamingly bright T-shirts and hoodies in vivid shades of magenta or neon yellow, often accented with leopard print and rhinestones. It's a far cry from the drab attire conjured by the phrase "garment worker." I had always, perhaps naively, taken these colors as a way of asserting individuality in the face of the numbing repetitions of factory labor. But this turned out to be only a minor concern in the complicated calculus of dressing oneself on a salary of around $80 a month.

*Wearing black-and-white cotton paisley pajamas.*

I was born in Prey Veng [a poor rice-farming province on Cambodia's eastern border]. My parents were farmers, but they died around sixteen years ago. I also used to work in the rice fields before starting as a construction worker. After I got married and had my first child, I quit my job at the construction site because I thought working at a garment factory would be easier. First I sewed seams for warm jackets. It was really hard to learn to sew seams. I couldn't do it in a straight line in the pattern that was needed, and I would come too far in or too far outside the line. When I did that, I would always get blamed.

My husband is still a construction worker, and we have two sons, aged sixteen and thirteen. I want my kids to have a better life than me, so I had my older son quit school and enroll in a training course for television repair. The younger son is in grade 7. I would never allow my children to work at a garment factory. I am just working there because I have no other option. I have no idea what my future will be like—not just my own future, but all my colleagues' futures—because we're exposed to lots of chemicals where we work, and we don't make enough money to buy nutritious food. We don't eat for health, just to fill our stomachs.

I have been at the factory for two years. I work from 7 a.m. until 6 p.m., Monday to Friday, and 7 to 4 on Saturday, and make around $119 or $120 per month including overtime pay. Until the union was created, we worked until 6 p.m. on Saturdays. We have two lines where the garment workers sit to sew seams and each line has around twenty seats with sewing machines. In between the two lines there is a long table, and they put piles of fabric and jeans for us to sew seams on the table. There are two of these double lines, with around eighty to a hundred workers sitting around each table. It's really hot, because there will be 1,500 garment workers inside these big halls. Most of the workers need to wear long sleeves, because there are always fibers in the air. If they land on our skin, it makes us incredibly itchy.

The work is really boring, but I have to make a living, so I have to sew seams every day. I make jeans for Gap, Levi's, and a company called ATM. Even though I work at a factory that produces jeans, I don't like wearing *khao kaboy* ["cowboy pants"]. Usually when I'm at home I like dressing this way [in cotton pajamas], because it's cooler and the fabric is soft. Mostly I buy clothes that are sold along the street, because I don't have the money to afford expensive ones. Sometimes they set up the umbrellas in front of garment factories. Because we don't have the money, we don't think a lot about the style of the clothes. We just try to find something. Generally, the *kaohaov krom chhat* ["clothes under the umbrella"] cost around 10,000 riel [$2.50] for one

pair, and I'm wondering how those people afford those expensive jeans while my salary is so small. I sometimes wonder how I could ever afford them. They look beautiful, and I think how beautiful I would be if I wore them. Once I met an official from a clothing company and they told me that the jeans they wore cost $120. Sometimes we feel like our hearts hurt, because the Chinese staffers and superiors at our factories will tease us. They'll say that our salary is not worth a pair of their shoes.

o°₀°o

shirt or sometimes one pair of pants, and they're all very bright colors. I really love soft colors, they're more attractive, but the kinds of clothes that have nice colors are expensive. Here's an example of the clothes I bought under the *chhat*. This kind of fabric makes you cool.

*Did you buy this shirt because it says Chanel? That's a well-known brand in Europe.*
I never knew this Chanel. I cannot read, so I don't care what it means, personally. I'm never interested in brands. The most important thing for us is the price. If it's cheap, we buy it. I think the others are not different from me and would have the same thought: If it's cheap, we don't care about the brand. Actually, even though it arrives with the name of a brand on it, the fabric is not good and that's why it is cheap.

When I'm sewing seams, I always think that these jeans must be very expensive, they cost at least $40 to $50 per

### VANTHA

*Wearing jeans, a black knitted sweater with rhinestones on the front, a purple-and-white scarf, and a large black flower-shaped hair scrunchie.*

I entered garment factories more than ten years ago. Soon it will be my eleven-year anniversary. I first came to Phnom Penh from my home in Svay Rieng [a poor border province] in 1993. I decided to come because our family was very poor. I had eight siblings, but my dad couldn't afford to treat us well and we always had to borrow rice from our neighbors so we could eat. I first started working at a factory that made flour for bread. It was very dusty and smoky there, and my health was getting bad, so finally I decided to quit my job there and jump to a garment factory.

First I started sewing T-shirts and warm jackets, the kind that have a zipper in front. For T-shirts it was kind of like short- and long-sleeved shirts, but with split ends at the bottom. Now I work at a jeans factory, and my job is doing what we call double-sewing. My unit is called the final processing unit, meaning that we sew designs on the pockets of jeans and reinforce certain areas of the pants so they don't rip. You can see this kind of sewing I do here *(points to a yellow reinforced stitch on the side of my jeans)*. My group works longer hours than other units at the factory, usually twelve hours per day. Sometimes I can make $130 or $140 per month since we work more than other units, but if we're sick, then there is no money. Whenever we get sick, we always borrow from our landlords. The most sick leave we are ever granted is two days. Even then, we have to bring a doctor's note proving we are getting medical treatment. It's not easy to prove this, so usually our wages get deducted.

I am single. This was a choice. Because I am from a poor family, I was afraid that if I decided to get married, my husband wouldn't be a nice person, and I wouldn't be able to help my parents anymore. In the past, I used to send $10 or $20 to my parents in my home province, but lately I've been giving my money to help my brother, who was in a traffic accident during Pchum Ben [the Festival of the Dead]. He was impaled by a piece of iron.

The black sweater on my body now was bought under the umbrella, and it cost $5. The jeans were given to me by my niece, and she also gave me this scarf when she noticed I don't have nice clothes, so she wanted to help out. We never really decide to go shopping for new clothes, but when we get free time we might see clothes being sold under the umbrella along the street and in the spur of the moment decide to buy it. Sometimes, if I am interested in the style but don't have money in my pocket, I stop to bargain the price. Luckily, clothes *krom chhat* are cheaper than the same quality of fabric at a shop, like some might cost 15,000 riel [$3.75] in a shop, but *krom chhat* they charge us only 10,000 riel [$2.50]. Sometimes I might only have 10,000 riel in my pocket, but a shirt or something will be so nice that I'll just pay for the shirt and not buy food. Everyone loves good material and nice things to wear, and sometimes we workers really want to buy expensive or interesting styles, but we cannot afford it because we have small salaries, plus we need to adapt to the environment at the factory, which is very hot. We need the material that makes us coolest. I can wear this sweater today because it's my day off.

Even after working in factories for so many years, I have no savings. Nothing! I don't want to spend the rest of my life in a garment factory. I dream of having my own business. I would sell noodle soup. But I can't afford it right now. Every month, I find that I don't have enough money to put any away for savings. That's why I stick with the factory.

## LEAP

*Wearing a bright pink top with ruffles down the front and gathered sleeves, and a skirt printed with butterflies and strewn with glitter.*

I started working when I was twenty-two years old, and now I am thirty-five. Because we were poor and my family had only a small plot of land for doing rice farming, and especially because I was single and had no husband to feed me, I left my home province.

Since then, I have jumped from one factory to another. Now I'm at a factory producing underwear and bras, where I have worked for just over four months. I work between eight and ten hours a day at a factory owned by Koreans. It produces underwear for export, but I don't know the brand of bras I make since I can only read Khmer. I just know it is expensive, since it's a world brand name. I'm in charge of sewing a row of double stitches on the underside of the bras, like the bottom part of the cup. I make around $110 each month, which is my salary plus overtime.

I'm a widow. My husband passed away about three months ago and left me behind with two daughters. They stay with my mother in my home province, Kompong Thom. Of course it's not a happy life being separated from my kids, but I have to have a job to make money to send home and support them. I rarely meet them in person, but I talk to them on the phone a lot. The last time I saw them it was during Water Festival [about four months ago]. I go home in a tourist van [a twelve-seat van crammed with twenty or more passengers—a common means of rural transportation].

Farming rice is physically more difficult than garment work, and it can be uncertain, but at the end of the rice harvest we usually have some stock left over. As a garment worker, we have a secure long-term job, but it doesn't seem to make life better—there's not enough left over at the end of the month to save. Being here, everything is money. My salary goes to utility fees, accommodation, and transportation to the factory. After all my spending, I can usually send my family only 60,000 or 70,000 riel per month [$15 to $17.50]. I don't have a bank account, so I send it through a taxi driver, who charges 5,000 riel [$1.25] to take the money to Kompong Thom. The worst is that I have to live separate from my children. But I can't go back yet. I want to have money to buy a plot of land first. I just want to get a little savings so I can get back home with my family and my children and buy a small plot of farmland and rely on farming to feed my children.

My own everyday clothes I buy from street markets or *krom chhat*—I sometimes joke and call them "clothes on the ground," because even though they're under the umbrella, they're piled up on the ground. They usually sell them in this area on the weekend only, since on workdays we're too busy and nobody would buy them. When I go shopping, I don't prefer any design or style, but I look for cheap clothes that are not sexy. I mean, I want them to cover my entire body. I want decent clothes. I am a Khmer woman, and it doesn't look good to show off my top or my bottom, my chest or my hips.

My clothes are simple. I have around ten shirts, including T-shirts, and around five pairs of pants. I have three skirts. My favorite and most expensive outfit is the one I'm wearing today. I love the style of the ruffle on my shirt, and the bright color. It cost 8,000 riel [$2.00]. My skirt cost 10,000 riel [$2.50] and I got it at the market in Kompong Thom. I was attracted by the sparkles near the hip and the butterflies. My other clothes are just ordinary fabric with no specific sparkling materials.

I don't wear the bras I sew, I just buy the cheap ones from *krom chhat*. I pay around 2,500 riel for a bra [60 cents]. It's new but not a quality bra. The bras I sew and the ones I wear are quite different. I sew my bras very carefully and the stitches are very tiny and strong with good-quality thread. But the bra I wear is very bad quality and the thread is not double-stitched. It's sewn with larger stitches. Because I sew every day, I know that the quality is totally different.

While I am sewing bras, I often think about whether or not I could ever wear a bra like the ones I make. The bras I make are very beautiful with a variety of quality fabric and I sew them very well. The fabric is good, it's so soft, and it will make the person who wears it feel cool and comfortable. I used to think that if I could have one quality and beautiful bra like I make, I would be really happy and I would be very beautiful. But it's impossible. These bras are for export, and the price of one of the bras I make is almost equal to my salary. While working, I hold the bra up in front of my face, then I ask myself who is the woman who will wear the bra I am sewing. I also wonder how the women in those countries are so rich and lucky to wear these expensive bras while the person who makes that bra just wears a very cheap one bought from the pile of clothes on the ground under the umbrella. So I feel jealous. ✕

# WEAR AREAS | JILL MARGO

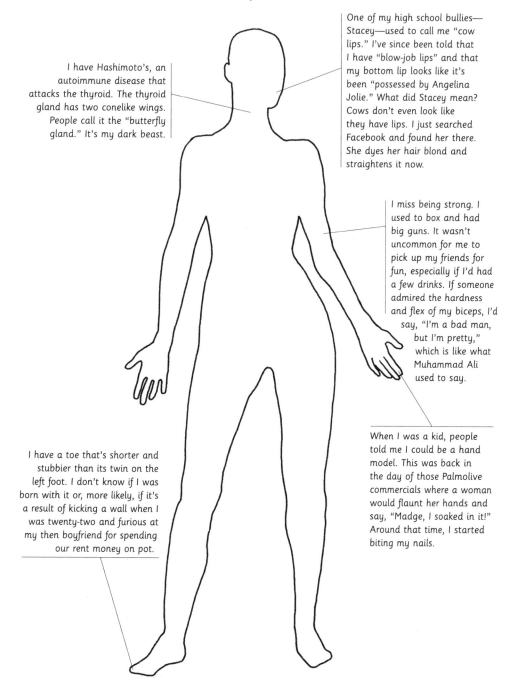

I have Hashimoto's, an autoimmune disease that attacks the thyroid. The thyroid gland has two conelike wings. People call it the "butterfly gland." It's my dark beast.

One of my high school bullies—Stacey—used to call me "cow lips." I've since been told that I have "blow-job lips" and that my bottom lip looks like it's been "possessed by Angelina Jolie." What did Stacey mean? Cows don't even look like they have lips. I just searched Facebook and found her there. She dyes her hair blond and straightens it now.

I miss being strong. I used to box and had big guns. It wasn't uncommon for me to pick up my friends for fun, especially if I'd had a few drinks. If someone admired the hardness and flex of my biceps, I'd say, "I'm a bad man, but I'm pretty," which is like what Muhammad Ali used to say.

When I was a kid, people told me I could be a hand model. This was back in the day of those Palmolive commercials where a woman would flaunt her hands and say, "Madge, I soaked in it!" Around that time, I started biting my nails.

I have a toe that's shorter and stubbier than its twin on the left foot. I don't know if I was born with it or, more likely, if it's a result of kicking a wall when I was twenty-two and furious at my then boyfriend for spending our rent money on pot.

# **POSTURING** | LEANNE SHAPTON *featuring* ZOSIA MAMET

*Poses from fashion media. Photographs by Gus Powell*

ZOSIA MAMET, SEPTEMBER 2013

*VOGUE PARIS,* JUNE 1975

*PEOPLE,* MARCH 1980

*AQUATIC WORLD,* MAY 1974

*BLACK BEAUTY,* NOVEMBER 2013

*BUST,* OCTOBER 2013

*CHEAP DATE,* SUMMER 2004

*VOGUE ITALIA,* APRIL 2000

*THE GENTLEWOMAN,* SPRING 2010

*COLORS,* WINTER 1991

COUNTRY LIFE, MARCH 2011

ELLE QUÉBEC, MAY 2011

VOGUE, OCTOBER 1952

FRANK, MARCH 1999

GQ, OCTOBER 1992

GRAZIA, MARCH 2012

HOLIDAY, APRIL 1963

HARPER'S BAZAAR, SEPTEMBER 2005

LADIES' HOME JOURNAL, MAY 1963

*HARPER'S BAZAAR UK*, SEPTEMBER 2008

*HEALTH*, OCTOBER 2013

*i-D* MAGAZINE, SUMMER 2010

J.CREW CATALOG, AUGUST 2013

*VERY*, DECEMBER 1988

*VOGUE*, OCTOBER 1930

*TEEN VOGUE*, NOVEMBER 2013

*MOTION PICTURE*, JUNE 1967

*VOGUE*, DECEMBER 1973

*HARPER'S BAZAAR,* MARCH 2009

*LADIES' HOME JOURNAL,* JUNE 1950

VERMONT COUNTRY STORE CATALOG, FALL 2013

CREATURES OF COMFORT WEBSITE, 2013

*VOGUE,* JUNE 1988

*DAZED & CONFUSED,* SEPTEMBER 2003

*VOGUE,* JULY 1952

*HELLO,* DECEMBER 2011

*VOGUE PARIS,* AUGUST 1971

WOMAN WITHIN CATALOG, FALL 2013

*ZEIT MAGAZIN,* JANUARY 2011

*JACQUES,* WINTER 2010

*GLAMOUR,* AUGUST 1968

*VOGUE ITALIA,* DECEMBER 2003

*i-D* MAGAZINE, SUMMER 2010

*PURPLE,* NOVEMBER 2004

*TATLER,* MARCH 2013

*VOGUE,* OCTOBER 1952

*VOGUE UK*, MAY 1996

*VOGUE PARIS*, MAY 2009

APHRODITE OF KNIDOS, 4TH CENTURY B.C.

*VOGUE PARIS*, DECEMBER 2007

*SHAPE*, NOVEMBER 2013

*BENEDICTE PINSET*'s white canvas sneakers

# MOTHER, DAUGHTER, MUSTACHE

CHRISTEN CLIFFORD

### ONE

I bought it at Halloween Adventure. It cost $6.99. A bright blond natural-hair mustache, with a net, that you attach with spirit gum to either side of the philtrum, that dip above the lips. I couldn't smile very much, or the mustache would start to peel off. Maybe that's why I felt so much less feminine. I couldn't smile.

It's wonderful to be a woman if you are young, thin, and pleasing to men. Otherwise there's not so much that's wonderful about it. We were told to be sexy, that without children we wouldn't be fulfilled as women, but raising them in decent conditions is practically impossible. It seems essential to capitalism that women be made to feel that they are failing all the time. Every choice is the wrong choice. I wanted to break free of convention.

### TWO

My husband has long hair. When we met, we both had long hair, mine a few shades blonder than his. We would walk the streets in matching leather jeans, and when we went to brunch at Teddy's the hostess would say, "Here you go, ladies."

"Does it bother you that people think we are both women?" I asked him while we were dating.

"Not really," he said. Sometimes it made me uncomfortable on his behalf, sometimes I was proud of how gender-bendery we were.

### THREE

We got married in Sydney, on his home turf, and when he said, "I take you as my husband," everyone twittered politely, thinking he had made a mistake. When I said, "I take you as my wife," our guests realized it was a joke of sorts and laughed.

When I told my shrink there was women's underwear in his drawer, she said, "Well, there's a few possible scenarios. One, he's a cross-dresser. Two, he's just super-careless and messy and doesn't even realize they are there. Or three, he's seeing someone now. I bet it's one or two."

I was like, Huh, okay. I have no problem with that.

If you dress up in women's clothes, who am I supposed to be?

### FOUR

The night my daughter was born, at home, she nursed and sucked her thumb and slept, curled in my arm. She was perfect and pink and I was not worried about her health. I was worried about her growing up with me as a mother. My self-loathing came bursting out. I thought all night, "Am I a good enough feminist to be a mother to a daughter?" I barely slept. Never mind that this question would have been just as valid had I asked it when her brother was born five years earlier. I spent all night in an extended anxiety attack. "I'm not a good enough feminist. I've stayed home with my son, he hasn't seen me work very much, and my daughter needs a stronger role model." It all boiled down to that familiar feeling: "I'm not good enough."

### FIVE

When my daughter was one, and my son was six, and my husband was forty-seven, I was thirty-eight, in the throes of my midlife crisis.

"You're too young to have a midlife crisis!" a well-known academic in his fifties crowed to me while we visited his summer house in the Catskills. "Life doesn't even begin until you are twenty!"

I just laughed and said something like "My life expectancy as a white woman with a master's degree in NYC is seventy-six, I think, so I'm right on time!" But what I really wanted to say was, "I was raped when I was fifteen, so you can believe my life started way before twenty. By the time I was twenty I had already been to orgies and had a few female lovers. So don't tell me when I'm allowed to have a midlife crisis. And stop dyeing your hair, dude, it doesn't make you look any younger."

### SIX

I was so good at being sexy I should have been a sex worker. I was good at 1980s sexy—a bob, tight short skirts, red lips. I did everything right to be a woman. I was told to be sexy, get married, have babies. I did it all.

### SEVEN

I don't care about being pretty. Because pretty makes me feel like it's something I owe to the world. I have to be pretty.

Now, *attractiveness* is real. Popular science shows that good-looking people get more attention, and are therefore smarter, whatever. So it's not like I want to give up my symmetry. I just gave up on colorful floral patterns, girly decorations, and the idea of youthfulness.

### EIGHT

I'll be *jolie laide*.

### NINE

Maybe the mustache is a preemptive strike. My mother spent many hours in front of the TV with her magnifying mirror set in a white beaded glass dish, her tweezers plucking valiantly, trying to eradicate the mustache and beard that appeared as her estrogen declined. I thought I would take hormones to stay juicy as I got older, but in the last year, two of my three sisters have been diagnosed with breast cancer, so now I don't think I'm going to do that. I'll grow a 'stache and wear tailored suits and look like Peggy Shaw.

## TEN

Becoming less feminine isn't a decision. It's happening. I see it. I feel it. I will never be as good at yoga as I was at twenty-eight, my chin has flesh under it, that deep crack between my eyes only goes away after a nap. It's not a decision to not be pretty. I'm not pretty. Aging is real. I am entering my Artsy Lady phase. I buy asymmetrical clothes in good fabrics that I can wear forever.

"Why are you doing the supershort-hair-big-glasses thing already? You still have a few years of pretty left in you."

Thanks. A lot. Seriously, thank you. Unfortunately, that still means something to me.

## ELEVEN

I was pretty. Weird pretty. I did some modeling in my teens when weird blondes were kind of in. I had a platinum bob, was tall, and had attitude. At thirteen, I was a local winner of a *Seventeen* magazine Look of the Year contest. I modeled in suburban department stores in and around Buffalo, bridal wear, even lingerie. I went to try my hand in New York and did a runway show. "Make love to the coat!" a man with an indistinguishable accent told me as I teetered up makeshift

stairs behind the curtain that led to the runway. I was thirteen. I did not know how to "make love to the coat."

## TWELVE

Giving up femininity is a relief. It makes me less eager to please. By not dressing in a traditionally feminine way, I have been able to stop making everything better for everyone else.

To give myself the entitlement of a man, I have had to look like a man. I don't feel the need to live as a man, or dress like one all the time, but I like being able to play with it. And yes, it does feel dirty, like I'm getting away with something that other people can't. I wouldn't recommend it to anyone, but it has worked for me.

## THIRTEEN

When I dress in drag, I take up more room at the bar when I order a drink.

When I order a drink as a woman, I often put my elbows on the bar, my shoulders are hunched, my upper arms pushing my small breasts into a bit of cleavage, on my tippy toes even though I'm tall, my hands clasped together with a twenty, an expectant, searching smile on my face. It's as if I am silently saying "Pick me" to the bartender, as if my getting a drink faster will prove my worth.

When I order a drink as a man, I don't give a shit what the bartender thinks of me, if he is silently laughing because I don't really look like a man, if he thinks I'm a freak. I stand looking out at the room, one elbow on the bar, shoulders wide, feet planted, a twenty casually in front of me. I don't think about changing my posture. I just do.

### FOURTEEN

"You still read very feminine," a friend said recently.

"Well, I don't feel very sexy lately. I don't like my body right now, I don't like that my weight goes up and down. I don't feel like I look good in my clothes."

I'm on my way to being a sexless woman in khaki capri pants. And yes, I am being judgmental. Short gray hair, no shape, boxy bright T-shirts, sneakers. A wacky piece of jewelry. My worst nightmare. Or, god forbid, Eileen Fisher. Mud-colored linen.

### FIFTEEN

I didn't try to look more masculine.

All these years of mothering a daughter, of dealing directly with her femininity, with her eventual womanness, of looking at her tiny labia and using unscented wipes and thinking, "Please god, don't let her get raped," even though I don't believe in god and even though that's a terrible sentence, it's what came to me then. And figuring out what it meant to me to be a woman, what femininity meant to me, what feminism meant to me, what being female meant to me, what it meant to be a cis white female, a cis white queerish female with kids, and on top of all of this dealing with the Princess Industry (not buying that pink plastic crap for my house; she can play it with her friends but I won't do it—when little girls want to play princess with me I tell them I am a King).

Age was creeping up on me, and I had all of this art in my head that I loved—I *loved* the women performance artists of the late '80s and early '90s. I really needed to do this idea I had in my head about using my Rape Tape (an actual audiocassette on which my attacker's friends made a recording of themselves mocking the attack). I guess I wanted to explore this fear of my daughter being raped, though I wouldn't have said that even a few years ago. I was thirty-eight, I had a daughter, and I couldn't hide from myself anymore.

I started doing remixes and mash-ups of feminist performance art with my own work. Carolee Schneemann, Yoko Ono, Annie Sprinkle, Ana Mendieta, Kara Walker, Yayoi Kusama, Holly Hughes, Karen Finley, Lenora Champagne, Barbara T. Smith, Penny Arcade.

My biggest fear is of my daughter getting raped.

I was raped at fifteen and again in my twenties. I don't want history to repeat itself. Yet what I did to stave off my fears of history repeating itself was to repeat history.

And here we delve into psychoanalytic theory; everything is repetition, from Freud on.

### SIXTEEN

I had an older boyfriend who liked to be humiliated; he was forty-three to my eighteen. His cultural references were different. To him, being humiliated was being forced to dress as a woman.

When men want to dress as women, they want to be the sexy version, in lace. Men never want to be a stay-at-home mom still in her period underwear and nothing else at four p.m., nursing a baby and zombie-ing her way through the house, not picking up anything, crying in front of the dishwasher.

### SEVENTEEN

Before I started dressing like a man in public, I had a cock in private. I had experience fucking. Like a man, but not. A strap-on. Well, a few actually. There's the leather dildo harness that my partner had when I met him, and the simple black one we bought together, and the silver glitter one (comfy and sparkly), and the RodeoH underwear, black and gray with a cock ring attached. These are good, because they make the cock so close to my body that it feels warm and a part of me. But it doesn't fit a double dildo. For that I need the leather one without the backing snapped in. Then I feel like we are fucking each other. It's pretty amazing.

### EIGHTEEN

When I was in London recently, as an actor in a play, I was the Chechen whore. "Typecast as usual!" I laughed with my martini. I walked by a bar at night. It was a pub on one of those small cobblestone alleyways off an alleyway not far from St.

James's Park. It had open windows, and a small shelf outside. Men in dark suits and white shirts and ties—youngish, rakish— were standing in the alleyway, drinking and smoking, leaning on the shelf. I walked by, so attracted to that scene. I went back and tried to find it. Did I want to be a young woman in a sexy dress, getting their attention? In a previous life, yes.

I went back and ordered a drink. I sat inside at a corner table, my bags on the stools nearby (a lady never puts her bag on the floor!), solemnly drinking my pint.

I wanted to be them. I wanted to be one of them, dressed so, well, Britishly, with that easy laddish behavior. At one point one of them took off his shoe and threw it at the building across the street and they all laughed. A dare? A bet? A girl living there? I wanted to be like them, like with that downtown writer I dated. I didn't want to date him; I wanted to *be* him. I still kind of do.

### NINETEEN

Maybe I will take testosterone someday. The great thing about being a woman and knowing I will go through menopause is that I kind of feel like I will get to be both sexes, naturally. Like, "You aren't losing femininity, you're gaining masculinity!"

### TWENTY

I'm always telling my kids they can change genders when they get older. "You're weird, Mom," my son said.

"Yes," I said happily. "I am." ╳

# HOW TO DRESS
## IN OUR NEW WORLD

### BY MARGAUX WILLIAMSON

1. We see now that every part of our lives needs cleaning up for the new world—for the contemporary situation. Like what we wear.

2. We can just start here. We can see what we have. Recent face science has shown us that our faces communicate almost everything we thought we were hiding or enhancing with our clothes.

3. The new face science has shown us that most communication happens with the twitches of our muscles, with the way we move our eyes and lean our heads in. We have learned that people see who we are before they even look down.

4. There used to be seminars on how to dress like a strong woman, how to dress like a deer. We used to dress to show the real us, or the other us, or of course to stay warm or without shame; to show our sex, our carelessness, our professionalism, our nihilism, our money; to be camouflage, a glossy magazine, a protest sign. But now we see—this old game is only a game of playing matchy-matchy with our souls.

5. The new game is to be misunderstood. And the new challenge is to learn how to be misunderstood.

6. Being misunderstood makes everything easier. It makes clothing acquisition less time-consuming. The contemporary situation is taking up plenty of your time, no time to waste.

7. Getting dressed used to be a game that happened too quickly, lasted forever, and was boring to win. Like Monopoly. But things are different now. Things are worse, but also better.

8. The stores are dying, or being killed. It is a new time of not so many private helicopters to take you to old ground, not so many fur coats on racks so far away from the forest, not so many black-and-white balls where we pour champagne down the gutter in the ceremony to remember where we came from. We must find new ways to acquire clothing, new ways to show we are both of the sky and of the earth.

9. So now, if you find a T-shirt on the street and it is 100% cotton, maybe it is time to put it on. That is a great find, to find cotton on the street, so far away from the fields. And though it probably advertises a bad system that you don't believe in, everyone knows from your face what's in your heart. And besides, our personal investigations are as valuable as our speeches. See what it is like to match your face with the bad system. There are not so many vacations anymore, but we still must go places.

10. If a kindly older woman gives you a coat that makes you look like you're on the wrong side of the money wars, wear that coat to your comrade's or nemesis's dinner party. If we can't practice our beliefs and our empathy and our experiments over dinner, what is the point of dinner?

11. It might seem like, in the new world, clothes are nowhere to be found, but they are everywhere. In the desert, at the funeral home, in the garbage.

12. There will never not be enough clothes. We made so many. Galaxies of factories were born in the name of individuality. Our person-to-clothing ratio spiraled out of control and the resulting great piles of clothes made more visible the meaninglessness of our individual lives on earth.

13. Stores were built up with marble bricks and were filled with empty clothes. They were guarded by kindly workers or menacing security guards in an attempt to show that a dress was still hard to come by, still meant, maybe, just for you.

14. But they needed the marble again, for the marble wars, so the game now is to make meaning of that more visibly depressive pile of production.

15. Now, we must remember, the less effort we spend before that pile of production, the more meaning. It is not about finding the perfect you in that garbage heap, it is about economical movement and effort—what we can find here, at our feet. Since you are very much you, and anything else is, again, a juxtaposition, a gift.

16. So now, if you easily come across a dress that fits you like a glove, but makes you look like a stranger, remember, this is a fortune-telling game of meaning and ease—we must turn in the direction of what fits.

17. If you are worried you might be inappropriately dressed, just keep in mind there is always a funeral somewhere.

18. What we love now are worn things, things that have made it through experiences with what appear to be travel scars and thick skin. We think, these dull blue boots are strong, I can tell they have been to the woods and the jungle and the floods and the dinner. Maybe we can't tell what the shoes mean, since we haven't been there, but we know they are still here. Sometimes, not knowing the meaning is not meaninglessness, but love.

19. We get dressed now like we are in love. We don't need mirrors anymore, or the sides of the old shiny buildings or the placid lake, to see what is good. Mirrors are for amateurs, for people from the old tragic mirror era. We can use our bodies to feel what's happening.

20. What we are talking about is something we have always known but have forgotten: Our bodies are smarter than our eyes. Our bodies are the newest mirrors and the ancient way.

21. Also, don't look down. We now know that clothes can't change the information on our face, but what we do with all of the time we have saved can. There used to be secret meetings about how to get people to look down, they always want you to look down. But we know, and maybe always knew, that looking down is more time-consuming than heroin, academia, or beer.

22. Wash but do not make alterations.

23. This is not a make-work project. Make no adjustments beyond what scissors can do. If the shirt is too big, you will look young and poor. If the shirt is too small, you will look big and strong. If the shirt is much too small, leave it on the street for a smaller hunter.

24. We are not talking about comfort here, we are not advocating fleece. We must always be a little bit uncomfortable. We are, are we not, part of this world? We have to be alert here, we can't get too comfortable. As they say, if you are going to go anywhere, you mustn't get too comfortable.

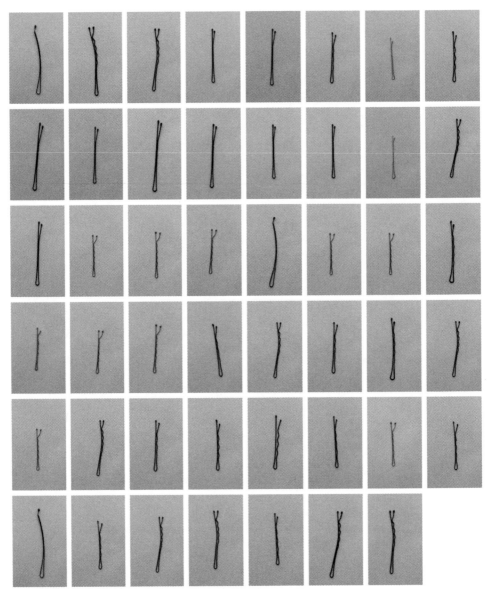

*AMY PINKHAM*'s bobby pins

# HANDMADE

*"When I was about nine, my mother hand-sewed a* Little House on the Prairie–*style dress for my birthday, and a matching dress for my Barbie."*—TANIA VAN SPYCK

**EDIE CULSHAW** When my great-grandmother was in her thirties during the Second World War, she was in the Women's Royal Naval Service. She was so horrified by the quality and cut of the uniforms that she had hers remade, by hand, by her tailor.

**COLLEEN ASPER** I am an artist. This means appearance is an occupational concern. Many artists take this literally and seem to match their work, but with the exception of Yayoi Kusama, I usually think it's more interesting if someone doesn't look like what they make.

**MOLLY MURRAY** I do something to alter everything that comes into my closet—cut off embellishments, change a seam or hemline, wear it back to front—though I don't do it as much or as well as my friend Jane, an artist with great style who is the undisputed master of clothing modification. I also compulsively remove all identifying tags and labels from my clothes. In some superstitious way, I feel like this allows the clothes to become more fully themselves, to speak with their material and cut and color and shape, rather than for a shop or designer.

**BRITTANY BROWN** My mom was a seamstress who worked in a warehouse sewing the garments doctors wear. She constructed the uniforms to withstand gushes of blood and ultraviolet light. She would also pick out fabric and make me a shirt or dress. One day I was with her in the warehouse, sitting at a sewing machine by myself and my shirt caught on something—a splinter of wood, a tiny knob, I don't remember what exactly. The thread from the sleeve's hem unraveled and I remember thinking this would never have happened if my mom had just bought my clothes at a store instead of making them with her own hands. I remember distrusting everything she ever made and therefore everything I wore, all of it concocted by the unskilled craftsmanship of my mother. From then on, I rebelled against everything she made me wear.

**MARGARITA TUPITSYN** Most Russians were really poor, so they couldn't afford to wear the high fashions of the West. My mother, grandmother, and aunt compensated by making things for my family and me to wear. Russian avant-garde artists like my aunt believed that fashion should be egalitarian, part of everyone's life, and that all things should be beautiful and aestheticized. They were against fashion as elitist. But after Stalin's regime, this sensibility was lost.

**RACHEL KUSHNER** My mother is a southern Protestant beatnik who wove see-through tank tops on her loom and wore homemade pleather hot pants. No bra, never shaved her legs. She has waist-length bright red hair. DIY was instilled in me, I guess.

**FELIZ LUCIA MOLINA** My parents are Filipino immigrants who came to L.A. in the late '60s.

They were hippies and kept a lot of their clothes. At a young age, I instinctually wore their old clothes. In college, I cut up some of my mom's old dresses because the patterns were cool. In the '80s, they owned and managed board and care homes (where my family lived) for the physically and mentally handicapped. One of the patients taught me how to tie shoelaces.

**ZIVA SERKIS-NAUMANN** I have twenty or thirty Bedouin dresses. One is so fine I'm donating it to a museum after I die, and they are waiting for it. I like all things handmade and hand-embroidered. Years ago, I realized it would be a lost art, because it takes so long to weave the cloth. Now you can't get them—just imitations. I got it in the market in Hebron. I've had the dress for forty years or more. I wear it maybe twice a year.

**IVY ARCE** My cousin has made clothes for me from scratch. He made my wedding dress and my husband's suit, vest, and pants. In his suit there was a fabric accent of my dress and vice versa. My cousin has been my best friend since childhood. I keep everything he has made me.

**HEL GURNEY** People say, "I love your shirt." I thank them and sometimes proudly add, "I made it myself." Ten years on, it's still the best-loved thing in my wardrobe. It's my go-to for formal and semiformal events, costume parties, and on days when everything about my body screams wrongness. When I made it, I had no idea how important it would become. I was fifteen. Most of my textiles classmates were making prom dresses, but with startling prescience, I knew my wardrobe needed something different, something that expressed the sort of dandified masculinity to which I was increasingly drawn. The town goth shop had a few extortionately priced ruffled men's shirts that clung awkwardly to my hips and chest, and my next pilgrimage to Camden was months away. So I made my own. Constructing the shirt was beyond exasperating, the silky fabric was slippery, and much of the detail needed hand-sewing. But the finished product was a labor of love. When I wear it, I feel proud, not only of how damn fine I look, but of that early instance of (literally) taking my gender presentation into my own hands.

**RUTH SATELMAJER** In our community, all the kids belonged to the 4-H Club. Since my mother taught the 4-H Sewing Club, I belonged to it. My mother said, "At least you know how, and one day you will be glad for what you have learned." When I got engaged, my husband-to-be bought me a sewing machine. My husband was a pastor, and we got by with my making all of our children's clothes, as well as my own. Also, there were several young people who made their home with us, and I often sewed for them.

**MARLENA KAESLER** My Oma is from Prussia and had to abandon everything when Russia invaded in 1945. She lived in Germany during her teens. She was a seamstress and made almost every piece of clothing she owns, but arthritis has prevented her from doing so the last ten years. Last year, she showed me a sweater she knitted fifty years ago, when she was twenty-two. She got her seamstress internship with it. She says that there is a "curse" in the family, and she calls it the "Jordan Curse," and it's because that part of her family are all obsessed with clothing or are mechanics. The people who have the curse cannot do anything but produce work. Some are successful at it and make it their living, but some are debilitated by it and it takes over their lives.

**SASHA WISEMAN** I finally bought a new winter coat, after six years of wearing my old one. I found the old coat in a lost-and-found bin at a fancy restaurant where I worked as a hostess, and I spent weeks painstakingly altering it to meet the standards I had for beauty (sewing patches of floral silk onto the edges, painting a pattern with acrylics onto the back, even trimming the fur hood with mink pelts, and sewing in small jewels in geometric patterns). Over the years, I stopped feeling that these adornments had anything to do with me, and every time I put on the coat I kind of cringed, though I could barely admit to betraying my former self. But I think it's important to view your style as fluid.

<u>CLARE NEEDHAM</u> I once found this little-girl's dress, and having fallen in love with it, I took it to an Indian seamstress who has a shop in Kensington Market filled with saris and beaded scarves. I had fabric added to it so I could fit into it. Years later, when I weighed less and lived in Buenos Aires, I took it to a *costurera* from Armenia whose shop, and later my dress, reeked of cigarette smoke, and had some fabric removed. It goes without saying that it's my favorite dress. ✕

## "BRA"

*Changing room of New York City gym.*

**WOMAN:** Can I ask you an indiscreet question?

**LISA:** Sure.

**WOMAN:** Where did you get your bra? It's so beautiful. The lace . . .

**LISA:** I know! I just got it to replace a favorite one that wore out. It's so great, isn't it? And it's navy.

**WOMAN:** I have to get one.

**LISA:** It's from La Petite Coquette on University.

**WOMAN:** I'm gonna go get one right now. Thank you so much.

**LISA:** No problem, I would have done the same thing. ✕

*MELINDA ANDRADE*'s aviator sunglasses

# FLOWER X

SMELL SCIENTIST **LESLIE VOSSHALL** SPEAKS TO **HEIDI JULAVITS**

**HEIDI:** Is smell a language?

**LESLIE:** I think it's absolutely a language. But the lexicon for most people is really, really narrow. Once you start paying attention to it, you learn the nuances. You know, one can identify different kinds of fire: electrical fire, rubber fire, paper fire, wood fire—they all smell different.

**HEIDI:** Did you start paying attention at a young age, or is it something you concentrated on more when you started studying it?

**LESLIE:** I've always paid attention. I've always smelled stuff. Even body smells. I know the smells of different farts. Whenever I pee, I pay intense attention. Um . . . I'm sorry.

**HEIDI:** No! I think it's really fascinating.

**LESLIE:** Urine changes entirely based on your health and what you've eaten. I've always been an acute observer of smells that I generate and the perfumes people wear.

**HEIDI:** Personal body smells can be a language, right? I remember the first time I went out on a date with this guy I ended up with for a few years, and at one point I got this whiff of spoiled meat.

**LESLIE:** Was this at the beginning or the end of the relationship?

**HEIDI:** This was our first date! And I had a moment of "My nose is telling me to back off!" I just wonder—if he knew I wasn't attracted to his smell but I otherwise loved him, is that something he could change?

Or is smell part of your genetic identity?

**LESLIE:** Your hair smells different from your neck, from your underarms, from your pubic hair—from, obviously, your genital area—from your feet. All those things smell different because of different bacteria. So the bacteria call the shots as to what you're gonna smell like in those areas. And then there's your genetics. Your genetics you basically can't change.

**HEIDI:** Do you inherit the way you smell?

**LESLIE:** In some sense. Then perfumes are a way to change how you smell. But it's unpredictable, because every perfume smells different on different people, right? Because of how oily their skin is, or because of the bacteria—they're gonna chew on the perfume in different ways.

**HEIDI:** I love online customer perfume reviews for that reason. A person will say, "It starts out nice, but after fifteen minutes on me it starts to smell like glue."

**LESLIE:** Those blogs have completely disrupted the fragrance industry. It used to be that the manufacturer told you what it smells like. But the perfume bloggers have much more nuanced opinions, and everybody has a slightly different opinion of what something smells like.

**HEIDI:** Because it smells different on each of them.

**LESLIE:** Yeah, because they will have done some surgery on the perfume just with their body. I love a lot of perfumes, and I buy a lot of them, but I generally ignore the manufacturers' descriptions because they're total bullshit. They'll always say a perfume smells like flower X, which actually has no scent—that's very typical. Like a daisy is almost scentless. Many orchids are almost scentless. The people who sell the perfumes are in general such morons; they'll say, "Do you like lemon, or do you like woody?" They're untrained and they're idiots.

**HEIDI:** I read that you said that most people think they're better smellers than they are.

**LESLIE:** The context for that quote was a really big smell study. Ten out of five hundred people, their answers were completely random. They're very expressive and very excited, like, "Oh, I really like that," but the data proved that they're basically blind to smells. It would be like a blind person going to a museum and saying, "I really like the colors of that one," while standing in front of the elevator.

**HEIDI:** What's happening neurologically? Are they actually smelling something, do you think, like having a scent hallucination?

**LESLIE:** I think they're bluffing. I would say that in general people are not well trained. You need to be experienced with smell, and recognize and learn, and train yourself, and then this whole world opens up where, you know, strawberries—there isn't just "a strawberry scent." Depending on ripeness, there are thousands of different strawberry scents. I find that so exciting.

**HEIDI:** How do smells become culturally meaningful? How do we culturally agree on what a smell means or what's a desirable scent?

**LESLIE:** I think that every single smell that someone in America can identify and put into a category—like beer, vinegar, apple, fire—is something that we've learned. From the earliest age your parents are teaching you smell identification and smell categorization. Babies start out with this blank slate: they haven't learned what the associations are, but they're interested in all the smells. So—poop. They learn to hate the smell of poop only because of the actions of their parents—you know, if they're changing a diaper, the parents are always verbalizing, or scrunching up their faces, and saying, "Don't touch it." That's an extreme example, but in every case, you're associating a smell with an object. But if you go overseas, to Africa or Asia, where they have unfamiliar things, and you ask yourself what does something smell like, you'll be completely tongue-tied. You can't even say "It smells like" because it's so unfamiliar, right? You can't physically put a description on it.

**HEIDI:** Are there fashions in perfume?

**LESLIE:** Definitely. There are a few key moments when a perfumer will make something revolutionary. Perfumers are very creative, so they make something, and they find it fantastic, and they put it out there, but the public has to be ready for it. The fragrance White Linen is an example of a very musky, powdery fragrance.

**HEIDI:** People didn't like it at first and they learned to like it?

**LESLIE:** It wasn't a style in perfume before, but everything started smelling the same and people were a bit sick of it, and then this new, musky, powdery fragrance came out, it took off, and for the next ten years everybody was copying it.

**HEIDI:** It seems like there was a vanilla perfume moment and then there was a fig perfume moment and then there was a vetiver perfume moment . . .

**LESLIE:** Absolutely. Whenever I go to airports, I spend a lot of time in the crappy duty-free shops smelling the crappy perfumes, they're all powdery, floral crap, and I'm just waiting for that moment when the next big perfume hits and shifts it. It's not that different from music. I grew up as a teenager in the seventies and early eighties, and I remember when everything was disco, and then some door opened and disco was killed. Then it was Depeche Mode and the Psychedelic Furs. I think perfume parallels that. Fashion also. People just get sick of things.

**HEIDI:** But perfume feels different from fashion trends. It seems much more self-erasing to go out and buy the same perfume that you know many other people are wearing.

**LESLIE:** I think it depends on the temperament of the person. Some people like being part of the herd and wearing things that are recognizable and somewhat generic. There's some comfort in that. Whereas I've always been a contrarian. I have in my collection of perfumes some of those signature perfumes that everybody wears, but I would never wear them myself.

**HEIDI:** Why own them then?

**LESLIE:** I guess I'm just a perfume fanatic. I sometimes want to see, Why do people like this? There's a fantastically famous perfume called L'Eau d'Issey. At a certain point one in ten people in New York were wearing it. So I wanted to own it to see what it smelled like on me. But I would never wear it outside the house.

**HEIDI:** Some perfumes you wear only around your house? Like sweatpants or something?

**LESLIE:** Sometimes I'll try things out, yeah. There's a lot of stuff I really love that my husband hates, so I can't wear it unless I'm traveling. Scent is important in relationships because why are you wearing it? Are you wearing it for yourself, or are you wearing it for your partner? Ideally there's some consensus.

**HEIDI:** True.

**LESLIE:** It's a beautiful art form and form of human expression. There are certain people who wear a lot of cheap perfume—I think men are much more guilty of that than women, you know, the men who are putting on Axe. Cheap aftershave has given the whole industry a bad name. In general the perfumes marketed to men are just gross. Historically men used to wear much more floral scents. In the days when men were wearing those beautiful high-heeled buckled shoes and frilly blouses and powdered wigs, they were not wearing Eau Sauvage. Most men's perfume and aftershave and cologne today is leather, tobacco, citrus. Really idiotically simple. No nuance. Sharp to the nose, and to me really horrible. I like men who cross-dress with the perfumes, because a lot of women's perfumes are really great on men, and vice versa.

**HEIDI:** It's interesting that there are certain specific moods that are evoked by specific smells and how that gets decided. How are emotions controlled by cultural consensus?

**LESLIE:** The effect of culture is very strong. My favorite perfumes as a kid were Love's Fresh Lemon and Love's Baby Soft. They're tiny, one-note perfumes, and they do evoke specific moods, and those moods are related to context, to how you've been trained to feel about them. So Love's Baby Soft—

**HEIDI:** Is that still available?

**LESLIE:** I wish it were. They reformulated it. I should go on eBay and try to buy some unsealed original. But the association with Love's Baby Soft is that it smells like babies, it smells like baby powder. So it puts us in the mood of cozy, warm, enveloping cotton.

**HEIDI:** I didn't use baby powder on my kids. I wonder if they'll have that association.

**LESLIE:** Exactly. Maybe not. The current fashion in perfumes I find very depressing. A lot of people smell like vanilla blackberry ice cream: very vanilla, very musky, but with fruit layered on top.

**HEIDI:** So how do you break those down, moodwise? Musk is sex. What's vanilla?

**LESLIE:** We did a smell test with hundreds of people, and we determined that vanilla was the number-one favorite fragrance among New Yorkers.

**HEIDI:** I hate to tell you this, but I'm wearing a vanilla scent. It makes me feel like a cookie. A happy cookie.

**LESLIE:** Yeah, that's the association, because people think of ice cream and baked goods and pudding. It's warm and sweet. I buy a lot of avant-garde perfumes that you can't categorize. Frédéric Malle made a perfume with Dries Van Noten—I mean, he made it, but it's called Dries Van Noten—and to me the notes are phenol, which is an industrial solvent, and burned rubber. It's objectively the nastiest, most disgusting thing, but I love it because it's very strange, it's original, and it's the farthest thing from all those horrible cheap celebrity perfumes, like the Nicki Minaj and Britney Spears; they're all making the same thing: musk, vanilla, berries.

**HEIDI:** How much of it is education and how much of it is scent exhaustion—that you've smelled so much you just want something new to happen to your nose?

**LESLIE:** That's what happens! My perfume cabinet's a bit like an archaeological dig at the back. I have a bottle from my grandmother and a bottle from my deceased mother-in-law that are just historical items. And then I have—

**HEIDI:** Do you ever smell them?

**LESLIE:** They're pretty oxidized at this point. Perfumes do have a shelf life.

**HEIDI:** But would you ever do a little spritz in the air just to have a moment with them?

**LESLIE:** It's a good idea, like it's a ghost. The truth is they're so far gone that they're not pleasant to smell anymore. Just like with clothes, you may have a few pieces that you go back to all the time, but there are certain things at the back of the closet that you don't wear. Perfumes are the same way. If you have only three perfumes then you're stuck, because it would be like having only three outfits in your closet—of course you get sick of them. You need to diversify. Get samples.

**HEIDI:** So when people choose those musk, vanilla, berry scents, what are they saying?

**LESLIE:** The vast majority of Americans put no thought into what they wear, fashion-wise, or what perfumes they wear. A lot of people just lead functional lives. A lot of people don't know what they're doing when they buy perfume, and the people selling perfume to them don't know what they're doing, either. So people will buy Britney Spears's perfume because they like Britney Spears, and it's the biggest piece of shit ever. They're not really choosing it to match their personalities. If you want to be serious about it, you have to spend some time and explore by yourself. With fashion, you have to have a personal vision of what you want to wear, and mix things together. It's the same with perfume.

**HEIDI:** Here's why I never had an interest. My mom used to wear Lauren by Ralph Lauren, so when I was a kid I would try to wear that perfume—

**LESLIE:** That's actually a pretty good one.

**HEIDI:** Well, it gave me a migraine every time I wore it. As a result my curiosity shut down. I thought, Okay, perfume makes me sick, I guess that's just not going to be part of my world.

**LESLIE:** You have to get there. You have PTSD for perfumes.

**HEIDI:** I do!

**LESLIE:** It's possible to get beyond that. I think you can get beyond it. ✕

# THIS PERSON IS A ROBOT | LESLIE VOSSHALL AND HEIDI JULAVITS

*A smell scientist sniffs coats in a busy New York City restaurant's coatcheck closet.*

❧

*(A night in February, sleeting, twenty-two degrees)*

### TICKET #410

**WOMAN'S SHEARLING-LINED
GRAY WOOL JACKET**

*I think this is a thirty-five-year-old woman who's coming in from New Canaan or Westport. I smell cigarette smoke in the pocket. Maybe she's a secret smoker. But it's not obvious on the coat, it's almost like she must . . . There's something she puts in the pocket that has cigarette smoke on it. I think people know this is happening.*

### TICKET #391

**WOMAN'S BROWN PUFFER
WITH FAKE-FUR HOOD**

*This one's really coconutty. This is someone who wants to be in the Caribbean right now. She wants to be transported by a smell that makes her think of sunscreen.*

### TICKET #418

**WOMAN'S BLACK ELIE TAHARI PUFFER**

*This person is a robot. A lifeless robot just walked in here. I don't smell anything. This person is probably like one of those people in the movie* Safe *who are chemically sensitive. It's like unscented soap, scentless, dye-free, fragrance-free deodorant, fragrance-free laundry detergent. It's a complete absence of anything. Let me see if her friend is also a robot.*

**WOMAN'S BLACK WOOL
KENNETH COLE CAR COAT**

*Oh my god, this smells like it's been in an attic. Smell the armhole there. Really, really musty. It's been in storage with a bunch of old clothes, or it came from a Salvation Army. They don't wash those clothes, I know because I buy a lot of clothes from Salvation Army, so everything acquires exactly the same scent. Yeah, so who is this person? There's the robot friend or partner who's afraid of scent, and then there's this person who doesn't realize that she smells moldy, so I guess I would question whether she has a sense of smell at all. It's the woman who's afraid of smell hanging out with a woman who can't smell.*

## TICKET #398

### WOMAN'S DOUBLE-BREASTED
### OLIVE WOOL JACKET
### WITH BABY-BLUE-STRIPED SCARF

*This is suffused with the classic musky—the current fashion—musky, vanilla, with a lot of blackberry. This would be someone under thirty. I would have to say this is a woman, or a man who's cross-dressing.*

☙

## TICKET #412

### MAN'S BLACK PUFFER
### WITH LEATHER TRIM

*(Coatcheck woman
comes to claim coat.)
That was an original classy scent that I would need to sniff out a little longer to identify. It smelled like class and money. Like the leather on a Rolls-Royce. Goddamnit, I need the coat back!*

☙

## TICKET #401

### MAN'S BARBOUR OILSKIN

*Oh, this is terrible. This is a deeply conventional man, this is exactly what I was complaining about. The terrible, conventional men's aftershave called Axe. It's the biggest blockbuster. The old generation, people in their sixties and seventies, buy Old Spice, but Axe is marketed to teenage boys. Then they grow up and keep wearing it.*

### WOMAN'S TAN WOOL J.CREW COAT

*This smells like really powdery violets. This is someone who is refined and subtle. It's a very nice scent. I think she's with the wrong guy. Yeah, I feel for her. It's gonna end in . . . They'll probably make it until the kids are out of the home, and then she'll realize that there's really no reason to stay married to him.*

💧

## TICKET #397

### WOMAN'S NAVY BLUE WOOL DUFFEL
### AND STRIPED WOOL SCARF

*This coat smell has a base of bananas. This is another one of the trendy fruit-cocktail perfumes. It's like banana and vanilla yogurt, it's what young children smell like. The scarf is sour-smelling. It's like hay, sour hay. This is probably someone who lives in Warren County, New Jersey. The perfume ran out of juice long before the evening was over. But the hay is just natural.*

## WOMAN'S BROWN WOOL ANDREW MARC COAT WITH FUR HOOD

*This is a sweaty person. Something's a little bit more real. Stale perfume and sweat, and the perfume is so degraded you can't really identify it. So I would say this is a young lady who goes out a lot and either doesn't have time or doesn't care about her hygiene. Who doesn't make any attempt to use deodorant or wear perfume.*

## WOMAN'S TOPSHOP CAMEL BOUCLÉ COAT

*This woman doesn't wear perfume, she uses only a very basic soap or bodywash. It smells like someone who showers a lot, blow-dries her hair a lot, doesn't wear perfume—doesn't make a big impression. The coat is kind of beige, the scent is kind of beige. Someone who's not going to go into a room and dominate it.*

## MAN'S NAVY G-STAR RAW PEACOAT

*It's a pretty clean scent. Yeah, it's a good smell. Subtle. I think this is a good guy. It's not disgusting aftershave, it's a pretty clean avant-garde scent. It goes away after smelling. I would say this guy is gonna be a quieter, more thoughtful person. He uses scents but doesn't douse himself, so he's not trying to draw attention to himself, but he is thinking about it.*

## MAN'S NAVY WOOL COAT WITH HOOD

*Ugh, this is like the airport, the cheap airport. Yup. This is definitely a deeply conventional scent that men put on these days, in huge quantities . . . With men you can't tell, because a lot of the deodorant also has that vile smell, so I can't tell if it's . . . it's in the body of the coat, too, so I would assume that it's maybe a combination of deodorant and cologne. And it's pretty consistent, so it could be someone who really likes this stuff and has bought the whole line—lots of it. When you shake the coat you get another big bloom. He wants to be the big man in the room.*

## MAN'S BLACK WOOL COAT

*This is cleaner. . . . These kinds of scents are more popular in Europe. It's pretty nice. It's spicy-citrus-powder, rather than tobacco-leather-citrus. It's baby powder with a little citrus on top. I think we have the first guy who's super-subtle and quiet and thoughtful. It's a very smart scent, someone who's more of an intellectual. But I think all these guys are straight. And then there's the guy who just doesn't know better. He's a bore. And he loads himself up with the scent.*

## WOMAN'S BLACK DKNY COAT AND
## BRIGHT BLUE KNIT HAT

*The hat smells of strawberry shampoo. On the coat, this is another deeply conventional raspberry-blackberry scent I'm picking up. So this is like some twenty-something office girl. But still kind of a kid, because of the hat that smells like a kids' strawberry shampoo.*

## WOMAN'S PLAID WOOL GAP JACKET

*This is another robot. There's nothing. She's one of those people who's so clean, and who uses only unscented products. There's a little bit of a smell of the other woman's coat on this coat, and that's the only thing. This Gap lady is just a total cipher. But she hangs out with a young woman who has a little bit of something going on.*

## WOMAN'S BLACK WOOL COAT
## WITH FUR COLLAR

*Oh my god! This is someone who cares. This is someone who really cares. It also helps that it's real fur, because fur holds the perfume much better than wool. There's no smell in the coat, so I think that she put the coat on and then sprayed perfume as she was going out the door. I'm guessing it's someone who's busy, busy social life, changes coats all the time. Probably has a lot of coats and spritzes as she's on the go. So that's why the coat doesn't have a personality. The coat is like a dead coat that's never been worn, but the fur collar has a lot of smell on it. The scent is gardenia, very sophisticated. The fur collar has lots of smell personality.*

## WOMAN'S BEBE
## BLACK-AND-WHITE-PLAID COAT
## WITH BLACK-AND-WHITE WOOL SCARF

*There's definitely a high-end perfume in here
I can't identify. But this is someone who cares,
who's put some thought in. Again, powdery-
musky is the dominant scent. She's been spraying
it mostly on her arms, because there's nothing
at the collar. Maybe a little bit here, a little bit
of perfume at the front of the placket. You have
to guess that she grew up with parents, like
a mother, who cared about perfume, so even
though she's probably twenty-three years old
and in some kind of entry-level office job, she's
put some thought into what she buys and wears.
You can tell she's kind of delicate and classy. She
doesn't have a lot of money, but she's thought
about it, and the scent is very subtle—probably
grew up in private school, but her parents are
not giving her any money.*

### MAN'S ARMANI JEANS BLACK WOOL
### OVERCOAT

*Oh no. This is another bad match. This guy
has doused himself. I won't even make you
smell it. Enormous quantities of the cheapest
possible . . . It's the combination of aftershave
and a lot of soap. This guy's afraid of his body
odor and he compensates by dousing himself
in this stuff. She's delicate and thoughtful and
making the most of not having a lot of money,
and making good decisions. He probably has
more money, but doesn't think about things
very deeply, just grabs whatever.
He's also big in every way:
the coat is big, the smell is big.*

*TARA WASHINGTON*'s knitted hats

# 40s

*"I'm Korean, late forties. At my age you're an* ajumma, *you're supposed to get a perm and wear shapeless clothes accented with a visor."* —MARIE MYUNG-OK LEE

AMY MARTHA McGURK I always carry my Revlon Cherries in the Snow lipstick, even if I'm not wearing it, because I bought it in high school when I saw a model with coloring similar to mine wearing it. I mentioned it to my mother because I thought the name was kind of funny, and she got this weird look on her face and said that was my nana's (her mom's) signature shade, and she died with a tube of it in her purse. My mom still has that tube, and I hope it eventually gets passed on to me, but for now I have the same tube I bought in high school (I'm forty).

KRISTIN SJAARDA I remember someone saying to me, "After forty, it's time to up your game. You can't get away with just throwing something on." I think she was talking about expensive bras at the time.

UMM ADAM Since I turned forty, and my kids have grown older, I've had time to think about myself and my identity again, so I want to look good, wear more color and more trendy clothes. I bought some hot-pink and bright orange clothes to wear at home—colors I could never have imagined wearing in my youth—and I am still looking for the right clothes to wear outside the house, something trendy but modest and Islamically appropriate. Something that identifies who I am.

K. L. CANDELA In my second year of university, when my consciousness was raised, I dropped the nail polish, the makeup, and the dresses, and broke out the jeans and black T-shirts. As I've moved into my forties, however, I have that desire to return to the feminine, to wear makeup, to feel glamorous. I wish I could go back in time and use the beauty I had in my twenties and parade it, enlarge it. I feel a very strong inner metamorphosis brewing, and it's hard because now I look in the mirror and it's almost rearview.

LISA FRANZETTA I'm almost forty, but I still want to wear tight pants most days.

IVY KNIGHT I'm constantly worried about what I'm wearing because I'm nearing forty and I wonder if the clothes I choose are age-appropriate. My husband is in his fifties and he wears jokey T-shirts. He has a neon-green one with a picture of Jabba the Hutt and underneath it says "Original Gangster." He gets assaulted with compliments when he wears it. I don't think I could wear that out. I don't want to start wearing sweater sets and little white gloves, but I don't want to be in miniskirts and stilettos. I'm trying to straddle the line between how I was dressed when I was in my twenties—slutty—and frumpy.

STEPHANIE DINKMEYER When I was going through exposure therapy for a panic disorder, I wore a piece of old jewelry from my great-great-aunt Winnie. She didn't marry until her forties. She traveled to 126 countries. I needed her courage.

NANCY FORDE I am forty-six and a single mother of a four-year old. In my thirties, I liked vintage things, but since turning forty, I have veered more toward easy, athletic casualwear for comfort and practicality (as a single mum of a baby, then toddler). I tried for most of my thirties to have a child with my then partner, and the struggle certainly did not help make me feel attractive or womanly. I left my partner three days before I turned forty. A year and a half later, I pursued IVF on my own and gave birth at forty-two. In forty-one years I had never felt so attractive (in and of myself, not "for" anyone else). It was a time I was not trying to date or meet anyone. The joy I felt carrying a pregnancy to term contributed to my positive feelings. Nowadays, I don't look in the mirror much. If my clothes have no food on them, I can go outside.

CHRISTINE MUHLKE At a certain point I realized it was more punk to dress like a "normal" person and infiltrate the world from the inside than to have everyone treat you like a freak. Now I'm just a bougie mom with an Hermès bag who talks about how she had a nose ring in 1987.

LINDA HESH I grew breasts at age forty. Might be a thyroid thing.

ANITA DOLMAN My favorite shirt has a lot going for it. It's soft and flannel and my favorite shade of blue. But none of this is why I love it. I love it because I'm turning forty this year, and it reminds me of how much I have learned in that time, and what it means to be comfortable. I saw it on the rack this winter. It was $8, which clinched the sale, because one of the many things about myself I have grown comfortable with is my frugalness.

KATJA PANTZAR I recently started a new gig as a broadcast journalist and have had positive feedback about how I look on camera and in general. This is a surprise, because at forty-three, I think I'm sort of a late bloomer for a TV career, especially in a country (Finland) full of beautiful women. When I was hired, one of the things that I was told was that they liked my "look."

BAY GARNETT I think women are forced into reassessing and reevaluating how they look when they reach forty in a way that men don't have to. As you get older you become curious about lots of different things because you become more humble and less self-involved to an extent, and I think that goes into a lot of different areas. ✕

# OH MY GOD, WHO WEARS THAT?

ENGLISH LITERATURE STUDENT **JAGODA WARDACH**
SPEAKS TO **SHEILA HETI**

**SHEILA:** You live in Poland but you have traveled in New York and around Canada. I wonder if you notice differences in the way people dress in these places.

**JAGODA:** Yeah, sure. Basically the biggest difference between Canada and the U.S. is that in the U.S. you have more access to clothes. They are much cheaper, you have better brands, and they have Marshalls everywhere. You can get really cheap and famous clothes. Here, in Toronto, I haven't found any places where it would be possible. Even outlet stores are much more expensive. It's reflected in the way they are dressing. In the U.S., in the streets, you see a lot of brands, even handbags. Almost everyone has at least one designer handbag. Here people have more like, I don't know—

**SHEILA:** Tote bags.

**JAGODA:** Yeah, tote bags. Canadians have a more humble way of dressing, I think? But also in the U.S. you have huge discrepancies. You have a lot of people dressed in beautiful, luxurious clothes, but on the other hand, you have more people wearing rags. Here society is more homogeneous—people on the streets look more or less the same.

**SHEILA:** Does it feel different to be in a place where you see people with designer handbags beside people in rags?

**JAGODA:** I think in a more homogeneous place a person can feel more comfortable. Because when you are there, you are always looking up at the people who have better things, and you envy them, and you crave it.

**SHEILA:** How about back in Poland? How do people dress there compared with here?

**JAGODA:** For example, I was at the University of Toronto yesterday. When I am back at my university, if I would like people there to look like people here, my advice would be: Go to the secondhand store, pick up the most crazy things, and wear those. One girl yesterday had a blue coat with people—Eskimos—dogs, an iceberg, and a white fur hood. Oh my god, you look like a girl from kindergarten, you look like a baby!

**SHEILA:** You're going to laugh, but look at this. *(goes to closet)* This is my mom's coat! *(pulls it out—the same coat Jagoda is describing, but green)*

**JAGODA:** *(tight voice)* Oh my god, that's great!

**SHEILA:** It's a very traditional Canadian kind of coat! Put it on.

**JAGODA:** *(laughing)* Okay! That's awesome! I really appreciate it. To allow me to wear your mum's coat. So yes. Another girl was wearing the bottom of her pajama, I think. In Poland, you would be put on the spot instantly.

**SHEILA:** What do you mean?

**JAGODA:** People would be like, Do you feel okay? Why do you wear pajamas? People are more concerned in Poland with wearing clothes that indicate their status. It's a bit like in the U.S.

**SHEILA:** Can you talk more about feeling envy in America?

**JAGODA:** I know a girl in New York, she

works in an office, and she's younger than me, she's about twenty. She has a lot of clothes. She already has her Louis Vuitton handbag, so for a girl her age, in terms of fashion, it's an accomplishment. And she told me, "Oh, but I would like to have this Chanel 2.55." I thought, "Okay, but you are young, you still have time, you don't have to be so stressed," but for her it's important. She's from Poland, so that would elevate her position among her friends, when she would be hanging out with a Chanel 2.55 bag. Maybe it's also a case of being an immigrant, that you want to keep up with Americans.

SHEILA: Did you buy anything in New York?

JAGODA: Every time I go there I buy some things that I'm really satisfied with, because I'm a hunter. When I went there, I saw how much they are really worth. When you can buy a Gap T-shirt from an outlet for five bucks, and you go to Gap, and you can have the same thing for twenty, you see that you don't have to spend that much, because it's a rip-off. You are just putting your money into the pockets of the owners of the company. So I realized that clothes are not worth a lot, so I don't like to spend a lot on them. But I'm very concerned with the quality of the textiles, because I'm very irritated when I put something on and the quality is getting worse and worse. What else? I couldn't be hipster—I would never be able to go hipster because I don't like ugly things.

SHEILA: Do you think they buy things they find ugly?

JAGODA: I think so. It's a bit like recycling. To use the things again, to give them new meaning, that's a cultural concept, but on the other hand, American Apparel and Urban Outfitters—they are preying on young people and the need to be not that mainstream. They want to look different from their peers, but these brands are creating something artificial. I like to window-shop at those stores but I have never, ever found anything.

SHEILA: No? Why?

JAGODA: It all lacks something. The clothes make you look awkward. I found this maxidress, it was turtleneck, but with the proportions of my body I look like a nun.

SHEILA: When you say they lack something, what do you mean?

JAGODA: They were like . . . unfinished. They don't have the twist.

SHEILA: So with the shirt you're wearing, the twist is the little gold studs?

JAGODA: I think so. I wouldn't buy this shirt without it.

---

SURVEY  *Please describe your mind.*

Right now especially, my mind is mush. —RANDI RIVERA • Romantic. —EMILY RABOTEAU • High levels of comprehension but lower levels of production. —GLORIA ARMINIO • I would like to think of myself as intelligent and quick. I am very analytical, and 75% of the time, I turn things into humor. —ALEXANDRA KERN • I have a tendency to favor my imagination, and it can lead me to worry sometimes. Worry is the dark side of the imagination. I counter the neurosis with work and practicing art, cooking, fencing, and other activities. —KARIMA CAMMELL • I am always thinking of the next thing that needs to be done. I am extraordinarily efficient but not especially compassionate. I generally believe, however, that most people are alike and this gives me comfort. I am able to get through difficult situations by remembering "This too shall pass." —CAITLIN VAN DUSEN • Works well most of the time. —JEANIE KIMBER • Pessimistic, sarcas-

SHEILA: Where did you get it?

JAGODA: In Bluenotes and it was cheap. When I posted a picture on Facebook, and got my flatmate's seal of approval—I like your shirt!—I thought, Okay, that was a good choice. I wouldn't want to wear something to be invisible in the crowd.

SHEILA: You don't want to be invisible?

JAGODA: No no no no no. It's not like me. Maybe I want to be anonymous, but I don't want to be invisible. I would like people to notice me maybe?

SHEILA: You like to see them noticing you?

JAGODA: Yes—and I like to look at people. Maybe that's what I want—this exchange. 'Cause I like to observe people. And I'm really grateful when they give me this aesthetic pleasure, when I have something nice to look at. That's why I love public transportation—

SHEILA: Is it women or men you like getting looks from? Or both?

JAGODA: Both. I don't really perceive it in terms of sex. I think I'm more likely to notice a beautiful woman dressed in the way I like than to see a man dressed beautifully.

SHEILA: So it's not sexual pleasure, it's more aesthetic.

JAGODA: I think so. Because, of course you look at the person who's wearing this clothes, but this pleasure is made of some items. When you like the shoes, you look at the shoes. You also look at the face of the person and at his or her body, but it's only a tool in conducting this message.

SHEILA: Do you try to show things about what your body is like when you dress?

JAGODA: Sometimes. I used to be plump, to put it straight. So when I lose some weight or when I exercise a lot, I like to show how my body looks. But normally I use clothes to hide, to deceive people. Maybe that's why I like clothes so much—because I'm never satisfied with how I look without them.

SHEILA: Do you like lingerie?

JAGODA: Yes. My mum, she says, "Oh my god, kid, you're sick in the mind! You have so many bras in your closet!" But I like them! The same is true in the case of swimsuits. I really have a lot of them. I have pieces—for instance, only the bottom and not the top part, because in the U.S. a couple of years ago, I think it was at the beginning of the crisis, you could buy a lot of things very cheap. So I managed to buy pieces from Calvin Klein and Victoria's Secret for one dollar. They were so beautiful that I couldn't help it, and I was buying them, hoping I will find something similar, just to make a whole one. So now

---

tic, sensitive, paranoid. —ANNE LAURENCE GOLLION • Healing from an emotional two years of loss with my mother's passing and a benign tumor that wreaked havoc on me that just so happened to be in my mouth. —CARLA DU PREE • My mother says I am "very strong-minded."—JODIE YOUNG • My mind feels feminine and masculine at different times. —FELIZ LUCIA MOLINA • Troubled. —GABRIELLE BELL • My mind is what I turn to and take seriously. —ANNIKA WAHLSTRÖM • My mind is clear and I know what I want. —GAIL O'HARA • I am a sensitive and creative person with sometimes-occurring dark thoughts that I mostly manage to spit away with the help of my positive and optimistic cells. —GINTARE PARULYTE • I have really bad memory due to medication. —IMOGEN DONATO • I like my mind about as much as I like my body; I'm aware of my limitations as well my strengths. I've been lucky to be able to play to my strengths. —FAITH HARDEN • Curious, bright, searching. —RAISEL BRUNO • Peaceful, quiet, aware, focused on the

I have a bottom from Victoria's Secret with gold things, or I have one from Juicy Couture with beautiful hearts—and even if I find the top in normal, regular stores, it will be okay because I paid just one dollar for the bottom. But it never happened. So I have a huge box in my closet with those pieces that I will never wear.

**SHEILA:** Are you going to throw them out?

**JAGODA:** No no. They can stay, because I'm fortunate enough that I have a room at my parents' house and I also have my flat in the city where I'm staying, so I have two closets. Talking about clothes, when my grandmother was living in the U.S., she was sending us parcels. I was twelve years old. I was excited and so looking forward to some nice clothes to show off at school, but every time she was sending something I was so heartbroken, because it was so her, it was completely her grandma style, and when I was opening the parcel, it was like, I don't know, a red shirt with a glittering star, oh my god, who wears that? And my mom was like, You don't need clothes, because Grandma is sending them to us.

**SHEILA:** So you had to wear your grandma's stuff?

**JAGODA:** Yeah, basically. I was not like the rest of my teenage colleagues that were so concerned with designer clothes, that were making a drama at home for their parents just to buy something. I was more peaceful. I was like, Okay, I will suffer in silence. But it's funny. Some of these odd things my grandma was sending, at the beginning I found them crap, but now some of them, they are real gems. Like the white leather pencil skirt? It's gorgeous. Unfortunately, I'm not that skinny to wear it, but if I were, I would definitely do that now. . . . It sometimes doesn't seem a good thing to talk about clothes.

**SHEILA:** Because people will have the impression—

**JAGODA:** Yes, that I'm stupid, and I don't have any other things in my life to think of. It's a general view that you should be more concerned with the inside of you than the outside layer. People probably think I'm stupid and I just have this outer layer and I don't have anything inside my head. I don't know, maybe it's just because I was brought up in a Catholic country, so this is a part of their thinking, that you shouldn't show off and be concerned about worldly things. When you think about your clothes, you're automatically thinking about yourself, and you are evil. I don't know. ✕

---

moment. —JESSICA JOHNSON • Intelligent. Anxious. Careful. Ambitious. —JILL GALLAGHER • Analytical and poetic. —CYRENA LEE • Content. I've just had a very busy month and don't have anything to plan or do for a few weeks. —CRYSTAL MORTGENTALER • I am very content with my life, I feel blessed to have a very loving and sweet marriage, good health, a good job, and close friends and a terrific family. I look forward to retirement in the next couple of years and hope to volunteer and help others. —DENISE MINEO • My ego is very easily inflated and deflated, and I have OCD/body dysmorphic tendencies I struggle to keep under control. I have high standards for my understanding and analysis of the world. I try to be ever aware of what's going on inside me so that I can always be in the process of improving. It's all interesting to me. —AMANDA M. • Chaotic, lazy. —EVELIJN MARTINIUS • Sound. —CHARLOTTE BOYD ✕

## THE OUTFIT IN THE PHOTOGRAPH | II

**DENISE MINEO (RIGHT):** I remember feeling very grown-up on my tenth birthday. It was 1962 and our family was celebrating my twin brother's and my birthday by dining at a classic old New Orleans Creole restaurant. We dressed up for the occasion. I thought I was mighty cute and I just loved that dress. The fact that it was sewn by my mom was fine, that was the norm. Paired with a pretty, white blouse, I felt very stylish, at least by my standards. And those shoes—two-tone, pointy, and very modern, even with socks. I had a matching two-tone purse to round out the ensemble. I wasn't dressed like a little girl anymore. My aunt Kate is standing next to me. We were in awe of her—she had such confidence and she dressed very stylishly, even if her clothes were not expensive. She was a rebel, a free spirit, a divorcée. Her clothes were form-fitting and she wasn't at all afraid to show off her best assets. She used Maybelline cake mascara, drew on her eyebrows, then completed the look with bright red lipstick.

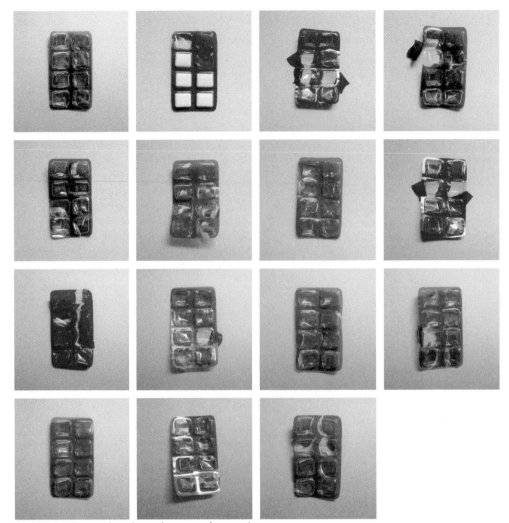

*KRISTIN GORE*'s gum chewed over the course of one week

# SHOPPING

*"I don't 'go shopping.' If possible, I happen upon things to wear in more interesting ways."* —MOLLY MURRAY

CAMILLA GIBB I have a bad habit of shopping after therapy. I don't know if this influences the choices I make, but I like that time to wander alone, idly scanning racks and shelves, meditating. The only problem with this is that I have recently started psychoanalysis, which means being on the couch a minimum of three times a week. That's a lot of shopping.

ALEXI CHISLER I can get very stressed out and confused when I'm shopping. This can result in my buying things I later realize I don't like. So a rule I have is that I go into a store only if I like the majority of the clothes they have in the window. I have to trust their "curation" of clothing, so that even if I am disoriented inside the store, I can still come out with something good.

ALISSA NUTTING For many years, I was addicted to shopping. I'd shop until my car was full of clothing, my closets overflowing, my bank account empty and my credit cards maxed. I did this for the better part of a decade and tried and failed to quit on several occasions. It took therapy and a twelve-step support group for me to stop shopping compulsively.

EILEEN MYLES I've had a lot more success shopping when someone else is shopping or when I'm in a rush to go somewhere and shouldn't look. I like shopping out of the peripheral vision.

MARSHA COURNEYA When I have bought a dress to wear to a gala or a party, I can't help feeling embarrassed by the idea that I am excited enough or nervous enough to use clothes as a way to cast a spell over myself, so that I might feel special. When I look at photos of myself wearing something I bought especially for an occasion, it's hard because I have to relive the memory of things not going as I had hoped, because they never do.

CLAIRE CAMERON My desire for nice clothes feels at odds with the financial needs of my family. I've since thought, Fuck that.

AURORA SHIMSHAK Once in a while, my boyfriend's mom takes me shopping. I love shopping with her. It's not completely guilt-free. There's a bit of a nagging in my stomach that probably comes from the fact that I'm taking money she could be spending on herself. But it's still much lighter than spending my own money on clothes. Recently, I figured out that she likes to see things after I try them on. She's quite generous with compliments. *Yes! Let's get that. How often do you find a perfect fit like that?* Shopping with her gives me a high that lasts for hours.

ANNETTE CARGIOLI I made a decision this year to not shop for clothing and to use what I have.

AMANDA STERN More often than not, I do my best shopping off other people. I often find myself asking women where they got their shoes or their bag, willfully ignoring that how good it looks on them is not indicative of how it will look on me. I want the item, as much as I want the specific way it drapes on their body, or as much as I just want their body, or their way. I shop based on the false premise of being granted an entire promise, and I am almost always disappointed when the promise falls short.

**CASSANDRA LEVEILLE** Being working poor, I never have a ton of money or opportunities to shop. When I do have money, a great resource has been finding fashion blogs that link to good Etsy shops. I usually wait until there are sales, or I use coupon codes, which many shops give to customers for their first order. I feel like I buy items only a couple of times a year.

**ESTELLE TANG** I'm weaning myself off cheap and cheerful purchases made on sunny days filled with ice cream and sheer delight, or miserable rainy evenings after a shitty day. These are quick, guilt-free fixes I justify to myself as not breaking the bank. But the pale yellow cardigan I never wore, the *two* cheap cardigans in the same cut, and the shirtdress that never quite sat properly around my hips are all sobering reminders that quick and thoughtless buys are rarely a good idea.

**BLAINE HARPER** I avoid shopping with a sense of desperate need or desire, in the same way that one might avoid visiting the supermarket on an empty stomach.

**CHRISTINE GIGNAC** When I was younger, I went shopping more often but bought cheaper items. Now I shop less often, but spend more on each piece. It probably evens out to about the same amount.

**AMY TURNER** Buy the dress, the place to wear it will follow.

**CATHERINE LITTEN** I dislike shopping. I'm on the large side (for many years a size 14 or 16, but recently a 12 or 10), and it can be discouraging to try on tons of clothes that weren't made for my body type. So when I shop, I have a battle plan: This is what I want to get, and I will find it.

**JACKIE SORO** When I shop at thrift shores, I feel I've taken a big step away from the sweatshop production cycle. That's the reason I get so many of my clothes from friends. I like to imagine why someone parted with the lovely flannel I'm wearing now.

**CARMEN JOY KING** This is weird: every time I close a dressing-room door, I have to pee.

**AUDREY GELMAN** I think, "Can I imagine wearing this in five years?"

**BONNIE MORRISON** I've tried to be more mindful as I have gotten older, because if you shop regularly, you end up with stuff you'll never wear, because are there even that many events or occasions in a normal person's life? What did you buy all those hats, parasols, bangle bracelets, opera gloves for? Now you're just old and crazy and live in a rat nest of weird items you never used.

**GILLIAN BLORE** I have a constant series of lists of things I want/need/desire: perfect knee-high black boots, a trench coat, a bathing suit . . . Some things have been on the list for over a decade. Then the stars will collide and I'll find a pair of boots that tick all the right boxes and I'll throw down my credit card for what would seem to be an unduly large expenditure.

**ANN IRELAND** How come all these young women are laden down with bags from snazzy shops? Where do they get the money? I start to feel pissed off. To hell with the whole concept of shopping. Who needs clothes? ✕

# I REFUSED

MANSOURA EZ ELDIN

One must choose when to rebel with clothing. Three years ago, I participated in the anti-government demonstration known as "Friday of Rage," which turned out to be the most important and violent day of the January revolution in Egypt. I carefully dressed before going to demonstrate against Mubarak's regime: a light brown sweater, a blue shirt with blue stripes, and jeans and sneakers to permit me to run if the police force attacked our demonstration. I wrapped a *keffiyeh* (scarf) around my neck to protect my face, to lessen the effects of tear gas in our clashes with the Central Security Forces. I put on a bit more makeup than usual to suggest to the police that our participation in the demonstrations was not just an everyday activity.

My friends and I rode the metro to the Amr ibn al-Aas mosque. The demonstration was scheduled to begin after Friday prayers. At the last stop, my friends urged me to use the scarf wrapped around my neck to cover my hair. I refused. My friends thought entering the mosque without a headscarf would draw the attention of the police. I stuck to my refusal—it had been years since I had worn a headscarf, and I refused to put any covering on my head, even for a minute, as compensation for the many years I had unconsciously covered my head as an innocent girl.

We exited the metro and instantly ran into Central Security Force officers hiding behind their shields. I quickly put the scarf on my head to avoid any trouble.

I remember the first time I walked outside without covering my head. It was winter in Cairo. I was thirteen. The headscarf had evolved over time to become part of my body. Then I realized I could shed it, as it no longer expressed me or my thoughts. That night, as I walked through the streets in the middle of the city with my hair showing, I was overcome with the feeling of being watched, as if I were walking completely naked.

People who watch you in the streets see you differently from how you see yourself. In 2009, while visiting Algeria, I stopped in front of a store that sold silver Berber jewelry. I was fascinated by the inscriptions in the metal. It seemed like an entry into a world of seductive promises. I chose a necklace and a bracelet, and wore them immediately. As I walked down Didouche Mourad, passersby started to talk to me in a language I did not understand. I responded in Arabic. Then one man started to yell at me. A stranger who knew from my accent that I was Egyptian told the man this. He slunk away after stealing one last look at my silver necklace. My savior explained to me that the angered man assumed, because of my jewelry, that I was Berber, so he had spoken to me in Berber. When I did not respond, he thought that I was denying my identity and trying to take on a different one.

I once unthinkingly went out in a red sweater when the Al Ahly Sporting Club (the most famous Egyptian soccer team, the Red Devils; they wear red uniforms) was playing. I received many flirtatious comments in the street about my red clothing: "Al Ahly is iron," "My darling, my Al Ahly fan," "I love the Red Devils." After that, I stopped wearing red on big game days.

There was a red, short lace dress I owned when I was seven years old. I loved it because it made me feel like a hero in a film. I wore it once to my Quran lessons with Sheikh Abdul Rahman. During that lesson, he looked at my dress with contempt. He approached me at the end of the lesson to hear the verses I had memorized, then pulled me toward himself and scratched me on my arms with his pen, to punish me for not respecting the Islamic dress code. "Wrong! You will go to hell!" he yelled.

I did not say that his own daughter—who spent most of her days on the balcony facing the room where we studied—wore pretty, elegant clothes that complimented her skin.

After that, I no longer attended his lessons. Free from his gaze, I continued to wear short dresses.

Today, I am going to meet with several writers and publishers in one of the foreign cultural centers in Cairo. I must walk ten minutes from my house to the main street, where I will take a coach. Since I will be in the streets, I cannot wear anything too revealing or short, in order to avoid any trouble or commotion.

Deciding what to wear, I stand before my armoire, confused. I do this every day—enter into complicated negotiations with myself.

When I was younger, I would grab the first thing that looked good on me, put it on, and go out.

# MY OUTFITS | THESSALY LA FORCE

### JANUARY

"The Love Child of Shackleton
and Pocahontas"

*Deep, dark Iowa winter. Late for Marilynne
Robinson's writing workshop.*

Boyfriend's grandfather's tan shearling coat
Khaki green pants over yoga pants
Faux-shearling-lined knee-high snow
boots
White wool neck scarf knitted by my
mother
Gloves
Many sweaters
Two hats

### FEBRUARY

"A character cut from the publishing house
scenes in *The Last Days of Disco*"

*California winter day. Sixty degrees. Going to
the DMV to renew my driver's license.*

White, billowy, sheer men's dress shirt
Light blue jeans rolled at the cuff
Pony-hair leopard-print oxfords
Blazer
More makeup than usual

### MARCH

"Princess Di at a grunge concert"

*David Hockney sky. Thirty degrees. Viola
lesson.*

Black beanie
Ballet flats
Long pleated skirt
Large sweater
Rose-gold rings under my mittens

### APRIL

"Joan Didion in Santa Monica
on a cloudy day"

*Fifty-four degrees. Nothing could go wrong.
Buying groceries from the food co-op in Iowa
City for the Russell Banks potluck.*

Black turtleneck
Denim
Trench
Brown loafers
Sunglasses
Hair parted down the middle

### MAY

"Channeling Michelle Obama"

*Sixty-one degrees. Just a touch too hot for a
coat. Job interview.*

Neon and blue floral silk dress
Low gray suede heels
White blazer

## JUNE

"Anthropologist at her going-away party—
Elsa Rush meets Jane Goodall"

*First real summer day. Handing in my thesis.*

Tan silk drawstring pants
White button-down
Turquoise-and-tan gladiator sandals
Silver necklace
Bare face

## JULY

"Sandra Bullock of the nineties"

*Hot summer sun. Can't think. On a date
to see* The Artist Is Present *at Film Forum
with my friend.*

Black silk dress
Birkenstocks
Sunglasses
Black bucket bag
Denim jacket

## AUGUST

"Someone in Tilda Swinton's
intimate circle of friends"

*Sweltering. Midday sun is oppressive.
US Open.*

Green jacquard capri pants with gold
threaded embellishment and zippers
Pink and white sleeveless tunic printed
with small people all over
Slingbacks
Very firm brown leather bag
Blow-dried hair

## SEPTEMBER

"Winona Ryder, the morning after"

*Crisp. Feel the need to buy firewood. In a
cabin in Callicoon, upstate, at my friend's
birthday.*

Body-conscious black maxidress with
spaghetti straps
Cropped sweater
Gold loafers
No makeup except what mascara stayed on
overnight
Messy ballerina bun

## OCTOBER

"Francesca Woodman at home"

*Sunny but air-conditioned. The office.*

Navy floral skirt
Black sweater with open back
Black lace bra
Pink-nude ankle boots with wooden heels

## NOVEMBER

"A Greta Gerwig character on a first date"

*Rain, damp streets. Gallery opening
in Chelsea. Followed by friend's choir
performance uptown.*

Ecru and silver coat over a long pink silk
dress with thin satin straps
Ballet slippers that cross around my ankles
Glossy lipstick I love but always forget to
wear

## DECEMBER

"Patti Smith at a book signing"

*Strangely warm. Book party at Brooklyn
Brewery.*

Black tunic
Baggy black jeans
Black flats
Bracelets

# BALM

*"I usually wear what's on the chair from the day before. It's been tested already, and I feel good in clothes I know the effect of."* —RACHEL KUSHNER

**RAMOU SARR** I like to come home and deep clean in the tub, soak for a bit with a bath bomb, moisturize the hell out of myself, then lounge for an hour in a sheer dashiki before passing out.

**HEATHER LOVE** I use clothes to calm myself down, for sure. My kids always comment on how "comfy" I look and how weirdly soft my clothes are. My girlfriend refers to my style as "Build-A-Bear." I think she is trying to get at how these clothes are not only comfortable for me but comforting to her.

**CATHERINE ORCHARD** I was in a sailboat that tipped over when I was a kid, a very minor thing, but it was startling and cold. I remember walking back and dropping all the freezing, heavy-soaked clothes on the floor, running my feet under hot water, and putting on my pajamas and feeling very calmed. I still like a full men's pajama set—I find it comforting and calm.

**LILI HORVATH** I like looking at and fondling my mother's clothes when she's away. It's comforting to run my fingers across them and bury myself in something comforting and familiar.

**ELLEN RODGER** Coming home and putting on sloppy layers of clothes is calming.

**LENAE DAY** I love to swim, but even more than swimming, I love to sit, wet, by the water. Owning so many swimsuits makes me feel like I will always be close to water, which is a thought that calms my soul. There is something about the fit of a one-piece swimsuit—the way it hugs the stomach, hips, groin, and heart—that is akin to swaddling. I feel safe in a swimsuit, like nothing is going to fall out or get out of control—like organs or wayward emotions or that burrito I just ate.

**STELLA BUGBEE** I spent a week in the hospital for abdominal surgery. Each morning, despite terrible pain, the nurses would make me get up and walk so I didn't get too weak. The hospital gowns depressed me, so I'd slowly pull a striped Breton dress over my head, brush my hair, and put on bright red flip-flops and lip gloss. My friend had given me a giant Missoni robe, and I'd pull that on and make my way around the recovery unit. By taking the extra step of wearing clothes that made me feel "normal," I felt like I wasn't giving in to my illness. It was one of the few times I used clothing to calm myself.

**BRONWYN CAWKER** I went through a major episode of manic depression in my early twenties, and was given an oversized men's sweater from H&M called the "old man's sweater" by my best friend, Dustin. When I felt really upset, we would get stoned, put on our old-man sweaters, drink tea, and watch bad movies. We live in different cities now, but when I want to feel calm or closer to him, I wear mine. ✕

# BAG DANCE | LEANNE SHAPTON *featuring* HEIDI JULAVITS

*Photographs by Gus Powell*

*GINA RICO*'s hairbrushes and combs

# I HAD A LITTLE PEGBOARD

### ARTIST **CINDY SHERMAN** SPEAKS TO
### ACTOR & WRITER **MOLLY RINGWALD**

**MOLLY:** You've always been such an icon for me in terms of how I want to look. You're very fashionable but you never look like you're a slave to it. You just have this flair. What is your first clothing memory?

**CINDY:** Oh gosh, I was maybe eleven or so. And because I loved paper dolls, I made paper-doll versions of all the clothes I would wear to school. I had a little pegboard with days of the week, and on the weekend— Sunday night, I guess—I'd figure out my outfits for the whole week ahead. I think it was because of a math teacher I had, and I was amazed at how she seemed to be wearing different outfits every single day, never repeating for months at a time. I mean, you'd see the same skirt show up, or the same sweater, but she would always work it with a different configuration. I was so impressed with that. I think that's what inspired me to do these little cut-outs.

**MOLLY:** That's so sweet. You probably don't have them anymore.

**CINDY:** No. But when I was in college, I remember thinking about it, and I did an art-project version of the same thing, only without the days of the week. I just made a doll of myself with my underwear, and photographed all my clothes, and made it into a little children's book of school clothes, play clothes . . . Then I made an animation from it. It's sort of how a lot of my work evolved, out of that.

**MOLLY:** When you first started making art and taking photographs, did you know that it was going to be only you in the pictures? Did you ever think you were going to include other people?

**CINDY:** I don't remember thinking about it one way or another, but I didn't expect to be doing basically the same thing for thirty years. I guess in the beginning I thought, I'm doing one project that is using myself, and who knows what I'll do after that? I did try shooting other people at times—friends or family members. I even paid somebody to model, but it made me so self-conscious. I just wanted to entertain the person.

**MOLLY:** That sounds exhausting.

**CINDY:** Yeah. Because when I'm on my own, I will just push myself. But I didn't want to impose on other people, so I'd sort of rush it along to get it out of the way, and I wasn't happy with the results.

**MOLLY:** You've told me that you see yourself as a blank canvas in a way. Do you spend the same amount of time with each transformation? Have you gotten to the point where you think, "Oh, this one is going to be really time-consuming," or are you constantly surprised by how it ends up?

**CINDY:** I guess it's a crapshoot. With some of those history portraits, I feel like I just whipped one out in a couple hours. Then there are others where I think I know what it is I want and I'll work at the same thing for days, and maybe never really feel satisfied. It's always different.

MOLLY: When you're thinking of a new character, do clothes always play a part?

CINDY: A lot of times the clothes actually determine it. When I did the clowns, I was researching them online. I didn't want to just buy clown outfits, which you can easily get. The imagery online that I was interested in, or influenced by, was of clowns who looked like do-it-yourself clowns. People who just looked funkier appealed to me because I started to wonder *(laughs)*, Is that an alcoholic hiding behind this clown mask? What's under the clown makeup and the funky costume? So I would go online, like on eBay, and look up, I don't know, colorful clothes, and I found square-dancing dresses with these crazy ruffles and everything. Or I'd go to the Salvation Army and get a bunch of brightly colored striped T-shirts. I would amass all this stuff and then play with it, mixing things up, and then from that I would figure out what the clown should look like, and have more of an idea of the personality of that clown.

MOLLY: When you do a portrait, do you feel you know the character—in terms of biography? Or is it more the essence of somebody?

CINDY: It's more like an essence. With some of the society portraits, as I'm shooting them, as the character is evolving, I will start to feel I know the character, or maybe I'll realize the shots that work the best are the ones where she looks very haughty and bitchy and distant and cold, and that will help inform the character even if I didn't plan on making her that way. Some of them look more haunted and sad and are trying to put up a good front. But it's always a surprise to me when I see the results in the tests. Then I realize, "That's the one that works."

MOLLY: I think I've told you this before— but when we were working together on the movie *Office Killer*, I remember thinking about my character's clothing, and I had this idea that she was going to be very New York and wearing all black, you know, because she was written kind of bitchy. And when you came in you were like, "No no no." You were very forthright: "Wrong, wrong, this is not right, she's colorful, she has to have really bright colors." I hadn't thought of it that way, but as soon as you said that, and we started to build the character around these colors, it really changed the way I saw the character, and she ended up being a lot more funny and interesting. She was still really bitchy, but the color really informed my interpretation of her. It's something I've thought about a lot since then.

CINDY: I like to make characters who are not supposed to be frumpy—to dress them up frumpy and take it in an opposite direction.

MOLLY: Do you ever find yourself wanting to photograph people you see on the street, like, Oh I have to remember that outfit?

CINDY: Sure, yeah. And I've tried to do it surreptitiously. Usually the person's approaching me and I'm trying to find my phone really quickly and then I pretend I'm just looking at my phone, and usually the picture is way out of focus or I catch the person from the side or the back. Recently I was in Venice and a bunch of us were having lunch and there was this waitress who was incredible—I have never seen anybody with so much mascara on. It was as if she used a whole thing of mascara in one sitting. It was caked on in the most outrageous way! I wish I were one of those people who don't mind going up to a stranger and saying, "Wow, can I take your picture, you look great!" That would make sense if they're really attractive, but if they're very strange-looking . . . maybe they don't know that they're strange-looking. It might be a little insulting or something. So I make mental notes.

**MOLLY:** I feel that every time one goes out it's a transformation—I certainly don't look the same when I go out as I look in the morning. We all transform and we all have this idea of what we want to look like when we go out. Do you ever wear the same clothes as your characters? Or are those things totally separate?

**CINDY:** There are some things I could see wearing. Sometimes what's more scary is that I will be getting dressed to go somewhere and then I'll look in the mirror and I'll realize I've actually become one of my characters. Then it's like *(laughs)*, "Okay, it's time to change something."

**MOLLY:** *(laughs)* Yeah, scale it back a little.

**CINDY:** I do feel about getting dressed to go out that it's a totally different thing from my normal daytime self. I enjoy putting a lot of makeup on to go to some function, and wearing something I wouldn't normally wear during the day.

**MOLLY:** Do you feel women in general take enough risks with what they wear?

**CINDY:** Well, I don't think celebrities take enough risks—especially celebrities who have a creative side and probably know exactly what they feel good in. But that's because they get torn apart in the press so much they're afraid of taking chances. So everybody just looks very tasteful and kind of all the same.

**MOLLY:** Yeah, bland.

**CINDY:** Yeah. So for somebody who likes to watch celebrity events, it's sad to see everybody look the same. But the general public? I think most people see themselves one way, and that's how they always see themselves, even as they get older, like wearing the same hairstyle forever. They hit a certain look when they're twenty-five and continue to look that way until they're old. Men and women.

**MOLLY:** Most fashion people actually counsel you to do that—to keep one hairstyle, like Anna Wintour or Jacqueline Kennedy Onassis. They really picked a look and didn't deviate very much.

**CINDY:** That's true.

**MOLLY:** I don't feel I can do that. That's one of the reasons why I won't get a tattoo, because I feel I'd want to change it up too much.

**CINDY:** I love tattoos. I've always fantasized about having one big tattoo all over my back or something—I love it, it's like clothes.

**MOLLY:** I would hate to have to wear the same outfit every day. It would feel like a uniform.

**CINDY:** But I could see becoming one of those people who just keep adding more and more tattoos.

**MOLLY:** I do think tattoos are beautiful, but I don't think they're for me. I guess that's what it is—it's art that continues to grow and transform and it just happens to be on your body. I've always felt I can do that with clothes. It doesn't have to be ink actually on my body. Which women make you the happiest to look at?

**CINDY:** I think women who look like they're going against style but look super-confident in what they're doing, like they don't care what the fashion magazines say, they're just out there and happy about it. I'm aspiring to that as I get older—to just not care and go with it.

**MOLLY:** It's hard, though, when you're in the public eye. I feel I took way more risks as a young person. I'll look at old photographs of myself—or even old movies, because that had a lot to do with my clothes—and I'll think, "Wow, I was really bold, I was really going for it there." I never really thought in terms of what other people were going to think. Now I'm not a neutral dresser, though I certainly don't take the risks I used to take. Do you find you've gotten riskier as you've gotten older?

**CINDY:** I think so, because when I was younger, especially when I was starting to get more successful, I felt so guilty about it that I didn't want to stand out. I'd go to an opening and just try to blend in. Now it is what it is. And I can afford to experiment more with shopping and purchases, so I definitely feel more playful.

**MOLLY:** I feel like you're a lot sexier.

**CINDY:** Ha! That's nice.

**MOLLY:** I always thought you were great-looking, but you were more . . . I don't know . . .

**CINDY:** I was tomboyish, I think.

**MOLLY:** And cute! I wonder if that had anything to do with . . . Well, you were at the tail end of not such a happy marriage. Do you feel your clothing is influenced by the person in your life?

**CINDY:** Yes. Although I think what also happened is I became single again and I was starting to get older, and I wanted to recapture some femininity I felt I lost through the unhappiness of the marriage or my youth going away. I also was so much more insecure about my body then, and I felt so much better about myself after the divorce that I didn't mind letting more of my femininity come out.

**MOLLY:** It was really interesting to see that transformation. It's also great for me to know somebody who looks better as she gets older *(laughs)* rather than the other way around. Because I think aging is really, really rough.

**CINDY:** It's scary, yeah.

**MOLLY:** It is! It's fucking scary! There's part of me that wants to say, "I'm deeper than that, this shouldn't matter, think about the roots of the tree rather than the flower." And I do. There's a part of me that really believes that.

Then there's the other part of me that's just like, "Fuck, it's only going to get worse."

**CINDY:** I know, it's really scary.

**MOLLY:** But in a lot of ways, I'm better-looking now than I was in my thirties. I'm more confident, my body is better because I think about it and work on it.

**CINDY:** I totally agree.

**MOLLY:** How do you feel about the way culture sees and presents women to women?

**CINDY:** I think it's scary what the fashion world presents as women. But I also know that when I've had my picture taken and they've done a tiny bit of retouching, I actually am thankful. They show me the before and it's like, "Oh god." But it's these models, I think. It's not so much the retouching, it's the choice of models. They could still find really beautiful people who weren't necessarily so skinny, or they could find really interesting faces that weren't classically beautiful.

**MOLLY:** They don't look quite human to me. I feel like I'm conditioned like everybody else to think, "Oh, that's pretty, that's beautiful, they're so elongated," but when I really think about it, they're just not like anybody else.

**CINDY:** Yeah, they're freaks of nature compared with the rest of us.

**MOLLY:** And freaks of nature that go in one direction rather than another. Fashion's always been around, but there's a lot more pressure on girls to look a certain way. I love your centerfold pictures, because most centerfolds are so fake and the women don't look real.

**CINDY:** I made them for a magazine as a response to the idea of a centerfold. But I wanted it to feel like you were intruding on somebody's intimacy, rather than feeling like you wanted to gawk. I wanted it to make you feel like, "Oops, I better turn the page." ╳

# SISTERS

*"When I was seven, I stole the side–part hairstyle from my sister for a school picture.
Household drama ensued."* —DAPHNE JAVITCH

**ALISSA NUTTING** There was an oatmeal-colored oversized T-shirt nightgown patterned with bow-tie-laden teddy bears. It belonged to my older sister, whom I adored, and I received it as a child when she discarded it. Wearing it I felt this nearly cannibalistic pleasure. It was this combination of feeling that I'd become her, that she was with me, that we were the same person, and that I looked great because she looked great. I still wore it in college. It was soft and very short on me by that point, and I felt sexy in it. But I got rid of it a few years later when I was attempting to have a ubiquitous level of sophistication in my life. I wanted to look put-together even at bedtime, partially to impress the guy I was with. It didn't take long for me to realize this was a really stupid notion, but by that point it was too late. I'd already gotten rid of it. I remember how comfortable I felt when I put it on. It was like transdermal Valium.

**MAEGAN FIDELINO** The first outfit I remember clearly is the polka-dot dress I wore to the hospital when my sister was born.

**SARA K.** I can't stand borrowing clothes from people and nearly have panic attacks when I find out that a new girlfriend is one of those oh-I-had-sisters types who starts rummaging through my closet and pulling shit out. To me, clothes are really personal, so I'm offended that someone would think that she and I are interchangeable.

**CAITLIN VAN DUSEN** I talk to my sister often about clothes. We once distinguished between people who are "ball" (they look consistent from day to day, neither extraordinarily good nor bad) and people who are "bat" (sometimes they look drop-dead gorgeous and other times frumpy; their appearance varies a lot from day to day). I don't know where those terms came from, but they stuck.

**LENAE DAY** I am constantly giving my younger sister clothing items and then, much to her chagrin, taking them back. I figure if it wasn't a birthday or Christmas gift, it was really only ever borrowed from me.

**ZENDA SHIMSHAK** My sister gave me a ring for Christmas one year that I wore every day until I got engaged, at which point I switched it for my engagement ring. It was very hard to take it off. It meant so much to me.

**MELISSA HENDERSON** I love giving gifts. I recently gave my sister a necklace of music notes. She likes to sing. She wears it all the time and cherishes it more than her other jewelry. She still has the special box. It's not from a popular designer, but I picked it out especially for her and I didn't care how much it cost because it screamed her name.

**JOSS LAKE** I don't generally give gifts of clothing or jewelry anymore. I gave my sister a beautiful coat a few years ago and she never even wore it as a courtesy gesture, so I'm done.

**LILI OWEN ROWLANDS** On school photo day, my sister and I were dressed in identical stripey tops. We were supposed to be taken in for our individual and class photos in the morning, then siblings were paired up in the afternoon for family photos. During lunch, I had put on my fleece because I was cold. When the order forms and sample photos marked PROOF arrived, my mistake was obvious to all. In our individual portraits, my sister and I looked sisterly. But in our joint photo we looked chaotic and a little sad, and you could see cat hairs speckling my fleece. I think this was probably PROOF of something.

**JOHANNA FATEMAN** I remember desperately wanting all kinds of outfits and shoes, especially things my older sister wore. I have a clear memory of standing at the top of the stairs in the white patent-leather Mary Janes that she'd outgrown. It was an ecstatic moment, feeling like a sophisticated, older girl in my sister's party shoes. They were like the key to a fairy-tale realm.

**KIMBERLY JEAN SMITH** While still a child, my sister underwent radical brain surgery. As a result, she had lots of cognitive and physical disorders and died at age forty-two. But even at that age she looked like a small child. My mother often dressed her as one, choosing clothing that drew no attention to her, because my sister was bald due to her treatments, and thin, and sat in a wheelchair. For most people, she was already a strange sight. But I liked to buy her bright things, things to accentuate the color of her rosy cheeks or draw attention to her big brown eyes and long dark eyelashes—like red caps, and rose-printed jackets in fashionable cuts from trendy designers. It gave me great pleasure to see her wearing these things. I think she enjoyed them too, as much as she could, I suppose, as she seemed mostly to live beyond such trivial things.

**SAGAN MacISAAC** When I was fourteen, my sister moved out to go to university. During the time she was away, I got into vintage/Value Village dressing and liked to match all sorts of colors and patterns. I looked really hippie-ish. When my sister came home after being away for a few months she said, *"What are you wearing?"* My mum was in the room and leaned over and whispered (but I heard), "That's how she dresses."

**AMY LAM** My friend Zeesy told me a story about how a girl I don't know lied about where she got a piece of clothing. This girl told one of our friends, Yuula, that she got the piece of clothing from Value Village, then later on, in a different scenario, told Yuula's sister Xenia that she got it from a dumpster. Zeesy said the girl told Xenia she got it from a dumpster because Xenia is slightly cooler than Yuula.

**RAISEL BRUNO** Once while we were swimming, one of my sisters said to me, "You're ugly." She said I had beady eyes. Another time while we were swimming, another sister said, "Raisel's pretty." I took both things to heart.

**GAYLE DAVIES** I was wearing a pink dress and was about four years old. My mother had taken me and four of my sisters to the Lutheran church in a small country town. I crawled into the pew next to my sister, aged nine, who in no short order informed me that I was NOT to sit next to her because my pink dress would clash with the red one she was wearing.

**SHAYLA CROWEL** I love getting hand-me-downs from my older sister. We have similar tastes in clothing, so I was really happy when, after she had her first baby and was not able to fit into some of her clothes, I was able to take some things of hers I've always liked.

**NAOMI ALISA CALNITSKY** The borrowing of clothing remains a contentious issue in my family with the dangerous potential to deeply damage my relationship with my little sister, whose sense of style and intuitive fashion sense remain far superior to mine.

**MAIREAD CASE** My sister and I don't live in the same city anymore. Once I needed a new coat and we went out together and she helped me find a good one. It was the most expensive item I ever bought, $130, on the sale rack at Macy's. I wore this wool coat every winter day for years and, maybe this is lame, I cried when it got moth holes.

**REBECCA SALERNO** There was this knit linen sweater that my sister and I fought over for several months, and her best friend was also fond of it, so all three of us were wearing it and stealing it from one another.

**RACHEL PERRY WELTY** My sisters and I use a form of shorthand in our own language to describe clothing-related things. CPW stands for "Cost per Wear," which is a term I believe I read in a funny little book from the '80s on how to dress. We use it to justify purchases. If a sweater is $500 but you think you'll wear it three times a week all winter, then the CPW is low and the sweater is a good buy. Another term is PL, which means "Permanent Loan," and is used when you want to give something to your sister or friend, but you want the right to ask for it back. As far as I know, in the history of the PL no one has ever asked for anything back. I think it just helps us part with things, knowing it's not forever.

**HOLLY MERRITT** My little sister has been instrumental in helping me with makeup. She shuddered when she saw I owned only two eye shadows.

**TALATA BOWSER** My mother used to dress me and my sister, who is two years younger, the same. I remember an outfit from when we were six and four. It was shorts and a sweatshirt with a bright hearts pattern. I asked my mother why we had to wear the same outfit, as if we were twins. From then on, I tried to be different from my sister, even though we were still dressed the same way for many more years.

**JENNIFER WINEKE** One of my fondest early memories is from when I was seven, and my sister, who was nine, either found a jellyfish in her shoe or was irrationally terrified of finding a jellyfish in her shoe. My mom sat us down and had us write and illustrate little books about finding jellyfish in our shoes to work through our anxieties about jellyfish.

**GLYNDA ALVES** When I was going through a difficult phase with my body, my eldest sister said, "Your body is changing from a girl to a woman. You need to dress for it." I was twenty-two at the time. It put things into perspective.

**NICHOLE BAIEL** I passed on a ring to my sister that meant a lot to me, but I wanted her to have it because she was going through some pretty hard times, and it was my way to always be there with her. ✕

*EMILY SHUR*'s prescription eyeglasses

# WHAT I SPENT | EMILY STOKES

*April 1–September 30*

**RENT: $1,000/MONTH**

**NUMBER OF CLOTHING ITEMS PURCHASED: 36**

**NUMBER OF ITEMS RETURNED: 8**

**TOTAL SPENT ON SHOES/CLOTHING: $1,858.07**

**TOILETRIES ETC.: $245.78**

**HAIRCUTS AND PEDICURES: $86.32**

**TIGHTS AND UNDERTHINGS: $158.45**

**DRY CLEANING, COBBLER, ALTERATIONS: $390.95**

## APRIL

**4.1** I am cleaning out my wardrobe in preparation for the spring. Going to the Salvation Army are the following items: Three small tweed jackets with three-quarter-length sleeves—each jacket is from a "petite" line—the kind of jacket that has large buttons that make the petite person look like a Borrower. I probably bought them only because they fit; I am 4 ft 8. • G. H. Bass brogues and four pairs of ballet flats—my right leg is shorter than the left by 5cm as a result of my having broken it so many times (I have brittle bones). It would therefore be advisable for me to wear an orthotic in my right shoe with an extra raise, which would mean a larger shoe. It has always seemed unfortunate that I should have to wear large shoes, as I am very small and would like to look dainty and nicely proportioned. For this reason I tend to look for shoes that I think make my feet look as small as possible—mostly ballet flats. I bought the brogues because they seemed like the sort of invisible, hardworking, no-nonsense footwear an editor should wear, but they have become worryingly foot-shaped. • Four cream-colored tops—each is now threadbare in the same place. I use a cane to walk, and the wrist holding the cane rubs against my left hip. At the last minute, I decide to keep the tops. After cleaning, I order two 4.2 oz bottles of Clinique Dramatically Different Moisturizing Lotion from Sephora. **$54.44**

**4.2** On the way to a Passover seder, I worry that my top is see-through, and so buy a singlet from Forever 21. When I eventually change into the singlet (which claims to be XS), I find that the straps come to below my bra and the bottom of the vest reaches my knees. **$2.99**

**4.8** I spill salad dressing down one of my cream silk tops at lunchtime, so buy a white T-shirt from Muji. My idea of a perfect white T-shirt is the one my father wears: starchy, wide, with a crew neck and longish sleeves. I have spent a lot of time trying to find a man's T-shirt in my size. **$14.95**

**4.16** I am pining after a denim skirt from A.P.C. It looks like a child's drawing of a skirt: A-line, cut just below the knee, with buttons down the front. It is very expensive—$225—but I justify the price by telling myself that I could wear it all the time. I often fantasize about items of clothing I could wear every day, like the mustard-yellow "It-Doesn't-Matter Suit" in Sylvia Plath's children's book. **$0**

**4.19** I go to the Jil Sander sample sale at the recommendation of the managing editor of the magazine where I work. He dresses many female friends and sells many items on eBay. On the way back to the office, another colleague and I visit my A.P.C. skirt, which surprises me by being too big and not very nice. **$0**

## MAY

**5.1** Duane Reade: shampoo. **$8.98**

**5.9** I need a summer dress to replace last summer's, which is faded and smells. I buy a dress from Steven Alan online before work. Steven Alan is comforting to me because the clothes are preppy and a bit British. The clothes remind me of my older sister's, which are classic and expensive-looking. When I think of her, she is ironing cotton. **$245**

**5.11** I am "in conversation" with Lydia Davis at the Frieze Art Fair. I dress in black trousers, black ballet flats, and a white shirt, like a cater waiter, and borrow a gold 1950s men's wristwatch from the managing editor, in order to keep track of time without a mobile phone onstage. The black cane gives the look an edge; my friend organizing the event tells me I look "dapper." **$0**

**5.12** I am high with relief after the Frieze event. I see a shop called Eponymy with dresses in the window, which reminds me of the two weddings I must attend this summer. I try on several dresses that don't fit, and then a skirt that is more promising: below the knee, pleated, with a hectic pattern. I buy the skirt, which I imagine will make me appear spontaneous. I have a theory that most of the clothes I pick out in stores have ur-versions from my childhood. The ur-version of this skirt, I realize when I get it home, is a blue Liberty-print skirt that my sister called her magic skirt. She would pick out shells from the pleats during magic shows she would put on for me while I was in the bath. **$78**

**5.13** The Steven Alan dress arrives. I try it on and look like a child wearing a hospital gown. Why do I buy clothes online that most likely will not fit? I am avoiding trying things on in the shop—trying to postpone their not fitting me. Later, I go to the Comme des Garçons sample sale at the behest of the managing editor. He points me in the direction of a tiny gold leather jacket before returning to the office with several pairs of women's polka-dot plimsolls. I spot a navy blazer for $60, but something about the loud music and the shoppers here makes me feel very self-conscious. I try it on and take it off too quickly to see how it looks. Pick up dry cleaning. **CREDIT, $245; $11.50**

**5.14** Managing editor e-mails me a link to a white-and-orange-striped Breton sweater on eBay for €12. Stripes are my bread and butter. I tell him to make a bid for me. He wins. **€12**

**5.15** I buy two pairs of trousers online from Urban Outfitters: one in beige with a floral design ($39.99), and one in bright red, also with flowers ($29.99). Perhaps I won't have a need for a summer dress. Perhaps floral cocktail trousers will become my signature look. **$69.98**

**5.16** On the subway to work, I decide that the Eponymy skirt was a mistake. After work, I go to a dance performance with a friend and wish I were wearing something in a neutral color made of a natural fiber. **$0**

**5.18** My computer knows that I am looking for a summer dress. I see a Macy's advertisement on my screen, click it, and purchase an ivory-color broderie anglaise cotton dress with three-quarter-length sleeves. **$88.95**

**5.19** The trousers are too big. It is not to be the summer of the floral cocktail trouser after all. **CREDIT, $69.98**

**5.20** Macy's dress is pretty and meant for someone else. I add this to the Steven Alan dress and the Urban Outfitters pants also to be returned. **CREDIT, $88.95**

**5.21** I go to the Tibi sample sale at the recommendation of the managing editor. It is the first sample sale I have ever been to that has so many appealing options that I must make decisions about what I would like to buy, rather than have decisions made for me by the scant availability of items in my size. I try on a white long-sleeved silk dress with small black stars, before realizing that I am drawn to the dress because it is like a wizard costume I had as a child. I also try on a black dress made of thick, firm, stretchy material, with long sleeves. It will look good with thick black tights and, I imagine, trainers, which I have resolved to buy and wear for the sake of my feet. ● I try on a white silk shift dress. I wonder if you can wear white to a wedding if it is a gay wedding? ● I try on a sweater that is neon orangey-pink and great. It makes me want to wear a lot of mascara and let my hair get greasy. • I try on a knee-length skirt—white with a thick stripe along the bottom, as if it has been dipped in a vat of blue paint. It gives me a waist and hips. • In the line to pay for the white dress, the black dress, the skirt, and the sweater, I get cold feet about my vast spending, and leave the sweater behind. **$332.98**

**5.22** In preparation for my work trip to Venice for the Biennale, I buy a 1.7oz bottle of Fracas Eau de Parfum Spray by Robert Piguet from Amazon, which is the only place I can find it now. I have worn Fracas since I was 16. It smells of tuberoses. The only reason I do not wear Fracas to work every day is that the receptionist in my office is allergic to roses. The last time I worked the phones while wearing the perfume, he had to go to the ER. • I buy a Travel Smart by Conair 1875-Watt Mini Hairdryer ($27.47). • I am suffering from intense regret about buying the Tibi skirt rather than the sweater. I feel very ashamed at having recently bought two ugly skirts. **$101.71**

**5.23** My concern about having the appropriate toiletry supplies for Venice has grown into a general anxiety about the state of my entire wardrobe. I have been so excited about this trip for such a long time that I have started to imagine myself walking around Venice with matching luggage and themed outfits like a character from a Wes Anderson film. On my way to work, I go to a shoe store near the sub-

way where I purchase a pair of Clarks ballet flats. • I also go into a shop I have walked into many times without success because everything there has only been nearly nice. I try on a white-and-blue knee-length shift dress. It is quite cheap—$62—so I buy it. **$152**

**5.24** I have had three dresses altered at G&G Chinese Laundry on Grand Street. Unbelievably, this is the first time I have ever had clothes, or anything else in fact, altered to accommodate my small size. When I try on the dresses at home, I experience a revelation. I am no longer limited to buying dresses that fit me. I had never noticed before that by wearing too-big clothes, I was limiting my movements and gestures to hold the clothes in place—to avoid showing my bra in a low-cut neck or an underarm, or by keeping too-long sleeves rolled up. • The blue-and-white shift dress, on the other hand, is not good. The pattern is too big and bold, like wrapping paper, and the fabric is slightly shiny, suggesting that it or I will melt in the heat. **$75 (ALTERATIONS)**

**5.25** A few hours before my flight, I go shopping for a pair of trainers. At DNA, a discount shoe store, I try on a pair of fluorescent-yellow ones; they are not my usual style but I am channeling an image of a very beautiful thirty-something Italian gallerist I saw at the Frieze Art Fair who wore colorful Nikes with jeans and a blazer. A friend meets me in the store and suggests that Supergas

would be smarter and easier to wear with skirts. The Supergas are less supportive and comfortable than the yellow trainers but they are pretty and Italian. • A few hours later, at JFK, I notice that my new Supergas are pinching my toes. I should have bought the 7.5. I am stressed because I have forgotten to pack an important folder with information about the artist I am supposed to be interviewing in Venice, and the too-small shoes make me want to weep. **$48.95**

**5.26** At 4 a.m on my way to Venice, I am sitting in the Refuel Café at Dublin Airport. I am in a state of anxiety and fear, which has funneled into an intense regret about my packing. I wish I had brought fewer clothes with me. My bag is too heavy to carry over the bridges on the way to the hotel, so I will have to rely on strangers to help me. I wish I had brought warmer clothes with me. I wish I had brought my big, comfortable knitted sweater. I wish I hadn't bought too-small Supergas. • I think about how, even at 27, I have not yet learned to buy a pair of shoes that fit me and how, over the years, I have bought many pairs of shoes that have made me hobble— I have doubly crippled myself with shoes. • I go to the sport store in Dublin Airport that is somehow open at this early hour. I buy a pair of Converse All Stars in navy blue, which is the only color they have in 7.5. I feel strongly that Converse are best in white or not at all. However, the feeling of wearing the right-size shoes is wonderful. I feel the depression lifting at the relief of having found a solution. **€54.99**

### JUNE

**6.1** The man I would like to be dating is in Milan for a conference. He is coming to Venice and we are having supper (or maybe he is coming to Venice to have supper with me?). I wear my newly altered red dress with tights, ballet flats, and my black leather jacket. I have always been wary of the jacket, which felt not quite mine. Tonight, the leather jacket is useful. I rise to its sense of occasion. **$0**

**6.3** Pick up dry cleaning. **$64**

**6.7** Duane Reade: toothpaste; soap. **$8.15**

**6.13** Victoria's Secret: four pairs of knickers. **$28**

**6.14** I am looking for a smart jacket to wear with the white dress to the wedding. Comptoir des Cotonniers is my favorite shop. The clothes are beautifully designed and they come in small sizes for skinny French people. The only thing that puts me off is the staff, who are too friendly; they hug me when I walk in, when I would rather browse quietly. • The shop assistant today, however, is excellent. She understands the urgency of the situation, and brings me several jackets. I try on a white and neon-orange blazer and a light green jacket with a round neck. I am dithering. The orange one looks better with my coloring, but it is very

bold and, as the shop assistant says, the kind of item you have to be careful not to wear too often because everyone will remember it. I don't think I have a big enough wardrobe for memorable clothes, so I go with the green. • I also buy a beige mac, which I want to wear immediately and every day. The ur-mac is one that lived on the clothes peg in my childhood home in North London, which my mum and dad shared. This one is mini. As my mother would say, it's a classic. **$390**

**6.15** I am looking for shoes to wear for the wedding that are not ballet flats. In Steven Alan, I find a pair of white leather sandals with espadrille-style soles. I buy them with my credit card, forgetting that I still have to return the Steven Alan white-and-blue dress. **$120**

**6.16** Day of wedding. Wake up, go to French Sole, buy silver ballet flats. **$175**

**6.25** In an attempt to find a replacement summer dress, I go to Steven Alan with the $245 dress and the $120 white shoes I want to return. I am too late to get a refund on the dress, but can exchange it. I try on three other dresses (all far too big) and a pair of white denim trousers. I ask the assistant if he thinks the trousers are too big. He says, thoughtfully, that there is a difference between big trousers and trousers that are too big. Then he says, "If I saw you walking down the street I wouldn't stop and be like,

'Your trousers are too big.'"
**CREDIT, $120**

**6.26** Abby at Arté Salon gives me a free between-cuts trim. She says, "Do you have a hot date tonight?" **$30**

**6.27** It occurs to me that the man finally kissed me last night because I turned up at the restaurant with my top accidentally inside out, and having forgotten to wear makeup. I had finally stopped trying to impress him. • In the morning, on the way to the subway, we pass the dry cleaners, and I pick up my clothes, which includes a dress to change into at the office. He says, "Do you always take so many clothes to work with you?" **$42.50**

**6.28** The Mizuno Wave Rider 16 running shoes worn by Texas state senator Wendy Davis during her 11-hour filibuster of the Republicans' antiabortion legislation remind me of how attractive it is to look comfortable. **$0**

**6.30** I go to see if I can find anything to buy with the store credit from the white-and-blue dress. I try on a wraparound dress in a black and white stretchy fabric. It has the kind of high V-neck I seek out to hide the fact that my neck is angled due to scoliosis. • At home, I try on the dress again and feel less sure. Can you get store credit on something that was bought with store credit? **$104**

**6.31** I wake up feeling insecure. The man has gone away for two weeks, leaving me to fret.

I decide to wear the ugly Eponymy skirt to work. The skirt gets a lot of compliments. My colleague Sam says, "That's a cool skirt." I say, "It's kind of ugly," and he says, "Yeah, but it's cool." **$0**

## JULY
**7.1** Managing editor has found me a pair of Selima Sun for J.Crew sunglasses on eBay. They are perfect: big but not silly. **$60**

**7.2** Duane Reade: conditioner; floss **$11.52**

**7.4** On the way to London for my stepsister's wedding, I buy a bright red lipstick by Dior called Addict Extreme 639 (Riviera) at JFK Duty Free. It is the first lipstick I have bought for myself. I usually rely on fashion-editor friends to give me their hand-me-downs. **$31**

**7.6** After a late night at the pub I meet my sister, Polly, at our local hairdresser before our stepsister's wedding. She tells me that I look rough and that I smell of wine, and suggests I get a blow dry. **£20**

**7.19** I take Friday off work to spend the day with Polly, who is visiting from London. Our aim is to buy summer dresses and also to try to spend my credit vouchers at Lily's and Steven Alan. We try on many things at Lily's but nothing works. Polly advises that I save the voucher until I need to buy someone a birthday present. • On Atlantic Avenue we discover a shop that sells vintage dresses. Polly picks one out for me that is dark green, purple,

and pink, with a wide skirt at the mid-calf. I put on the dress and she nods slowly. The dress is $98. I buy it and feel very certain about it. I always feel certain about purchases that are approved by my sister. That is why I should not shop with her too often; it becomes hard to shop without her. • At Steven Alan, Polly suggests that I buy a pair of diamond earrings from the jewelry counter. I worry that there are more urgent gaps in my wardrobe, but Polly is very persuasive and says that, at $270, these diamond earrings are very good value. I put them on and everything shines. It feels like a celebration of something, so I buy them. • On a high from the diamonds, we go for pedicures ($24). I sit next to my sister and the man scrubs my feet very hard. My sister says, "I think he thinks you're really dirty." **$388**

**7.22** Pick up dry cleaning. **$56.50**

**7.29** I discovered Worishofer shoes last year. They look very German but not unattractive. The problem is that the cork soles disintegrate—particularly, in my case, the sole of the left shoe, which carries more weight. I buy a new pair of Worishofers from Amazon in size 7, which I resolve to take to the cobbler immediately. **$50.80**

**7.31** DNA has a sale. I go in to check that I bought the correct size Worishofers; I am always doubting the size of my feet, probably because one foot is bigger than the other. I end up buying a second pair of Worishofer shoes. **$48.99**

**8.4** Cobbler. **$22**

**8.7** My bras are a bit gray-looking, so I order a new one from Amazon—a blue lace Freya bra ($49.49). My friend Beka and I discovered Freya at a tiny Dickensian shop in the Angel, NW London, that specializes in fittings; the shop has been there for decades, and is run by an elderly woman who wears shockingly threadbare velvet leggings. My size was ascertained to be 28DD. This sounded to me ridiculous, but the woman was so adamant that she made me leave behind the 32B bra I had been wearing. The bras I wear now are very push-up and tight around the chest, so that they leave a mark, which is apparently how they should be. I also buy some more Clinique Dramatically Different Moisturizing Lotion ($31.97). **$81.46**

**8.15** I might have found the perfect T-shirt—from Everlane, online, for $15. It is boyish: short and wide, with a pocket. I buy three. **$45**

**8.16** Perhaps I am happier, or perhaps because I am dating a man who is largely uninterested in clothes, I am spending much less time wondering about another, more quirkily dressed version of myself whose clothes the real me finds hard to wear, and thinking about things I could use, such as tights, or an umbrella, or an overnight bag. • The managing editor sends me a link to a Fjällräven backpack which is 70 percent off. When the bag arrives, I find that it is small as a child's. I wonder whether the managing editor thinks that, because I am small, I can pack light. **$29.98**

**8.18** CVS: cold and flu medication; prescription for antibiotics. **$32.03**

**8.19** Still groggy with a cold, I take off my diamond earrings in the bathroom and drop one of them down the sink. I am not grown-up enough to have a pair of diamond earrings. I write an e-mail to Steven Alan in the hope that it is possible to buy one earring; I know from past experience that I must replace the earring as soon as possible so as not to get mired in regret. It then occurs to me that I could take apart the sink. I ask my downstairs neighbor to help; he wrenches open the P-trap; the earring drops out. **$0**

**8.28** Cobbler. **$32**

**8.29** I am about to go away for the weekend to Martha's Vineyard with Ben, who is now apparently my boyfriend, hence going away for the weekend with him. On the way to work I buy a top from Urban Outfitters without trying it on. The top—white, cotton, milkmaidish—isn't that nice. So I return it. I must be wary of my need to buy unnecessary things before going away. **$0**

## SEPTEMBER

**9.10** My Everlane T-shirts have been lost in the mail! **REFUND, $45**

**9.7** A store on Atlantic Avenue has a luggage sale. There is a Fjällräven duffel bag reduced from $150. The managing editor approves, thank goodness. **$75**

**9.13** Polly has been telling me about the pleasures of her Wolford tights. I order some from Amazon. They are indeed magnificent. **$46**

**9.15** Alterations and dry cleaning. **$84.45**

**9.17** Rite Aid: deodorant, soap. **$13.49**

**9.20** I am looking for a pair of Chelsea boots to wear with my dresses and tights, but when I try on a few pairs, I find myself wanting something more supportive. I see a pair of G. H. Bass black suede shoes with navy soles, which will look good with a new COS dress my mother bought me, although I worry that they will not be right with my black Tibi dress. Why do I feel that, in order to be worth buying, these shoes ought to go with everything I own? **$79**

**9.25** Managing editor sends out a link to a Tretorn sale online; I buy a pair of all-black Skerry Wellington boots. Useful. **$30**

**9.30** I have cleared the summer clothes from my cupboard and moved my sweaters back in. The cupboard looks sparse, but when I open it in the morning, I see my new COS dress, which I have had altered to fit me, and my mac. Plus I have tights, and nice comfy new Bass shoes. I could wear this outfit all fall. **$0** ✕

---

SURVEY *What was the first "investment item" you bought?*

A Prada wallet my one-year-old daughter plays with now. —SARAH ILLENBERGER • I bought a Martin Margiela sweater when traveling in Italy ten years ago, probably cost me a month's rent. I still have it and wear it. —TRISH EWANIKA • A blue J.Crew sweater. I used to wear it with red jeans. It got eaten by moths in Cairo. — SOFIA SAMATAR • Black Versace sunglasses I bought at seventeen. I still have them, don't wear them anymore. —RACHEL L. • I bought this gorgeous satin gown on an impulse. I didn't need it, but it was so glamorous and fit so well I've worn it twice recently for performances, and I will wear it again. The style is ageless and it's so soft against my skin. —MONIQUE AUBÉ • I bought $200 jeans and I thought it was a big deal. They were great for a few months and I started to think they were worth it. Then they ripped in the butt and I have maybe had my heart broken in the jeans world. —NICOLE LAVELLE • A golden bracelet. —SATENIK AVAKIAN ✕

PROJECT

## WEAR AREAS | ANNA BACKMAN ROGERS

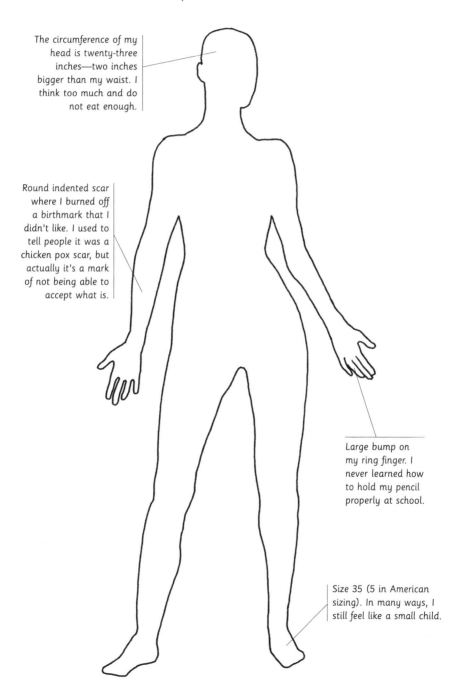

The circumference of my head is twenty-three inches—two inches bigger than my waist. I think too much and do not eat enough.

Round indented scar where I burned off a birthmark that I didn't like. I used to tell people it was a chicken pox scar, but actually it's a mark of not being able to accept what is.

Large bump on my ring finger. I never learned how to hold my pencil properly at school.

Size 35 (5 in American sizing). In many ways, I still feel like a small child.

*MOLLY MURRAY*'s vintage three-inch heels

# YOU REALLY ARE THE MOST DISAGREEABLE GIRL

## PHOTOGRAPHER LUCY BIRLEY SPEAKS TO LEANNE SHAPTON

LUCY: I always feel much more comfortable dressing the way I want to dress if I know I'm not going to be photographed. Knowing that you might be photographed is a real bridle, like having a martingale on. I don't want to be revealed to the world in this, but I'm very happy to be revealed to my friends in this.

LEANNE: Do you always know when you might be photographed?

LUCY: If you're going to somebody's house, or somebody's birthday that's private, you can have much more fun than if you're going to some party where they're going to come up with a flash. I'm really allergic to it and I can actually sense where they are in the room, so when they're coming nearer, I look down or avoid.

LEANNE: It's like an animal sense.

LUCY: It feels like being hunted, I hate it.

LEANNE: Have you ever dressed to calm yourself or gain control over a situation?

LUCY: Yes. When I got divorced, I bought a pair of steel-toe Manolo Blahniks to face the lawyers. I needed those.

LEANNE: Have you seen the armor for women at the Wallace Collection? It's sort of a corset thing, with room for boobs, amazing. Constricting yet protective.

LUCY: It sounds like McQueen. I think Alexander dressed women to go out into the world to do battle. He was all about giving women strength to go out into the fight, all about making them stronger.

LEANNE: How did you come to know him?

LUCY: I once lost this coat that I loved. I was at a party that a friend gave, but after about ten minutes suddenly the walls came up and there were hundreds of hookers all throwing cream pies at everybody, and it turned into this massive food fight. It was so hilarious, it was such fun, I absolutely adored it. But I was actually very pregnant, and I was really scared I was going to slip on the floor because the whole floor was covered in cream, so I hid under a table for a bit. Then everybody left covered in stuff. Most people were furious, actually, it was so weird. When I finally got out, my coat had disappeared.

LEANNE: What was the coat like?

LUCY: It was a red alpaca Dior with a fur collar. Very '50s, A-line, lovely. Very light.

LEANNE: Nobody steals a red coat by accident.

LUCY: It was maroon, it wasn't really a bright red. But I loved it. So my friend Issy Blow said, "I've just met this guy Alexander who has just come out of art school, maybe he can replace it and make you a new one. I'll get him to come round." So I was at home, doorbell rings, and this little skinhead-looking guy walks in with jeans and shaved head, book under his arm. We started talking and he said, "So what was this coat like?" I said it was alpaca, red, fur collar, and it was this kind of shape, and he went, "Okay, right." Then he said, "Do you want to see what I'm into?" And I said sure, and he got this book out and I opened it and it was all pictures of, um, Vietnamese children who'd been disfigured by napalm, and people running out of towns during the war in disarray and bombs going off, and I just shut the book and I said, "I see." I was so fazed, because I was expecting a lovely sketchbook with lovely pictures and drawings of coats and dresses, and I was so weirded out, but I thought, Well, whatever. I was embarrassed, and then he said, "Well, I need some money to get the material," so I said, "Okay, how much do you need?" and he said £300, so I wrote him out a check and gave it to him and said good-bye, and he started making it. I didn't hear from him for a long time, so I called him up and he said, "Yeah, the coat's at Elizabeth Street, finished and everything." I went round to Elizabeth Street, and the day before, the house had collapsed. It had fallen down. So I never got the coat. For years after that, whenever I'd see him we'd just go, "Alpacaaa!! Where is the fucking coat?!" But he actually did give me loads of stuff after that.

LEANNE: Do you remember the first time you were conscious of what you were wearing?

LUCY: It was a shift dress with strawberries on it. I must have been about four. I just wanted to wear it all the time. I think I wore it running through the fields and whenever I could.

LEANNE: When do you feel the most attractive?

LUCY: When I'm in the country and I get up in my nightie and go out on a summer morning with my gun and shoot rabbits. I love that combination of being in a nightdress and having a gun.

LEANNE: What are you trying to achieve when you dress?

LUCY: Well, it depends where I am. If I'm in the country, I'm dressing to keep warm and dry, or be able to ride or do some gardening. If I'm in town, I'm trying to look as if I'm in control of my life, tidy, and like I'm not completely mad.

LEANNE: Whenever I see you there's something you're wearing that refers to some inner life, like you're doing something just to please yourself.

LUCY: I want people to realize I'm not a square, but I don't want to look like everybody else, and I also want to feel comfortable and that I'm not going to get freaked out. So that might involve wearing something I love that has got me through some tricky situations before, almost like a talisman.

LEANNE: The red velvet piece you're wearing today does that.

LUCY: It's funny you should say that, because I probably haven't worn this in three or four years. I like to throw it. Always.

LEANNE: Tell me about being photographed by Mapplethorpe.

LUCY: Well, he had been over to the house a couple of times, and he was going to do a picture for this Butler & Wilson shop in Fulham Road. They used to have a photograph on the side of the shop that they'd change every six months or so. I think when they found out he had AIDS they canceled it, but we did the picture anyway. I went down to 14th Street in New York, and I got out of the cab on the wrong side, and I'd been smoking a joint, and I nearly got run over by a lorry! So I was quite freaked when I got there. We sat and smoked a bit beforehand, and then he wanted not to see my body at all, so somebody in the studio had a black jumper that I put on. He had a little handheld Leica and he just said, "Right, okay," and

I sat down and he wanted me to move my head around, and he was kind of going around me. We were quite stoned so it was very relaxed. It was very quick. I don't think he was that interested in taking the picture. He was like, "Okay, I think we got it." I think he shot two rolls. Then he said, "Oh, I really want to show you my bedroom, come have a look," so we went down a passage and into this room and the whole room was covered in different crucifixes and some weird African masks, quite threatening-looking things, almost devilish. It was a really intense room, there was a real juxtaposition between good and evil. And he said, "What do you think? Which side do you like?" And I was actually kind of freaked that he'd asked me that question. I said the crucifix side, and when I said that I thought he seemed relieved. Reassured. I felt he was looking for the right direction in some weird way.

LEANNE: That's intense.

LUCY: He was very intense, but he was like a very, very clever naughty teenager. So quick. Very much the same kind of mind Alexander had. Very naughty, very confrontational, very funny, and moving so fast.

LEANNE: Did your parents teach you anything about dressing?

LUCY: No, they were too crazy. But my mother was very elegant and ladylike and always wore tweed skirts and jackets and headscarves and gloves. And the top drawer of her chest of drawers had sort of silky things and her jewelry and her scent bottle and all her feminine things, but I was never allowed to look at it. That was quite hurtful. I always felt that her femininity and her sexuality were things she cut off from me. And having three brothers, I grew up in a very male environment, and that's kind of sad—I wish I'd had more of a girly relationship with my mother. But she used to lend me things. She had this beautiful pair of bright pink court shoes with great big buckles on the front, they must have been her best shoes in the '50s for going to parties in. And I really wanted to borrow them. I must have been about sixteen, and she said, "Yeah, but please look after them." And I went out to a punk concert in the Hammersmith Odeon, in probably fishnets and a short skirt, and they got absolutely trashed, covered in beer, mud, ash, really trashed. And she said, "Oh, how could you do that, you really are the most disagreeable girl."

LEANNE: What is your relationship to lingerie and feminine things now?

LUCY: I don't indulge myself in that way. I would love to have beautiful frilly knickers with lovely lace and satin in sort of beautiful colors, but I don't allow myself that. Maybe if I was in a relationship with somebody where that was really important to them I would, but I'm not. (laughs) Actually, I remember going round to [Issy's] flat after she died, with Lee and Philip Treacey, and we had to choose something for her to be laid out in, and there were three or four rails of clothes, and I remember Lee opening this drawer and there was all this amazing underwear in it, it was like a sweet shop or something. And Lee said, "Take it, take it all!" But I didn't feel I could.

LEANNE: When did you meet Isabella Blow?

LUCY: I think when I was fourteen or fifteen at a party in Oxford. It was one of those friendships that click instantly, which doesn't happen so much later in life. We were best friends from the moment we met. She came to live with my mother because she'd been kicked out of her own home and left school. We didn't have any money, and we used to go down to

Kensington Market, to all the vintage shops in the King's Road. We did a lot of shoplifting. At least I did. She wouldn't have the guts.

LEANNE: Was she doing her own thing then?

LUCY: She dressed in a much more overtly sexual way than I did, and she was a great encourager of making you push it in that way. She'd go, "Oh, pull your skirt up, ohh you're really gonna get lucky tonight!" She was very sexually motivated in her dressing, and she always wore stockings and suspenders, or no tights. So we didn't dress in the same way. But we used to go out together, and we had boyfriends who were friends before we both got married, so we used to go off to shooting meets and things together a lot. *(cries)*

LEANNE: Sorry, Lucy. If it's painful to talk, we don't have to.

LUCY: No, it's okay, I'm fine, honestly, it's just that growing up with somebody like that is not anything to do with fashion, you know, we just had a great time. We had a great time.

LEANNE: Do you think she was an artist?

LUCY: Well, we did a sculpture course together in New York, but we smoked so much dope before we went in that we couldn't stay in the class, we were just hysterical with laughing. But yeah, she was very motivated by art, history, literature. And she loved Scotland, the moors and the big landscapes, the freedom. She was one of those people who'd get into a taxi in the middle of Cheshire and start talking to the driver about his family, his wife, and the guy would be completely bowled over by her. She just had this way of connecting with people, a totally genuine energy of wanting to know about people and what made them tick and what made them laugh, and it was such fun.

LEANNE: So much is made of her depression and demons.

LUCY: That was a tiny bit at the end. But as a teenager I remember my mum saying to me one day, "You know, with Isabella it's either hundred-miles-an-hour fireworks and fun or she's in bed with a hot water bottle having to have soup. There's no middle ground." So you would just wait for her to rest and recuperate and then it would be the sports car going again. She had this extraordinary energy and imagination and daring. I don't think she had the discipline to sit down and concentrate on anything, really.

LEANNE: What do you think gives people the motivation to dress to their own standards?

LUCY: I think it's part of being a creative person. I think you have to have the imagination and the vision and be able to visualize stuff. I think that a lot of people don't. Not everyone is artistic or creative or thinks in that way. It's easier for them to be told what to wear, and that's fine, it doesn't matter.

LEANNE: I want to ask about your friendships with women.

LUCY: My girlfriends have always been really important to me. I've got the same friends now that I had when I was a teenager. Sadly, a lot of my friends aren't here anymore, because I'm obviously drawn to extreme people who burn out. I love being around my female friends who have daughters, and watching what goes on, because I never had a daughter. Four sons.

LEANNE: What's the situation with your hair?

LUCY: Oh my god. I cannot believe that my state of mind is so dependent on what this stuff on my head is looking like. I just find it absurd, but I've accepted that if I feel that it looks terrible, then I'm going to feel terrible.

LEANNE: It's increments I would never notice.

LUCY: You'd notice if it were greasy, because I've had a problem with greasy my entire life.

LEANNE: Having very dry hair, I envy people with greasy hair.

LUCY: But you've got so much volume!

LEANNE: That's what I hate, no control whatsoever. I love the idea of hair being close to your head, or when you can see the shape of a woman's skull.

LUCY: I'm obsessed with hair. If I go to the opera, I look at people's hair and I give them marks. I go, "Oh, she should have that much off, or She's definitely been to the hairdresser this morning." And I get really bad hair envy. Oh my god, I envy my cousin's daughter's hair. She's probably twelve. She's got russet Pre-Raphaelite hair. Bunches of it. Ohhhhhhh God. I would love to be able to lie in bed naked with my hair covering my bosoms and going down between my legs. The feeling of having really long hair on bare skin must be so amazing.

LEANNE: Do you dress for men or women?

LUCY: Oh, definitely for women. About six months ago, I was getting up and I saw my wedding dress in its box and I thought it would be fun to try it on. So I put it on and I went into the kitchen to make breakfast and I thought, He's going to say something in a minute, and he didn't notice. So from my point of view, dressing for men is completely pointless. I think most men don't want the person they love to stick out or be noticed, they're uncomfortable with that. But I would say I dress for other women in order for them see that they better not try and come get my man, because I'm just as attractive as they are. Like, recognize me and don't mess with my man. I've got moon in Scorpio, and I don't like other women going near my man or flirting with him and stuff, and considering he spends his entire time in a nightclub, I'm under quite a lot of pressure. I'm joking, but yeah, there's an element of that.

LEANNE: How do you shop?

LUCY: I have to be in the right mood, but I don't really need more clothes. I've got loads, so it's dangerous for me to go into a shop because I could get overexcited and blow a lot on something I don't need. It'd be pure extravagance and self-indulgence. I find there's far too much fashion everywhere, and I don't know whether that's the reality of the situation or if I've been around that scene for so long, but it seems to have become very obsessive and has invaded so many areas of life it wasn't ever part of. I get to the point where I don't even want to know about it—take it away!

LEANNE: When did you go from shopping in vintage markets to buying designer clothes?

LUCY: I didn't have money to buy expensive clothes until I started going out with Bryan [Ferry], and he was very generous and took me shopping and gave me money to buy the things I wouldn't have been able to afford. Unfortunately what I wanted to wear at the time, in the '80s, was Comme des Garçons, black things with holes, and Bryan would say, "Why are you wearing those widow's weeds?" Very expensive widow's weeds was not his idea of what he wanted me to wear at all. ✕

## PLASTIC BASKETS |
### JOSH BLACKWELL

*Cut, collaged, and
hand–embroidered discarded
plastic shopping bags
found on the streets of
New York City.*

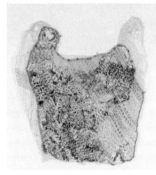

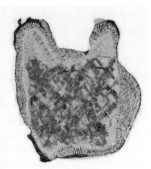

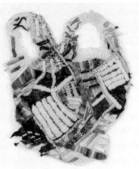

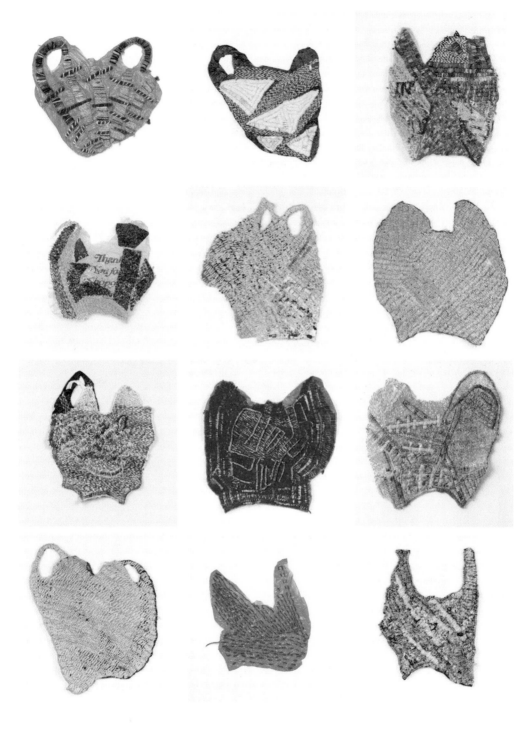

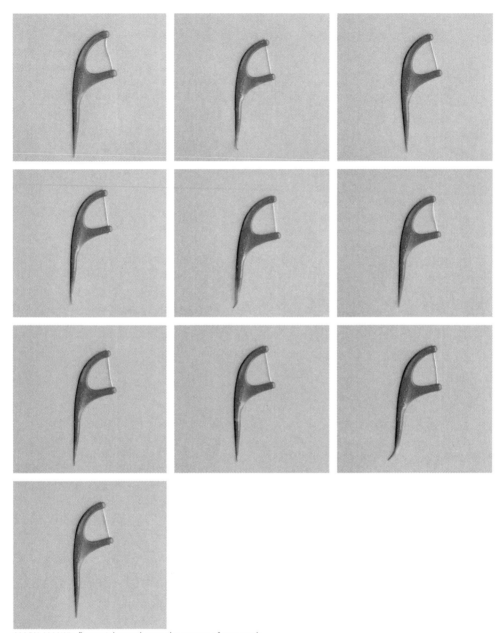

*MARY MANN*'s floss sticks used over the course of one week

# whatever closeness you felt was based solely on the assumption that everything he expressed was an accurate representation of something his brain produced within the privacy of his own skull and surrounding skin

MIRA GONZALEZ

arrive in a new city with a suitcase full of oversized sweaters
and allow the outside world to establish control of your youth

say, "motion is only possible by displacement," then,

know that everything is moving apart slowly,
one second at a time, forever
each second we forget another second

that night in mid-July, our cabdriver told us,
was the hottest night in three years

I didn't mention that my stockings were full of pebbles,
or that you had torn a hole in my floral dress

when you pushed my face against that wall in your closet
and promised there was something more for me

I became capable of existing as one thing
but simultaneously being nothing particular

this was the month we gave up on doing laundry
and stopped allowing thoughts to control our emotions

how can they say the relationship was doomed to fail?

I could feel love fading out of you
like the barely visible sweat stains on my black cotton shirt
but even then, there was too much restraint

I will consider our relationship beautiful in terms of distance

years from now I will tell myself I am thankful,
for the time you spent, for giving me the opportunity

for the beer stains on my favorite yellow coat
and for the bloodstains on your sheets

now we have learned to live with the burden
of being somehow in the aftermath of events
that never occurred in our own lives

when I am alone I wear your clothes
and allow you to die, gracefully
despite the inescapable knowledge that we don't want to feel better

# PUT ON A TUX AND GO

CHOREOGRAPHER/DANCER **MONICA BILL BARNES** & DANCER **ANNA BASS**
SPEAK TO **LEANNE SHAPTON** & **HEIDI JULAVITS** ABOUT THEIR COSTUMES

**SUDDENLY SUMMER SOMEWHERE**
*(linen dresses, vintage overcoats)*

**ANNA:** One of the first visual inspirations for these costumes was—what is the sculptor's name?

**MONICA:** Ron Mueck. We really wanted to be able to shift from male to female, imagery-wise. We wanted our figures to be masked in the boxy shape of the coats.

**ANNA:** He did an exhibit at the Brooklyn Museum of all of these lifelike sculptures of varying sizes.

**MONICA:** Incredibly lifelike.

**ANNA:** Super-detailed. And there were these two old ladies in housecoats.

**MONICA:** I was so affected by the entire exhibit, and I just loved these two women. By their proximity to each other it was clear that they were incredibly intimate. They aren't looking at each other, and it was fascinating to think, God, you get to that point where you've spent so much time with somebody that you actually

don't need to look them in the eye. And it mimics something Anna and I do a lot in rehearsal, where we don't actually square off and face each other. We spend a lot of time . . .

**ANNA:** . . . just feeling each other. And actually, this is funny, smelling each other, too. All of our costumes have been previously owned.

**HEIDI:** So they smell like other people's perfumes, or body odors?

**ANNA:** Both. They're heat-activated.

**MONICA:** One of the reasons the costume designer, Kelly Hanson, is drawn toward pre-owned clothing instead of building new costumes is that she is always costuming us to look like real people and real people seldom have clothes that fit perfectly. There is always something a little off or unique that tells you who that person is.

**LEANNE:** Do you take the coats off during the performance?

**MONICA:** At the very end I take my coat off and put it on the ground in an old-fashioned gesture, the way men used to do over puddles, which actually seems like the most ridiculous thing you would ever do. Like, wouldn't you just step over the puddle? Would you actually drench your own coat?

**HEIDI:** And what do you do afterward? Do you pick it up and put it back on?

**LEANNE:** Leave it there for other women.

**HEIDI:** When you come up with a dance, are

you already thinking about the costumes?

MONICA: Kelly is a part of the conversation from the very beginning. Kelly will watch us and say, "I wonder what they would look like in a sequined dress," or "How about we try that dance on a dining room table?" We have been working together for so long at this point. The conversation started fifteen years ago and it has never really stopped.

**MOSTLY FANFARE**
*(feather headdresses, white feminine undershirts, black wool skirts)*

MONICA: Some of the inspiration came from silent movies. Kelly and I loved the idea of headdresses, but we wanted to counter the image of showgirls, so she took all the color out of these costumes. The costumes are always referring to something that the audience is familiar with. Also, we are always looking at costumes, and one of the first questions is: Is there any way this is coming across as sexy? and then, How can we strip that?

LEANNE: I want to hear about the rejection of "dancer sexy."

ANNA: We grew up doing tap-dance, ballet. I remember one of my tap costumes, it was a high-cut red leotard. And it had a tie. My mom was like, "I'm not sure who picked this, but we're gonna have to pull that leotard down." That was my one sexy moment. Twelve years old. Haven't had one since.

HEIDI: You're never as sexy as you are at twelve. So at what point did you guys decide that you were against that variety of sexy?

MONICA: There's something you figure out early about the way you're being perceived. As soon as somebody finds you attractive, you immediately think: You're not totally paying attention.

HEIDI: You lose respect for them?

MONICA: Not exactly. It's just that there is nothing surprising about a pretty woman, it is such a known entity. In that sense, you're unoriginal. And you're not funny. That was the other key: in movement terms, it's hard to be attractive and funny. There's just a way in which those two physical impulses counter each other, because there is an inherent grace to beauty, and humor requires a certain force, a physical force. You can't physically be lackadaisically funny. To be funny you have to be quick, twitchy.

LEANNE: That's fascinating.

HEIDI: Fascinating and also sort of depressing.

LEANNE: Maybe when an audience is seduced by beauty, something switches off, and the performer doesn't have the same kind of attention.

MONICA: As soon as you present yourself as really pretty onstage, you lose a certain amount of power. You're safer. You're admired. And then people feel comfortable with you.

**ANNA:** They know who that is.

**HEIDI:** Right. I wonder if age isn't somehow coming into this decision-making process, because that kind of beauty and that kind of sexiness have such a shelf life, but humor doesn't.

**ANNA:** Yeah. Dance has a very narrow, very small shelf life. We've already expired, but we're still going.

**MONICA:** *(laughs)* Also we're both small, and to have a physical impact we have to be aggressive. One thing both of us have done all our dancing lives is try to be bigger. Honestly, that was the original inspiration for wanting to wear a headdress—I wanted to be taller.

***I FEEL LIKE***

*(wool turtleneck sweaters, brooches, plaid wool skirts)*

**HEIDI:** I feel like this costume needs so much unpacking, because you are playing to a sexy stereotype here, right? Yet the brooch is saying: grandmother.

**MONICA:** If this costume fit better or the skirt was shorter, it would look like a Catholic school uniform. We are always struggling against these costumes, like the moment where we pull our thick turtlenecks down to lick our shoulders. Kelly and I always discuss the underwear at length. For this duet, it is really important that the underwear is black and substantial, so when you see any of it you're like, "Oh my god, they're in big black underwear." Somehow what we're wearing underneath is the least sexy thing that could be there.

**LEANNE:** Do you rehearse in leotards, pink tights, you know what I mean?

**MONICA:** No, we do not. I've never seen Anna in pink, ever.

**LEANNE:** Is it track pants and tank tops?

**MONICA:** Yeah. And the worst part is, you're looking at yourself so often.

**ANNA:** That's how we've spent our entire lives. Looking at ourselves in the mirror. We will try to spice it up a bit. I started cutting a small V-neck in the men's undershirts I always wear.

**MONICA:** But it is pretty hopeless. I mean, our hair is matted and sweaty and all our rehearsal clothes are worn-out. I will put lipstick on if it gets really bad.

**ANNA:** We actually use lipstick as a "You know what we need?"

**MONICA:** We will have breaks when we just walk away and put lipstick on.

**HEIDI:** I completely understand. Recently I had to Skype with someone, and I was nervous about Skyping with them, so I put on perfume. But back to the wool skirt/ sweater. It seems to me that the dance came about with the costume. From the costume we expect you to behave one way, but then you behave this other way.

**MONICA:** I feel the relationship is cyclical, like the dance informs the costume and then the costume informs the dance and that goes on forever until we premiere the dance. The audience is so profoundly influenced by what we are wearing; so much of the humor is in the costume design, which allows the audience to see the humor in the dance. It's amazing how funny clothes can be.

**LUSTER**
*(vintage-inspired sequined dresses, running shoes, purses)*

**LEANNE:** Okay, let's talk about the sequined dresses . . .

**MONICA:** This is going to be a sad statement. Those were the most attractive things we've ever worn. They're beautiful. They were actually made for us. All the bad smells are our own.

**ANNA:** We loved the way it looked under stage lights, and Kelly really loved that it felt like a layer of armor. And the running shoes are key. They undercut the sequins.

**LEANNE:** There's also that female stereotype of the woman wearing her tennis shoes commuting in her work clothes.

**MONICA:** We're the exact reverse of that stereotype, we dress up for our commute and then change into our dingy rehearsal clothes when we get to "work." I mean, I only get to wear my outfit for the subway ride and the walk to rehearsal, then I have to take it all off.

**HEIDI:** So you need a tear-away outfit.

**ANNA:** Yes. That would save us hours of time. Sometimes I feel, Why am I even bothering wearing real clothes?

**LEANNE:** Who are you in those two hours?

**MONICA:** The good news is that we can get at least two or three days' use of one outfit, because it is only on our bodies for a few hours each day. So we save money on laundry.

**ANNA:** Yes! And if it is a day that we have to have a business dinner or a gala event, then we have our "fancy" outfits all balled up in the bottom of our bags.

**HEIDI:** So what do you wear for those events?

**ANNA:** Tight pants and a top with a little edge.

**LEANNE:** But not a dress.

**ANNA:** Very rarely.

**MONICA:** We were just at a gala event and I wore really thick and wide-legged wool pants and a turtleneck and a scarf, and I somehow thought it was gonna look classy. And then I just felt like I was buried in wool, which is funny because many of our costumes are wool.

**HEIDI:** So you always carry a wardrobe of clothes around?

**MONICA:** Carrying things around is just a central part of our artistic life, whether we are on tour or not. And then that part of our life ends up being in the dances. In "Luster," we carry a six-foot-tall proscenium set around and I was like, I love the idea that we are carrying our own stage around wherever we go, it's just like our real lives, but it turns out that lugging that fifty-pound stage is not fun. So I feel responsible for causing us a certain amount of suffering.

**ANNA:** Yeah, but dancers are a hardy bunch.

*EVERYTHING IS GETTING BETTER ALL THE TIME*
*(men's rip-away suits, sleeveless undershirts, wool athletic shorts)*

**MONICA:** These are men's three-piece suits that are tricked out to rip away in one motion—like the Chippendale tear-away. We rip them in the middle of the dance, and underneath we're wearing old-fashioned boxing shorts, like you'd wear in gym class in 1972. They're itchy, they're thick—

**ANNA:** The crotch is too high.

**MONICA:** And we use batons. It's the most ridiculous piece, but also one of the edgiest things I've ever made, because I'm dealing with entertainment in such a gross way. It's aggressively—

**ANNA:** Aggressive entertainment.

**MONICA:** Kelly said, "I think we should try it in men's suits, but not like you are wearing your dads' suits, but like you are in the Midwest at a conference for insurance and you're going to the hotel bar for a night." I feel like I am this particular guy who is wearing his favorite suit.

**LEANNE:** What do you notice when you look at men and women on the street?

**HEIDI:** Do you pick up movements?

**ANNA:** I rarely look at women. I look at men a lot.

**HEIDI:** That's so interesting! I never look at men. Do you?

**LEANNE:** I look at both.

**MONICA:** I look at both. Also, kids are really fascinating movers. I've spent a lot of time watching people dancing at weddings. My dad is a minister, so I went to a lot of weddings growing up. Some of the choreography for this dance came from watching people dance at weddings. Social dancing looks funny in formal clothes. I feel like we're gonna be in suits again soon.

**HEIDI:** And then, after the show, you dig out your fancy outfit from the bottom of your bag. Is that hard?

**MONICA:** Sometimes.

**HEIDI:** It seems weird, like expecting a professional swimmer to get out of the pool and put on a tux and go.

**ANNA:** It's fascinating to switch from performer to human being after a show.

**MONICA:** Not to mention that you've been sweating buckets for hours and your hair is hairsprayed into a helmet.

**ANNA:** Then we're like, "You know what we need? Earrings." We both have earrings in our bags.

**MONICA:** Emergency earrings.

**ANNA:** And lipstick. ✕

*HEATHER O'DONNELL*'s Catholic jewelry

# THE PANTSUIT ROTATION

## ALEX WAGNER JOURNALIST AND TELEVISION ANCHOR
## SPEAKS ABOUT HER WORK CLOTHES WITH LEANNE SHAPTON

**LEANNE:** Tell me about your flannel shirt.

**ALEX:** I have three flannel shirts. I wear them to work with my jeans and I literally wait until the very last moment to change into my work clothes. I bring my work outfits with me, I have a garment rack in my office. The show is live every day from four to five p.m., so wearing my flannel shirt, I go get hair done around midday, and then edit scripts until 3:15, then I put on my dress, run down to makeup, and then run to set. I'm always late. As soon as the show is over I run back upstairs, take off the makeup, take off the dress. As soon as I can physically get out of that clothing I do.

**LEANNE:** Describe the shirt.

**ALEX:** It's awesome, actually. It always happens that I get caught in the rain after I get out of my shrink's office, and so I go to Urban Outfitters, which is right around the corner, and inevitably I find something good. I have this one electric-blue flannel sort of Native American–motif shirt. Women have come up and asked me if it was Isabel Marant and I'm like, No, it's whatever the fucking Urban Outfitter tag says, "Blue Dog" or whatever. It's super-soft.

**LEANNE:** A lot of women seem to go shopping after their shrinks.

**ALEX:** You're in a good mood! You worked it out!

**LEANNE:** How do you avoid repeating the outfits you wear on screen?

**ALEX:** We're instituting a new system where I have a little tag or piece of paper that I tape to the outfit so that I know when I last wore it. The volume of clothes needed for TV . . . Chris Matthews told me a couple weeks ago: "I wore the same blazer three days in a row and nobody noticed!" I was so jealous and outraged. It's ridiculous. You have five suits and that's all you wear, all year long. Women in television need to have at least three or four weeks' worth of dresses where there are no repeats, which is a lot of clothing. And then, depending on the season, it's an insane amount of wardrobe. You really do lose track. I have a hard time recalling what was on the show the day before. And I certainly cannot remember what I wore ten days ago. Hillary Clinton, notoriously, on her plane had taped to one of the walls of her wardrobe the pantsuit rotation. Literally, the first of the month is the pink pantsuit, the 17th of the month is the green pantsuit, the 20th of the month is the blue pantsuit. I remember first being sort of aghast and then thinking, Eureka, that's exactly what I need to do.

**LEANNE:** Was she back-dating them or forward-dating them?

**ALEX:** Forward-dating. They were on rotation.

**LEANNE:** Wow.

**ALEX:** And the press on the plane were like, "Well, it's the seventeenth—that means the green pantsuit!"

**LEANNE:** That's amazing. So organized. Has anyone ever called you out on wearing the same thing?

ALEX: Once, when I was just starting on TV. I didn't have a show yet, I was a contributor. I had a button-down silk shirt. As reporter, you didn't know if you were going to be on TV, so I wore the same shirt two days in a row, not in real life but for TV purposes. My friend Chris Hayes texted me, "I saw that shirt yesterday," and I remember being mortified because Chris is not a sartorialist and if he noticed then other people did too. That was my first glimpse into thinking I had to be more cognizant about never repeating things two days in a row.

LEANNE: How different do you feel in the clothes you have to wear for work?

ALEX: I definitely feel more focused. The pieces are more body-conscious than the clothes that I would wear in life, so I pay attention to my posture and my shoulders being back and that in no small part has to do with the fact I'm on TV. The clothes convey a message, they establish a physical consciousness I don't have in my everyday clothes. The clothes are nicer. They're not Urban Outfitters "Dog Whatever," they're more tailored and more fitted and you can't loaf around in them.

LEANNE: How have you made those clothes "you," either by personalizing or by rebelling in small ways?

ALEX: I think on some level I personalize by the kinds of designers I pick. Once in a while I'll find myself in a newscasterish dress and it feels spiritually apocalyptic. I do try to make a conscious effort to pick from lines that are more creative. There's a public side of it—can anybody tell the difference between that Row dress and J.Crew—probably not, but there's the personal satisfaction one gets from just knowing that this is from a different place. It's not just about price, it's about the thinking that went into it. I'm a bit reliant on that private knowledge. In a lot of aspects in TV, I know that I'm presenting myself as this public person, but privately I know that I'm actually like *this*.

LEANNE: Has anything really backfired?

ALEX: Volume. There was this beautiful Jil Sander dress that was one of the first purchases I made. Like a trench dress, beautiful, but totally did not work on TV. I remember just being devastated. It was expensive and I thought, This is the kind of clothing I'm going to wear and it's going to be my identity. And it just did not work at all. Now it's part of my wardrobe. My work clothes exist. . . . I literally cannot wear them unless I'm in front of the camera.

LEANNE: Tell me about shopping. Do you shop with someone?

ALEX: When I first started in TV, I shopped with a personal shopper at Barneys. And I did my first big wardrobe purchases with her. Her name is Laura Mannix, and she's great, really talented. She works with a lot of people in TV and is a serious fashion person in a lot of ways but understands the profession. One issue with shopping with Laura is that she always picks out incredible pieces, but sometimes they are just too sophisticated for television. And there's a limiting nature to the shot—I'm at a desk, as opposed to, say, the *Today* show, where you see more of the anchors' bodies; they're standing up, they're sitting down, there's more room to be creative, and people can really see the silhouette of a dress. Whereas for an anchor at a desk, lines have to be sharp and standard. I now use Laura for special things. When I was on Conan O'Brien's show we worked together and she got me a great outfit for that. But now I shop with my executive producer, Dana Haller, a lot, or do a lot of shopping on my own. I've sort of figured out what works and what doesn't. Dana is really good—she has beautiful taste in clothing that's very different from mine and we'll look at stuff together. It's like shopping with a sister insofar as we have a shorthand. She'll pick out stuff that I would not pick out for myself. But I'd say I shop half-half, sometimes by myself, sometimes with Dana.

**LEANNE:** Do you notice women on the street?

**ALEX:** Women are so used to being given the once-over. I know what that feels like, as every woman does, so I don't want to do that to other women, but I definitely notice them. I never ask people where their outfit is from, but I will definitely think, Oh I need to be wearing more white sailor pants or whatever, then I go home and do that weird thing where I try and duplicate what I've seen. It never works.

**LEANNE:** How do you feel when you see footage and photographs of yourself?

**ALEX:** It's by far been the most traumatic part of the whole thing. I'm always like: Pull the camera back! Lower the lights! And they're like: You're not doing fucking radio, Alex, this is television. It's a weird thing to be something that people watch every day and that people have opinions about. You know what struck me as crazy: One time a producer said, "Oh, my mom called. She loved your haircut." And it dawned on me that it was not only my mom that was looking at my haircut, it was other people's moms. Moms I don't know about. Moms all over the place that may have opinions about my haircut. If I think too much about that, I get really freaked out. That said, I can see a transformation in myself looking back to when I first started doing TV and the way I carry myself and the stuff I wear. I'm more comfortable having my picture taken, but for someone who is on live television every day I am remarkably awkward still. ✕

COMPLIMENT

## "SCARF"

*Mid-November, 10:30 a.m. A university in southern Ontario. The elevator is going down. A twentysomething woman with dark skin and green eyes wears a brown leopard-print scarf around her neck. It's an indoors outfit, an indoors scarf.*

**SHEILA:** That's a nice scarf.

**WOMAN:** Oh, thank you!

*(They giggle. The woman searches for something to say.)*

**WOMAN:** They sell so many beautiful ones down here [in the lobby of the university commons].

**SHEILA:** Is that where you found it?

**WOMAN:** I got this— I was in Spain last year, and I picked it up, but I've been seeing them all around everywhere.

**SHEILA:** Really? I actually haven't seen anything . . . It's such a nice color.

**WOMAN:** Thank you. Yeah, I've seen one just like this. There's a lady who has a scarf stand—

**SHEILA:** Oh, yeah?

*The elevator doors open. They exit and walk into the foyer.*

**WOMAN:** I haven't seen her for a little while but—

*She points at a pink scarf hanging on a scarf stand in the lobby.*

**WOMAN:** I feel like this one right here is the opposite color. Well, different color. So check it out!

**SHEILA:** I will! Thanks! *(They part.)* ✕

*CHARLOTTE YOSHIMURA*'s navy blazers

# AN OLDER WOMAN GOING THROUGH HER CLOSET

**PAMELA BAGULEY** *as told to Leanne Shapton*

This cream one I bought in Turkey on holiday with my mother. It was in a shop window near the hotel for £30. John's mother, when she came to stay, always used to go through my wardrobe, which was in the spare room where she slept. She was very nosy, and she didn't like me, horrible old bitch, so on the price tag I added a zero so it read £300. She'd tell John how extravagant I was.

That one I bought in a market in Italy. When I bought it, my friend Frankie said, "What have you bought that for?" but then she admitted it didn't look bad when it was on. I wore it once. It's got horses on it, so I wore it when I went to an evening that was about horses—about horse racing. I've never worn it since, because another friend said, "Oh, you can wear that when you're ninety." That put me off.

This was my outfit for my fiftieth birthday. I bought it in Harrods. It's Max Mara. We went with some friends to hear Gerard Kenny at the Café Royal. It was a great night, but the trousers sort of stick to you, they're not right.

Most of these I've only worn once.

This I wore when I met Margaret Thatcher. It must be over thirty years old. I'll never wear it again because I won't go sleeveless. My arms have had it.

That I had made in Egypt. I'd wear it, but the dye comes off. I put it on once and thought, "Hmmm, what's all this black?" They used cheap vegetable dye.

This is all evening—that's my ballgown. I've only worn that once. I love the color.

This I have never worn, ever. It's far too big. God knows what possessed me to buy it. Helen McAlinden is a designer—an Irish girl who has a shop. I honestly must have been . . . I mean, look at the size of it! I honestly. I have never, ever. It just hangs there. I've never worn it.

That's my lovely dress that I love. I feel good in that. Don't look at the price. £545. If anything happens to me just make sure my clothes are looked after, will you? Don't put them in a bin bag.

Gill gave me this suit because it didn't fit her anymore. The skirt was really long, grandma-y, and actually I didn't like it that much, but when I tried it on I thought I looked good in it and I liked it and have actually worn it quite a lot. But I had the skirt shortened. Gill said, "You've had that skirt of mine shortened!" And I said, "You gave it to me!" And she said, "I wanted it back." She said she gave me the jacket but lent me the skirt. She knew that I had this large microwave plate, and she said, "Well, you can give me that microwave plate for it." And then she said, "You'd better buy me a decent Christmas present."

This is what I want to surprise Noel in, with a sexy red skirt. I'll have to get some really nice black shoes, very high, to go with it. If I could just get to see him . . .

That I've only ever worn once. I bought it in Hong Kong in 1972. I'm saving it for when I'm with somebody really nice. I wore that when I was with Sugar. Sugar was the love of my life. There was an eightieth-birthday party for a friend of ours, Bobby, and I said to Vicky, "I hope Sugar's not going to be there." And she said, "Oh no, he's not friendly with Bobby, he won't be there." Anyway, when I got there I went to sit with some friends, and as I was sitting there somebody said, "Sugar's here with his wife." So I felt really, really strange and I avoided looking. But I felt I looked okay, I was happy, I was slim. Anyway, a bit later on I went to the ladies', and as I came back he was standing at the bar on his own, so we started to talk and a lot of people were noticing because everybody knows how he felt about me and how I felt about him. People were looking and nodding. It got a little bit embarrass-

ing. There were things I wanted to say to him about what had happened—that I wanted to say I was sorry for. Anyway, his wife came over, little thing, unattractive, and Sugar said, "Oh, this is Pam." She said, "Oh, you're the ex." And Sugar said, "We've been married for thirty-three years, it was thirty-odd years ago!" It was just the way she said it, she just looked me up and down. After thirty years, for heaven's sake! So then I wandered over back to the bar, excused myself. And it was strange . . . I knew the way Sugar was looking at me. You never, ever . . . *(starts to cry)* Anyway, I went back to the bar and Howard, who is an evil toad, said, "Oh, he should have married you, she's awful." But we couldn't. He was Jewish. I couldn't have converted. And I wasn't nice. I was horrible, you see, that's what I'm sorry for. That's what I wanted to say. We were in the South of France and I said some really horrible things about his mother, and I never should have said them because they were hurtful and horrible. His mother had given up everything for him, his sister wasn't well. But I just couldn't see. You know, nobody's ever loved me like Sugar did. He knew how selfish, mean, spiteful I could be—all the bad things about me— and still didn't care. And now as one gets older, you hide those things. You'd think as you get older . . . *(cries)* ✕

# Souvankham Thammavongsa

*When do you feel most attractive?*
After I have written something I really like. It makes me feel so beautiful and timeless. Also, after I come out of a salon. It reminds me of being a child, when my mother used to cut my hair or give me baths. Having someone else groom me makes me feel attractive. Being clean makes me feel attractive.

*Are there any clothing items that you have in multiple?*
I don't have items in multiple, but I do wear the same outfit on several occasions. What I seem to be wearing a lot right now is a navy blue or brown skirt with a black top.

*What is your process getting dressed in the morning?*
I think about what I'm doing for the day and who I might be meeting and the weather. I think about the neighborhood, and if I feel safe there or not. I think about the kind of transit I will be in—subway, train, bus, a taxi—and what I will be carrying around with me. That will determine the kind

of shoes I will wear. If I don't know the neighhorhood, flat shoes are a must. I always wear a skirt and flats with a black top in different variations. I have three or four items I change around to make it look different, but if you paid attention you can tell I only have three or four things.

*Is there anyone you talk to about clothing or style?*
A good friend of mine had expensive taste, and when I spent time with her, she would take me into all these stores I would be too afraid to go into, and she'd tell me to try things on. She would order people around to bring me clothes. Then we would go to other stores and find items that were similar to the expensive ones we liked. But we had an idea of what "good" clothing was like. She showed me what looked good on me and what colors worked best, and she wasn't afraid to say to me, "Are you wearing your ugly sweater again?" She also taught me what to expect from clothes, and what it should feel like when you are wearing good

clothes. Quality clothes are expensive, but they also last forever. She taught me to care about my body—to keep it healthy, to go to the gym, because then whatever you put on, cheap or expensive, it will look great on you. Always have your clothes tailored if they don't fit right, and save money by taking sewing classes. She taught me to care for my hair and skin and nails. You can put on the fanciest thing, and if you don't take care of those things, nothing will look good. She also helped me throw away clothes. Some items are too full of memories of who you were and who you were with, that to move on, you have to throw them away. I bought this beautiful dress once, hoping to wear it for a special occasion with the person I loved, but then he stopped loving me before we had an occasion to go to. Every time I opened the closet and I saw this dress, I was reminded that I wasn't loved and the occasion I was waiting for never happened. So I threw it away.

*Do you think you have taste or style? Which is more important?*
I think I have taste, and I try to choose things to fit that taste. My taste is often informed by things I like to read and look at. I think taste is more important than style. Style can change and be influenced by trends, but your taste is like your soul and it's forever. I think taste is like the bubble in the level. You measure everything else by that. Style is a thing that's outside you, changing and flowing like clouds and weather.

*When you see yourself in photographs, what do you think?*
I hate to see myself in photographs because I think I'm prettier and more charming in real life. A photograph never catches the life-force I have when I look in the mirror and can see myself. In a photograph, I think my cheeks are really big, like I am hoarding nuts for the winter, and I am always scowling and looking un-friendly or sad. Sometimes I think my head is so big and round it looks like a vol-leyball. I'm loyal and warm and funny, and a photograph never catches that.

*What are some things you admire about how other women look?*
I admire the way they walk in a crowd. I always step out of people's way or am the one holding doors for others. I wish I could be that person who walks through the door or leads the pack, the one who expects the other person to move out of the way on a narrow sidewalk. I also admire the ones who make demands and get upset when someone treats them terribly in the service industry. I wish I was brave like that.

*Have you ever stolen or borrowed dressing ideas or items?*
I've taken some of my husband's sweaters and his colorful socks. Also, I've worn my mother's dresses for special occasions when I grew to be her size—ones she made herself. I hated all the prom dresses that were out there. They were too expensive or looked terrible on me. The dress I wore for prom was my mother's dress. There was a time when my best friend dressed like me, or I, like her. We even had the same haircut.

*Are there any dressing rules you'd like to convey to other women?*
Always wear a bra in an office environment. I don't think it's appropriate to have it all hanging out there. It's fine if you are on vacation or at home, but in the office, I don't want to see your hard nipples. And never wear those thermal T-shirts that change color. I once wore one for a school presentation

and only the breast area changed color. I was very embarrassed.

*How and when do you shop?*
I like to shop on my own. I don't like to go with other people. I take a long time to choose and I like what I choose to be a surprise to the people who see me. I shop four times a year but only to add a small item to update what I already have. Some-times that's one sweater, a shoe, basic tops, socks.

*How does money fit into all this?*
I don't have a lot of it for clothes. I usually wait for things to go on sale. If they don't have it in my size, I tell myself it wasn't meant to be, or I buy it and tailor it myself. I also shop at thrift stores. I pay attention to fabric and how it is sewed. I don't like fabric I can't take care of, and I don't like things I can't mend on my own. I never use my husband's money. It feels weird and inappropriate, even though I've seen other women in stores be "treated." I take great pride that I buy my own underwear and clothes with the money I made, however little that is.

*Was there a point when your style changed dramatically?*
I used to wear beautiful dresses my mom made for me. When I grew breasts, I stopped wearing them. Part

of the reason was that they didn't fit anymore and showed too much. I started to wear sweatshirts or big sweaters to cover my breasts after that. Then, when I got married, I wore less of those big sweaters because I felt safe and like I didn't have to be the only one protecting myself.

*Can you describe what you own, clothing- and jewelry-wise?*
My only jewelry is my watch and wedding ring. I used to live in a dangerous part of Toronto, so not wearing jewelry became a habit.

*What is your closet like?*
I have three shelves on the left-hand side, for winter clothes, summer clothes, and underwear/bras. The clothes on the hangers are those that fit the season. If they are not the current season, I put them in another closet in the hallway. On the floor are my fancy shoes in boxes. There are four. Then I have a black suitcase. There is one purse.

*How does how you dress play into your ambitions for yourself?*
I tend to feel more ambitious than the way I dress.

*What is your background, and how has that influenced how you dress?*
I'm Laotian, and when my family came to Canada, our papers said we had "nil" in money. I think this makes me feel like I don't deserve nice clothes, and I feel guilty for having them, like I'm forgetting where I come from, my roots. There are beautiful dresses which I've never worn called *sinh*. I remember my mom wearing one to the temple, but you can't just go out to a store to buy it. You have to get the fabric in Laos or Thailand, and my mom had so few.

*Can you recall some times when you have dressed a particular way to calm yourself?*
Yes! I am really scared of doing public readings. If it's in a bar I'm afraid a drunk person will tell me to show them my tits rather than listen to what I have privately written, so I'll wear a sweater over whatever I'm wearing even if it's really hot. Once, I dressed like a teenager because I was staying out late to give a reading. I thought this would prevent men from approaching me in a bar, and it did work. Then, when I was walking home, a car full of young men started to call me "Sexy" and talk about my body. That made me feel scared. So I turned to them and said, "I'M TWELVE!" They rolled up their windows and drove away embarrassed. I felt in control. Also, sometimes with some friends I won't wear nice things because I'm afraid it will make them feel bad about themselves or jealous. A person once stopped being my friend for that reason, and her friendship, at the time, was important to me.

*Do you have any dressing tricks?*
I think you can buy cheap clothing but make it not look cheap if you have nice shoes. And when I work out and keep fit, then everything looks good on me.

*Is there any article of clothing, makeup, or accessory you carry or wear every day?*
I moisturize my skin a lot— so lip balm and sunscreen. I put on concealer under my eyes and wear a cheek stain. The cheek stain is a lot easier to apply because you don't have to think about contoring or shaping, you just put a dot on your cheek and rub it in. It's really easy. I generally don't like makeup because it takes up a lot of time and it's expensive. I think if I take care of my skin then I will look good.

*Do you care about lingerie?*
No. Because it all comes off anyway. I like to buy things I can wear for a long time.

*Do you have style in any areas of your life aside from fashion?*
I try to keep it simple and to do the best with what I know and with what's in front of me. It's also important to me that in my relationships and friendships things are kept

simple and honest. When I first met my husband and was beginning to like him, I asked him, "Are you a one-at-a-time kind of man?" The answer to this was important to me. I once dated someone who was not, and I felt like I was interchangeable with the other women, a thing to have for one night and dump into the laundry basket another night. He said he took on the personality of whatever woman he was with, the way a person might feel about clothes. There was always someone more beautiful, younger, smarter, talented, cool, or just plain new, or someone coming who was going to be that. No matter what I wrote, wore, or thought, it never made me feel beautiful, attractive, or timeless. I wanted to be chosen, to be that bubble in the level. At the time, I thought what we had was profound and different, but love that was just for me, that fit me no matter the occasion, seemed to be more profound, and when I figured that out I went to find it, even though nothing about the universe at the time said I would. And when I did, it took only two weeks to decide the rest.

*What would be a difficult or uncomfortable look for you to try to achieve?*
I think the stripper look would be too difficult for me. I already feel people are looking at me too much.

*How is this stuff important?*
I used to think clothing didn't matter, but it does. People respond to you differently. In jeans I look like a kid, but if I wear a pencil skirt and heels, then people start calling me "Ma'am" and I like that. Also once someone didn't want to go out with me because I looked like a kid. I was always really sore and sour about not having a boyfriend in high school, but when I look at pictures of myself, the big sweaters, the unplucked eyebrows, I feel like I was hiding and no wonder no one was looking.

*Please describe your body.*
I'm short. I am four feet, eleven inches. I think I have big breasts, but I am told they are not all that big by my friends. I have a nice collarbone and long, graceful fingers. I could have been a great pianist but I'm an excellent typist instead. My toes are nice. I have thin ankles. My skin is nice.

*Please describe your mind.*
It's very quiet. Not because it isn't thinking but because it is, and when it is it's quiet.

*Please describe your emotions.*
I feel like a jellyfish. I try not to think in ways that undermine myself or to feel too much that things are unbearable. I like the jellyfish because it has no

brain or heart. It's just a thing that takes in the ocean through its mouth. I like that kind of ambition and simplicity.

*What makes you feel presentable?*
I need to shower at least two times a day.

*What are you wearing?*
I am about to go to bed. I have on a recovering serum. Moisturizer is too oily for me. If it's cold I wear a heavier moisturizer, but if it's hot like it was today I wear the serum. I washed my hair yesterday and it is swept to the side. I am wearing cotton because it's good for my pores and I worry a lot about yeast infections.

*Where and when were you born, and where do you live now?*
I was born on August 13, 1978. I was born in a Lao refugee camp in Nong Khai, Thailand, and raised in Toronto. I now live in Stouffville, Ontario.

*What kind of work do you do?*
I work for a company that publishes financial advice and newsletters. I also write poetry and create art with PowerPoint and paper clips.

*Are you single, married?*
I am married. I don't have kids.

*Please say anything you like about yourself for context.*
When I was a child, my parents only had two outfits for me to wear. We were poor and they said whatever they bought for me I would outgrow anyway. My parents rarely dressed me. I dressed myself, and having to choose between two outfits made things easy. I care a lot about being clean and feeling clean because when I was a teenager, my parents sold our home and we lived in a van until their sign-making business started up. I remember not having a shower and having to wait to go to school to brush my teeth. My mother wasn't very strict with me about grooming or clothes. I didn't know I was supposed to shave my legs until in gym class a guy who I was sitting next to looked down at my legs and said, "Yo girl, you gotta shave that thing. I couldn't tell which were my legs!" My mom didn't take me to buy a bra. I had to ask her to after a guy at school said my tits were really big and I needed support. When I had my period, when I was nine years old, I thought it was a leech and asked my mother to take it out for me. She took one look at me, turned back to her cooking, and with one loud hack of a cleaver said, "You have your period. Go put a pad on." She also always had cheap maxipads. The kind that got wet and

then the glue would come undone. I had one fall out during gym class. It wasn't until I was fourteen that I discovered there were such thing as pads with wings that protect the underwear and also secure it all there. They came in a pink box that we all had to buy in grade nine. Inside was also shaving gel and deodorant. My mother used soap to shave and just wiped her armpits with soap rubbed into a cloth. There are some people who don't need to use deodorant, but I'm not one of them. I need a serious one. Although it might shock other women or make them judge my mother for not taking me aside to tell me how to groom myself or tell me about my period and celebrate it or teach me how to cook and clean the house, I think my mother loved me deeply and gave me something by not doing that: a strong and bright mind of my own. I could lend it space for other things. To my parents, success was the simple act of living and being able to live. It wasn't clothes or furniture or the house to own or the china set on display. Those things are great to have, but just living, when it's hard, is good enough. I used to have a friend who would, over the course of a meal, pick on the way people dressed in the restaurant and imagine what their lives were like outside that. I don't think everyone

gets a chance at having access to nice clothes. I think about my "ugly sweater" and the times I just had a simple wish for a shower. No one at school knew what was happening at home, but I never felt judged or teased for what I was wearing. I'm grateful for that. I dressed the way I dressed because that's what I had and that's what made me feel good.

*Please include a picture of your mother before she was a mom.*
I don't have pictures of my mother before she became a mom because everything was lost when she and my dad built a raft made of bamboo to cross the Mekong River and live in the refugee camp. I doubt what she looked like is much different from now. She wore what she wanted and she made it herself. It didn't matter.

Here's a diary entry I found from when I was twelve years old.

*Dear Diary,*
*Today I wore my new jeans and nothing happened. I really hoped something would happen. But I loved wearing them. They felt so comfortable. I LOVE MY NEW LEVIS JEANS.*

This is what I believed about clothes then—that they had the capacity to "make things happen." ✕

## SHOPPING TRAILS | KATE RYAN

*The paths made while walking through various stores.*

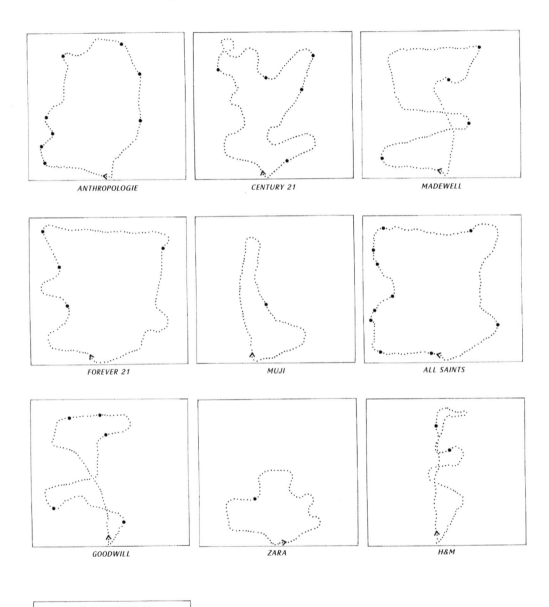

ANTHROPOLOGIE

CENTURY 21

MADEWELL

FOREVER 21

MUJI

ALL SAINTS

GOODWILL

ZARA

H&M

• STOPPED TO TOUCH AN ITEM

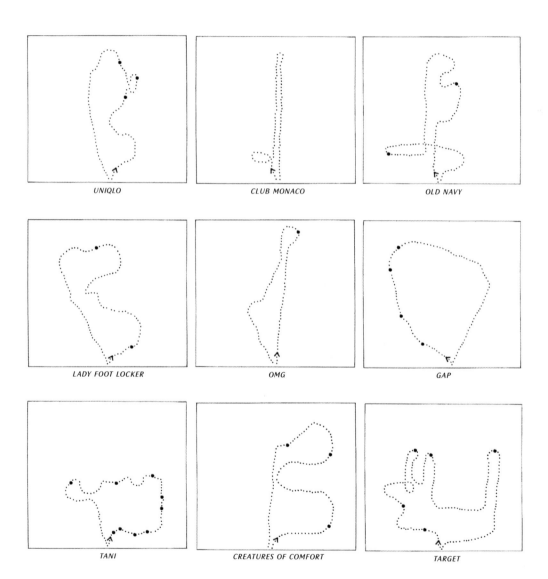

UNIQLO

CLUB MONACO

OLD NAVY

LADY FOOT LOCKER

OMG

GAP

TANI

CREATURES OF COMFORT

TARGET

*HEIDI SOPINKA*'s Levi's

# MEN LOOKING AT WOMEN

*"As he was selling me a piece of halibut, my fishmonger said, 'Your bangs are too long, why are you scared of showing your real face?'"*—KATHRYN BOREL

SZILVIA MOLNAR Recently, my partner gave me my first pair of sneakers (high-tops) and as practical and unromantic as it sounds, I found it so endearing that he wanted to get me a pair of shoes that offered comfort. For so many years I've squeezed my toes and heels into tight spaces and I never allowed myself to find style in comfort, but it means a great deal to me now.

SARAH GERARD When I first moved to New York, I worked for a thriller writer near Grand Central. I'd spent the last three years in my hometown of Tampa and was accustomed to dressing in a revealing way, and perhaps a little shabby. One day, I came to work wearing a short dress and no tights (I never wore tights). He told me I should never walk around Midtown with bare legs, that I should always have tights on.

LUCIE BONVALET I remember talking with my Japanese boyfriend ten years ago when I was living in Kyoto. He said that the most erotic, sensuous part of a woman's body in Japanese culture is the nape of the neck, and traditional fashion aims at thousands of different ways to reveal it. He also said that in medieval poems the perfect woman's body is compared to the weeping willow. The conversation helped to break, deepen, and rebuild my seeing the body as art, art in motion.

JUDY REBICK Once when my nephew lived with me and I was working on television, I asked him what he thought of an outfit I had put on to appear in on TV (usually I sat behind a desk, but this time I would be filmed standing) He said, "You look like a mushroom." I changed, and after that I always consulted him, 'cause he's honest.

ERIKA THORMAHLEN I feel most attractive when a male European tourist passes me on the street and gives me the once-over. Maybe he'll say something like "bella" (it happened once).

CLAUDIA DEY A man said once: If only you would brush your hair! Another man said: If only you would wear your hair off your face!

GRACE DENTON Some days I ask my boyfriend for a word to get dressed to, like "yellow" or "garden" or "Settlers of Catan." He's pretty good at it, and it gives me some inspiration.

JENNIFER WINEKE I don't like when dudes say, "I prefer girls who don't wear makeup." It's based on the assumption that girls are using makeup to correct flaws and present themselves more ideally to dudes, and the guy is saying, "Hey, no worries, you don't have to do that for me." There are so many cool things you can do to your face. Saying you prefer girls with no makeup is almost a weird arrogant pressure-statement, like, I want you to be naturally beautiful and confident about it all the time, and also not have fun expressing yourself.

AMY LAM My hair is long now for the first time ever in my life. I started growing it four years ago—when the relationship I'm in first started. Because the boyfriend likes it! Haha! I am not emancipated. I always used to have short hair, some kind of weird haircut with too many ideas. Now it's long and people always remark on it. People say it makes me look like a woman, and I believe them! I guess out of principle I should cut it off.

**MELANIE PAGE** Shopping for plus-size clothing is a nightmare. It's a niche market, so stores take advantage and charge a lot of money for something an average or petite woman would not be charged. Recently, I discovered a resale store that has beautiful clothes. The most I ever paid for one item there is $20, and that was a whole dress. Now that I've found a store that's run by a woman who empathizes with the plus-size shopping experience, I buy something nearly every week. My husband doesn't say anything about the money, because it is inexpensive, I am happy, and I feel better at work.

**TALATA BOWSER** Most of my hijabs are pashmina shawl types, and I use the wrap-and-tuck method. I accent them with cheap rayon scarfs. I wear conservative skirts, long sleeves, and loose pants. This came about after my first two or three years of marriage because my husband did not like some of the pieces in my wardrobe, and it became a source of contention. He decided to buy me new clothes and I became more practicing, and this led to a shift in how I dress.

**ANDREA MICHELLE STEELE** My husband said you should dress for the job you want, not the job you have. After adopting this philosophy, I have doubled my salary in the past year and a half.

**MIRANDA FISHER** My favorite dress might be this coral-and-yellow floral minidress from Forever 21 that cost $8. The first time I wore

it, I interviewed one of my musical heroes, and he complimented both the interview and the dress. Another time I wore it the first time I was in the same room as a guy I ended up dating. Later he recognized me because of the dress and told me that the first time he saw me he thought, "How can a person be so beautiful?" which is so nice that I'm choosing to believe it.

**JILL MARGO** I had a friend who was always looking at and talking about and panting after women of a body type that is the polar opposite of mine. Even though I wasn't interested in him sexually, his range (or lack of it) kind of pissed me off. I thought he watched too much porn and was too hard on women. Then one day he said, "I love looking at you." I said, "No you don't." He said, "Yes, I do! I love the way you look." I guess I'd been measuring how appealing I was by whether or not someone wanted to shag me. It perfectly matched growing up in a household where I was told I'd never get a husband if I was too overweight.

**PAMELA BAGULEY** My boyfriend John and I had been out for lunch and we were at the traffic lights in Huddersfield. There was a very nice ladies' dress shop on the corner, and a very special blue dress in the window. John saw it and said, "Oh, that's nice, it would suit you. Go and get it and I'll buy it for you." I liked it, it was a nice dress, and it was £200. That was in 1980, so that was a lot of money. I paid for it and he never gave me the money, which is how I remember exactly how much it was.

**ELEANOR WEST** Since I tend to date people who are as immature as I am, if a guy says something about my looks, he usually means it as a comment on how he feels about me, and it's usually something along the lines of "I'm disappointed in you." A guy I was dating once told me that my breasts "could be bigger." I think what he meant is that he'd imagined dating me for a long time, fantasizing about what it would be like, then it turned out to be different, with smaller breasts. Probably after so many years of dating jerks, at this point, I would take any comment from a boyfriend about my looks as a comment on our relationship.

**KARIMA CAMMELL** In my family, I was known for my "sausage fingers." There was a family friend I really respected, a father of one of my friends. One day in the summer when I was reading on the couch, just being an awkward teen and feeling really ugly, he walked through the room and said, "You have the hands of the Madonna." I realized that we tell ourselves stories about how we think we are. It's better if it's a nice story.

**LENAE DAY** When I got married at eighteen, I went from having a free-spirited '70s style to shopping exclusively at places like American Eagle and Hollister for low-cut jeans and super-tight tank tops. I was super-depressed. I bleached my hair and grew it long. I was embarrassed to shop at thrift stores and wear the "crazy" or "over-the-top" things I used to, because my husband thought it all too loud and embarrassing. Then I started making art, cut off all my hair, and began making my own dresses and shopping for vintage pieces. And I left that husband.

**HIKARI YOKOYAMA** I bring out my sexy lingerie if I need a boost, imagining my boyfriend will gently strip my clothes right off me inside the doorstep to discover this naughty present, but instead I'm always wearing it the night we get home late and just go to bed.

**RACHEL SIGNER** Recently, when I broke up with my boyfriend of two and a half years, I confessed that one of the reasons I'd stayed with him for so long is that I'm self-conscious about how attractive I am to other people. He said, "Well, honestly, I think you really need to dress better." The next day, I went out and spent $250 on clothes.

**BONNIE MORRISON** Sometimes I get ensnared in thinking I should try harder to be more attractive to men—more fitted clothes, heels. But I have mostly accepted at this point that I'm not really that type of woman.

**NANCY FORDE** I was sexually assaulted when I was thirty. It affected how I dressed—not that I was dressed in a particular way when I was assaulted. But after, I found myself buying clothes that did not hug my body. I have always argued with the notion that women are sexually assaulted because of their attire. I say, "Yes, that grandmother and that little girl of six should have been more modest, right?" So it was strange to see myself change how I dressed as a result of the assault. I didn't want to give any man "out there" the "pleasure" of picturing my body.

**ANA ZIR** Here I am, it's the 1970s, I'm newly married, I have on this killer black sexy silk nightdress I had just bought. My significant other comes home from work, I approach him in this seductive attire. What happens next? Nothing. No notice, no comment, nothing. Zip, invisible, waste of money, what was I thinking, unbelievable, don't ever do this again.

**AURELIA BELFIELD** I was at a wedding in Manhattan, and I had on this new dress that I'd just bought, and it looked great. It was a black Kate Spade sheath dress with big white bows printed all over it, and I was running like mad to catch the train, and there was this man who stopped me, and I thought he was gonna hit on me, I thought we were going to have a problem, but he just said, "You know what? That is a really nice dress." And I said "Thank you, sir," and ran and got the train. ✕

# MOTHERS AS OTHERS | PART 2

*Send a photograph of your mother from the time before she had children and tell us what you see.*

HYON LEE

SUSANNE MUNDHENKE

This is a photo of my mom on her honeymoon in Tahiti in 1983. She is wearing a dress that my grandmother and aunt made together. Every time people see this photo of my mom, they say, "I can't believe how much you look like your mom!" And I always reply, "No, she is so much prettier than I am." I do see the resemblance, but in truth, she is much more striking than I am, her features more symmetrical. When I see this photo, I see a sexy, punchy, funny girl. And carefree. I wish I was as outgoing as she looks in that photo. I got married at the same age, twenty-eight. Many of her friends asked if they could borrow her wedding dress for their wedding. She always obliged. One friend returned it completely altered. I regret not trying it on during my dress search, even though I would not have worn it. But it would have been fun to uncover it, to see how my mom and grandma would have felt. **LAUREN RO**

This is a photo of my mom at twenty-four, five years before she had my sister and eight years before I arrived on the scene. It was probably taken by my dad. I see many elements of my mom that have gone unchanged, such as her love of puzzles and obscure art books (under the box, behind her arm), as well as her beauty. She was never "mom-ish" in the ways my friends' moms were. Her rich inner life is something I sensed as a child and always respected. In the picture, she is wearing a gold Rado watch given to her by a suitor. I got the impression from the stories of the women in my family that in order to become a fully grown woman, one had to reject at least one marriage proposal as a sort of rite of passage. This photo shows the strongest resemblance between me and my mother that I have ever seen. Many people who look at the photo (which we keep on the fridge) have mistaken me for her, and I find this very complimentary as I think she looks like an off-duty model with a penchant for Escher puzzles. **MARSHA COURNEYA**

*DENISE DAMA*

*OKHEE KIM*

This photo has been with me through six different towns and many more apartments, so it looks a lot older than it is, but I kind of like that. It was taken in the mid-seventies in North Carolina, and I think you can tell by the way she's handling that snowball that this is one of the first times she's encountered snow (she grew up in Panama City, Florida). She looks happy and healthy. This was before she had kids or a husband, and before she decided to become a nurse. At the time, she was living on a farm and dating a guy who kept beehives in his car. I love her corduroy peacoat and her center-parted hair. **MARY MANN**

Aside from her youth, I'm struck by how round and full her cheeks are (for as long as I've known her, she's had high, prominent cheekbones). There's a softness to her face, but her expression is direct and quite steely, and I see a determined set to her mouth, which isn't quite smiling. When I look at those arched, partial eyebrows (which my older sister inherited), I remember the expert way she filled in the rest with her eyebrow pencil. None of us got her large, deep-set eyes. I have her full lips, but I resemble my father, and though he was a handsome man, as a child I always felt disappointed when people told me I looked like him and not her. **CHIN-SUN LEE**

PACITA PACIFICADOR

ELIZABETH LEILA SHARPE

She always hated her chin. When she looked at herself in the mirror, she would jut it out in a way that was unsettling to me. When I look at these pictures, I see my mom as she wanted to be seen—admired—and I see a private, ambitious side of her she didn't talk about or show me. Sometimes, in old photos of her, I can sense a strength and stubbornness I like. **LEANNE SHAPTON**

My parents at their wedding. I'm dying to know why my mom chose to wear black. I love the square neckline on her dress, its three-quarter sleeves, and the great fit. What I see is all the good intention and hope that infuses a wedding, yet I'm acutely aware of the knowledge I possess now about what happened. My mother looks elegant to me, poised, great bone structure. She's trim and tall, or taller than I am. Her face and her body eventually succumbed to the effects of medication, and her life succumbed to the incredibly unfair and tragic conditions that so many with mental illness are confronted with. So in this picture I see promise. I also see spirit—that black dress (maybe chosen to hide me growing underneath it)—and spunk—the woman who dared wear that black dress, and who dared have a child in adverse circumstances, and who then dared raise that child in even more adverse circumstances. My mom was going to return to her maiden name after her divorce, but she decided to stay with Welch so that she and I would have the same last name. When I married in 2001, I was going to take my husband's last name but my son protested and I instantly understood that I needed to keep my last name for my child, just as my mom did. **ZOE WELCH**

FAYE BINGHAM

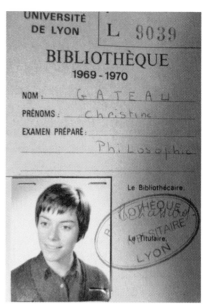

CHRISTINE GATEAU

This is my favorite photograph of my mother as a young woman. In it, I see a young and relatively carefree woman who likes to have fun, act childish, and take silly photographs. It reminds me a lot of myself. Her underwear is nearly showing (like mine, in countless photographs posted online by friends). She looks great. I love the nod to bougie-rich '80s culture, but the headband? It's just so good. This is a woman's idea of what it is to be sexy—a woman who, very much like me, is uncomfortable being sexy, and so we do it as a joke. **LENAE DAY**

I used to work part-time in the library of the English department at the University of Strasbourg, where I also went to school. One of my favorite aspects of the job was to read students' library cards and know what books they were reading, what their middle names were, and look at their pictures. I felt like I was getting to know them intimately. Around the same period, I discovered my mother's library card from the time she was a philosophy student in Lyon, and I have kept it with me ever since. But unlike my fellow students in Strasbourg, she has remained a complete mystery to me, and the longer I stare at this picture, the more mysterious she becomes. **LUCIE BONVALET**

OLGA FAB

TIGER KEOGH

My mother was very young here, maybe in her early twenties, maybe younger. She had been in the United States less than a decade. She and her family were Jewish immigrants from Ukraine, but she decided early on that she wanted a glamorous life, and actively sought one. I think she was eager to begin a new life away from her past as a refugee and immigrant. She was not exactly innocent but certainly hopeful and full of yearning. I admire the simplicity of her white shirt and the beauty of her profile. I always loved and envied her nose. I think she knew how beautiful she was, and was beginning to learn how to use that beauty to her advantage. I wish I had asked her a lot more questions. She was not like her sisters who became quite conventional housewives. My mother invented herself when she came to America. **RUTH GAIS**

My mom is on the far left in this picture. She's a teenager, standing there with her mom and sisters. It's probably 1970. She grew up in Moab, Utah, and the family was working-class. Odds are good that someone in the photo sewed her coat—they all were and are capable seamstresses, probably proud of their skills and style. I know my mom really felt the restrictions of that small, conservative town, and was eager to get out and see the world. **MOLLY DOVE KEOGH**

*DENESE CHARLES (on the right)*

*MARJORIE BANKS*

It's '60s–'70s in the Caribbean. She's about six feet tall. You can't see her feet but she has size 13 triple E feet. She's carrying a Bible and a songbook, which means she's going to church, and she probably made that dress herself, with the long collar. She was a seamstress. And she's not really looking at the camera, which is exactly right for her. I think she was probably very shy and still is. She was always proud that I could read. The only time she wouldn't let me read was when I was cooking. She made me wear socks and shoes in the Caribbean in the frickin' heat. Later I understood, it was because she had such big feet she couldn't buy shoes, and so she had to stop going to school. She didn't tell me this until much later. It made me really sad. For her it was pride that her daughter was going to school and she could provide socks and shoes. The thing I remember the most are those long legs. I just remember being around her legs all the time. **DORLA McINTOSH**

I can't find a picture of my mom, but this is my grandmother on my father's side. She joined the British Royal Air Force because she liked the outfits better than the outfits in the Navy or the Marines. She told me she wouldn't have married my grandfather—a Canadian she met during the war—if premarital sex had been acceptable. **MEGAN FRANKLYNE**

*GENISTA STREETEN*

*JENNY PHANG*

My mum was in her thirties here and lived in a block of one-bedroom flats in Holland Park. Most of the residents were single and they called themselves the Swinging Singles. She ran her own theater PR company and enjoyed all the parties this involved. The man in the photograph was a neighbor, and they used to meet for a little nightcap after their various nights out, and if she was too drunk he would help her pull her boots off. I like this photo because it shows the fun and carefree life she was living, but also shows a hint of her vulnerability. **POPPY TOLAND**

This photo was taken in the late sixties in Hong Kong, when my mum was in her early twenties. The hand my mum is holding is my dad's—they'd just started dating. She looks happy and nervous and naive. She had just broken up with her first serious boyfriend and my dad was a bit of a rebound, but she fell desperately in love with him all the same. When I look at this photo, I can see that her sense of style is pretty unchanged. She still likes to take risks, and wearing a dress that short would have been risqué then. The photo also makes me a little peeved, because she's always told me to dress reservedly, and here she is flaunting those legs in platform shoes. **MICHELLE LAW**

ANNE PERRIE

SUSAN JEAN KLINE

My mum on Lake Muskoka, circa 1965. I didn't quite inherit her long, lean legs, or her chic sense of style. I could never, for example, have gotten away with plaid slacks, as she could. **SIOBHAN ROBERTS**

I see a beautiful and vibrant woman who was halfway through her college career, had just met her life partner, and was overjoyed to be with her older sister on spring break. Her style is fully seventies, which means I currently would covet everything she is wearing. This was my mom's face when she laughed. Knowing that my mother knew how to cut loose and really burst with happiness solidifies to me that I am her daughter. **REBEKAH AMBJOR**

FRANCES STRAUSS

LYDIA GLICK

When I asked my mother about this photo, what she remembered best was her car, which she was very proud of owning. It was the seventies. I don't think anyone wore a bra. Besides that, she was very independent. In this photo she's about twenty-seven years old. She's almost a decade away from having me. She's in between traveling stints and doesn't have a boyfriend. My mother didn't think of herself as attractive, and I think that her insecurity inhibited her a little bit, which is a shame. I think she looks very beautiful. **SARAH STEINBERG**

My grandfather is holding my mother in this picture—she's the baby with her little hand held out. Honestly, when I think of style, I think of her older sister, my aunt Elizabeth (Libby), who is standing to the right of my grandfather and wearing glasses. My mom's side of the family is Mennonite. The kids in this picture grew up on a dairy farm in North Dakota. Aunt Libby told me that they weren't allowed to wear jewelry, yet she wanted some kind of decoration, so she faked having bad eyes until my grandparents got her some glasses. She'd sit there squinting at her book going, "Uhhh, uhhh, I can't see." She told me, "I wanted glasses so badly! They were like jewelry!" So when I look at this picture, I see my aunt, this young girl in glasses. She's triumphant. **SOFIA SAMATAR**

*SUSAN ELIZABETH TROUP*

*FUSAE KISHIMOTO*

Though my mother was model-scouted once in Bermuda, I don't think she had any idea that she was beautiful, or if she had an idea, she didn't much care. She rarely wore makeup or fussed over her clothing. Her hair, for the entirety of my childhood, was cut in this style, known as a "Dorothy Hamill." Hers was maintained monthly by a Rod Stewart ringer named Claude. Claude was her beloved hairdresser. I asked Claude to cut my long hair exactly like hers. For months afterward, I was mistaken for a boy. I learned, through similar missteps, that she was more effortlessly beautiful than I was and that I couldn't follow her lead. What our faces have in common, however, is this: When happy, we both look like dogs with our heads thrust out the windows of a speeding car. **HEIDI JULAVITS**

I love this picture of my mother. She was twenty-three, traveling through Thailand with a friend. In this picture, she has just gone parasailing and has landed on the beaches of Pattaya. Her hair is a mess but she is happy. I have always looked up to my mother for being the adventurous and courageous woman that she is. In this picture, I imagine she feels liberated and full of life, traveling the world. A couple years after this, she will meet a foreign man and fall in love, give birth to a daughter, then be widowed. She raised me on her own and I have taken in many of her core values. I am just as happy and adventurous as she is in this picture, and it's all because of her.
**STEPHANIE MIKI ARNDT**

*MANIA CIUPKA*

*DOLORES GRIEGO*

My mother was a beautiful woman and I have tried for a long time to model my look after this photo. **M. WHITEFORD**

My mother died on February 20, 2012, at the age of seventy-nine. I miss her very much. My mother was from a beautiful family, they only had love. She married my dad when she was seventeen and had eleven kids. My mother was left-handed and ten of her children are left-handed. She worked caring for her family all her life. She only had a sixth-grade education. She hated school because they were very prejudiced and hateful to the Hispanic kids. She quit school to go to work in the fields with her dad to help her family. I think my mother was a beautiful woman.

**CHRISTINA GONZALES**

EIRA ROBERTS

VALERIE ANNE FRASER

I love this picture of my parents because it's taken in front of one of the most romantic buildings I know of, the Taj Mahal. They're looking so young. They've swapped cultures. Dad in suit, mom in sari. They look utterly free and besotted and with their whole lives ahead of them. I imagine they felt like that then, and it's what I see. Two beautiful people beginning their lives. **TISHANI DOSHI**

Here is the best picture of my mother. At the time, 1980, she was around fifteen years old and probably pregnant with my older sister. The theme of this particular Polaroid was "Valerie in front of her friends," and it's basically the same as an accompanying Polaroid, "Valerie in front of her parents," where she's sitting on the couch in the same outfit but without makeup on. I use this picture of my mom to explain my family to other people. It makes me laugh. She is the exact same person in many ways today. My mother adores this picture of herself. **WEDNESDAY LUPYPCIW** ✕

343

*CHRISTINE MUHLKE*'s identical dresses in different fabrics and patterns

# I STOPPED BY
# THE STORE EVERY DAY

### IDA HATTEMER-HIGGINS

Morrissey sings: *I would go out tonight, but I haven't got a stitch to wear.* I bet Morrissey would agree that the man who is speaking probably has not too few clothes, but too many. He defeats his evening in advance by thinking too much about their effect— about their future.

Recently, I was engaged to be married. Right away, I put a lot of thought into a dress for the wedding. I wanted something old, something very specific. I put more thought into the dress than I've ever put into any single other item of clothing. During my search, my future was never more vividly imagined, never more desirable, and, of course, never more manhandled.

A few months later, the engagement was called off in a manner both stubborn and violent. Gradually it became clear that everything I had thought was my life was not my life. I had thought I would soon be living in Portugal. Suddenly I would be neither living in Portugal nor adopting any of its worldview. I had thought I would be the wife of a Russian. Suddenly I was not going to be linked to Russia in any way at all. My daily routine, the deliberate shaping of my tastes, my identity, collapsed. I was left futureless.

Among much else, this posed a specific handicap, in that when I buy clothing, I resist the idea that I'm buying for the present. It pains me to imagine that any piece of clothing is not meant for eternity. New clothes feel like a hand one reaches forward into the folds of a later time. You touch a piece of fabric, and in doing so you touch a future occasion, a future city, a future life. New clothes are the solid tip of the future.

Because I resist the ephemerality of clothing, I make grandiose demands of it: a garment must touch on all that I have ever been and will be. The irony is that for all my grasping at eternity, in the end, I almost never wear any item for more than a few months.

So it was not just the wedding dress I could no longer touch. I could no longer touch the specific destiny surrounding it, and all the clothes that went with it. There was no replacement destiny. The life I thought was coming, with its particularities of mood and thus style, vanished without a trace. It was lurid to watch as its deep contingency was suddenly exposed.

In the last days of the relationship, when it was already far too late to do anything about the implosion, I went to Athens to visit my ex-fiancé, to wander the ruins of love, and make some kind of halfhearted inventory of loss, as you see survivors of an earthquake do—moving in shocked, fascinated circles around the vacant space where a home once stood. As it happened, we found very little to say to each other.

Every day I took a long walk near Omonia Square, among the heroin addicts, illegal Pakistani immigrants, police in riot gear, and fat old posturing pimps standing around the magazine kiosks. Not far off from this action and to some degree within it, I found a large, old, decrepit store in the colonial style, once grand, with ragged bunting now hanging flaccid over a protruding lip of iron filigree.

The entrance to the store was draped with merchandise on racks facing the sidewalk, apparently aimed at a population of tourists at once greedy and slightly stupid: new T-shirts grimed by the street, army-navy gear, knock-off jeans, shoddy camping equipment, football jerseys without official license.

Once inside, however, sunlight sliced by narrow, weak beams fell onto high-ceilinged rooms, and under the layers of dust was a grand old sartorial shop, a merchant's palace filled with ancient dead-stock, tailored prêt-à-porter—mostly for gentlemen, but plenty for ladies as well. Clothing designed in London, Paris, and Milan, forty, fifty, sixty years ago. Jackets, trousers, wool-and-felt hats, broadcloth shirts, and ties still in their rotting white boxes, each labeled by size and style with a yellowed sticker on their thin edges. A few garments lay on the floor where they had fallen. It seemed like they had been lying in the same slatternly constellation for a long time, as though the former owners had abandoned the store hastily a few days ahead of an advancing army.

The jackets—tweed, wool, gabardine, of fine cuts and colors—hung on long racks, their hues softer along the ridges of shoulders and crests of lapels, blanched by the light and the dust.

Without any evident pattern, the eccentric owners were mixing new clothing into the racks—articles made in China, with the names of sports teams and designer brands in large plastic letters across the chest. These things looked clean, shiny, and very much like garbage, while the old things appeared dignified, honorable, dirty, and diseased.

During my stay in Athens, I stopped by the store every day. In the beginning, I only pulled at the edges of interesting fabrics that I saw poking out from the bins at the front, where odds and ends had been thrown together and were being sold for one euro an item. Sometimes their yellowed tags were still attached; they had mod fonts on heavy card. Every day, it seemed the piles were slightly different. On my first visit, I saw a little boy's shirt made of fine silk paisley, beautifully tailored, with square buttons made of bone, but the next day it was gone. I didn't imagine for an instant, however, that it had been sold. The shop seemed almost completely unvisited. It was far more likely that the shirt was swallowed up in the turning of the piles, which fell round and round as in a washing machine, shifted constantly by the old woman.

The old woman was not so old, really, but the lines of her face were flamboyant, almost like an alligator's, framed by hair clearly dyed its brick color. Under eyes outlined in kohl, she wore a black leather jacket and a polyester turtleneck. She shifted the clothes with a casual hand, strong and indifferent, a cigarette burning in her other hand, ashing regularly onto the piles of clothing. With her free arm, the one without the cigarette, she made suggestions, pulling out items for me to try on with a breezy majesty—things invariably grotesque and inappropriate.

On the first day, I found a deep green pencil skirt of delicate wool twill, made by Yves Saint Laurent circa 1965, sewn to simulate a wrap. The closure was held by dark gold buttons made of military braid, which ran all the way down its length. When I tried it on, the skirt clung to me as if it were liquid. I bought it.

The next day, I found a linen dress with three-quarter-length puffed sleeves and two concentric Peter Pan collars, one on top of the other. At first I thought it was made in the eighties, but then I saw the hook-and-eye closure, and the straightness of the hips. It could not date later than 1939. Because it was the color of sea glass, I bought it, too.

I bought some ladies' button-down shirts in salmon, indigo, and turmeric silk. I bought a short dove-gray swing coat, closely fitted in the shoulders, with massive cuffs and a collar stiff enough to stand up around the ears. I bought a camel coat of a rare, almost mustard tone that was lined in scarlet paisley brocade.

I kept buying clothes. But for perhaps the first time in my life, the purchases were without consciousness: I did not imagine wearing them. There was no plan of any kind. When it came to my future style of dress, I could not imagine anything at all. It was as if a great gourmand had suddenly lost his appetite, but kept eating nonetheless, making himself sick.

Still, to go to this place every day—to have something to bring home for a euro, something to put into the bathtub with detergent, to run the water, looking on with vain satisfaction as the water turned black from the filth; to rub the fabric against itself, jealous of its age, its delicacy, and, when it was clean, to have something to take into the sunlight on the terrace, at the top of that tall building sitting kingly at the almost highest point of one of the highest neighborhoods in Athens, from which one could see beyond the Parthenon all the way to the port of Piraeus, and watch as the sea became paler and more reflective as the sun descended—this was not an altogether bad thing.

I stood for long spells in this way and thought not of the future, not of my life, but rather of Pasolini, of Charles de Gaulle, of Tegel Airport when it was still young—of what it would have done to redeem a person's humiliation to walk across the tarmac and up the stairs of a commercial airplane while wearing, say, this dress.

The romance of clothes is one of the few aspects of life I love. Or rather, one of the few aspects of public life I love. I see the world as an execrable place, lurking with humiliations, and dressing to go out is the last link to a fantasy I once had of what going out would be like— indeed, the only shred remaining of an early promise that the world would not be bereft of the feelings I had learned to desire from it in movies and books.

But I don't think I dress well. And these same fantasies may be standing in the way of my putting myself together beautifully. I seem, to paraphrase Chekhov, to be asking more from fashion than it can give, because the source of my fascination is a dream.

I was once entranced by the connection between proper, girdled undergarments that altered the figure, and a story by Nabokov, "That in Aleppo Once." At its climax, we read:

*Some time later, as I sat on the edge of the only chair in my garret and held her by her slender young hips (she was combing her soft hair and tossing her head back with every stroke), her dim smile changed all at once into an odd quiver and she placed one hand on my shoulder, staring down at me as if I were a reflection in a pool, which she had noticed for the first time.*

When I think of my hips, the question arises of whether it is possible to be subject and object at once. I try, with my elaborate 1930s clothing, to be the woman in the Nabokov story, but as I play her, I also play the story's narrator, and in my efforts to approximate the consciousness that invented these lines, I also play Nabokov. I'm overworked and underperceived, like an actress—like an actress in a one-woman play with no audience.

---

SURVEY *Do you consider yourself photogenic?*

I do not consider myself photogenic in any way, shape, or form. I look much better in person than in any picture. —NATASHA MOLETTA • Didn't used to, but I do now. I'm considered to have a "winning smile." —KAREN GARBER STEPHENS • No. —KELLY WILSON • I do believe that I am photogenic, although I feel awkward saying so. —JYTZA GUZMAN • I am photogenic, and to save myself from being labeled as conceited, I'll explain that I love being in pictures—often sporting a goofy face. —KRISTY HELLER • Yes, yes, and no. I have three selves in photos. Two are photogenic. One is not *at all*. Horrible. —GILLIAN SCHWARTZ • Yes, but only if I smile my head off. As soon as I stop smiling, I look devastated. —SOFIA SAMATAR • Depending on my mood, I can feel at ease in front of the camera; other times, complete distrust. It all depends on my confidence. —CHRISTY-CLAIRE KATIEN • Not at this stage. —PAULINE SMOLIN • Yes, if you mean do I use my digital camera's delete button religiously. —DANKA HALL • For an author shot I have to have hun-

At the northwestern corner of Omonia Square, there is a hotel called Hotel La Mirage. The name is spelled out in giant sans serif capitals on the roof, each letter as tall as a person. One day, while I was gazing up at the roof as I sat in the square, it occurred to me that I could release my grasp on the things I owned and everything they implied about the future I thought I'd lead, and just move to Paris.

It's amazing how quickly my extravagant consciousness returned. A new future flashed toward me. I would pack away my life in Berlin, bringing only the tall wardrobe, the oak desk, the sleigh bed, the citrofortunella tree, and my books of German philosophy. I would sell or throw away my wedding dress, and perhaps all of my other clothes, too, keeping only what I had bought from the decrepit shop in Athens. Sitting in a café on Odos Athinas that had wireless, I found an apartment on a Parisian real estate website that looked very nice. On a Listserv, I saw a job I wouldn't mind.

I envisioned how my things would look in that living room there, and how they would appear to a person visiting— not to a friend, but, crucially, to an acquaintance, someone who was still trying to understand me. I saw how I would seem to someone who would spot me from a passing car the moment I emerged from the entryway of that apartment in the 10th—me, a sudden movement under a cloudy sky, hues of blue and graphite, a dark green skirt of wool twill with military braid. My adequate future was clear.

This avid consciousness that forces me to see myself and be seen by myself in a constant, grinding feedback loop, which makes the future a monstrous presence elbowing disproportionately for itself, did not slacken after the breakup. In fact, it was the only thing that remained. Destinies rise and destinies fall. Yet I still reach toward the outline of an absence, and dress to go out tonight—interesting to myself and myself alone, deep in a dream. ✕

---

dreds of pictures taken to find one I like. I think people who like to have their picture taken or are photogenic settle on a face and make that when the camera points. I have never found that face. —EILEEN MYLES • Not at all. A former roommate who was a professional photographer tried to use me as a test subject and we had to stop because I'm so unphotogenic. —BRYENNE KAY • Yes. Very. I once dated a sociopathic photographer and he would take pictures of me anytime, without notice. I can pose within milliseconds once a camera is whipped out. —MARI SASANO • No. Oh god no. And I think that if you aren't photogenic, the worst thing you can do is to try to work on being photogenic, like developing some mannered pose or facial expression. Everyone hates that person. Just look like you're having a good time. No one can criticize you for that because it's endearing. —BONNIE MORRISON • No. My features are too light to register well with a camera. —CLARE NEEDHAM ✕

*MELISSA WALSH*'s scrubs

# STRANGERS

*"A young gay man on the street waved his finger from my head to my toes, approving of my look. I felt damn good that day."* —MALWINA GUDOWSKA

**MAIA WRIGHT** I called up a guy who was selling a bike on Craigslist. I wasn't sure if the frame was the right size. He asked how tall I was and what my inseam was—explaining it was the distance from the floor to my crotch. I got out a tape measure and told him. He exclaimed that I had very long legs for my height, and that I must be a runner. Far from it. I've never considered myself long-legged—I've always thought of myself as short-waisted. Ever since then, though, I have thought of myself as a long-legged person, which has made such a difference in the way I dress. I really delight in wearing tailored pants in a stripe or bright color.

**CARMEN JOY KING** I wish I didn't need to wear makeup all the time, but I do. It just feels completing and reassuring. I noticed that in Paris, the more pared down and simple my look was, the more attention I got. I find the opposite in Montreal. If I'm not wearing makeup, no one looks at me. Do I need people to look at me? Yes. I mean, what's the point of being in the world if we're not looking at one another? You don't have to want to fuck me, but I want you to notice me.

**JENNIFER WINEKE** I dyed my hair cotton-candy pink yesterday. The lady behind the counter at my coffee shop complimented me on it. She basically compliments me every morning, even when I'm wearing yesterday's clothes and no makeup. A stranger saying, "Hello, beautiful," to you at six-thirty a.m. is the best.

**AMY BRILL** All my life I've been subjected to comments about how tiny I am. How petite. How small. Even when I was pregnant, I had strangers approaching me and telling me that I couldn't possibly have a baby in there. "I have an eight-pound baby in there," I wanted to say, and often did. I think this lifelong diminution fostered in me an aggressive presence, a persona that favors appearing "tough" as opposed to fragile—leather over lace.

**SOOK-YIN LEE** I have found it helpful to dress like a saint because then strangers are nicer and more respectful to me, and I am never cruised by annoying men.

**FATIMA G.** I once met an elderly woman on an airplane and we started talking. I told her how much I liked her outfit, which I can't remember in detail now but which I definitely remember as being quite fabulous. She thanked me, then said, "Every morning that I wake up and realize I'm not dead is a chance for me to say 'Fuck it.' So I dress like this."

**RITA TRONTI** Now that I am out there on the Internet on account of a book I wrote, and I see misogynistic comments going both ways (she's getting attention because she's photogenic, because she's *not* photogenic, etc.), my inclination is to be more self-confident and self-protecting, and to bury my own dislike of how I look in pictures. I'm more inclined to be easy on myself, now that I'm being exposed to the judgments of strangers.

**HILARY PROSSER** In 1993, when I was working in France, an elderly lady who was a friend of my client arrived, then went straight out shopping. She returned from her shopping trip and handed me a ring which she thought was perfect for me—Art Deco–ish, brass, set with three bits of diamond-shaped black-and-turquoise Bakelite. It is still my favorite piece of jewelry.

**PENELOPE C.** In my early twenties, I was walking down a street in Sydney with a female friend and we were holding hands. A man walked past and said, "Who gives it and who takes it?" So I said to my friend in all innocence, "What does he mean?" She said, "I think he means you'd take it because you're short, and I'd give it because I'm tall." I said, "I'm not short." But as the words came out, I looked up at her and it was as if she grew taller before my eyes. Suddenly, I was painfully aware that she was really tall (six feet) and that I was really short (just over five feet). It was as if I never knew how short I was until then. It was a sad moment. I lost some confidence that I've never gotten back.

**VANESSA BERRY** A few years ago, I was in Berlin and was wearing one of my great dresses—a black dress with big red poppies printed on one side, and big white polka dots on the other. I passed a woman who met my eye with a warm, happy look. She said something I didn't understand (I don't speak much German), but I knew she was trying to communicate that she loved my dress. My dress made her happy that day. I felt released from the lonely anonymity of being in a city where I knew almost no one.

**AURELIA BELFIELD** I want to insinuate myself in somebody's life, no matter how I look. A stranger doesn't even have to speak to me—I just need to know that I look good enough that you are now thinking about me. Like, you've fallen in love with me a little bit. You're maybe not creepy enough to write a Missed Connections, but you thought about it for a second.

**MEG BARKER** I bought my favorite cap for £10 on Shaftesbury Avenue. As a kid, I wasn't strongly identified with femininity or masculinity, it wasn't possible to hang out with the boys who were interested in the things that seemed exciting to me—drawing, computers, role-playing games. And I had little in common with most of the girls. After moving to a single-sex school where there were girls who were more like me, I found my way toward versions of femininity that fit me better, and I adopted a uniform of jeans, baseball boots, a red-check shirt, and a denim cap with a hole for my ponytail. In recent years, I've moved away from a "feminine" appearance toward being more masculine-of-center and nonbinary. The cap is read in different ways. A quick glance often gets me a "guv" or "sir." A smattering of those, mixed in with "lady" and "madam," feels good enough for now in a world where I can't just be seen as a person.

**HALEY MLOTEK** As a child I insisted on wearing dresses and skirts every day. Once, another mother, a total stranger, confronted my mother on the playground. She said that her daughter was only allowed to wear dresses on Fridays and that her daughter was complaining that I was allowed to wear dresses every day, and could she please stop me from wearing dresses every day? I don't know what my mother said exactly, but I'm pretty sure it was along the lines of "What the fuck are you talking about, my daughter can wear whatever the fuck she wants," because that's how I've dressed myself ever since. ✕

## WEAR AREAS | MARGO JEFFERSON

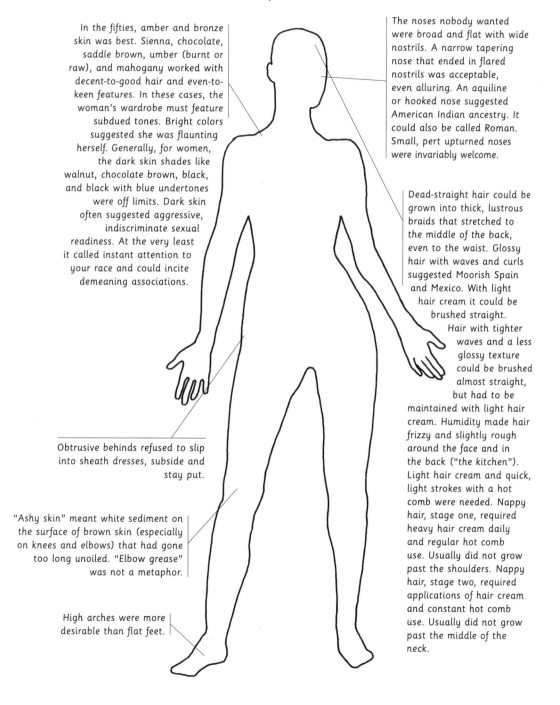

In the fifties, amber and bronze skin was best. Sienna, chocolate, saddle brown, umber (burnt or raw), and mahogany worked with decent-to-good hair and even-to-keen features. In these cases, the woman's wardrobe must feature subdued tones. Bright colors suggested she was flaunting herself. Generally, for women, the dark skin shades like walnut, chocolate brown, black, and black with blue undertones were off limits. Dark skin often suggested aggressive, indiscriminate sexual readiness. At the very least it called instant attention to your race and could incite demeaning associations.

The noses nobody wanted were broad and flat with wide nostrils. A narrow tapering nose that ended in flared nostrils was acceptable, even alluring. An aquiline or hooked nose suggested American Indian ancestry. It could also be called Roman. Small, pert upturned noses were invariably welcome.

Dead-straight hair could be grown into thick, lustrous braids that stretched to the middle of the back, even to the waist. Glossy hair with waves and curls suggested Moorish Spain and Mexico. With light hair cream it could be brushed straight. Hair with tighter waves and a less glossy texture could be brushed almost straight, but had to be maintained with light hair cream. Humidity made hair frizzy and slightly rough around the face and in the back ("the kitchen"). Light hair cream and quick, light strokes with a hot comb were needed. Nappy hair, stage one, required heavy hair cream daily and regular hot comb use. Usually did not grow past the shoulders. Nappy hair, stage two, required applications of hair cream and constant hot comb use. Usually did not grow past the middle of the neck.

Obtrusive behinds refused to slip into sheath dresses, subside and stay put.

"Ashy skin" meant white sediment on the surface of brown skin (especially on knees and elbows) that had gone too long unoiled. "Elbow grease" was not a metaphor.

High arches were more desirable than flat feet.

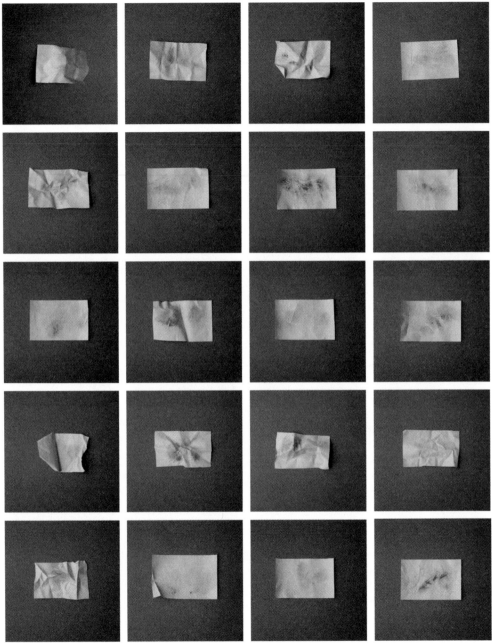

*ALICIA MEIER*'s blotting papers used over the course of one week

# AT THE CHECKPOINT

### SHANI BOIANJIU

Here are my ten fashion Dos and Don'ts for the teenage Israeli female soldier.

T—T—T—T—T—T—T—T—T—T—T—T—T—T—T—T—T—T—T—T—T—T—T—T—T—T—T—T—T—T—T—T

1. Don't wear lipstick. It's not allowed. It will get stolen. You're no Angelina Jolie. Your guy is no Brad Pitt. He is a dude whose interests are balancing plastic spoons on his nose and clapping. Above all, this is a guarding post, not the red carpet. Wake up and smell the ninety-two-year-old construction worker peeing on your spare helmet.

2. Do lick your lips every ten seconds when you are stationed in the eastern guarding tower. It'll make the eight-hour shift pass more quickly, and thanks to the hot air and strong winds in the tower, your lips will swell up and their color will transform into a luscious cherry red.

3. Do keep a Zippo lighter in your pocket. Nothing is hotter than you, bending over to light his cigarette when you two finally sit down at three a.m. after everyone has left the checkpoint gate. Particularly if it's a full-moon night, and particularly if it's windy and your hands meet as you shelter the fire.

4. Don't smoke like a chimney. Nothing is less attractive than you, dead. It's as simple as that.

5. Do wear a linked dozen 7.62 bullets as a necklace. You'll look tough, confident, and maybe a little like the Terminator, but in a fun way. Your dark hair will glow against the golden sparkles of the dirty-copper color of the bullets. To make those bullets really shine, you might want to spray them with water. You risk ruining 200 shekels' worth of ammunition, but war is too retro anyhow.

6. Don't place the strap of your rifle on the back of your neck like they tell you to. It will mess up your posture and clash with your bullet necklace. Sure, carrying your rifle any other way will make it harder to aim and fire in case you have to respond quickly, and will seriously risk your life. But just think—what a way to go! You'll forever be remembered as the supercool girl who got a bullet in her head because the strap of her rifle got all tangled because she didn't carry it around her neck because it looked so lame. In short—a legend.

7. Do wear the strap of your rifle diagonally across your chest, right in the middle. Make sure the strap is a bit tighter than it ought to be. That way you're emphasizing what might be left unnoticed in the uniform—you are a female! Call it cheap, call it low, call it silly, call it "I look so hot and I don't look like I am trying," call it brilliant. Whatever you call it, it works.

8. Don't eat. We have yet to meet the girl who can keep down a rotten egg and a ten-day-old bean soup. Even if he volunteers to hold your hair when you throw up, everyone will get grossed out by you. Yes, even the Palestinian with the spiky mustache will give you a nasty look.

9. Do smile. You are beautiful when you smile. Dare to be different. Smile like you know all of your dreams are going to come true, like a better tomorrow is only a day away.

10. Don't actually believe your dreams will come true. Look at you, you are so dirty, even mosquitoes stay away. Look around. Do any of the adults seem like their dreams came true? Face it, you are eighteen, a grown-up, over the hill. Come on, girl, don't tell me you really think you are going to "make it after all," or do you? ✕

# THE MOM COAT

AMY FUSSELMAN

I'm a stay-at-home mom, so I don't dress for any other milieu. I dress in what I think of as my mom clothes, for my mom job.

I have created a uniform for myself. I wear cotton because it's easy to clean, pants because they are easier to move in. I have a few T-shirts in my drawer and I wear them until they are full of holes and then I get new ones. If Jackson Pollock were a mom, he would wear my clothes.

I don't like any kind of language or insignia on my clothes, yet for a while I wore a pink T-shirt emblazoned with the logo of a New York theater company I very much admire. It was light pink with a small black unicorn head and NYC PLAYERS in small lettering. No one ever asked me about it, but I liked having that connection to this theater company in my uniform, especially because so much of mothering involves dealing with children's playing in a way that is like being a stagehand or a director to their ongoing improv. So I was a New York City Player, in my way, in that shirt.

I also have a Mom Coat. The Mom Coat seems unavoidable here in New York City. I wear it as part of my uniform from November till March. I have very mixed feelings about the Mom Coat, which is a down coat that has a hood, completely covers your ass, and is black, gray, or gray-black.

The Mom Coat is a sleeping bag you walk around in. It turns you into a pod. I almost cease to be human when I wear it: I am just a shroud with pockets. And of course, because I have kids, my pockets are always stuffed with Kleenex, hair clips, Goldfish, et cetera. The Mom Coat is like a minivan in that way. You are inside and piloting a receptacle for your kids' stuff.

I wore my Mom Coat every weekday morning this winter during the fifty-block commute I did with my kids on the subway. My kids are eleven, nine, and four, and for the first four months, from September through December, my daughter (the four-year-old) would start asking me to pick her up after we had walked a mere half block. (It's a block and a half from our apartment building to the subway.) In the beginning, a lot of the journey was about not picking up my daughter, then it was about not buying the children candy, even though our commute included a waiting period near an underground newsstand with an enticing display. I was toeing the no-carrying and

no-candy lines (although we occasionally bought cough drops because of their
medicinal properties), and that was hard
enough. Then you throw in the wind, cold,
rain, snow, and finally the other things
you couldn't prepare for—like the week
when a giant, candy-eating homeless man
started occupying "our" bench. He would
sit there like Jabba the Hutt, eating nois-
ily from a jumbo bag of M&M's. (Did he
know our no-candy rule? Was he taunt-
ing us?!) I had to keep my daughter from
eating the stray pieces he was spilling on
the platform. Then there was the man we
walked past daintily as he squatted by a
garbage can and defecated.

I was even jealous, some days, of moms

We had many adventures, let's leave it
at that.

Climbing into my gray Mom Coat
every morning felt like hunkering down
to get through this journey. This part of
my day, from 7:45 to 8:45 a.m., was always
gray, black, or gray-black, and I needed all
the Kleenex, Altoids, and Squinkies I had
floating around in every one of my Mom
Coat pockets to get through it.

I was even jealous, some days, of moms
above me, on the street, driving minivans,
because I imagined that the minivan freed
them from the Mom Coat. The minivan
itself served the Mom Coat purpose.
Those moms could step out of their minivan in some little Chanel jacket because
they had twenty-two cupholders full of
crap nearby, double-parked.

All of which is to say that I think
of this uniform—the chinos, the Mom

Coat—as temporary. There will be a day
when I no longer wear this, and I have
started collecting pieces for that time.
When I am older, I am going to wear
only Comme des Garçons. I will have a
correction for this time when I was lost
in a lollipop-and-tissue tornado. I will
wear clothing that makes people's heads
hurt with difficult questions: Why must
a pair of pants have two legs? Is a lumpy-
sculptural shirt beautiful? Are two halves
of two different shirts stuck together a
whole shirt?

Writing this makes me realize that I
am a bit like someone who is on a very
strict diet, who is craving things that are
off the diet, and I wonder if that's not a
sign to ease up. I am not really sure who
is being helped by my uniform. It's not
my kids, I don't think. I wore a cocktail dress one evening recently, and my
younger son saw me and declared, "You
should wear that every day!" My kids
are in on the severity of my uniform,
and really, how does severity ever help
anyone? Yes, cotton is easy to clean, but
who cares? Why don't I wear my shirt
that is two half-shirts stuck together
and ask my kids difficult fashion questions on our way to school? Didn't I come
to New York in the first place so I could
be around freaks—people dressed in plastic bags directing traffic? Didn't I come
here so I could have the freedom and
courage to be the freak that I am? So how
is it that I now find myself so deep inside
my Mom Coat?

I think this is something that happens as you get older—you begin to think that fashion, like so much else in life, is only for young people. I am from Ohio, and one thing I love about the Midwest is how the middle-aged moms there bedazzle themselves. The holiday season, in particular, is a time to bring out a whole range of sweaters and sweatshirts adorned with rhinestones and other sparkly gems. Sweatshirts and sweaters with football or hockey team logos on them—also with gems, where possible—are accepted as casual and even semiformal wear anytime of year. This is a very different approach from my mom-community in New York, where women wear a lot of black, and gems are not fun or fake or splattered all over your Pittsburgh Steelers sweatshirt. Gems are on your fingers or in your ears, and they are real and serious.

I think what I am facing now is the fact that I need to get the "Player" off my mom uniform and into my life. I need to get back to bedazzling—not because a bedazzled Pittsburgh Steelers sweatshirt looks better than a black cashmere sweater, but because bedazzling is itself a beautiful activity.

I'm reminded of Emily Dickinson's words, "Beauty—be not caused—It is." I think this speaks to the trickiest thing to embrace about fashion and style, which is that the product of all the effort is ultimately not that important. This is hard to accept because it's absurd. But I think it's the truth: you can't actually make yourself beautiful.

It's similar to writing: what's beautiful about writing is not the words. The words are a recording of the beautiful thing. The words are a recording of the beautiful thing in the person, the thing that becomes beautified only by action, and ultimately becomes most beautified only by the most beautiful action of all—love. This thing, this transmitter of beauty, is ultimately unadornable and undecoratable. It is invisible and it bedazzles. That we can't see or touch it should not stop us from paying homage to it, and we do this by imitating it. We do this by sincerely and wholeheartedly beautifying to no end. ✕

*LORNA SHAPTON*'s tsinelas

# GUT FEELING

*"I cried many, many tears while buttoned up into a Laura Ashley dress."*—ALLISON D.

STEPHANIE P. My grandma's favorite outfit was a light-blue-and-tan sleeveless dress and coat to match, that she wore when seeing *Hair* on Broadway (in the '70s, I guess) with her then boyfriend, Morris, a great jazz musician. She had clear ideas of when she looked pretty. She said that in Germany, before the Nazis, when she was nine, her mother had a seamstress make her clothes, but that the clothes only reflected her mother's tastes. One day, she was given a wine-colored skirt with a wine-colored scalloped bolero jacket, a very pale pink scalloped shirt, and a wine-colored velvet hat. My grandma didn't hate the clothes, but she hated the hat, so she refused to wear it. Her mother gave her such a beating that she peed in her pants. But she didn't wear the hat.

MARSHA COURNEYA If someone feels very strongly that she should wear one thing and not that other thing, she should certainly be allowed to without feeling judged on her "level of taste."

MELISSA HENDERSON Black girls get hit the hardest with trying to be molded into Western images of beauty. It's bullshit. No one cares what your hair looks like when you get outside the U.S. as long as you are comfortable. I was reminded of this when I traveled to Norway to see a dear friend get married to a Norwegian. I washed my hair and wore it wild for three days. I felt completely comfortable, beautiful, and attractive around a bunch of alluring Vikings and pirates. I love the laissez-faire attitude about my hair when it's just "being."

MALWINA GUDOWSKA My grandmother, who gets minimal pension payments from the Polish government, gave me some birthday money one year and told me to buy myself something nice. I tried to refuse the gift but she insisted, going as far as to say that she would be insulted if I didn't take the money. I went to a jewelry shop so at least I could have something forever that would symbolize her selflessness and love, and bought myself a ring with the money. I've worn the ring only once, and for some reason it doesn't represent my grandmother in my eyes at all. Perhaps it's because I chose the ring over a gold necklace. I still think about that necklace today, wishing I had bought it instead.

MELISSA ABE I lost my shit in the car on the way to school because I couldn't stand wearing my bright white sneakers with brown jodhpurs. They just didn't go together.

KATE McMULLAN I know what I like. When I veer from my instincts, that's when I make mistakes.

CATHERINE STOCKHAUSEN My early memories of clothes are mostly negative. At five years old, I found a spider in the roll of my rolled-up jeans. I did not wear jeans again until junior high. I also hated the feeling of tights, I think because I was tall and they were always slipping down. I also hated my Brownie uniform. I couldn't formulate my feelings, but I knew the material was cheap and it gave me an emotional rash.

**AMY TURNER** My favorite piece of jewelry is a gold heart that I got in upstate New York. I never have distinct or clear feelings, but when I saw it and put it on, I knew unwaveringly that it was for me. At the time, I was with a friend I'd become close to over a year of writing e-mails, and in our first exchanges, I knew she was for me, too. Now when I put the necklace on, I think of her, and I think of what it feels like to know something clearly in my gut.

**EILEEN MYLES** I remember a gay man I knew going on about how he resented how straight men just let themselves go and got big bellies and wore dirty clothes and the same clothes day after day and were rewarded for their gross behavior by getting great and beautiful girls. This was transformative in that I thought, You're right! It's not that I want a big belly, but I want a piece of that freedom to be a pig.

**SASHA GORA** I bought a black leather jacket when I was sixteen, working a summer job as a janitor at a tennis tournament. It was $400 and I saved up. I was at a party in Montreal years later and someone tried to steal it. I sensed it immediately and chased them down the stairs.

**RUTH MILLS** The piece of clothing that makes me feel most comfortable in my gender identity is the headband I currently wear—out of necessity, to hide a receding hairline. I transitioned in 2013, at age thirty-nine, though I wish I had done so years before then. I work in IT, and it was always a worry that transitioning would seriously harm my career. Since transitioning, I have felt so much

more confident. I am finally happy in the present, rather than feeling my life whizzing past me. Now I can just *be*, in a career I love, while experiencing life as the woman I know myself to be.

**LINDY WILSON** When my mom would take us to Walmart for groceries, I'd always go to the girls' section. I coveted almost every piece in the Mary-Kate and Ashley clothing line, and was always picking out things I wanted and putting outfits together, though I knew I wouldn't be allowed to get them.

**ROXANE GAY** Rompers are not ever going to be on my body.

**PETRA KRUIJT** When I was twenty, I did an internship at a women's magazine. Since I was still a student, I didn't have much money. One day, when the weather got colder, I wore a cashmere scarf that I had bought for ten euros. It was awesome: deep green, so large I could use it as a blanket, and softer than anything I had ever felt before. When I walked into the office wearing it, the colleague I despised most said, "What a nice scarf. That really is a statement piece." I thanked her, and that is when I realized: If I love what I'm wearing, other people will notice it, too.

**CLEO PERRY** If I find a piece I like, I buy it, even though I may not wear it for months. My friend's mother did that with what became her wedding dress. She was single at the time and found something she thought would do the job should the day ever come. She put it in a plan chest and dug it out years later. That tale struck me as crazy at the time, but perhaps not. She had found something that would be perfect for an occasion that might happen, and it did. ✕

# TOO MUCH OF ME

VEDRANA RUDAN

A woman is never thin enough. I have a double chin, I shove my tits into minimizers that minimize nothing, I get into Levi's designed to flatten the tummy and lift the ass, but my ass and stomach are immune to the intention of the jeans. I am a cow! A dull creature with tits who lives in Croatia. You don't know where Croatia is? It's a small country in the sticks in which all the women nevertheless want what the women in New York or Paris want. We want bodies without a single hair. We want to be skeletons covered with thin, white skin.

One of us succeeded. A famous TV talk-show host who's been on the covers of all the Croatian magazines for months now. After a number of battles lost, the woman has won the war. Spreading her arms wide, jumping high in the air, screaming: "I can fit into a skirt I wore when I was eleven! I can get into pants I wore when I was ten!" If you don't look like a minor in your fifties, your life has no meaning. The Croatian talk-show host I'm referring to became a human being when she squeezed into that tiny dress. She's been giving interviews, showing tits that are irresistible because they're nonexistent. Her legs are the sticks that every woman dreams of. She created herself out of two hundred pounds of fat. She melted away in order to exist.

Who likes women? Who likes women as fat as me? Why do all men who live with famous skeletons as a rule fuck their children's heavy-breasted nannies? Who do we, bones and future bones, want to seduce? Women are our targets. Our only and eternal real enemy. We feed off their jealousy, their angry looks. Men interest us only as objects with which we prove our normalcy. They're so irrelevant they'll do in whatever shapes they come in. That's why no fifty-year-old man even thinks of trying to force his body into pants he wore playing in the sandbox, even though his mother has kept them.

It should, however, be noted that we women, no matter how desperate, never lose hope. We look at our childhood dresses, stamping on the floor, hissing: "Become something, become something, bitch!" Most men don't give a fuck what they look like. They carry their beer bellies with pride.

Will I ever become a doll? Will I ever be a happy human being who will dangle her bones happily in the faces of the sad human beings of my gender? At the moment I'm trying to fit into my maternity dress from 1975. Can't do it. There's too much of me. That's why I don't exist. ✕

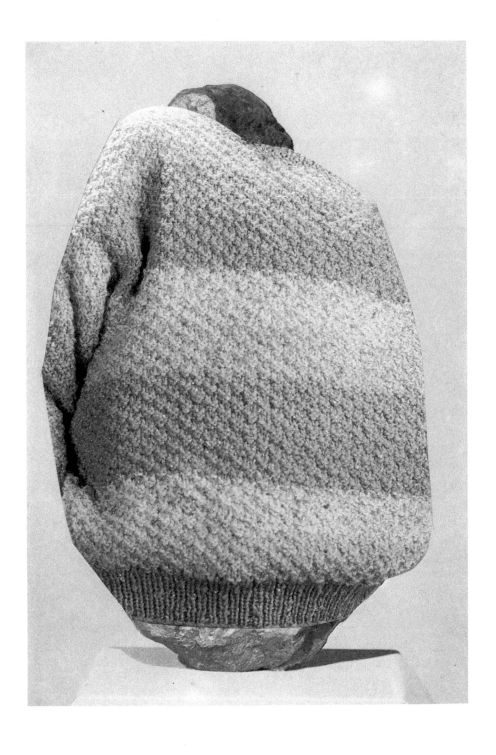

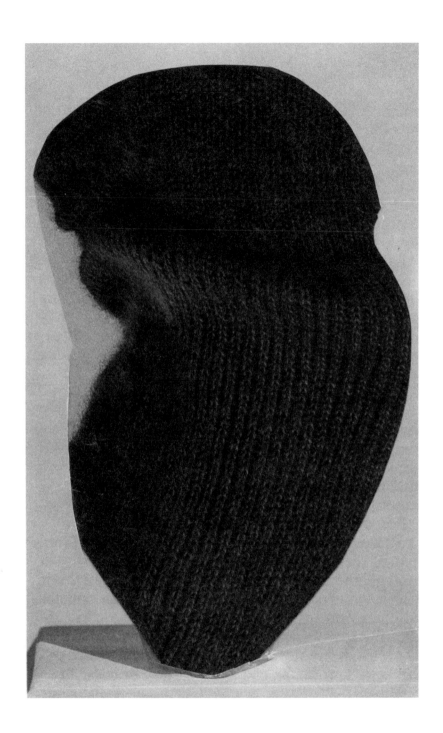

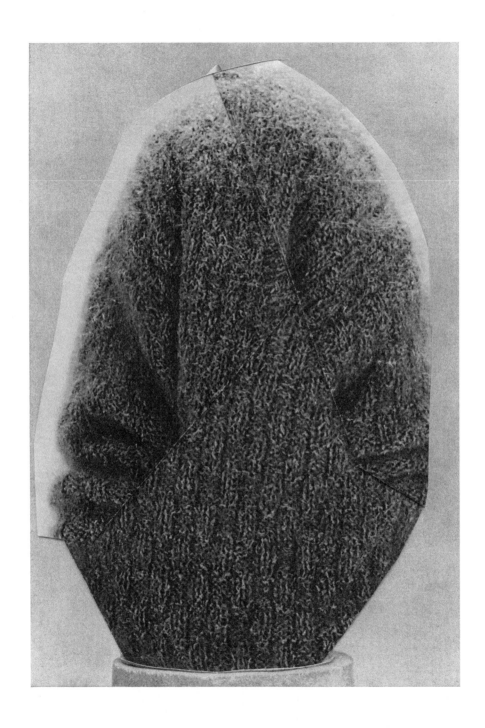

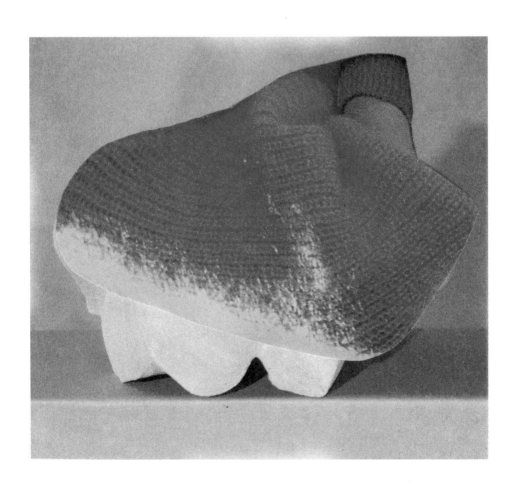

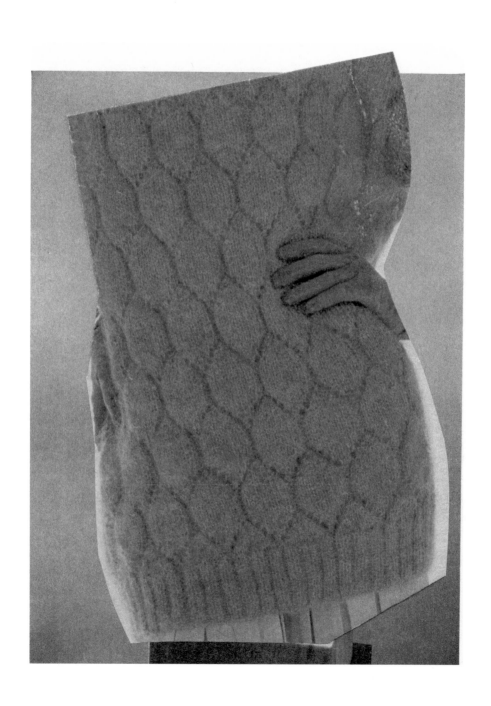

1.

2.

3.

4.

5.

6.

## COLOR TAXONOMY | TAVI GEVINSON

*Illustrations by Sarah Illenberger*

### 1. BLACK

Black is often seen as negative space, a blueprint you wear when you want people to focus on a more interesting article of clothing, or on your character. On the contrary, black should be considered a complete look all on its own. It is the uniform of New Yorkers and goths alike, confusing sophisticated intellectuals with disaffected teenagers. It can be seen on the red carpet as either sultry (Angelina Jolie at the 2012 Oscars) or not-giving-a-fuck (Lorde at everything). Though I'd imagine Stevie Nicks's actual favorite color is something like purple, she sports all-black in all performances, presumably for its witchlike mystery and ability to command an audience. Black is, in the words of a very poetic Wikipedia editor, "the color most commonly associated with mourning, the end, secrets, magic, power, violence, evil, and elegance."

### 2. WHITE

Although white is thought to be immovably holy for its role in weddings, it has been ostracized as an everyday color for its reputation as unflattering. In doing this, however, we forget what white does better than any other color: lace. The sleekest kinds of leather. Pristine Seinfeld sneakers. If one must avoid wearing white on one's body—despite the potential to feel like an ice queen—I strongly advise exploring it when it comes to accessories and embellishments. If you're a clumsy eater, remember Vivienne Westwood: "Stains are decorations." If you just detest the association with purity, dig up a few kinderwhore references.

### 3. GRAY

Gray was made for nice sweaters and gross sweatpants, thus covering both ends of the Sunday-spent-at-home spectrum: productive lazy (tea, reading) and plain lazy (junk food, TV).

### 4. RED

Red is infallible when it comes to power-dressing, as proven by the high school hierarchy in the 1989 film *Heathers*. It is categorized as a warm color, but it is not soft, the same way Heather Chandler is an alpha female, but not feminine. In fact, red translates femininity to power, according to a thing I once watched about how red lipstick makes people think of vaginas and that's why it's thought of as sexy and as inappropriate to

7.

8.

9.

10.

11.

12.

wear to the office. One master of turning the feminine into a source of power is Taylor Swift, whose music utilizes girly emotions to assert ownership over the unfortunate history of a romantic relationship. This talent is best showcased on Swift's 2012 album, *Red*.

### 5. BLUE

The conceptual opposite of red, blue is categorized as a cool color, but it is not hard. It is the sky, the water, and Joni Mitchell. It is a little hippy-dippy. It is hard to read as a word without hearing Beyoncé crooning the name of her baby in that video where they're on the beach. Baby blue is great for a poodle skirt or a Margot Tenenbaumesque Lacoste jumper. Regular blue is the shade favored by sports teams and Mrs. Peacock. Navy blue was outed in Mindy Kaling's 2011 memoir as a crutch for stylists trying to slim down their clients without going for the obvious color choice of black. (In navy blue's defense, it is the best color for a peacoat.) All in all, blue is okay, but never lasts as anyone's favorite color past the age of nine.

### 6. GREEN

Type "yellow-green" into Google, and the first three suggestions are "mucus," "urine," and "vaginal discharge." With "dark green," you get "stool," "diarrhea," and "vegetables." Emerald, however, is a universally perfect shade, and Tippi-Hedren-in-*The-Birds* mint is possibly the best color visible to human eyes. If green were a film character, the actor would be Oscar-nominated for tackling such a multifaceted role.

### 7. PINK

Pink is not a real color. It is not on the spectrum of light, and was not visible in the world until UV rays, radio waves, gamma rays, and other signifiers of the planet's eventual demise came into existence. But despite this troubling history, pink is thought to be the most nonthreatening color, which may explain its assignment to the female gender. It's frilly and inconsequential, and best known for its appearances on princesses, dolls, and blushing faces. Sometimes I wear lots of pink, to show that girliness and intelligence are not mutually exclusive. Sometimes I never wear pink, to show that some girls don't identify with the idea of girliness. Pink is fraught with politics, and I still haven't even gotten to *Pretty in Pink*, the 1986 John Hughes film; Pink, the Victoria's Secret juniors line; or P!nk, the pop vocalist.

### 8. YELLOW

While green may be cursed with an association to bodily functions, yellow gets away pretty easily. It's bold yet sweet, and the color of one of the most well-known plaid looks from the 1995 film *Clueless*.

### 9. PURPLE

The 2000s failed purple. After American Apparel V-necks tainted it with faux differentness, Justin Bieber took a stand in restoring it to innocence and even gender neutrality, but dropped the ball once he felt the need to defend his manliness with steroids and subsequent shiftlessness. What purple needs to do is take a page from *Walden* and go live in the woods, where it can be judged free of any cultural associations.

### 10. ORANGE

While many avoid orange in a solid-colored garment for fear of looking like an actual orange, it can do a lot for a print. See: '60s–'70s Pucci, the music video for Solange's "Losing You," and any space dye worthy of a *Freaks and Geeks* appearance.

### 11. GOLD

Gold has been rightfully monopolized by disco, *Dynasty*, and the Illuminati. Gold can be legitimately glamorous, but is most fun in windbreaker form.

### 12. SILVER

Silver has been rightfully monopolized by New Year's Eve, *Zenon: The Zequel*, and Beyoncé's "Single Ladies" robot hand. Silver can be legitimately classy, but is most fun in sequin form. ✕

# GLAMOUR

*"The sound of my mother's heels used to scare the living shit out of me. I rebelled against her glamour by looking like a tramp."*—LISA GUNNING

MEGAN HUSTAD My aunt wore silk Gloria Vanderbilt blouses and worked as an attorney downtown. Her purse was always Coach and her pens Cross. Evenings, while relaxing, she played with her shiny brown hair, forming a lock into a tiny curl and staring off into the middle distance, smiling about things she didn't wish to speak of. If it was possible to exude more glamour, I had no direct experience of it.

ROSALBA MARTINNI When I was twelve, I bought two sets of jewelry: pearl earrings and brooch, and crystal earrings and necklace. They made me feel grown-up and glamorous. Decades later, I still sometimes wear them.

GILLIAN SCHWARTZ My late friend Annabel Tollman taught me about impetuous glamour and being impractical. Through her, I realized that while being "done" may not be the fashion of our time, it is such a stylish and transformative choice. I admire women who look glamorous always. I wish I followed this rule through my life, but I can't seem to change. The jean jacket always comes out, the lipstick wiped off, heels switched for flats.

CARRIE MURPHY My Italian grandmother was incredibly stylish, even into her eighties. Imagine a thinner, smaller, less overtly sexy Raquel Welch. She was glamorous but approachable, with a look wholly her own. If there was something I wanted to keep, I'd ask her, and she always let me have it.

HIKARI YOKOYAMA Once I was chatting with Charlotte Tilbury and she said, "There are no ugly women, just lazy women." She was referring to makeup, but the mantra extends to dress as well. It takes a bit of time and effort, but I love the time it takes, especially in the magic hour between work and going out at night. I put on music, zone out, and make a big mess. It's like being in the studio—meditative and creative.

GILDA HABER I was seven and about to be a bridesmaid at my wicked aunt Mitzi's first wedding. I was thrilled to be wearing a dress held up by thin satin straps over my titless body. I wondered how the older bridesmaid with breasts held up their strapless bodices. I was aware that my mother and her sister, Aunt Mitzi, were bitter enemies, but I didn't care, I wanted to be as glamorous as my glamorous aunt, and still do. Another time, aged sixteen, and just back from wartime evacuation, my mother bought me my first postwar, unrationed beautiful white dress, which showed off my new, gorgeous figure. She refused to let me wear it to go to tea with an editor. She made me wear my horrid school uniform. The young, handsome editor expected a glamorous teenager. Tea was a disaster. I was so angry with my mother that I risked a slap in the face. Right then, I decided to leave home and come to America, which I did.

ALI COTTONG When I was in middle school, I went with my mom to a talk at SFMOMA with the designer Zac Posen. The talk was about glamour and living glamorously. I remember he said that you should always find some way to make your life glamorous, even if it's on the cheap side, like buying nice stationery.

**MASHA TUPITSYN** The kind of dresses you see Sophia Loren wearing in neorealist Italian films had elegance despite being a hyperfeminine exalting of the female form. You see this in Fellini films, too, though Fellini had a kind of early-Gaultier approach to beauty ideals. He made everything beautiful, grotesque or strange. He deformed beauty.

**JUSTIN VIVIAN BOND** I have an ill-fitting vintage '60s puss-print coat that I might wear once a year because it makes me feel like Jeanne Moreau in Roger Vadim's 1959 version of *Dangerous Liaisons*. I keep it as a reminder of how utterly glamorous and jazzy she was in that film.

**TRISH EWANIKA** I'm drawn to the kind of glamour that gives women strength, with an elegance that is understated. Foremost would be Coco Chanel. Jacqueline Onassis figured large in my childhood because I was born just before John F. Kennedy was assassinated. And Grace Kelly. Then there was Greta Garbo—not so much for her style, as she is famously known for being inept at choosing her own clothes—but for her way of inhabiting clothes. The closest person I admire today who can do this is Tilda Swinton.

**MAIA WRIGHT** When I started dating my girlfriend, I realized I could do better when it came to dressing myself. She has a great eye, and is so effortlessly glamorous. It's been a process over the past ten years, but I think she's definitely improved me in that department.

**AGNES BARLEY** My grandmother and her friends were the most stylish women I have known. They were so elegant and ladylike that they float in my mind like film icons of another era. They were exquisitely presentable at all times, and represented my ideal of beauty and womanhood. They were each so capable, so pretty, so delicately scented, so carefully dressed. I did not realize until I was much older that I had been admiring them in their fifties.

**LIANE BALABAN** The word "glamour," in its original 1700s definition, means "magic" or "spell." So it seems that for hundreds of years, our way of thinking about beauty and desire has been linked to revelation, insight, and knowledge. I think a lot of what we're doing when we put on clothes, or create a personal aesthetic, has to do with the idea that we know something others do not, that we have a unique and sacred lens for seeing the world. When we see people who are put together in a certain way, it's like they have their own special lens as well. Maybe they know something we would like to find out about, too.

**EDIE CULSHAW** My British great-grandmother used to have enormous, glamorous parties, once turning her garden and house into New York for the night. The waiters were dressed as cops, and I've been told there was a real New York taxi as a prop.

**ELISE PETERSON** Growing up, it was just me and my mom for a while. We were constantly together, and she was still really hip, I always thought she was so fashionable. She was a babe in the '90s—had that whole Whitley Gilbert meets Lisa Bonet meets Jade thing.

**KARIMA CAMMELL** If you look at the history of art and at pictures of women around the world, lots of archetypal women wear long single pieces of fabric—in India, Africa, Eastern Europe. That's what I do, too. It seems a pointless practice in our modern age of waste, but the rationale is that by dressing in one long piece we're conserving fabric for future purposes—the uncut panels can have many lives. Everywhere I go, people stop me and say, "I wish I could wear long flowing skirts like you do," and I think, Why don't they just go put one on? Some people have a fantasy of something romantic, but they end up wearing something conventional. There are some people who hide their inner life, and others who don't have trouble letting it out.

JILLIAN TAMAKI My grandmother, who was a belly dancer and nightclub owner in Montreal, was an extremely glamorous, incredibly beautiful woman. I remember showing friends old promotional photos of her lying seminude on bearskin rugs, and we had some of her dancing garb in our dress-up box. I was proud to be related to such an interesting, sexy woman. As I grew up, however, I started to recognize a dark side to my grandmother's glamour, including a dependence on male attention, even when she was in her seventies. She made ultrafemininity look really hard and sad. ✕

**SURVEY** *I feel most attractive when . . .*

Honestly? When I'm drunk. —JENNIFER CROLL • When I'm slightly intoxicated. —ALEX • After I have had a few drinks with friends, I go to the bathroom and glance in the mirror while I'm washing my hands. —LARA AVERY • When my hair is clean and my hormones have agreed to let my skin be clear and glowy, and I've had maybe two large glasses of wine and I have matching underwear on. —ANA KINSELLA • When I let my concerns go and just own the outfit and the moment. This is usually accompanied by a dress and a cocktail. —ADRIEN J. • When I'm wearing a twirly skirt and liquid eyeliner, and after one glass of wine. —BRYENNE KAY • After a few glasses of wine. —DANKA HALL • When I'm half drunk. —AMY KEY

The day after I have had good sex. —SUSIE GREEN • After having sex. —MADELINE SMITH • I feel like a beautiful queen when lying naked after perfect passion. —DOROTHY DENISOFF • When my hair is nice, and I am wearing a comfortable, swishy dress, and I've just had some good sex. —RACHEL PRINTZ • When I have the softness of face and hair after a good nap—or that lazy calm after sex. —CHRISTY-CLAIRE KATIEN • Post-coitus: when I'm naked in bed with someone I find rampantly attractive, who plainly finds me the same way. —CLAIRE O. ✕

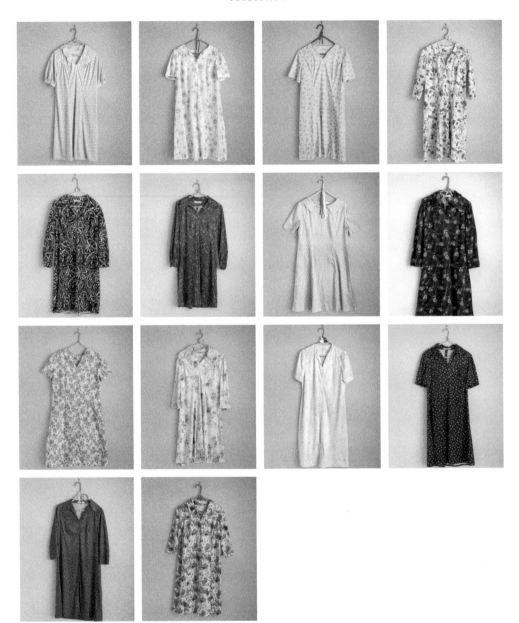

*SARAH BRUBACHER*'s handmade dresses

# A PERFECT PEACH

AUTHOR & FORMER RESTAURANT CRITIC **RUTH REICHL**
SPEAKS TO *HEIDI JULAVITS*

**HEIDI:** You used to disguise yourself to review restaurants. What would you do? Wear different outfits? Wigs?

**RUTH:** All of it. My mother had a really good friend who was an acting coach, so I called her and said, "I need to get a wig." She said, "I'm coming over. But it can't just be a wig—if you're going to do it, you've got to do it right. Who are you gonna be?" I hadn't thought about it, so I just pulled someone out of the air—my ex-mother-in-law. I said, "I'm gonna be Molly Hollis." The acting coach made me get clothing. I went to thrift stores, bought rings, watches, everything. Then, when I was finally decked out as Molly Hollis, she got a makeup person to come and do wig and makeup and transform me completely.

**HEIDI:** That's so interesting, to be shopping for another person, basically. So you would have her in your mind—would you think, "What would she like in this store?"

**RUTH:** Yeah. And I would pad my body. I'd wear layers and layers of clothes so that I was much bigger. Then that person got known, so I had to do new people. I knew this wig person and I would go in and say, "I wanna be a redhead," and she'd say "What kind?" and I'd say "I wanna be this wild . . ." So she would give me this wild red wig and I would go buy hippie clothes—really colorful clothes. I would decide who all these people were going to be and then I'd go mostly to thrift stores. Then there was a moment when I said,

"Everybody wants to be a blonde, I want to be a blonde." It was the only time I bought a really good wig—real human hair. It was this pageboy, amazing.

**HEIDI:** So what did she wear?

**RUTH:** I still have her suit. I wear it all the time, actually. I found it at Michael's, a fancy resale store on the Upper East Side. I got this cocktail suit, black, by Chloé. So I named her Chloe.

**HEIDI:** Did she have a last name?

**RUTH:** I can't remember what her last name was. They all had credit cards. I had this incredible, beautiful black cocktail suit. Then, you know, she had to have nails, so I got extensions, and it was amazing to me because I'm not a clothes person, really.

**HEIDI:** But you obviously notice how an identity might be formed through clothing.

**RUTH:** Oh yeah—you're in control of your image and people respond to who you make yourself. Before that job, that was just something I'd never really thought about. It was, ah, you are who you are. But doing those disguises while I was at *The New York Times*, I suddenly understood: You totally control how the world sees you, and they buy it, completely. Whoever you present yourself as, they reflect. For me, what was interesting was that you become that person, and people respond to you as that person, and then you respond back, even though you're not that person, and suddenly you become that person, because that's who people are seeing. The power of one's image became really clear to me. I was on a bus one day and a woman got on—a bag woman, essentially—and she was old and she looked tired and she was carrying all these bags, and I got up to give her my seat and she said, "Oh, thank you, nobody ever gets up for me, I feel invisible." And I thought, that's what I want to be. Invisible. She got off and I followed her and I saw—she really was invisible. I watched her go into a store, and nobody paid any attention to her. I thought: This is the perfect disguise. So I got some Enna Jetticks shoes, and this really frumpy dress, and this shlumpy gray wig, and I made myself completely shapeless. I went out as "Betty" and it was really pathetic.

HEIDI: Was Betty the only time you aged yourself?

RUTH: No. I also did my mother—

HEIDI: Did you wear your mother's clothing and jewelry?

RUTH: Yes. And my mother had beautiful silver hair. I never thought about how much I look like my mother, but I sent a photograph of myself dressed as my mother to my brother, and he said, "I've never seen that picture of Mom."

HEIDI: Wow.

RUTH: She didn't wear makeup, she didn't wear wedding rings. She was unconventional. She didn't wear *(whispers)* underwear! I remember once when I had friends over when I was in high school, she was standing at the sink in a wraparound skirt and it blew open and she was wearing no underpants. It was like *(gasp)*! She was not middle-class conventional. My mother went out and people paid attention. She didn't take any shit. But Betty was just . . . pathetic. When I went as her to restaurants, anybody with me was instructed to call me Aunt Betty, and I would tell people, I'm not going to look at the wine list, so you order the wine, and you

pay the bill, and I'll pay you back. Betty just totally faded into the background. No one ever noticed her.

HEIDI: Did you feel any residual effects from having been treated this way?

RUTH: It was a relief not to be her anymore. I had two feelings: one, enormous pity for her, and the other was, You don't have to take that.

HEIDI: You were mad at her. You wanted her to take a little more charge.

RUTH: Part of it was that I was feeling better about my mother, who was such a squeaky wheel. I felt that if you have to be one or the other, be the one who's out there saying, "Pay attention to me!"

HEIDI: It feels like something more people should do—dress up like their mother and go out as their mother into the world.

RUTH: Yeah. Inhabit your mother and you understand her, in a way. Scary, uncomfortable, but I really began to appreciate her. She knew how to take pleasure in things.

HEIDI: What kinds of things?

RUTH: Really good restaurants, which I had become completely oblivious to. Being her, I would go to a great restaurant and it was suddenly: Ahhh! She was so happy to be there.

HEIDI: So you were able to become her emotionally, too?

RUTH: Yes. And I became mean like her. I channeled her and I was able to be the pain in the ass that she was, which I don't think I am in real life, but I was also able to experience the kind of pleasure she took in things, which I don't have so much.

HEIDI: Was she usually very well dressed?

RUTH: She was bipolar, so it depended: she was Betty half her life—her weight would go up and down. But really she was enormously flamboyant the rest of the time. Wore big hats with color. I wouldn't say she was fashionable, but she enjoyed fashion. She dressed to be noticed. I mean color! She'd get off a plane and you wouldn't miss her.

**HEIDI:** You must think differently now about how people see you when you're just being you.

**RUTH:** I wish I had a better fashion sense. Having been in the counterculture for a long time, there were "the hippie years." And then the Berkeley years, when we didn't have three cents and it was kind of an antifashion time. Then we moved to L.A., and L.A. is such a weird place for people who don't have a lot of money. We were two working journalists, it was around '84, and we'd walk around Beverly Hills and look in these stores with this ludicrously expensive stuff and I felt completely left out. Then we came to New York, and we were trying to figure out how to make ends meet, and my sense of New York was going into fancy stores and feeling embarrassed, feeling so uncomfortable in Saks and Bergdorf's. I would walk in and wander around, thinking, "I wish I knew what to buy, I wish I knew how to dress, I wish I had some sense of this," but I didn't really. Then, when I went to Condé Nast, suddenly I had a clothing allowance. I didn't know what to do with it!

**HEIDI:** Did you have to have someone take you shopping?

**RUTH:** I should have done that, but what I really did was spend all my money on, basically, art. I bought all these Edwardian clothes, beautiful things. And things made in the 1890s, the 1930s. I spent my money on clothing that felt like art to me.

**HEIDI:** Do you think back to times in your life and say, Oh wow, if only I'd owned that situation differently, if I had dressed differently, been more confident . . .

**RUTH:** Yeah. I feel I was good in the hippie years. I had a lot of fun and it was fine—I wore mismatching socks, I did all that. But I would have had a better time in L.A. if I had defined my look better. I couldn't tell you a single thing I wore in the ten years I lived in L.A.

**HEIDI:** Really?

**RUTH:** When I got to Condé Nast I didn't even know that I could have my hair blown out. I'd never heard of it. My PR person, in my first few months there, said, "Who cuts your hair? Who does this?" She took me to a salon and I came out and I had straight hair. Which, for me, was heaven. I didn't know I could have straight hair. It was life-changing.

**HEIDI:** I know you as somebody who has curly hair.

---

**CONVERSATION** *A brief conversation about dressing.*

**SHEILA:** It was so hard to decide to buy that leather bag, but you were so encouraging. Of course, I wanted it because you have the same one. But I still can't look at the stain at the bottom. I have to avert my eyes from the body of the bag. Even though I take it everywhere and I think it's the perfect bag. **LEANNE:** But mine is in worse shape than yours, no? **SHEILA:** You have to tell me how I *cannot* have a bad feeling because of the stain. It makes me feel dirty and schlubby! **LEANNE:** Describe that. **SHEILA:** Well, it makes me feel like I'm a sloppy person. And a dirty person. Like I don't notice there's a stain. It feels like I've got something on my face. **LEANNE:** Look at me! *(pulls at her sweater—it has moth holes and a rip, held together with a safety pin)* **SHEILA:** But the holes looks so artful! **LEANNE:** No. It makes me feel like—not caring. And I like not caring. I care so much about so much stuff that when I have something on me that says "Fuck it," it gives me more confidence. **SHEILA:** Really? **LEANNE:** Yeah, and it makes the item blend in because it's not spanking new. There is some part of me that feels rootless. My mother

RUTH: Also, before I got to Condé Nast, I never had my makeup applied, ever. My first week there they have a party and my publisher says, "We'll send a makeup person." I got to know this makeup person, and she was at my house once a week, and suddenly I've got makeup! I'd worn makeup to do the disguises, but never in my real life.

HEIDI: Did it make you feel like you were wearing a disguise when you put it on?

RUTH: Oh yeah, after three hours of makeup, I look like another person. It's great that you can do that. It's fun. But when I left Condé Nast, my makeup lady and the people who came to do my hair in the morning went away. Once you realize all the things people can do to themselves, you could spend your entire life worrying about your nails, your heels, your toes. But come on, we've got to have better things to do with our time than deal with all this stuff. Life is a choice. Who knows how it happens, but you decide that you're going to focus on one thing. I'm not conscious of having decided to focus on food, but there's no question.

HEIDI: Did you eat differently as your characters? Did they have different food identities?

RUTH: They did. Part of being a critic is that it's not about what you like, it's about the food. When I was Chloe—

HEIDI: *(laughs)* She was watching her figure?

RUTH: She was! You can't understand what it's like to momentarily be the shiksa goddess. So there I am, I've just come from having my nails and makeup done, and I'm sitting in a bar having a drink by myself and this guy picks me up. And I'm thinking, Oh, this is perfect.

HEIDI: What kind of guy was he? Was he the kind of guy who had never hit on you before?

RUTH: Guys didn't hit on me. I wasn't that kind of person. But I was this blonde and it was like a dream. I mean, I was married and I was going to have a meal by myself, which I did a lot as a critic, and this guy comes up and says, "Will you join me for dinner?" He was a complete jerk, but it was too delicious, because he really thought I was that person! So Chloe has dinner with him, and I suddenly turn into this ridiculous ditz! I'm *(lowers voice)* talking in this breathy little voice, and he's coming on to me, and suddenly I'm saying, "I'll just have the filet of sole." That's the thing. We can disguise ourselves. And we do it every day. We're these fragile little creatures behind these façades, trying to make our way through the world, and one of the ways we do it is with the clothes we wear, which say: Pay attention to me.

---

isn't from Canada and we had very few traditions, so I want things that have some affectation of legacy or tradition. **SHEILA:** Like somebody handed down that sweater to you. **LEANNE:** Exactly. Even though nobody did. I went out and bought it. So I'm a total poseur. **SHEILA:** Did you rip it? **LEANNE:** No. I got it at a flea market. It was already ripped. But it's something I'm attracted to. Maybe if you feel so strongly about something, you're trying to conceal something. If I feel so strongly about things that look as if they've been worn and used and passed down through generations, it makes sense: I'm a first-generation Canadian. **SHEILA:** But I'm first-generation Canadian, too! **LEANNE:** I know. But did you grow up with a lot of used things? **SHEILA:** No. And I don't think that's the explanation in your case. With you I always think of that Italian word *sprezzatura*. **LEANNE:** But if you saw me carrying the bag, would you go, "Ew, it's stained!" **SHEILA:** No. But all your choices seem so deliberate to me that I'd never question it. **LEANNE:** That is insane! Maybe you give people too much credit. **SHEILA:** Of course I do. I know I do. **LEANNE:** That's a lovely, generous thing, too. **SHEILA:** I know, but I should see that the same thing

Be nice to me. Don't look at me, I'm tough. I'm vulnerable. Whatever. Most of the time it's unconscious—but there's no question that we see ourselves on a stage.

**HEIDI:** Obviously, with food there's literal taste, but what's the difference for you between style and taste, in terms of food? I feel that in the fashion world it's confused. Would you rather have good taste or good style?

**RUTH:** With food it's so clear—good taste in a heartbeat. Style in food is just pretty. Style, in terms of food, is pretentious. It's just how it's arranged on the plate. As opposed to taste, which is real and honest and inherent.

**HEIDI:** That's interesting.

**RUTH:** In fashion terms, if something is tasteful, you think, "I don't want to be tasteful in terms of my clothes, but I really want to have a style. I wish I had a style." But with food, taste is the honest thing. Style is the pretentious, put-on piece of it. Because food is about flavor. Flavor and taste are synonymous. All food has taste, and really good food—like corn—you get a great ear of corn, it just comes out of the earth, and it tastes wonderful. You can play with something and can make it stylish, but you can never make it taste great. Taste is natural.

**HEIDI:** But there are people who have cooking styles, right? You might say that a certain chef has an identifiable style.

**RUTH:** Absolutely. They have a style and that's fine. There are two major opposing styles now. One is the molecular fucked-with, and you manipulate food in every possible way. And the other is the Alice Waters, where the best food is the most natural, perfect stuff that was just harvested, just came out of the earth, and you do as little as possible to it, and it tastes of itself. Both of them are current and accepted.

**HEIDI:** You live in both worlds. You have these costumes you put on, but also, right now, here beside me, you're an ear of corn.

**RUTH:** I'm an ear of corn. And really, I just want to be an ear of corn. Or a perfect tomato, just picked off the vine. Or a perfect peach. That's the hardest thing to get. You get one every ten years or something, but when you get a great peach . . .

**HEIDI:** What's the last great peach you had?

**RUTH:** Oh god. It came from Frog Hollow Farm in California. But a perfect peach—it's really hard to get. Yeah. That's what I want to be. ✕

---

applies to me. **LEANNE:** Yes! You don't have the Japanese version, *wabi-sabi,* and you're not minimalist, but your clothes don't look like they came from anywhere specific, which is a good thing. You look clean, so I can see how something stained would make you feel like there's an unraveling. **SHEILA:** Like there's food on my face. **LEANNE:** But remember when we were in Montreal and you had that parka? Like a secondhand parka? **SHEILA:** Oh yeah, Martha's. **LEANNE:** There was something about it. One dirty thing is kind of lovely. And maybe it gives you this little question. Like, is there a sentimental story behind that thing? It adds a little mystery. That's why I like used stuff. It's my obsession-with-ghosts thing. You really like new things—new art, new forms. It gives me security to have old crap on my body. I think you should get the purse cleaned and see how you feel. **SHEILA:** I don't know if you can clean leather. **LEANNE:** You can clean leather. **SHEILA:** But we were talking about going outside our comfort zones. . . **LEANNE:** Why? Someone saying, "I'd never buy it—there's a stain," I can totally respect that! **SHEILA:** No. I think I have to keep it and adapt to it. ✕

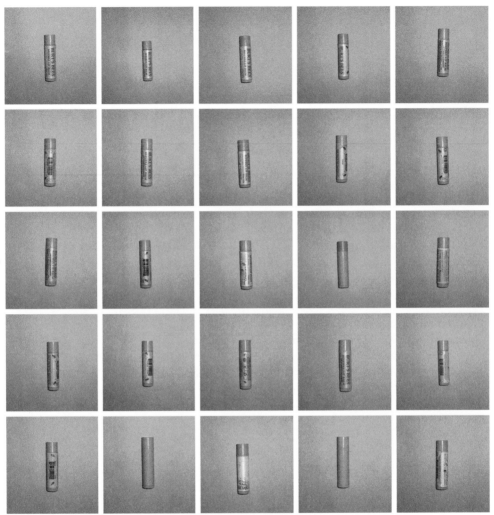

*JANE LARKWORTHY*'s lip balms

# SMELL

*"Every once in a while I smell my kindergarten teacher and when I turn around I'm a bit disappointed it isn't her."* —STAR SPIDER

**LAURA SNELGROVE** I wear perfume every day, and rotate through three lovely fragrances. Two of my regulars were gifts. The third I smelled on someone at a house party in Berlin. I deduced it was the hostess who smelled so incredible, and proceeded to smell all the bottles in her bathroom until I located it. Then I bought it immediately at the duty-free on the way home.

**LAUREN SPENCER KING** After my mum died, for four years I preserved her closet exactly as she left it. Sometimes when I was home, I would just go in there to look around, or have a good cry, because it still held her smell.

**KARIMA CAMMELL** I used to be a huge fan of Laura Biagiotti's perfume Venezia. As soon as I had kids, though, I realized that so much of our communication was based on scent. I wanted my kids to know what I naturally smelled like. As they get older, I think about exploring perfumes again.

**AMANDA STERN** Everything my best friend Stephen Hara wore and owned, I wanted. I coveted even his personal scent (Derby by Guerlain). He was a beautiful boy, and I coveted him, too, but he was gay and unavailable to me. We had clothing swaps, and when I was at his house, I'd steal things from his closet and shove them into my bag. Soon enough, I had to go through a Stephen Hara security checkpoint before leaving. He died of AIDS in the late '90s, and when I discovered eBay, I found three bottles of Derby by Guerlain and bought them so I could smell like Stephen Hara whenever I wanted.

**DAPHNE JAVITCH** My perfume has been tragically discontinued. I'm down to my last few bottles. I treasure it. I like to spray a little in my hair before bed.

**FRIEDERIKE GIRST** Since I was fifteen, I always wear the same perfume. It is Jil Sander. I always admired Jil Sander. Of course I could not afford her clothes back then. The olfactory should not be underestimated. I love it when people tell me I still smell the same.

**STEPHANIE DINKMEYER** I love perfume cautiously. I am hyperaware that whatever perfume I'm wearing will be forever inextricably tied to whatever happens to me that day. I could tell my whole life story with a trail of perfumes. I've gladly abandoned many scents throughout the years.

**SANCHARI SUR** Perfume is so bourgeoise. I have never bought perfume for myself. The perfumes I own have all been gifts.

**HALEY MLOTEK** Buying the Embryolisse moisturizer felt like paying a membership renewal fee. I used it when I was studying to be a makeup artist, and it smells exactly the way I remember it, like eight a.m. classes, and having another student brush it on my face, and smelling traces of it under my fingernails after class. Makeup school was the first time I'd ever done something really creative instead of mostly cerebral. I miss it.

**MIMI CABELL** My house burned down (it was arson) when I was in grade ten, and my mother wore this vanilla oil for the six months following the fire. That was fifteen years ago, but whenever I smell vanilla oil I am instantly transported back to the rental house we lived in while our home was getting rebuilt. I reexperience the feelings of suppressed rage and sadness I felt about losing all of my things.

**NINA MOOG** I own a wax-covered coat that reminds me of Scotland. It smells of outdoors and sheep and rain, rain, lots and lots of rain, and black coffee.

**HEATHER BLOM** Like lingerie, perfume is the icing on the lady-cake. Some women just smell SO GOOD.

**BRITTANY BROWN** Scent really can change the way I feel or the way I present myself. I have a ton of different oils with different scents and combinations. I find it exciting when I choose something and let it be the theme of the day. I'm currently wearing one that's called "Sacred Whore of Babylon."

**SHALINI ROY** My maternal grandmother greatly influenced my sense of style. She wore beautiful chiffon saris and printed silks in the hot days, and heavier materials at night. I played with her cut-glass necklaces. My favorites were the midnight-blue and the aqua-and-pink refracted ones. She had a dressing room and it smelled like her soaps and perfumes and talcum powders. She was the owner of Calcutta Chemical, a toiletries manufacturer.

**CARLA DU PREE** I always wear a hint of cologne in all the right places. I like for my husband to find my scent, even when he's not looking.

**CLARE NEEDHAM** I regularly rip out the sample perfume strips from magazines and put them in my drawers, but I've never purchased any expensive perfume. I've worn The Body Shop's White Musk for over a decade, and love it because while I can't smell it on myself, other people can smell it on me. A friend of mine told me it makes him hungry, and taxi drivers and people on metros around the world have correctly identified my scent as White Musk.

**RUTH GAIS** I've worn White Musk bath oil from The Body Shop for years now. It's the only thing I've ever worn that people ask about all the time. The downside of it for me is that I can't smell how nice I smell. It's a very soothing and affectionate scent. My mother always wore Joy by Worth. She said that it was the one fragrance that cabdrivers always asked her about.

**LEAH DIETERICH** When my husband and I lived apart for two years, I began wearing his Old Spice deodorant. Partly because it smelled like him and that was comforting, partly because I liked smelling like a man, and partly because I had just transitioned from my old antiperspirant (because of the aluminum-cancer correlation) and it was easier to use his than to find a new brand for myself. Four years later, I'm still using it. It's a part of my scent now. I also have a men's cedar-scented cologne that's made in Bermuda. It reminds me of the smell inside churches there—my family used to go to Bermuda every summer. One of my other perfumes is also from the Bermuda Perfumery, made with frangipani, which I believe is in the jasmine family.

LISA GUNNING I wear perfume, but not girly perfume, more unisex things that smell like leather, incense, old libraries, or dubious sexual parts.

ALEXIA CHANDON-PIAZZA I am afraid my sense of smell is not refined. Most scents, when put on my skin, incommode me, as if I had the smell of someone else stuck to my body.

TAYLOR SMALL Once—I think I was sixteen or seventeen—I made a friend smell every perfume I owned and tell me which ones turned him on the most. We were just hanging in my bedroom, getting ready to go out. I put on Daisy by Marc Jacobs while I finished getting ready. He remarked on how I smelled. He focused on how the way I smelled was different from me as a person. He said that the smell specifically turned him on, not me. It didn't prompt me to change perfumes, but I think that I do usually wear Marc Jacobs for dates now.

HENRIETTA ALTMAN Perfume is a must! Even to bed!

LINDSAY PAGE I wear perfume but I never want to be someone whose fragrance announces my presence. My current boss leaves a trail of something that smells like W hotels for about ten minutes before and after her. This triggers a tremendous anxiety in me, knowing that she is on her way, or was just near.

PETRA KRUIJT When I know that I smell good, it gives me self-confidence. Also, I love the moment when I smell myself and think for a split second: What smells so good? Then: That's me! ✕

COMPLIMENT

## "WALLET"

*One p.m. on a Saturday at a Staples store in downtown Manhattan. Kate is paying for batteries.*

WOMAN: Oh, I like your pink wallet.

KATE: Thank you!

WOMAN: Do people comment on it all the time?

KATE: Yes, sort of.

WOMAN: It's great—so fun. You should get a lipstick that matches it. And some shoes . . . no, that would be too much, maybe just the lipstick. You know how it's nice when there's just one little thing that matches, and people can't tell if you meant it or not.

KATE: You're right, I should!

WOMAN: You could find one at Sephora. They have them in Pepto-Bismol pink too, but this color's more . . .

KATE: More of a neon, with some orange in it.

WOMAN: Yeah! My friend has lipstick like that. She has a darker complexion than me, so she can wear it. And you have a lighter complexion than me, and it would look good on you. But on me . . . no.

KATE: You can have your own color. Maybe . . .

WOMAN: I like burgundies and maroons on me. I don't even wear lipstick, but if I did, that's what I would wear.

KATE: You should get one for yourself! It would look great. ✕

391

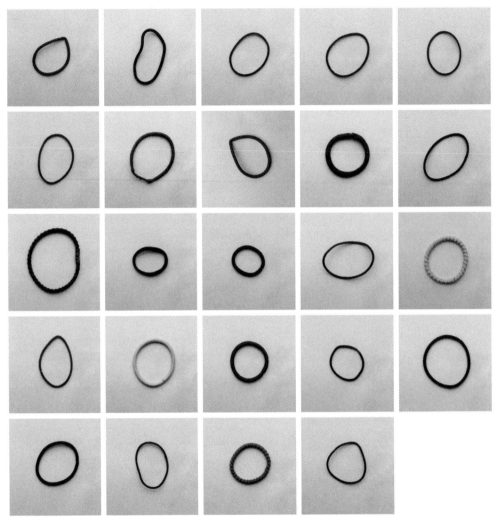

*PAULA BLACK*'s hair elastics

# SURVEY DIARY NO. 2

MARY MANN

### JUNE 17

When I'm reading surveys, the calmest ones come from women who know their real bra size because they've been fitted. It's lulling, the idea of having this one basic thing nailed down. So between looking at surveys I looked at lingerie websites. I thought this would make me feel better, like I was getting a handle on adulthood, but instead I felt worse, like some weirdo looking at porn on a weekday afternoon. Why are lingerie websites so porny? I imagine it's women mostly shopping for lingerie, but maybe not.

### JUNE 24

There were a handful of surveys today from women who hold up their dads as style icons. They have shopping traditions or clothing conversations or maybe they just admire their style. It's nice and sad for me to read. My dad and I don't have a relationship like that. As a preacher, he had a uniform for work: robes every week, three different kinds—cassocks, surplices, and chasubles—and black shirt, black pants, and a white collar underneath. He always smelled like the myrrh they burned in church. The vestments are such an important part of religious ritual, and it's funny to think that so much is invested in them— heavy embroidered fabrics, gold thread on the stoles, the bishops' crazy hats. These fancy clothes sort of legitimize the rituals, and the rituals legitimize the religion.

One woman wrote that she chooses her underwear to give her extra oomph for what she needs to do that day, and different pairs of underwear bring different kinds of luck. My underwear is all just different color variations of the same thong that I bought from Lululemon back when I worked there and it was cheap. But that was two and a half years ago! While I worked on my computer today, I kept taking "underwear breaks" and Googling to see if I could find some really nice-looking stuff that wasn't too pricey. Later I asked my boyfriend if he had preferences in the realm of ladies' underwear. He said he liked what I have. I said, "But if I had all the kinds of underwear there are, what would you like to see me in the most?" He said, "I don't know, the sexy kind," which doesn't mean anything. When I pressed him he said, "Maybe red?"

No surveys today, which feels weird. I've gotten used to the survey responders keeping me company as I work from home, but today the only voice in my head is my own. After a few hours of work I went to a yoga class. The class was wonderful. I even managed a handstand—I felt so strong. I sweated right through my black tank and leggings, and afterward changed into a loose white dress and tied my sweaty hair back and felt like a hundred dollars.

A survey arrived from my mom today, and I had lots of trepidation about opening it. I put it off almost all day. What if it said something I didn't want to know or revealed something distasteful through her writing? But when I finally read it I found it to be pretty cute. She's a sweet lady, and it was a relief to see that she is also sweet on paper.

Living with a partner means that he sees you looking not so hot sometimes. Over the last week or so I've been thinking about this, and worrying that maybe the romance will get lost in the mix of smelly exercise clothes and eyeglasses and dry feet. I had always felt sort of judgey of women who dress for men, yet the other night I told him that I was concerned that seeing me with zit cream on or whatever would make me less attractive to him. He said: "But that's the real stuff."

The surveys go both ways on this issue: (a) Dress nice to keep the romance alive; or (b) Be sloppy because it's more real. I don't agree that the equation is as simple as sloppy = real, but it does seem nice to share a whole spectrum of my ways of being with this person I care about. This morning while he got dressed for work, I put on a black sundress to work from home and some mascara. He noticed and remarked that I looked good. I told him he looked good, too (in a black collared shirt and tan pants). It was nice being barefoot and admiring of each other at seven a.m.

### AUGUST 2

Feeling attractive, according to one survey, comes down to being tan in a foreign country and not having anything to carry. I told this to my boyfriend as we headed out for the night and he was struck. "Not having anything to carry . . ." He said it slowly, frowned, then nodded seriously. We decided that for the rest of the summer, whenever we go out on Sunday night, we will leave our phones and bags and purses and books at home.

### AUGUST 24

We have so many surveys now. I can't believe I've read all of them, and can even quote from some. There are 400, at 4 pages average each, so 1,600 pages, longer than *War and Peace*. Most of the surveys teach me something, which is pretty amazing. The ones that speak to me the least are the ones where the respondent is crafting an image. They make an attempt to conceal flaws or give off a sexy or cool vibe that doesn't sound true, but I understand the impulse. I have it, too. But the really sexy and cool ladies seem pretty flawed on paper. ✕

*Apfel*

*Lethe*

*Freud*

*Parsley*

*Birdcage*

*Improper*

*Arabeske*

*Honey bunny*

*Dancing women*

*Mothballs and sugar*

*Strawberry thief*

*Rose & lily*

*Soup can*

*Aspirin*

*Oomph*

*Sarah*

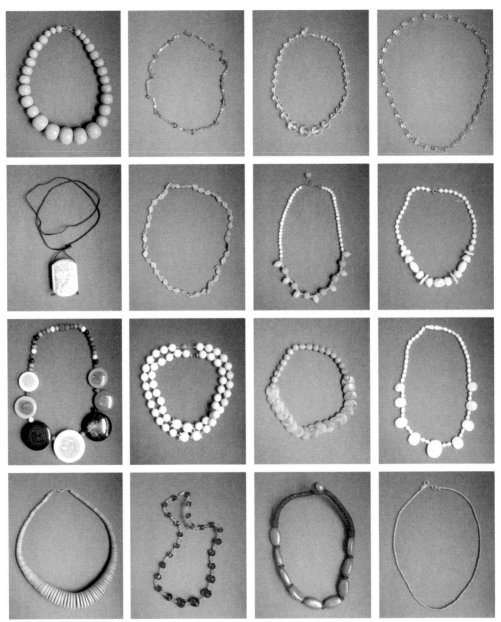

*MITZI ANGEL*'s unworn necklaces

# FILTHY WHITE DAISIES

CHRISTA PARRAVANI

My identical twin, Cara, wore plastic flowers in her hair. She favored stiff pink roses and filthy white daises. We were born in 1977, but she was kin to Ophelia, Cordelia, and Persephone. Her soul sisters in tragedy dressed in ceremonial garb. They shared a broken, frilly look that Cara called "romantic." Her closet was filled with floor-skimming skirts, and peasant tops she laced so tight it was hard for her to breathe. Fake flowers fastened into her hair, a crest of faith. Cara's bouquet attempted to conceal invisible filth. Hidden beneath cheerful immortal blooms: the unwashable mark that had been left after she'd been raped at twenty-four. A rainbow of gaudy jewelry helped make her trauma feel survivable. It made her beautiful.

Identical twins are analyzed for their differences. Cara and I were scrutinized down to every barely different feature: My nose has a bump. It is larger than hers was. My legs were thinner, gangly beside her shapely ones. Cara's cheeks were full, and her chin sloped closer to her neck than mine. Her hair was lighter, curlier, and bouncier. She was the pretty twin. But we were also so much the same. Strangers couldn't tell us apart. Except for our dress: I was fashionable.

We were lumped together, as twins often are. When Cara wore something absurd, I had it on, too, by proxy, even if I was perfectly well dressed and put-together. Twins are bound, like runners in a three-legged race. We were perceived as one, struggling because we were actually two. So if Cara was wasted, or dressed in a purple gown for a casual dinner, or wore a navy mesh blouse and sailor pants, arms sleeved in elbow-length black wool gloves with the fingers cut off—I was wearing it, too.

Everything she wore hung oddly. She was that woman: the one whose dress was just a little too low-cut, or hiked up where it shouldn't be. The person with an outfit that never matched the occasion, that clung to her like Saran wrap. She was often seen in a corset laced so tight her breasts were lifted in a provocative hello. She'd wear it with ill-fitting jeans and low-top Converse All Stars. It sounds hideous, it does. But these outfits were also charming, the way a velvet painting or an ornate frame around a badly painted picture is.

o—o—o

Cara died from a heroin overdose on our mother's bathroom floor. She probably died in her pajamas; she'd fixed early in the morning. The dose had been too strong and stopped her heart. She'd just moved back home with our mother to save money, her dissident wardrobe in tow. I'll never be sure what she was wearing the day she died. I can't bring myself to ask.

Eight years later, Cara comes to me in flashes. It can be hard to remember her eyes, how they seemed both bold and broken, so brown and clear in the sun. Or her pleased, half-lipped smile that showed just a sliver of teeth. But I can't forget her clothing. She'd had lovers who'd asked her why she did not dress like me, in pencil skirts and slim belts, in too-tall feet-killing heels. She tossed those men aside like heavy cargo on a sinking ship.

She hadn't wanted to get older, be old. Those flowers in her hair kept her young.

Cara had hoped years would bring children, a writing career, and maybe a home in the redwoods of California. She fully expected wrinkles, and disappointments, and even the pessimism that comes with taking your hard knocks. She was a realist, but she also believed in fairies and tarot and polyester. They were her religion as much as Mom had asked that Jesus Christ be, or so many of her New Age boyfriends had hoped of the Buddha. Her clothing was her way of keeping optimistic. Her sense of humor was her way of spitting in the face of a lousy life. She was in charge.

Cara liked baby-doll dresses, too,

though she coasted thirty and it was 2006. Her clothes could also take a turn for the dark. She owned an extensive collection of subversive, curve-hugging ringer T-shirts.

Her favorite was really an advertisement, a throwback television-cartoon owl licking his red sucker, a Tootsie Pop. Her rape had made her both timid and bold. How many licks to get to the center? The wry smile she wore with the owl atop her breasts, it was nearly convincing: How many knocks of the headboard till my sweet spot opens? I dare you to find out. I dare you to want me after I cry.

I own a stash of her clothes now, closets full. I have palazzo pants. Too-long and low-cut hippie dresses with dusty hems. Pilling synthetic sweaters that were meant for one season of wear. They're what I have left: cheap garments that Cara had hoped were merely transitional, a wardrobe that would accompany her to better stead. Now Cara's clothes are a symbol of her, her eulogy. They define the person that she was: Silly. Hopeful. Careless. Poor. Sentimental. Always looking back. Forever tacky.

o—o—o

Mom worked for years as a waitress at the Dry Dock when we were young, slinging hush puppies and popcorn shrimp. Her hair smelled of the fryer when she came home. She wore a white tuxedo shirt with shiny gray snap buttons, and a scratchy black apron and skirt, and a silky clip-on bow tie looped under her collar. Wearing formal attire to serve always seemed less dignified to me than being naked. I wanted to cover Mom whenever I saw her in her uniform, hand her something comfortable and venerable to wear.

She'd married badly, twice, and moved us so many times that by our thirteenth birthday the number of schools we'd attended outnumbered the years we'd lived. On that account, I sought order. I learned to groom and dress myself with the kind of conviction usually reserved for obsessive-compulsives, though I was not one.

I thought I wanted to be beautiful. That quality, the collection of features I possessed that seemed to make men desire me, they were my way out. Men had been Mom's primary problem. Her selection of the wrong partners had her pulling double shifts, covering her bruised cheeks with pancake makeup so she could serve with a smile. The women in our line were long-suffering secretaries, house cooks, and young widows, expert knitters who developed early cancers. Mom's mother was a farmhand, stripping an upstate orchard heavy with fruit with her calloused hands. She didn't care one iota to be fuckable.

Passage out of my family was assured, I thought, with the right getup, to attract the right man. I saw it that way for a long time, into my late twenties. Before Cara died, a lover finally questioned my fashioning of myself. "I want to look behind the armor," he'd said, "the you you're covering." I wanted to protect myself. I wanted to be in control, too. I was more like Cara than I knew. It was just that my shell was hard and hers was soft. It had never occurred to me that a girl could win her freedom through her mind.

Shakespeare was useless to me. (Cara had that on me. Taking the long view, I see her wardrobe was striving to be academic—the robes, the charming oddness.) As a girl, I carried copies of *Vogue* and *Glamour* stuffed in my knapsack. I learned to canvass the rack at Salvation Army. I constructed the woman I most wanted to be. Wild but perfectly groomed, with wine-colored suede pumps, and dresses that skimmed her knees. I wanted to be sexy but modest, tailored with an eye toward chic. I was part Stepford wife, part *Reality Bites*, and part Kewpie doll. I knew by heart which lipstick shades blushed the lips to look bee-stung or beard-brushed. I dressed myself until I was no longer Cara's twin, and we resembled one of those *Cosmopolitan* city-girl salon makeovers, only a shadow of our twinned selves. Cara hated every minute of my escape through lipstick and A-lines, fur-trimmed coats and lacy stockings. And how could she not? For every piece of cheap finery I owned, I'd betrayed her, our birthright sameness. To her, I'd left her alone in the dark in the rooms of our childhood, badly dressed.

I had, of course, imagined taking Cara's wardrobe and setting it on fire in our mother's front yard after she died, for all of suburbia to see. Or I might have given it to Goodwill to dress the needy. That's how angry I was at Cara. But I wore her clothes instead, like so many grievers do, until the fabric no longer smelled like Cara's fruit perfume, but like me, the bastard version of her. The contours of that gaudy fabric lay against me until it was a cover that belonged as much to grief as it did to either of us. And I looked ridiculous, just as she had, but even more so. And for the first time I understood her, in a way I never could while she was alive. I looked at myself in the mirror after she died and couldn't help noticing how much alike we'd looked. Her plastic and silk flowers brought color to my cheeks. Cara couldn't die. As impossibly as daisies growing on a snow-covered meadow, she was alive in me. ✕

# LOST MITTENS

### HEIDI JULAVITS

**1**

I cannot bear to lose clothing. I refuse to accept as fact its loss. A misplaced sweater turns me into an obsessive, a paranoid, a believer. I fixate. I sleuth and accuse. I experience flights of ingenuity or madness (the categories, when a missing sock is on the line, so often blur) as I try and try to find it.

**2**

The other day I lost my mittens. The disappearance of a full pair seemed against the mitten odds. Initially I blamed my parents. They'd been in town for a woman's funeral. I thought, *Maybe they accidentally packed them*. I sent my parents an email. I padded my mitten query with heartfelt things I would have said, that I'd wanted to say, about the woman who died. I did not want to appear insensitive or accusatory. I wasn't implying that my parents had stolen them.

**3**

Unless they had. I'd snapped at my father that morning when he asked (I was trying to get to the library) if I might quickly speak on the phone to my ninety-two-year-old grandmother. Maybe my parents were angry and, no longer having any jurisdiction over me, decided to punish me the only way they could. Also my parents had been spending time in a Gullah community in South Carolina that sold bone jewelry and believed in voodoo. And my brother had told me that weekend at the funeral that I talked too much. Maybe my parents also thought I talked too much (though not enough to my grandmother). Maybe they were taking the mittens to a Gullah witch doctor. Soon I'd be unable to speak at all.

4

I returned to the library. Maybe my parents hadn't packed my mittens. Maybe I'd left them here. They were not under the desk where I'd been working. Perhaps someone had stolen them? They were quite worth stealing. I'd bought them at a flea market in Berlin; they were bright yellow and brown, hand knit by the market stall owner's Polish grandmother. A German woman advised me to buy this pair over a red pair. She'd said, "If you buy the yellow all the women on the street will look at you and wonder, *Who is she?*" Maybe another woman wanted people on the street to wonder who she was. I imagined spotting the thief wearing my mittens along Broadway. I ran through a few confrontation scenarios. I needed to be prepared in the event.

5

I returned home. I dug through my kitchen trash (digging through trash is the highest form of cosmic due diligence—when I want something to reappear in my life, I dig through my trash). No mittens. They were not in the laundry or between the sweaters or trapped under the blanket that hides the stains on the couch or in the Dutch oven. They were not, clearly not, in the apartment. But they were in the building. Somebody had them.

6

I asked one of the building porters. He said, as though in a trance, "I seem to have a memory of maybe seeing some mittens like that." I made "Lost Mittens" signs. I posted them around the building. I offered a reward. Then I walked in and out of my building, reenacting the loss of the mittens. I narrowed the viable loss sites to three—the lobby, the elevator, the third-floor hallway.

7

But why, if they'd been found in the lobby or the hall, hadn't they been put on the doorman's desk? Or pinned to the tenant bulletin board? Why were they being withheld?

8

I suspected the third-floor neighbor who fried fish for breakfast. I was often vocally (because I talked too much) expressing my unhappiness with the Fish Weather System that hovered in our hallway. Perhaps this neighbor heard me complaining about the greasy low-tide smell coming from her apartment; maybe she had kidnapped my mittens and intended to sell them on eBay (because I'd said on my sign "VERY VALUABLE"). I imagined finding the mittens for sale and bidding two million dollars for them (just to make sure I won). I would walk across the hall and tell my neighbor—luckily for her, she didn't have to pay for shipping.

### 9

It was also conceivable that a busy, tired person had taken his dog for a walk, and the dog had snagged the mittens off the lobby floor, and the person hadn't realized until they were already at the park, and the mittens were already filthy and saliva-covered, at which point the tired person had, not without a little guilt, pried them out of the dog's mouth and thrown them in the trash. I forgave this person. I was tired, too. But not so tired that I did not plan, after work, to walk to the park, poke through the wire rubbage bins with a stick.

### 10

(My finding mania at this point was so primal and intensely preoccupying that I'd begun to confuse myself. It was as if I were the thing that had been lost. I had a friend who lost himself in the Sierra Nevada Mountains for three days. He built snow caves and made SOS signs from old railway ties. He survived, he said, by always having a plan. This was me, always having a plan.)

### 11

While I was at work, the porter had a memory breakthrough. I returned home to find one mitten on my doorstep.

### 12

One mitten! One mitten found! Normally this would have provoked even greater regret—what is more heartbreaking than one mitten, one sock, one earring? It is not a glass half-full, it is a broken fucking glass. It is a nagging reminder of loss. Except that I had just been to the funeral of this woman. I had spent time with her husband. He was what remained of a pair. He wasn't a painful reminder of her disappearance, he was such a welcome human symbol that she once, also in human form, existed. Because of him, I did not worry about her as I occasionally worried about my mittens when both were still missing— that maybe they'd never existed at all.

### 13

I decided (cosmic due diligence) to "move on." I emailed a friend in Berlin to arrange for a replacement pair of mittens. I described the mittens as *yellow and chestnut brown, wool, with what looks to be an icelandic/norwegian design all over*. I described where the mitten stall was located (*near goltzstrasse, in front of the church*). I made a joke to distract my friend from my potential crazy-seemingness over the loss of my mitten. I said of the stall guy, *he also sells wool socks. apparently all were made by his polish grandmother. who is locked in a room in his apartment. churning out these socks and these mittens.* After sending, I worried if my joke was in poor taste. Implying that a German man might capture a Polish woman and force her to do manual labor. With the Germans, with everyone, I am always worrying that I have said the wrong thing while trying to trick them from noticing that I am, for reasons that cannot be explained (especially when discussing a lost mitten), distressed on a molecular level.

### 14

Immediately after arranging for its replacement, I deduced the location of the missing mitten. It was at the bottom of my building's elevator shaft. This was less a clairvoyant experience than it was a hunch so unlikely that it did, true, carry the whiff of a psychic revelation. *I know where the body is hidden.*

### 15

I gathered recruits for the mission. Two children held the elevator doors open while I, on my knees, peered through the crack between the car and the floor. I saw nothing but paint chips. The mitten might (as it fell) have slipped beneath the elevator and out of view. I remained convinced it was there, possibly because it eased my mind to think that, even if it remained forever inaccessible to me, at least I knew where it was.

### 16

On my way to teach the next day—I wore my one found mitten with a mismatching mate (on the street I saw more than one person look at my hands and wonder, *Who is she?*)—I mentioned to the porter my suspicions about the mitten and the elevator shaft. He promised that the next

time the elevators were inspected, he'd make sure to look for it.

### 17

Obviously his curiosity was piqued. Or maybe he saw my sign advertising a reward.

### 18

In the middle of my class, during which I spoke the phrase, "You don't want to institutionalize the hurt," my husband texted me. *Your other mitten was found! Under the elevator, just as you suspected.* I tried to create a teaching moment from my astonishment and happiness. This is what it's like when you're writing a novel and—oh, fuck it. I bragged. I told my students the story of losing and recovering my mittens. I touted my master sleuthing skills. I vowed to quit the immaterial joys of the writing life and follow my true calling, retrieving through invincible logic and willpower objects that appear irretrievably lost. I find things that should never be found. I force a reckoning. I oblige them back from the abyss to rejoin the world and me.

### 19

After my elation waned, however, I worried about the implicit downside to my gift. I worried about my ability, in the future, to accept that sometimes things or people are simply gone. It cannot be healthy, can it? It cannot be. To so confidently believe: I can conquer loss. I can love a thing so hard it must always come back to me. ✕

# THE WETSUIT IS NOT FASHION

**RENATE STAUSS** *as told to Heidi Julavits*

From the moment we're born, the world is mediated through textiles. We have bed linen, we're being swaddled. The act of getting dressed involves feeling your body boundaries through dress. *Thérapie vitale* in France uses dress as a weekly form of therapy for young patients with eating disorders. They enter a room where they find wardrobes filled with garments. There's a therapist and a big mirror. It's like a dress library. The patients can check out clothing, try it on, talk to the therapist. The emphasis is on bringing culture into the hospital, rather than removing the kids from their lives and exiling them to a place where they're out of school, out of touch with their friends, and don't go shopping. One therapist took the stylist approach, saying things like, "That looks lovely on you, maybe you should try that." She hired a professional stylist to come to the sessions, one who normally styles editorials for fashion magazines. In another clinic I visited, the wardrobes had signs "S" and "M" and "L" on them. For an anorexic, being forced to wear a size M or L . . .

At the same time, clothing doesn't give a clear message. I wear all-black clothing, but that can mean different things. Clothing is context-dependent, it's culture-dependent, it's class-dependent. Dress is not a language you learn to speak and then everybody understands you. Because of this, clothing is more of a code—like music—that alludes to things; again, it is context-dependent, it has underscoring. If therapists are taking cues from the dress of the patients, they're probably going to get the meaning wrong a lot of the time. There are certain elements in dress that we can read, but strictly speaking, we shouldn't dare. A German sociologist, Niklas Luhmann, said that ninety percent of human communication goes wrong. I'd say that ninety percent of human communication based on clothing goes wrong.

In the 1960s, the San Francisco Mental Health Association sponsored a fashion group to go into a mental hospital and do a series of classes with the patients—makeup classes, comportment classes, dressing classes. The program was called "The Therapy of Fashion." Every woman had to design and sew her own dress. At the end, there was a fashion show. The doctors who supervised the project wanted to create "healthy feminine characteristics" in the women. Women were taught that they have to make an effort. They have to beautify themselves, dress well, do chores, fulfill a role for the husband, the household, the family. It was very much of its time. The goal was to use dress and fashion to move these women toward the role they were expected to fill in society. Still today, fashion magazines are implicated in this sort of "help" culture. You can't help wondering, How far have we come? In a PC world, we don't want to say that we're trying to create "healthy feminine characteristics" in women, but in many ways that's what we're doing.

I've been looking at something called sensory stimulation therapy. Haptology is the science of touch. A haptology professor in Leipzig did tests where you feel an object without looking at it, then draw what you feel. The drawings done by anorectics were really off. In the same way they had an inaccurate perception of, say, the size of their own thighs, they could not accurately feel or draw the shape of an object. His thesis: In anorectics, body perception is disturbed in such a way that they can't *feel* what they look like. He wondered whether you could remap their body image to make it more realistic.

He came up with a neoprene wetsuit. His patient would wear this for one hour a day, then three hours a day—so there's the constant stimulating touch of the wetsuit. The results were incredible in terms of weight gain. This method, which is now being used in other hospitals, simulates one's body boundaries.

Of course, the wetsuit is not fashion. In a way, it's dress at its purest. And it really highlights the sensory function of dress. We get dressed with this sensory function in mind. Do we want to feel our body boundaries or not? To me, this is the therapeutic approach that holds the greatest potential, because it moves away from fashion, and it's not about size or knowing what's trendy. The wetsuits are made-to-measure for the patients. They don't come with the value baggage that other forms of dress come with.

If you look at the past hundred years, fashion has become increasingly accessible. It's twenty percent cheaper than it was even eight years ago. In combination with a society that's very focused on appearance, where media often replaces language with images, fashion becomes ever more important in our social interactions. Even nuns' uniforms have changed to be more relevant to society. Police uniforms, post office uniforms—they're being revised by fashion designers to be more relevant to the societies in which they're worn. It seems that nobody's outside fashion nowadays. If you can't rely on nuns being outside fashion, I don't know who you can rely on. ✕

# THE DRESS GOES OVER YOUR HEAD

## SCULPTOR **MICHELE OKA DONER** SPEAKS TO WRITER **FRANCESCA MARCIANO**

**FRANCESCA:** First of all, how did the idea of having only one type of dress come to you, and when?

**MICHELE:** The idea of having one didn't arrive. It evolved. I had many beautiful dresses, I've always loved dresses, and I found a dress in a shop in Rome in 1987, and this dress looked so Roman, yet it was embellished. I bought it, and when I returned to the city, I called the store and they put me in touch with the designer, I called him and said: "I love the design. How does the fabric arrive?" He said: "All white, and then I modify it." I said: "Can you just make me an all-white?" So then I had this dress the way I liked it, and when I would go to get dressed, over and over again it was what I wanted to wear. And over the next five, six, ten years, this was the go-to dress that made me feel so comfortable I never had to think about how I was going to look or what to wear with it.

**FRANCESCA:** Can you quickly describe what the dress looks like?

**MICHELE:** I would say it's a cross between a caftan and the Renaissance robe you see on Cosimo de' Medici in the Uffizi. As it turns out, the person who designed it began to think about it in Tunisia in the sixties, and ended up in the Uffizi looking at the portrait of Cosimo de' Medici.

**FRANCESCA:** Let's go back a minute. I think you told me you wear this dress almost every day, right?

**MICHELE:** Yes.

**FRANCESCA:** So to me you're the woman with one dress, because since I've known you, I've seen you in that dress. I think you said that whoever makes the dress for you sends it in a box that arrives to your house in New York. Am I right?

**MICHELE:** Yes.

**FRANCESCA:** So what makes this dress so perfect? I think you also said something about the dress not having any buttons or hooks or anything.

**MICHELE:** Yes, the dress goes over your head, and what's so wonderful about it—besides the one size fits all—is that it cloaks me from the outer world. That's the advantage when I'm out, and when I'm home it allows me to move freely without being bound by the feeling of elastic. It keeps me warm or it keeps me cool, depending on what I put under it. So it allows me such great freedom.

**FRANCESCA:** How many of the dresses do you have in your closet?

**MICHELE:** I have about forty of them.

**FRANCESCA:** For both seasons, right? And different fabrics—is that how it works?

**MICHELE:** Yes, for Miami I have lots of white ones, and then in New York I have black ones. I have one or two grays because I realize it's sometimes nice to have a transitional piece, and then I have silk, velvet, and he tried cashmere.

**FRANCESCA:** I remember once you said he sent . . . Actually I even remember the cashmere. It was years ago in New York, it was a dark brown, and you thought it was quite daring. You weren't sure about it, but it was actually fabulous.

**MICHELE:** Yes. Yes. Yes. He was a remarkable and interesting designer, and the dress has served me so beautifully. I've gone to several photo shoots where they've asked me to bring clothes, and I show up with that dress and they say, "Stop right there."

**FRANCESCA:** Do you ever get bored with wearing the same thing over and over?

**MICHELE:** Not at all. No. No. No. It's just the opposite. It becomes a blank canvas, and I can change earrings, or if I put on nail polish, it has a connection. It looks more vibrant. It shows off any little whim or thought I have.

**FRANCESCA:** So you carefully choose what is around the dress, from nail polish to shoes to one piece of jewelry?

**MICHELE:** Yes. Because I want an accessory if I'm going someplace that requires an accessory, and it allows me—how do I say it?—to showcase something very, very wonderful. Even kelp! I once did kelp, a necklace pulled right out of a lake in Maine, and I put it on.

**FRANCESCA:** Yes! *(laughs)*

**MICHELE:** Then I went out to dinner. The dress doesn't fight anything. It's soft, and the neckline is soft, there's no sharp V, there's no tailoring, no hard angles. This is the key point, I feel: There's a softness. Not only has the shape of it allowed me the freedom to move around, but the softness has allowed me to age gracefully. Because I'm getting softer.

**FRANCESCA:** *(laughs)* Of course. But also it is genius because it's a dress that can be worn in the morning, in the daytime, and it's perfect for the evening. Did you ever think of changing any tiny detail of it, with time?

**MICHELE:** Designers I know are always trying

Michele Oka Doner's dress.

to update it. So I give them one to copy, and they design it with pockets—which then accentuates the hips, which I don't love. One designer shortened the dress, which wasn't bad but made it something that I wouldn't wear every day. People have tried to do different things. Many designers. Everyone asks. It's a challenge for them, because they see I'm very content, and they feel they can do better.

FRANCESCA: Did anyone ever try to copy it?

MICHELE: People have asked me to have it so they could copy it, yes. And they've tried to—they've aggressively followed me down the street, actually, to have it. I don't understand it, quite frankly.

FRANCESCA: And how do you fend them off when they ask?

MICHELE: I laugh and say it's really nothing special, or the person has the copyright and I can't . . . Even though he's living in a trailer in upstate New York and not doing very well.

FRANCESCA: Is it true that he lives in a trailer, or you're saying that to scare them off?

MICHELE: No, he does, he lives in a trailer, and he's had a lawsuit with his neighbor over a cat. He sends me letters on occasion.

FRANCESCA: Amazing, so you're like his number-one client.

MICHELE: I'm his number-one client. When I wore it in *The New York Times* in a feature on beautiful faces, I got a call from a woman who said she made the pattern, and she won the Golden Thimble Award at Parsons. I said, "What? What about Tunisia and Cosimo de' Medici?" She said, "Oh, he was my partner and he was seductive, and it was terrible, he stole it from me." So I don't really know who made it. I have two who claim it. I'd have two problems if I ever gave it away.

FRANCESCA: Right. So do you break the rule of wearing that dress, every now and then?

MICHELE: Sure. I had a black-tie gala opening at a museum in Miami, and I wore a Morgane Le Fay dress, low-cut, with a wide skirt. It looked like a Goya painting. I've had that dress for fifteen years.

FRANCESCA: You must be very picky. Every time you step out of the dress, you must want to step into something that doesn't make you feel too different.

MICHELE: Correct. What I've bought recently are some summer color things that break it up a little.

FRANCESCA: Right. Maybe more than different shapes, maybe you miss wearing colors sometimes?

MICHELE: I don't miss it, but I see that it's beneficial to break things up. Being monolithic about everything forever—it's good to let other things flow through. It's like diet. You can eat mostly one kind of thing, but it's nice to vary it.

FRANCESCA: One word that you use a lot, which has been my mantra, stolen from you, is: edit.

MICHELE: Edit, yes. That's a wonderful thing. We're all drowning in our own excess. I say we. Our culture. And consumerism turns out not to be a worthy altar. The most interesting thing I read—I can't place where I read it, but I haven't forgotten it—is that there are five stages of luxury: aspirational; acquisitive; curatorial; experiential, meaning: my walls are filled with paintings, my closets are stuffed, I'm gonna be dropped off on the Great Wall of China by a guy and there'll be somebody waiting for me every two miles with a water bottle; and then, finally, where you find me, transcendent. The dress is transcendent. It's the real luxury. ✕

# FIXES | RACHEL PERRY WELTY

*Grooming in public without the help of mirrors or cell phones.*

BRUSHING TEETH WITH
FINGER WHILE DRIVING

CHECKING TEETH IN
KNIFE REFLECTION

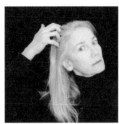

COMBING HAIR WITH
FINGERS

PINCHING CHEEKS FOR
COLOR

FEELING LASHES FOR
MASCARA CLOTS

ADJUSTING PONYTAIL
FOR VOLUME

FLOSSING TEETH WITH
BITTEN FINGERNAIL

BLOTTING OILY FACE
WITH TOILET SEAT COVER

STAINING LIPS WITH RED
WINE

BREATHING INTO HAND TO
CHECK FOR BAD BREATH

BRUSHING SHOULDERS
AFTER SCRATCHING HEAD

TAMING EYEBROWS WITH
LICKED FINGER

# DAUGHTERS AND SONS

*"I have a very fashionable daughter. From the time she was five she was full of advice, 'You should wear more red. You need more high heels.' She's right."* —ELISSA SCHAPPELL

**TRISH KALICIAK** Shopping for my kids has become a fun part of my life. Oddly, I find a lot of enjoyment in stocking their closets with cool items and then seeing how they put them together.

**SASHA ARCHIBALD** I sometimes feel pressure to dress more like the other mothers at my daughter's school. They wear expensive casual clothes, like expensive T-shirts and expensive flip-flops, and really expensive jeans. Understated luxury. I prefer the opposite: cheap, not-casual clothes. Sometimes I feel gaudy around them, and immature.

**MARILYN BOOTH** My daughter and I bond over buying clothes, maybe more than we should. Maybe it substitutes for other things, but it's fun, and in some ways replicates my relationship with my mother. She and I still get along best when we are either shopping or knitting together. It's not as if I would or could ever tell my daughter what to buy or wear, but there is nice bonding in "You look good" and "I'll buy that for you, it's great on you!" I always remember, with fondness, taking her out to buy a dress for a wedding when she was three, and she said, "No, Mom, I won't wear that." You learn a lot about style from three-year-olds, I think. But I would also say that it's tough in our Western consumer culture to convey to children, "No you don't have to have a seventy-quid pair of jeans. Go to the charity shop and you'll find the same." So for me "style" is also about thinking carefully about consumerism and trying to pass that on.

**SHALINI ROY** I talk about clothes most often with my seven-year-old son. He won't wear the rainbow trousers I bought him. My husband says he is not part of Wham! so this makes sense.

**KARIMA CAMMELL** I overheard one of my daughter's preteen friends bemoan how she didn't feel beautiful. I told her that beauty is not innate but is actually a magic charm, something that's passed along to young girls from grown women. So I took her shopping for a magic spell that could help her feel beautiful.

**AURELIA BELFIELD** A few years back, my mother and I got into it over this tentlike swing dress I had bought to wear to a party. I thought it was great, my mother thought it was matronly, and I was not having it. After a while, it finally came out that she thought I was hiding my body, and it was true. So we cried and we hugged and she helped me get past whatever quasi-dysmorphic fit I was in the middle of, and convinced me to wear this great black dress and lime-green paisley tights. I convinced her to wear this bandage dress she'd been avoiding, and we both looked great and had a great time.

**PEGGY BURNS** My Librairie D&Q tote bag enrages my six-year-old son, who wants me to have "a pretty purse, not a sack for food."

**LORI HANDELMAN** I was belittling my body, and my second daughter, Marnie, called me out on it, saying our bodies are similar so putting mine down put hers down, too, and how did I think it made her feel to hear that? It struck me like a bolt of lightning, and ever since, not only have I quit talking smack about my body, I've started caring about how I dress. After the conversation with Marnie (when I was fifty-one) I started buying outfits, "pieces," combinations. I started thinking about how I wanted to look, how I wanted to present myself. Clothing became something entirely different from what it had ever been before, just something to cover my body.

**RAINBOW MOOON** My mother saw her daughters as extensions of herself and how she was perceived, not just by the neighbors, but especially by church folks. It was her reigning concern. We were never allowed to get dirty or mussed in any way at any time for any reason. My mother was a beautician and believed that if we didn't have a certain image, it would affect her business. She was also divorced and seriously concerned that people would see her as less than capable if we didn't look well kept. Monday, her day off, she'd religiously take us shopping to buy new clothes so she could appear to be sufficiently well-off. Our hair also had to be immaculate. My memory of being overconcerned about my appearance includes being traumatized when, in third grade, I tripped and fell and tore my dress on the way home from school. I knew there was no way to hide the tear and rushed home to attempt to mend it. Though adequately repaired, it was only a matter of time—when she washed the clothes—before she found the mend and punished me for damaging something she had spent good money on. Her regularly announced effort to work hard to make us look good was an overriding concern for her and the source of much of the abuse I incurred.

**MONA KOWALSKA** We went into a store once when my daughter was small and she saw this belt—it was hideous: wide, purple elastic, with a big, lumpy buckle. She was like, Ding! The guy in the store said, "You know, I don't think anyone's ever gonna like this belt as much as you do. Here, have it." She wore it for years. For years! It was her thing. It's a big deal for her to get clothing from me that I've designed, but it's also a big deal for her to say, "I don't want that." She's in between those two feelings. She wants to be her own person. And I understand.

**SARA HABEIN** I have a gold dress that I wore to prom when I was sixteen, and again for Halloween as a Dead Prom Queen when I was around twenty-six. It's a muted gold and it's beautiful. Even though I don't fit into it anymore, I love it too much to get rid of it. Who knows, maybe my daughter will wear it.

**LIZ LERMAN** My daughter, Anna, spent a lot of her early life in rehearsal studios, backstage in dressing rooms and hallways, and on airplanes and buses while I was on tour with the dance company I founded twelve years before she was born. When she was a baby and then a toddler, I played a little choreographic game with myself. The task was to get all my dance bags (with rehearsal clothes, music, books, and food) and all of her bags (with a change of clothes, toys, diapers, and food) out of the house and into the car in one trip. Of course, I also had to carry her or hold her hand as she got older, and this last lovely detail, along with managing the keys to lock the house and then the keys to open the car door, made for a lively, rhythmic urgency. The whole thing was an excellent choreographic task. It included weight sharing, sequence, balance, effort, strength, even love—all part of the essence of making a dance. ✕

# IT'S A GOOD FLEECE

**KERRY BARBER** *as told to Sheila Heti*

There's a thrift store in Dawson City, Yukon, then there's a free store. The free store's by the dump and the thrift store is run by the Anglican church. It's the same-quality stuff. The guy who runs the free store, he works there all the time, but there's volunteers that go out there and sort. Everyone likes going to the free store, but you have to have a vehicle to get there because it's out of town. You can find good stuff all the time, like I find my baby Old Navy and some Gap clothes at the free store, and same thing at the thrift store. All the kids' clothes are free up to age two, so everyone recycles. Everyone recycles clothes. That's because kids don't get things dirty. Little kids, babies, they just lie there and don't do anything.

You can find good stuff at the thift store. I found a Mountain Equipment sweatshirt that was a nice color, and a lot of people go there for Halloween. And if you know the thrift store lady, you can say, "I'm looking for this"—maybe you want navy cords—and she'll search in her brain and find it for you in a couple of days and bring it to you. Sometimes you get a good score, like Carhartts—someone drops off Carhartt pants, those are a good score for Dawson because they're like carpenter pants. The thrift store has lots of toys for kids, and books, and videos, and cassette tapes. There's lots of kitchenware, lots of sheets and linens, there's maternity clothes in the back, there's little rubber boots for kids, and snow pants and mud pants, and there's lots of material at the front, lots of purses and shoes—women's shoes, like high heels. If you want them, just grab them, buy them for two bucks, and the next day you can bring them back if you don't want them.

You can always find someone there, and all your friends are there on Saturday. It's open Tuesday and Saturday, and the first Saturday of the month, if you fill up a grocery bag—you know, those little plastic bags—you can buy it for five dollars. So everyone's stuffing their grocery bags on the first Saturday of the month.

So that's the hub. Then there's a store called Miss Kittie Galore's—she just opened a couple years ago, that's kind of American Apparel–looking clothes and they're expensive. There was another store, but they closed down because they didn't have very much business because it was all gaudy, kind of sparkly old-woman clothes. Oh! And Raven's Nook has sports clothes, like North Face and Columbia. She also has bras for the local women that never leave Dawson, like the First Nation women who kind of never leave.

She's a local, she grew up in Dawson, so everybody knows her.

Also, everyone online-shops at J.Crew, the Gap, Old Navy . . . A lot of people shop at Old Navy because they have a good return policy if it doesn't fit. It's free. One year I ordered three different coats from Mountain Equipment because I wanted to try them on and see what the style was, and I rejected three of the coats, but I had to pay fifteen dollars each to send them back and I still didn't find a good coat—so I just gave up. One of them I was too lazy to send back so now I'm stuck with it. A red, boxy coat. It's hard to shop online because you don't know if it'll fit or not, so the return is the key. Oh, and I shop at American Eagle, because they have nice clothes and cheap, and they go up to size fourteen, like if you're fat, that extra-large shirt is good for you.

In terms of style, the joke is "If it's a good fleece . . ." It's a more practical kind of look. It's warm, it's fleece, and everyone has the latest fleece. No one really dresses up. A friend was visiting Dawson, and he felt weird going to the bar The Pit because he didn't have a plaid shirt, and everyone here wears plaid, all the men do, and some women. So it's more practical clothes we wear, warm and stuff. In the summertime, it's summer clothes, but most people are working really hard, so everyone's wearing Carhartts and stuff. *(sighs)* I don't know. If you go to a wedding, you dress up. *(laughs)* ✕

## "COAT"

*New York City street corner. Mild winter day.*

**LEANNE:** I like your coat.

**WOMAN:** Thank you, I like yours, too!

**LEANNE:** Is it vintage? Or new? It looks like a Courrèges . . .

**WOMAN:** I hate to admit it's new. But it's warm. Even though today I don't need it to be warm.

**LEANNE:** Bye.

**WOMAN:** Bye. ✕

# OW OW OW OW | KATHERINE BERNARD

*What women say as they get their hair braided.*

Do you know that girl? Basically, she's the one who wants this to happen, and it's happening. It was the first one that was approved by this vast machinery of approval, and she went on this rampage about it. She was like, "Well, what do you think? It's atrocious, isn't it? Isn't it horrible?" I'm really nervous because I sent e-mails that are like, "I really like this, fuck her." Well, I just hope that shit doesn't hit the fan.

I noticed Y was following me on Twitter, so I followed her back, then she started copiously liking and favoriting things. I know she has a boyfriend, so it's not anything. Then she tweeted about animal rape, and I had been doing this research on duck rape—one third of all duck sex is rape. And ducks have these insanely evolving genitalia because the females are constantly evolving to avoid the rape, and the men are evolving to thwart the avoidance. So I went to tweet that back and then I was like, I don't want to tweet this about duck rape. Is this a DM moment? I felt really jazzed about it. So I DM'd her and was like, I felt compelled to share this with you, and she was like, I want to send you something but it's too risky for the Internet. And I was like, Here's my number, and we had the most bizarre text chat two people who don't know each other have ever had about rape. Then it was like, G'night! I was really titillated by it. I'd like to never talk to her again and let it just be that, just let it exist in time as a perfect thing.

It's so surreal coming home. And then to be back in the office, it's just strange because everyone's been doing the same thing every day the whole time, and then you're back and you've been through this whirlwind, and there's no way to explain it. Everybody always asks, "Oh, tell me a story!" and I'm like, "I actually can't tell you a story right now. I can't. I don't even know what you're asking me for."

Sometimes I feel that people— like, I just shut myself up around certain people. I also maybe declare myself a little too much, so maybe people feel like, "There's no room in the conversation, she's already decided." I don't know. I guess I sometimes feel like I have to be a little quieter if I want to have a pleasant dinner.

I'm on the last leg, but I'm rewriting two chapters. Z read the whole thing. It was good. He hadn't read any of it before. If we'd been dating longer, I'm sure he would have. I haven't read his new book, but I read his old book before I knew who he was. I remember thinking, "I bet this guy is short like his main character." But yeah, he's tall. No one needs to be that tall. He's six-three.

Before I came here, I had coffee with a book agent. I don't really want to do a book, it was more like a "Let's say hi." And he was very complimentary, so now weirdly at this moment in time I don't feel stressed about work. The agent was like, "Now you can do anything. There's nobody that would say no to you. You're doing everything right." Then I spilled iced tea on him. I had a dream last night that I just remembered. I was sent to interview the Olsen twins, and I walked into a giant industrial space, and they were sitting, sharing a chair at this big desk. I was completely unprepared. I knew nothing about them, which is untrue in real life. Like, I feel like I'd be able to wing it in real life. Then I woke up.

Now it's like, ow ow ow ow, is it possible for me to see the project outside of it being a product? Ow ow ow! And it becomes hard to remember what *is* true to the project. Sorry, no, it doesn't hurt. Then you start working around what you DON'T want it to be, and then you just end up boxing yourself into a place that doesn't exist—some imaginary ideal that's neither stuffy nor silly nor snarky nor pretentious nor too funny. But now my head's like: I want to make movies! Ah, ah, ow. Like, these unmarketable movies! The advice I've been getting is to just ah ah have fun with whatever is happening, and have that be the only guiding force.

This woman's ear is always peeking out of her hair and my coworker said, "I think she does it because it makes you look like a teenager." It was the craziest, most absurd thing anyone has ever said. "Why is her ear always exposed like that? Is her hair just thin? Why!" She theorized that it was this very useful, premeditated thing. A guaranteed way to look young and careless. She said she was tempted to make a Tumblr of pictures of her ear peeking out from her hair.

*(looks in the mirror)* Is it okay if I undo it?

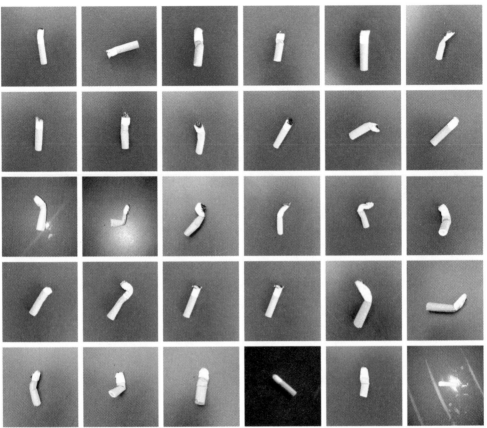

*JENNY SCHILY*'s cigarettes smoked over the course of one week

# YOU'RE LYING WITH YOUR FACE

## WRITER **AMY ROSE SPIEGEL** SPEAKS TO **MARY MANN**

**AMY:** I go camping a lot, and I'm not the kind of person who adjusts my beauty routine. I will bring pairs of fake eyelashes into the woods and layer them.

**MARY:** I want to talk about this! When did you start wearing the eyelashes, and how did you hear about them?

**AMY:** I don't know how I heard about them. I remember I was sixteen, and I started putting on individual ones with tweezers— like that you buy in the drugstore for four dollars. I put them on with this permanent glue but it rips out all your eyelashes.

**MARY:** Oh my god.

**AMY:** You have to use the strip glue, but I didn't know that at the time, so I basically just wiped out my eyelashes and they haven't come back since. But that's fine because I wear the fake ones all the time.

**MARY:** Did you freak out?

**AMY:** No, because it was like falling in love, this instantaneous . . . It was like when I dyed my hair blond. It was something I had been waffling on, then when I did it I was like, Why didn't I do this from the beginning of time? When I started with the eyelashes, I guess I had just been reading about beauty on the Internet, and it was weird because I didn't wear a lot of makeup, but I was really getting into the idea of building my face. As a teenager, you often don't like what you've been given. Around this time I also saw fake nails. I tried those, and they didn't work out; I wasn't good at them, they would fall off. But when I wore fake eyelashes it changed the way I

looked entirely, so I just never stopped. It feels like me, who I'm supposed to be. When I don't have them on I feel uncomfortable.

**MARY:** Do you sleep in them?

**AMY:** Yeah. And I go out into the world without them very, very rarely. The last time was last summer. I took them off while I was at work—I had this part-time job in a coat store—and I took them off in the bathroom and wore my face without them for, like, an hour. Then I put them back on. I was like, Uh, no. Without my eyelashes it feels like something essential is missing.

**MARY:** How long does it take to apply?

**AMY:** If I'm concentrating, probably fifteen minutes.

**MARY:** That's quick. If you walk into a drugstore, are you like, I'll just check out the eyelashes?

**AMY:** No, not unless I need them. *(pulls out three-inch piece of plastic covered in tiny clusters of lashes)* This is a packet. It's three dollars at a drugstore.

**MARY:** How long will this last you?

**AMY:** That's maybe one and a half applications. I freshen them up probably every three days. I go through them pretty quickly. The strip ones, I keep them clean and reuse them. But it's like being a smoker—you have to constantly be buying this thing.

**MARY:** Do you find the ritual part of it relaxing?

**AMY:** Now that I have a job, I find it pretty

annoying. Well, no, maybe "annoying" is the wrong word. I love putting on makeup, but I'm often rushed, so it's less of a ritual than it used to be. It's not like the means to the end is the enjoyable part. When it's over, and you're done and you're changed, and you're new—that's the good part.

MARY: What other kind of stuff do you do?

AMY: I'm really into really elaborate kinds of makeup application, like contouring, or special things you can put on your face to make your lips look more 3-D, or different kinds of eyebrow shapes. Tricks. Anything that feels like a trick. Anything that feels like you're lying with your face, I'm into that. *(laughs)*

MARY: It's like magic.

AMY: Yeah, exactly. And I really enjoy the act of sharing it—it's like sharing a secret: "Oh, if you wore lipliner . . ." People don't understand that lipliner is helpful. I like the feeling of sharing this magic.

MARY: Did your mom wear makeup, and would you watch her put it on?

AMY: My mom does wear makeup, and she does it very well, but she wears makeup in an entirely different way from how I do. My mom never really got the maximalist way that I wear makeup. She wears really tasteful mascara, and tan and pink eye shadows and really pretty lip gloss. It's very mom. Actually, she's really extremely beautiful, and is able to wear minimal makeup because that's what works for her, but that's just never been my bag. I don't like the barely there.

MARY: How does your boyfriend feel about the eyelashes?

AMY: He loves them, because he knows how important they are to me. Every other person I've been with has done that incredibly annoying thing of "Oh, you look so much better without makeup, I want to see the real you." But this is the real me. I think he understands that. He thinks I'm

beautiful without the eyelashes, but he understands that this is what I prefer, and this is how I feel comfortable. He's really respectful of that.

MARY: Did any of your friends start wearing them after you did?

AMY: No, but I did notice that it changed the way people saw me. People suddenly saw me as more attractive, which is definitely a big part of it.

MARY: Specifically dudes, or did you also get compliments from women?

AMY: Both. It was just the right thing to do for my face. I felt it immediately, then the positive reinforcement that really nailed it down.

MARY: What do you feel it communicates about you?

AMY: This really rabid femininity that I'm really into. I'm into the idea of projecting undeniable, unimpeachable femininity. That's problematic, though, because that can mean a lot of things. I'd just like to be a cartoon.

MARY: You said "cartoon" and you said "feminine." Where do those connect? Is it more of an exaggerated form? Is that what you mean?

AMY: Yeah, it's an exaggeration. I understand that not all women embrace this exaggerated, stereotypical, Western femininity, but I find a really great power in embodying that. Because I used to deny it completely. I used to not wear makeup at all, and I thought that to look like a woman is to not look smart, which I think a lot of women feel. I think to align yourself with really straightforward femininity can be a way of almost inviting people to take you less seriously. And I like to buck that. I want to be taken very seriously, but I also want to be this . . . *(gestures at herself)* you know what I mean. For me it's a steadfast desire to make it a both instead of a versus. To be both of those things is a sort of power for me.

**MARY:** Do you feel it's something you're ever going to stop?

**AMY:** No, this is forever. I cannot envision a future where I wouldn't do it.

**MARY:** What else comes with being an eyelash enthusiast? Do you look at other people's lashes?

**AMY:** Yeah, totally. There's a code. If your waitress has them, or someone on the subway has them, or someone else out there has them, you have to talk about it. You absolutely have to. It's really friendly and sweet. It's spotting out your crew.

**MARY:** How does that go down?

**AMY:** Sometimes it's subtle, but usually it's to the tune of "I like your lashes." "I like *your* lashes." Or we'll talk about it. I was interviewing some teenage girls once at an IHOP, and one of them pulled out her makeup bag and she was wearing them, and we ended up just tabling the interview and getting into our eyelashes for the rest of it. Oh! And it happened on the way home today—on the subway. You just big up somebody, like, "What's up?" *(nods chin).*

**MARY:** And you've been wearing them for how many years now?

**AMY:** Six years now. It'll be funny when I reach the period of my life where I realize that I've been wearing them for longer than I haven't. I know that it's coming, somewhere in the future. I look forward to that day.

**MARY:** Will you celebrate?

**AMY:** God, what would I do? Get some sort of eyelash cake?

**MARY:** Have an eyelash party?

**AMY:** I feel like my whole life is an eyelash party. ✕

**SURVEY** *I feel most attractive when . . .*

As dependent and shallow as this sounds, I feel most attractive when my boyfriend says I look beautiful. —JANICE CHAN • When I'm getting undressed in front of a man I'm with and he's acting all amazed and enchanted by my body. —CAILIN HILL • When I'm around someone I'm flirting with, or who I sense is attracted to me. —CAITLIN VAN DUSEN • Why am I finding this so difficult to answer? Because I don't want to admit that I feel most attractive when someone else is finding me attractive? —SUSAN SANFORD BLADES • In my husband's eyes. —LUISA B. • I feel most attractive when I'm happy with my appearance and my husband confirms his happiness with my appearance after seeing me. —REBECCA SALERNO

The time I felt the most attractive (though I attracted no one at that time) was when I was pregnant. My hair was thick and full, I didn't have to worry about having a belly! I felt fabulous. —NANCY FORDE • I've never felt as beautiful as I did in the days after giving birth to my daughter. In the days that followed, I felt transformed. I had also never felt more myself. So much about feeling beautiful revolves around transformation: the way we look in different clothes, a different hairstyle. When I became a mother, I didn't become someone else. I simply encountered a version of myself that had been hidden from me until my daughter burst into the world. —ARIA SLOSS ✕

## THE OUTFIT IN THE PHOTOGRAPH | III

*Mika Mulligan and Emily Schuller with their dates, Virginia, 2000*

**MIKA (SECOND FROM LEFT):** This photo was of our seventh-grade formal—seventh grade was the first year we had a formal dance. We were still in a phase when boys had cooties.

The vertical lines on the photo are creases from where I folded the boys out, so that only Emily and I would show. It seems like a mean thing to do, but we were just in a very awkward stage. It was awkward being put into a formal situation with my friends.

My mom got my dress for me from Express. I didn't like dresses or shopping. She would buy a few dresses, I would try them on at home and go with one of her choices, and she would return the others.

Before the dance someone's parents drove us out to eat. At first I remember feeling awkward in a dress-and-date situation. Someone broke the ice by referencing a popular commercial. We would roll down the window and take turns asking people at stoplights, "Pardon me, but do you have any Grey Poupon honey mustard?"

I did like the dress I ended up wearing, though. It was a solid green underneath with a sheer overlay that had flowers on it. It seemed simple and natural. I still try to dress simply and naturally today. I saved that dress through high school. As I grew older, so did the fit of the dress. Toward the end of high school I parted with it.

**EMILY (SECOND FROM RIGHT):** I remember getting this dress at the exchange on the air force base where my dad worked. I don't remember too much about picking it out, but since our school colors were maroon and gold, I'm sure that ended up influencing my decision.

# SUMMER DIARY

HEIDI JULAVITS

I went to my friends' house for dinner last night. These friends are family to me, but the wife and I can be affectionately hostile with each other. I am told I look thin as an accusation. She's said to me numerous times after giving me a compliment, "I hate you." I understand that she loves me when she hates me.

She is the mother of four children, and she runs a very tight domestic scene. Her children are never in stained clothing; their faces and hands are clean, their hair is brushed. Her floors are dustless and she is always folding laundry. I try to wash my children and myself before going to her house so that I don't offend her, or make her feel like she has to wash her house after we leave it. Tonight I washed my hair for the first time in a week; I didn't bother with my children's hair, because one was planning to swim at her house (she has a pond) and the other colored his white hair with a red Sharpie and it's never coming out, so what's the point?

I was running late; I didn't have time to comb my hair. I thought the huge knots wouldn't be obvious, but then I also forgot a hair elastic to bundle the mess into a bigger mess on top of my head. We ate dinner. After dessert, my friend—who was sitting at the opposite end of a long table—stood up and said, "I can't stand it anymore! I can't stand looking at that bird's nest in your hair!" She grabbed a brush and sat next to me. She isolated the biggest knot cluster and said, "Hold this!" She worked her way around my head while the rest of us talked about whatever we were talking about. I felt ashamed, happy, infantilized, adored. How long has it been since another person—aside from a hairdresser (whom I visit roughly seven times a decade) or my daughter—had brushed my hair? Decades. This ritual felt so intimate that we couldn't have done it without other people around to ease the intensity. And I know it's ridiculous to read into these things, but as she brushed my hair I felt a level of acceptance—her of me—that I've never fully experienced before, though we've been friends for ten years. She wasn't criticizing me by brushing my hair—I am forty-five years old, and might really feel insulted by her implication that I couldn't brush my own hair—she was taking care of me.

.....

Yesterday I swam the length of the harbor, and along the Reach, and around a point, and to the beach where my friends are renting a cabin. I felt every different temperature ribbon of water flow past me. I felt the ocean like a garment. I started to think of different outfits I could wear that could approximate the garment feel of the ocean when, in two weeks, I'm no longer able to swim in it because we're going back to the city. I thought about the used wool sweater I bought with the too-tight arms, and how it might feel like the cold closing in (cold can feel like oppressive warmth). I thought about the white dress Sheila and Leanne bought me at a sample sale, and how its swishy, cool

sheets feel on my legs approximated the warmest patches of water, the ones you can't believe you've found out here in the icy Atlantic.

The older I get, the less interested I am in how my clothing looks, and the more interested I am in how clothing feels on my body. And by "feel" I don't mean how I feel in clothing, as in "I feel confident"— I mean literally the feel registered by my body when I put clothing on it. Soft or warm or tickly or whatever. I've started to seek out sensory experiences in hopes that I might replicate them, or memorialize them, in clothing.

When I got to the beach, I lay front-first on the hot rocks. These rocks are the size of walnuts; they mold to your body. They felt like little suns. When my body cooled them off, I'd shift a few inches to the left and soak up the heat again. I thought, Why doesn't anyone make dresses that feel like smooth, hot rocks against your skin? This struck me as such a colossal oversight. People design clothing that makes you imagine you might be the sort of person to lie on a beach of hot rocks—a frequenter to St. Tropez— but they don't design clothing that makes you feel like you're lying on a beach or swimming in salt water. Why not? Why doesn't clothing take greater advantage of the fact that it touches your body? When I'm in the city I don't want to pretend, through my clothing, that I'm walking by the sea. I want to believe I'm swimming in it. ✕

# GENTLE, CONSERVATIVE STYLES

TAILOR **MONIKA CHHY** SPEAKS TO PHOTOGRAPHER
**ANNA CLARE SPELMAN** & TRANSLATOR *JENNIFER LIEBSCHUTZ*

**ANNA**: I'm sorry, how old are you?

**MONIKA**: Fifty-three.

**ANNA**: No you're not! *(laughs)*

**JENNIFER**: You look so young!

**MONIKA**: Ah! Thank you.

**ANNA**: So what are you considering when you're choosing the clothes you wear every day?

**MONIKA**: I like to be pretty because I'm a tailor, and I want to have a nice style so when the customers come, they'll say, "Oh, she looks nice."

**ANNA**: It's good advertising. If you look nice, then people will buy your clothes.

**JENNIFER**: And she makes all her own clothes.

**ANNA**: How long have you been a tailor?

**MONIKA**: I started when I was twenty-one, 1979. No European customers, only Khmer. The shop used to be on the riverside in Battambang. In 1981, I came here, to this shop. I've been in this shop twenty-eight years [on the bottom floor of her house in Phnom Penh].

**JENNIFER**: And when did you start to have Western customers?

**MONIKA**: 1993.

**ANNA**: That makes sense—the UN entered Cambodia in 1992.

**MONIKA**: I like cotton. And I like to wear comfortable clothes! Europe, not tight. Khmer, tight clothes.

**JENNIFER**: Do you think Western people wear clothes that are more comfortable than the clothes the Khmer wear?

**MONIKA**: Yes. Because Khmer want to be more pretty. More interesting. So tight you cannot move. But at home, Khmer people like to wear comfortable clothes.

**ANNA**: Do you think most Cambodian women think fashion is important?

**MONIKA**: They wear different clothes for different occasions: to go to a wedding, to go to the *wat*, to go to the market, to go to sleep. You need different clothes for each place.

**ANNA**: Where do people here buy their clothes?

**MONIKA**: The seller, they buy from Thailand and they sell.

**ANNA**: Oh, in the markets. Or in the stores.

**MONIKA**: Mm-hmm.

**JENNIFER**: Is fashion more important in Cambodia now than before?

**MONIKA**: Yes, because of TV. Internet.

**JENNIFER**: People take many pictures of each other now. Do people care more about fashion now, because they take so many pictures?

**MONIKA**: Yeah, I think so. They care.

**ANNA**: Is there anything else you want to say about clothes or fashion?

**MONIKA**: The older people can't change styles. They still wear gentle, conservative styles like before.

**ANNA**: Can we ask you a little bit about your business? Who works for you?

**MONIKA:** Now business is good. I want more workers, but there are no more. They do not know how to make clothes.

**JENNIFER:** So you'd have to teach them.

**MONIKA:** Now many people work in large factory because so easy, easy, easy, easy.

**JENNIFER:** They don't have the skills to tailor.

**MONIKA:** Yes. And you have to think a lot to do this job. Many styles.

**ANNA:** I see, so it's difficult to find people to work here. Because it's a difficult job.

**MONIKA:** Yes.

**JENNIFER:** And because they go to Thailand or Korea to work, or they work in the factories.

**MONIKA:** The last one, she married—left. ✕

## "SKIRT"

*Children's section of a bookstore. Woman crouches down, reshelving books. She wears a tight cotton skirt with a print that from a distance looks like a drawing made with a pen but is actually sewn-on pieces of silk-screened fabric.*

**STARLEE:** I like your skirt.

**WOMAN:** Oh, thanks.

**STARLEE:** Did you design it?

**WOMAN:** Oh, no. I wish I could design stuff like this.

**STARLEE:** It looks like your tattoo.

**WOMAN:** Oh? *(looks confused, since the tattoo is of a rose and the design on her skirt is of birds)*

**STARLEE:** I don't know. What are they—birds?

**WOMAN:** Yeah, a bird here and then a bird right here.

**STARLEE:** It's nice.

**WOMAN:** Thanks. ✕

# CLOSETS

*"Trying to describe my closet stresses me out."*—AVA V.

**MELISSA SMITH** My closet is like a museum. Everything is in its place. I arrange my tops by sleeve length (spaghetti straps, tanks, short sleeves, quarter-length, long sleeves). The dresses follow and are arranged in a similar order. Skirts follow dresses, short to long. Once this system is in place, I organize each top by color of the rainbow. It helps me keep track of my clothes. I know when a friend has a piece of mine or something is in the dirty pile. It also helps me when I'm half awake in the morning, trying to get ready for work in under ten minutes.

**JOWITA BYDLOWSKA** Every few months I go through my closet and get rid of items I haven't worn in more than a year. The exceptions are clothes that are too pretty or carry a sentimental value or are what I call "clothes I'd like my future daughter to have." (I don't have a daughter.)

**RACHEL PERRY WELTY** My friend's grandmother used to say, "It owes me nothing," when she was ready to divest herself of an item in her closet.

**FARAH BASHIR** I have multiple jeans because they never go out of style, and jeans are a "safe option" when one lives in South Asia. I also have multiple sleeveless tops, as I love my shoulders, but for the last year I have hardly had the "societal permission" to wear those. I have to depend on occasions when I go out with my husband to enjoy wearing those tops. Last week, I gave so many

clothes away to my maid for her daughters as I couldn't afford to just look at them sitting unused in my closet, making me feel miserable and helpless and without any control over the basic right and freedom to wear what I want, when I want.

**ROXANE GAY** I'll stand before my closet and look at all the clothes I'm too shy to wear, and pretend for about three minutes I might do something different, and then reach for one of the ten or so outfits I wear regularly.

**CATHERINE MAROTTA** I'm a compulsive Goodwill donor. If something has hung in my closet unworn for a month, it's out the door. I have been caught donating my friends' items that they have left at my house.

**BETH FOLLETT** I have a vintage clothes rack, which I found one garbage night in the Annex in Toronto. Beloved clothes in my wardrobe were found in other people's garbage also.

**CAITLIN ANN HARRINGTON** I have a clothes rack. Everything that isn't on a hanger is lying in messy piles below the hanging clothes. I hate doing laundry, so I just constantly buy more underwear and rewear my clothes until they smell, are stained, or stretch out. I think not washing clothes might be good for them, though. Not sure.

**NAN KEVIN GELHARD** My daughter-in-law said, "Why are you keeping clothes you don't like

427

and don't wear? It is okay to admit mistakes." And we cleared out the closets.

**KIRSTIN CORCORAN** The way I dress, along with my occupation, is a direct representation of me. I never wanted to have a separate wardrobe for work, so there is no differential between what I wear to work and what I would wear after six p.m. or on the weekend.

**NINA MOOG** I am thinking of the chair in your room that acquires the function of the wardrobe, where you pile dresses, shirts, sweaters, and pants as you rummage through your closet to find an item. I noted the chairdrobe in almost every bedroom I entered throughout university.

**AMANDA MILLER** My closet is so large it could be a bathroom. My bathroom is so large it could be a bedroom. My apartment has no bedroom, though, so the closet is host to many things besides clothes and shoes and jackets and boots. I'm a Virgo, therefore there is a place for everything and everything is in its place. I could tie a blindfold across my face, switch off the lights, and remove a specific garment from my closet without ruffling the adjacent blouses.

**SASHA GORA** I grew up with older cousins, which meant I was rich in hand-me-downs. I remember being in elementary school and counting how many bottoms I had in my closet. This was the nineties, so leggings counted as pants. I counted more than sixty bottoms and was shocked and impressed. I brought it up the next day in the schoolyard. My intention wasn't to brag (at least not to brag too much), but my claim was met with grave suspicion. My friends thought I was lying, something I didn't realize at first. But then a few days later, when I was wearing the same pair of pants for I guess too many days in a row, a friend cruelly asked why I

was wearing them again when I had sixty-plus options.

**KELLEY HOFFMAN** While I was in New York, I thought the designer clothes I'd bought were beautiful. But then I'd see these pieces that seemed so nice trampled on the floor at the Barneys Warehouse Sale, or I'd find them being sold on eBay for $30 a few years later, or they would sit in my closet until I started to notice that maybe they weren't that well made despite the label. You get tricked by the magic of it.

**CARRIE MURPHY** My grandmother had this big, custom-made octagonal closet, painted bright fuchsia pink, stacked with hat boxes and glove boxes and clothes from the 1960s. It smelled like her, it was pretty like her, and it was my favorite spot in the house. When I knew her, my grandmother wore silk blouses, lots of gold jewelry, and comfortable poly-blend pants, but her closets were full of the more dramatic clothes she used to wear: paisley caftans, a suede coat with fur cuffs that she had promised to my older cousin (damn!), pillbox hats, everything you can think of. I idolized her, so you can imagine what it was like for a young girl to have free rein in the magical closets of a woman she loved and admired.

**SARAH MANGUSO** My clothes are divided into inside and outside wardrobes. I teach one day a week, so when I use my outside wardrobe, it's an occasion.

**THANDO LOBESE** I clear out my closet when I feel claustrophobic. Then I feel so light. It might feel like you're losing your identity, because you've worn this dress so many times, but now you have to move on to another level. Instead of dragging the whole closet with you. ✕

# A "MUFF DOG"

GILDA HABER

Sumptuary laws have, throughout history, been used to permit, forbid, or enforce the wearing of clothing or identifying marks among specific groups of people, including women, the lower class, and minorities. Sumptuary laws were (and still are) enforced, and transgressions against them are punished, but women often have found ingenious ways to circumvent them.

The Greek statesman Solon, in the sixth century B.C.E., ordered that women not wear more than three garments at a time in public.

In 215 B.C.E., a law was passed that forbade Roman women from possessing more than half an ounce of gold. In Florence in 1536, peasant women were prohibited from wearing any gold.

Julius Caesar prohibited women from wearing pearls. In Venice in 1306, a sumptuary law forbade women from wearing pearl ornaments in their hair. Servants couldn't wear pearls at all.

Nobles' belts were heavily jeweled in Europe. In the eighteenth century, watches were hung on these belts or girdles. Women were forbidden to carry gold or silver watches on their belts, and in Nuremberg, they were forbidden to carry more than one watch.

In sixteenth-century England, Queen Elizabeth I permitted starched ruffs, a new invention, to nobles only. The size of the ruff depended on the wearer's rank. Royal guards closely monitored the use of ruffs.

European lower-class women were forbidden to wear linen. When linen became easily available, the rank at which linen was permitted was lowered. When muslin was invented, only upper-class women were permitted to wear it, and it was forbidden to the lower class.

*-*-*-*-*-*-*-*-*-*-*-*-*-*-*-*-*-*-*-*-*-*-*-*-*-*-*-*-*-*-*-*-*-*-*-*

Silkworms were smuggled from China to Byzantium around 552. In fourteenth-century Nuremberg, women were not allowed to wear silk garments. So they wore silk linings. They were then forbidden to wear silk linings.

In the sixteenth century, the French king Henri III allowed only the highest-ranking female aristocrats to carry a fur muff. Other women had to make do with velvet. A lower-ranking woman might therefore wear a velvet muff, inside of which she carried, for extra warmth, a tiny dog, which was called a "muff dog."

In eighteenth-century Bern, some maidservants were permitted to wear a fur cap, but only if it was made of skunk.

Venetian aristocrats of the fifteenth century forbade women to ride in carriages. Women countered by wearing *zoccoli*, platform shoes that raised them as many as twenty inches from the street mud, but wearers of these shoes required slaves on each side to support them. A sumptuary law then forbade the use of *zoccoli*, piously claiming that pregnant women might fall. However, women had the last word. They requested that their *zoccoli* be buried with them, a symbol of freedom.

In medieval England, lower-class females more than fifteen years old had to wear dun, brown colors. Later, Queen Elizabeth I forbade the new crimson to all but nobles and cardinals.

In Zurich in 1390 and 1744, laws forbade lower-class women from showing more than two inches of skin, especially at their throat or shoulders, so as not to tempt men of the upper classes.

Nobles were absent from their wives for long periods of time, carousing at castles, in debauchery, off hunting, or at war. Many were killed in battle, or in jousts or tournaments. Noble wives were locked into chastity belts during their husbands' frequent absences. These often caused infection, since the women could not clean the vagina. Inbreeding between nobles may also have reduced fertility and increased infant mortality. Many noble houses died out for want of heirs.

Male noble rulers passed sumptuary laws and appropriated for themselves all innovations, such as starched ruffs, watches (miniature clocks), and the color crimson, forbidding their use to others. One innovation they did not appropriate was gunpowder, as it was considered dishonorable to royalty, who honored face-to-face fighting. This, in part, caused their demise and the rise of the wealthier among lower classes.

For the most part, sumptuary laws on clothing are not currently practiced. However, ranking by clothing may have been transferred to ranking in bureaucratic location and office furnishings. A high-ranking man, particularly in private companies, will have a fancier office location, better furnishings, and a better-marked parking space than women of the same rank. Female colleagues, grateful for their own high rank, will rarely complain about this discrimination, or about their lower pay for doing the same job as a man, or poorer working conditions, even in our society, which is proud of its equality and democracy. ✕

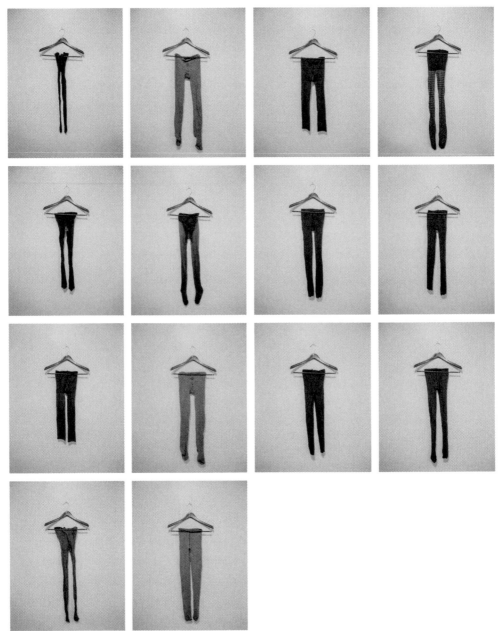

*KIM BOST*'s tights

# COVET DIARY: REGARDING THE DRESS OF ANOTHER

LEANNE SHAPTON

I saw a dress on a woman at a party and wanted it for myself. It was a long, printed dress. It looked comfortable and light and cool and inscrutably chic. When I asked the woman about the dress she said it was Isabel Marant. She said it sort of apologetically, acknowledging with a faint, resigned smirk that while it looked vintage—could have been '70s Yves Saint Laurent or handmade—by being off-the-rack designer it was less interesting, cheating somehow. The fact that this was communicated so quickly and silently was interesting. It must have been then that I realized that I, too, might one day own the dress.

Later that day I was with a friend, C, and saw the woman again and spoke to her. C knew her a bit. She lived in the country but worked as a stylist in the city. I admired her hair: worn loose, flecked with gray, and her manner: warm, thoughtful, sincere. She wore no makeup, and the dress, which was sacklike, lent her a modesty I liked. We spoke about our children. Then, in a lull in the conversation, I came back to the dress, complimenting it again. She nodded, knowing. Then I did something that surprised me: I leaned down and picked up the edge of her skirt and touched it, marveling aloud at the light, smooth fabric.

I have never touched another woman's dress like that before. A fur sleeve once, but I've never had that grasping, clutching impulse. I wondered if it had something to do with my post-pregnancy confusion about my body, its new aches and shapes. My breasts are mysterious, they have moods and urgency and look like sea creatures. My body gives off new smells

433

and I picture an orangutan when I think of my nursing posture. Though my pre-baby weight is within spitting distance, my relationship to clothes has shifted. I don't know quite who I am anymore, and yet I am more defined than ever. In the past, when I looked at clothes, I'd imagine a version of myself in them. Some part of me has always thought I could wear almost anything and look good, but photographs of me always disappoint. The dawning knowledge of my asymmetries and lumps, my perceived flaws, has been somehow kept at bay until now. Now I see them and accept them, I'm just not sure how to dress them.

I touched this woman's dress and marveled, then the moment passed, the sun went down, I changed my daughter's diaper and headed home. A week and a half later, after thinking about the dress in an abstract way on a regular basis, I typed "Isabel Marant dress" into eBay. After a few pages of scrolling I found it. It was $360, marked down from $1,200. I checked the return policy—fourteen days—and bought it.

I felt weird after clicking BUY IT NOW. The whole process went so fast. Seeing the dress on another woman, ascertaining its provenance, touching it, then going after it. I'd never bought something like that before, never had that "It could be mine" feeling about the clothes of a woman I'd met. I had that feeling after seeing things in print or on people I did not know, but I'd always felt it was only fair to let a woman, from vaguely one's own social circle, own the dress if she found it first. Maybe it's my competitive-

The coveted dress.

swimming background, but I go around thinking in terms of firsts. It's only fair.

Was it to do with childbirth, this slackening of my own rules? After depending so heavily on other women, more than I'd ever had to before, was I coming to realize how shared an experience mothering was, and so didn't feel so bad copying another one? I've always been interested in how women mimic and copy one another. I'd copied things I'd admired before: cumulative lessons in being myself. I copied the way a friend placed tulips in a beer stein in 1993, the way another woman sitting in front of me on an airplane wore men's trousers in 2001 (it turned out to be Phoebe Philo). The way yet another said "Please" when ordering in a restaurant in 2007.

I wondered if my feelings also had something to do with admitting I want something. I've struggled with admitting what I want most of my life, not admitting until the last possible moment that I wanted a child. Admitting I flat-out wanted this dress was new to me. I was nervous.

When the dress arrived I laid the small package on the bed and looked at it. I still felt it was someone else's discovery. I wonder if the lovely woman had any sense of how much covetousness her dress inspired, that in fact I would hunt down and capture her dress. Would I have still wanted it if she'd been unfriendly? I wondered if men did this to other men's women. Or if women did this to other women's men.

I opened the package. All folded up, the dress looked deflated. On the woman's body it had been large, airy, and flowing. The fabric was very fine and thin, so the entire thing squashed down to a little pancake. I fluffed it out. It was still great. I put it on. I loved it anew.

I kept the tags on in case I changed my mind. But the next morning, in a rush to get to the passport office, I threw it on. It felt soft and cool against my skin. The cut felt above par for so uncomplicated-looking a garment; there wasn't too much material across the shoulders, chest, and arms, but plenty from the armpits down. I

---

**SURVEY** *Please describe your body.*

I have an amazing body! I won the genetic lottery. Do I sound like a horrible asshole? I don't mean to be a bitch, I mean to be infinitely grateful for the body I was born with. I am tall and have a tiny little rib cage, nice hips, perfect breasts on the large side, small waist, long legs. I am curvy and feminine. I do struggle with being heavier now that I'm a mom with kids, and I miss being thirty pounds lighter, as I was in my twenties, and I now have a dimply thing happening in many locations that is pretty horrifying in a bathing suit, and sure, I am critical of many features. But really, I have nothing to complain about, and I thank God for this body every day. —VALERIE STIVERS • Small and strong. —AMY BRILL • My husband says I still have good-looking legs. —CAROLYN F. • I have a scar running down the left side of my face from a traumatic train-hopping accident. —SARAH GERARD • Feminine. —ANNA WEBBER • I am short and of average weight. I try every day not to obsess over it or my diet. I like to run a few times a week so I can eat what I want and not give it too much thought. — KERRY CARDOZA. • I have fairly pronounced muscles, presumably from my field-dwelling ancestors. My

435

was worried about the size, but it fit perfectly. I slung my baby into her carrier and set off. By the time I reached the passport office I was sweating and my daughter had drooled down my chest. The dress was giving off a "new dress" scent: something gluey; sizing and thread and tarpaulin. I worried about my daughter sucking on it and moved it away from her face, then worried about her breathing in factory fumes and regretted I hadn't washed it before wearing it, something I usually do with my new clothes.

After the passport office, I walked to my designer friend R's studio to pick up a tape recorder. We stood chatting and passing around the baby. While I was talking to another woman, I felt R touch the dress. When I got home I washed the dress, then put it straight back on.

I wore it the next day to get an ice cream cone with a friend. And the day after that, to a show in Brooklyn and a late dinner.

On both of these occasions I felt good. The good of knowing I had on something that was attractive to me. It didn't matter if I thought I looked attractive in it. In fact, I think I looked merely okay in the dress. I wonder what wearing a designer piece bestows on the wearer, because what I was feeling I can describe only as designer security. I was leaning on the fact that I'd paid a lot for this security. The "thingness" or value of the dress made me feel protected and attractive in a lazy way—the mass security of doing what other people do, or buying into the "Expensive is good" mindset. I suppose I expected the dress to do some of the heavy lifting.

The specifics of the dress: It is a long-sleeved, printed dress, made of a silk and cotton blend. The colors are olive greens and navy blues and the print is imperfect and messy, an Indian/Liberty pattern that includes tiny pomegranates and vines. There are a number of pin-tucks across the shoulders in the back and along the collarbone, making the top part tidily but comfortably tailored. The dress unbuttons to the belly and has a tiny frilled collar. The sleeves have

---

sister and I both have bendy legs (hyperextended), which are often caught in photos we send to each other. Self-love and good food is the right path, surely. —ALEXA S. • My body can do things, it can run, and lift, and push, and pull, all of which usually makes me pretty happy with my body. —CAROLANN MADDEN • Tall, slender, a pleasant derriere. —JENNA KNOBLACH • Old. —PAT JONES • My body resembles a Coke bottle, the three-liter size. It used to be like the old small glass bottles, not far from the 36-24-36 ideal of the fifties. I now resemble something closer to a nude bather from an eighteenth-century painting. —DEBORAH KIRSHNER • Sometimes I think my body looks like a T. rex. I have a small upper body, small breasts, small waist, and a decent-size butt and thigh region. I'm not very tall (five-four). I think I have a slightly athletic build, pretty curvy, fair skin. —LINDSAY ALLISON RUOFF • I have lost my girlish figure. "My chest has fallen into my drawers," as they say up north. My flat rib cage has gone, my waist, too. I need to sit most of the time. It's a long time since I wore high heels: joint replacements make them unsafe and uncomfortable. I seem to have assumed someone else's body, one that is sagging and stooped.

short, buttoning cuffs. It has two hip pockets and a drawstring. It delivers a demure, feminine, slightly hippie feeling and falls to just above the ankles. It's sensuous, with its almost transparent fabric. It has a quality I love in clothes—of being a platonic ideal of an image of something, an illustration. It evokes David Hamilton photographs, Wales in the '60s, Woodstock, early Laura Ashley, libraries and flea markets. There is something gauzy and French '70s about it, like it should smell a little, and warmly, wonderfully, of b.o.

There is reliable drama to the idea of two women wearing the same dress. It's considered a faux pas, documented in movies and stories as a mortifying event, and more recently and efficiently in the cruel "Who Wore It Best?" features in celebrity weeklies. A woman need only own the same expensive dress as another, and wear it weeks and miles apart, to be shamed in a photographic comparison.

What I felt in the dress was a deep dread of running into the woman I had coveted the dress on, and also C, who was with me when I first saw it. It's hard to explain this dread other than that of being caught red-handed, of appearing to not have my own mind when it comes to dressing. As these things go, on the fourth day of possessing the dress I ran into C at a coffee shop where I was meeting another friend, A.

When I saw C across the room I felt a jolt of panic before relief that, finally, I could make my confession. I pointed at the dress as she approached and said "I found it!"

She said in reply: "You found it." Then told me she had looked for it online for my birthday. She touched it and asked if she could borrow it someday. We told A about the dress at the party. She admired it and declared that it looked perfect and she wanted it and was going to look for it, too.

That night, I wore it to a farewell party for a friend, P. She and I had had a strained relationship for the past year, and in deciding what to wear that night I chose the dress as a sort of protection.

---

—ANITA ABRAMS • Waistless. I am straight with overall softness, which translates as not one particularly slim or special body part. —AGNES BARLEY • When I was a child, people said "big-boned," but I knew what they meant. I grew up to have an hourglass shape—big bust and hips, small waist. I like my shape and think that it, in part, explains my love of vintage clothing, as it is often designed for women of this shape. How I perceive my body changes depending on my mood. Sometimes I'm surprised to see my body when I'm naked and look at myself in the mirror. It looks so small and pale to be the vessel for all my wild feelings. —VANESSA BERRY • It's never been in better shape. —SARAH MOSES • Tall and slim with great curves and proportions. Flaws include visible varicose veins on the surface of my legs and a dimple from a partial mastectomy in 2008 due to a breast infection. —ANN BOGLE • Small-framed, sloping shoulders, swan neck. Sort of lumpy thighs, awkward knees, coarse hair, nice feet, on the slender side but never quite in shape. —KATHARINE HARGREAVES • On a harsh day, I describe my body as a hot dog on a stick. —ANNA COSTLEY • My back has scars. When I see other women's backs with such beautiful smooth skin, I feel like an alien. —ALISSA NUTTING • Five-eight.

I went to the party carrying my daughter in a sling, which provided a little more armor, too. The heat of her little body was comforting, and the thin material of the dress kept the inevitable sweatiness manageable. On arriving, P told me that a man I'd been involved with ten years before would not come to her party if I was there, that he was waiting until I left. On top of the existing tension between P and me, this cast an uneasy feeling over the evening. My daughter fell asleep against my tense chest. I stayed for an hour longer, growing defiantly aware of some tension my presence was creating. When I saw P and another woman look at me and whisper into each other's ears, I left, feeling downcast. Walking home, I texted two of my friends, who were in Korea, and told them I missed them. When I got home I bathed my daughter and put her in her crib, took off the dress, and pumped breast milk.

The next day involved a long drive, stopping to breast-feed at a gas station. I put on the dress once more. My husband and

I met a painter friend, J, for lunch, and we talked about discernment and nostalgia. I told him about the dress, that I was disappointed I didn't uncover it in a vintage store but bought it for its approximate qualities to a perfect version of a dress you'd find in a vintage store. He immediately said the colors of the dress were ideal for me. As we were leaving, he touched the dress and said it really was a very good dress.

We arrived at a friend's house in the early evening, in the rain. By this time the dress felt like a part of me. I'd forgotten about it, which I took to be a sign of its true integration into my wardrobe, the way that, in "Bernice Bobs Her Hair," F. Scott Fitzgerald has a character say something like: If you are conscious of what you are wearing at a party, you made the wrong choice. The material soothed me, and the cool, wet breeze blew the skirt out in gentle billows. I knew it smelled of milk and baby vomit and me and car, but I wore it for a few hours more, dropping some pulled pork and slaw onto it, finally taking it off for a bath before bed. ✕

---

Medium build. At its best—lean, fit, and muscular. —METIS RYER • I'm seventy-five percent legs. My butt likes to take up some space and my waist is narrow. I have spiderlike arms, which I've always liked, and breasts that are larger than a pair you can cup. —SZILVIA MOLNAR • I have a protruding stomach. I do not exercise intentionally. My body is nice, my skin is smooth. I have an autoimmune illness of the eyes called uveitis and it requires the use of steroids pills and immunosuppressants. These have physical ramifications such as weight gain, glassy-looking eyes, hair loss on the head, and hair growth on the face. Perfection. —SHALINI ROY • I have one bunion, the other one was removed in January. My fingers are very long and crooked. — KRISTINA ANNE GYLLING • Underweight. Short-torsoed. Long-limbed. I slouch, and apparently when I walk, I bob like a cobra snake. —NATASHA HUNT • My husband sees his body as himself, and as a tool to do what he wants to do. I see my body as a case for my self, which lives inside my body. I think of my body as my adversary, something that often keeps me from doing what I want to do. —REBECCA SCHERM • Not bad for an old broad. —LAUREN REITER ✕

# MESSAGES

*"Clothes seem like literature to me. The text of a dream."* —EILEEN MYLES

LARA AVERY My mom and I are in Kohl's discount department store in Topeka, Kansas, the only place she would buy my clothes that wasn't a secondhand store. I am twelve or thirteen.

ME: I want to get this spaghetti-strap tank top.

MOM: Why?

ME: Because everyone wears spaghetti straps and I like them.

MOM: Spaghetti straps send people the wrong message.

ME: What message?

MOM: That you want them to see your skin.

ME: . . .

MOM: Do you want people to see your skin?

ME: I don't know.

MOM: My mother always told me that if you can't wear it to church, don't wear it all.

ME: Fine. Whatever. They're just clothes. Not messages.

MOM: You're getting older. They're messages.

NATALIA ELTSOVA Sometimes you can see women who wear something that doesn't give you any information about the body, you can hardly say if a person is fit or not, or what shape. I pay attention to how others dress. It doesn't mean you can judge a book by its cover, but you can make some conclusions about a personality.

ERIKA THORMAHLEN I heard Maria Shriver give an interview once about her late mother, Eunice Kennedy Shriver. Her mother always picked her up from school in a convertible with the top down. Her mother would wear a cashmere cardigan, looking very classic New England. But the twist was that Eunice always had all these handwritten notes pinned to her sweater, things she didn't want to forget, to-do lists. I greatly admired that anecdote, its mix of timeless style with a haphazardness and air of no-nonsense practicality. There was nothing curated about those notes, but it was the most memorable image of a woman's style I ever heard.

BETH FOLLETT Before I started my publishing company I worked as a therapist, most often with women survivors of sexual and other forms of physical abuse. During my practice I saw hundreds of women who carried deep shame in their bodies, broadcasting that shame and confusion in their gestures, habits, and ever-changing manner of dress. I believe all women carry shame to some degree, and it has been my practice to explore where and how mine resides in or moves through my living body. I would rather not hide the facts of my living self through tricks.

SADIE STEIN The politics of a clothing exchange with women are complex. *Here, this will look good on you,* someone might say. But they are also saying, *I am rejecting this. And I am choosing what you wear, and what the world sees.* Now that I think about it, although I always take large armfuls of clothing to swaps, I never come away with much. I've never found it as satisfying as being able to choose who gets what, deciding what will flatter them, or what, in my opinion, they should be wearing.

**CARISSA HALSTON** My tattoos have proven more valuable the longer I've had them. What they've meant to me has changed as I've aged, but they remind me of who I am, which is like finding a cheerful letter you wrote to your future self.

**AMY ROSE SPIEGEL** My boyfriend drew a heart on my thigh in black pen.

**EMILY BROTMAN** I was smart enough to understand what all the girls in my school were saying with their mismatched sneakers and racerback bras, but I didn't have the means, the mother, the magazines, to ask them, in that same silent language, "Am I cool, too?"

**JENNIFER ARMBRUST** I feel most attractive in clothing that fits well, wears easily, and conveys the desired emotion. I feel best when the clothing acts as a second skin, a visual representation of my inner landscape.

**AMY BONNAFFONS** My mom grew up in the South with the dictum "You can tell a lady by her hairbrush," and though she escaped most of the trappings of her upbringing, she continued to carry the idea that it was some kind of moral failure to look slovenly. The idea was: It's inconsiderate to dress sloppily, because other people have to look at you.

**REN JENDER** When the war in Iraq started, I went to a protest march and decorated the back of my black vinyl motorcycle jacket with yellow electrical tape so it became a sign—PEACE LOVE AND PVC. I kept the tape on the jacket for years afterward. I think I figured I would take off the tape when the war ended, but I never did.

**EVA SCHLESINGER** After I was sexually harassed at a job, I made a shirt that said "Stop sexual harassment now!" I enjoyed wearing it to my place of employment.

**CARLA DU PREE** I would never want to return to the civil unrest of the '70s, way too horrific to relive those critical times, but I remember wearing my black-fist earrings, and loose-fitting gauze tops and embroidered tote bags, and the freedom that came with being different and stating poetically what was with an armful of bracelets and puka-shell necklaces and bolder shoes.

**TANIA VAN SPYCK** Charm is the antithesis of cool. We lost a lot when we lost charm. Cool is dull because it's pretty uniform. Charm is that specialness—the little extra thing, the detail and thought. Charm can be sexy, but not always. It's about interest in things and details and creativity and a playfulness with taste. There is so much detail to the best items.

**JOHANNA ADORJÁN** I used to be a blonde for some years. I got the idea when I first saw the video for "Don't Speak." Then I wrote a book about my grandparents, Holocaust survivors from Hungary who late in their lives killed themselves. Typical first book: you investigate your own roots, wanting to understand where you come from. Halfway through, I suddenly decided to go back to my natural, darker hair color. I do see a connection. ✕

# WEAR AREAS | ALICIA BERNLOHR

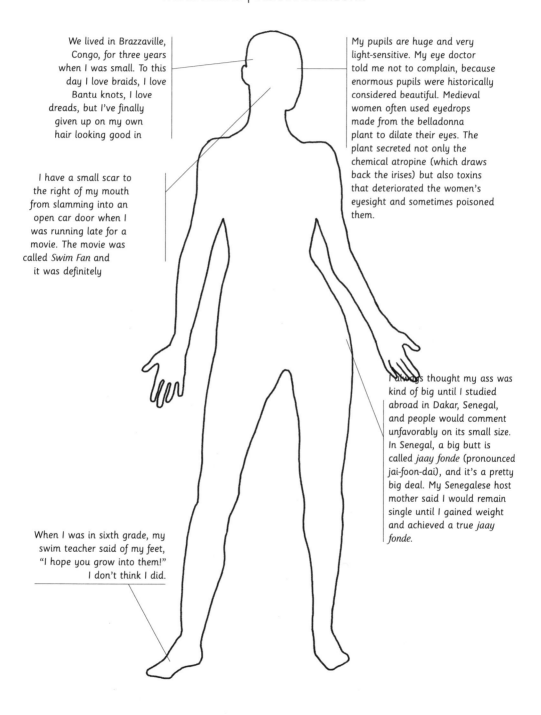

We lived in Brazzaville, Congo, for three years when I was small. To this day I love braids, I love Bantu knots, I love dreads, but I've finally given up on my own hair looking good in

I have a small scar to the right of my mouth from slamming into an open car door when I was running late for a movie. The movie was called *Swim Fan* and it was definitely

My pupils are huge and very light-sensitive. My eye doctor told me not to complain, because enormous pupils were historically considered beautiful. Medieval women often used eyedrops made from the belladonna plant to dilate their eyes. The plant secreted not only the chemical atropine (which draws back the irises) but also toxins that deteriorated the women's eyesight and sometimes poisoned them.

I always thought my ass was kind of big until I studied abroad in Dakar, Senegal, and people would comment unfavorably on its small size. In Senegal, a big butt is called *jaay fonde* (pronounced jai-foon-dai), and it's a pretty big deal. My Senegalese host mother said I would remain single until I gained weight and achieved a true *jaay fonde*.

When I was in sixth grade, my swim teacher said of my feet, "I hope you grow into them!" I don't think I did.

*RACHEL HURN*'s shirts stolen from her boyfriend

# AN OUTFIT FOR A TURTLE

COSTUME DESIGNER **THANDO LOBESE** SPEAKS TO **HEIDI JULAVITS**

**HEIDI**: So you grew up in your Xhosa village playing with only boy cousins. Did you dress like a boy when you played with them, and does that still influence how you dress?

**THANDO**: Of course I did dress like a boy, you know? We all used to play athletics, go cycling together, running and playing crazy sports, so I had to look like one of them. I was the only girl, so I had to be tough. It does influence my style of clothing. It has for many years.

**HEIDI**: How so? Do you feel more comfortable if you're wearing a tough outfit?

**THANDO**: I don't know if I should call it tough, but even with heels, the masculine side comes out. It has influenced me big-time. Even the way I dance. I used to do break dancing.

**HEIDI**: Really? I guess you can't wear a dress for that.

**THANDO**: No. You know how girls move, like the video chicks nowadays? I don't really move like that. I have a certain way of moving because I'm comfortable. I don't want to attract unnecessary attention, I guess, from the male side.

**HEIDI**: How do you move your body that doesn't attract the "male side"?

**THANDO**: Well, less playing with my ass and my boobs.

**HEIDI**: You don't wear clothes that accentuate your ass and your boobs so much. Or do you?

**THANDO**: Of course I do! But in a way that

I'm comfortable. So as much as you can see everything, it's very comfortable.

**HEIDI**: So this is your outfit for—you're in Johannesburg and you're going to work?

**THANDO**: Yeah. I want to be able to run if I want to run. And because I work in theater, when we have setups, I have to be able to go onstage and not get hurt. I can't wear heels in the theater.

**HEIDI**: Do you ever wear heels?

**THANDO**: Yeah, I do.

**HEIDI**: I was trying to figure out why I don't like to wear heels—and I do wear them, I do—and I realized it's because I can't run if someone's chasing me! I feel unsafe.

**THANDO**: I can dance in heels, I don't mind. And there are moments when I go to a club and I'm not wearing heels and it changes dynamics. When I'm dancing with flat shoes, I feel like I'm too short and I can't move properly.

**HEIDI**: I want to talk a little about your mom, because you mentioned that she wanted you to be more girly and feminine, and you didn't want to be.

**THANDO**: I was born in Johannesburg, and until I was three, she was always there. Then she took me to the country because she had to work. So I was brought up by my grandparents and my cousins and everyone else. She used to be a model, so you can understand how she dressed: she was a lady. When we went to live with her again, my brother and I—at the time I was eight—we were not used to the lifestyle that she lived. We were carefree, and then suddenly, whoa, there were responsibilities, and you can't do this, you can't do that. She worked in a rape clinic, and at the time you were told, "You can't play with boys like this." Now it was: Don't sit like that with your legs open, sit like a lady, do this and that. And I didn't like it. My mother was more of a lady than I was. She still is. But I'm starting to appreciate my womanhood. It happened at a time when she'd lost hope, if I can put it that way.

**HEIDI:** Right. How old were you when she finally lost hope?

**THANDO:** I don't know, she never said it out loud.

**HEIDI:** You could just see the hopelessness in her eyes. Just total hopelessness.

**THANDO:** Yeah, I could. I'd go visit her wearing All Stars, and very dirty, and she's like, "Oh god, no no no no, you must wash your shoes, please, the least you must do is wash your shoes." And now when I go to see her, she's so happy. I'm also glad I didn't change because of what she wanted, it had to come from within—that's where accountability comes. The beautiful thing is, we somehow have the same sense of style.

**HEIDI:** Really!

**THANDO:** I know! And now she's not so hectically into being a lady and glamorous and all of that. Me, my image, it changes all the time. I have different hairstyles, I don't know how many hairstyles I've done. When I'm done with a show, it just happens. I change my hair color or dread it or whatever. And each time I change my hair, I change my wardrobe. Because I couldn't have silver hair and wear a pink shirt, you know? It wouldn't make sense! So I'm always aware of the colors. When I had silver hair, I used to wear mostly black, and it also looked very nice with white shirts,

neutral colors. Then I had red hair. It's just playing around, and I like it.

**HEIDI:** Let's talk about costumes. How do you go about designing a costume for a play?

**THANDO:** I have to read the script, of course, and understand the character. What I like to do with my research—I like to see the person playing that character, to meet them in person. Or if I don't meet them in person, if I have their photograph, I can actually tell the personality and then I can combine it with the character, and then design around those elements. So it helps to see, Okay, Heidi is skinny, Heidi is fat, Heidi is tall, Heidi has dark eyes—those things really help.

**HEIDI:** That's why costume design is so fascinating, because it takes what you do every day, to your own body, to the actual art level.

**THANDO:** The most amazing thing was having to convince people, This is what you're going to wear. It's no use if you can't convince actors as a costume designer. The first production, my budget was nothing, it was three hundred dollars.

**HEIDI:** For how many costumes?

**THANDO:** Six people. I had to make something, create my own tribe, people who live in the desert and then they go search for water. I decided, I'll take old T-shirts—white—and dip them into dye and make them look old. Then I made these . . . not panties, not napkins, something like that.

**HEIDI:** Really short shorts?

**THANDO:** I'll show you. They were like panties, but I made extra fabric, so they can play with them. For the girls, I was happy they had small boobs. I wanted them to wear spoons to cover their boobs. So I made them wear spoons.

**HEIDI:** They could have worn ladles, if they had big boobs.

**THANDO:** *(laughs)* And then I used leather

straps, I made bras from that. I cut their hair in different styles. That's how I created the tribe. It was so beautiful that I could convince them, and they were so easygoing and excited about it. I don't think I've had any moments when people were not happy with their garments.

**HEIDI:** Would you ever wear anything that you designed? Do you ever design things for people who are in plays and then think, Oh, I would actually love to have a spoon bikini.

**THANDO:** I think I . . . would? Let me see . . . It goes the other way around. I've had people from other productions say, "Oh Thando, you must make this for me." A writer came to see a show, and she was like, "I want you to make that outfit for me." It was actually an outfit for a turtle.

**HEIDI:** *(laughs)* Did she know it was for a turtle?

**THANDO:** Yes, I made a jumpsuit, green, the color of a turtle, and then I made layers, for the hands and for feet. And then I made a backpack—the shell—and pleats, to accentuate the shell.

**HEIDI:** It pops out!

**THANDO:** You couldn't see any of her fingers. I made a cowl neck, so when she's sitting you see just the eyes.

**HEIDI:** I would wear it.

**THANDO:** Yeah, you would love it!

**HEIDI:** Do you help people choose "costumes" for their everyday lives?

**THANDO:** *(laughs)* Well, I look at people, you know? My friend's boyfriend, I could tell his style. He loves leather jackets and has his own style. He only wears black. I was shopping with my friend and I said, "Oh, those shoes would look so good on him," you know—because I do that every day. I don't think she liked that. Ever since that experience, I keep my mouth shut. ✕

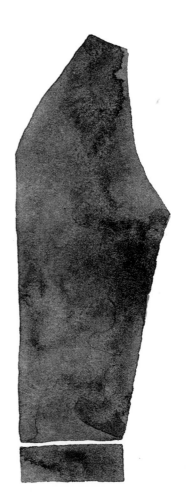

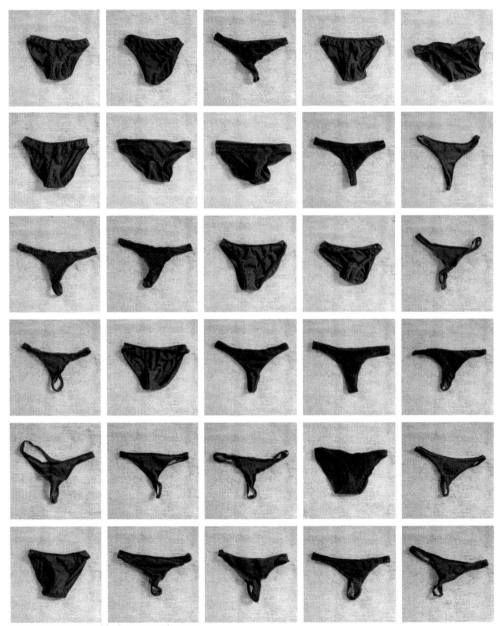

*CONSTANCE STERN*'s black cotton underwear

# THE DELIRIUM OF DESIRE

### FASHION MAGAZINE EDITOR **MIRANDA PURVES**
### SPEAKS TO **LEANNE SHAPTON**

**LEANNE:** When I first met you I was interested in you because you were this brainy academic who wore clothes in a way I hadn't seen; and when I went to your house for the first time I saw you owned Miu Miu and Prada shoes, and I had never met anyone who owned designer clothes before. I wondered how it was that they had a place in your life. I remember some caramel loafers.

**MIRANDA:** I have always had an incredible drive for what I guess you might call a status object. As long as I can remember, I've always known the "important thing to have now." When I was five, Kork-Ease, the wedge-heeled cork shoes, came out with kids' Kork-Ease. I don't know how I knew it or why I knew it, because my mom was a feminist who wouldn't buy me Barbies or think it appropriate for me to be wearing heels. I said, "I will do anything for these." She said, "If you keep your room clean for six months you can have them." She just assumed I would forget because I was five and never kept my room clean, and six months to the day I said, "I kept my room clean, I want them now." And she got them for me. I've always wanted to have the thing and had to have it first. It was like a talisman. If you know and you have that thing, you have some power. Obviously as I've gotten older and understood the horrors of the luxury business and mass-produced clothes, it's all become so tainted. It's complicated. Being an old person who chases trends is just *Death in Venice*.

**LEANNE:** What else did you want?

**MIRANDA:** I was the first girl to wear leg warmers at Seaview Elementary School, in Lantzville, British Columbia, the tiny town we moved to. I was mocked, in that way that fashion people are always mocked as freaks. I don't even know where I saw leg warmers. We didn't have a TV. Lantzville was a desert.

**LEANNE:** When I met you, you were twenty-seven and a student. How did you afford those Prada shoes?

**MIRANDA:** My first car was a Corvair convertible. I think it was $1,500, and I sold it for $3,000. I put that money in an American account, and when I'd visit my brother in New York, I'd spend the money on shoes. That was before the meme of girls being into shoes. Carrie Bradshaw came along and made it a thing. But that's always been countered by my snobbery of not wanting to look obvious or like I'm trying too hard.

**LEANNE:** You worked the expensive shoes into your wardrobe pretty seamlessly. I was impressed.

**MIRANDA:** But I'm still that five-year-old girl. These jeans are a Margaret Howell collaboration with Edwin. I saw a woman wearing them at the fashion shows and I was eagle-eyed. *What are those?* I was ashamed to ask, but I broke down and did ask. I had an associate editor on a press trip to England, and I interrupted six hours of my workday to try and remotely ferry these jeans to her London hotel room. Some people are snotty about telling you what they're wearing. Some women will go: Why

447

are you clocking my shoes? Working at *Elle* was crazy like that. These girls would be wearing straight-off-the-runway head-to-toe outfits and then act all ruffly and huffily if you said anything about it. Maybe because by noticing it, it degrades it? Don't you think?

**LEANNE:** It's probably more like a British thing, that by noticing it, it degrades *you*.

**MIRANDA:** Successful vanity seems so magical—it's you, it's not something to be parsed and identified, so the minute you're called out for your vanity, it's shameful. Old-school fashion people don't want to say what label. The red carpet "What are you wearing?" has made it more acceptable.

**LEANNE:** I want to talk about your experience working at fashion magazines.

**MIRANDA:** At *Elle* I was doing interiors and food and entertaining and travel, so I was the redheaded stepchild in that world. When I interacted with fashion people, there was a real divide.

**LEANNE:** Did the fashion people feel they were running it because it was all about attracting ad pages?

**MIRANDA:** The kind of people who are attracted to being in a fashion department— market editors, stylists, fashion directors— not always, but in general, tend to be snobs. A real awareness of hierarchy, a lot of paranoia: it's a dark world in ways that surprised me. Very competitive. It's bitchy.

**LEANNE:** Why?

**MIRANDA:** If you looked at individuals, you'd find something redeeming in all of them, but en masse there is a definite trauma bitch factor. It's terrible to say something so clichéd, but the values of that world are the values of the surface. If you are trying to attain or create a surface, that has to be based on judgment and snobbery, because without those things it all dissolves, there's nothing holding it up. Your entire identity is meaningless. So that's not ground anyone wants to stand on. You're defensive.

**LEANNE:** Who are fashion magazines speaking to?

**MIRANDA:** The question that comes up over and over is, How much does the reader want to know about anything, or do they just want to look at shiny, glittery shoes? That is a conflict in fashion magazines because a lot of the women who work at these magazines are really intelligent writers and thinkers and want a forum for that, but they've been steered into fashion magazines because that's where you can get jobs. There's always a conflict in thinking readers just want pretty things and shopping pages and presenting them with a fantasy of acquisition. Then, on the next level, people get analytical about it and say we want to empower women to make their own creative decisions. It's a time of chaos because the old diktat model has been called into question. Editors are a bit at sea as to what readers want, but the idea is to give them that frisson of shopping. You want to ignite their interest in clothes and style. Every magazine is different. At *Flare* I wanted to think that there was a reader I could attract who wanted to self-style and didn't want just prescription. That might not be the case. The shopping pages at *Elle* are tremendously popular. *InStyle* is consistently the best-selling fashion magazine out there, and the most anodyne. To me it's the deglamorizing of fashion. Whether it's *Vogue* or *InStyle*, all fashion magazines are—any month— working with the same shoes and bags, they all have this tiny basket of clothing and are just manipulating it with some visual rhetoric, some fantasy of what the fantasized reader wants. It's like formal poetry.

**LEANNE:** To build a house for advertisers to live in, though, really.

**MIRANDA:** Yes and no, though more and more that's the way it is. Advertisers count every single mention they get. And they take the editor to task. But creative people work at magazines, and if you have to write about a Chanel watch that's based on the shape of Coco's living room, within that you say, How can we do something fun?

**LEANNE:** What was the first time you were conscious of what you were wearing?

**MIRANDA:** My grandfather's family all worked in the garment district in Montreal, and a cousin of my mom's who owned a kids' clothing factory came over with clothes. I remember these red pants with a matching mod-style tunic, and being so excited, then putting them on and thinking: There is something wrong with these. It was because they were polyester. It just did not feel right on my body. One day at school I was feeling this polyester feeling way too much and I realized I'd forgotten to wear underwear. I thought, How am I going to get through the day? It wasn't embarrassing, it was sensory. Other things would feel so good. I had these baby-blue cord culottes that felt right. I was born a snob. But I fancied myself too snobby to be a snob. You should read Proust on snobbery.

**LEANNE:** Would being a snob make you feel attractive?

**MIRANDA:** I wanted to have the special item that someone would notice. I've got this bag now that's made of teddy-bear fur and I get so many compliments on that bag. From women. All kinds of women. There is something democratic about fashion. Like from a woman in an airport, and it's a moment of connection. But it's a funny way to get your power, from owning something that few people can have.

**LEANNE:** Vanity can be healthy.

**MIRANDA:** But I wonder if I can give it up. I'm forty-three, I've got children. It's hard to respect women who are too fashionable after a certain age. Why does it give you power to have that thing? I get scared about getting old and losing my sense of what is important. I have a fantasy of outwitting it all by having a uniform that then requires you to buy more things for your uniform, so you're actually not outwitting any of it. But I also think there is something about my relationship to my sexuality and what I feel safely contained in. I want clothes that won't make me feel shame.

**LEANNE:** What kind of clothing makes you feel shame?

**MIRANDA:** Anything overtly sexy make me feel shame.

**LEANNE:** Exposed or shame?

**MIRANDA:** Shame to not have the body to put those clothes on. I know enough about my body that it's not that mold. So if I tried to put clothes on it that were for that mold it would be like having egg on my face.

**LEANNE:** Who do you talk to about clothes?

**MIRANDA:** Sometimes I get a bit resentful because I'm the person my girlfriends talk to about clothes. I'm in a phase where I'm slightly less interested and I don't want to go through their permutations of angst about whether or not to buy something. Although as soon as I'm interested again, I'm the first to suck some poor friend into the loop of madness. I went to a bitch-and-swap the other day and I was marveling at how supportive everyone was being.

**LEANNE:** There's so much to go around now.

**MIRANDA:** Yes, maybe it's because we're older or because there is more stuff everywhere, but now the relationship with bitch-and-swap is the sense that you hope it doesn't look good on you, "Oh no, here I am trying it on, oh no, here I am taking it!"

**LEANNE:** Can you remember a transformative conversation you had with someone about clothes?

**MIRANDA:** I have satisfying conversations with my friend Morwyn about the slippery slope into the delirium of desire for these clothing items, the craziness of it. It usually has to do with the specifics of something we didn't buy. We can still to this day reignite the knife-in-the-gut pain of not buying these Oscar de la Renta paint-splattered dresses a year and a half ago. They were on sale and we didn't get them because it seemed like $700 was a lot to pay for a dress, but we will have those girl conversations: "But we would have worn them all the time!—But remember, they were $700! That's a lot of money to spend!—Not for a great dress!—Yeah, and those really were great dresses!—Maybe they didn't look that good on us and we can't remember?—No, actually, they looked really good and would have come into their own." You know, someone who understands the patheticness of it all. Clothes are so fundamental as a way to be aesthetic that is both serious and light. You couldn't talk about art that way.

**LEANNE:** What do you do about being conflicted over fashion and sweatshops and all of the politics that go into it?

**MIRANDA:** In my last editor's letter I featured our receptionist and pointed out that she got all her clothes at Goodwill. It was my final word: Goodwill! Get it secondhand! Not that it was a message that could breathe in that environment in any sustained way.

**LEANNE:** Do you think the answer is secondhand shopping?

**MIRANDA:** Yes, that's what we should do at this point. Right? There is no reason to buy anything new. With globalized non-union labor, the new has become the shabby.

**LEANNE:** What math do you do in your head when you get dressed? Do you do aesthetic and ethical math?

**MIRANDA:** I have all these rules I'm constantly breaking that I try to live by. 1. Buy vintage. 2. Buy only locally made clothes and sustainable-processed clothes. 3. Spend more for the piece that has those qualities. 4. Buy fewer things. 5. Don't interlard with J.Crew. I do see it as social injustice to have a garment that was made in a sweatshop. I don't understand when peers say they can't afford to buy organic milk. You can afford to buy ten pairs of cheap shorts at Old Navy and some toxic flip-flops, but you can't afford to buy from a humane farm? It comes between me and my friends sometimes, but if we're not all making these changes, then what hope is there for anyone? What hope is there for people who really can't afford it? It's easy to be judgmental, harder to act right. I don't think anyone who is really into fashion is making those sacrifices fully, me included.

**LEANNE:** Today as I was looking at some clothes in a vintage store I realized that the way I see clothes is in a moment—a dress might be two minutes, a sweater is ten seconds. I imagine where I would wear it and I see an image of myself and what I'm doing—paying for a coffee, waiting for the train, hunched over my desk, carrying my daughter on my hip—and I realize these little films starring these articles of clothing unfold within a space of time. Time doesn't exist, so I thought: What am I doing with so many clothes; what am I clocking with these clothes? They are unnecessary, but there's so much meaning I place in them.

**MIRANDA:** But it's also a way of tricking time. I go into an altered state when I'm looking at clothes. It becomes a different kind of time. It's a profoundly and fundamentally narcissistic experience. ✕

# STYLE AS CHARACTER

*"In my '70s fox-fur-collar spy coat I feel like a badass from a blaxploitation movie, like Pam Grier."*—ELISE PETERSON

MARSHA COURNEYA Knowing that the most valuable, courageous, and intelligent women of Tolstoy, Fontane, Hugo, and the Brontës wore finery at their finest moments has led me to feel empowered by feminine dresses. I often feel like my strength of character at any given moment is directly related to how close I feel to the heroines of literature I idolize.

SASHA GREY On an adult film set, you always bring your own clothing. Only occasionally are clothes provided. When I was acting, I wanted to distort the perception of the kind of girl I was. The more I saw how effective this was, the more I wanted to try different things. I could vacillate between the white-trash doll, the goth dom, and the classy pinup. I think this led to a lot of confusion and mystery.

ANISE LEANN I call it my "Margot Tenenbaum" when I wear the same thing every day, which I do often. If I could have it my way, I'd wear a ballet top with skinny jeans always. It makes me feel sexy, artistic, and I love wearing my hair up and feeling like a dancer.

MASHA TUPITSYN I admire a stubborn yet effortless style. Joan Didion had that, and my teacher, the scholar Avital Ronell. There is a uniform/structural quality to people who have real style. It's like a form of discipline. When you see that something unique and personal is going on with someone's relationship to aesthetics and their body, it's fascinating. Style, as opposed to fashion, is standing your ground, which at the end of the day is what individuality and intelligence are for me. You remain who you are—loyal to an identity that you've formulated for yourself. It's neurotic to a certain extent.

SZILVIA MOLNAR I love the simplicity of a white T-shirt and blue jeans, and the straight angles that they create. I would also enjoy growing a thick beard and walking around, stroking it.

MOLLY RINGWALD If I'm playing a character, I don't feel bad in her clothes, because I'm acting. But wearing clothes I don't like as myself just feels depressing.

JENNY TROMSKI All of my force is gathered into the daylong internalization of whatever character I've become.

ALISSA NUTTING "I am an artist!" I felt the need to scream a few weeks ago, and maybe, I reasoned, people would get that more if I bought some Jeffrey Campbell troll-fur wedge sneakers and lots of clothes with donuts and googly eyes on them, and wore jewelry made from ethically sourced taxidermied animals. Except, you know, "I'm also an academic!" So when I went to buy a suit jacket for a conference, I was overcome with the need to have a great many outfits that could voice my professional drive and ambition (but in a slightly edgy and eclectic manner), so I bought tailored polka-dot dresses and plaid silk conical vestments and asymmetrical blazers and earrings that looked like vintage beaded nipple tassels.

LENAE DAY A smear or an overdrawing of the lips goes a long way toward not taking yourself so seriously. I have found that I am a lot funnier, therefore I feel more attractive, when I look like Lucille Ball.

CLAUDIA EVE BEAUCHESNE One of my role models is the "Charlie Girl" from the Charlie fragrance ads of the seventies and eighties. She embodies everything I want for myself—confidence, personal and financial independence, a "sunny disposition," a fulfilling career, friends, fun, beautiful lovers, et cetera. I don't like the way the perfume smells and I would never wear it, but I still aspire to be a Charlie Girl. I even listen to the TV jingle ("Kind of young, kind of now . . . kind of free, kind of wow") to psych myself up before important meetings.

ALICIA ELLIOTT When I was in high school, I sold tickets at a speedway that also sold bright orange sweatshirts. At the time, I was in love with Clementine Kruczynski in the movie *Eternal Sunshine of the Spotless Mind*. For me, she was encapsulated in all her flawed and charismatic glory by the bright orange sweatshirt she wore. I wore my speedway sweatshirt half convinced that her awkward charm would manifest itself beneath its sleeves.

ANU HENDERSON When I was studying communications, I would go to the library and borrow films about Marshall McLuhan and Glenn Gould, and I'd listen to Glenn Gould on the record player, to make sure there was a harmony in my studies and in my environment. And at the time I would also dress like Glenn Gould, wearing overcoats and fingerless gloves.

IVY KNIGHT I have lots of black tights because I'm a lazy loser who wears such things.

CHRISTY-CLAIRE KATIEN Often I am inspired by a movie or a photograph that resonates with my mood. I will challenge myself and my wardrobe with that emotion. For example, this past October, I discovered a photo of my grandmother from the seventies, wearing her hair in a chignon, a beautiful beige dress, and brown heels. Throughout the following week I wore my hair in that style and an item of clothing that was brown or beige, in homage to my grandmother. Emotional connections make getting dressed very easy.

LILI HORVATH In my teenage years, I spent about fifteen minutes each morning trying to assemble an outfit that would communicate who I was that day. When I was thirteen, in the morning my brain probably went, "Okay, so today I want to express that I am sad, I am angry, and that I fancy that boy in English class. Navy skirt for sad, oversized KoЯn T-shirt for teenage anger and . . . errm . . . let's paint my nails pink to look feminine."

ANITA ABRAMS When having outfits made, I tend to hark back to Edwardian style, with lots of buttons down the back and on the sleeves, nipped waist, hip-covering jacket, and a curvy look, from well before the liberation of Chanel and the flapper styles. I associate this look with the elegance of the suffragettes and George Bernard Shaw's heroines. I also keep buying shoes with a heel and "Oxford" detail on them. They have a kind of Edwardian elegance, something like a feminine version of a man's formal shoe. Am I trying to convey that I am in a man's world but there's a female way of doing this? ✕

# I'M NOT A FUCKING D

## MUSICIAN HELEN KING GOES BRA-SHOPPING WITH SHEILA HETI

SHEILA: Oh my god, there's so many bras in here. Have you ever had a bra-fitting?

HELEN: *(laughs)* No!

SALESLADY: We'll do it this time, but you definitely need to make an appointment.

HELEN: Okay, thank you. Do we have to get naked?

SHEILA: Well, you probably do, but I'll sit out here. I'll close my eyes.

SALESLADY: I'm sorry, my hands are a bit cold. This one that you've got on is too tight.

HELEN: Yeah, a little. I've put on weight recently.

SALESLADY: *(measuring)* You're in between sizes 34 and 36. Would you like to try on something like this?

HELEN: Yes, one like this would be fine.

SALESLADY: I'll bring you the first 34D . . .

HELEN: D?

SALESLADY: Yes.

HELEN: Oh my god.

SALESLADY: Well, sometimes it depends. It can be C as well, it just depends how the cup is. *(leaves)*

HELEN: Oh shit. I brought a white bra because I've been going to these sex parties in the suburbs . . . it's really bad. I don't understand how I'm a feminist, and yet indulging these scenarios in which random men tell me what to wear. . . . *(laughs)*

SHEILA: Oh my god. Strange men?

HELEN: Yeah. And the three that have done it are really fat. *(laughs)*

SHEILA: Is it a turn-on?

HELEN: Totally! I wouldn't do it if it wasn't. One of the guys was like, "I would like it if you wore white knickers." And I was like, Okay, I don't normally do that, so maybe I need to get a white bra to match it.

SALESLADY: I brought three different sizes.

HELEN: I'm not a D, am I?

SALESLADY: It's better to try on, because sometimes it will surprise you.

HELEN: I'm not a fucking D!

SHEILA: What are you?

HELEN: *(laughs)* As far as I know, I was a B, right?

SHEILA: That's a big difference.

HELEN: I'm not a fucking D! You're a D!

SHEILA: I'm a B, maximum.

HELEN: I am not a D!

SHEILA: Do you feel excited that you're a D?

HELEN: No, I feel ashamed.

SALESLADY: Are you going to try? You can try.

HELEN: I am not a D!

SALESLADY: Try C, then.

SHEILA: D is really big. But I think they just changed the sizes recently, so everyone's a size bigger, because they have to do double A's and triple A's.

HELEN: If I'm a fucking D I'm going to kill myself. My whole life I've been fighting against the family curse of massive tits. *(laughs)*

SHEILA: Why is it a curse?

453

HELEN: Because then I'll be fat and depressed!

SHEILA: You said your breasts grew because you started drinking milk.

HELEN: I didn't drink any milk, I just ate pizza that had milk in it. Oh shit. What the fuck is this? I never wanted to be fat and now I am.

SHEILA: You're not fat at all.

HELEN: I am.

SHEILA: Oh my god, you're not fat at all.

SALESLADY: Let's have a look. It's a good fit. Do you feel all right?

HELEN: What size is it?

SALESLADY: Right. So that's 34C.

HELEN: It feels good.

SALESLADY: But it's not a bit tight on your back?

HELEN: I don't mind. Well, it is a bit.

SALESLADY: Let me try something else.

HELEN: If they tell me I'm a D, I'm gonna kick them in their . . . face. Honestly, this fetish website I've been going on . . .

SALESLADY: Try these on, see if you can get any more comfort from one of them.

HELEN: So the fetish website I went on, I was really stupid when I first went on it. I had some guys asking me, "How tall are you? What's your bra size?"

SALESLADY: How's that one. Better?

HELEN: Yeah.

SALESLADY: What I've done is I've gone up on your back and down on your cup.

HELEN: Yeah, that feels good.

SALESLADY: Because you're between a 34 and a 36. So I gave you a 36B. But really you're 34C.

HELEN: Okay. Brilliant. Thank you. So what do I do to buy one of these? ✕

*A fish is a fish is a fish*

*Femme écoutant*

*Farmer's dinner*

*Savage parade*

*London wall*

*Light bulb*

*Black goose*

*Mr. Man*

*Ballerina*

*Radishes*

*Acrobats*

*Coupons*

*Palisade*

*Poppies*

*Melons*

*Grapes*

*Iberia*

# MORE ADVICE AND TIPS

*"Try not to eat cake every day."* —FRIEDERIKE GIRST

**COLLEEN ASPER** The only thing I can imagine recommending that every woman do is to work to destabilize the category "woman." This doesn't really translate into clothing advice, though. At various points it has translated into things like "Wear trousers," but that seems awfully literal to me.

**RACHEL L.** If I can answer yes to the question "Could I wear this in any capital city and still look the part?" then I'm happy with my style.

**NICHOLE DELAFIELD-BROMME** It's very helpful to take a picture of yourself in clothing when you plan to wear it to something important. Wedding, reunion, some other event where you especially care about your appearance. What we see in the mirror is NOT how we really look. Having a photo to look at helps pick out little details like: the hemline on that dress should be a little longer, the belt or shoes aren't quite right. I once wore an evening dress and thought it was smashing, then later saw a picture and realized the neckline wasn't fitting right. I could have easily fixed that had I bothered to have someone snap a quick pic on my phone a few days before.

**PATRICIA MARX** My mother told me to stay away from plaids based in white.

**PENELOPE C.** A trick is to not have full-length mirrors. If you can't see yourself, you spend less time being critical of yourself, and that's important.

**TRISH KALICIAK** The smartest thing I ever did was hang twenty-four hooks along my wall. That's where my most-worn clothes live. Sure, it looks like a hallway at a primary school, but it keeps my stuff off the floor, where it used to live.

**LEORA MORINIS** I admire the unapologetic. I admire women who have a sense of humor about the whole thing. I mean, about our lumpy little bodies roaming around the planet, covered in bits of woven cloth.

**CHRISTINE MUHLKE** I like things to be casual but special. Like if I have a dinner party, I want the best food, but the most relaxing way of eating it.

**SARA FREEMAN** My friend Julia is probably the best-dressed person I know. She told me that a couple of years ago she decided to stop buying things simply because they were sexy or alluring. She wears beautiful, functional clothes every day and she always looks amazing. Before our conversation, I'd only bought clothes because they made some part of my body look good. After, I started thinking about clothes as things to wear to do certain activities, instead of things to wear to make my breasts look bigger and rounder, or my thighs smaller, or my waist thinner.

**MARGARITA TUPITSYN** If a shop assistant tells you that you look good in something but you don't feel it, it doesn't matter. It's a sales pitch.

**GILDA HABER** I use very little makeup—only eyebrow and eyeliner, lipstick, and a spot of lipstick spread on cheekbones. I wear my hair with long side curls like a Cossack to make my face look thinner and fiercer.

**GINI ALHADEFF** No synthetics. They are hot and cold. They are treacherous. The wife of the film director Francesco Rosi, who was a friend, went up in flames when a spark from her cigarette landed on her synthetic caftan.

**RAMOU SARR** Spanx are probably killing me and I do not give a shit.

**AMY TURNER** If it's over a hundred bucks, wait twenty-four hours. Money is freedom. Don't give away your freedom for assimilation.

**GILLIAN SCHWARTZ** My mom says, "If you see a cashmere sweater, buy it." It's good advice. I wear my three cashmere sweaters more than anything else in my closet. She says the same thing about extension cords.

**KARIMA CAMMELL** Wearing an apron renders everyone incapable of processing your outfit. When I get dressed, nine out of ten times I realize, "The apron is missing." So I add it. The outfit works and other things happen. I meet strangers and they assume I don't speak English—that I'm not from around here. But generally speaking, I think, "If the outfit's not working, add an apron." ✕

## WEAR AREAS | ANNIKA WAHLSTRÖM

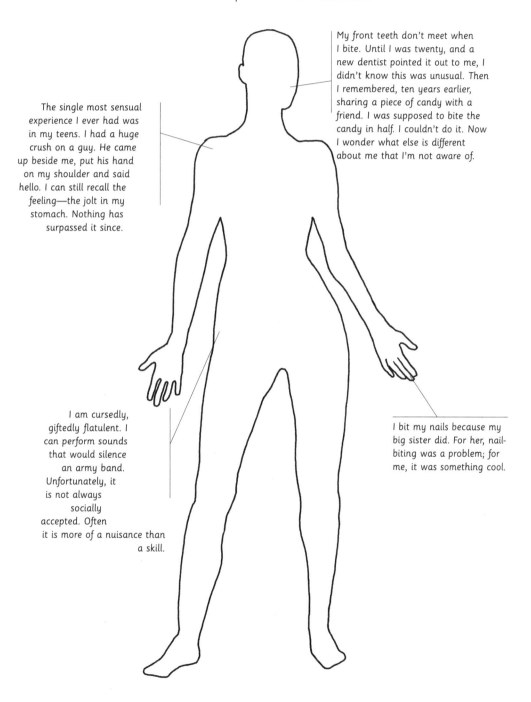

My front teeth don't meet when I bite. Until I was twenty, and a new dentist pointed it out to me, I didn't know this was unusual. Then I remembered, ten years earlier, sharing a piece of candy with a friend. I was supposed to bite the candy in half. I couldn't do it. Now I wonder what else is different about me that I'm not aware of.

The single most sensual experience I ever had was in my teens. I had a huge crush on a guy. He came up beside me, put his hand on my shoulder and said hello. I can still recall the feeling—the jolt in my stomach. Nothing has surpassed it since.

I am cursedly, giftedly flatulent. I can perform sounds that would silence an army band. Unfortunately, it is not always socially accepted. Often it is more of a nuisance than a skill.

I bit my nails because my big sister did. For her, nail-biting was a problem; for me, it was something cool.

# WARP & WEFT NOs. 1–6 | KARIN SCHAEFER

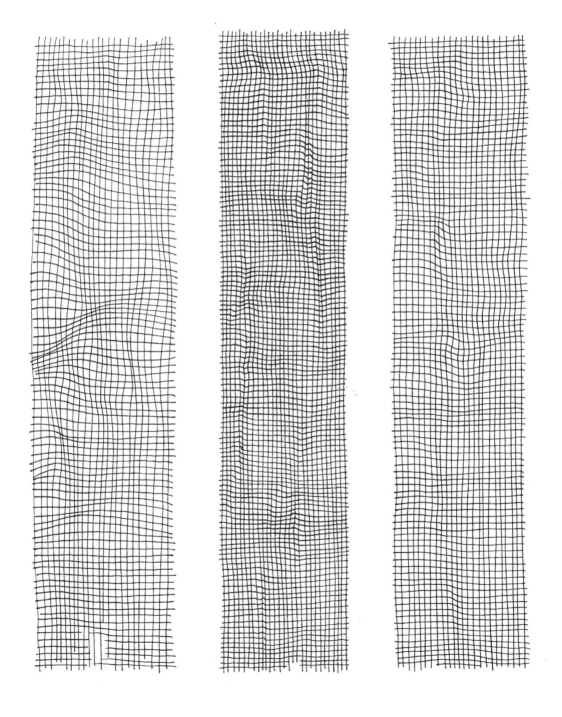

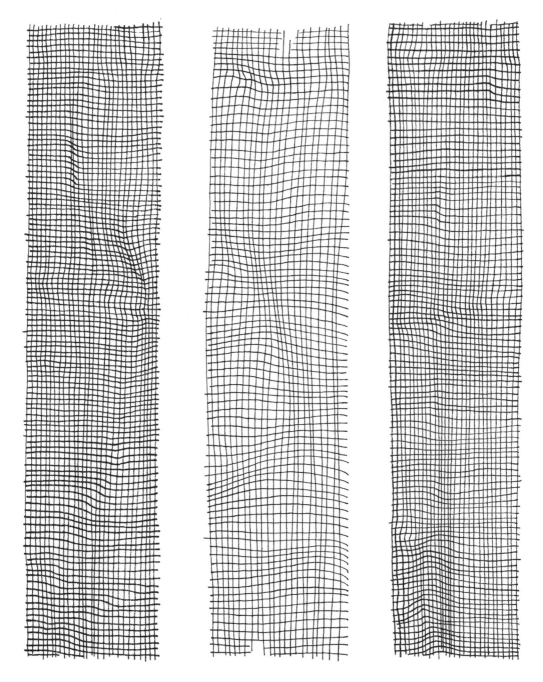

*IVORY SIMMS*'s aprons

# A FRENCH GIRL HOEING

## FARMERS **BARBARA DAMROSCH** & **ELIOT COLEMAN**
## SPEAK TO *HEIDI JULAVITS*

**HEIDI:** I'm wondering about the romance of dressing for certain careers. Did you harbor any style romance about being a farmer?

**BARBARA:** I was completely into the romance of it. Utterly. I basically left the academic life because of the whole back-to-the-land thing.

**HEIDI:** What year was this?

**BARBARA:** Oh, good question. It was like '77 or something. The clothing that reflected that romance for me was overalls. Since I was cutting my own wood and all of that, I ordered some red suspenders from a company and they said "Logger's World" on them. This was when I was changing oil in my truck myself.

**HEIDI:** What had you been wearing when you were an academic?

**ELIOT:** Miniskirts.

**HEIDI:** Miniskirts?

**BARBARA:** Absolutely. I got into trouble for teaching in micro-miniskirts. I also got in trouble for seizing a building.

**HEIDI:** You seized a building in a miniskirt? Double violation.

**BARBARA:** I'd been at a poetry reading and I had an all-night babysitter because of the reading, and the students had seized a building, so I went in.

**HEIDI:** Let's talk about what you decide to wear when you get dressed in the morning to go to work. What's the process? Do you have a uniform?

**BARBARA:** My outfits are very weather-dependent, but they also rest a lot on comfort. I don't like baggy jeans, I like tight jeans, but I don't like to feel constrained when I'm squatting a lot, so I'll wear things like Garnet Hill leggings, or old beat-up jogging pants. Sometimes stretch jeans or stretch pants or something like that. The one thing I never, ever wear is boxy T-shirts.

**HEIDI:** Why not?

**BARBARA:** I don't like boxy on me. So I'll wear fitted T-shirts like the one I'm wearing now, or ones I've worn out or that have gotten irreparably stained or something. What I'm wearing at the moment would be my "going to town" outfit—clean jeans, a clingy top, sleeve three-quarter length, depending on the weather. And I'm big on layers. You go outside to work in Maine, you could start in your parka, then strip down to a flannel shirt, then have a tank top underneath in case the sun comes out.

**HEIDI:** Have you ever stolen a style idea from one of your farmhands? You're known around here for having a very attractive and stylish staff.

**BARBARA:** Their sense of style is only one of the many, many reasons we love living surrounded by twenty-somethings. Everything about them is fresh and fun and challenging. Diane has an incredible sense of style. A natural grace.

**ELIOT:** As does Vera.

**BARBARA:** Vera wears little, cut-on-the-bias, longish fifties skirts, and her guy wears red suspenders all the time. The person I think was the most inspirational was a woman named Lydia. I would note things she did, like wearing underwear showing, or integrating something lacy and nightgowny into a tailored outfit. That's been around a long time, but she did it better than anybody.

**ELIOT:** I thought you were gonna talk about Aubrey.

**BARBARA:** Well, Aubrey was in a class by herself. Aubrey would be sitting around on the grass after work in a little black dress and a heavy gold necklace.

**ELIOT:** Aubrey was the queen of the little black dress.

**HEIDI:** She would wear that to work?

**BARBARA:** She wouldn't actually garden in it, but once she wore jeans and a white, clingy, translucent tank top, with a black lace bra underneath, at the Brooksville farmers' market. She was just the best.

**ELIOT:** You have a bunch of hand-me-ups from my daughters, don't you?

**BARBARA:** Oh yeah. Like a thrift shop, only free. I have a Betsey Johnson dress that Eliot's youngest daughter outgrew in high school that I wear still. I call it my hooker dress.

**HEIDI:** The way you dress is very contra how people expect farmers to dress.

**BARBARA:** I don't think people expect . . . Well, okay, when we go to organic conferences, I don't look like the women there.

**HEIDI:** What do those women look like?

**BARBARA:** What would you say, Eliot?

**ELIOT:** Dowdy.

**BARBARA:** Totally utilitarian. I think the way I dress is utilitarian, too, but I always have to look sexy.

**ELIOT:** With many back-to-the-landers, that's not the case.

**BARBARA:** There's always exceptions—you'll see some farm chick who really knows how to tie a muffler. They can do a nice thing with a scarf. Actually, here's my favorite farmette story: I'm in France, we're at a museum that's a medieval monastery, and it's a plant museum where they've got historical gardens from all the different eras, and antique herbs and vegetables—

**ELIOT:** Their gardens were pre-Columbian. So no tomatoes . . .

**BARBARA:** So there's a vegetable plot out there with a French girl hoeing it. And she was wearing green velvet pants. Clingy bell-bottom green velvet pants to garden in. It

---

**SURVEY** *Do you ever wish that you were a man, could dress like a man, or had a man's body?*
If I were a man, I would want to be a very specific type of man—a twink, I guess, is the word. I would want dark hair and olive skin and big dark eyes. And I wouldn't want it to last very long, maybe a week. —ELEANOR WEST • Yep. About once every couple months or so I decide it's a boy day, and I'll wear trousers and a collared shirt buttoned all the way up, and often a vest, too. Just escaping, a little bit at least, being a woman, for a little while. I think it's a seriously sad thing that men can't do the same thing without stigma. —EMMA HOOPER • Not really. I guess maybe a boy who is slim and has a flat stomach, but I wouldn't want any of the other parts belonging to a man. —ALEXANDRA KERN • I would like the ease that a man has. —CHRISTINA GONZALES • I never wished to be a man or have a man's body. To be a woman who can be in love with men and women is the best of both worlds. —FELIZ LUCIA MOLINA • I think that if I were a boy, I would be the most stylish guy in the world. They have it so easy! It's only a choice between tops and bottoms—not skirts or

wasn't that she was trying to be medieval. She was just French.

ELIOT: Now, I was there with her and I don't remember that at all, so this is something only a woman would notice.

BARBARA: They were probably pants that she'd trashed in a rainstorm or something, you know?

HEIDI: Why is it important for you to look sexy?

BARBARA: Why not? Some people don't consider it important to look attractive to the opposite sex, and I just don't think I will ever be that way. I think I'm going to be one of those 125-year-old slow drivers and still dress the way I do now.

HEIDI: Do you feel like you're dressing for men rather than women?

BARBARA: I wouldn't say I dress for men. It's just the way I like to think about myself.

HEIDI: What about the sauna?

BARBARA: Oh yeah, the sauna.

HEIDI: You host regular naked coed saunas that have become pretty famous. Who comes to them?

BARBARA: Our workers, our neighbors, our guests. Sometimes it's just me and Eliot. It's just a holdover from the sixties. I had my first nude sauna in 1970 when I was on the faculty at Middlebury, and there was a rock quarry where faculty and students swam naked—it was just what you did in the sixties and seventies.

HEIDI: What happens when people are uncomfortable being naked around strangers or friends or bosses?

BARBARA: We try to explain that it's not obligatory. We have not been able to predict who's gonna dig it and who isn't. That is what's really, really interesting— you'll find somebody who's a complete suit but who embraces the birthday suit just as readily, whereas somebody who you think is going to be very open to it is like, "Oh my god, no no no." You never know. Often with a couple it's one and not the other. But if somebody is uncomfortable with it, I don't remember once feeling judgmental about it. It's just: Oh, that's who you are, that's fine, that's how you feel.

HEIDI: Let's talk about Helen and Scott Nearing, whose property this once was. They were married, and they were the preeminent back-to-the-landers with a very specific style. Was Helen an inspiration to you?

BARBARA: Aesthetically, what was wonderful about Helen was that she had a Dutch background, so her garden didn't look like a hippie garden. It looked like a European garden. It was tidy, well grown, she had this

---

dresses or tights. —IMOGEN DONATO • I do own clothes that men typically wear. —NICHOLE BAIEL • All the time. I aspire to be a lanky, skinny dude constantly. —ARIEL GARFINKEL • I've wished that I could dress like a man, although I've never wished to be a man. —ARIEL N. KATES • No. —MEGGIN HAMMILL • I have sometimes wished I could be a man so that I could act as aggressively as I wanted and not be judged for it. But I really have never wanted to dress like a man or wanted a man's body. Women's clothing is so much more fun and varied. —CHIN-SUN LEE • I'm not envious of men's clothes so much as men's lack of curves. I would like to sometimes feel that a shirt was hanging on my shoulders rather than on my breasts. —SASHA ARCHIBALD • I objectively prefer women as a crowd. I have never looked at a man and thought, "That's it, I want to be that, that's what's wrong." That would have been so easy!—KARI LARSEN • Freshman year of high school, I mistakenly thought that if I dressed like the boys I found attractive, they would realize how much we had in common and fall in love with me. I wore a lot of denim vests. This is not a successful mode of seduction. —CAMILLE

stone wall around it. She was a stonemason. She was the one behind all that stone building, not Scott. I loved that about her. But she dressed kind of . . .

ELIOT: . . . as if she didn't care.

BARBARA: Really didn't care. And she chopped her hair short as if she didn't care. I did see her with makeup on once, and I thought, "Oh, that's so cool, she does have that side to her." I saw her once in a green silk dress that she'd gotten at a thrift shop—I forget what that was all about, what occasion that could have been. She liked flowers. I would sometimes go and help her with her kitchen garden, and she would say, "I've let the poppies come in," or "I've let the lupines come in. Scott would never have let me do that." She was quite constrained by his severe socialist aesthetic and lifestyle.

HEIDI: Talk to me about your farm, about how the land looks.

ELIOT: This land was all wooded when I came here in 'XX. I had a blank canvas and I was able to do anything I wanted with it. We've often thought about some of the farmers of the past whose operations were described in France as *ferme ornée* [ornamented farm]. It wasn't that they were frilly—they were practical farms that were beautiful. The decorations weren't pasted on, they were integral to farming well.

BARBARA: A lot of the English estates did the ornamented farm, but they would glue on the cupola effect. Thomas Jefferson wanted the true *ferme ornée*—instead of making the farm estatey, he made the estate farmy. Here's my take on it: Any beauty our farm has comes out of its utility. Everything we do to make the crops grow better at the same time makes it more beautiful. The rows are straight because it's easier to grow that way, easier to harvest, everything. All of our choices are completely practical, and because we adhere to them religiously, there's a uniformity to the farm. It's not haphazard. It's never haphazard. There's never any distinction between beauty and utility at this farm.

HEIDI: Do you have any meaningful or special tools that you use?

BARBARA: I have my pet tools. I have one that Eliot designed—he made it for me with an extra-long handle and a pistol grip, and the hoe itself, the blade, is sharpened on both sides. It's lost. The other one is a trowel that has a nice wooden handle and a very strong cupped narrow pointed blade. I love that trowel. It's also missing.

HEIDI: Oh no! *(laughs)*

---

CAMPBELL • Why wish? Gita Bellin has a great quote that I like to think about: "If you know you want it, have it." In other words, I don't wish for a male form because I contain the male form—my body is home to both. I think this is true for everyone. I have rejected my "maleness" in the past out of fear that I would be seen as less attractive. But now that I honor this aspect of my beauty and being, I feel more whole. —KATHARINE HARGREAVES • Sometimes I wish I could walk down the street like a man and not be scared of other men. Which is not really wanting to be like a man. I just don't like men staring at me on the street or making comments. I would probably dress sexier if men didn't exist. —RACHEL ANDES • Not really. The only thing I would like about wearing men's clothing is that it's often better made than women's. —SHELLEY LONG • My first conscious memory was of wishing I was a boy so I wouldn't have to give birth. I've always wanted to get my little girl body back, but I've never felt any particular affinity to the male form, more just a slight aversion to being a woman. —SARAH WHIDDEN • I would like to try everything! —LUISA B. ✕

**BARBARA:** I still have my favorite little snips, for when you don't need the strength of a pruner. I love those.

**HEIDI:** Can you see any connection between how you dress, how your garden looks, and what you cook?

**BARBARA:** I don't know, earthy and pleasure-loving? A lot of people think the way we eat is a little decadent because we tend to make a big deal of meals. We have a fairly substantial meal in the middle of the day. None of this "Grab a sandwich." Everything else about our life is sort of frenetic—and that's the one still point in the turning world.

**HEIDI:** Are there any clothing rules you follow around animals? I know you're not supposed to wear red around bulls, for example.

**BARBARA:** The only time I ever thought of anything remotely like that was when I was researching which colors biting insects are repelled by or prefer. One day in the garden, Aubrey said, "They hate beige." I would certainly wear a beige hat if I thought bugs wouldn't bite me.

**HEIDI:** Otherwise you haven't really changed your color palette for the sake of bugs?

**BARBARA:** For the sake of bugs, no. ✕

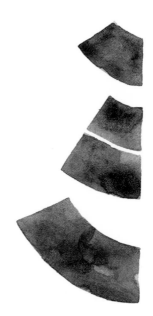

*ARIA SLOSS*'s white nightgowns

# THE FACTORY COLLAPSED

*Reba Sikder, an eighteen-year-old garment worker and survivor of the Rana Plaza collapse in Dhaka, Bangladesh, talks to Sara Ziff. Kalpona Akter, executive director of the Bangladesh Center for Worker Solidarity, translates between Bengali and English.*

**SARA ZIFF**

**REBA SIKDER**

Can you tell me from the beginning what happened at Rana Plaza?

So on that day the 23rd of April, I came to my work, and after doing two hours of work I saw my coworkers rush to escape from the factory, and then our general manager said that we have to leave the factory now. I didn't even know why—then I went outside. When I was outside I came to know that some workers saw a crack in the building, and sand and concrete had fallen on one worker's hand. The factory managers said that we should go home and come at two p.m. to the factory again. We went home, and when we came at two p.m., our factory managers said that the building owner told the factory owner that the engineer has inspected the building and it's fine. It's safe for running the factory, we can work. So the management told us to go home and come the following morning.

The next morning when I came, I saw that many of my coworkers are standing outside the building and everyone is in fear—whether they should go inside or not. I was standing with them outside, too, and some of them were going inside and then our middle management, they started screaming at us, yelling, "Just go inside! Why you are standing here? You have to go inside." One of our production managers was slapping female workers—Go inside—and they're threatening us that if we don't go inside, we will lose our job and they will not pay our salary. And then we went inside, and I saw that nobody even started work because the people were talking more . . . What is going to happen? There was a crack in the building. Then our general manager announced that everybody should go back to their machine and start work because there is a rush for shipment—the buyer is putting pressure. He says that we have to hit our production target, then we can go home. We start work because, you know, they're shouting at us, and I think I worked twenty minutes and then the power was gone. And within two or three minutes they start the generator, and when they start the generator I hear this huge sound, like BOOM, and everything collapsing. My coworkers ran to the stairs and I was following them, and then I fall, and I'm stuck under a machine.

I don't know how long I was unconscious—and when I got conscious, I was feeling that somebody's head was on top of my head, and my whole body's wet because the blood is coming from him. He was stuck under a beam and column. And I found my feet were stuck under a machine—maybe there was a stool or something—and he was asking for help and screaming for water and to save his life, and he was pushing me, too—he could move only his hands. He was my coworker who was working beside me. When he was pushing me and asking for help, I said, "Brother, I cannot help you. There's no way I can help, because my feet are stuck, too." He was able to speak to me for a few minutes and then he died. Aminul—my colleague's name was Aminul.

So when he died, I got unconscious, and I don't know how long it's been, and when I got conscious, I thought, There is no hope that I can escape. But still I wanted to give all effort to escape from that place. And I started kicking the stool, but my feet were stuck. I was able to free my leg. And then I saw there is a tiny place, and I start crawling toward the screams I was hearing from my coworkers. A kind of room or pocket had been made, when this beam and column had fallen. And when I went there, I saw another thirty workers trapped, many of them dead, injured, and everyone is screaming. I saw my other coworkers stuck—many of them thirsty and crying for water—and I saw one of my coworkers drinking her own blood from her injured area, because she was so thirsty and there is nothing she can get.

I got unconscious many times, and when I got conscious I felt I am so thirsty, and I was crying and screaming for water. Then my coworkers replied that they cannot give me anything because there is no water, and I said, "Whatever you have, please give me, because I'm dying." And one of my coworkers, she gave her own urine, which I drank. And I found that, meanwhile, it is two nights and two days since the factory collapsed—it was through my coworkers I came to know. Then I know that we're all stuck, but four of us among all these survivors, four of us who are skinnier than others, we try to find a way to escape. So we were crawling every single way. We saw there is a tiny way to go. But wherever we would go, it was dark. And when we were crawling to the other area, we saw one of the female workers, she is stuck under a machine, and she said, "Please help me—please save me," and we replied to her, "Sister, there is no way we can help you, because the way you're trapped, it is impossible to help you, the ceiling is coming down every single second." And then she said, "Maybe I will not survive, maybe you cannot help, but I can tell you how to escape from here because I saw—many of the workers went through this area, and I believe they escaped from this building." Then we started crawling toward that place. But we haven't found any way to get out, so there is one dark place, four of us sitting and crying, and we thought, There is no hope that we can get out. I cannot tell how big it was—maybe we just crawled in the same place many times because we don't know where we are going.

So when we were sitting without hope in a place in the dark, and thought maybe we will not survive, suddenly one of my coworkers felt some air that is coming from outside, and then we thought, There is hope. We started crawling to that place where air is coming. And when we're close to that place, there is a huge sound. We are hearing that people are breaking the wall, breaking the rubble or the concrete. So we started screaming and asking for help. Finally he heard our voice, and he saw us, and he said, "Please stay here—I will not be able to rescue you, because I don't know how to, but I can call the army, who are doing rescue." So he called the army, and after half an hour or so, the army came and they rescued the four of us. One machine has fallen on my back, and my neck has been cut up, so there is a screw in my neck; in many, many places in my body there is a screw, and both ankles were injured.

I wanted to say that I worked for this factory and this company, and I was making—including my overtime—$90 a month, but I had to work eight a.m. to ten p.m., sometimes overnight. That was seven days a week, thirty days a month. I want to say that I didn't receive any compensation. Moreover, I cannot say how many coworkers I left in that building, how many of them I lost. It was more like brothers and sisters, because we worked together. I can remember one whole line of sewing workers, they were just trapped—I saw them falling.

I lost many, many of them. So I want compensation, and I want a safe working place for our workers. Just think about those workers who lost their limbs—how they will live. And think about those families who had only one person to earn, and they lost that person.

Were the workers afraid that morning when they were told they had to go into the factory?

Yes we were afraid. We knew that this building would collapse. But we had to go because the managers said they will not give us our salary. We need to feed ourselves. So that is why we had to go.

What would be in the rubble?

If you go to the factory area you will see all these fossils, they're still in there. The rubble might be removed to other places, but people can find all the fossils inside. So it means that the death toll is not eleven hundred thirty-four, it is more. Many families, they're coming with pictures and say that they didn't find their bodies. They didn't find their beloved.

How does it affect you now, almost one year later?

I couldn't recover from that. What I went through. When I see my coworkers who lost their limbs, that reminds me of so many things. All the time I remember those faces I left behind, and especially when I see those mothers, or the family members who bring their pictures with them, looking for their family members. If I died in that rubble, my mother would be bringing my picture—coming and going around and asking for me. ✗

# WEAR AREAS | LITHE SEBESTA

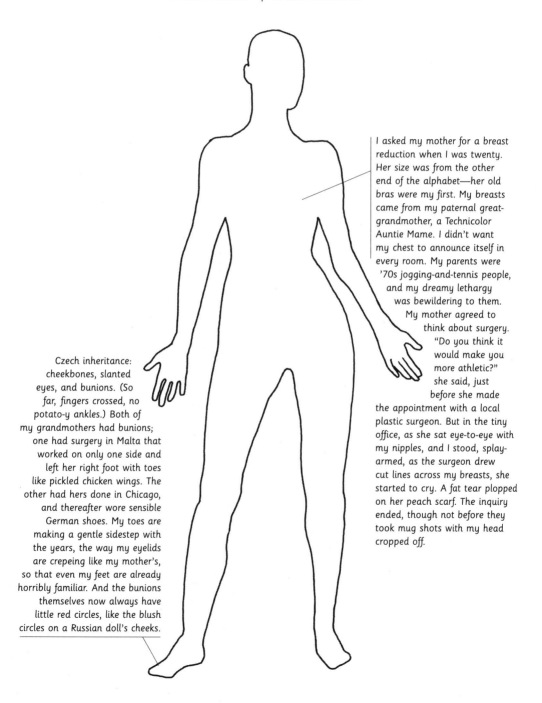

I asked my mother for a breast reduction when I was twenty. Her size was from the other end of the alphabet—her old bras were my first. My breasts came from my paternal great-grandmother, a Technicolor Auntie Mame. I didn't want my chest to announce itself in every room. My parents were '70s jogging-and-tennis people, and my dreamy lethargy was bewildering to them. My mother agreed to think about surgery. "Do you think it would make you more athletic?" she said, just before she made the appointment with a local plastic surgeon. But in the tiny office, as she sat eye-to-eye with my nipples, and I stood, splay-armed, as the surgeon drew cut lines across my breasts, she started to cry. A fat tear plopped on her peach scarf. The inquiry ended, though not before they took mug shots with my head cropped off.

Czech inheritance: cheekbones, slanted eyes, and bunions. (So far, fingers crossed, no potato-y ankles.) Both of my grandmothers had bunions; one had surgery in Malta that worked on only one side and left her right foot with toes like pickled chicken wings. The other had hers done in Chicago, and thereafter wore sensible German shoes. My toes are making a gentle sidestep with the years, the way my eyelids are creeping like my mother's, so that even my feet are already horribly familiar. And the bunions themselves now always have little red circles, like the blush circles on a Russian doll's cheeks.

*MARLENE BARBER*'s furs

# SEAMS, HEMS, PLEATS, DARTS

LISA COHEN

Last night I dreamt a friend was cold; she's not my mother but I wish she were, so gallantly I draped her with my coat. You know: My coat is unconditional.

*Do not tremble. If she had an institution it is the one excluding her mother. Her native land is not beautiful. She likes the poet to mutter.*—Gertrude Stein, "Advertisements"

This is a story of grammar and glamour. First: A systematically composed body of words. Then: A systematically clothed body of love. Fascinated and impatient, I watched her anoint herself, make up, and dress. Visions of elegance, brushes with fabrics, fashion circa 1962–79. I wait for her. I do not know what waits for me. I cannot stand that we'll be late.

Mutter mutter.

A certain instinct, a certain gesture, a feel, a flair, an eye, a rage for femininity.

Sometimes it still causes me to tremble, tremble.

Grammar is a system of basic rules by which words in a language are structured and arranged. Language is a set of basic rafts by which I stay afloat. Clothing and its sentences were her bag, her boat.

Including: what's right for girls; what's meant for boys. ("Shirt" or "blouse"? "Pants" or "slacks"?)

Clothes as exhortation and admonishment.

The summer of 1974: Hot, horrible August; the resignation speech. We mocked Richard Nixon—my mother, my sister, and I—as he cried about his mother on TV. *My mother (sob, sob), my mother was a saint.* It was the end of Our Long National Nightmare. It was just the beginning.

Clothes as control, as correct order. Ardor. Asserted and undone. What I wore was everything to her.

But if I said that she wanted me to wear *this*, and I wanted to wear *that*, what would it prove?

Clothes also as pure description. Her marriage was over. I found the yellowed newspaper announcement of her wedding: *The bride wore a short gown of Chantilly lace over blush peau de soie in bell silhouette.*

My first word, I was told repeatedly, was "shoe."

*Captain, I have to go back inside my mother's mind. It's the only way we're ever going to get any answers.* —Counselor Troi to Jean-Luc Picard, *Star Trek: The Next Generation*

Her mind and mine, so intertwined. "My mother," or: "My mother's." "My mother _____," and "My mother's _____."

I went back inside her purse. I came alive rifling through that bag, feeling for the charged surfaces of paper money, for tissue scented with perfume, for the box of gum with a hard candy coating. I listened in on phone calls, probed the bedside tables, read the appointment book, eavesdropped from the second floor to a room below. I watched the rain scar the windows, rain darken the brick, rain sound like relief and then regret. The pitch of traffic rises in the rain. Look: A child composed of fear, of reverence, and disdain.

*I love the lie and lie the love, A-hangin' on, with push and shove.* Over and over lifting the needle and dropping it—to get caught again in the pulsing momentum of the piano, the tough voice of the sax, the long traveling cry of Les McCann and Eddie Harris's "Compared to What." (They were Live in Switzerland; I was live in the living room, crouched next to the turntable.) I love so much I cannot breathe. I love her white wool sweater from Greece. I love her short-sleeved dark paisley shirt, the pattern's hidden meaning. I venerate the rare perfume from Paris. I believe in her belted white trench coat, large dark tortoiseshell sunglasses. I understand brown suede two-strap sandals with a heel just right; elegant arch of the instep, poise of the feet.

The composition is always complete. It explains itself. It is a view of the whole world. And when it slips I know that something bad is going on.

Standing at the door to the bedroom I could see into her closet, the closet, her closet: eternally inadequate, neither deep nor wide enough.

She had been a fashion journalist.

I learn: Seams, hems, pleats, darts, and bias tape.

In the beginning (was I four years old?) red stretch stirrup pants, a red-and-white-striped jersey, red leather oxford shoes. I admire the outfit and would almost dress this way now.

Age ten or eleven, Watergate era, before breasts: A blue-and-white wide-striped T-shirt with a torn pocket, very tight. A pumpkin-colored T-shirt so loose and long it came to my mid-thigh.

The struggle: To wear that, to look like what, like me, or you, like her, like everyone, like no one else.

*Tryin' to make it real—compared to what?*

Unharnessed torment in a thing I'd begged her not to buy. Synthetic velour, green that offended me, a plaid component. A maxi-skirt or dress; my meticulous and wild distress. The push and shove. I caused a scene? I refused. She caused a scene. We caused a scene. It made us late—to a wedding.

Such bitter conflicts over my clothes, cited years later (by my father) as evidence of trouble between us—her and me—of long duration. I had forgotten it all. I remember only some of it now.

I wore it, in the end.

For I did love a pair of maroon corduroy tapered Levi's, worn low on the hips, when I had no hips, with cheap gray fake-suede sneakers. (This at the dawn of fancy running shoes.)

I did adore my short- and long-sleeved striped Marimekko T-shirts, and one in thick plackets of color that I later swiped from her. I indeed participated in the interesting "Norwegian workshirt," the blue-and-white vertically striped Greek blouse (or smock, or something worn on top). Clothes from elsewhere, from the world.

For I am referring to white jeans, slightly belled, with matching white jean jacket: the only mother-daughter outfit I recall. Confused dismay, minor pleasure. Cease-fires in this tiny war at home. Or we just wore each other down. Or: rhythms of aggression and capitulation. Note subsequent high-waisted wide bell-bottoms, two tiny welt pockets in front; in back the smooth expanse of navy blue or dark brown corduroy round ass. Brown leather clogs that hurt, even when I didn't run in them. Polyester patterned shirts in which I sweated. And other awkward, sleek expressions of the age.

There is no explanation.

The clothes weighed so much, wet wool trousers in the snow, heavy with clogged and clotted feeling, with all of the not-feeling I was busy feeling. The lie, the love: perfect submission, mastery; trying to see; a being seen that was, also, striving for invisibility.

Something someone covering me.

Do clothes make the woman. Clothes made my forgetting, a deep and wide vacancy. The asthma of memory, the burlap curtains of memory, the rasp of breath, the scratch of textiles.

Clothes were signs so clear I could not read them. As in: The things she left hanging for years in what had been my father's closet: his white wool turtleneck, seersucker jacket, olive-drab wide-wale corduroys. Later I wore the sweater, almost a dress on me (irony I did not see).

She said: Now you'll divorce me too.

To wear that, to look like that, like me, or you, like her, like us, like everyone, like no one else, like what and whom you love.

Grammar deals with rules for word order, verb forms, plural and singular nouns, and parts of *her shoulder-length veil*. A basic rule of English grammar is: *A cascade of white sweetheart roses and ivy.*

I did not ever say the following: I leave you your house and several things I loved or understand. I steal myself. I steal away. I steel myself. I keep the things I keep.

Was there a set of rules that governed her veil, which was *caught to* a nonbinding contract and to *a crown of seed pearls,* or that regulated her bouquet?

Clothes, the source of it all, don't matter at all.

Compared, compared, compared to what?

Nonstandard usage: I done it. I seen it. I worn it. And finally. ✕

## A MAP OF MY FLOOR | SHEILA HETI

**OCCASION** *Onstage book reading at a literary festival in Cologne, Germany. The final performance of a three-week tour in Europe. Flying home in the morning. The hotel room floor displays the following tried and discarded items:*

**1** Silvery shirt with three-quarter-length sleeves. Bought secondhand in Berlin on this trip. A possibility. **2** Blue-and-yellow-patterned silk Rachel Comey top, no sleeves. Would be great in the middle of summer, but it's March and cool. **3** Light pink bra. Can't remember where this came from, but when I bought it I was skeptical. Now it's my favorite bra. **4** Gray Topshop sweatshirt. Too informal and it stinks. Needs a wash. **5** Black leather shirt with three-quarter-length sleeves. Bought secondhand in Paris. I really shopped a lot on this trip. Wore it for an interview the other day, and those people will be there tonight. Need something different. **6** Red cashmere sweater. After three weeks in a suitcase, it's lost its shape. **7** Deep purple silk Chanel top, from my boyfriend. Wore this onstage in London, but it's too dressy for my current mood. **8** Thick gray wool skirt, long and close to the body. I was going to wear this with the silvery shirt until the last second, when a small voice in my head said, "Don't wear this outfit." I think that it felt too conservative. **9** Pale blue silk blouse. I packed it to wear for just such an occasion, but when I took it out of the suitcase, I noticed a stain on the front, from the last time I tried to iron it and it got wet. **10** J.Crew cords. I like them but suspect they would look sloppy onstage. **11** Also from Berlin, a black semi-sheer shirt from COS. As yet unworn. I didn't notice it in the also-black suitcase. Wish I had. It would have been just right.

**WORN** *Black leather oxfords with a slight heel, no socks. Tight black jeans. The pink bra. A snug long-sleeved cream-colored Isabel Marant shirt, with red and blue stripes. Suspect I wear this outfit too often. I wish that was more acceptable.*

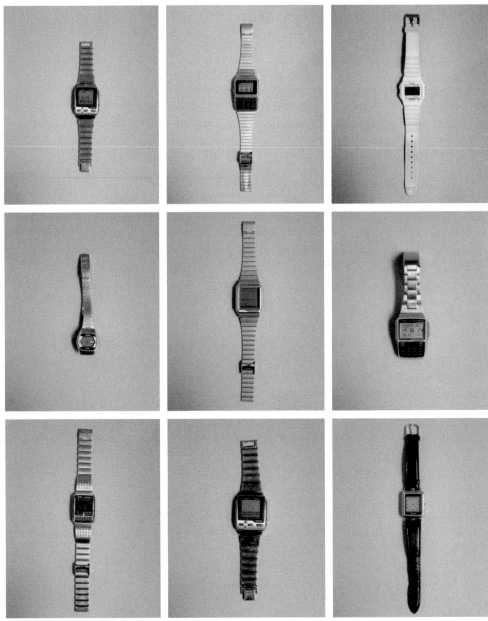

*SENAMI d'ALMEIDA*'s digital wristwatches

# FATHERS

*"My dad came back from a trip to America and said to me, 'I saw this big, marvelous magazine, so I thought I'd get you a subscription for it.' I was ten and it was W magazine."* —BAY GARNETT

IVY KNIGHT When I was ten, my dad (my real dad who lived in Ontario, not the dad who raised me) gave me a gold ring with a little heart and my initial inscribed in it. When I saw the little gold sticker that said "18 karat gold" I figured it was a really expensive piece of jewelry. I had heard about karats in the People's Diamond commercials on TV. I now know that the ring was probably worth about twenty bucks, but it made me feel like a little millionaire.

BIANCA HALL I keep all of my jewelry in a big tool box that has eight drawers. My father was a contractor and he bought it for me when he saw how vast my accessory collection had grown. He painted it and lined all of the drawers with felt. He generally rolls his eye at feminine opulence, so it was sweet and funny of him to make it for me.

EUFEMIA FANTETTI I spent a year in track pants as a depressed student, failing university, which forced my father to ask me politely, "Can I ask you something? Don't you want to look nice?" I yelled, "Who am I supposed to look nice for? Every man on the street?" "Why not?" My dad shrugged. "What's wrong with that?"

ALICIA BERNLOHR In 1981, my parents had just started dating, and my dad was the proud wearer of bright green corduroy bell-bottoms with a matching jacket. He'd just gotten back from three years with the Peace Corps on a tiny island in Southeast Asia. He had missed out on much fashion news. Power dressing was in, and hippie and disco styles were out. "Tomorrow," my mom said to him, "I want you put on your green bell-bottoms and catch the tram. Ride it all around San Francisco. Look at the people inside the tram, and then look out the window. See if you see anyone still wearing an outfit like that." He stopped wearing the green bell-bottoms in public, but did not give them away. I think he would be wearing those green bell-bottoms today if he had been allowed to do so.

ELEANOR JOHNSTON For years I wore a white lightweight Egyptian-cotton bomber jacket that had belonged to my father. He'd been in North Africa in World War II, but probably bought it in London afterward. It had secret pockets, buttoned and zipped a dozen different ways, an articulated side latch, a shoulder flap. Best article of clothing ever.

STEPHANIE WHITEHOUSE When my dad was dying, I dressed up like I was going to work every time I visited him. Somehow being presentable in that situation gave me a sense of dignity and respect for him that made me feel strangely like things were a little under control.

CLAIRE O. I imitated my dad's walk when I was six. I remember copying him when we went fishing and he was loping along in his gumboots. Nowadays when I dress like a boy, I lower my center of gravity a lot and walk from my hips, with an upper-back slouch to hide my breasts.

**RAINBOW MOOON** I was in my twenties and trying to reconnect with my father. He wanted me to go out on a date with his boss, the captain of a police division in Chicago. I put on one of my favorite pantsuits for the occasion, and both my dad and his boss insisted I go change into a miniskirt. I was uncomfortable the entire evening and furious with my father.

**JUSTIN VIVIAN BOND** When I was old enough to walk, I was at the grocery store with my father and he looked down and couldn't find me. He rushed around the corner, and there I was in the next aisle, trying on a lady's high heels! Seeing my father's confusion, she said, "He was so adorable and he asked so sweetly, I just had to say yes!" I don't use the pronoun "he" anymore, but I still like the story.

**MEGAN HUSTAD** My father said nothing regarding clothes. His proud announcements that he left all wardrobe decisions "up to Karen," my mother, gave me the idea that there was something masculine, i.e., powerful, in not caring about clothing, or at least in making as few decisions about clothing as possible.

**RUTKA ABRAM** My dad was an accountant at a big fashion house in the New York City garment district. In high school, during the summers, I worked in his office, on Broadway and 36th Street. At lunch he would say, "Let's go window-shopping to see what the windows look like. Let's wander through to look at the new styles."

**CLODAGH DEEGAN** My father was a pattern cutter and my mother made a lot of our clothes. We never had any money, so caring for our clothes was very important. At the same time, I have a simultaneous, contradictory attitude of "Easy come, easy go" because Dad would sometimes bring home samples. My sisters and I were often the most fashionable girls in the neighborhood, but we'd have had our electricity cut off for not paying the bill.

**ARIEL GARFINKEL** Once my dad gave me this very furry Elmo-ish red chenille sweater. It was hideous, but I knew he had tried, and when I opened the box, I just cried because it was so ugly and I felt so bad for hating it.

**ALICIA ELLIOTT** When I was a teenager, my father once told me I should dress more feminine. This stuck with me. If my own father, a man of limited and dubious taste, thought I dressed terribly, what must everyone else think?

**CARISSA HALSTON** My father spent an exorbitant amount of money on clothes for me, clothes that girls my age didn't wear: pantsuits in pre-adolescence, power suits in my middle teens. He was buying my way into womanhood. When I was fifteen, my father suggested my nose be "fixed." Twice! Years later, my nose is still asymmetrical. I'm almost certain my father was disappointed with the result. Before he was married, my father was a fashion model. It was implied that this was de facto proof that he knew what beauty was.

**EMILY HEMSON** One year for Christmas, my mom told my dad to go out and buy something else for me. So my dad went out and bought a silver necklace with a butterfly and small diamonds in it. It's my favorite necklace, though it's not really my style. But I'd always thought it was so sweet that my dad tried to find something nice for me. At some point I started imposing things onto the necklace. I'm terrified of flying, so when I do fly, I wear this necklace. I even started wearing it when people I cared about travel. ✕

# THE EIGHT-YEAR DRESS

*I met the painter Kate Shepherd at a wedding in the summer of 2013. I noticed her from across a wide lawn. I said to my husband, "Don't we know her?" And he said, "Yes, I mean no, she's a famous actress, isn't she?" She isn't; but something about the dress she was wearing—it was flat, gunmetal gray, and looked to be either vintage or a party dress a ladylike robot from the future might wear—made her seem both familiar and untouchable. She told me that the dress was the result of an ongoing eight-year collaboration with her good friend Nellie Davis, a master printer. Many months later—it was deep winter by then—we all got together and talked about the dress.* —HEIDI JULAVITS

**NELLIE:** I was a Russian major in college. I was also interested in puppetry, so I went to Moscow for a few years. I always made clothing for myself.

**KATE:** Miles's sister was getting married, and I thought, I don't want to go buy a dress, so I said to Nellie, Let's just whip one up together.

**NELLIE:** My wedding dress was the first thing that I spent a lot of time doing finishing work on. After that I started doing a wedding dress every year for a friend, or for a person I wanted to be my friend.

**KATE:** I gave her a Butterick pattern from the '60s, just as an idea. It was meant to be a thirty-hour project.

**NELLIE:** Wedding dresses start with what each woman thinks looks good on her, which I'm not sure is a good place to begin. People don't necessarily have the best judgment about what their body looks good in.

**KATE:** We both think sculpturally about clothing. And we both have unusual noses. When you have an unusual nose, you have to accentuate.

**NELLIE:** When I first met Kate, I was wearing really insanely bright colors like chartreuse and poison red. Then I moved to a bad neighborhood and had children.

**KATE:** It's a very intense, scrutinizing moment to try to design the ultimate dress for yourself.

**NELLIE:** My intuition is to add pleats, add smocking, add embellishment. Kate's aesthetic drive is minimalist, toward clean lines. Her influence was constantly paring down my impulses. Distilling, I would say.

**KATE:** With Nellie and me there's an enormous amount of intimacy. I can pretty much go into her bedroom and get naked and we start picking away at something.

**NELLIE:** Kate puts on all my dresses backward.

**KATE:** She made a muslin version of the dress first, before even touching the fabric.

**NELLIE:** Women's bodies are incredibly different. I've never made a dress for anyone based on measurements that fit her in any way that was flattering when I put it on her the first time.

**KATE:** Nellie tailors everything. She's tailored my bras.

**NELLIE:** I think we flipped the dress around as we were trying it on. Suddenly everything changed.

**KATE:** I really like it when clothing looks like it's drawn as in a coloring book. I like for the silhouette to always be one of the most present things you see.

**NELLIE:** In my ideal world I would be covered head to toe in a headscarf. That's just what I'm driven to wear.

**KATE:** And then I said, Let's turn it inside out. I thought, that's the decoration of the dress—the making of the dress—as opposed to the decorating of the dress.

**NELLIE:** Particular things about the garment bothered her that I never would think of with other people. So some of the details, like the cap sleeve, weren't purely aesthetic. They were also driven by how the dress felt, how she felt in it.

**KATE:** You have to be there as a spiritual object, and that's the hardest part. The clothing has to support you in being that thing. I really try to just listen to my physical body and see what it wants to wear.

**NELLIE:** The fastenings took a long time to resolve. I'm still not sure they're resolved.

**KATE:** When I first wore the dress at said wedding, it fell off. I was topless coming out of the ceremony.

**NELLIE:** The dress hung in my closet for many years. I was looking for the perfect zipper. I thought that would be ideal, if I could find a beautiful zipper. I just never found it.

**KATE:** In all those years the dress didn't change. It's not like, oh you age and you need a different dress. It's always the same dress you need. Maybe I'd like to cover my arms a little bit more now, but other than that it's the same.

**NELLIE:** We talked about putting hooks

The eight-year dress.

and eyes on it, but Kate thought it was too fussy. Now I think that would have been fine.

**KATE:** Then she tried covered buttons and I was like, No no no. A lot of the process was her doing some really ravishingly beautiful work that I undid.

**NELLIE:** I don't know where it would go next, but everything that I make feels transitional. Nothing is ever finished.

**KATE:** Thinking back to the initial impulse to make the dress, there was a moment in fashion that's over now that I probably wanted to harness and copy. Before certain designers started making so much money on handbags, they made extremely sophisticated and sensitive and artful clothing. But I didn't want to spend $3,000 on a dress. I just wanted to spend eight years. ✕

**SURVEY** *I feel most attractive when . . .*

When I'm alone. —GABRIELLE BELL • I feel most attractive when I'm alone. Specifically, I feel most attractive in front of a mirror, pouting and being lit in a specific way that shadows certain portions of my face. It is a personal dreamworld, without the scrutiny of anyone. —NORA PALEY • When I am staying at a hotel, on a trip, away from home and all its responsibilities and complications. —RITA TRONTI • When no one sees me, generally right before I go to sleep. —ELISSA SCHAPPELL

When I'm exercising. —NAOMI ALISA CALNITSKY • I feel at my most attractive after a run—like I'm strong and look really healthy. —DORETTA LAU • When I've spent a leisurely day outdoors, hiking, walking, gardening, and have showered and changed and am hanging out with my husband. —STEPHANIE WHITEHOUSE • I love the glow after exercise and the way that makes me feel. —POPPY TOLAND • After Bikram yoga class. —PEGGY BURNS • After I exercise my body well. —PAULINE SMOLIN • When I'm biking in shorts and a tank top, and I'm in full control of how I propel myself— how fast, how aggressively, and to what end. —SASHA PLOTNIKOVA • After a long run, I feel strong and attractive from the inside out. —MONICA MCCLURE ✕

# THE OUTFIT IN THE PHOTOGRAPH | IV

*Fashion designer Rachel Comey and photographer Willy Somma have been friends since 1990.*
*The two discuss Rachel's outfits in pictures Willy has taken over the years.*

**1**

**RACHEL:** Oh my god, what is that? I made that.

**WILLY:** It's an art piece.

**RACHEL:** I kept it for years. It was really just to hang on a wall. Absurd. With a hole in it.

**WILLY:** Isn't it beautiful?

**RACHEL:** I just wanted to see stripes with bows on top of them, I don't know. I wanted to see fabric draping. It was before I made clothes.

**WILLY:** It's really more of a sculpture.

**RACHEL:** I remember the first time I met you, at the University of Vermont. I got in your car— what year was that Cadillac?

**WILLY:** It was an '86 Fleetwood. An inheritance from my rock-'n'-roll dad.

**RACHEL:** It was a huge-ass Cadillac. Anyway, you were adorably dressed as usual, and interesting, and there you were, driving your black Cadillac, and I just thought, "Who IS this girl?" I don't think you remember meeting me that time.

**WILLY:** I don't. But I remember you being very certain about your ideas, which I found really inspiring, as they were always big ideas, big plans.

**RACHEL:** I had big plans to get outta Dodge. You have to have some kind of dream.

**WILLY:** I remember one of the first times I went to your house and looking through your closet of vintage clothes, going through every single thing and analyzing it. We'd pick apart the things that were good about it, the things that weren't, put it on, decide what kind of girl would wear it and for what reason. We were there for hours. Hours and hours.

•

**2**

**RACHEL:** That's my Ferrari jacket. Nylon.

**WILLY:** And some kind of necklace.

**RACHEL:** Looks like I have hat head, hair dyed black.

**WILLY:** You had another nylon jacket, a red one, that I used to borrow a lot. It was amazing. It was your Joan Jett jacket, though on me it looked less Joan Jett, more Blondie.

**RACHEL:** Looks like we're on the Lower East Side somewhere. I think in those days I was just trying things out.

**WILLY:** But it wasn't just tough; under it you were wearing a blue button-down ruffle blouse.

•

**3**

**RACHEL:** Bill Cunningham took my picture that night.

**WILLY:** It was at the Whitney Biennial.

**RACHEL:** I still have that mini-hat. I hadn't heard of Cunningham. It was in the paper the next week and someone told me about it. He was a hat designer originally, so he loves a hat. Wills, what did you wear that night?

**WILLY:** Oh god, I don't know. I was really into yellow tights during that period.

**RACHEL:** You were a mastermind of color. To this day. I remember always being really blown away by your color mixes. Crazy palettes. Beautiful.

**WILLY:** But what was I thinking with yellow tights? I was going for mod '60s but it was more like, Hello bumblebee.

**RACHEL:** Well, you probably had a lavender leather skirt on.

•

**4**

**WILLY:** Mona the two-legged dog was part of your wardrobe in those days.

**RACHEL:** That was my most expensive purchase ever. A Tracey Feith dress. My dog is tied to my waist, on my most expensive dress, with a piece of ribbon.

•

**5**

**RACHEL:** I don't know where I saw this cape originally, but I special-ordered it. I had to wait months for it and I saved up for it. Yellow pigskin. Wore it quite a bit. Had an unfinished hem. I think this was at a Bad Seeds concert.

•

**6**

**WILLY:** I actually think this is my dress.
**RACHEL:** What dress?
**WILLY:** That vintage dress from the '40s.
**RACHEL:** Pretty.
**WILLY:** Seemed to work with your mustache.

•

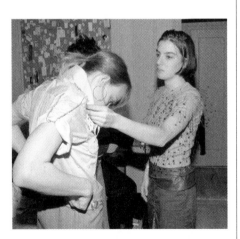

**7**

**WILLY:** This one is amazing, Rachel.
**RACHEL:** Oh. My. God. Can you see what's happening there?
**WILLY:** It's tags. Hang tags.

**RACHEL:** I had a tagging gun and I tagged it.
**WILLY:** Look, you also did it in the background.
**RACHEL:** That was a canvas I tagged. It was all the clothes I bought that year. All Salvation Army. The whole year I retagged. And just kept going and tagged the sweater, also bought at the Salvation Army.
**WILLY:** And you had a crazy leather belt. Was it attached to the pants?
**RACHEL:** I think it was. Nice color palette, yellow, brown, and olive. Remember I made that other dress where I got latex from Canal Rubber. I made latex tags and used the tagging gun and tagged a cocktail dress. Who knows what's up with my hair.
**WILLY:** You were really into wearing your hair in a pompadour for a while.
**RACHEL:** That looks good on me. I should do that more often. To get away from these eyebrows.

•

**8**

**RACHEL:** Where did those jugs come from?
**WILLY:** Seems to be what this photo is all about.
**RACHEL:** I was probably experimenting with some undergarments too. I think that's a feather hat. I used to carry a plastic bag around as my handbag. I look so young and fresh.

**WILLY:** I think those are Alpana Bawa pants.

**RACHEL:** Oh yeah. I love Alpana Bawa. All Indian-dyed, made in India.

**WILLY:** Really, really interesting, colorful fabrics. All ethnic, used to be on First and First.

**RACHEL:** But all these style tips I got from you and Rachel Grady and all the girls here in New York before I moved here. They'd just tell me where to go and I would go there. Rachel Grady told me—I'll never forget it—that in high school she cut the tops of her Converse All Stars off and then safety-pinned them back onto the soles and wore them like that. I was like, That is pretty much just the coolest thing I've ever heard. And then Heather Hernan, she used to take Esprit labels out of her garments and sew them onto the outside of other garments. She'd "Esprit-ize."

·

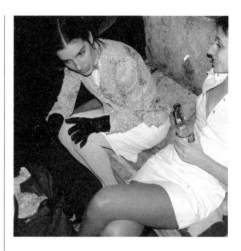

**10**

**WILLY:** You were SO into that shirt.

**RACHEL:** I love it. You've had to bite your tongue all these years. "Man, you were really into that shirt!"

**WILLY:** No! I loved that shirt too and tried to borrow it on numerous occasions.

**RACHEL:** It was that really slippery polyester.

**WILLY:** And you were wearing polka-dot white tights, red shoes, a white skirt, and black gloves.

·

**9**

**WILLY:** This was in Maine, 2002.

**RACHEL:** That trench coat was so versatile. You could wear it out and it could be dark and moody, or you could wear it on an island in Maine. The thing about this trench coat was the proportion. I think it was a kid's trench coat. It was small.

**WILLY:** You didn't customize it?

**11**

**WILLY:** This was one of my beginning stabs at portraiture, I was experimenting with lighting people indoors and you posed for me in your apartment on Elizabeth Street. You had your workshop in that room. It was that time in our lives of, Here's me "the photographer" taking a portrait of my friend Rachel "the designer." When we were just starting to inhabit those roles, even if it still felt kind of abstract.

**RACHEL:** I made that top. So this was after I started the women's line. I remember that table.

•

**12**

**WILLY:** Isn't that great? Look at this amazing thing.

**RACHEL:** I got that in Brighton Beach. I'm in the back of a cab. The shawl would dazzle up any old cheap outfit.

**WILLY:** This isn't your usual look.

**RACHEL:** But in those days we'd change several times a day.

•

**13**

**WILLY:** You were really into making watch-fob necklaces back then.

**RACHEL:** I kinda look hot. This kitty-cat shirt was from—this is embarrassing—from a field trip with my Ultimate Frisbee team, somewhere in the South one spring break and I reshaped it.

**14**

**WILLY:** Look at your braids with the bathing suit. It's pretty awesome. Come on, you look amazing.

**RACHEL:** The suit's Norma Kamali. She's so cool. Rob Pruitt gave me that towel.

**WILLY:** You were really proud of purchasing that suit.

**RACHEL:** Hell yeah, it's a good suit.

**WILLY:** That was the two-second moment when you were single. Not even, really.

•

**15**

**RACHEL:** That's my own dress. I think this is between breakups. I look thinner.

**WILLY:** Yep. You look very skinny. And you have two drinks.

•

**16**

**WILLY:** This is Todd's fiftieth.

**RACHEL:** I love that dress, actually. It's a dress where we got the cutting ticket wrong in the factory. The underlayer was made out of sheer mesh and the skirt had a flap front and back, so we made a matching panty. It was a happy accident. ✗

489

*TANIA VAN SPYK*'s dress sets part II

# Tryntje Kramer

*Tryntje Kramer (née Elgersma) was born in 1919 in Friesland, the Netherlands. She lives in Grimsby, Ontario, in Shalom Manor nursing home. She was a homemaker and was married to Juke Kramer, who died seven years ago.*
—KRISTIN SJAARDA

*When do you feel most attractive?*
When I have my blue-colored clothes on.

*Are there any items that you have in multiple?*
Purses.

*What is the most transformative conversation you have ever had with someone on this subject?*
Grace, my daughter, did my colors. Then I always chose clothes within that palate.

*What are some dressing rules you wouldn't necessarily recommend to others but you follow?*
The colors should go together.

*Do you have taste or style?*
Both! To get nice clothes during the war, I would barter or trade. Butter or milk could be exchanged for material or sewing. A trip back to Holland meant I could buy new clothes. I took really good care of them. I had a good figure. We had money in Holland, and I had a seamstress there during the war, but I didn't have many clothes because of the war. I was interested in style. Two weeks before I got married, I got a new dress in a beautiful green. My wedding dress was white with all these little buttons down the front. It was unusual during the war to have white.

*What do you admire about how other women present themselves?*
In Jarvis church—the church we used to belong to when we got to Canada and bought a farm—I was the one they admired. Mrs. Kray had a nicely decorated house. She was a real lady. Dressed nicely. Behaved like a lady. Was not an immigrant. We went there often for coffee.

*Are there any women in culture whose style you admire?*
No one from TV or movies. Now, from *Wheel of Fortune*, Vanna looks good. She can pick whatever she wants to have on. She's wealthy. And she has a good figure.

*Do you take after your mother in any way?*
I didn't know my mom, but she was very beautiful and stylish. I know that from pictures. She died when I was nine. Once I took the boat from Canada to Holland, and my father was there when I disembarked. He said, "You are just like your mom." I had on a beautiful coat fitted with buttons and orange polka dots. So my mom must have had good taste, too. There is only one picture of her, from approximately 1900, and indeed, she is very dressed up.

*When you see yourself in photographs, what do you think?*
Plain housewife. Nothing special. But I always had good clothes on. In a picture with friends in Niagara Falls, I had a blue-and-white polka-dot dress. It fit me so well. I had

seven or eight kids then. I still had a good figure.

*How do you shop for clothes?*
I went once to Hamilton with a friend who lived close by. She lived with her dad and siblings and ran the house. Now sometimes a lady comes to the auditorium of Shalom with clothes to sell. But I don't often buy because there are so many of the same things. And I don't want to look like the other residents. There are ladies who buy, but maybe they are not as picky as me.

*How does money fit into all this?*
If I can get it on sale, I will, but it's not always possible. My sister says I can smell the sales.

*What is your favorite piece?*
My blue sweater. And I have a coral brooch about two hundred years old. My husband bought it for me. And a gold pendant necklace.

*Was there ever an important purchase in your life?*
Mostly my jewelry.

*How does the way you dress play into your ambitions for yourself?*
What a funny question. I don't think much about my ambition.

*How has your background influenced how you dress?*
I'm Frisian. A Dutch immigrant. I prefer European materials and styles and quality.

*What would be a difficult look for you to achieve?*
I would have trouble wearing something dowdy.

*How is all this important?*
For my feelings. I like the details.

*Do you have routines?*
I go to the hairdresser every week to get it washed and set. No makeup. For my age, my figure is pretty good. On my body I put good-smelling cream. With clothes, I pick the ones that look good. Before, I had a better figure, but that's okay. I have a skirt in black with a little movement that's my favorite.

*If you had to wear a "uniform," what would it look like?*
A purse. And I always wear gold pendant of a Huguenot cross, night and day.

*Do you have any powerful clothing memories?*
I once had an apron with long sleeves to bathe a boy with diphtheria. A boy from Scheveningen who was staying with us during the war. He would have starved back at his home. He stayed in bed always.

*Are there any tricks that make you feel like you're getting away with something?*
I was kind of shy. If I had to go into a room full of people, I didn't go in first. ✕

# LOST

*"My dog ate my shoes. I liked them. I want them back. I want my dog back."* —ALEXA S.

**SUSAN SANFORD BLADES** During my childbearing and married years, I think I lost my style. I lost a lot of myself. I became a jeans-and-T-shirt mom. My husband was very conservative, judgmental, and jealous, and thought any expression of myself was a deviation from the marriage. One day when he picked the kids up, I was wearing shorty-shorts with tights and moccasin boots, and he said, "Say hello to your colleagues downtown for me." It wasn't until we separated that I regained my style.

**KIRA JOLLIFFE** I've lost too many things I've loved. These losses plague me, some even twenty years later. When I get a new piece of clothing I love, I grieve its future loss.

**ELEANOR WEST** There's a dress I didn't buy for prom, a gold gown from Screaming Mimi's. The top was silk and the bottom was taffeta. All my friends thought it was hideous, and maybe it was, but I remember it fondly. Sometimes I miss things that I didn't buy.

**DALE MEGAN HEALEY** I always lose black cardigans, especially during the winter, because when I take my layers off it's easy to remember my coat and harder to remember I was also wearing the black cardigan. I've lost two in two months. I lost the first one at a party. Earlier that day my California friends and I wrote fortunes to each other and pulled them out of a hat. My fortunes were: "You'll be reinvented completely" and "Someone will want to interview you and you will have a compulsion to lie."

**STAR SPIDER** My wedding tutu and veil were made by a friend who is no longer a friend. They hold memories that are both unbearably bitter and wonderfully sweet. I keep the tutu although I lost the friend who made it.

**ELENA MEGALOS** I had this embroidered purple shawl that my mother bought me on a trip to Copper Canyon, Mexico. An old roommate borrowed it without asking, and later admitted that it had been stolen at a bar. She was very apologetic and acknowledged that the piece was irreplaceable. It had been an accident, but I felt sorry for myself. I would have liked to participate in the item's fate. At the very least, I wanted to be the person who lost it.

**JOANNA CORNISH** I was quite a bit heavier when I was in my later years of high school and through university. I was very distant from my body and lived mostly in my head. When I turned twenty-four, I lost sixty pounds, which I've mostly kept off for just under a decade. As a result of this weight loss, it's less of a struggle to find clothes that fit me and shopping is more fun. I dressed like a homeless person when I was a teenager. Not "cool" hipster homeless like kids now, but actually homeless.

**JOHANNA FATEMAN** I found a fitted black jacket on the street in my early twenties. I was on some kind of desperate errand for my boss and opened a cab door into a bank of trash bags on the Upper East Side. The jacket was laid on top of the garbage and sort of fell into my arms as I squeezed out of the car. It was originally probably very expensive, but a little threadbare by the time I got it, which actually made it better, punker. It was vaguely military, somehow French, and it had a secret pocket. Even rich people complimented me on it. I loaned it to a friend who took it somewhere to have the lining repaired for me and I never got it back. I want it back because I would still wear it. I have the superstitious conviction it was intended for me, a gift from the universe.

**CARLA DU PREE** During our courting of eight years, before being married for twenty-five and then some, my Big Al gave me two bracelets that his beloved mother, Vonda, owned. She passed away when he was a mere seventeen-year-old boy. Both were gold: one charm bracelet with a jade Buddha, and the other a large, heavy link bracelet, something I wore for years before someone stole them both.

**DEBORAH KIRSHNER** I used to love the things that transformed me from an unmade bed into a thing of perfection. These items no longer do the trick—they either are too old or don't fit anymore—including some really lovely pieces of jewelry. Also lately, certain colors and patterns that once looked good don't seem to suit me. The truth is that I'm having a hard time with my newfound body. It is nothing like the old one. I can't get used to it and I can't redesign it, no matter how hard I try.

**ASHLEY C. FORD** I can't recall ever feeling there was an article of clothing I wish I could have back. By the time I give something away, I'm truly done with it.

**MARGARITA TUPITSYN** One of the reasons Winona Ryder and Johnny Depp once had

interesting style has a lot to do with the '90s—the last moment for alternative culture in America. They obviously had great, raw taste, and when they wore those clothes, they were open to possibilities. Today, everyone, artists included, aspires to be part of the mainstream. There is no alternative culture. No outside.

**STEPHANIE RUSSO** For a girl with glasses, the perfect pair of glasses are as elusive as they are to be treasured. Mine were so amazing. Perfectly suited to my face, they looked so natural that it was like I wasn't even wearing glasses. Then one day I sat on them and snapped one of the arms. I still think about those glasses.

**KATHRYN DAW** I dearly miss my black leather Hermès Cape Cod watch. I sold this beautiful watch in Paris on Craigslist so that I could remain in my rented apartment for another few months while freelance work was minimal.

**MARGARET HULL** I evacuated to Florida from Louisiana for Hurricane Isaac. The last night of evacuation, my friends and I went dancing and drank too many gin and tonics. I woke up the next morning and realized I wasn't wearing my great-grandmother's gold padlock charm. I looked in the car, all over the house, and I was so uncomfortably hungover I went back to bed. I was heading back to New Orleans that day, and though the bars were forty-five minutes away and I had my cat in the car, I had a strong feeling that I should go back and look. The first bar had a large outdoor deck. I talked to a bartender and looked down where we stood. The padlock was at our feet! No chain, and the lock was a little scuffed, but it was there! Such adrenaline passed through me. I thanked her profusely. I love the charm because it has been lost and found (I lost and found it). It's small, it's scratched, and it connects me to my family.

**JACKIE SORO**  A couple years ago, in a rush to move out of my house and make it to the airport in time to fly back to the Midwest, I left a pair of glittery silver high-top sneakers in the front room. I only remembered in the car on the way to the airport, and I was tempted to break in through the window and get them, but I didn't want to risk missing my plane. Those shoes were awesome, though.

**SU WU**  A few years ago, I got an engagement ring. I didn't want to get married, but the ring was just right—asymmetrical and chipped and old. It sat in a box for more than a year, feeling too delicate and heavy all at once, before I started wearing it. It got a lot of compliments. One day my boyfriend and I went surfing. I was about to go under a wave when I saw a fin. Shark, I thought. I flipped underwater in a ball. When I came up, there was a school of dolphins swimming against the sunset. When my boyfriend and I got home, I realized I had lost the ring in the ocean. My boyfriend said, "It's good to know there are treasures out there." He was the real treasure, blah blah, I know, but I still think about the ring.  ✕

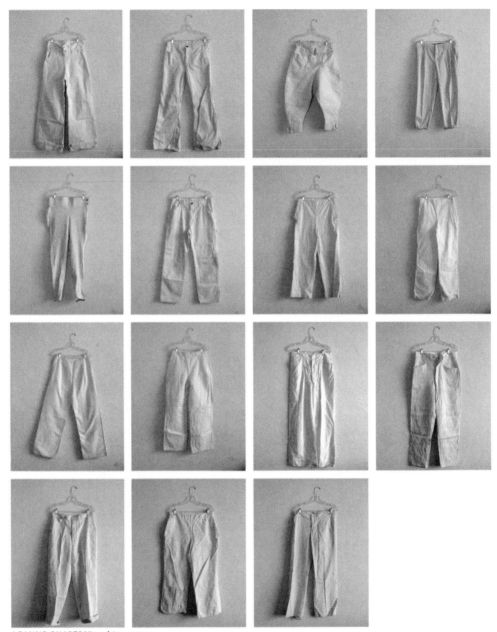

*LEANNE SHAPTON*'s white trousers

# NOTHING

## LISA ROBERTSON

Because nothing was thick enough, nothing was light enough, nothing was supple enough, nothing was orbiting enough, nothing was scathing enough, nothing was touching enough, nothing tried enough, nothing was thinking enough, nothing laughed enough, nothing kissed enough, nightly wasn't enough, not puffed enough, not long enough, not pelt enough, not loving enough, not liking enough, not dressing enough, not velvet enough, not raining enough, I need a feathered dress for reading Pessoa, I need violet platform pumps for reading Mouré, I need powder and high socks for reading Agamben, I need a Bordeaux batwing shantung jacket for Benveniste. I go on the websites of everything. I'm just someone living in 2014. I'm searching. I'm beginning.

There was the blue crepe knee-length frock printed with comets and rockets, with a wide décolleté. There was the pale pink and black taffeta circle skirt worn with flat sandals and a cropped mohair top in electric blue. There was a broad-shouldered very long 1940s swing coat worn with a string of ivory beads and jazz shoes. There was the teal silk gauze oblong printed Japanese scarf and matching beret. There were brown silk paisley pajamas good for dancing at Les Bains Douches. There were silver bangles and ivory bangles and plastic bangles and wooden bangles. There were lined hand-stitched pigskin gloves. There were gray and yellow floral cotton off-the-shoulder summer dresses. There were pointed shoes and the worn-in ink-marked saddlebag. There were satin-back black crepe Sonia Rykiel hip-huggers cropped above the ankles to show patent leather Doc Martens. There was a honey-colored deep V-neck dress with ruching at the waist and flared skirt. There was the jagged hemmed Japanese thrift skirt worn with brand-new Belgian small-shouldered jacket, ripped tights, and bucked boots from Camden market. There was the equestrian time, the time of little '60s ladies' suits worn too tight with boots, the time of jeans torn right and bleached-out platinum hair. There was the discovery of intense red lips, first shiny, then matte, then shiny again. There was dark green mascara. There was the squinting with no glasses, then the tortoiseshell retro glasses. There was the fluid drape of the amazing Demeulemeester overcoat courtesy of Cambridge University Faculty of English. There was the curator friend's mother's Comme des Garçons kimono-sleeved taupe knit tube dress with motorcycle boots. There was extremely short hair cut at the barber's or shaved by boyfriends. There was the '50s suede pilot-style zippered bomber jacket with knee-length tight plaid skirt and laced ankle boots. There was the high-slit heathered Harris tweed pencil skirt with black stay-ups. There were the twin sets and the off-the-shoulder black sweatshirts and the backless white summer wraparound dress with fine black trim. There were often green shoes. There was the first bottle of black-red nail polish, the big fake-fur coat with high flaring collar worn over the very short skirt with garters showing, there was the black lace knee-length dress with little velvet bolero bought for standby seats at the opera, there was my grandmother's raw-silk pale yellow skirt suit from 1962. There were the flesh-toned fishnets. There was gingham, alpaca, beading, asymmetrical hair and long hennaed hair. The skull ring. The little kilts with tailored '40s jackets. The dark green '70s trench coat with cropped plaid '50s trousers.

All of this was necessary for reading.

The rules: Awkward proportions, tomboy wears femme or femme wears tomboy, something must be worn-out and frayed or mended, most outfits will reference the history of female genius in their cut, fit, era, or accessories, one pair of good boots is basic to living decently, the bag will always contain several books and many lipsticks, designer is better thrifted, hair should be inappropriate, toenails always painted, tailoring, eBay occasionally for Comme des Garçons.

When I get dressed I'm inventing concepts, in the way concepts are invented. To steal, to layer, to shorten, to mend, to mix eras wrongly, to patiently elaborate a proportion, to not care and to care a lot, to exaggerate and to curtail and to misquote and to buy when a grant comes in to make my girlfriends smile.

# ACKNOWLEDGMENTS

Thank you to all our wonderful contributors, and to all those who filled out a survey for the book. We wish we could have included everyone. We'd like to thank all those who helped spread word about this project, in particular Sona Avakian, Juliet Jacques, Tyler Perkins, and Nafeesa Syeed. We'd like to especially thank Miranda July and Sarah Nicole Prickett for early editorial input. Also thank you to Rebecca Nagel, Jim Rutman, and Andrew Wylie, and to our editors, Helen Conford, Sarah Hochman, and Friederike Schilbach, for their trust in our vision. Thank you to our families and friends for their love and support. We couldn't have made this book without the excellent work of our associate editor, Mary Mann, and assistant designer, Kate Ryan.

Leanne Shapton would like to thank Katherine Bernard, Josh Blackwell, Kim Bost, Semi Chellas, Claudia Dey, Bay Garnett, Kuch Naren, Gus Powell, Tom Schierlitz, Jenny Schily, Michael Schmelling, Kristin Sjaarda, Willy Somma, Heidi Sopinka, Luise Stauss, and Rachel Perry Welty for additional photography, and Lisa Naftolin for consulting on the design. Miranda July would like to thank Jona Borrut and Ari Seth Cohen for their support of her project. Thanks to Jennifer Armbrust and Max Fenton for website design. Special thanks to Kathryn Borel, Tom Consiglio, Beth Ficzko, and Claire Vaccaro. Thank you to the women who participated in the Katherine Bernard piece: Irina Aleksander, Rachel Antonoff, Joana Avillez, Durga Chew-Bose, Audrey Gelman, Julie Houts, Alexandra Kleeman, Thessaly La Force, Lucia Della Paolera, and Julia Wideman. Additional illustrations are from *Hebrew Through Pictures*, *The New Encyclopedia of Modern Sewing*, *Key to the Native Trees of Canada*, and *Basic Field Manual: Conventional Signs, Military Symbols and Abbreviations*.

# CONTRIBUTORS

**ABI SLONE** (p. 123) is an editor in Montreal. **ADA EZE** (p. 100) is 19; she studies in Turkey, lives in Maine, and wears green lipstick. **ADINA GOLDMAN** (p. 75) is an editor and Web producer in Toronto, where she lives with her partner and son. **ADITI SADEQA RAO** (p. 209), 23, grew up mostly in Bombay and a bit in Saint Paul, and is now a law student based in London. **ADRIEN J.** (p. 381) is a young woman who lives in Los Angeles, working at a start-up company. **ADRIENNE BUTIKOFER** (pp. 123, 141) works as a designer in Toronto and is married with two children. **AGNES BARLEY** (pp. 87, 148, 380, 437 ) is an artist who lives and works in New York City. **ALESIA PULLINS** (pp. 17, 25, 133) is a professional lady who dwells on the West Coast. Her general interests are bronzer, Beyoncé, and making you feel uncomfortable as she loudly discusses gentrification in wine bars. **ALEX** (p. 381) works on screenplays and spends most of the year in New Orleans. **ALEX WAGNER** (p. 313) is a political analyst and anchor of the daytime program *Now with Alex Wagner* on MSNBC. **ALEXA S.** (pp. 134, 436, 493) is a 33-year-old film producer in London. **ALEXANDER NAGEL** (p. 187) is currently writing a book on orientation in art and an essay on art forgery. **ALEXANDRA JACOBS** (p. 112) is deputy fashion critic for *The New York Times*. **ALEXANDRA KERN** (pp. 266, 462) is a Brooklyn-based writer and performer. She is originally from Shaker Heights, Ohio. **ALEXANDRA KLEEMAN** (pp. 415–417) lives and writes in Brooklyn, New York, where she is completing her first novel. **ALEXANDRA ZSIGMOND** (p. 117) is deputy art director for the opinion section at *The New York Times*. **ALEXI CHISLER** (pp. 61, 124, 271), born in 1977, currently lives half the time in Brooklyn, New York, and half the time in hotels around the world while working for the American Museum of Natural History. **ALEXIA CHANDON-PIAZZA** (p. 391) is a French multidisciplinary artist and actress. She is studying to become an art therapist. **ALI COTTONG** (p. 379) is 24 and lives in San Francisco. **ALICIA BERNLOHR** (pp. 102, 135, 178, 207, 441, 479) is a writer and artist who lives in New York. **ALICIA ELLIOTT** (pp. 452, 480) is working on her first screenplay and lives in Brantford, Ontario, with her husband and daughter. **ALICIA MEIER** (p. 354) studies writing and translation in New York City. **ALISSA NUTTING** (pp. 271, 285, 437, 451) is author of the books *Unclean Jobs for Women and Girls* and *Tampa*. **ALIYA JACOBS**'s (p. 101) second book, a collection of poetry, was released this year. She is married and lives in South Africa. **ALLISON D.** (pp. 73, 148, 361) is a writing professor in Iowa, where she lives with her husband and dogs. **ALMITRA COREY** (p. 136) is 34 and lives in Los Angeles, where she works as a production designer. **ALY MARGARETS** (p. 125) is 23 and lives in Hamilton, Ontario. **AMANDA M.** (pp. 19, 268) is an editor in Chicago. **AMANDA MILLER** (pp. 74, 100, 428) lives and works in Toronto. **AMANDA STERN** (pp. 271, 389) is the author of the novel *The Long Haul* and eleven books for children. She founded the popular Happy Ending Music and Reading Series in New York City. **AMÉLIE SNYERS** (p. 87) is Belgian, 28, and lives in London. **AMY BONNAFFONS** (pp. 133, 440) is a writer and educator living in Brooklyn, New York. **AMY BRILL**'s (pp. 351, 435) first novel, *The Movement of Stars*, was published by Riverhead Books in 2013. **AMY FUSSELMAN**'s (p. 357) new book is *Savage Park: A Meditation on Play, Space, and Risk for Americans Who Are Nervous, Distracted, and Afraid to Die*. **AMY KEY** (p. 381) lives in London. Her poetry collection *Luxe* was published in 2013. **AMY LAM** (pp. 286, 327) is one-half of the performance-art group Life of a Craphead. She lives in Toronto. **AMY MARTHA McGURK** (p. 263) is a designer and single mom living outside Atlanta. **AMY PINKHAM** (p. 248) is a photographer. **AMY RUDERSDORF** (pp. 125, 177) lives in Wisconsin, where she works as a librarian. **AMY ROSE SPIEGEL** (pp. 72, 141, 419, 440) is a 23-year-old writer and story editor for *Rookie*. **AMY TURNER** (pp. 272, 362, 456) lives in Los Angeles. She has written for NBC, CBS, ABC Family, and *The Huffington Post*. She is working on a collection of essays. **ANA BUNČIĆ** (p. 153), 38, is an editorial assistant in Zagreb, Croatia. **ANA KINSELLA** (pp. 17, 381) is a 25-year-old writer and journalist living in London. **ANA OTTMAN** (p. 62) is a writer living in Los Angeles. **ANA ZIR** (pp. 98, 134, 329), 63, is a mother of four daughters and a hospice and palliative care RN in Tucson. **ANAHIT ORDYAN** (p. 61) lives in Yerevan and works at the American University of Armenia. **ANDREA MICHELLE STEELE** (p. 328) is married and living in Cambridge, Massachusetts, where she works in clinical research. **ANDREA WALKER** (p. 80) lives in Stamford, Connecticut, and is an editor in New York City. **ANISE LeANN** (p. 451) is 36 and lives in the San Francisco Bay Area, where she is a commercial photographer. **ANISSE GROSS** (p. 123) is a writer living in San Francisco. **ANITA ABRAMS** (pp. 437, 452) is a recently retired clinical psychologist. **ANITA DOLMAN'S** (p. 264) short stories and poetry have appeared in magazines, journals, and anthologies throughout Canada and the United States. She lives in Ottawa, where she is on the board of directors for *Arc Poetry Magazine*. **ANITA POWELL** (p. 134) is a radio and television journalist based in Johannesburg. **ANN BOGLE'S** (pp. 133, 437) stories appear in various print and online journals. Her clothes are shelved in four closets in St. Louis Park, Minnesota, one block west of Minneapolis. **ANN IRELAND** (pp. 17, 141, 272) is the prizewinning author of four novels and lives in Toronto. **ANN TASHI SLATER** (p. 46) (anntashislater.com) is working on a travel memoir set in India and a novel based on the Tibetan side of her family. **ANNA BACKMAN ROGERS** (p. 295) is a postdoctoral scholar in film studies at Stockholm University. **ANNA BASS** (p. 307) is a dancer and associate artistic director of Monica Bill Barnes & Company. **ANNA COSTLEY** (p. 437) lives in Wellington, New Zealand, and writes the Web comic *Anna-grams*. **ANNA LEE** (pp. 218–219) is 26 and lives in New York City, where she attends nursing school. **ANNA CLARE SPELMAN** (p. 425) is a documentary photographer from Silver Spring, Maryland. She is currently based in Phnom Penh, Cambodia. **ANNA WEBBER** (p. 435) is a literary agent in London. She is married and has three children. **ANNE LAURENCE GOLLION** (p. 267) is 26 and just moved from Paris to Jerusalem, where she works as a freelance writer. **ANNEMIEKE BEEMSTER LEVERENZ** (p. 147) is a graphic designer living in Brooklyn, New York. **ANNETTE CARGIOLI** (p. 271) is a natural health care doctor and educator in Indiana. **ANNIE REBEKAH GARDNER** (p. 221) lives between Cambridge, Massachusetts, and Cairo. **ANNIE McDONALD** (p. 76) is a writer and prop stylist who lives in Toronto with her husband and two small children. **ANNIKA WAHLSTRÖM** (pp. 267, 457) is a Swedish textile artist and bus driver. **ANU HENDERSON** (pp. 98, 124, 452) is a researcher and lives in Victoria, British Columbia, with her husband and baby. **AREV DINKJIAN** (pp. 18, 124) is 21 years old. She is currently studying elementary and special education at Providence College and hopes to become an elementary school teacher. **ARIA SLOSS** (pp. 421, 466) is the author of *Autobiography of Us*, which was published in 2013. **ARIEL GARFINKEL** (pp. 463, 480) is a writer from New Jersey. **ARIEL N. KATES** (p. 463) lives, works, and writes in New York City. **ASHLEY C. FORD** (pp. 36, 73, 494) is a 27-year-old writer from Indiana who lives in New York. **AUDREY GELMAN** (pp. 97, 125, 272, 415–417), 26, lives in Brooklyn, New York, and works as a political and public affairs consultant. **AUGUSTA LEE** (p. 207) is a model in New York. **AURELIA** (pp. 25, 221, 329, 352, 411) is a screen and stage performing artist based in the eastern United States, and cohost of *Black Girls Talking*. Parisian-born **AURÉLIE PELLISSIER** (p. 113) lives in New York, where she is senior art director at *T Magazine*. **AURORA SHIMSHAK** (pp. 54, 271) is 30 years old and teaches high school English in Oshkosh, Wisconsin. **AVA V.** (p. 427) is 38 and lives in Bilbao, Spain. She writes unpublished books and works as a hairstylist and makeup artist. **AVIVA MICHAELOV** (p. 114) is an art director at *The New York Times.* **BARBARA DAMROSCH** (p. 461) is a farmer and author of *The Garden Primer* and coauthor of *The Four Season Farm Gardener's Cookbook.* **BAY GARNETT** (pp. 220, 264, 479) is a contributing fashion editor at British *Vogue,* a stylist and thrift store devotee, and a former coeditor of *Cheap Date* magazine. **BEN** (p. 213) is an artist and engineer living in Winchester, England. **BENEDICTE PINSET** (p. 240) is an artist and mother. **BETH FOLLETT** (pp. 36, 427, 439) lives in St. John's, Newfoundland, where she is publisher-editor at Pedlar Press. **BETH STUART** (pp. 71, 124) is an artist who lives and works in Hamilton, Ontario. **BEV SANDELL GREENBERG** (p. 46) is a fiction writer, reviewer, poet, and editor living in the Canadian prairies. **BIANCA HALL** (p. 479) is 30 years old and lives in Toronto, where she works as a television news producer. **BLAINE HARPER** (p. 272) lives in San Francisco. She works on Alcatraz Island and is an intern for the Multidisciplinary Association for Psychedelic Studies. **BONNIE MORRISON** (pp. 75, 272, 329, 349) is a New York–based fashion publicist. **BRIAN McCLOSKEY** (p. 143) was born in Northern Ireland in 1969 and now lives in Southern California. **BRITTANY BROWN** (p. 390) is 26 and lives in Philadelphia, where she works at two independent bookstores. **BRONWYN CAWKER** (pp. 123, 277) is 27 and lives in Toronto, where she works as an administrative assistant and attends school part-time. **BRYENNE KAY** (pp. 123, 221, 349, 381) is 28 and lives in Moscow. **CAIA HAGEL**'S (pp. 142, 207, 451 [interviewed Sasha Grey]) personality profiles, fictions, cultural travelogues, and art+design thoughts appear in magazines, in advertising, and on social media internationally. **CAILIN HILL** (pp. 97, 123, 421) is a retired fashion model who now does everything *but* that to make ends meet. She is a freelance writer, hot wife, zine publisher, photographer, and founder of the blog Modelburnbook. **CAITLIN ANN HARRINGTON** (p. 427) is 26 and lives in Brooklyn, New York. She is a researcher on the Chuck Close catalogue raisonné. **CAITLIN VAN DUSEN** (pp. 266, 285, 421) is an editor and writer living in Brooklyn, New York. **CAITLYNN CUMMINGS** (p. 61) is a creative writer and administrator based in Calgary, Canada; follow her on Twitter @Tartaned_Maple. **CAITRIN LYNCH** (p. 36 [interviewed Rachel Weeks]) is an anthropologist at Olin College of Engineering and the author of *Juki Girls, Good Girls: Gender and Cultural Politics in Sri Lanka's Global Garment Industry.* **CAMILLA GIBB** (p. 271) has a Ph.D. in social anthropology from Oxford University and is the author of four novels, including *Sweetness in the Belly* and *The Beauty of Humanity Movement.* **CAMILLE CAMPBELL** (p. 463) lives in Los Angeles, where she writes screenplays and blogs at excellentnotion. com. **CARISSA HALSTON** (pp. 36, 440, 480) has been a prose editor at *AGNI,* and is currently writing a novel called *Conjoined States.* **CARLA DU PREE** (pp. 221, 267, 390, 440, 494) is the author of the novel *Where the Spirit Meets the Bone* and has been published in *Callaloo* and other literary journals and in the anthology *The Spirit of Pregnancy.* She speaks regularly at literary events and lives in Columbia, Maryland. **CARLY KATZ** (pp. 218–219) is 26 and lives in Washington, D.C., where she works on Capitol Hill. **CARMEN JOY KING** (pp. 272, 351) is a writer living in Montreal. **CAROLANN MADDEN** (pp. 51, 436) has an M.A. in English from Boston College, and an MFA in poetry from San Diego State University. She is working on a book of translations of Irish-language poetry. **CAROLINE EICK** (p. 87) is a writer and editor in New York City. **CAROLINE HIRSCH** (p. 107) is a photo editor who lives north of New York City with her beloved husband, Chihuahua, and tortoise. **CAROLYN F.** (p. 435) is a writer who lives in north central Washington state; she is married and has five grandchildren and one great-grandchild. **CARRIE MURPHY** (pp. 379, 428) is a poet and doula living in Albuquerque, New Mexico. Her first book of poems, *Pretty Tilt,* was published in 2012 and her second, *Fat Daisies,* is forthcoming in 2014. **CASSANDRA LEVEILLE** (p. 272) is 24 years old and lives on Long Island. She has interned at many feminist nonprofit organizations. **CAT TYC** (p. 124) is a new media poet/video artist whose music videos have aired on Logo's *NewNowNext* and mtvU. **CATH LE COUTEUR** (p. 211) is a filmmaker based in London. **CATHERINE CONNELL** (pp. 218–219) is an almost 30-year-old mental health clinician in Leyden, Massachusetts. **CATHERINE LACEY** (pp. 75, 125) is the author of *Nobody Is Ever Missing.* **CATHERINE**

**LITTEN** (p. 272) is 24 years old and an international education professional. **CATHERINE MAROTTA** (pp. 147, 427) is a teacher and graduate student living in Brooklyn, New York. **CATHERINE ORCHARD** (p. 277) is a graphic designer and illustrator in Brooklyn. **CATHERINE STOCKHAUSEN** (p. 361) is a Toronto television producer, photographer, and sometimes musician. **CATHY DE LA CRUZ** (p. 208) is a filmmaker and writer with an MFA in visual arts from the University of California, San Diego. She will soon have an MFA in creative writing from the University of Arizona. **CERIDWEN MORRIS** (p. 29) is a writer and childbirth educator. **CHANG SHIH YEN** (p. 47) is from Malaysia and currently living in New Zealand. She writes a blog about shoes at shihyenshoes.wordpress.com. **CHARLOTTE BOYD** (p. 268) is 23 and lives in Louisville, Kentucky, where she works as a Web producer at a news station. **CHARLOTTE YOSHIMURA** (p. 316) is an oncologist in Oklahoma. **CHIN-SUN LEE** (pp. 333, 463) lived in New York for many years, and is currently wandering the West and writing. **CHRISTA PARRAVANI**'s (p. 397) first book, *Her: A Memoir*, was published last year, and she is currently at work on another. She lives in Los Angeles with her husband and daughter. **CHRISTEN CLIFFORD** (p. 241) is a writer, feminist performance artist, actor, curator, professor and mother who lives in Queens, New York, and online at christenclifford.tumblr.com. **CHRISTINA GONZALES** (pp. 342, 462) is 50 and lives in Fort Sumner, New Mexico, and is working as a program technician for the USDA Farm Service Agency. **CHRISTINE GIGNAC** (p. 272) is 30 and lives in New York City, where she works as a creative director in advertising. **CHRISTINE MUHLKE** (pp. 91, 264, 344, 455) is the executive editor of *Bon Appétit*. **CHRISTOPHER BOLLEN** (p. 99) is a writer who lives in New York City. His first novel, *Lightning People*, came out in 2011; his second, *Orient*, will be out in 2015. **CHRISTY-CLAIRE KATIEN** (pp. 348, 381, 452) is a designer and photographer based in New York City. **CINDY SHERMAN** (p. 281) is an artist who lives and works in New York City. **CLAIRE CAMERON** (p. 271), author of the novels *The Bear* and *The Line Painter*, lives in Toronto. **CLAIRE COTTRELL** (pp. 216, 222) is a filmmaker and photographer living in Mount Washington, California. **CLAIRE GRIFFIN** (p. 47). **CLAIRE O.** (pp. 208, 381, 479) trained as a lawyer before going into teaching. She is 26, and lives in Melbourne, Australia. **CLARE NEEDHAM**'s (pp. 50, 221, 251, 349, 390) novella *Bad Books* will be published in 2015. **CLAUDIA EVE BEAUCHESNE** (pp. 50, 73, 452) is a Montreal- and New York–based art critic, curator, and film buyer. She is currently writing a book on the 1980s East Village art scene. **CLAUDIA DEY** (pp. 14, 327) has written plays and the novel *Stunt*. She makes dresses under the label Horses Atelier. **CLEO PERRY** (pp. 124, 362) is 37 and works and lives, happily, in London. **CLODAGH DEEGAN** (p. 480), 45, is a costume designer working in theater and opera, based in Dublin. **COLLEEN ASPER** (pp. 142, 249, 455) is an artist. **CONSTANCE STERN** (p. 446) is a student in Vienna. **CRYSTAL MORTGENTALER** (p. 268) is a 31-year-old film archivist from London. **CYRENA LEE** (p. 268) is a writer and anthropologist living in Brooklyn, New York. **DALE MEGAN HEALEY** (pp. 73, 147, 493) is a Brooklyn-based writer and teacher. Her work has appeared in *The Atlas Review, The Common, Diagram, Prick of the Spindle*, and elsewhere. **DANKA HALL** (p. 124, 348, 381) works in sexual health awareness. **DAPHNE JAVITCH** (pp. 215, 285, 389) created and designs TEN, an underwear line inspired by her spirit and style icons. **DEBORAH AUER** (p. 115) sings jazz and teaches music in New York City. **DEBORAH KIRSHNER** (pp. 436, 494) is a violinist, now retired from a long career of making music, and lives in Toronto. **DELIA MARCUS** (p. 132) is 10 years old and lives in New York. **DENISE MINEO** (pp. 268, 269) lives in the New Orleans suburbs, is happily married, works as an executive assistant, and has two grown sons and two cats. **DIANA BECKER** (p. 19) is a mother, wife, and marketing creative from California, currently living in New York City. **DINA GOLDSTEIN** (p. 127) is a preschool teacher and grandmother. **DONORA HILLARD** (p. 136) is a coauthor of *Covenant* and other collections of poetry and hybrid text. Projects she has been involved in have been featured on CNN, MSNBC, Lybba, and the Poetry Foundation. **DORETTA LAU** (pp. 61, 483) is the author of *How Does a Single Blade of Grass Thank the Sun?*, a short story collection. She lives in Vancouver and Hong Kong, where she works as a journalist. **DORLA McINTOSH** (p. 337) works at Columbia University and lives in New Jersey. **DOROTHY DENISOFF** (p. 381) lives on the Washington coast and is writing a memoir. **DOROTHY PLATT** (p. 38) is an environmental rights activist. **DURGA CHEW-BOSE** (pp. 415–417) lives and writes in Brooklyn, New York. **E. M. HECTOR** (p. 207) lives and works in the Sunshine State. She is married and has two grown sons and three grandchildren. Though clothing has never been her passion, writing has. Her work has appeared online and in print. **EDIE CULSHAW** (pp. 249, 380) is 26 and lives in London. **EILEEN MYLES** (pp. 124, 177, 271, 362, 439) is a poet, novelist, and art journalist who lives in New York. She is currently working on a dog memoir, *Afterglow*. **EITHNE BARRON** (p. 215) is an office worker; she is married and has two grown sons. **ELEANOR JOHNSTON** (pp. 222, 479) is a former bookseller and now a collection curator in Toronto. **ELEANOR WEST** (pp. 328, 462, 493) is 27 and teaches English in Nanjing. **ELENA MEGALOS** (p. 493) is 27 and lives in Brooklyn, New York, where she writes, draws, and teaches. **ELIF BATUMAN** (p. 15) was writer-in-residence at Koç University in Istanbul and wrote about Turkey for *The New Yorker*. **ELIOT COLEMAN** (p. 461) is a farmer and the author of *The New Organic Grower, Four-Season Harvest*, and *The Winter Harvest Handbook* and a coauthor of *The Four Season Farm Gardener's Cookbook*. **ELISE PETERSON** (pp. 380, 451) is a 20-something writer and graphic designer living in Brooklyn, New York. **ELISSA SCHAPPELL** (pp. 134, 411, 483) is a writer in Brooklyn, New York. **ELIZABETH KAISER** (pp. 61, 177) is a writer living in Savannah, Georgia. **ELIZABETH PERKINS** (p. 125) is a retired administrative assistant, and a wife, mother of twins, and grandmother of four. **ELLEN RODGER** (pp. 35, 277) lives in Sydney, Australia. Her novella *The Girls' Room* was published in 2007. **EMILY BROTMAN** (pp. 36, 440) is 22 and lives in San Francisco. **EMILY COYLE** (p. 56) studies early modern literature, theater, and performance. She lives in New Jersey. **EMILY GOULD** (p. 223) is the author of *Friendship* and the co-owner of Emily Books. **EMILY HASS** (clothing pattern illustrations throughout) is an artist who lives in New York City. **EMILY HEMSON** (p. 480) is a 27-year-old writer living in Portland, Oregon. **EMILY K.** (p. 149) is 36 and is a writer living in Los Angeles. **EMILY RABOTEAU**'s (pp. 216, 266) most recent book, *Searching for Zion*, was published in 2013. **EMILY SCHULLER** (p. 422) is completing her MBA at the Darden Graduate School of Business (UVA) and is still best friends with Mika Mulligan. **EMILY SHUR** (p. 288) is a photographer living in Los Angeles. **EMILY SPIVACK** (p. 148) is a Brooklyn-based artist, writer, and author of the book *Worn Stories*. **EMILY STOKES** (p. 289) is an editor and writer living in Brooklyn, New York. **EMMA HOOPER** (p. 462) is a viola player and author; she has a band called Waitress for the Bees, and her novel *Etta and Otto and Russell and James* will appear in 2015. **EMMA MADNICK** (p. 75) is a costume designer and vintage clothing specialist who lives and works in Brooklyn, New York. **ERIKA THORMAHLEN** (pp. 98, 327, 439) is a copywriter who lives in New York City. **ESTELLE TANG** (p. 272) is an Australian writer and editor who lives in New York City. **EUFEMIA FANTETTI**'s (pp. 207, 479) first book, *A Recipe for Disaster & Other Unlikely Tales of Love,* was released in 2013. **EVA SCHLESINGER** (p. 440) (redroom.com/member/eva-schlesinger) is the author of three poetry chapbooks and has completed a young adult novel, *Everyone Knows About Aleph*. **EVELIJN MARTINIUS** (p. 268) is 25 and lives in Amsterdam. She studies art and political sociology. **FAITH HARDEN** (pp. 87, 267) is an assistant professor of early modern Spanish literature and cultural studies at the University of Arizona. **FARAH BASHIR** (p. 427), a former photojournalist with Reuters, was born and raised in Indian-administered Kashmir and writes about her strife-ridden hometown. **FATIMA G.** (pp. 25, 351) is a writer and community organizer based in Canada and is a cohost of *Black Girls Talking*. **FELIZ LUCIA MOLINA** (pp. 249, 267, 462) is the author of *Undercastle* and a coauthor of *The Wes Letters*. She lives in Los Angeles. **FRANCESCA MARCIANO** (p. 407) is the author of four novels, a collection of stories, and several screenplays. She lives in Rome. **FRIEDERIKE GIRST** (pp. 389, 455) is a designer and professor and a co-owner of Studio Umlaut in Munich. She is the happy mother of three little children. **FRIEDERIKE SCHILBACH** (p. 56) is 33 and lives in Berlin and

Frankfurt, where she works as a book editor. **GABRIELLE BELL** (pp. 215, 267, 483) is a cartoonist and the author-artist of *Truth Is Fragmentary* and *The Voyeurs*. **GAIL COLLINS** (p. 118) is an op-ed columnist at *The New York Times* and the author of several books, including *When Everything Changed: The Amazing Journey of American Women from 1960 to the Present*. **GAIL O'HARA** (p. 267) is a writer, editor, and photographer who cofounded *chickfactor* magazine. Currently the managing editor at *Kinfolk*, she lives in Portland, Oregon. **GAYLE DAVIES** (p. 286) lives in San Francisco and taught English at San Francisco State University for thirty-two years. **GENEVIEVE FERRIER** (p. 133) is a pediatrician in New York City, and lives there with her husband, teenage son, and golden retriever. **GENISTA STREETEN** (p. 338). **GILDA HABER** (pp. 379, 429, 456) is a professor, author of *Cockney Girl*, and hat maven. Her website is at gildahaber.com. **GILLIAN BLORE** (p. 272) is a freelance writer from Vancouver, Canada. You can find her writing about film at malevolentandoftenright.com. **GILLIAN KING** (p. 141) is a painter and multidisciplinary artist, curator, and art educator from Winnipeg, Manitoba. Now living in Ottawa, she is the communications and special events coordinator at La Petite Mort Gallery. She also teaches painting. **GILLIAN SCHWARTZ** (pp. 348, 379, 456) heads a creative agency, Schwartz & Sons, and lives in Brooklyn. **GINA RICO** (p. 280) is a painter living in New York. **GINA SHELTON** (pp. 71, 208) is 30 and lives in the suburbs of New York City with her husband and kitty. She works at an academic library and is working on her master's degree in library and information science. **GINI ALHADEFF** (pp. 125, 456) has published a memoir, *The Sun at Midday: Tales of a Mediterranean Family*, and a novel, *Diary of a Djinn*. **GINTARE PARULYTE** (pp. 33, 267) is a 29-year-old actress and freelance writer. Born in Vilnius, Lithuania, she currently resides in both Luxembourg and Berlin. **GISELA WILLIAMS** (p. 61) is a writer who lives in Berlin with her husband and two daughters. **GLORIA ARMINIO** (p. 266) was born in 1984. She currently resides in Jersey City, New Jersey, with her cat. **GLYNDA ALVES** (pp. 125, 287) is 29 and lives in Mumbai, where she works as a journalist. **GRACE DENTON** (pp. 17, 57, 327) is a musician and artist. She lives in Bristol, England, and works at an independent movie house. **GUS POWELL** (p. 233) is an artist in Brooklyn, New York. He is married and has two daughters. **GWEN SMITH** (p. 176) is a mother and an artist based in Brooklyn, New York. **HALEY MLOTEK** (pp. 352, 389) is the publisher of *WORN Fashion Journal* and a freelance writer. Her writing has appeared in *The Globe and Mail*, the *National Post*, and elsewhere. She lives in Toronto. **HEATHER BLOM** (p. 390) is an arts and culture programmer, currently working in advertising and residing in Toronto. **HEATHER LOVE** (p. 277) is a professor of queer studies who splits her time between Philadelphia and New York. **HEATHER MALLICK** (p. 19) is an author and a staff columnist for the Toronto *Star*. **HEATHER O'DONNELL** (p. 312) runs Honey & Wax Booksellers in Brooklyn. **HEIDI HOWARD** (p. 98) paints portraits in New York City. **HEIDI SOPINKA** (p. 326) is writing a novel inspired by Leonora Carrington at ninety-two. She makes clothing under the label Horses Atelier. **HEL GURNEY** (p. 250) is a writer and activist whose poetry has been published in three countries. **HELEN DeWITT** (p. 19) is the author of several books, most recently the novel *Lightning Rods*. **HELEN KING** (p. 453) lives in London, where she makes music and writes about records and books. **HENRIETTA ALTMAN** (p. 391) passed away before publication; she was a mother and retired secretary. **HIKARI YOKOYAMA** (pp. 329, 379) is 31 and lives in London. She helped found the online auction site Paddle8 and earns a living as a cultural curator. **HILARY PROSSER** (pp. 208, 352) is an artist and lives in Bristol, England. **HILLARY SCHNELLER** (p. 136) is a lawyer from New York. **HIMANEE GUPTA-CARLSON** (p. 133) is a professor in Greenfield Center, New York. **HOLLY MERRITT** (p. 287) is a Toronto-based filmmaker and cofounder of Problem/Solution Pictures. **HONOR JONES** (p. 105) is an editor at *The New York Times*. **IDA HATTEMER-HIGGINS** (p. 345) is the author of the novel *The History of History*; her essays have appeared or are forthcoming in *n+1*, *London Review of Books*, and *Die Literarische Welt*. **IDA LIU** (p. 217) is a former investment banker and fashion executive and is now Head of the North America Asian Clients

Group for Citi Private Bank. She lives in Manhattan with her husband and daughter. **IMAN BIBARS** (p. 73) lives in Cairo and is regional director of Ashoka Arab World and vice-president of Ashoka Global. **IMOGEN DONATO** (pp. 267, 463) is a 23-year-old midwifery student in Brisbane, Australia. **INELL WILLIS** (p. 106) lives in New York City. **INGRID HAGEN-KEITH** (p. 36 [interviewed Rachel Weeks]) is a student of mechanical engineering at Olin College of Engineering. She is interested in fashion, ethical garments, and fabrication practices. **INGRID SATELMAJER** (p. 62) lives in Silver Spring, Maryland. **IRINA ALEKSANDER** (pp. 415–417) is a writer in New York. Her work has appeared in *Elle, The New York Times, The Atlantic,* and *Harper's.* **ISHA KAZEMI** (p. 147) is an attorney in New York City. **IVANA AMERL** (p. 363 [translated Vedrana]). **IVORY SIMMS** (p. 460) is an illustrator from Ontario. **IVY ARCE** (p. 250) moved from Bolivia to New York to become the loving mother of Ahimsa, the Atom, and Kokoro. **IVY KNIGHT** (pp. 87, 263, 452, 479) writes about food for *Vice;* her first two cookbooks will be published in 2014. **JACKIE SORO** (pp. 272, 495) recently received her bachelor's degree in history and in feminist, gender, and sexuality studies and is currently seeking gainful employment. **JACLYN BRUNEAU** (pp. 52, 125) lives in Vancouver, where she facilitates the work of contemporary artists and writers. **JAGODA WARDACH** (p. 265) is a student of literature, looking for her path in life. **JANE LARKWORTHY** (p. 388) is a beauty editor who lives in Manhattan with her husband and dog. **JANICE CHAN** (p. 421) lives in Toronto, where she works in strategic communications. **JASON BARKER** (p. 37) is a filmmaker who lives in the United Kingdom. **JEANA DelROSSO** (p. 101) is a professor of English at Notre Dame of Maryland University and is the author of several books about women and Catholicism. **JEANIE KIMBER** (p. 57) is a costume designer for film and TV who lives in Halifax, Nova Scotia. **JEMIMA TRUMAN** (p. 206) is an illustrator who lives in New York City. **JEN MAY** (p. 136) is an artist living in Brooklyn, New York. **JENNA KNOBLACH** (p. 436) is a visual artist who teaches third grade in New Orleans. **JENNA WORTHAM** (pp. 111, 136) is a writer who lives in Brooklyn. **JENNIFER ARMBRUST** (p. 97, 440) is an artist and creative consultant living in Portland, Oregon. **JENNIFER CARROLL** (p. 102) is 30 years old and works in the nonprofit sector in Toronto. **JENNIFER CROLL** (p. 49) is a Vancouver-based writer and editor; her book *Fashion That Changed the World* will be published in 2014. **JENNIFER LIEBSCHUTZ** (p. 425) has been living in Cambodia for three years and will be attending graduate school to study international development. **JENNIFER WINEKE** (pp. 287, 327, 351) is 25 and lives in Los Angeles where she is a writer. **JENNY DAVIDSON**'s (p. 221) latest book is *Reading Style: A Life in Sentences.* **JENNY SCHILY** (p. 418) is an actress, lives in Berlin, is married, and has two children. **JENNY TROMSKI** (pp. 74, 451) is a blogger, writer, and arts administrator living in New York City. **JESSICA JOHNSON** (pp. 125, 136, 222) is an award-winning journalist and copy director for Hudson's Bay Company in Canada. **JILL GALLAGHER** (p. 268) is an editor and writer in Boston, where she blogs at looksandbooks.com. **JILL MARGO** (pp. 17, 75, 231, 328) lives in Toronto, where she is working on her first novel. **JILLIAN TAMAKI** (p. 102, 381) is a Canadian cartoonist and illustrator living in Brooklyn, New York. **JINNIE LEE** (pp. 55, 185), 29, is a content writer and editor based in Brooklyn, New York. **JOANA AVILLEZ** (pp. 55, 75, 123, 415–417) is an illustrator living and working in New York. She recently illustrated Lena Dunham's book of essays *Not That Kind of Girl.* **JOANNA CORNISH** (p. 493) lives in London, Ontario, and works in PR. **JOANNA WALSH** (p. 133) is the author of *Fractals* and *Hotel* (forthcoming). **JODIE YOUNG** (p. 267) is a graphic designer living in Belfast, Northern Ireland. **JOHANNA ADORJÁN**'s (pp. 222, 440) first book, *An Exclusive Love,* has been published in eighteen languages. She lives in Berlin. **JOHANNA FATEMAN** (pp. 101, 286, 493) is a writer, musician, and owner of Seagull Salon in New York City. **JONATHAN GOLDSTEIN** (p. 127) is the host of CBC Radio's *Wiretap* and author of *I'll Seize the Day Tomorrow.* **JOSH BLACKWELL** (p. 302), an artist and teacher, has lived in and out of New York City since 1992. **JOSIE HO** (p. 125) is a recent graduate of graphics and marketing, aspiring to work for a fashion magazine. **JOSS LAKE** (pp. 18, 285) lives in Brooklyn and is an associate editor at *Conjunctions.* **JOWITA**

BYDLOWSKA (pp. 53, 427) is a Canadian writer whose first book is *Drunk Mom*. **JOYCE WALL** (p. 88) is a freelance editor. **JUDE STEWART**'s (p. 35) first book, *ROY G. BIV: An Exceedingly Surprising Book About Color*, came out in 2013, as did her son. She's now working on a second book, about patterns. **JUDY PACIFICADOR** (p. 150), 62 years old, retired UPS HR manager from Brampton, Ontario, spends winters in Florida, and is a dedicated quilt maker. **JUDY REBICK** (pp. 71, 327) is an author and activist living in Toronto. **JULIA LEACH** (p. 186), a design thinker, has a company called Chance and lives in New York and Los Angeles. **JULIA WALLACE** (p. 225) is a 29-year-old American writer and editor living in Phnom Penh, Cambodia. **JULIA WIDEMAN** (pp. 415–417) is a producer living in New York City. **JULIE HOUTS** (pp. 415–417) is a designer living in New York City. **JULIET JACQUES** (p. 89) is a writer based in London. Her book *Trans: A Memoir* will be published in 2015. **JULIET LANDAU-POPE** (p. 145), based in London, coaches busy people to manage time and space more effectively. **JUSTIN VIVIAN BOND** (p. 380) is a trans-genre artist living in the East Village, New York City. **JYTZA GUZMAN** (pp. 97, 348) is 23 and lives in New Jersey where she works as a freelance fashion stylist and writer. **KALPONA AKTER** (p. 467) is the executive director of the Bangladesh Center for Worker Solidarity. **KAREN GARBER STEPHENS** (p. 348) is a hospice nurse and middle-aged newlywed living in Petaluma, California. **KARI LARSEN**'s (pp. 142, 147, 463) first book is coming soon. **KARI MAH** (p. 136) is a software developer and writer in San Francisco. **KARIMA CAMMELL** (pp. 98, 266, 329, 380, 389, 411, 456) is an award-winning author, painter, and book publisher in Berkeley, California. **KARIN SCHAEFER** (p. 458) is an artist who lives and works in Brooklyn, New York. She shows with the Sears Peyton Gallery in New York and Los Angeles. **KATE McMULLAN** (pp. 49, 361) lives in Sag Harbor, New York, and is the author of many children's books. **KATE QUENZER** (pp. 218–219) is a Ph.D. student at the Centre for Arab and Islamic Studies at the Australian National University. **KATE RYAN** (pp. 32, 34, 218–219, 324, 391) is a designer in New York. **KATE SHEPHERD** (pp. 222, 481) is a painter who lives and works in New York City. **KATE ZAMBRENO**'s (p. 37) novel *Green Girl* was recently reissued. **KATHARINE HARGREAVES** (pp. 437, 464) is a writer, designer, and strategist based in Los Angeles. Her writing and other work can be found here: projektkatharine.net. **KATHERINE BERNARD** (pp. 415–417) is 26 and lives in Brooklyn, where she writes articles, stories, and, recently, a short film. **KATHERINE MIN**'s (p. 52) novel *Secondhand World* was published in 2006. **KATHRYN BOREL** (pp. 36, 327) is the author of the book *Corked*. She writes for television in Los Angeles. **KATHRYN DAW** (p. 494) lives in Toronto, where she works as a freelance consultant in branding; she is designing her first collection of clothing. **KATIE KITAMURA** (p. 69) is the author of *The Longshot* and *Gone to the Forest*. Raised in Canada, **KATJA PANTZAR** (p. 264) is a writer, editor, and broadcast journalist living in Helsinki. **KELLEY HOFFMAN** (pp. 18, 428) is 30 and lives in San Francisco. **KELLY WILSON** (p. 348) lives with her boyfriend and their cat in Brooklyn, New York. **KERRY BARBER** (p. 413) is a filmmaker from Dawson City, Yukon Territory, and is a mother to a daughter. **KERRY CARDOZA** (p. 435) co-operates Amigos, a small art press, and publishes *Girl Talk* zine. She is a graduate student in journalism at Northwestern University. **KERRY DIAMOND** (p. 91) is the editorial director and a cofounder of *Cherry Bombe* magazine. She also co-owns the Brooklyn eateries Seersucker, Smith Canteen, and Nightingale 9. **KIANA JANNESARI** (p. 218–219) lives in Albany, New York, where she is studying to be a school psychologist. **KIM BOST** (p. 432) is a designer in Brooklyn. **KIM GORDON** (p. 99), former vocalist for Sonic Youth, is a visual artist, fashion designer, and actress. **KIMBER HALL** (p. 157) is a storyteller living in Los Angeles. **KIMBERLY JEAN SMITH** (p. 286) is a writer and teacher. **KIRA JOLLIFFE** (p. 493) coauthored *The Cheap Date Guide to Style* and is now a counselor practicing in London. **KIRAN DESAI** (p. 41) is a novelist. **KIRSTEN SCHNITTKER** (pp. 136, 218–219) is a dancer, choreographer, and arts administrator living in Brooklyn. **KIRSTIN CORCORAN** (p. 428) is 33 and lives in Sydney, Australia, where she works in book publishing. **K. L. CANDELA** (p. 263) has returned to study at Queen's University, taking classes in creative writing; she lives in Kingston, Ontario. **KRISTI GOLDADE** (pp. 18, 63) is an associate editor at a distributed marketing firm in Manhattan. **KRISTIN ANTHONY** (p. 58) works at a surf shop in San Diego. **KRISTIN GORE** (p. 270) is a novelist and screenwriter. **KRISTIN SJAARDA** (pp. 102, 263) is a photographer and mother of three living in Toronto. **KRISTINA ANNE GYLLING** (pp. 35, 124, 438) is a content specialist by day and writer by night in Montreal. **KRISTY HELLER** (pp. 35, 348) is a 28-year-old artist working at Renaissance festivals across North America. **KUCH NAREN** (p. 225) is a Cambodian journalist who has reported on politics, land issues, and economic and social conditions in her home country for more than a decade. **LARA AVERY** (pp. 123, 381, 439) lives in Minneapolis, where she is an editor and contributing writer at *Revolver*; she is the author of *Anything but Ordinary* and *A Million Miles Away*. **LAURA PETERSON** (p. 136) is a consultant, editor, and curator in twentieth-century photography. She also explores fashion and mental health in her work with textiles, garments, and personal history. She lives in Santa Monica, California. **LAURA SNELGROVE** (pp. 135, 222, 389) is a fashion studies scholar from Toronto living in New York City. **LAUREN BRIDE** (p. 142) is a writer living in Toronto. **LAUREN MATTHEWS** (pp. 218–219) is an artist and designer in Los Angeles. **LAUREN REITER** (pp. 208, 438) is a 57-year-old practicing architect, formerly a resident of New York City, now living in Maine. **LAUREN RO** (p. 332) works in film and lives with her husband in Brooklyn. **LAUREN SPENCER KING** (pp. 177, 389) is an artist living in Los Angeles with her dog. **LEAH DIETERICH**'s (p. 390) first book, *thxthxthx: thank goodness for everything*, was published in 2011. **LEAP** (p. 225), 35, is originally from Kompong Thom, Cambodia, and sews bras at a factory in Phnom Penh. **LEIGH McMULLAN ABRAMSON** (p. 62) is a lawyer turned writer living in New York. **LEINI IRELAND** (p. 75) is an event planner and lives in Hong Kong with her husband and two children. **LENA DUNHAM** (p. 81) is a writer and filmmaker from New York City. **LENAE DAY** (pp. 277, 285, 329, 335, 452) is an artist and writer in L.A. Her third publication, *Day Magazine*, appeared this year. You can see her work at lenaeday.com. **LEOPOLDINE CORE** (p. 21) is a writer who lives in Manhattan. **LEORA MORINIS** (p. 455) is 27 and lives in Manhattan. **LESLIE VOSSHALL** (pp. 253, 257) is a professor at the Rockefeller University in New York City, where she studies the sense of smell in insects and humans. **LIANE BALABAN** (pp. 98, 380) is an actor and the co-creator of crankytown.com. **LILI HORVATH** (pp. 277, 452) is 21 and is studying menswear design at London College of Fashion. **LILI OWEN ROWLANDS** (pp. 18, 87, 286) is 21. She lives in Paris and studies literature and philosophy. **LINDA HESH** (p. 264) is an artist who exhibits internationally; she lives in the Washington, D.C., metro area. **LINDSAY ALLISON RUOFF** (pp. 102, 436) is a poet living in Portland, Oregon. **LINDSAY JOHNSON** (pp. 218–219) is a mariner and artist who lives with her husband in Haines, Alaska. **LINDSAY PAGE** (p. 391) lives in Toronto, where she works for a global nonprofit organization. **LINDY WILSON** (p. 362) is 24 and lives in Memphis, where she works as a clinical operations specialist in a doctor's office; she has one daughter. **LISA COHEN** (p. 473) is the author of *All We Know: Three Lives*, published in 2012. **LISA FRANZETTA** (p. 263) is an animal rights advocate living in Oakland, California. **LISA GUNNING** (pp. 75, 379, 391), based in London, is a film editor and director. **LISA NAFTOLIN** (pp. 64, 251) is a New York–based creative director. **LISA PRZYSTUP** (p. 210) is the owner of James's Daughter Flowers, a Brooklyn-based floral design company. **LISA ROBERTSON** (p. 497) lives in France and teaches in the MFA program at Piet Zwart Institute in Rotterdam. Her newest book of poetry is *Cinema of the Present*. **LITHE SEBESTA** (p. 471) is a writer and interior designer who lives in Brooklyn and Stuyvesant, New York. **LIZ LERMAN** (p. 412) is a choreographer, performer, writer, educator, and speaker based in Baltimore. **LORENE BOUBOUSHIAN** (pp. 218–219) is a performance maker, performer, and teacher originally from rural Texas (lorenebouboushian. com). **LORI HANDELMAN** (pp. 221, 412) is 55, travels the world, and has a brand-new grandson named Oliver. **LORNA SHAPTON** (pp. 150, 334, 360) is a wife, mother, grandmother, Hawaiian dancer, book lover, and fashion aficionado. **LUCIA DELLA PAOLERA** (pp. 415–417) lives and works in New York City. **LUCIE BONVALET** (pp. 327,

335) is a writer and French teacher in Portland, Oregon. **LUCY BIRLEY** (pp. 208, 297) is a photographer and mother of four sons. She lives in England. **LUISA B.** (pp. 421, 464) is the editor of *Mondobelo* magazine, mondobelo.com. **LUISE STAUSS** (p. 2) is a photography editor in New York. **LY KY TRAN** (p. 65) is 24 years old and working on a memoir titled *Tales from a Brooklyn Nail Salon*, detailing her struggles as a Vietnamese immigrant. **LYDIA BURKHALTER** (p. 20) lives in Los Angeles and works as a wardrobe stylist. **LYDIA JOHNSON** (pp. 48, 177) is a poet and writer pursuing her MFA in creative writing from Butler University. **M. WHITEFORD** (pp. 216, 342) is an artist living in Los Angeles. **MAC McCLELLAND** (p. 171) is an award-winning journalist whose first book was a finalist for the Dayton Literary Peace Prize. Her second book comes out next year. **MADELEINE STACK** (pp. 47, 61, 87, 148) is an Australian artist and writer living in New York and London. **MAE PANG** (p. 120) is a mother and writer. **MAEGAN FIDELINO** (p. 285) is a 25-year-old graphic designer living in Toronto. **MAIA WRIGHT** (pp. 351, 380) is a designer based in Austin, Texas, and a member of the art collaborative AK/OK. **MAIREAD CASE** (p. 287) is a writer living in Denver. **MAKIKO YAMAMOTO** (p. 77) is an artist based in Kyoto, Japan. **MALWINA GUDOWSKA** (pp. 74, 351, 361) is a writer and editor based in London. **MANSOURA EZ ELDIN** (p. 273) is an Egyptian novelist who lives in Cairo. She is the author of *Maryam's Maze* and *Emerald Mountain*. **MARGARET HULL** (p. 494) is an artist who works in textiles and thinks about legacy. **MARGARITA TUPITSYN** (pp. 249, 455, 494) is an art historian, critic, and curator. She will be curating the Russian Pavilion at the 2015 Venice Biennale. **MARGAUX WILLIAMSON** (pp. 97, 246) is a painter who lives in Toronto. **MARGO JEFFERSON** (p. 353) is a Pulitzer Prize–winning critic, the author of *On Michael Jackson,* and a professor at Columbia University. **MARI SASANO** (p. 349) writes for television and magazines, administers a short film compilation, and produces a festival for dogs in Edmonton, Alberta. **MARIE MYUNG-OK LEE** (pp. 36, 263) lives in New York City; her next novel will be published in 2015. **MARILYN BOOTH** (pp. 134, 411) holds the Iraq Chair in Arabic and Islamic Studies at the University of Edinburgh. **MARION LARSEN** (p. 177) is a retired addictions counselor in Sarasota, Florida. **MARJORIE BANKS** (p. 337) is an avid sewer, actress, artist, and musician living in Toronto. **MARLENA KAESLER** (p. 250) is an avid sewer, actress, artist, and musician living in Toronto, Ontario. **MARLENE BARBER** (p. 472) is an entertainer in Canada. **MARSHA COURNEYA** (pp. 271, 332, 361, 451) is a writer from Toronto. **MARTHA McCARTY** (p. 178) is a Kansas City writer whose memoir won a literary award, unexpectedly. **MARY DUENWALD** (p. 177) is an editor and lives in Brooklyn. **MARY MANN** (pp. 85, 218–219, 304, 333, 393) is a writer in New York City. **MARY PEELEN** (p. 74) is a writer and poet who lives in San Francisco. **MASHA TUPITSYN** (pp. 147, 380, 451) is a writer, critic, and multimedia artist. She has published several books, most recently *Love Dog*. **MAURA EGAN** (p. 110) is a writer and editor in Brooklyn, New York. **MAYA FUHR** (pp. 71, 87, 97) was born in Victoria, British Columbia, and now lives in Toronto; she is a photographer and actor. **MEG BARKER** (p. 352) is an activist, therapist, academic, and author of the book *Rewriting the Rules*. **MEGAN B.** (p. 141) is a musician and educator who lives in Toronto. **MEGAN FRANKLYNE** (pp. 123, 337) is an environmental consultant who spilts her time between Faro, Yukon, and Toronto. **MEGAN HUSTAD** (pp. 141, 207, 379, 480) lives in New York. **MEGAN PATTERSON** (p. 124) is a Toronto-based writer and the science and technology editor of Paper Droids, a geek culture site for women. **MEGGIN HAMMILL** (p. 463) is a high school teacher in North Carolina. **MEGHAN BEAN FLAHERTY** (pp. 35, 101) is a writer of nonfiction. **MELANIE PAGE** (pp. 101, 328) runs the women's book review site Grab the Lapels and organizes virtual book tours. **MELINDA ANDRADE** (p. 252) teaches at a boarding school in Mumbai. **MELINDA VICKERS** (p. 150) lives in Auckland, New Zealand, and is an avid hiker. **MELISSA ABE** (p. 361) is a creative producer who lives in Brooklyn. **MELISSA HENDERSON** (pp. 134, 285, 361) lives in New York City and works in digital marketing and writes on weekends. **MELISSA SMITH** (p. 427) is an administrative assistant at the University of Texas at Austin. **MELISSA WALSH** (p. 350) is an obstetrician-gynecologist who lives and works in New York City.

**METIS RYER** (p. 438) lives in New York City, where she works in the arts. **MICAH LEXIER** (p. 191) is a Toronto-based artist, curator, and collector. **MICHAEL SCHMELLING** (p. 157) is a photographer and graphic designer. He lives in Los Angeles. **MICHELE OKA DONER** (p. 407) is an artist who lives in New York City. **MICHELLE BERRY** (p. 100) has published eight books. She lives in Peterborough, Ontario, and teaches creative writing. **MICHELLE GARRETT** (p. 178) is the operations director for fashion designer Rachel Comey. **MICHELLE LAW** (p. 338) is a writer and screenwriter based in Brisbane, Australia. Her first book (coauthored) is *Sh*t Asian Mothers Say*. **MIKA MULLIGAN** (p. 422) is 26 and an ESOL teacher in the Washington, D.C., area. **MILENA ROSA** (p. 183) is a 5-year-old and lives in Los Angeles. **MIMI CABELL** (pp. 36, 147, 390) is 32, lives in Germany, and is an artist. **MIRA GONZALEZ** (p. 305) was born in 1992 and is a writer in Los Angeles. **MIRANDA FISHER** (p. 328) lives in Austin, Texas, where she edits the music magazine *Rubberneck*. **MIRANDA JULY** (p. 157) is a writer, artist, and filmmaker. She lives in Los Angeles. **MIRANDA PURVES** (pp. 200, 447) is a Canadian-American writer, editor, and mother of two sons. **MITZI ANGEL** (p. 396) was born in London and works in publishing in New York City. **MOLLY DOVE KEOGH** (p. 336) divides her time between Accra, Ghana, and Los Angeles. She works with clothing and costumes in both places. **MOLLY MURRAY** (p. 296) is a professor in the English Department at Columbia University. **MOLLY RINGWALD** (pp. 157, 281, 451) acts, writes, and sings jazz. **MOLLY YOUNG** (p. 136) is a writer in New York City. **MONA KOWALSKA** (pp. 29, 148, 263, 412) is a clothing designer and founder of A Détacher. **MONICA BILL BARNES** (p. 307) is the artistic director of her own dance company. For more than fifteen years she has been in a collaborative conversation with her costume designer, Kelly Hanson, about what to wear onstage. **MONICA McCLURE** (p. 483) works on projects for Patagonia and lives among the orange blossoms in Ojai, California. **MONIKA CHHY** (p. 425) is a tailor who owns and runs her own business in Phnom Penh, Cambodia. **MONIQUE AUBÉ** (pp. 222, 294) is a 24-year-old flutist from New Brunswick studying for her master's in music performance in Toronto. **NAN KEVIN GELHARD** (p. 427) lives in Akron, Ohio, and does performance automotive advertising and PR. She is married, and so is her only son. **NANCY FORDE** (pp. 264, 329, 421) is a Waterloo, Ontario–based photographer and lucky mother to one son. Her photos have been published in *Grand* and *Green* magazines. **NAOMI ALISA CALNITSKY** (pp. 287, 483) lives in Winnipeg with her partner and enjoys crafting, building gardens, history, and playing with her cat. **NASRIN HIMADA** (p. 136) is a writer and curator from Montreal. **NATALIA ELTSOVA** (pp. 147, 439) is 29 years old. She was born in Novosibirsk and moved to Saint Petersburg four years ago. **NATASHA HUNT** (pp. 222, 438) is in her twenties and lives in Toronto. She focuses on the philosophy of fashion. Her ambition in life is to be Kanye West's in-house cultural theorist. **NATASHA MOLETTA** (p. 348) is 27 and lives in Youngstown, Ohio, where she is finishing her master's in education for counseling. **NELLIE DAVIS** (p. 481) is a fine-art needleworker and silkscreen master printer. She lives in Brooklyn with her husband and two sons. **NENE PACIFICADOR (BALMER)** (p. 150) is 68 years old and retired. She loves to cook, garden, and travel. **NICHOLE BAIEL** (pp. 287, 463) is a user-interface designer for a technology company in Chicago. **NICHOLE DELAFIELD-BROMME** (p. 455) is an artist and designer. She teaches art in Florida, where she lives with her husband and three children. **NICOLE LAVELLE** (pp. 136, 142, 294) is an artist who lives in California. **NIKKI HAUSLER** (p. 151) is a 42-year-old whose passions include ranching and animal control. She is one of two animal control officers for the city of Hays, Kansas. **NIKKI WOOLSEY** (p. 136) is an artist living in Toronto. **NINA MOOG** (pp. 221, 390, 428) lives in Rome. **NORA PALEY** (p. 483) is a film student in Ontario. **NYJIA JONES** (p. 157) is a filmmaker and writer who works in reality show casting. **ODETTE HENDERSON** (p. 28) works in not-for-profit publishing. **OLIVIA S.** (p. 177) is a writer living in Washington, D.C. **OLLA NAJAH AL-SHALCHI** (p. 18) teaches Arabic at Smith College, and is married with three children. **PAIGE V. LYNN** (p. 135) is a 28-year-old lawyer in Los Angeles. **PAMELA BAGULEY** (p. 317) lives in the beautiful Vale of Belvoir, England. **PAT JONES** (p. 436), 66, lives in Prairie Village,

Kansas, and is a retired schoolteacher. **PATRICIA MARX** (pp. 97, 455) is a staff writer for *The New Yorker*. **PAULA BLACK** (p. 392) lives in New York and is a mother. **PAULINE SMOLIN** (pp. 348, 483) is a playwright living in Cincinnati. **PAVIA ROSATI** (p. 144) is the founder of the travel website Fathom. She lives in New York City. **PEGGY BURNS** (pp. 411, 483) lives in Montreal with her family; she is the associate publisher of Drawn & Quarterly. **PENELOPE C.** (pp. 352, 455) is a writer based in Melbourne, Australia. **PETRA KRUIJT** (pp. 87, 362, 391), 27, is a writer and journalist from the Netherlands. **POPPY TOLAND** (pp. 61, 125, 338, 483) comes from London and is currently working on her Ph.D. and translating a novel from Chinese. **RACHEL ANDES** (p. 464) is a graduate student at an East Coast university. **RACHEL ANTONOFF** (pp. 415–417) designs clothing in Manhattan. **RACHEL AZZOPARDI GRUET** (p. 136) is a pie baker who lives in Toronto with her husband and two sons. **RACHEL COMEY** (p. 484) is a clothing designer who lives in New York City. **RACHEL HURN** (p. 442) is a writer in Brooklyn. **RACHEL KUSHNER** (pp. 71, 75, 249, 277) is a writer living in Los Angeles. **RACHEL L.** (pp. 294, 455) is a stylist and student living in Melbourne, Australia. **RACHEL NACKMAN** (pp. 218–219) is a curator and editor living in Brooklyn. **RACHEL PRINTZ** (p. 381) is a kayak instructor. **RACHEL SIGNER** (p. 329) is a writer living in Brooklyn. **RACHEL TUTERA** (p. 73) makes clothes for women and lives in Brooklyn with her fiancée. **RACHEL WEEKS** (p. 36) is the founder of fair-trade clothing manufacturer School House. **RACHEL PERRY WELTY** (pp. 287, 410, 427) is an interdisciplinary artist who works in New York City and Gloucester, Massachusetts. **RAINBOW MOOON** (pp. 101, 412, 480), 67, is a spiritual crisis counselor and philosopher of integral yoga living in Kansas City, Missouri. **RAISEL BRUNO** (pp. 267, 286) is a data analyst in Boston. **RAMOU SARR** (pp. 25, 277, 456) is a writer in Boston. **RANDI RIVERA** (pp. 218–219, 266) is a touring theater artist and native New Yorker. She is 27 years old. **REBA SIKDER** (p. 467) is a former garment worker from Bangladesh. **REBECCA ACKERMANN** (pp. 75, 134) is 31 and lives in Brooklyn, where she works as a UX strategist. **REBECCA SALERNO** (pp. 287, 421) is a creative director at the Indiana University Kelley School of Business in Bloomington. **REBECCA SCHERM**'s (p. 438) first novel, *Unbecoming*, will be published in 2015. **REBEKAH AMBJOR** (p. 339) is a massage therapist, cooking instructor for children, and aspiring children's book author who lives in Brooklyn with her husband and baby boy. **REN JENDER** (pp. 36, 208, 440) is a queer writer-performer-producer. She's on Twitter @renjender. **RENATE STAUSS** (p. 405) is a fashion theorist and lecturer at the RCA London. **RENEE GLADMAN** (p. 131) is the author of eight works of prose and poetry, most recently the novel *Ana Patova Crosses a Bridge*. **RESHAM GELLATLY** (pp. 136, 218–219) is a photojournalist working on a book about *chai wallahs*, or tea vendors, in India. **RITA TRONTI** (pp. 351, 483) is a writer on the West Coast. **RIVKA GALCHEN** (p. 103) is a writer, most recently of the short story collection *American Innovations*. **ROBERTA ZEFF** (p. 109) is a copy editor at *The New York Times*. **RONNIE ANGEL POPE** (p. 133) is a high school student from Britain who aspires to work in the fashion industry. **ROSALBA MARTINNI** (pp. 136, 379) is an actress who works in theater, film, and television. She lives in Toronto. **ROSE WALDMAN** (p. 39) teaches academic writing at Columbia University and is completing her MFA there. **ROSEMARY HOCHSCHILD** (p. 157) is an actor and importer of South African accessories. **ROXANE GAY** (pp. 37, 221, 362, 427) lives and writes in the Midwest. **RUTH GAIS** (pp. 50, 336) is a rabbi and a hospital chaplain in New Jersey. **RUTH LA FERLA** (p. 108) writes about fashion and style for *The New York Times*. **RUTH MILLS** (p. 362) is 40 and lives in Shropshire with her wife and seven cats and one pug. She is a freelance IT consultant and Web developer. **RUTH REICHL** (p. 383), former *New York Times* restaurant critic and editor of *Gourmet* magazine, is the author of many books. **RUTH SATELMAJER** (p. 250) lives in Maryland and is a grandmother and retired educator. **RUTH VAN BEEK** (p. 365) is a visual artist; her book *The Arrangement* was published in 2013. **RUTKA ABRAM** (p. 480) is a doula. **SAADA AHMED** (p. 63) is 26 and lives in Brooklyn, where she works in production curation and events. **SADIE STEIN** (pp. 59, 196, 222, 439) is a writer from New York. **SAGAN MacISAAC** (pp. 125, 286) lives and works in Toronto. **SANAA ANSARI KHAN** (p. 177) is a lawyer and clothing designer (Haute Heritage) in Washington, D.C. **SANCHARI SUR** (p. 389) lives in Canada, where she is working on her first book and attending grad school (sursanchari.wordpress.com). **SARA FREEMAN** (p. 455) teaches writing at the Fashion Institute of Technology in New York City. She is working on her first novel. **SARA HABEIN** (pp. 142, 412) is the author of *Infinite Disposable* and the editor for Electric City Creative. She is a staff writer at *Persephone Magazine* and lives in Great Falls, Montana. **SARA K.** (p. 285) is a filmmaker who lives in Memphis. **SARA ZIFF** (p. 467) is a fashion model, documentary filmmaker, and labor activist. She is the founder and executive director of the Model Alliance, a nonprofit for models working in the American fashion industry. **SARAH BRUBACHER** (p. 382) is 97 and lives in St. Jacobs, Ontario, where she still wears her handmade dresses daily. **SARAH GERARD**'s (pp. 327, 435) novel *Binary Star* is forthcoming; her chapbook *Things I Told My Mother* was published in 2013. **SARAH ILLENBERGER** (pp. 75, 294, 375) is a multidisciplinary artist based in Berlin who works at the intersection of art, graphic design, and photography. **SARAH MANGUSO** (pp. 147, 428) is the author of several books. She lives in Los Angeles with her family. **SARAH MOSES** (p. 437) writes about health and works as a translator. She is from Toronto and now lives in Buenos Aires. **SARAH NICOLE PRICKETT** (pp. 98, 121) is a writer, a contributing editor at *The New Inquiry*, and the editor in chief of *Adult* magazine. **SARAH STEINBERG** (pp. 178, 340) is a writer and editor. Her first book of short stories was published in 2008. She lives in Toronto. **SARAH WHIDDEN** (pp. 87, 462) is 38 and lives in Montreal. **SARAH WILLIAMSON** (p. 119) is an illustrator and artist who lives in Brooklyn. **SASHA ARCHIBALD** (pp. 17, 207, 411, 463) is a writer and curator in Los Angeles. Originally from Toronto and now based in Munich, **SASHA GORA** (pp. 97, 362, 428) works as a curator and writer. Since leaving the adult-movie world at age 21, **SASHA GREY** (pp. 142, 207, 451) has starred in HBO's *Entourage*, published the photobook *Neü Sex*, penned the novel *The Juliette Society*, and deejayed internationally. **SASHA PLOTNIKOVA** (p. 483) is 24 and lives in Houston, where she studies architecture. **SASHA WISEMAN** (pp. 148, 250) is a 27-year-old undergraduate studying nonfiction writing. She lives in North Bennington, Vermont, and Cobham, Virginia. **SATENIK AVAKIAN** (p. 294) is a librarian and works at the American University of Armenia. **SEMI CHELLAS** (p. 197) is a writer and co–executive producer for *Mad Men*. **SENAMI D'ALMEIDA** (p. 478) is a writer and actress living in New York City. **SHALINI ROY** (pp. 390, 411, 438) is a full-time freelance writer and the mother of an 8-year-old. **SHANI BOIANJIU** (p. 355) is the author of the novel *The People of Forever Are Not Afraid*. She lives in Israel. **SHAYLA CROWEL** (p. 286) is 21 and lives in San Diego, where she is studying art history. **SHEILA O'SHEA** (p. 154) is a public relations executive experienced in book and magazine publishing. She lives in New York City. **SHEILAH RAY COLEMAN** (p. 74) is a writer and occasional musician, based in Boston. **SHELLEY LONG** (p. 464) is a "woman of a certain age" and the author of the blog *Forest City Fashionista*. **SHERWIN TJIA** (p. 155) organizes quirky events like Slowdance Nights, Strip Spelling Bees, and Crowd Karaokes in and around Montreal and Toronto and is the author of a Choose Your Own Adventure–style book titled *You Are a Cat!* **SHIRLEY WONG** (p. 136) is a postdoctoral fellow in the English Department at New York University. In fall 2014, she will join Westfield State University. **SIBYL S.** (p. 215) is 29 and lives in Baltimore. **SIOBHAN BURKE** (pp. 218–219) is a writer and dancer based in Brooklyn, New York. **SIOBHAN ROBERTS**'s (p. 339) book *Genius at Play: The Curious Mathematical Mind of John Horton Conway* is forthcoming. **SNIGDHA KOIRALA** (p. 116) is a Web editor at *The New York Times*. **SOFIA SAMATAR** (pp. 75, 149, 294, 340, 348) is the author of the novel *A Stranger in Olondria* (2013). She lives in California. **SONA AVAKIAN** (pp. 61, 147, 439 [interviewed Anahit Ordyan & Natalia Eltsova]) lives in San Francisco. **SOOK-YIN LEE** (p. 351) is a filmmaker, musician, actor, visual artist, and radio and TV broadcaster based in Toronto. **SOPHAL** (p. 225) is a 41-year-old garment worker who sews seams for jeans in a Cambodian factory. She is also a union representative at the factory. **SOPHIE ZEITZ** (pp. 62, 101) translates novels and lives in Berlin. **SOUVANKHAM THAMMAVONGSA**'s (p. 319) third poetry book, *Light*, was published in 2013. **STAR SPIDER** (pp. 389, 493) is a writer from Toronto, where she lives with her awesome husband. **STARLEE KINE** (pp. 63, 130, 426) is a writer who lives in New York and Los Angeles. **STELLA BUGBEE** (pp. 18, 277) is the editorial director of The Cut, a fashion and style website. **STEPHANIE MIKI ARNDT** (p. 341) is a fiction writer from Kobe, Japan, and is in New York working on her first novel. **STEPHANIE AVERY** (p. 87) is a Toronto-based artist, art director, and adventurer. **STEPHANIE COMILANG** (pp. 77, 136) is a Canadian filmmaker based in Berlin. **STEPHANIE DINKMEYER** (pp. 263, 389) lives in Washington, D.C., with her tiny black cat. **STEPHANIE P.** (pp. 74, 136, 361) is a documentary film producer and freelance writer who lives in Brooklyn. **STEPHANIE RUSSO** (p. 494) is a lecturer in English literature in Sydney, Australia. Her research interests include the politics of clothing in eighteenth-century literature. **STEPHANIE STUDENSKI** (pp. 218–219) is a physician who conducts research on aging in Baltimore. **STEPHANIE WHITEHOUSE** (pp. 479, 483) is a designer. She lives in Winnipeg with her husband and daughter. **SU WU** (p. 495) is a writer in Los Angeles. She runs the inspiration blog *I'm Revolting*. **SUSAN GLOUBERMAN** (p. 73) is a psychoanalytic therapist living in Toronto. She was raised in Montreal and taught literature in London and Toronto. **SUSAN SANFORD BLADES** (pp. 421, 493) lives in Victoria, British Columbia, and writes short stories, some of which have been published in *Numéro Cinq*, *filling Station*, and *Grain*. **SUSAN SWAN** (p. 62) is a Toronto writer. Her next novel is *The Dead Celebrities Club*. **SUSIE GREEN** (p. 381) is 34 and is an artist and musician. She lives in Newcastle upon Tyne, England. **SZILVIA MOLNAR** (pp. 19, 36, 327, 438, 451) is 29, lives in Brooklyn, and works as a foreign rights manager at a literary agency. **TABATHA RAJENDRA** (p. 157) works as a background extra. **TALATA BOWSER** (pp. 287, 328) is an educator and is blessed to live with three generations of her Muslim Ghanaian-American family in the suburbs of Washington, D.C. **TALITA S.** (pp. 35, 102, 213) is 20 and lives in Winchester, England, where she works as a nursery teacher. **TAMARA SCHIFF** (p. 35) is a southeastern transplant living in Portland, Oregon, where she works for a nonprofit. **TANIA VAN SPYK** (pp. 10, 490) is a barber living in Guelph, Ontario, with her husband and two cats. **TARA WASHINGTON** (p. 262) is an art director from Toronto. **TASHA COTTER** (p. 61) is the author of the poetry collection *Some Churches* (2013). She lives in Lexington, Kentucky, where she is at work on a novel. **TAVI GEVINSON** (p. 375) is a writer, actress, and editor in chief of *Rookie*. **TAYLOR SMALL** (p. 391) is currently working toward her B.A. in English literature at the University of Waterloo (Canada). **THANDO LOBESE** (pp. 428, 443) is a costume designer and visual artist living in Johannesburg. **THERESA PAGEOT** (pp. 75, 222) is a 27-year-old performer. She has lived all over Canada and, for the past year, in Berlin. **THESSALY LA FORCE** (pp. 275, 415–417) is a writer living in Manhattan. In 2012, she edited *My Ideal Bookshelf*; she currently is working on a collection of short stories. **TIFT MERRITT** (p. 140) is a musician, writer, and North Carolina native who lives in New York City. She collects vintage ribbon and sews guitar straps in dressing rooms while on tour. **TISHANI DOSHI** (p. 343) is a dancer and the author of four books of poetry and fiction. She divides her time between Tamil Nadu, India, and elsewhere. **TRISH EWANIKA** (pp. 294, 380) is a designer and purveyor of goods with a thoughtful sense of beauty. **TRISH KALICIAK** (pp. 411, 455) is a marketing professional and mother of two in Toronto. **TRYNTJE KRAMER** (p. 491) is a mother of nine children and a grandmother and great-grandmother of many more. Her grandkids call her "Beppe." She lives in Grimsby, Ontario, Canada. **UMM ADAM** (pp. 19, 137, 263) is a homemaker and home-schooler of four children. **VALERIE STIVERS** (pp. 71, 435) is a writer living in Brooklyn with her husband and two children. She blogs about her reading list at anthologyofclouds.com. **VANESSA BERRY** (pp. 17, 71, 352, 437) is a writer and visual artist from Sydney, Australia. **VANTHA** (p. 225) is a 43-year-old garment worker from Svay Rieng, Cambodia. She sews seams for jeans. **VEDRANA RUDAN** (p. 363) is a Croatian blogger and novelist whose books have been translated and adapted for the stage. **VERONICA MANCHESTER** (p. 96) is a journalist. **VICTORIA HAF** (p. 142) is a 26-year-old designer-illustrator currently living in Mexico City.

**WEDNESDAY LUPYPCIW** (pp. 221, 343) is a manual laborer and has a performance and textile art practice in Calgary, Alberta. **WILLY SOMMA** (p. 484), a photographer who lives in Brooklyn, New York, has been an artist-in-residence in locations around the globe. **YOUNG KIM** (p. 201) lives between New York and Paris, working in the worlds of art, fashion, film, literature, and music, as well as looking after the Estate of Malcolm McLaren. **ZARA GARDNER** (p. 35) is an illustrator who lives in Norwich, England, with her toddler daughter and partner of 18 years. **ZENDA SHIMSHAK** (p. 285) works in early childhood education in Madison, Wisconsin. **ZIVA SERKIS-NAUMANN** (pp. 157, 250) is retired from the nonprofit law firm she founded. **ZOE DANIELS** (pp. 218–219) is a writer and comedian who moves to a new city every eight years. **ZOE WELCH** (p. 334) makes women's clothes, and makes photographs. She lives in Vancouver but is planning a getaway. **ZOE WHITTALL** (pp. 75, 134) is the author of two novels and three collections of poetry, most recently the novel *Holding Still for as Long as Possible*. She lives in Toronto and works as a TV writer. **ZOSIA MAMET** (p. 233) is an actress-musician who lives in Brooklyn, New York, with her boyfriend and her two goldfish.

**The Blue Mountains Public Library**
L.E. Shore Memorial Library
Thornbury, Ontario N0H 2P0